D1267540

DEMOLISHING THE MYTH

THE TANK BATTLE AT PROKHOROVKA, KURSK, JULY 1943: AN OPERATIONAL NARRATIVE

Valeriy Zamulin

Translated and edited by Stuart Britton

Helion & Company Ltd

Helion & Company Limited
26 Willow Road
Solihull
West Midlands
B91 1UE
England
Tel. 0121 705 3393
Fax 0121 711 4075
Email: info@helion.co.uk
Website: www.helion.co.uk

Published by Helion & Company 2011

Designed and typeset by Farr out Publications, Wokingham, Berkshire
Cover designed by Farr out Publications, Wokingham, Berkshire
Printed by Gutenberg Press Limited, Tarxien, Malta

Text © Valeriy Zamulin 2010. English edition translated and edited by Stuart Britton, © Helion & Company 2010. Maps © Barbara Taylor 2011. Photographs as individually credited.

Originally published as *Prokhorovka – neizvestnoe srazhenie velilkoi voiny* (Moscow: AST, Tranzitkniga, 2005). This English edition is based upon a revised and updated text from the author and also includes specially-commissioned maps and additional photographs and appendices.

ISBN 978 1 906033 89 7

British Library Cataloguing-in-Publication Data.
A catalogue record for this book is available from the British Library.

All rights reserved. No part of this publication may be reproduced, stored in a retrieval system,or transmitted, in any form, or by any means, electronic, mechanical, photocopying, recording or otherwise, without the express written consent of Helion & Company Limited.

Front cover: The 5th Guards Tank Army attacks! (RGAKFD). Rear cover: Armor of the German XXXXVIII Panzer Corps in the vicinity of the main road to Oboian'. (RGAKFD).

For details of other military history titles published by Helion & Company Limited contact the above address, or visit our website: http://www.helion.co.uk.

We always welcome receiving book proposals from prospective authors.

Contents

List of illustrations

Color Section

All images from the author's personal archive.

A German artilleryman's panoramic view of the Oktiabr'skii State Farm on the high ground in the distance from the eastern slopes of Hill 241.6, where firing emplacements of SS Division *Leibstandarte Adolf Hitler*'s artillery regiment were located.

The view from the same vantage point on Hill 241.6, now looking to the left toward the bend in the Psel River and the higher ground beyond, where Soviet forces were defending.

All that remains of the Soviet anti-tank ditch, 500 meters southwest of Hill 252.2, which SS Division *Leibstandarte Adolf Hitler*'s 2nd Panzergrenadier Regiment struggled to cross on 11 July 1943. In the distance is the upper portion of the Victory Memorial on Prokhorovka Field, which marks the summit of Hill 252.2.

Another view from Hill 241.6, where on 12 July 1943 the observation post for SS Division *Leibstandarte Adolf Hitler* was located. In the background on the right is the monument marking Hill 252.2, and on the left are buildings of the Oktiabr'skii State Farm.

The area of Storozhevoe: the hamlet itself is out of view on the left. The road in the foreground leads through Storozhevoe to the railroad crossing on Hill 252.2. In the background is the balka that runs through the Storozhevoe woods and extends toward the southern outskirts of Prokhorovka.

An echo of the past war: A Soviet anti-personnel RDG-33 grenade, found in the Storozhevoe woods on 17 April 2010.

A fraternal grave of Soviet troops in Storozhevoe.

The "corridor" between the Storozhevoe woods (on the left) and the belt of woods along the railroad, which a group of tanks from the 32nd Tank Brigade under the command of Major S. P. Ivanov used to break through to the Komsomolets State Farm on 12 July 1943.

A panoramic view of Hill 252.2 from the Stalinskoe Branch of the Oktiabr'skii State Farm.

First of a small group of photographs, taken by author Valeriy Zamulin from the top of the Victory Memorial on Hill 252,2, which rises 47 meters above the ground. This view is looking to the southwest across the lower slopes of Hill 252.2.

Another view from the top of the Victory Memorial. In the foreground is the railroad bed in the area of Hill 252.2. Beyond the field behind the wooded belt along the railroad are the Storozhevoe woods. The field is the "corridor" used by elements of the 32nd Tank Brigade to slip through the German defenses to the Komsomolets State Farm on 12 July 1943. Remember, this photo was taken from the top of the Victory Memorial, so the wooded belt along the railroad would have obscured the view of the corridor from Hill 252.2.

A third view from the top of the Victory Memorial, looking generally to the southwest from Hill 252.2: In the mid-ground, offset to the left, is the railroad crossing; the road running from it to the right leads to Prelestnoe. The road angling from it to the left into the trees in

In the center of the photo are remnants of the wooden bridge in the village of Rzhavets, over which *kampfgruppen* of the III Panzer Corps crossed to the right bank of the Northern Donets River.
View of the vicinity of the German crossing of the Northern Donets River in the village of Rzhavets and the heights rising above the opposite bank.
The monument in the center of Shakhovo to the Soviet troops who fell in the Battle of Kursk.
A T-34/76 is being moved into a new wing of the Prokhorovka Battlefield State Museum, where it is now on display, 30 July 2009.
The Military Museum in Prokhorovka.
The Church of the Holy Apostles Peter and Paul, built in memory of the Soviet soldiers who fell at Prokhorovka. Consecrated on 3 May 1995 by the Patriarch of Moscow and All Russia Aleksii II.

List of Maps

All appear in color section. All maps drawn by Barbara Taylor.

List of Tables

List of Abbreviations Used in Tables

AA	Anti-aircraft
AT	Anti-tank
Bde	Brigade
Bn	Battalion
Co	Company
Gds	Guards
Hvy	Heavy
Regt	Regiment
Sep	Separate

Publisher's Note

Bringing *Demolishing the Myth* to an English-speaking audience has been a team effort. I would like to extend my sincere thanks to the following individuals: Stuart Britton, this book's editor and translator, who has unfailingly answered questions and provided help and assistance above and beyond the call of duty, particularly with regard to the book's cartography; Valeriy Zamulin, the book's author, who answered all our questions, added photographs showing the battlefield today when requested, and has bore patiently the many delays as we strove to get this book 'right'; Barbara Taylor, the cartographer, whose knowledge of the topography and tactical movements across the battlefield must now be even greater than perhaps she hoped for when she began work on the maps, and who has unflinchingly got to grips with the complex task of bringing some order to the battlefield; David Glantz, who was able to help out with our request for orders-of-battle at short notice. Thank you, all of you.

Duncan Rogers, Publisher

Introduction

The Battle of Kursk was the most important step on the path to the victory of our people in the Great Patriotic War. It consolidated the strategic initiative in the hands of the Red Army command and decisively undermined the power of fascist Germany. After its defeat in July-August 1943, the *Wehrmacht* was no longer able to conduct another strategic offensive operation on the Eastern Front.

One of the key moments in the first stage of the Battle of Kursk was the victory of our troops in the area of the small Prokhorovka railroad station, which has entered history as the Prokhorovka tank battle. Unfortunately, as is the case with the majority of battles and clashes of the past war, the Russian reader knows about the events at Prokhorovka only from fundamentally "cleansed" and "polished," essentially superficial, memoir and historical literature. It is not surprising that for more than 50 years since the tank battle at Prokhorovka, historians continue to argue about a number of important questions: For example, when and on what ground did this tank clash occur? How many tanks and self-propelled guns took part in it? What were the losses on both sides? There is also not a uniform answer to the main question, "Who won the battle at Prokhorovka?" A number of foreign scholars continue to maintain that the German II SS Panzer Corps, which was opposing the Soviet armies of the Voronezh Front, emerged victorious.

It is impossible to investigate these questions without analyzing the primary sources – the combat documents generated by the formations of the opposing sides. Unfortunately, if abroad at least some of these materials have been published, in our country after the events of 1943, for many years access to the files of the Ministry of Defense's Central Archives, where the Red Army's documents are stored, was extremely limited – and this significantly complicated the work of scholars.

This situation changed to a great extent at the beginning of the 1990s. In 1993, a majority of the operational and summary documents of the Red Army's divisions, corps, armies and *fronts* that participated in the Battle of Kursk was declassified. I was fortunate to have an opportunity to work in the Russian Federation's Central Archives of the Ministry of Defense between 1997 and 2003, where I was busy with finding and systematizing the sources on the Prokhorovka battle. Over this time, I studied more than 60,000 pages from the archives of the 69th, 5th and 6th Guards Armies, 5th Guards and 1st Tank Armies, and the 2nd Air Army; six rifle, eight tank and three air corps; 12 rifle and airborne divisions; 25 tank, mechanized, motorized and destroyer anti-tank brigades; and those of several dozen separate units and subunits. As a result, a documentary foundation for the study of the battle took shape.

As a result of the analysis of the collected material, for the first time a study of the battle entitled *Prokhorovka – vzgliad cherez desiatiletiia* [Prokhorovka – a view through the decades] was published in 2002 by the State Military-Historical Museum "Prokhorovka Field" [known less formally as the Prokhorovka Battlefield State Museum] together with files of the *Narodnaia pamiat'* (National Remembrance) organization. Nevertheless, scholarly work didn't end with this. The possibility appeared to become familiar with foreign and other previously classified sources, which allowed a more detailed examination of both the key moments and several episodes of the battle. As a result, the initial study was significantly expanded and revised.

The present study before you represents an initial attempt to conduct a complete analysis of the Prokhorovka tank clash, to determine its place in the overall Battle of Kursk, to lay out the course of combat operations on a daily basis, to speak of the tragedy of the 5th Guards 'Stalingrad' Tank Corps, the encirclement of which on 6 July 1943 to a significant extent foretold the enemy's arrival at the third line of defenses on the Prokhorovka axis, as well as to define more accurately the territory upon which the Prokhorovka tank battle took place. Finally, this study attempts a fresh evaluation of the results of the battle, and their impact on the outcome of the entire defensive operation of the Voronezh Front.

The basis of this book is a description of the course of combat operations; however, in distinction from earlier publications, here the focus of the description of the events, which have traditionally been regarded as part of the battle, has been significantly expanded. Previously, authors have focused attention only on the study of the fighting on 12 July 1943 on the "tank field". However, in this book I take a detailed look at the defense of a 40-kilometer sector of the rear defensive line in the area of Prokhorovka Station between 5 and 16 July 1943 by Lieutenant General V. D. Kriuchenkin's 69th Army in concert with formations of Lieutenant General P. A. Rotmistrov's 5th Guards Tank Army and Lieutenant General A. S. Zhadov's 5th Guards Army, and track the connection between the Fourth Panzer Army's II SS Panzer Corps, which was attacking toward Prokhorovka Station from the southwest, and Army Detachment Kempf's III Panzer Corps, which was attacking from the south.

Unquestionably, the data published in this book about the number of tanks and self-propelled guns that took part in the Prokhorovka battle will attract the particular attention of readers. For a long time, legends have circulated on the pages of various publications about the 1,500 or even 2,000 tanks, which supposedly collided head-on on the field near Prokhorovka. In this book, for the first time documents from General P. A. Rotmistrov's army, as well as those of corps that had been placed under his operational command, have been collected and systematically analyzed, which allowed a more reliable determination of the number of armor vehicles that took part in the battle on our side, as well as the losses suffered by the Soviet forces not only in the course of the famous fighting of 12 July on the "tank field" (1.5 kilometers southwest of Prokhorovka Station), but also those incurred while attempting to localize the German penetration of the 69th Army's defenses (south of Prokhorovka), as well as in the battle as a whole, which stretched from 10 July to 16 July 1943.

A full analysis of such a massive event of the war is impossible without a study of the men (and women) of the Red Army who took part in it. The soldiers and officers of the Red Army were the genuine creators of the victory at Prokhorovka. Particular responsibility lay upon the command staff. To a great extent, not only the outcome of the fighting depended upon their skills, experience, and personal characteristics, but also something no less important, the cost of that victory – in other words, the level of losses. On the basis of personnel service records, the author has compiled the detailed characteristics of the command of our forces at the brigade, division, corps and army levels. The level of training of the personnel of both the Red Army and of the enemy has also not slipped the author's attention.

In order to understand the real capabilities of our tank and mechanized formations in the summer of 1943, it is necessary to know the structure of the formations, and the tactical-technical characteristics of the combat vehicles that equipped them, especially the weaknesses and strengths of the Red Army's "work horse" – the T-34/76 medium tank – as well as those of the enemy armor that opposed it. This information is included in the book, including the recollections of tankers and senior officers of the tank and mechanized corps, and summary reports from the formations. All of this allows the reader to take a fresh look at the bloody armored fighting that unfolded on the southern face of the Kursk Bulge, which was unprecedented in its intensity.

While working on the book, I used a vast amount of scholarly material, a significant portion of which is still not known to a wide circle of readers and academics. This includes declassified documents from the Central Archive of the Russian Federation's Ministry of Defense and from Russia's Federal Security Service, and previously unpublished recollections of participants in the fighting that are stored in the files of the State Military-Historical Museum "Prokhorovka Field". Moreover, with the aim of a more objective and well-rounded analysis, I have studied and used corresponding foreign publications, including a compilation of combat documents of the II SS Panzer Corps that came out in the Federal Republic of Germany in 1980. Information about the battle that I've discovered in these sources is also included in the book.

Because of the subject's complexity and lack of study, I have considered it necessary to include in this work, partially or in full, the orders, combat dispatches, operational summaries, and the transcripts of Voronezh Front command's discussions with the leadership of the armies. All of these documents have been written extremely laconically and are of a deeply bureaucratic nature. This language doesn't make for easy reading, but at the same time these documents give the discussion supporting evidence and contribute additional colors to the picture of the battle. They not only allow one to study the course of combat operations in detail, but also to perceive the gravity, and at times, even the drama of the situation and to sense the tension and emotional pressure on the event's participants.

At the same time, it should be considered that in documents written without delay after the events and in the summary accounts prepared immediately after the battle's conclusion, an inaccuracy can insinuate itself, or the discussion of the combat actions can be deliberately distorted, in order to cover one's own mistakes and miscalculations. Documents are frequently encountered, wherein the command of units and formations and at time even the armies, in attempting to shift the blame for the large losses or the failure to carry out an order onto a neighbor or onto higher headquarters, have falsified the combat operations beyond recognition. I have noted examples of such "creativity" in the book where they appear. Both sides sinned in this to varying degrees. As a rule, I have used sources in my analysis that give rise to suspicions only after carefully checking them against other sources. However, it is hardly possible to eliminate shortcomings of such a nature entirely.

The defensive operation conducted by the Voronezh Front in the summer of 1943, despite its lengthy period of preparation and successful conclusion, cannot be called a model. In the course of conducting it, a large number of errors in commanding the forces and in organizing the counterattacks are apparent. The use of the tank armies – at the time a new organizational form for the armored forces – also didn't occur without mistakes. The poor cooperation among our units and formations led repeatedly to unjustified sacrifices and the failure to carry out a combat order. I speak about these mistakes quite candidly in the book. However, all these shortcomings do not diminish in any way the significance of our victory at Prokhorovka. Despite all the difficulties, blunders and oversights, thanks to the courage and resolve, and in many cases the self-sacrifice of the soldiers of the 5th Guards, 5th Guards Tank and 69th Armies during the battle, the enemy's plan to destroy the Voronezh Front was decisively foiled, and with it the failure of the German army's entire summer campaign was made a certainty.

The given research does not at all exhaust the study of the Prokhorovka battle. This is only the first step toward a complete and detailed analysis of an episode of that war that has not yet been studied exhaustively. Difficult and very painstaking work still awaits future historians. I hope that this book will be of interest to both Eastern Front buffs and professional scholars.

I want to express my sincere gratitude to the director of the State Military-Historical Museum at Prokhorovka Aleksandr Ivanovich Anchiporov, to the staff of the Central Archive of the Russian Federation's Ministry of Defense, and to both Colonel (ret.) Lev Nikolaevich Lopukhovsky and Aleksei Valer'evich Isaev for all their guidance and assistance as I worked on this book.

1

The Situation in the Kursk Sector as of July 1943

By the end of March 1943, the winter campaign was grinding to a halt. Forces of both sides had settled into defensive positions, and a rare cessation in operations along the Soviet-German front ensued. Both sides strove to use the lull in fighting to replace their losses in personnel and equipment.

In the course of the winter campaign, attacking Soviet forces had created a large, deep bulge in the enemy's lines in the region of Kursk. The configuration of the front lines in this sector created an opportunity for the enemy to launch powerful flank attacks with major force groupings from the regions of Orel and Briansk in the north, and Belgorod and Khar'kov in the south, with a subsequent breakthrough into the Soviet rear areas. However, by the beginning of April 1943, the balance of forces between the two sides along the entire Soviet-German front had turned in the favor of the Soviets, who held a 1.1 to 1 superiority over the adversary in personnel, 1.4 to 1 superiority in tanks, 1.7 to 1 superiority in artillery, and had twice the number of combat aircraft.

Such superiority in strength could have been used to continue the offensive in one of several strategic directions. Some military leaders and front commanders proposed to forestall the enemy's summer plans by launching a pre-emptive offensive to exploit the situation that had developed and destroy the flanking German forces on either side of the Kursk bulge. However, the *Stavka* VGK [Headquarters of the Supreme High Command], in light of the fatigue of the troops, the fact that many formations were not at full strength, and the difficulty of moving supplies and material during the spring muddy season, rejected an offensive. Doubtlessly, a factor in this decision was also the failure of the Khar'kov offensive in May 1942, when attacking forces of the Central and Voronezh Fronts had scored deep penetrations in the enemy's defenses, but had wound up exposed to encirclement by the counterattacks of strong German formations on the flanks of the penetration.

On 12 April 1943, the *Stavka* adopted a preliminary decision to assume a prepared defense on the Kursk axis. Subsequent events at the front would show that this was the proper decision for the situation that it was facing by the spring of 1943.

Hitler's headquarters also desired to take advantage of the favorable situation that had developed for its forces around the Kursk bulge in order to conduct a major offensive designed to seize the strategic initiative and to change the course of the war in its favor. The plan for a general offensive on the Eastern Front in 1943 traveled a long and winding path up and down the chain of command and through the Reich's highest corridors of power. From its initial conceptions to the precisely formulated, laconically worded final order for the offensive, the operation became the *Wehrmacht's* final strategic offensive on the Eastern Front.

The commander of Army Group South, E. von Manstein, issues orders to one of his staff officers, July 1943. (RGAKFD, Russian State Archive of Film and Photo Documents)

It must be said that from the very moment the question arose in February 1943 about planning the *Wehrmacht's* summer campaign in the East, right up to the latter half of June, Hitler simply could not decide upon the optimal plan for the offensive. More accurately speaking, he was unable to reconcile his boundless personal ambitions to the more limited possibilities of Germany and its armed forces. The spring of 1943 was marked by disagreements at Hitler's headquarters over the further course of the war. At the same time, it was apparent that the acute pain of the Stalingrad catastrophe was fading among the top Nazi leaders, even as optimistic evaluations of Germany's potential and a tendency to underestimate the Soviet Union's possibilities were growing. In these arguments, the question of the usefulness of the Kursk offensive became fundamental.

Two groups, which had diametrically opposite points of view on the subject of the Kursk offensive, coalesced in Germany's political and military leadership. The opponents of pursuing a large-scale offensive were primarily a number of high-ranking generals, including Colonel General H. Guderian; the commander of the Fourth Panzer Army Colonel General H. Hoth; and the operations chief of the Armed Forces High Command (*Oberkommando des Wehrmacht*, or OKW) Colonel General A. Jodl. By the end of spring, the commander of Army Group South Field Marshal E. von Manstein came to share this point of view as well. They believed that the *Wehrmacht* was not ready for large-scale offensive operations, including in the area of the Kursk bulge, against a battle-seasoned Red Army. In their opinion, such an offensive could lead to the exhaustion of Germany's resources and drain the strength of its armed forces. Moreover, Jodl pointed to the danger that the British and Americans might open a second front in the West, and considered it inadvisable to use the limited reserves, which were being gathered with great difficulty, for an offensive. He proposed that the German forces on the Eastern Front instead adopt a defensive posture, straighten the lines wherever feasible, and transfer part of the forces thereby freed to the west, in order to strengthen the French and Mediterranean coastlines.

In the first days of April, fresh intelligence began to arrive, especially from aerial reconnaissance, which showed that the Soviet forces in the Kursk region were preparing a strong and deeply echeloned defense of the Kursk bulge, and that intensive work was underway precisely along the directions of the planned attacks. These preparations were obviously designed to reduce the pace of the German breakthrough efforts to a slow grind, and might eventually cause the complete failure of the offensive. However, Hitler just as before relied upon the shock strength of his panzer divisions, which had received new types of heavy tanks and assault guns, as well as upgraded models of the Panzer IV tank. The plans counted upon establishing overwhelming superiority over the defending Soviet forces in the designated breakthrough sectors, and rapidly destroying them before the arrival of reserves.

Hitler was still gripped by the experiences of 1941 and 1942, when Soviet defensive positions had collapsed under the concentrated blows of tanks and infantry, supported by the Luftwaffe. Moreover, the tasks of the main assault groups in this offensive were significantly more modest than in preceding operations. In addition, the political aspect of the future operation had a significant influence on the Führer's views.

On 12 April, Hitler spread out a prepared map of the operation's plan on a table before him. He had in fact just approved the plan earlier that same day. Within three days, on 15 April, the plan was put into motion by Operations Order 6, which laid out the goals and tasks of a summer campaign in the East, and spelled out the primary missions for both Army Group South and Army Group Center. The essence of the operation, which received the code name "*Zitadelle* [Citadel]," was by means of a concentric attack in the direction of Kursk from the region of Orel in the north and Belgorod in the south, to split the defenses of two Soviet fronts – Voronezh Front (commanded by General N. F. Vatutin[1]) and Central Front (commanded by General K. K. Rokossovsky) – and encircle their forces. The author of this scheme was General W. Model, commander of the German Ninth Army. The operation was planned as a simultaneous attack, designed to secure a rapid and decisive success, for which the attacking forces from the north and the south were given the mission to link up on the fourth day of the offensive east of the city of Kursk and thereby close a ring around the trapped Soviet forces. The eastern flank formations of the assault groupings had the task to create an outer shield for the pocket along the line of the Korocha River, Skorodnoe and Tim as quickly as possible, which would have in its rear the important lateral rail line running from Belgorod to Orel through Kursk. The plan also intended to use secondary forces of the assault groupings to guard the inner ring of the encirclement from breakout attempts, while at the same these covering units were to attack to reduce the enemy pocket. If the operation went smoothly, the plan envisioned a subsequent attack into the rear of the Southwestern Front. Here is an excerpt from this document:

> I have decided, as soon as the weather permits, to conduct '*Zitadelle*,' the first offensive of the year.

> This attack is of the utmost importance. It must be executed quickly. It must seize the initiative for us in the spring and summer. Therefore, all preparations must be conducted with great circumspection and enterprise. The best formations, the best weapons, the best commanders, and great stocks of ammunition must be committed in the main efforts. Each commander and each man must be impressed with the decisive significance of this offensive. The victory at Kursk must be a signal to all of the world. I hereby order:
>
> ... 3. Army Group South sets out from the line Belgorod-Tomarovka with concentrated forces, passes through the line Prilepy-Oboian', and makes contact with the attacking armies of Army Group Center east of and near Kursk. To cover the attack from the east, the line Nezhegol – Korocha sector – Skorodnoe – Tim is to be reached as soon as possible without threatening the concentration of forces on the main effort in the direction of Prilepy-Oboian'. Forces will be committed to protect the attack in the west; they will later be used to attack into the pocket.
>
> 4. Army Group Center launches a concentrated attack from the line Trosna-north of Maloarkhangel'sk with the main effort on the eastern flank, passes through the line Fatezh-Vereitinovo, and establishes contact with the attacking army from Army Group South near and east of Kursk... The line Tim – east of Shchigry – Sosna sector is to be reached as soon as possible. To protect the attack in the east, however, the concentration of forces on the main effort is not to be disturbed. Secondary forces will be committed to cover [the attack] in the west.
>
> At the beginning of the attack, Army Group Center forces operating west of Trosna to the boundary with Army Group South are to fix the enemy with local attacks of specially concentrated attack groups and then attack promptly into the forming pocket. Continuous ground reconnaissance and air observation is to insure that the enemy does not withdraw unnoticed. If this occurs, there is to be an immediate attack along the entire front.[2]

Of the twelve German armies and five operational groups present on the Eastern Front in the spring of 1943, the plan proposed to employ three armies (the Fourth Panzer Army, the Second Army, and the Ninth Army) and one operational group – Army Detachment Kempf – to implement Operation Citadel. The planned attacks were to strike rather narrow sectors, which comprised less than 14% of the entire length of the Soviet-German front.

Of the two assault groupings participating in the offensive, Army Group South was the primary one, and it was given the more complex and sizeable tasks. In order to reach the line where the two attacking groupings were to meet in the vicinity of Kursk, the forces of Field Marshal G. von Klüge's Army Group Center had to advance approximately 75 kilometers, while those of E. von Manstein's Army Group South would have to go much further, 125 kilometers. Accordingly, Army Group South had a somewhat more powerful strike force (nine panzer and motorized divisions) concentrated at its designated breakthrough sector in the Soviet defenses, while Army Group Center had only seven such divisions. Moreover, Army Group South was further strengthened on paper by receiving Brigade Decker (the 10th Panzer Brigade), which controlled two panzer battalions equipped with 200 of the new Panzer V Panther, 196 battle tanks and four recovery *Bergepanthers*.

A group of officers of the SS *Leibstandarte Adolf Hitler* Panzergrenadier Division. In the front row, second from the left, is SS *Obergruppenführer* 'Sepp' Dietrich, who on 4 July 1943 turned over command of the division to SS *Oberführer* T. Wisch, who appears over Dietrich's left shoulder. (RGAKFD)

Army Group South consisted of the Fourth Panzer Army, under the command of Colonel General H. Hoth, and Army Detachment Kempf, under the command of General W. Kempf.[3] The two commands had a combined strength of eleven infantry and nine panzer and motorized divisions. By the end of April 1943, Hoth's army had the following formations: the LII Army Corps (with the 57th 167th, 255th and 332nd Infantry Divisions), the II SS Panzer Corps (with the 1st SS Panzergrenadier Division *Leibstandarte Adolf Hitler,* the 2nd SS Panzergrenadier Division *Das Reich*, and the 3rd SS Panzergrenadier Division *Totenkopf*) and the XXXXVIII Panzer Corps (with the *Grossdeutschland* Panzergrenadier Division and the 11th Panzer Division). A short time later, the Fourth Panzer Army received the 3rd Panzer Division from the First Panzer Army, and it was assigned to the XXXXVIII Panzer Corps at the end of June. Army Detachment Kempf was weaker than Hoth's army, although it contained three corps: the XXXXII Army Corps, the XI Army Corps, and the III Panzer Corps. The III Panzer Corps was weakened when it lost *Grossdeutschland* to the XXXXVIII Panzer Corps in exchange for the weaker 19th Panzer Division under a reorganization prior to the offensive.

In addition to these forces, Army Group South had under its command the Fourth Air Fleet, commanded by General of Anti-aircraft Artillery Otto Dessloch. Dessloch had under his command the I, IV and VIII Air Corps. The latter Corps, during the course of the Kursk offensive, was placed in direct support of the Fourth Panzer Army and Army Detachment Kempf. The VIII Air Corps was commanded by General of

Colonel General H. Hoth, commander of the Fourth Panzer Army, observes the battlefield through scissor binoculars. (Private collection)

Aviation Hans von Seidemann, who in the spring of 1943 had replaced a favorite of Hitler's in this post, General Wolfram von Richthofen. At the start of the offensive, the VIII Air Corps had 1,112 aircraft on its roster, of which around 900 were operational.[4]

As has already been mentioned, Colonel General H. Hoth[5] was among the group of generals who did not believe the *Wehrmacht* was capable of encircling the forces of two Soviet *fronts*. Lacking the possibility to have any real influence on this decision, Hoth still persistently tried to advance a more realistic, in his view, goal for his army in the upcoming operation: the destruction of the Red Army's large reserves. He believed that already by May, the Soviet command had managed to amass significant strength in the region, and had readied up to ten large tank formations. Therefore he tried to convince the Army Group command to make the aim of destroying the Red Army's reserve formations the primary goal, if only during the initial stage of Citadel, and have this objective included in the process of operational planning. He searched for a suitable occasion, where he could thoroughly discuss this problem with Field Marshal von Manstein; such a meeting occurred on 10-11 May in the headquarters of the Fourth Panzer Army in the city of Bogodukhov in the Ukraine.

In the course of the discussion, Hoth managed to obtain Manstein's agreement to make significant changes to the existing plans of attack for the Fourth Panzer Army. Firstly, the boundary line between the Fourth Panzer Army and Army Detachment Kempf was shifted. Secondly, the XXXXVIII Panzer Corps was strengthened significantly. Under the original plans, prior to this meeting, the XXXXVIII Panzer Corps and the

SS *Obergruppenführer* Paul Hausser, commander of the II SS Panzer Corps. (Private collection)

SS *Sturmbannführer* (at the time of the Kursk battle SS *Oberführer*) W. Ostendorff, chief of staff of the II SS Panzer Corps (a captured 1942 photograph). (RGAKFD)

II SS Panzer Corps were to attack on a straight line from Belgorod to Oboian' across the River Psel, with no deviation toward the Prokhorovka railroad station. Meanwhile, the III Panzer Corps of Army Detachment Kempf was to shield the right flank of the II SS Panzer Corps, and in the course of the operation, it [the III Panzer Corps] was to take the railroad station at Prokhorovka and the area around it.

Now, however, after Hoth's persistent entreaties, the area west of and northeast of Prokhorovka was transferred from Army Detachment Kempf's responsibility to the Fourth Panzer Army. This change found its reflection on 31 May, in an order from the commander of the II SS Panzer Corps, *Obergruppenführer* P. Hausser to his corps. In it, he first indicated that upon penetrating the second belt of Russian defenses, the II SS Panzer Corps should direct its main effort "*south of the Psel, in the direction of Prokhorovka*" [author's emphasis].[6]

The underlying meaning to all these changes lies in the fact that Hoth was anticipating a decisive battle with the Soviet reserves in the vicinity of Prokhorovka some time between 7 July and 9 July, and that the results of this engagement would determine the further fate of Citadel. Moreover, Hoth hoped that even if he then had to curtail the operation, the Germans might still be able to claim a victory. His calculations rested upon the following, as recollected by his chief of staff, General F. Fangohr:

Hoth came to the conclusion that it was possible that the Russians had already learned about our plans, and it was precisely for this reason that they had shifted the location of their strategic reserve to the east, in order to hold them in combat readiness.

On the basis of this evaluation, General Hoth decided that the order to attack directly to the north, along the direct route through Oboian', should not be interpreted literally. In Hoth's opinion, the lay of the land and the deployment of the enemy's forces would essentially prohibit such an advance. About 20 kilometers south of Oboian', the ground sloped downward in the northeast and north directions toward the Psel River. It gradually rose on the opposite bank of the river, giving the Russians an excellent field of view in the direction of our advance. The terrain, cut by the River Psel around Oboian', was too narrow because of the large quantity of reservoirs, while the course of the river's flow made it impossible to avoid them. Any Russian division, driven away from Belgorod, nevertheless would be able to find a new natural line of defense behind the Psel River in both directions from Oboian' and to the southeast of the city, from where it would be able to inflict great losses on an attacker.

General Hoth also had to assume that Soviet strategic reserves – including several tank corps – would enter the battle by pushing quickly through the narrow passage between the Donets and Psel Rivers at Prokhorovka (about 50 kilometers northeast of Belgorod). If Fourth Panzer Army's spearheads were engaged in a difficult fight for the Psel crossing sites around Oboian', then a Russian tank attack would hit our right flank at exactly the moment in which the panzer divisions had their freedom of movement extremely limited by the Psel River. Because such a situation could quickly turn into a disaster, General Hoth realized that his plans must anticipate an engagement with the Soviet armored reserves near Prokhorovka prior to continuing the attack toward Kursk. He considered it vital to employ the strongest possible force in such a fight, so that we could compel the enemy to meet us on terrain of our choosing in which the panzer divisions could fully exploit their superior mobility, unhampered by the Psel River. Accordingly, following our penetration of the enemy's defensive belt, II SS Panzer Corps would not advance directly north across the Psel River, but veer sharply northeast toward Prokhorovka to destroy the Russian tank forces we expected to find there. Such a maneuver had the advantage that it would place us much nearer to the intended thrust of Army Detachment Kempf's III Panzer Corps, raising the possibility of the coordination of the two interior army wings on the battlefield. Such a prospect also led General Hoth to modify the mission of XXXXVIII Panzer Corps on our left flank. After its initial breakthrough on either side of Cherkasskoe, the corps would not push north to the Psel but keep abreast of the II SS Panzer Corps as it wheeled to the northeast. Such a maneuver would cover *Obergruppenführer* Hausser's flank as he advanced toward the decisive battle with the Soviet reserves and potentially provide additional reinforcements for that engagement. To be sure, we could not as yet determine the manner in which the XXXXVIII Panzer Corps might be committed around Prokhorovka, though in no event would we commit General von Knobelsdorff's corps to an attack west of this objective. No plan of battle could be made for the continuation of the operation after achieving a victory at Prokhorovka, but such a

> success would place us in the strategic divide between the Oskol, Donets, Psel, and Seim Rivers, from which we would be able to continue the advance in any desired direction.
>
> General Hoth also called Field Marshal von Manstein's attention to the fact that breaking through the Russian defensive system would be difficult, costly, and time-consuming. He did not expect Fourth Panzer Army to achieve strategic freedom of movement until we had penetrated the line Teterevino – Noven'koe, roughly 27 to 30 kilometers southeast of Oboian', where the third and final Soviet defensive belt was located.[7]

In this way, having agreed with Hoth's ideas, von Manstein also came to the conclusion that one of the culminating moments of the first phase of the offensive was going to be the engagement that would take place near Prokhorovka.

The second decision turned out to be no less important. Von Manstein didn't believe that Army Group Center's Second Army, which was situated on the left flank of Army Group South, would be able to cope with the task preventing Soviet forces from launching attacks on the XXXXVIII Panzer Corps' lengthening left flank as his armies advanced towards Kursk. His intelligence indicated that the Russians were already accumulating significant reserves south of Kursk, probably with just this idea in mind. These concerns compelled von Manstein not only to transfer *Grossdeutschland* to the XXXXVIII Panzer Corps, but also to concur with Hoth's request for the Panther-equipped 10th Panzer Brigade, a powerful new tank formation, to go to XXXXVIII Panzer Corps.

On 27 June, a number of additional important decisions were adopted in turn, all of which touched upon the future events around Prokhorovka. In essence, it was on this day that Colonel General Hoth finally agreed upon a plan of action with the leadership of Army Group South for his Fourth Panzer Army for the first stage of the upcoming offensive, and transmitted the final tactical orders to the commands of his two corps. To carry out the main task of the first stage of the operation – the destruction of Soviet mobile reserves near the Prokhorovka railway station, Hoth decided to use the II SS Panzer Corps. In the course of advancing on the station, II SS Panzer Corps' right flank would be covered by the 6th Panzer Division of Army Detachment Kempf's III Panzer Corps attacking northward on its right, while its left flank would be protected by XXXXVIII Panzer Corps' *Grossdeutschland* Panzergrenadier Division. Hoth was calculating that the decisive encounter with the Soviet reserve forces would begin in the period between 7 July and 9 July. It was anticipated that by this time, XXXXVIII Panzer Corps would be able to force a crossing of the Psel River south of Oboian', and having erected a blocking position there, it would pivot part of its armored forces, particularly the 10th Panzer Brigade's Panthers, to assist the II SS Panzer Corps in its struggle with the Russian tank reserves.

I emphasize that Hoth was expecting the approach of significant Red Army reserves and therefore wanted the commitment of forces from the XXXXVIII Panzer Corps and Army Detachment Kempf into the anticipated decisive engagement around Prokhorovka without fail. However, General W. Kempf's forces were significantly weaker than Hoth's, and only a great optimist could expect that Army Detachment Kempf would be able to able to keep up with the advance of the Fourth Panzer Army.

The final task lying before the Fourth Panzer Army, the most powerful German formation that took part in the Battle of Kursk, was formally attached to Order No. 6, which General Hoth signed on the next day, 28 June 1943:

> 2. The Fourth Panzer Army is taking part in the *Zitadelle* [Citadel] offensive, for the purpose of encircling and destroying the enemy in the Kursk bulge. To this end, on "X" day (5 July 1943) according to plan, the Panzer army is to break through the enemy's first line of defenses along the heights northwest of Belgorod and Korovino, having first seized the heights on both sides of Butovo and south of Gertsovka on the afternoon of day "X-1" (4 July 1943) with forces of the XXXXVIII Panzer Corps.
>
> The Army will quickly crush any opposition in the enemy's second line of defenses, destroy the tank forces which have been hurled against it, and then strike in the direction of Kursk and east of that place, skirting around Oboian' to the east. Army Detachment Kempf's attack is to secure the operation from the east. To implement this cover, Army Detachment Kempf will attack with its left flank (6th Panzer Division) from Belgorod through Sabynino in the direction of Prokhorovka.[8]

Consequently, the decision to drive towards Prokhorovka was not made "on the fly," as a response to the current operational situation, as has been the accepted view in Soviet literature on the battle. Rather, it was a task given to two formations of Army Group South, the II SS Panzer Corps and Army Detachment Kempf, even in the planning stages for Operation Citadel.

The *Wehrmacht* command was forced to take an unprecedented three-month lull in combat activities in order to create two powerful attack groupings on either side of the Kursk salient; to restore the combat potential of their panzer divisions after the winter fighting and to equip them with a great number of new tanks; and to prepare for the operation thoroughly and carefully. The point was that Hitler wanted panzer divisions equipped with the latest designs in tanks and assault guns, such as the Panther and the Ferdinand, to serve as the basis for his assault groupings. Meanwhile, the production of these new designs was behind schedule, and their arrival in the combat formations encountered numerous delays. In connection with this, Hitler postponed the start date of the offensive several times.

The *Wehrmacht* leadership took heightened security measures and tried to keep their preparations for the offensive secret. In order to confuse the Soviet command about the location and direction of the offensive's main blow, special measures were taken in Army Group South: demonstration reconnaissance and tank movements; the concentration of bridging equipment at various points; deceptive radio transmissions; the work of its network of agents; the spreading of rumors; and so forth.[9]

However, the enemy's plans were revealed early on. Hitler's command could not even count on the element of surprise, through which it had obtained success in the summer campaigns of 1941 and 1942. The excellent work of Soviet intelligence and the numerous delays with the start of the offensive contributed to the disclosure of Hitler's plans to a considerable degree. The Soviet command made maximum use of the three-month lull in fighting and managed to build a strong, deeply-echeloned defense, capable

	Soviet *Fronts*	**Opposing Army Groups**		
	Central, Voronezh	**Ninth and Second Armies, Army Group Center; Fourth Panzer Army and Army Detachment Kemp, Army Group South**	**Balance of Forces**	**Balance of Forces, including Steppe Front (a)**
Personnel (b)	1,336,000	900,000	1.4:1	2.1:1
Guns and Mortars (c)	19,100	Around 10,000	1.9:1	2.8:1
Tanks and Self-propelled Guns	3,444 (including 900 light tanks)	2,733 (including 360 dated types)	1.2:1	1.8:1
Aircraft (d)	2,172	Around 2,050	1:1	1.3:1

(a) On 5 July 1941, Steppe Front had 573,000 men, around 7,400 guns and mortars, more than 1,500 tanks and self-propelled guns, and around 500 aircraft.
(b) Including personnel of the rear units and facilities.
(c) Excluding rocket artillery, anti-aircraft artillery, and 50mm mortars.
(d) The number for Voronezh and Central Fronts do not include aircraft of Long-Range Aviation, Southwest Front's 17th Air Army, or the PO-2 night bombers. Including these forces, the Soviet Military Air Force presence at Kursk grows to 2,900 aircraft, which is 1.4 times greater than the German side's.

Source: *Velikaia Otechestvennaia voina 1941-1945, Tom 2, Perelom* [The Great Patriotic War 1941-1945, Volume 2, Turning Point] (Moscow: Nauka, 1998), p. 260.

Table 1: The Balance of Forces between the Opposing Sides on the Kursk Axis at the Beginning of July 1943

Commander of the Voronezh Front General of the Army N. F. Vatutin at his observation post, July 1943. (RGAKFD)

of withstanding a massed panzer assault. But the *Stavka* did not adopt the final decision to go over to a premeditated defense in the Kursk direction until June.

The *Stavka*'s plan foresaw a concentration of effort north and south of Kursk, where the main events should unfold. Having repelled the enemy's attack and exhausted his forces in defensive battles, the main formations of the Central and Voronezh Fronts would then go on the counteroffensive, complete the destruction of the opposing enemy groupings, and create the conditions for shifting to a general offensive.

The Central Front under the command of General of the Army K. K. Rokossovsky received the order to defend the northern face of the Kursk salient along a 306-kilometer front, repulse the adversary's attacks, and then by going on the counteroffensive together with the forces of the Western and Briansk Fronts, destroy the enemy's grouping in the region of Orel.

The Voronezh Front of General of the Army N. F. Vatutin was to defend the southern shoulder of the Kursk bulge along an extent of 244 kilometers, exhaust and sap the strength of Army Group South's attacking units, after which it was to go on the counteroffensive, and in cooperation with the forces of the Southwestern Front, complete the enemy's destruction in the vicinity of Belgorod and Khar'kov.

Behind the Central and Voronezh Fronts, the powerful forces of the Steppe Military District (as of 9 July, Front) were deploying, with the task of preventing any further advance of the enemy in case of a breakthrough. However, the basic intention for the

Steppe Front was offensive; once the enemy's offensive had been stopped during the defensive stage of the battle, it was to play a major role in the planned counteroffensive.

Thus, both sides set for themselves the decisive goal of destroying their adversary in the first summer operation of 1943. However, for the first time, the Soviet command deliberately handed the initiative over to the enemy, in order to use the advantages of a pre-planned and well-prepared defense, in order to grind down his tank force, and then, by introducing fresh reserves, complete the destruction of the attacking Army Groups. In spite of the disadvantageous balance of forces and means that he faced, Hitler nevertheless took the decision to attack, which from a military point of view was certainly risky to a degree. Doubtlessly, the failure of German intelligence to discover the presence of ten Soviet armies with the Western, Briansk, Central, Voronezh, and Southwestern Fronts, which eventually took part in the battle of Kursk, played a definite role in Hitler's miscalculation.[10] However, Hitler could not refrain from going on the offensive, since for him the implementation of Operation Citadel was based not only on military, but also political considerations.

As a whole, in the upcoming operational area, the balance of forces was far from in the favor of the Germans, especially if you take into account the forces of the Steppe Military District (see Table 1).[11]

Incidentally, the data in Table 1, which characterizes the balance of forces between the two opposing sides at Kursk, only became known significantly later, after captured documents of the Third Reich had been analyzed, and the military archives of the two sides had been declassified. At the time we are examining, however, the very decision of the Soviet command to adopt a premeditated defense contained its own amount of risk: in the preceding two years of war, the Red Army's defensive positions had not been able to withstand the massed blows of panzer groups of even smaller size.

2

Defensive Preparations of the Voronezh Front on the Southern Face of the Kursk Salient

The commander of the Voronezh Front, Gen. N. F. Vatutin, thought the enemy capable of launching simultaneous attacks from the vicinity of Belgorod in three directions: toward Oboian'; toward Korocha and Volchansk; and toward Novyi Oskol. Based on this belief, he decided to concentrate his main strength along a 164-kilometer sector of his *front*'s left wing. He placed the 38th, 40th, 6th Guards and 7th Guards Armies in the first echelon of defense, and the 1st Tank Army and 69th Army in the second echelon. Vatutin held two separate tank corps and one rifle corps in *front* reserve.

By the start of the German offensive, each army in the first echelon had constructed three defensive belts with a total depth of 30 to 50 kilometers. The first or main defensive belt extended for 244 kilometers. The second belt stretched for 235 kilometers, while the rear third belt spanned 250 kilometers. The three defensive belts encompassed all the enemy's potential avenues of attack. In addition, the Voronezh Front constructed three intermediate lines of defense at a depth of 180 to 200 kilometers behind the front lines. East of the Kursk salient along the line of the River Kshen', the troops of the Steppe Military District had prepared the first strategic line of defense, while the so-called State line of defense ran along the east bank of the Don River. Forces were occupying all the most important sectors of the lines.

When laying out the lines and fortifications, engineers first of all took into consideration the presence of natural barriers to tank movement, such as small rivers, ravines, ponds and reservoirs, and so on. Together with engineered obstacles (like anti-tank ditches and minefields) and anti-tank fire, these natural obstacles served to obstruct the advance of enemy tanks, or to channel them into kill zones. The armies' third line of defense, which lay approximately 20 kilometers behind the second defensive belt, made particular use of the Psel River, which was difficult for tanks to cross, while the higher ground north of the river offered defending forces an excellent field of view to the south.

Prokhorovka Station,[1] near where the tank engagement erupted, lay just behind the third (Army) line of defenses. The forward edge of this defensive belt in the Prokhorovka direction ran along the line Bogoroditskoe (excl.)-Teterevino-Zhimolostnoe-Novoselovka-Vypolzovka-Mazikino. Prokhorovka Station lay about 12 kilometers from the Bogoroditskoe (excl.)-Teterevino sector, 9 kilometers from the Zhimolostnoe-Novoselovka sector, and about 18 kilometers from Vypolzovka.

In the spring and summer of 1943, Prokhorovka was a supply terminal for the 6th Guards Army. A major army artillery munitions dump, No. 1383, under the command of Major Agafonov, was located on its outskirts. Two airfields for the 2nd Air Army – a real one and a dummy one – had been constructed nearby. The 27th Fighter Aviation Regiment (commanded by Colonel V. I. Bobrov) was stationed on the operational field at Grushki at the start of the Kursk offensive. The command post of the 2nd Air Army was operating just to the northeast of Prokhorovka Station in a protective forested belt; as the front lines drew near during the battle, it redeployed to a different location for security reasons. Between 11 July and 2 August 1943, the forward headquarters of the 5th Guards Tank Army operated in the village of Skorovka, 8 kilometers east of Prokhorovka.

In case the Germans managed to penetrate or break through the main (first) defensive belt, Voronezh Front's 38th and 40th Armies had constructed defensive switch lines and intermediary positions (with a total length of 134 kilometers), while the 35th Guards Rifle Corps occupied an intermediate line that stretched 86 kilometers. A switch line for the Voronezh Front as a whole was also constructed, which extended for 125 kilometers. In a critical lapse, however, the 7th Guards Army and 69th Army to the south of Prokhorovka Station failed to construct switch lines. Von Manstein didn't fail to take advantage of their absence: after breaking through the main line of the 7th Guards Army in the direction of Korocha, he turned the main forces of Army Detachment Kempf to the north, taking the defensive positions in the flank, and began to roll up the Soviet line of defenses.

The first two bands of fortifications comprised the tactical zone of defense, where the armies of the first echelon deployed the majority of their divisions' (corps') forces and weapons. The tactical zone had an elaborate system of trenches, communications trenches, firing positions, and other constructed emplacements. The depth of the tactical zone at Kursk comprised 15 to 20 kilometers, which was deeper than any previously constructed tactical zone.

Battalion defensive zones (2 to 2.5 kilometers of frontage and up to 1 kilometer in depth) represented the main defensive belt. Two or three such zones in one or two echelons made up a regimental sector (spanning 4 to 5 kilometers of frontage and up to 4 kilometers in depth). Three rifle regiment sectors constituted the defensive belt of the division.

In order to repel the attacks of tanks and mechanized infantry, a widely developed system of engineered obstacles was used, including anti-tank ditches, block obstacles, and both simple and controlled minefields. Special significance in the preparation of the defenses was given to building a complete network of earthworks, connected by communication trenches. They served as shelter against enemy artillery fire and air strikes, provided for rapid and protected maneuver both along the front and from its depths, and made it more difficult for the enemy to figure out the firing patterns. On certain lines of attack (for example, in the sector of the 22nd Guards Rifle Corps of the 6th Guards Army), the trenches were four layers deep. Depending on the terrain, the second line of trenches was 150 to 200 meters behind the first line. The distance between the second and third line of trenches was approximately 200 to 250 meters, while the fourth line of trenches lay approximately 150 to 200 meters behind the third. In this way, a network of trenches encompassed the entire depth of the company and battalion areas of defense. The rifle units had a variety of cover: slit trenches, shelters and dugouts. On average, each rifle division defending in the main defensive belt had up to 70 kilometers of trenches and communication trenches.

As a rule, submachine gunners and tank hunters occupied the first line of trenches. Heavy machine-gun emplacements, in particular log bunkers, were in the second line. In the sector of the 23rd Guards Rifle Corps' 52nd Guards Rifle Division of the 6th Guards Army, which had three and in some places two additional lines of trenches, extensive use was made of platoon-strength outposts and machine-gun emplacements in a security zone 100 to 150 meters in front of the first main line of defense. These positions were heavily camouflaged from aerial and ground observation, and were equipped with slit trenches and dugouts for cover. They were under instructions not to fire before the start of the enemy offensive and thereby disclose their positions, but after the enemy had worked over the forward edge of the defenses with a preparatory artillery bombardment and air attacks, and launched the attack, they were to open fire and reestablish the network of fire.[2]

The entire defense was built and organized to combat tanks to the full depth of the army's defense, but primarily in the main defensive belt. The basis of the anti-tank defenses consisted of: the anti-tank fire of artillery and tanks; barriers and natural obstacles linked with the system of fire; the timely maneuver of artillery anti-tank and tank reserves and mobile barrier units; and a system of observation and signaling.

In addition, the defending armies around Kursk built special anti-tank strongpoints designed to neutralize the enemy's tank force. In the Voronezh Front, these strongpoints were located as a rule in the company or battalion defensive areas. Usually, a commander of the destroyer anti-tank regiments commanded each such anti-tank strongpoint, but this decision created problems in the heat of battle. Though the rifle regiment commander was responsible for his sector of the defense, he had no direct influence over the anti-tank strongpoints in his sector. In turn, the strongpoint commander didn't always know the full situation in the rifle unit's sector, and could make a decision only on the basis of his own personal assessment of what he could observe from his strongpoint. The Central Front came to a more successful solution to this problem. There, the anti-tank strongpoints were part of the rifle regiments' defensive sectors and linked into anti-tank regions. The rifle regiment commander was placed in charge of the anti-tank strongpoints in his sector, and his deputy was the artillery regiment commander.

An anti-tank strongpoint was a well-camouflaged firing position for six to twelve anti-tank guns with wide fields of fire, and it had approximately the same number of anti-tank riflemen. The tank hunters were covered against the fire of Panzergrenadiers by up to a platoon of submachine gunners. In the sectors most vulnerable to tank attack, the number of anti-tank guns in the anti-tank strongpoint increased up to 30, and the number of anti-tank rifles, up to 32. Twenty anti-tank strongpoints were created in the 6th Guards Army's main defensive belt, and eleven more were situated in the second band of defenses. In the regions Vasil'evka, Korovino, Cherkasskoe, Kamennyi Log, Koz'mo-Dem'ianovka, Shopino, Khokhlovo, and Dal'niaia Igumenka, anti-tank strongpoint defenses were connected into anti-tank regions, and subordinated to the divisional commanders.

The army anti-tank reserve was located in the regions of Pokrovka, Syrtsevo and 4 kilometers southwest of the village Malye Maiachki. On the rear (Army) line, the 69th Army's belt of defenses contained 19 anti-tank strongpoints: seven in the 183rd Rifle Division, eight in the 305th Rifle Division, and four in the 107th Rifle Division.

Destroyer anti-tank regiments, consisting of five batteries of anti-tank guns, were designated exclusively for the struggle against enemy armored vehicles. The source of these regiments' power was the tightly concentrated, accurate and quickly directed fire of 20 guns. For this purpose, the regiments dispensed with the battalion level of organization. This not only economized on personnel, but first of all it simplified the fire control of the batteries and decreased the amount of time required to transmit orders and instructions, which given the increased tempo of tank battle was very important.

Clear instructions forbade the breaking up of the destroyer anti-tank regiments into individual batteries, which would immediately disperse the regiment's power and lose the effect of concentrated artillery fire. Unfortunately, in the heat of battle, commanders often ignored these instructions. Destroyer anti-tank regiments, which had been assigned to rifle regiments and divisions, were frequently split up into individual batteries and distributed among the rifle battalions in the first echelon in order to strengthen their defenses. For example, the commander of the 9th Guards Airborne Division, Colonel A. M. Sazonov, who had received the 301st Destroyer Anti-tank Regiment, didn't use it to create an anti-tank strongpoint in the vicinity of the important Hill 252.2 (3 kilometers southwest of Prokhorovka), but instead gave three batteries to the 26th and 28th Guards Airborne Regiments, and kept two in his own reserve in the region of Kusty.

A new type of shell, the armor-piercing discarding sabot shell, which began entering the service of the Red Army in 1942, significantly increased the effectiveness of our anti-tank guns in their struggle with enemy armor. These shells had high armor-piercing capabilities, but they were also expensive to produce. Thus they were manufactured in relatively small numbers, and given primarily to the destroyer anti-tank units. However, individual battery commanders often managed to obtain a small number of these shells for their batteries, as a "secret weapon".

Howitzer battalions and regiments, firing from concealed positions, increased the effectiveness of the anti-tank strongpoints. Along likely avenues of tank attack, the howitzers employed shifting and fixed barrage patterns of fire. Such fire not only threw the attacking units into confusion, but also separated the Panzergrenadiers from the tanks and inflicted significant losses on them. The net effect was to weaken and reduce the pace of the adversary's general attack. Deprived of infantry support, the tank crews normally stopped the attack or withdrew their vehicles to a safe distance, from where they would begin to conduct methodical aimed fire at the artillery positions from a distance of 1,000 to 1,200 meters, using their excellent guns and optics. In addition, all the howitzer and cannon artillery prepared lines and positions for conducting direct fire at tanks over open sights.

The next step in the matter of increasing the possibilities of the artillery in the struggle against tanks became the NKO (People's Commissariat of Defense) Order No. 0063 dated 10 April 1943, which authorized the creation of a larger anti-tank formation, the destroyer anti-tank brigade. The authorized strength of this unit consisted of two regiments of 76mm Model 1942 guns, and one regiment of 45mm guns Model 1937 or 1942. All the regiments consisted of five batteries, with four guns per battery. The Voronezh Front had seven such anti-tank brigades.

In order to elevate the role of destroyer anti-tank artillery, and to stabilize and strengthen them with trained crews who had combat experience against tanks, Stalin signed NKO Order No. 0528 back on 1 July 1942, which also renamed the destroyer artillery units as destroyer anti-tank artillery units. All commanders in the destroyer artillery units, from platoon commander to battalion commander, were placed under strict control, and henceforth restricted to posts only in the destroyer anti-tank artillery. Privates and sergeants, after convalescing in hospitals from wounds, had to be returned to their former unit in the destroyer anti-tank artillery. Stalin's order also extended certain privileges to the members of destroyer anti-tank artillery units. All salaries were increased by 50%; gun crews would receive bonuses for each destroyed tank credited to them; and gun crews could tally their victories with special marks on their gun shield. The gun layer and his assistant received promotions to the rank of sergeant and junior sergeant respectively. A new shoulder patch was created to distinguish the members of destroyer anti-tank artillery units – a black cloth rhombus trimmed in red, with the depiction of two crossed gun barrels stitched in gold thread.

The plans for Kursk drew in all types of artillery to combat tanks, including anti-aircraft and self-propelled artillery; Guards mortar units with rocket launchers; and tanks. For the first time, special instructions were worked out for the Guards mortar units for their own role in the struggle against tanks. All divisional commanders and higher had various anti-tank artillery reserves at their disposal, for which they prepared lines of deployment for conducting fire well before the battle started.

In order to repulse the enemy's massed tank blows and to increase the operational stability of the defense, the Kursk plans paid particular attention to the use of the Red Army's armored forces. Each *front* defending in the Kursk bulge received one tank army and two separate tank corps. The Voronezh Front acquired the 1st Tank Army under the command of Lieutenant General M. E. Katukov, the 2nd Guards 'Tatsinskaia' Tank Corps under the command of Major General A. S. Burdeiny, and the 5th Guards 'Stalingrad' Tank Corps under the command of Major General A. G. Kravchenko.

In addition, armies in the first echelon of defense received separate tank regiments and tank brigades for direct infantry support. Thus, the 6th Guards Army obtained two separate tank regiments, one mixed-composition self-propelled gun regiment, and one tank brigade. On 1 July, these units had a combined total of 168 tanks and self-propelled guns. The 7th Guards Army had 222 tanks and self-propelled guns under its operational control (see Table 2).

The tank forces of the *fronts* were echeloned in depth. A participant of the Kursk battle, at the time the commander of the 3rd Mechanized Brigade of the Third Mechanized Corps, A. Kh. Babadzhanian remembered:

> Separate regiments of self-propelled artillery and tank brigades comprised the first echelon. These were the mobile reserves for the army commanders, the commanders of the rifle corps and the divisions. Part of the tank regiments was used as anti-tank and defensive strongpoints, as well as to set up tank ambushes. Half of all the tanks, which the *front* had at its disposal, went into the first echelon.
>
> Tank armies and separate tank corps stood ready in the second echelon. They were positioned 30 to 50 kilometers behind the forward edge of the defenses and were designated to counterattack any breakthroughs by hostile groupings.
>
> The second, armor, echelon of the defense was the primary maneuvering shock element. With its help, the Soviet command counted upon changing and did change the course of the defensive battle in its favor.

Table 2: The Number and Types of Armor Equipping the Tank Brigades, and Tank and Self-propelled Artillery Regiments in the 6th and 7th Guards Armies, June 1943

Unit	BA-64	T-38	T-60	T-70	T-34	KV	Mk II Matilda	Mk III Valentine	M3 Stuart	M3 Lee	SU-76	SU-122	SU-152	Total
6th Guards Army (data for 1 June 1943)														
96 otbr[1]	-	1	3/8	5	44/8	-	-	-	-	-	-	-	-	53/16
230 tp	-	-	-	-	-	-	-	-	32	6/1	-	-	-	38/1
245 tp	-	-	-	-	-	-	-	-	12	26/1	-	-	-	38/1
1440 sap[2]	-	-	-	8/1	12	-	-	-	-	-	-	-	-	20/1
Total	-	1	3/8	13/1	56/8	-	-	-	44	32/2	-	-	-	149/19
% of total number of tanks		0.6	6.5	8.3	38.0				26.1	20.2				100%
7th Guards Army (data for 25 June 1943)[3]														
148 tp	3	-	1	11/2	33	-	-	-	-	-	-	-	-	45/2
167 tp	2	-	-	7	32	-	-	-	-	-	-	-	-	39
263 ttp	-	-	-	-	-	20/3	-	-	-	-	-	-	-	20/3
201 tbr	-	-	-	-	2/1	-	14/4	31	-	-	-	-	-	47/5
27 g. tbr	-	-	-	4	46/4	-	-	-	-	-	-	-	-	50/4
1438 sap	-/1	-	-/2	-/4	-	-	-	-	-	-	5/4	12	-	0/6, 17/4
1529 tsap	-	-	-	-	-	1	-	-	-	-	-	-	12	1, 12
Total	5/1	-	1/2	22/6	113/5	21/3	14/4	31	-	-	5/4	12	12	202/20, (29/4)
% of total number of tanks			1.3	12.6	53.1	10.8	8.1	13.9						100%

Note: Where applicable, the number to the left of the slash indicates the quantity of operational tanks, while the number to the right of it gives the number under repair.

Notes

Source: TsAMO RF, f. 203, op. 2851, d. 24, l. 51, 52, 299.

1 Editor's Note: Due to space constraints, I've had to employ the transliteration of the Russian unit acronyms: otbr – separate tank brigade; tbr – tank brigade; tp – tank regiment; sap – self-propelled artillery regiment; ttp – heavy tank regiment; tsap – heavy self-propelled artillery regiment.

2 By the start of the Kursk battle, the 1440th Self-propelled Artillery Regiment was fully equipped according to the table of a combined self-propelled artillery regiment, having received 21 SU-76 and SU-122 later in June.

3 The BA-64 armored cars were not included when computing the total number of tanks and self-propelled guns for the 7th Guards Army.

> I stress once again that the presence of such major formations as tank armies in the *fronts'* composition of forces was one of the decisive factors that made our defense insurmountable.
>
> The use of major formations and units of the armored forces while conducting a defensive operation to support the defensive belts in depth – the second and third defensive belts of the armies – was a new operational application of the tank forces, which sharply increased the stability of the operational defenses, and allowed us to repulse the massed attacks of enemy tanks, which attacked on narrow sectors of the front with groups of 200 to 300 armored vehicles.[3]

Engineers laced the elaborate system of fortifications with extensive minefields, closely tied in with the system of fire of all types, natural barriers to movement, and with other engineered obstacles. The experience of war had demonstrated that minefields in the depth of the defense were more effective than when laid out in front of the first or second defensive belts. If in front of the line of defenses it required 350-400 anti-tank mines on average to damage or destroy one tank, then in the depths of the defenses that number fell to 150-200 anti-tank mines. Such a difference is explained by the fact that mine emplacement in the depths of the defense occurred along lines of advance already revealed by the enemy. Along anticipated routes of advance suitable for tanks, the density of the minefield barriers for the first time in the war reached up to 1,400-1,600 mines per kilometer of front.

It is interesting that in addition to regular mines, the defenses made wide use of special crude, but highly effective incendiary high explosive mines. This type of mine was noteworthy for its simplicity in construction and deployment. It was nothing more than an ordinary wooden box filled with rows of half-liter incendiary bottles. The center bottle was removed, and replaced by a regular demolition charge or an anti-personnel mine with a blasting charge reduced to 100 grams. The engineers then propped up the box's lid with a small peg, so the box was not fully closed. They would place the box into a small hole in the ground, and then carefully camouflage the location. When someone stepped on or drove over the box, the peg would break and trigger the mine's explosive charge, which in turn would detonate the incendiary bottles. The resulting flames, fragments and shock wave effectively destroyed infantry and any vehicle within a 40-meter radius. The flames would reach 30 to 40 meters in height and then cascade downward upon targets in the area of effect.

A well-camouflaged minefield with these high-explosive incendiary devices was almost immune to mine clearing. They had a strong psychological influence on the enemy. As one captured member of the 11th Company of the 332nd Infantry Division's 676th Infantry Regiment, Private Rudolf Amstberg testified: "Sappers who took part in the offensive incurred heavy losses from exploding bottles, planted in the earth in beer cases."[4]

All commanders, from the regimental commander up to the *front* commander, had mixed-composition mobile obstacle detachments, whose job it was to mine the routes used by enemy tanks, and to destroy roads and bridges in order to delay the enemy.

Before the start of the Kursk offensive, one more NKO Order, No. 38, appeared on 24 June 1943. This order announced incentive payments for knocked-out hostile armor, which applied to the personnel of all artillery and tank units, and to members of anti-tank rifle units:

> With the aim of heightening the effectiveness of the struggle against enemy tanks, and to inspire the fighters and commanders for the combat task of destroying the enemy
>
> I hereby order:
>
> 1. The establishment of a bonus for each knocked-out or burned-out enemy tank caused by an anti-tank rifle team: to the team leader – 500 rubles, to his assistant – 250 rubles.
>
> 2. The establishment of a bonus for each member of a tank crew, which destroys an enemy tank: to the commander, driver-mechanic, and gunner or turret leader – 500 rubles each; to the remaining members of the crew – 200 rubles each.
>
> 3. The establishment of a bonus for each knocked-out tank by all types of artillery: to the gun commander and gun layer 500 rubles each; to the remaining members of the regular gun crew, 200 rubles each.
>
> 4. The establishment of a 1000 ruble bonus to each fighter and commander, who knocks out or burns out an enemy tank with the assistance of individual anti-tank weapons. If a group of tank hunters participates in the destruction of an enemy tank, then the sum of the bonus will increase to 1500 rubles, of which each participant will receive an equal share.
>
> 5. The Chief of the NKO's Financial Directorate will give instructions on the application of the given order.
>
> 6. The order becomes effective on 1 July 1943 and will be transmitted by telephone.[5]

The organization of the anti-aircraft defense received special attention. The multi-layered fire of anti-aircraft artillery, for the most part small caliber, covered more than 60% of the entire area occupied by the ground units. Even special air defense rifle units were organized to combat German air attacks. For this purpose, 2,380 heavy and light machine guns, and 2,169 anti-tank rifles were distributed among the troops of the Voronezh Front.[6]

Simultaneously with the improvement of the defenses, the troops of the Voronezh Front trained to defend themselves and to attack according to the plans for their units and formations. In order to eliminate so-called "tank fright", infantry rehearsed situations where they were overrun by their own tanks. They learned to conduct fire on the approaching tanks from the cover of their trenches, then after the tanks passed over their trenches, to resume fire on them from behind. Tank units trained to fire from dug-in positions, and rehearsed moving rapidly from these positions into attack formation and going on the attack in combination with the infantry and artillery.

The Soviet military-political leadership paid significant attention to the creation of reserves throughout the war. Accordingly, the *Stavka* took all necessary measures not only to strengthen the Central and Voronezh Fronts, but also to create a powerful strategic reserve in their rear. As early as 3 March, the *Stavka* had created a Reserve Front consisting of three armies and three tank corps. In April, two more regular armies and one tank army, and two tank and two mechanized corps, joined the Reserve Front. On

15 April the Reserve Front was renamed the Steppe Military District, which in turn became the Steppe Front on 9 July 1943. By 5 July, the Steppe Military District had on its roster the 4th Guards, 5th Guards, 27th, 47th and 53rd Armies, the 5th Guards Tank Army and the 5th Air Army, as well as three mechanized, three tank, and three cavalry corps.[7] These reserves would play a vital role in the conduct of the defensive operation and in the final results of the battle – the achievement of victory at the Battle of Kursk.

Of the formations in the Steppe Front, the 5th Guards Tank Army and 5th Guards Army would play the most active part in the engagement at Prokhorovka. I will now discuss the creation of these armies, the composition of their primary formations, and I will give short descriptions of the commanders, Lieutenant General P. A. Rotmistrov and Lieutenant General A. S. Zhadov, as well as other key commanders.

3

The 5th Guards Tank Army and its Commander, P. A. Rotmistrov

The experience of the 1942 winter campaign had demonstrated the need for powerful tank formations – tank armies – in order to resolve the tasks of the *fronts*, and moreover to execute strategic operations. Only tank armies possessed sufficient mobility, maneuverability, and great shock power to follow up tactical successes decisively and to expand the depth and breadth of operations.

The first tank armies began to organize back in May 1942. The stable growth in tank production by Soviet industry, which had resumed by that time, enabled the creation of such large tank formations.

Initially, the tank armies were of mixed composition: they were composed of three tank corps, a separate tank brigade, two rifle divisions, and other specialized units. However, the initial combat test of the tank army had already indicated the inadequacy of such a structure: they had been used in just the same way as the combined-arms armies. The tank armies were used to occupy positions in the first echelon of the *front*, which robbed them of maneuverability. On the attack, even if there was a breakthrough, the relatively immobile infantry units fettered the maneuvering of the tank corps and prevented the rapid exploitation of the initial success. The counteroffensive at Stalingrad, where the Red Army command first employed tank and mechanized corps to develop the initial breakthroughs, plainly demonstrated the inferiority of the mixed-composition tank army. However, despite the problems, the new tank armies had yielded a glittering success even in the difficult winter conditions of the operation.

The changes and improvements in German defenses, which had become noticeable by the end of 1942, also gave a nudge to the leadership of our armies to search for new ways of organizing the tank formations. In 1941-1942, the adversary had based his defenses on isolated strongpoints and focal points of resistance, constructed on the most important directions of advance, without building an elaborate system of trenches and major fortified works. This permitted our rifle units, bolstered by tanks in a direct infantry support role, to penetrate the enemy defense with relative ease. After Stalingrad, the German command went over primarily to a defense along the entire German-Soviet front. From this time until the end of the war, the Germans sought mainly to improve this form of defense. The Germans switched to continuous lines of entrenchments, deeply echeloned, with numerous minefields and fortifications. To break through these defenses required a new instrument.

The discussion of the organization of tank armies and the new structure for them occurred not only in the General Staff and the Main Auto-Armored Directorate of the Red Army. *Front* commands became extremely interested in this question as well. A variety of opinions were offered, often contradictory in their details. However, on one main point they were all in agreement: the tank armies should be the force for exploiting the *front's* initial successes, and thus they should have operational self-sufficiency. For this purpose, the tank army should have a homogenous composition and be freed of the non-motorized rifle formations, while the artillery units and the rear units needed greater mobility. This would permit the tank armies' wide maneuverability during deep penetrations into the enemy's rear, and would improve the handling of the entire formation.

At the end of January 1943, a meeting took place at the headquarters of the Southern Front. As P. A. Rotmistrov, who subsequently became Chief Marshal of the Armored Forces, later recalled:

> To discuss this question, I was invited to meet with the commander of the Southern Front, Colonel General R. Ia. Malinovsky, and with a member of the Military Council, Lieutenant General N. S. Khrushchev. I gave the tankers' opinion that it was necessary to organize and improve the mass employment of tanks, for which it was necessary to create tank armies of homogenous composition, and to reexamine their use on the battlefield. My views met with approval. At the conclusion of the meeting, N. S. Khrushchev said that he would call I. V. Stalin and ask him to consider my proposals for the creation of tank armies of a new type. Soon I traveled to Moscow with a report on the question of building up the 3rd Tank Corps, which I was commanding at the time, into a new-type tank army with additional men and material. Stalin received me and listened to me attentively. He then approved all my proposals. Several days later, the decision to create the 5th Guards Tank Army took place.[1]

This was not Rotmistrov's first meeting with the Supreme Commander. They first met in the first half of November 1942, when Stalin had summoned Rotmistrov, at the time the commander of the 7th Tank Corps, for a personal discussion. Stalin had taken an interest in this man. He recalled the name of the commander of one of the first Guards tank brigades, which had received this designation after successful combat in the harshest conditions of 1941. He liked that this frontline combat general worked to share his combat experiences (an article by P. A. Rotmistrov had been published in *Pravda* on 24 June 1942). The Supreme Commander knew as well about the favorable description given to this corps commander by the Main Auto-Armored Directorate: "Competent, he handles his formation with a firm grip, and is dedicated to the Party of Lenin and Stalin." Probably, Stalin personally liked this short, bespectacled tanker. Thus it was not an accident, when at the start of 1943 the question arose about who should command the Guards tank army of a new type, the final choice fell upon Rotmistrov.

By this time, Rotmistrov already had proven himself in combat in command of large tank formations, although he came to the tank service at a rather late age, when he was already 36. After graduating from the M. V. Frunze Military Academy in June 1931, he received assignment to the city of Chita as the Chief of Operations for the 36th 'Zabaikal'skii' Rifle Division. Within a short time, he had climbed to the relatively lofty position as Chief of Operations for the Special Red Banner Far Eastern Army, commanded by V. K. Bliukher. In June 1937, in order to gain command experience, Pavel Alekseevich received assignment as commander of the 63rd Red Banner Frunze Regiment of the twice Red Banner 21st Maritime 'S. S. Kamenev' Rifle Division.

During the years of Stalin's unjustified repressions in the Soviet Union, the young, ambitious officer was accused of associating with "enemies of the people". Rotmistrov was dropped from the Party's membership rolls and even subjected to arrest. However, he never lost hope, and wrote a letter to the Party Central Committee, in which he expressed his disagreement with this decision. A short time later, they summoned him to Moscow, where the Party Control Commission reexamined his personnel file and readmitted him to the Party.

However, this episode unquestionably had an adverse effect on his career – such were those times. Despite this highest Party reaffirmation of his reputation and status, in January 1938 Rotmistrov was demoted, and became a tactics instructor at the I. V. Stalin Military Academy of Motorization and Mechanization. Within a year, P. A. Rotmistrov defended his dissertation and obtained the degree of Candidate of Military Sciences.

In November 1939, the war with Finland began. So there was nothing surprising when the academy professor turned in a formal request for transfer to one of the combat units. He received the appointment to command a battalion in the 34th Light Tank Brigade on the Kola Peninsula, but a short time later he became the brigade's chief of staff. For successful combat operations in this "Winter War", the brigade earned the Order of the Red Banner, while Pavel Alekseevich received the Order of the Red Star. This was actually his second combat decoration. His first, the Order of the Combat Red

Commander of the 5th Guards Tank Army Lieutenant General P. A. Rotmistrov (center) studies a map of the operational situation brought to him by a staff aide. On the left is N. S. Khrushchev. Photo taken in the area of Prokhorovka Station, 12 July 1943. (Author's personal archive)

Banner, came for the courage he had demonstrated in the storming of Fort No. 6 during the suppression of the Kronstadt Mutiny in 1921.

In December 1940, Lieutenant Colonel P. A. Rotmistrov became the deputy commander of the 3rd Motorized Corps' 5th Tank Division in the Baltic Special Military District. Since the division commander was away studying in Moscow, during his prolonged absence Rotmistrov carried out the duties of the division commander.

At the beginning of 1941, the leadership of the Red Army decided to resurrect the tank and mechanized corps. Each of these formations was to have more than 1,000 armored vehicles under its control. The deployment of these major formations required the preparation of a large number of officers. At that time, there were not many officers with combat experience. Accordingly, having not spent even six full months in the 5th Tank Division, Lieutenant Colonel (as of July 1941, Colonel) P. A. Rotmistrov received a new appointment, and became the 3rd Mechanized Corps' chief of staff.

From the first days of Germany's attack on the Soviet Union, the 3rd Mechanized Corps had to experience the hardships and bitterness of retreat and losses. At the war's outbreak, the 3rd Mechanized Corps was located in Lithuania, in the vicinity of the cities Kaunas and Alitus. It was equipped with only light tanks. Already by the fifth day of the war, the Germans had surrounded the Corps' administrative offices and the headquarters of the 2nd Tank Division. Rotmistrov together with a group of officers and soldiers spent more than two months making their way out of encirclement through the forests of Lithuania, Belorussia, and the Briansk region. As Pavel Alekseevich later recalled, these were his most difficult days of the entire war.

After successfully reentering the Soviet frontline, the entire group, but especially the senior officer staff, underwent severe interrogation by the organs of military counterintelligence. At those times this was a quite serious matter, but Rotmistrov managed to pass through the ordeal relatively quickly. It was in their favor that the group had managed to escape encirclement together with their weapons and documents. It is probable that Rotmistrov's old friendship with the deputy chief of the Red Army's Main Auto-Armored Directorate, Lieutenant General Ia. N. Fedorenko, also played a significant role in his escape from under a cloud of suspicion. At that time, Fedorenko offered Rotmistrov the position of chief of staff to the Directorate, but in the words of Pavel Alekseevich, he turned down the offer and requested to be returned to the front.

On 23 September 1941, Colonel P. A. Rotmistrov took command of the 8th Tank Brigade of the Northwestern Front's 11th Army, which was then forming up at Valdai (120 kilometers northwest of Moscow). This formation became a genuine school of combat experience and the art of command for the future army commander. The warriors of the 8th Tank Brigade performed well along the Kalinin axis of operations, where the chief of staff of the Northwestern Front, N. F. Vatutin, had created an operational group under his command. It was near Kalinin in September 1941 where Rotmistrov's acquaintanceship with Vatutin began.

There followed the battle for Moscow. The steadfastness and courage demonstrated by the men of the 8th Tank Brigade in the fighting for Moscow was recognized on 11 January 1942, when the unit was renamed the 3rd Guards Tank Brigade, while the brigade commander himself received the Order of Lenin. The distinguished record of the 8th Tank Brigade in such a critical battle, as the Battle of Moscow was, gave a major boost to Rotmistrov's career, when the NKO assigned him to command the 7th Tank Corps, which was organized in March 1942 around the 3rd Guards Tank Brigade.

Already at the end of June, in connection with the enemy's breakthrough in the region of Ostrogozhsk and the threatened capture of Voronezh, the *Stavka* rushed the 7th Tank Corps by rail to the region of Elets and placed it under the command of General A. I. Liziukov's 5th Tank Army. That army was to launch a counterattack upon the enemy's panzer group, which was threatening Voronezh. However, because of the clumsy and hasty organization of the counterattack, it did not achieve its aim. Three well-equipped and fully-staffed tank corps were committed into the battle piecemeal over the span of two days, and failed to halt the enemy drive on Voronezh.

Because of this costly failure, the *Stavka* removed General F. I. Golikov from command of the Briansk Front, and the General Staff itself took control of the operation. It was while his 7th Tank Corps was unloading in Elets that Rotmistrov became acquainted with the chief of the General Staff of the Red Army, Colonel General A. M. Vasilevsky, who had arrived so as to give the order that placed the 7th Tank Corps under the 5th Tank Army in person. It was an auspicious meeting for Rotmistrov, and afterward the two men met frequently. On New Year's Eve 1943, the chief of the General Staff visited Rotmistrov to congratulate him upon the successful completion of the Kotel'nikovo operation. The acquaintanceship served Rotmistrov well, for according to Rotmistrov himself it was Vasilevsky who would step in to defend him in July 1943 against Stalin's wrath over the heavy losses of Rotmistrov's 5th Guards Tank Army at Prokhorovka.

In hard fighting on the Voronezh, and then later the Stalingrad directions in the summer of 1942, Colonel P. A. Rotmistrov, just as in the summer of 1941, had to taste the bitterness of defeat. Once again, he clashed with the punitive organs and felt the chill of distrust. At the beginning of September 1942, the 7th Tank Corps, now as part of the Stalingrad Front's 1st Guards Army, was participating in a counterattack upon the German armies that had broken through to the Volga River, and was trying to reestablish connections with the 62nd Army, which had been cut off in Stalingrad. The situation was becoming critical, and it had become extremely important to try to divert German forces from Stalingrad to relieve the pressure on the defenders there. The *Stavka* was prodding the *front* command to act quickly. Therefore the attack began without sufficient preparation, and the attacking Soviet forces lacked air cover; the 1st Guards Army did not have even a single anti-aircraft regiment. As Rotmistrov later recalled, "We suffered heavy losses, especially in T-60 and T-70 tanks, which had light armor. It was calculated that just in the course of one day, the enemy air force conducted up to 2,000 sorties against us ...In this fighting, we lost 156 of the 191 tanks that we had at the start of the combat operations near Stalingrad."[2]

The failure to breakthrough to the 62nd Army and the extremely heavy losses placed Rotmistrov once again under the unwelcome scrutiny of the punitive organs. The NKVD [People's Commission of Internal Affairs] sent the following dispatch to the State Defense Committee and the General Staff:

> The NKVD of the USSR is dispatching a report from the Stalingrad Front's Special Department:

Personnel and Equipment	Soviet Tank Corps	German Panzer Division	Ratio, Tank Corps to Panzer Division
Personnel	7,800	16,932	0.46
Field Artillery	24	58	0.41
Mortars	52	54	0.96
Anti-tank Guns	12	101	0.12
Anti-aircraft Guns	20	63	0.32
Tanks and assault guns	168	200	0.84
Trucks and cars	871	2,147	0.41

Source: *Voenno-istoricheskii zhurnal,* No. 3, 1995.

Table 3. Comparative TO&E Strength in Personnel and Equipment between a Soviet Tank Corps and a German Panzer Division, 1 January 1943

> Over the last three days, the 1st Guards Army and the 24th Army have tried unsuccessfully and with great losses to break through the enemy's line of defense and linkup with the Stalingrad forces.
>
> An investigation has established that the gap between our northern and southern forces was not 1-2 kilometers, as previously indicated, but up to 8 kilometers.
>
> In the last three days, despite a number of orders from *Front* headquarters about the offensive … leading workers in the headquarters do not believe in the practicability of their very own orders, and think that the troops in their present condition cannot break through the enemy's defenses.
>
> For example, the *Front*'s deputy chief of operations Lieutenant Colonel Kramar declared: 'I don't believe in the feasibility of the order.'
>
> Losses are heavy in the divisions of the 1st Guards Army. The 7th Tank Corps, committed to battle on 7 September with 180 tanks, suffered great losses, and today has only 15 vehicles. The materials of the investigation, testifying to the fault of the commander of this corps Major General ROTMISTROV, have been submitted to the office of comrade Malenkov.[3]

The Special Department report resulted in an investigative commission, headed by G. M. Malenkov. The commission recognized that the 7th Tank Corps had failed in its assigned mission, and at the same time it had suffered very large losses. However, the commission's practical conclusions, as often happened after such investigations, were never followed up. The *Stavka* and the General Staff considered the complexity of the situation, in which the command of the attacking forces had found itself, and assumed part of the responsibility for the failure. This saved the future of the first Marshal of the Red Army's Armored Forces, but added to Rotmistrov's gray hairs.

In reality, Rotmistrov's golden hour struck during the successful November Stalingrad counteroffensive. After encircling von Paulus's Sixth Army and the enemy's Fourth Panzer Army, the forces of the Stalingrad and Southwestern Fronts went on a decisive offensive, in order to give the Germans no possibility to free their encircled group. Between 12 and 30 December 1942, the forces of the Stalingrad Front conducted a successful operation aimed at the destruction of the hostile Kotel'nikovo grouping. The tank and mechanized corps played an important role in developing the offensive on this axis of advance into the operational depth of the enemy's defenses. Hard, bloody fighting for the possession of the well-fortified railway station and village of 'Kotel'nikovskii' (today the city of Kotel'nikovo) continued for forty-eight hours. Rotmistrov's corps played the primary role in the battle. At the concluding phase of this operation, at 4:00 P.M. on 28 December, part of his force – the 87th Tank and 7th Motorized Rifle Brigades – managed to overrun the German airfield located a kilometer from the village. The attack was so impetuous that the enemy was unable to offer serious resistance. German airplanes, returning from missions, continued to land at the now Soviet-controlled airfield. The troops of the corps distinguished themselves in these battles, so on 29 December the formation was renamed as the 3rd Guards Tank Corps, to which was attached the honorific title "Kotel'nikovskii".

The bold advance of units from the 7th Tank Corps to the village of 'Kotel'nikovskii' demonstrated how the generalship of Major General P.A. Rotmistrov had matured. His strong performance in this operation earned Rotmistrov a promotion to Lieutenant General of Tank Troops, the Order of Suvorov 2nd Degree, and command of the first tank formation of homogenous composition – the 5th Guards Tank Army.

On 27 January 1943, the NKO Decree No. 2799 authorized the formation of tank armies of homogenous composition. This document completed the nearly year-long process of creating formations that would have three primary qualities: powerful armament, mobility, and the ability to combat the enemy's anti-tank resources.

Personnel and Equipment	Soviet Mechanized Corps	German Panzergrenadier Division	Ratio, Mechanized Corps to Panzergrenadier Division
Personnel	15,018	16,932	0.89
Field Artillery	36	58	0.62
Mortars	148	54	2.74
Anti-tank Guns	36	101	0.36
Anti-aircraft Guns	36	63	0.57
Tanks and assault guns	204	200	1.02
Trucks and cars	1,693	2,147	0.41

Source: *Voenno-istoricheskii zhurnal*, No. 3, 1995.

Table 4. Comparative TO&E Strength in Personnel and Equipment between a Soviet Mechanized Corps and a German Panzergrenadier Division, 1 January 1943

According to the decree, a tank army should include: two tank and one mechanized corps, one motorcycle regiment, one anti-aircraft artillery battalion, one destroyer anti-tank artillery regiment, one howitzer artillery regiment, and one Guards mortar regiment (equipped with *Katiusha* rocket launchers); as well as support units (a signals regiment, an aviation signals regiment, an engineer battalion); rear service units and facilities (an automobile regiment; two recovery-repair battalions; medical, rations, and field train facilities; units for gathering, processing, and evacuating captured items; fuel and oil units; artillery supply; signaling and chemical facilities), and others. The total number of officers and troops in a tank army should comprise approximately 46,000 people, and it should have 648 to 654 tanks.

The tank corps consisted of a corps headquarters, three tank and one motorized rifle brigades; mortar, anti-aircraft artillery and destroyer anti-tank regiments; and reconnaissance, sapper and signal battalions. Certain corps used separate armored car battalions and an element of U-2 biplanes for reconnaissance purposes. The tank corps also included rear and technical service units.

Altogether, the tank corps in the second half of 1942 according to its Table of Organization and Equipment (TO&E) had 7,800 officers and troops, 168 tanks, 52 guns (including 20 anti-aircraft guns), 44 mortars, and 8 rocket artillery vehicles. Future evolution in the organization of the tank corps all aimed at increasing its self-sufficiency, striking force and firepower.

Comparing the number of men, vehicles and weapons of the Soviet tank corps to the German panzer division (see Table 3), we'll note that the Soviet tank corps was inferior in men by 2.2 times, in field artillery by 2.4 times, and in tanks by 1.2 times. However, the number of anti-tank guns in the German panzer division exceeded the number of such guns in the tank corps by 8.4 times (101 guns to just 12)! This was an important difference.

The tank brigade, after its strengthening in January 1943, was to have according to TO&E 1,058 men and 53 tanks (32 T-34 and 21 T-70). It consisted of a headquarters company; two tank and one motorized rifle-machine gun battalions; a battery of anti-tank guns (four 76mm guns); a mortar company (six 82mm mortars) and an anti-aircraft machine gun company (nine DShK heavy machine guns); an anti-tank rifle company; a maintenance company; a medical sanitation platoon; and a Special (counterintelligence) Department.

The motorized rifle brigade had no special configuration and was structured just like a regular rifle brigade. It included three motorized rifle battalions and one mortar battalion, an artillery battalion, a headquarters company; companies of submachine gunners, anti-tank riflemen, anti-aircraft machine gunners, engineers, and reconnaissance troops; a medical sanitation platoon, a captured goods department, and a Special Department. A motorized rifle brigade numbered a total of 3,281 officers and troops.

A mechanized corps was distinguished from a tank corps only by its greater number of motorized infantry. This increased its self-sufficiency both on the attack and when on the defense. Motorized infantry were necessary not only to support the attacking tank units, but even more so for holding on to the ground seized by the tanks. Accordingly, mechanized brigades formed the basis of the mechanized corps formation. By norm, they were formed of motorized rifle brigades, with the inclusion in each of a tank regiment consisting of four tank companies and, as a rule, 39 tanks. In addition, in order to strengthen it, each mechanized corps received one separate tank brigade, which consisted of three tank and one motorized rifle battalions and had 65 tanks.

It should be noted that a Red Army mechanized corps on 1 January 1943 was significantly superior in strength to a German motorized division and was approximately equal to a *Wehrmacht* panzer division, but significantly yielded to them both in anti-tank gun strength (36 guns against 73 in the case of the motorized division, and 36 against 101 guns in the case of the panzer division; see Table 4)

As the former commander of the 2nd Guards Tank Army, General A. I. Radzievsky observed:

> Tank and mechanized corps, acting as operational-tactical formations, could independently accomplish a variety of combat tasks. … They could exploit success into the operational depth, pursue a retreating foe, seize important lines and objectives, attack a hastily-defended position, and engage the enemy's tank and motorized formations. When strengthened with rifle formations, howitzer and heavy artillery, heavy tanks and engineer units, they were additionally capable of breaking through the enemy's prepared field fortifications and defenses. Taking into consideration the intensity of combat, the availability of fuel and ammunition, and the character of the operations, these corps could advance constantly for five or six days at a pace of 50 to 60 kilometers a day or even more, and find themselves 30 or 40 kilometers ahead of the army's main forces.[4]

Thus, the beginning of 1943 marked a key moment in the development of the Red Army's tank and mechanized forces.

The date of origin for the 5th Guards Tank Army can be considered 22 February 1943. On this day, the NKO issued a directive authorizing the formation of two Guards tank armies, the 5th Guards Tank Army and the 3rd Guards Tank Army. The directive specified that the 5th Guards Tank Army was to form in vicinity of Millerovo and be ready for combat operations by 25 March 1943. It was to consist of the 3rd Guards 'Kotel'nikovskii' Tank Corps, the 29th Tank Corps, and the 5th Guards Mechanized Corps.

In order to increase the mobility of the new tank armies, they were reduced in size by 15-20% in comparison with tank armies of mixed composition, primarily by excluding the rifle formations. Nevertheless, by the time of the Prokhorovka battle, the 5th Guards Tank Army numbered more than 41,000 officers and troops.

Since the 5th Guards Army was organized around the 3rd Guards 'Kotel'nikovskii' Tank Corps, it was primarily the officers and generals of this corps that filled the leadership positions on the Army's staff. Moreover, they all knew they had the personal trust of the army commander – after all, he had gone through two hard years of war together with them. Thus, the former deputy commander of the 3rd Guards 'Kotel'nikovskii' Tank Corps for engineering, Engineer Colonel S. A. Solovoi, became the Chief of Armor Supply and Maintenance in the new tank army – a very important position and a real "hot seat".

On 21 March 1943, the chief of staff of this corps, 34-year-old Colonel Vladimir Nikolaevich Baskakov, became the chief of staff of the new army. He had been called into the Red Army in 1931, under a special mobilization ordered by the Party Central

Committee, from his first year at the Nizhegorod Machine Building Institute. After graduating from the Saratov Armor School in 1932, he served as an instructor, the commander of a tank platoon, and then tank company commander in the K. B. Malinovsky Mechanized Brigade. In November 1935, from his post as tank battalion commander in the 13th Mechanized Brigade, he entered the I. V. Stalin Military Academy of Motorization and Mechanization. After graduating from it in May 1941, Captain V. N. Baskakov received an assignment to the Kiev Special Military District, as the commander of a battalion of medium tanks in the 8th Tank Division's 15th Tank Regiment.

From the beginning of the Great Patriotic War, Captain Baskakov participated in the border battles as part of this regiment, and distinguished himself while leading a counterattack in the area of Berdichev. In July 1941, Baskakov took command of the 15th Tank Regiment. As part of Colonel E. G. Pushkin's 8th Tank Division, Baskakov's regiment conducted heavy defensive fighting in the area of Uman'. In August, the division as part of the Southern Front defended Dnepropetrovsk, and in September resisted the onslaught of Army Group South in the vicinity of Pavlograd. On 23 September 1941, Baskakov was promoted to command of the 130th Tank Brigade of the Southern Front's 8th Tank Division. The Brigade distinguished itself in the Barvenkovo-Lozovsk offensive operation. Dating from 15 February 1942, he became commander of the 62nd Tank Brigade, which entered the roster of the 7th Tank Corps that was then forming up.[5] It was from this time that military fate brought Vladimir Nikolaevich Baskakov and Pavel Alekseevich Rotmistrov together for the next two years.

In the 7th Tank Corps' very first battle, attempting to sever the lines of communication of the enemy columns rushing toward the Don River, Lieutenant Colonel Baskakov's brigade distinguished itself. By July 1942, Baskakov was now the 7th Tank Corps' chief of staff. However, one of the Corps' first major operations, in which Baskakov participated in his new role, was the failed, costly operation to break through to the bleeding units of General V. I. Chuikov's 62nd Army in Stalingrad. Together with the 7th Tank Corps, Baskakov experienced the painful retreat to the Volga and the Don, and later planned the breakthrough and liberation of the village 'Kotel'nikovskii'.

Baskakov's rapid career rise, from brigade commander to the chief of staff of a corps, to finally army chief of staff and the rank of major general, testifies to his superior commander's satisfaction with his combat work. Probably, a relationship of mutual understanding and respect had developed between Rotmistrov and Baskakov. Harmonious work between an army commander and his chief of staff is always important to the stable and productive work of a formation's headquarters. Analyzing Rotmistrov's and Baskakov's joint work, one can say with confidence that their cordial relationship in those difficult times was fruitful. Of course, it must be acknowledged that it was not easy for Baskakov to maintain an independent stance in such relationships.

Despite the fact that almost all the primary positions in the new 5th Guards Tank Army's leadership had been filled by this time by senior officers and generals, the "settling in" of the command continued until June. Major General I. A. Pliev had been appointed as the first deputy commander of the army. However, on 9 May 1943, he transferred to the position of deputy commander of the Steppe Military District's cavalry.

The 41-year-old Major General K.G. Trufanov replaced Pliev as the army's deputy commander. Kuz'ma Grigor'evich was born in Voronezh Oblast. In 1918 he entered

Units	Personnel	T-34	T-70	BA-64	Mortars		37mm AA guns	25mm guns	DShK Heavy MG	122mm howitzers	45mm AT guns	Anti-tank rifles	Submachine guns	Rifles	Machine Guns		Radios	Vehicles				Tractors
					82mm	120mm									Light	Heavy		Motor	Lend-lease	BA-10 armored car	Motorcycles	
Corps Headquarters	209												35	124	1							
363 Sep Signals Battalion	252	3		10									100	73			14	55	8			
193 Sep Sapper Battalion	399												88	309	2			27				
31 Fuel and Oil Supply Co.	107												8	90				50	1			
188 Med-Sanitation Platoon	41													5				3				
157 Mobile Field Bakery	69												1	37	1			7	1			
Total	1077	3		10									232	638	4		14	142	10			
25 Tank Brigade	1119	32	39	3	6		3		1		4	19	324	453	21	4	11	96	6		14	1
31 Tank Brigade	1072	32	39	3	6		2		2		4	18	314	413	21	4	9	91	24		6	2
32 Tank Brigade[1]	1193	64		3	6			3			4	24	441	459	28	4	8	99	5		12	3
53 Motorized Rifle Brigade	3031			17	30	6			12		12	81	1253	1184	109	45	30	281	1		11	
1446 Assault Gun Regiment	266									9/12			114	111			7	26	3			
38 Sep Armored Car Btn	131		7	10									9	16			14	13		12	3	
Total, Tank Forces:	6812	128	85	36	48	6	5	3	15	9/12	24	142	2455	2636	183	57	79	606	39	12	46	6
108 Anti-tank Regiment	268										8		32	193	5		2	11	27			
271 Sep Mortar Regiment	783					36						36	83	583	17		16	32	44			
169 Repair Base (tanks)	71												10	38	2			15			1	1
272 Repair Base (vehicles)	68								1				6	40	2			11				
Aerial Signals	10												3	4								
Total for Corps:	9089	131	85	46	48	42	5	3	16	9/12	32	178	2821	4132	209	57	111	817	120	12	47	7

Table 5. Personnel and equipment in the 5th Guards Tank Army's 29th Tank Corps for 9 July 1943

Source: TsAMO RF, f. 29 tk, op. 1, d. 36, l. 28.

Notes

1 In addition to the indicated tanks, the 32nd Tank Brigade also had 1 KV-1 tank and 1 captured Pz-38(t).

the ranks of the Red Army, and participated in the fighting against Denikin's forces and Nestor Makhno's partisan bands. As part of M. S. Budenny's 1st Mounted Army, Trufanov took part in the Soviet-Polish War in 1920. After the conclusion of the Russian Civil War, he continued to serve in the cavalry, advancing from platoon commander to command of a squadron of cavalry cadets in the Tver' Cavalry School. From 1935, he commanded a reconnaissance battalion, and then served as an inspector of the cavalry forces of the RKKA [Workers' and Peasants' Red Army]. He participated in the battles in the region of Lake Khasan in 1938. In June 1940, Trufanov accepted the post of commander of the 7th Tank Corps' 9th Motorcycle Regiment. He participated in combat operations from the very first days of the war, but Kuz'ma Grigor'evich didn't manage to fight long in 1941. In July while serving with the Western Front, he received a serious wound.

After his recovery in a hospital, Trufanov was appointed chief of the new Tashkent Cavalry School: he formed it, organized the training process, and oversaw the preparation of cavalry officers. In March 1943, Major General K. G. Trufanov was transferred to the 5th Guards Tank Army. He would command the Army's forward detachment as it moved out for the area of Prokhorovka Station in July 1943.

Major General P. G. Grishin was appointed member of the 5th Guards Tank Army's Military Council. Petr Grigor'evich was born in 1906 in Tula Oblast. He was at the front from the first months of the war. In the autumn of 1941 as commissar of the 108th Tank Division, he took part in the defense of Tula. He came to the 5th Guards Tank Army from his position as deputy commander for political affairs for the 1st Tank Army's 6th Tank Corps.

On 6 March 1943, in connection with the Red Army's failure at Khar'kov, the 3rd Guards Tank Corps under the command of Major General I. A. Bobchenko was removed from the roster of the 5th Guards Tank Army and transferred to the Voronezh Front. Thus, only two corps remained as part of the Army – the 29th Tank Corps and the 5th Guards Mechanized Corps.

As P. A. Rotmistrov later recalled about this situation:

> It must be said that these two corps were different in strength, combat experience, and combat potential. The 5th Guards Mechanized Corps … had proven itself in the Stalingrad fighting, especially at Zimovniki, Tsimlianskaia, in the area between the Rivers Don and Volga. However, after hard fighting in the region of Rostov, the Corps was short 2,000 officers and soldiers, and 204 tanks. I had to restore the combat power of the formation in a very short time, and train the new replacements using the experience of past battles, in completely different combat conditions.[6]

I will now discuss the commanders and primary combat units of these two corps of the 5th Guards Tank Army.

The 29th Tank Corps

The 29th Tank Corps was organized in February 1943 at an armor-training center near the city Naro-Fominsk. It had under its operational control the 25th, 31st, and 32nd Tank Brigades and the 53rd Motorized Rifle Brigade, as well as an assortment of specialized units under corps control. The strength and combat composition of the 29th Tank Corps as of 9 July 1943 are shown in Table 5.

Major General F. G. Anikushkin was the first commander of the 29th Tank Corps; his chief of staff was Colonel E. I. Fominykh. It was intended for the 29th Tank Corps to be the larger and more powerful of the two corps remaining in the 5th Guards Tank Army. All of its brigades had two tank battalions, one medium and one light (each with three tank companies), both of which were equipped with more tanks than the authorized strength of 31 vehicles. Thus, the 25th and 31st Tank Brigades each had 32 medium T-34 tanks and 39 light T-70 tanks, while the 32nd Tank Brigade, as the designated shock formation, had two medium tank battalions (of three tank companies each) totaling 65 T-34 tanks.

One of the main problems confronting the 29th Tank Corps command immediately after the corps' assembly in Voronezh Oblast was the fact that all of its constituent tank brigades had previously operated independently, primarily as direct infantry support formations. As Rotmistrov wrote:

> The corps commander and his staff had to mold the brigades into a single combat organism, capable of operating boldly and decisively in the operational depth after a breakthrough, but most importantly, capable of launching concentrated tank blows on the enemy's tank formations in meeting engagements and attack operations. To solve these tasks, it was not only necessary to change the tactical approaches to using the tanks in battle, but also to prepare the personnel of the brigades psychologically for new forms of battle.[7]

By 17 March 1943, 29th Tank Corps headquarters and part of its combat formations had completed a move by rail to the city of Ostrogozhsk (90 kilometers south of Voronezh). But even before the corps had begun moving out, on 2 March 1943 Major General I. F. Kirichenko had replaced Major General Anikushkin in command of the 29th Tank Corps.

Ivan Fedorovich Kirichenko was born in Kiev Oblast in 1902 to a peasant family. He took part in the Russian Civil War. Like many other Red Army commanders of his generation, he did not manage to complete his primary education. The only specialized military education that he completed before the war with Germany (other than some previous evening vocational schooling and a short series of military political classes) was a set of courses at the Leningrad Armor School in 1932.

After completing these courses, he was sent to the Ukraine to the Kiev Military District. Between March and October 1937, he carried out the duties of chief of staff of a separate tank battalion of the 44th Rifle Division, and then from December 1937 to 30 January 1938, he was in command of the same battalion.

In March 1938, Major I. F. Kirichenko was sent to Mongolia as a military adviser, where he served as an instructor of tank forces. He was stationed in the cities of Ulan-Bator and Tamnyk-Balane. Between February and September 1939, Kirichenko participated in the battles at Nomonhan and at the Khalkin-Gol River. For his successful fulfillment of orders during the course of the fighting with the Japanese, Kirichenko received the Order of the Red Banner from the Mongolian People's Republic.

In May 1940, Kirichenko's mission to Mongolia concluded. A month later, he received a promotion and traveled to Kishinev to serve as deputy commander of the 11th Tank Division's 22nd Tank Regiment. He served in the acting army from the first days of the war with Germany. From 26 June until the end of September 1941, his regiment conducted hard defensive fighting on the Southern Front's sector (in the region of Khristinovka and Uman'). His superior officers took notice of his tenacity and ability to make correct decisions in difficult situations.

Accordingly, by 29 September 1941, Kirichenko had earned promotion to brigade commander, and took control of the 9th Separate Tank Brigade. In this position, he particularly distinguished himself in the fighting for Moscow. Testimonial records from this period point to "a serious, seasoned, disciplined officer, who is demanding both on himself and on his subordinates." At the same time, however, there was mention of a certain indecisiveness and "timidity" in battle; that is, a lack of necessary boldness in certain situations. Subsequently, higher command would more than once point to these negative qualities of Ivan Fedorovich as a commander, as well as his tendency to underestimate the adversary. Nevertheless, as part of the Western Front, Kirichenko's brigade successfully routed the enemy, with particularly positive results in the region of Mezen' and Maloiaroslavets. I. V. Stalin himself took note of this. For successful operations in the course of the defense of the capital, in February 1942 Kirichenko's formation, the second among the tank forces of the Red Army after Katukov's renowned brigade, was awarded the title "Guards", while the brigade commander himself earned the Order of Lenin and received a promotion to lieutenant colonel.

From December 1942 until March 1943, Kirichenko, now as a colonel and the deputy commander of the 2nd Mechanized Corps, participated in the repulse of von Manstein's attempts to free the trapped Sixth Army in Stalingrad, engaging and defeating German groupings in the region of Manych, Staro-Cherkasskaia, and Tormosin. In March 1943, Kirichenko was awarded with a leadership post, and took command of a major combat formation – the 29th Tank Corps. It was fated for this formation to receive its baptism of fire at Prokhorovka, where in the course of a few hours it would be almost fully consumed in the famous counterattack of 12 July 1943. Despite the fact that it failed in its mission there and suffered very heavy losses in troops and tanks, the command of the 5th Guards Tank Army considered Kirichenko's actions successful. In a testimonial in the fall of 1943, the Army's Military Council noted:

> During the enemy's summer 1943 offensive, as commander of the 29th Tank Corps, [he] received the major blow of the enemy's attacking mechanized-tank group, numbering up to 700 tanks, and together with other units stopped it, after which he went on the attack.
>
> In the Belgorod operation of 1943, attacking in the first echelon of the 5th [Guards] Tank Army, he managed successfully to organize the introduction of his tank corps into the breakthrough. As a result of his skillful actions, the enemy's reserve forces were crushed. Subsequently, the 29th Tank Corps under Kirichenko's leadership operated successfully in the Khar'kov offensive operation of our forces.

The reason for such a flattering review, which in all honesty was not fully objective, lay in the fact that the Army leadership was itself forced to defend its performance after the serious miscalculations that the Voronezh Front leadership and the General Staff had made while organizing the *Stavka* Reserve's commitment into the Prokhorovka fighting, which had resulted in such tragic consequences. The commander of the neighboring formation, B. S. Bakharov, was made the scapegoat in this difficult situation, but that story will come later.

In the middle of 1944, Major General Kirichenko became deputy commander of the 5th Guards Tank Army, and from February 1945 on, he commanded the 9th Tank Corps. For his skillful leadership of this corps and his personal display of courage in the Vistula-Oder operation, on 6 April 1945 Kirichenko was awarded the title "Hero of the Soviet Union".

After the war, Ivan Fedorovich would complete the primary course of the Voroshilov Military Academy and take command first of the armored forces of the Northern Group of Forces, and then those of the Moscow Military District. In 1956, Lieutenant General Kirichenko traveled to China as an advisor to the commander of the Chinese People's Liberation Army. He retired in 1964. The general passed away in Moscow in 1981.

In March 1943, the chief of staff of the 29th Tank Corps was the 36-year-old Colonel E. I. Fominykh. He was a trained staff officer (he had taught tactics in the 2nd Khar'kov Tank School) with combat experience. Between 1941 and 1943, he had commanded a tank battalion and tank regiment in the acting army, and then became the chief of staff of a tank brigade. He also served for a time as the senior assistant to a tank corps' chief of operations. Moreover, Evgenii Ivanovich had fine qualities as a commander. Therefore it was not coincidental that it was Fominykh who took command of the 29th Tank Corps when Kirichenko was summoned to Moscow, and in December 1944, he was transferred to an equivalent position in the 25th Tank Corps. His formation fought successfully in the Sandomir-Silesian, Lower Silesian, and Berlin offensives. For successfully carrying out the duties of command during the fighting for Berlin, Major E. I. Fominykh was awarded the title "Hero of the Soviet Union".

As previously noted, the 29th Tank Corps had four primary combat formations under its command: the 25th Tank Brigade, the 31st Tank Brigade, the 32nd Tank Brigade, and the 53rd Motorized Rifle Brigade. I will now briefly discuss the leadership and combat record of each of these units.

The **25th Tank Brigade** formed up between 1 October and 20 October 1942 in the city of Novoe-Sormovo in Gor'kii Oblast. It then became part of the Western Front, and sent to the region of Istra, where it became part of the 16th Army's 7th Motorized Rifle Division. Between 24 October and 18 December, the brigade fought along the Solnechnogorsk axis near Moscow. On 26 December 1942, it relocated to Voronezh Oblast near the town of Shubnoe, where it passed to the control of the Reserve Front. On 28 February 1943, it became part of the 29th Tank Corps of the Fifth Tank Army. Between 8 September 1942 and 28 September 1943, the 33-year-old Colonel Nikolai Konstantinovich Volodin commanded the brigade. Before this, he had held the position of chief of engineer services in the 34th Motorized Rifle Brigade.

N. K. Volodin was one of the youngest tank brigade commanders in the army. However, he had good professional training – in 1940, he graduated from the I.V. Stalin Military Academy of Motorization and Mechanization. Major Mikhail Fedorovich Mashkov was the 25th Tank Brigade's chief of staff between 14 December 1942 and 24 March 1944.

The **31st Tank Brigade** first organized as part of the Southwestern Front on 3 September 1941 as the 1st Separate Tank Brigade. However, by 2 November, having come under control of the *Stavka,* it received a new designation as the 31st Tank Brigade. Several days later, on the overcast morning of 7 November 1941, the honor fell to its officers and men to participate in the famous parade on Red Square, which demonstrated to the entire world the courage and determination of the Soviet people to defend their country. The next day, 8 November, the 31st Tank Brigade transferred to the control of the commander of the 1st Cavalry Corps, General P. A. Belov. After five days of defensive fighting, the brigade, having completed a 270-kilometer march to the region of Klin, came under the control of the Western Front's 20th Army. The brigade operated in various formations of the Western Front up until the end of February 1943, including the 16th Army, the 20th Army, Group Remizov, and the 8th Tank Corps, pulling back periodically into reserve to rest and refit. The 31st Tank Brigade took part in defensive battles in the region of Volokolamsk and Meshchevsk, while in August 1942 it participated in the encirclement and destruction of the enemy Kamarovo grouping west of Moscow. On 7 March 1943, it transferred by rail to the vicinity of the village Grushevaia Poliana in Voronezh Oblast and became part of the 29th Tank Corps. There between 25 March and 6 July 1943 it was in *Stavka* Reserve, where it underwent refitting and combat training of its personnel.

Incidentally, back on 22 January 1943, when the brigade was still part of the Western Front, near Naro-Fominsk on a ceremonial occasion the brigade had received a column of tanks, which had been built through the donations of workers from Krasnaia Presnia. The turret of each tank bore an inscription in white paint, "*Moskva* [Moscow]". A short time later, the brigade moved into *Stavka* Reserve, and it took no part in any fighting right up until the start of the Kursk battle. Thus the "*Moskva*" column of tanks first entered battle on the famous fields near Prokhorovka on 12 July 1943.

The 47-year-old Colonel Stepan Fedorovich Moiseev commanded the brigade between 20 January and 8 August 1943. He joined the Red Army in 1918, and served in the fighting against Poland as a company commander. In 1919, he completed the "*Vystrel*" ("Shot") courses. In the 1930s, he had served as the commander of a rifle company and as chief of staff of a rifle battalion. After finishing a course of advanced studies on armored warfare for officers, Moiseev commanded separate motorized and armored battalions in the 170th Motorized Rifle Division and the 16th Tank Division. At the outbreak of war with Germany, he was serving as the assistant chief of the auto-transport services of the 18th Mechanized Corps. In the period August-October 1941, he was the chief of operations for the auto-armored forces of the Southwestern Front's 6th Army. Later he commanded the 10th Tank Brigade, and then the 243rd Tank Regiment.

The most powerful formation in the 29th Tank Corps was the **32nd Tank Brigade**. It was fully equipped with only T-34 tanks. The brigade formed up between 5 and 25 October 1941 on the basis of the 32nd Tank Regiment in the city of Vladimir, Moscow Oblast. That regiment had organized in the latter half of the 1930s and had participated in the invasion of Poland following the Ribbentrop-Molotov Pact of 1939. In the first months of the war with Germany, its tank crews had fought in Moldavia, defending Kishinev and Kotovsk, and then in the Ukraine.

On 28 October 1941, the brigade moved by rail to the city of Tula, where it became part of the Western Front. From that date until the end of October 1942, the brigade fought as part of the 50th Army (in the Bol'shaia Iarovaia, Ovsiannikovo, and Tikhvin regions), the 10th Army (in the area of Kirov), and the 16th Army (defending along the Zhizdra River). On 30 October 1942, the brigade moved into *Stavka* Reserve around Kubinka. By 12 March 1943, the brigade was concentrated in the region of Nizhne-Mitiakino in Voronezh Oblast, where it joined the 29th Tank Corps. In May 1943, the brigade was reorganized as a Guards unit. More than a third of its tanks, 27 armored vehicles were built through the donations of workers of the Urals and arrived in the brigade on 23 February 1943 as part of the "Sverdlovsk *Komosomol* Member" column of tanks. Ten of these tanks comprised the 1st Company of the 1st Tank Battalion, which was commanded at the time by Captain I. L Svetiuk, while the remainder went to other units in the 1st and 2nd Tank Battalions as replenishments.

One veteran of the 32nd Tank Brigade, N. Ia. Vishnevsky, recalls an interesting detail. When the brigade had been serving with the Western Front, it had received new tanks built on the financial contributions of collective farm [*kolkhoz*] workers from the Naro-Fominsk, Zvenigorodsk and Mozhaisk Districts of Moscow Oblast. However, after the brigade had received the order to relocate to Voronezh Oblast, all these "Moscow *Kolkhoz* Worker" tanks were transferred to a different tank brigade, which was operating west of the capital. In turn, the 32nd Tank Brigade received its "Sverdlovsk *Komsomol* Member" tanks after its arrival in Voronezh Oblast.

The 40-year-old Colonel Aleksei Alekseevich Linev, a native of Voronezh Oblast, commanded the 32nd Tank Brigade after 8 January 1943. From the middle of 1919 on, he had participated in fighting on various fronts of the Russian Civil War. After the civil war ended, he served as a political instructor in a training tank regiment in the Moscow Military District, then as the commander of a tank company, a tank battalion, and as the chief of staff of a tank battalion in the Separate Far Eastern Red Banner Army. Here he became acquainted with and served for a short time together with the commander of that tank battalion at the time, Lieutenant Colonel P. A. Rotmistrov.

In January 1937, after completing tactical and technical training classes at the Red Army's Academy of Motorization and Mechanization, A. A. Linev was appointed chief of staff of the motorized and armored forces of the 18th Rifle Corps in the Far East. Prior to his arrival in the 29th Tank Corps, between 26 January and 12 October 1942 he had occupied the post of deputy commander of armored forces of the Far Eastern Front. Judging from the actions of the 32nd Tank Brigade on 12 July at Prokhorovka, Aleksei Alekseevich was a decisive and resolute officer, who kept firm control over his formation. On 26 August 1943, Colonel A. A. Linev was killed in action during the liberation of the Ukraine.

The **53rd Motorized Rifle Brigade** formed in November 1942 in the woods around the city of Vladimir on the basis of the 353rd Reserve Regiment, which was composed primarily of officers and men from the Pacific Ocean Fleet and the Amur River Flotilla. It was originally known as the 53rd Mechanized Brigade. On 28 February 1943, the brigade became part of the 29th Tank Corps of the 5th Guards Tank Army. The brigade had initially traveled by rail to Rostov Oblast in March 1943, but then it was ordered to move to the region of Ostrogozhsk in Voronezh Oblast to join the 29th Tank Corps. The brigade traveled by both rail and road convoy, but in the conditions of the spring thaw, which dissolved Russian roads into a sea of mud, the movement experienced significant delays, with units of the brigade arriving piecemeal between 28 March and 14 April

1943. Because of the poor organization of the movement, the 5th Guards Tank Army's Military Council decided to remove Lieutenant Colonel I. S. Breslovets from command of the brigade, and Lieutenant Colonel N. P. Lipichev assumed command. On 2 May 1943, the brigade was reorganized along the lines of a motorized rifle brigade and became known as the 53rd Motorized Rifle Brigade. Prior to the battle of Prokhorovka, the units of this brigade had seen no combat action.

Lieutenant Colonel N. P. Lipichev was born in St. Petersburg in 1907. He received a secondary school education. Prior to his call-up into the Red Army in 1929, he was managing a post office in Leningrad Oblast. In 1937, he graduated from the prestigious Frunze Military Academy. Lipichev served in the Soviet-Finnish War of 1939-1940. From the start of fighting on the Eastern Front and until January 1942, he commanded a mechanized battalion in Northern Front's 40th Tank Brigade, then a rifle regiment in the Kaliningrad Front's 158th Rifle Division. As commander of the 13th Tank Corps' 62nd Guards Motorized Rifle Brigade, he took part in the Battle of Stalingrad. He was twice seriously wounded, and in July 1942, he received the Order of the Red Banner. His last assignment before his transfer to the 29th Tank Corps was as commander of the 11th Guards Motorized Brigade in the 5th Guards Motorized Corps.

The 29th Tank Corps continued the process of building up to its authorized strength until the middle of May 1943. A number of new combat and supply units and subunits were created especially for it. For example, the 75th Motorcycle Regiment completed its formation on 25 January 1943. It drew its personnel from soldiers and officers of the 14th Separate Reserve Motorcycle Regiment, while its equipment (motorcycles and armored personnel carriers) came from the Likhachev assembly plant. One battalion of this regiment was designated to become the 29th Tank Corp's reconnaissance unit, so it trained for this role. Another attachment destined to play a major role in the fighting at Prokhorovka was the 271st Mortar Regiment. It was organized on Iagra Island in the mouth of the Northern Dvina River on 10 February 1943. It was comprised primarily of troops from reserve units of the Arkhangel'sk Military District, while 70% of its officers came from the Penzensk Artillery-Mortar School.

In addition to these units, the 29th Tank Corps received the 1446th Self-Propelled Artillery Regiment, the 366th Light Anti-aircraft Artillery Regiment, the 76th Guards Mortar Regiment (of *Katiusha* rocket launchers), the 38th Armored Car Battalion, and the 363rd Separate Signals Battalion.

The 5th Guards 'Zimovniki' Mechanized Corps

An NKO directive dated 26 November 1942 established the 5th Guards 'Zimovniki' Mechanized Corps. Originally known as the 6th Mechanized Corps, it formed on the basis of the 17th Tank Corps over a period of five days. After participating in the battles that routed the 'Kotel'nikovskii' grouping of German forces in December 1942 and the liberation of Zimovniki on 9 January 1943, the formation was elevated to Guards status and began to carry the honorific title 'Zimovniki'. After a period of rest in the Southern Front's reserve, at the end of February 1943 the corps shifted to Voronezh Oblast and became part of the 5th Guards Tank Army as that army was forming up. Here the corps underwent refitting and conducted combat training exercises. The corps consisted of the 10th, 11th and 12th Guards Mechanized Brigades and the 24th Guards Tank Brigade.

On 2 March 1943, Major General of Tank Forces B. M. Skvortsov assumed command of the 5th Guards Mechanized Corps. Boris Mikhailovich entered the tank forces in 1931, and for four years he taught tactics at the Kazan' Higher School for Technical Staff of the Tank Forces. In 1936, he graduated from the Red Army's Academy of Motorization and Mechanization. As commander of a tank battalion in the 11th Tank Brigade, he had distinguished himself in the fighting on the Khalkin-Gol River during the conflict with Japan. At the height of the battle, the brigade commander had been killed. Skvortsov assumed command of the brigade, and in a concerted action with other units, they managed to encircle and annihilate an enemy grouping. For his skillful handling of the brigade, Skvortsov received the Order of Lenin. He next commanded the 61st Tank Division. By the start of the Great Patriotic War, Colonel Skvortsov was the deputy commander of tank forces of the 17th Army. Since August 1941, that army had been part of the Zabaikal Front defending the border with China and Mongolia. Later he commanded the 7th Mechanized Corps as it was forming in February 1943 in the Moscow Military District. Skvortsov died on 12 May 1946 after a serious illness.

The corps' chief of staff, Major General I. V. Shabarov, also came from Rotmistrov's 3rd Guards 'Kotel'nikovskii' Tank Corps. Before the war, Ivan Vasil'evich graduated from the Red Army's Academy of Motorization and Mechanization, where he remained to teach tactics for a number of years. In 1942, he was appointed to command and led successfully the 87th Tank Brigade, which eventually became part of the 7th Tank Corps.

The **10th Guards Mechanized Brigade** (formerly the 51st Mechanized Brigade) was formed in September 1942 in Gor'kii Oblast. Between 9 January and 6 February 1943, as part of the 6th Mechanized Corps under operational control of the Southern Front's 2nd Guards Army, it engaged in fighting along the Sokorevka-Kalach-'Kotel'nikovskii' axis. Between 7 February and 27 March, it was in the Southern Front's reserve, but on 28 March, now known as the 10th Guards Mechanized Brigade, it was transferred with the rest of the 5th Guards Mechanized Corps to the control of the 5th Guards Tank Army. Prior to 6 July 1943, it was staging near the village of Korpenko in Voronezh Oblast. I. B. Mikhailov commanded the brigade.

The **11th Guards Mechanized Brigade** (formerly the 54th Mechanized Brigade) was formed in the middle of September 1942. In January 1943, it took part in the fighting for Rostov; in the period 9-17 February 1943 as part of the 5th Guards Mechanized Corps it supported the 2nd Guards Army's offensive in the direction of Tsimlianskaia Station. After this it moved into reserve, but in March it became subordinated to the commander of the 5th Guards Tank Army. The former director of the Chkalov Tank School, Colonel N. V. Grishchenko, assumed command of the brigade.

A Hero of the Soviet Union, Colonel G. Ia. Borisenko, stepped into command of the **12th Mechanized Brigade** (formerly the 55th Mechanized Brigade). He had earned this high honor for successful combat actions against the Japanese aggressors on the Khalkin-Gol River in August 1939, when he was commanding the reconnaissance battalion of the 1st Army Group's 6th Light Tank Brigade.

Lieutenant Colonel V. P. Karpov commanded the **24th Tank Brigade** (prior to 13 March 1943 – the 52nd Guards Tank Regiment). At the same time, the 53rd Guards Tank Regiment under the command of Major N. A. Kurnosov was taken from the 5th Guards Mechanized Corps and placed under the direct control of the commander of the

5th Guards Tank Army. When the army moved out for Prokhorovka during the battle of Kursk, this regiment was part of its forward detachment.

The artillery of the 5th Guards Mechanized Corps consisted of: Major S. S. Belenky's 285th Mortar Regiment, the 409th Separate Guards Mortar Battalion of *Katiusha* rocket launchers, Major V. F. Gaidash's 1447th Self-propelled Artillery Regiment, and the 104th Guards Destroyer Anti-tank Regiment, under the command of F. Z. Babachenko. Fedor Zakharovich Babachenko had distinguished himself during the 1939 Winter War with Finland. As the chief of reconnaissance for an artillery battalion in the 123rd Rifle Division's 323rd Artillery Regiment, he had successfully scouted out the locations of the enemy's firing positions prior to the assault on the city of Vyborg, for which in April 1940 he received the nation's highest honor, "Hero of the Soviet Union".

The 18th Tank Corps

With the German Kursk offensive looming, and the 5th Guards Tank Army, the Steppe Front's key strike force, still lacking a major component of its combat strength after the removal of the 3rd Guards Tank Corps from the army, it was clear that the 5th Guards Tank Army needed a replacement tanks corps. On 5 July 1943, by order of the Steppe Front commander, the 18th Tank Corps joined the roster of the 5th Guards Tank Army. By this time, this corps already had extensive combat experience. The corps headquarters had been formed at the Moscow Armor Training Center in the course of two weeks on the basis of an NKO directive dated 15 June 1942. The corps initially consisted of the 110th, 170th and 181st Tank Brigades, and the 18th Motorized Rifle Brigade. The formation received its baptism of fire during the Voronezh-Voroshilovgrad defensive operation.

At the end of June 1942, the German command launched its summer offensive under the code name of Operation *Blau* [Blue]. Its aim was to crush the forces of the Southwestern Front and reach the Volga River, then turn southward for a drive into the Caucasus. On 28 June 1942, the German Sixth Army launched two powerful blows from the regions of Volokonovka and Kursk in the direction of the Don River. By 3 July it had already broken cleanly through the Southwestern Front's defenses at the boundary between the 13th and 40th Armies. Partially destroying and partially encircling divisions of the 21st and 40th Armies, the Sixth Army approached Voronezh.

Striving to prevent the enemy from further developing his offensive, the Soviet command began to gather all its mobile reserves, first of all its tank formations, to the region of Voronezh. The 18th Tank Corps found itself among those rushing to defend the city. Its leadership received the assignment from the Voronezh Front command to prevent the German tank divisions from seizing Voronezh and forcing a full-scale crossing of the Don River in the 40th Army's sector. The trains ferrying the troops and tanks of the corps approached the city of Voronezh as savage fighting was already going on inside it.

Staff documents of the 18th Tank Corps note:

> On the night of 2/3 July, the first train with tanks began to unload at the Voronezh station. Immediately after unloading, the tanks deployed into combat formation and entered the battle from the march. The Germans launched fierce counterattacks upon the city several times a day. Hundreds of fascist planes were

constantly bombing the handsome city, which was still bathed in the verdant colors of summer. In three days and nights of constant fighting, the troops and tank crews of the formation, under the command of its first corps commander, General I. D. Cherniakovsky, repelled the uninterrupted hostile attacks.

Through enormous exertions, the enemy was stopped. For the successful execution of a difficult mission and his skillful handling of his formation, the corps commander of the 18th Tank Corps, Major General of Tank Forces Ivan Danilovich Cherniakovsky, future twice-Hero of the Soviet Union and *front* commander, was shortly later promoted to command the 60th Army.

The corps continued to conduct heavy defensive fighting around Voronezh until the end of September. During this period, its brigades and regiments suffered significant losses, which were impossible to replace through the meager trickle of incoming companies of draft recruits. Therefore at the start of October, the corps was withdrawn into reserve in order to bring it back up to strength, and on 4 October it traveled by rail to the Tatishchevo tank lager in Saratov Oblast for reorganization.

However, already by 24 November, the headquarters and the 110th, 170th and 181st Tank Brigades, along with the corps' service and supply units, began moving by rail to rejoin the acting army on the Don River. By 11 December, the corps had fully reassembled in the region of Nizhnii Mamon (375 kilometers northwest of Stalingrad), where it became part of the Southwestern Front under the command of Lieutenant General N. F. Vatutin. However, it arrived without its "own" 18th Motorized Rifle Brigade, which had been detached from 18th Tank Corps' command prior to departure. Therefore, the Southwestern Front's command decided to place the 32nd Motorized Rifle Brigade under the operational control of the 18th Tank Corps' commander, General B. S. Bakharov. After 16 December, the 18th Tank Corps as part of the 1st Guards Army took part in Operation Little Saturn, the main aim of which was to crush the enemy's Bokovsk-Morozovsk grouping and to disrupt Army Group Don's attempt to free Field Marshal F. von Paulus's trapped Sixth Army at Stalingrad.

Having crossed the Don River on the morning of 17 December from its jumping-off positions around Osetrovka, the 18th Tank Corps was supposed to follow the attacking forces of the 1st Guards Army after they had cleared a path through the enemy's defenses. The corps was then to attack in the direction of Millerovo, thereby striking the flanks and rear of the enemy's encircled forces at Tormosin. However, the 38th Guards Rifle Division proved unable to penetrate the enemy's defenses and failed to create a sufficient opening for the introduction of the 18th Tank Corps. The 1st Guards Army's commander General V. I. Kuznetsov decided to commit the tank corps to break through the enemy's defenses. Thus, from the operation's outset, the 18th Tank Corps had to contend with a different set of problems that it had not planned to meet, and considering that there had already been one failed attempt to break the German resistance on this sector of the front, this controversial decision implied heavy tank losses. However, it should be noted that at this time, in effect, the 1st Guards Army was still in a process of reorganization (its second), and the mechanisms of supply and command and control had not yet been fully worked out.

The 18th Tank Corps launched a powerful attack, but the enemy put up stubborn resistance. Frigid temperatures and a strong snowstorm, which created problems with the delivery of fuel and ammunition to the fighting units, aggravated the situation. The 18th Tank Corps became bogged down in heavy, prolonged fighting, and made slow headway only with great effort. In this difficult situation, the army command decided to lay the responsibility for the corps' slow progress on its commander, and removed Major General B. S. Bakharov from command of the 18th Tank Corps. It appointed the corps' chief of staff, Colonel Gushchenko, to take over the responsibilities of corps command.

The leadership of the Southwestern Front, which at that time was commanded by General N. F. Vatutin, supported the decision to dismiss Bakharov. However, Bakharov was not only relieved of command; he was even placed under arrest, even though there were no strong justifications for this at all. Bakharov protested his dismissal and arrest. As a result, B. S. Bakharov's personal relationships with both 1st Guards Army's commander V. I. Kuznetsov and the Southwestern Front's commander N. F. Vatutin were ruined, which would later significantly affect the conclusions of the government inquiry into the Voronezh Front command following the Prokhorovka battle in July 1943.

Having completed a two-day lunge of almost 140 kilometers through the harshest winter conditions, the spearhead 170th and 181st Tank Brigades seized Meshkov, thereby cutting the Italian 8th Army's line of retreat to the south. Under the blows of Soviet rifle formations, numerous, disorganized fragments of the German 9th, 52nd, and 292nd Infantry Divisions and the Italian 3rd *Ravenna* Division, trying to break out in the direction of Millerovo, overran the settlement of Pozdniakovo and split the 18th Tank Corps into two separate combat groups. One of these groups, composed of the 110th Tank Brigade and the 32nd Motorized Rifle Brigade under the leadership of corps' chief of staff Major Gerasimenko, pushed the enemy back upon Pozdniakovo with its tanks. The second group, comprised of the 170th and 181st Tank Brigade under the overall command of Colonel Gushchin, stubbornly clung to Meshkov.

The enemy made desperate attempts to gain control of this city. On 20 December, they delivered a heavy attack from the north. On a hill near the church, the motorized rifle battalion of the 181st Tank Brigade, which at that moment numbered only 64 men, became encircled. Casualties mounted. Despite the enemy's numerical superiority, the battalion managed to repulse several attacks. At a point when ammunition ran out, the surviving 23 troops, under the command of Senior Lieutenant Frolovsky, mounted a resolute counterattack and managed to seize eight light machine guns and ammunition for them from the enemy, and with their use the motorized riflemen continued to hold on to the hilltop. Finally at day's end, the tanks of two brigades, supported by the forward detachment of the 152nd Rifle Division, arrived and drove the dwindling number of enemy out of the city. The savage fighting in the city center and on its northern outskirts left behind around 400 corpses, and 3,500 Italian, Romanian and German soldiers and officers surrendered together with all their weapons.

Gerasimenko's group near Pozdniakovo met with success too, although it had to contend with a significant portion of three retreating armies, concentrated on a narrow sector of the front. Using their advantage in numbers, the enemy even launched massed infantry attacks in the direction of Khlebnoe designed to shake the defenders psychologically, which primarily struck the positions of the 32nd Motorized Rifle Brigade. A staff account of the action from the Brigade's headquarters stated:

> The enemy had crowded up to 18,000 men in a confined area, together with artillery, vehicles, and field trains. Too cramped to maneuver, and enduring enormous losses in men and equipment from the fire of our tanks and artillery, they were forced to lay down their arms. As a result of uninterrupted fighting that continued for twenty-four hours, the Germans and Italians lost up to 5,000 men killed and wounded, and almost 11,000 as prisoners with all their equipment and supplies.[8]

This success came at a high price; Major Gerasimenko died in the fighting, the commander of the 32nd Motorized Rifle Brigade Major Serdiuk was wounded, and both brigades suffered significant losses in personnel.

By the morning of 22 December, the destruction of the Axis grouping north of Meshkov-Khlebnoe was complete. At this point, their forces along the Upper Chir River began to withdraw to the southwest in the direction of Millerovo. Trying to disrupt the enemy's intentions, the Southwestern Front command issued an order to the 18th Tank Corps to block the path of the retreating Italian *Sforzesca* Division and the units of the Romanian 7th and 9th Infantry Divisions moving with it in the vicinity of Verkhne-Chirskaia. That afternoon, the 110th Tank Brigade reached the station at Verkhne-Chirskaia, where the enemy had already set up a blocking position with anti-tank guns.

Using a rapid maneuver, the tank of Junior Lieutenant G. G. Kalinin of the 441st Tank Battalion burst into the station. The enemy anti-tank artillerymen could offer no resistance to the impetuosity and resolve of the Soviet tankers. Taking advantage of the anti-tank guns' deployment in line, the tank crew drove their tank right up to the anti-tank gun positions and destroyed nine guns in one swift blow. Continuing to push ahead, the tankers overran two mortar batteries and scattered approximately a company of enemy soldiers. By evening, the station was fully in the hands of the 110th Tank Brigade, and having camouflaged their armored vehicles among the sheds and other outbuildings in the town, the crews waited for the enemy's approach. As twilight fell, the retreating enemy columns began to enter Verkhne-Chirskaia. Bitter fighting erupted, which continued all night. At dawn, recognizing the hopelessness of their position, the enemy command decided to surrender. According to staff records of the 18th Tank Corps, more than 3,000 men marched into captivity.

The 18th Tank Corps also faced hard fighting for Millerovo. Reconnaissance reports indicated that the enemy had created a strong anti-tank defense there out of its retreating units, which included armor. Taking this information into account, the Soviet command decided to envelop the hostile garrison with a synchronized attack: from the northwest by rifle formations, and from the southwest by units of the 18th Tank Corps. Simultaneously, other units would feign a direct attack on Millerovo from the direction of Novo-Spasskoye.

On 2 January 1943, the Soviet forces launched the attack. The main forces of the 18th Tank Corps moved on Kamensk. With a decisive dash, the 181st Tank Brigade bypassed the city from the south and drove the fascists out of the villages of Ivanovka and Grekovo-Stanichnoe, thereby cutting the Millerovo-Kamensk railway. Exploiting this success, by dawn of the next day, the 18th Tank Corps had occupied a number of small villages and stations along the rail line, including Verkhne-Talovyi, Nizhne-Talovyi, Staraia Stanitsa and the "*Zovet Lenina* [Call of Lenin]" commune, while rifle divisions of the 1st Guards Army took the railroad station at Krasnovka. The German units defending Millerovo found themselves caught in a trap.

However, the enemy refused to budge and continued to defend desperately. Fighting for the city continued until 18 January. On this day, the defenders managed to overrun a screen of infantry units attempting to hold the pocket closed and broke out toward Krasnovka. The enemy was plainly trying to withdraw its trapped forces in Millerovo in the direction of Voroshilovgrad. The 18th Tank Corps command reacted quickly to the breakout. The 110th Tank Brigade attacked the Krasnovka station and regained possession of it. Part of the forces fleeing Millerovo, primarily the tanks, hastily retreated to Chebotovka, a major settlement and a large railway station.

A blizzard began, but the corps commander, hoping to surprise the Germans with a night attack and drive them out of Chebotovka, threw his brigades in pursuit of the Germans through the driving snow and trackless snow drifts. However, because of the poor weather conditions and a lack of coordination between the brigade commanders, a tragedy occurred.

At the designated hour, only the noticeably worn-out 170th Tank Brigade found itself in position to attack, while the 181st Tank Brigade and the 32nd Motorized Rifle Brigade were still *en route*. After conducting a quick assessment of the situation, Colonel Durnev, the 170th Tank Brigade's commander, decided to attack without waiting for his neighboring formations to come up. He was counting upon the element of surprise and the exhaustion of the enemy soldiers, who had settled in for sleep after the hard march. In fact, at the start of the battle the German and Italian soldiers began to flee in panic toward the southern outskirts of the village, but then resistance began to grow, while the brigade's strength inexorably dwindled. By the middle of the night, all of the brigade's tanks had been either destroyed or disabled. Having created a strong screen of forces in the center of the village, the enemy launched a flank attack and emerged in the rear of the brigade. Here, the attackers came upon the building that was housing the headquarters' operational staff group. The officers took up an all-round defense. For twelve hours, bloody fighting raged in the village as the 170th Tank Brigade sought to hold on while the ring tightened around its remaining points of resistance. Finally, at 1300 on 18 January, the operations group headed by the brigade commander S. A. Durnev and the commissar N. E. Lysenko led a desperate counterattack in the attempt to break out of Chebotovka, in the course of which nearly the brigade's entire command staff perished.

The corps headquarters had failed to organize the attack on Chebotovka properly. The commanders of the brigades involved in the attack had not conducted any meeting to discuss the plan, as was the normal practice prior to an attack. Absent from this planning session, because the brigade headquarters had no reliable communications among themselves, the commanders had been unable to exchange operational information, and they didn't know the full situation in the attack sector. Each brigade commander made decisions independently, without coordinating their actions with their neighbors. As a result, while Colonel Durnev's brigade poured out its lifeblood in its struggle with the enemy in Chebotovka, Major Cherdiuk's motorized riflemen were in column on a road just outside the station, fully prepared for battle! However, the 32nd Motorized Rifle Brigade never received an order to enter the fight and failed to render the tankers any form of assistance.

Unit	Personnel	Tanks			BA-64	Mortars		37mm AA	76, 85mm AA	DShK 39 AA	45mm AT guns	AT rifles	Submachine guns	Rifles	MG		Radios	Vehicles	
		T-34	T-70	Mk-4		82mm	120mm								Light	Heavy		Trucks, cars	BTR
Corps HQ	239	5	-	-	-	-	-	-	-	-	-	-	29	15	1	-	-	-	-
419 Sep Signals Btn	247	2	-	-	10	-	-	-	-	-	-	-	78	156	-	-	7	88	-
115 Sep Sapper Btn	478	-	-	-	-	-	-	-	-	-	-	-	97	353	-	-	-	40	-
Fuel/Lubricants Co	114	-	-	-	-	-	-	-	-	-	-	1	44	111	-	-	-	70	-
Medical Pltn	30	-	-	-	-	-	-	-	-	-	-	-	3	6	-	-	-	8	-
Mobile field bakery	51	-	-	-	-	-	-	-	-	-	-	-	31	-	-	-	-	6	-
Military post office	4	-	-	-	-	-	-	-	-	-	-	-	-	-	-	-	-	-	-
Total:	1163	7	-	-	10	-	-	-	-	-	-	1	251	673	1	-	7	212	-
110 Tank Bde	1145	32	21	-	3	6	-	-	-	9	4	24	317	445	20	4	5	106	-
170 Tank Bde	1026	32	21	-	3	8	-	-	-	9	4	24	298	508	20	5	9	100	5
181 Tank Bde	1094	32	21	-	3	6	-	-	-	9	4	6	355	490	20	4	9	101	-
32 Mot Rifle Bde	2629	-	-	-	7	34	6	4	12	-	12	81	1279	1335	112	44	16	261	4
36 Gds Tank Regt.	248	-	-	21	3	-	-	-	-	-	-	-	36	22	-	-	1	41	-
78 Sep MC Btn	284	-	-	-	10	4	-	-	-	-	-	-	135	82	16	-	3	17	-
29 Sep Recon Btn	205	-	-	-	24	-	-	-	-	-	-	20	71	67	44	-	20	28	20
1000 AT Regt	304	-	-	-	-	-	-	-	12	-	8	-	96	200	13	-	2	53	-
292 Sep Mtr Regt	691	-	-	-	-	-	36	-	-	-	-	22	392	377	19	-	18	94	-
1694 AA Regt	385	-	-	-	-	-	-	16	-	16	-	-	126	258	-	-	1	38	-
Total:	9174	103	63	21	63	58	42	20	24	43	32	178	3356	4457	266	57	91	1051	29
104 Mobile Repair Base	70	-	-	-	-	-	-	-	-	-	-	-	-	57	-	-	-	22	-
139 Mobile Repair Base	73	-	-	-	-	-	-	-	-	-	-	-	6	72	1	-	27	72	-
SMERSH	54	-	-	-	-	-	-	-	-	-	-	-	-	-	-	-	-	-	-

Source: TsAMO RF, f. 18tk, op.1, d. 93, l. 122.

Note: The 18th Tank Corps also controlled three U-2 airplanes that served as aerial signal links. BTR – armored transporters.

Table 6. Composition and Strength of the 18th Tank Corps, 5 July 1943

By evening of 18 January, the 170th Tank Brigade had been fully routed, all pockets of resistance had been mopped-up, and only a small group of scouts and motorized riflemen headed by Captain P. M. Levchenko managed to breakout of the encirclement. According to the testimony of local residents, after the battle the enemy committed atrocities, finishing off the wounded Soviet soldiers they came upon in the streets, and going from building to building, they tossed grenades into the basements where wounded men might be hiding. In the course of this cruel action, many peaceful residents, especially children, were killed or wounded. In this battle, Soviet soldiers who had just been liberated from a prison camp in Millerovo fought heroically.

Despite this terrible setback, the remainder of the 18th Tank Corps attacked again and routed the enemy from Chebotovka, which cleared the way to Voroshilovgrad. By 21 January, the 18th Tank Corps, sweeping aside minor rearguard detachments, had seized Kondrashevo and Luganskaia Stations and had emerged on the left bank of the Northern Don River. For the successful combat operations on the approaches to Stalingrad and for the liberation of Millerovo, the 18th Tank Corps received the recognition and personal gratitude of the Supreme Commander [Stalin] himself.

On 29 January 1943, the forces of the Southwestern Front launched the Voroshilovgrad offensive. By this time, the enemy on the southern wing of the Soviet-German front was in full retreat; the forces of the Southern Front had already taken the major cities of Rostov-on-Don and Shakhty. The 18th Tank Corps, operating as part of the Southern Front's Mobile Group under the command of General M. M. Popov, went on the attack towards Krasnoarmeisk, Proletarsk, Artemovsk, and Mariupol', with the aim of cutting off the enemy's path of retreat from the Don Basin. By 18 February, the 6th Army and the 1st Guards Army had reached the outskirts of Dnepropetrovsk, but there they were stopped by stubborn German resistance. The attempt by General M. M. Popov's Mobile Group to develop the offensive to the south met with failure. On 21 February, the Germans struck a powerful blow with fresh reserves at the boundary between the Voronezh Front and the Southwestern Front. The 18th Tank Corps was caught in a pocket, and retreated towards Barvenkovo in savage fighting. By 23 February, the main forces of the corps had broken out of encirclement and had taken a defensive position 70 kilometers to the west of Kramatorsk. The 181st Tank Brigade together with the anti-aircraft regiment managed to break out of the pocket a day later.

By the beginning of March, the 18th Tank Corps had been removed from General Popov's Mobile Group and was assembled in the area of Izium. For more than a month, the formation had seen constant fighting, had lost almost all of its armor and heavy weapons, and a significant share of its personnel. A number of mid-level and high-ranking officers had been killed, including two chiefs of staff, Major Gerasimenko and Colonel I. A Gushchenko, and the commander of the 170th Tank Brigade, Colonel Durnev.

However, by early March the situation around Khar'kov had become acute. The German Army Group South was persistently pressing the forces of Voronezh Front. Accordingly, on 10 March General Bakharov received an order to move to the region of Khar'kov (Russkiye Tishki) with his available forces and the attached 141st Tank Regiment (with 4 T-34 tanks and 6 T-60 tanks) and the 879th Destroyer Anti-tank Artillery Regiment (with just 4 anti-tank guns). By this time, the 170th and 181st Tank Brigades totally lacked tanks, while the 32nd Motorized Rifle Brigade had only 250 men, 3 guns and 14 mortars. Therefore, all the remaining armor in the corps (4 T-34 tanks and 15 T-70 tanks) was concentrated in the 170th Tank Brigade, and together with the remnants of the 32nd Motorized Rifle Brigade, they were sent to the assistance of General P. S. Rybalko's 3rd Tank Army, which was holding out with its last remaining strength against Fourth Panzer Army's attack from the region of Krasnograd. Having completed a 150-kilometer march across nearly impassably muddy terrain, on 13 March the detached formation of two brigades entered the city of Khar'kov, where it became involved in costly defensive fighting near Rogan' and in Staryi Saltov until the end of the Khar'kov operation.

On 23 March, corps elements were withdrawn into *front* reserve in the region of Rossosh'. There the corps underwent refitting and combat training until the start of July. By this time the corps consisted of three tank brigades (the 170th, the 181st, and the 110th) and one motorized rifle brigade. Table 6 shows the combat strength and composition of the 18th Tank Corps on 5 July 1943.

The **170th Tank Brigade** began to organize as a separate tank brigade on 15 February 1942 in Sokol'niki Park in the city of Moscow. The men of the brigade came primarily from the Kazan' Tank School and the armor training grounds around Gorokhovetsk. Two of the brigade's battalions were initially equipped with a mixed composition of three tank types: the Soviet T-34, and British Lend-Lease Matilda and Valentine tanks. This aid program also delivered American Studebaker and Ford trucks, which served as transportation and towed the brigade's guns. On 23 April, the brigade commander Lieutenant Colonel M. I. Rudoi received the order to have his brigade loaded on trains at the Riga Station by the end of the next day, and to depart for the Briansk Front, where it would come under that *front*'s command. By 26 April, the men of the brigade had already started disembarking from troop trains at three railway stations: Gorshechnoe, Kastornoe, and Staryi Oskol. Forty-eight hours later, the brigade was assembled in the cover of overgrown gullies 12 kilometers north of Staryi Oskol, where it entered Briansk Front's reserve.

After the start of the enemy's summer offensive toward Voronezh, the brigade became involved in heavy fighting in the regions of Oboian', Staryi Oskol, and Kastornoe Station. With defensive fire and sharp counterattacks, the brigade delayed the German advance, thereby helping to extract the rifle formations of the 40th and 21st Armies from encirclement beyond the Don River. Then until October 1943 it participated in the defense of Voronezh, coming under the control of the 18th Tank Corps during this period.

According to the recollections of veterans, the 170th Tank Brigade was considered the hard luck unit in the 18th Tank Corps. In the first four months of fighting from the moment of its arrival in the corps, the brigade had to replace its complete command staff, including its brigade commander, twice. There followed its crushing defeat at Chebotovka. The brigade suffered equally heavy losses at Prokhorovka as well.

At the start of the Kursk battle, the 47-year-old Lieutenant Colonel V. D. Tarasov commanded the formation. Vasilii Dmitrievich was a veteran of the Russian Civil War, and had been wounded in the fighting against General Denikin's forces in the south in 1919. In the period between the wars, he graduated from the Riazan' Infantry School (1921), and later completed a series of command staff training classes (1929-1930), as well as the Leningrad armor courses (1932). From 1921 until 1930, he at various times served as a platoon commander and a company commander, as well as an instructional commander at the Riazan', Ivanovo-Voznesensk and Nizhegorod Infantry Schools. Then for almost the next four years, Tarasov was a battalion chief of staff at the Gor'kii Auto-Armored School, and commanded a battalion of the 22nd Mechanized Brigade. During the 1939-1940 Soviet-Finnish War, he served as the chief of auto-armored services in the 95th Rifle Division. For the courage he displayed in battle, he was awarded with the Order of the Red Star. In February 1940, Tarasov was transferred to the Department of Special Assignments of the Chief Intelligence Directorate of the Red Army's General Staff.

When the war broke out, Tarasov was at the disposal of a district Military Council, and soon became deputy commander of the 205th Tank Brigade. He served in the acting army from 1942 on, and on 22 July 1942, he received appointment to command Western Front's 255th Tank Brigade. Lieutenant Colonel Tarasov arrived in the 18th Tank Corps on 8 May 1943, from his position as deputy commander of the 9th Tank Corps'187th Tank Brigade. He was killed in action in the fighting at Prokhorovka on 12 July 1943, when a shell scored a direct hit on his command tank.

The **181st Tank Brigade** began forming in Saratov on 19 June 1942. On 4 July, it joined the 18th Tank Corps in the region of Voronezh. Three days later, together with the rest of the tank corps, it was placed under the command of the Voronezh Front and took part in the Voronezh-Voroshilovgrad defensive operation. On 21 September, the 181st Tank Brigade transferred to the command of the 38th Army's mobile group, which was operating on the right bank of the Don River. Then together with the 18th Tank Corps, it took part in the hard fighting to smash the enemy grouping, which was trying to break through to assist the trapped Sixth Army in Stalingrad. At the end of March 1943 the 181st Tank Brigade was located in the region of Rossosh' in Voronezh Oblast.

On 21 January 1943, Lieutenant Colonel V. A. Puzyrev was named as acting commander of the 181st Tank Brigade. He was one of the youngest brigade commanders in the 5th Guards Tank Army. His life and military service were connected with Siberia. Viacheslav Alekseevich was born in 1911 in Novosibirsk. Having completed a seven-year school in 1929, he served in the Zabaikal Military District's 50th Training Tank Division. After his demobilization from the army, he completed vocational-technical training, and began to work at a railroad depot in Novosibirsk. On 5 July 1932, Puzyrev was called back into the Red Army during a Party mobilization drive, and he was sent to the two-year Ul'ianovsk Armor School. In 1934, he returned to the Trans-Baikal Military District, where he served in turn as a tank commander, a tank platoon commander, tank company commander, and as battalion assistant chief of staff. After completing the first year of the M. V. Frunze Military Academy (by correspondence) in 1940, he was appointed deputy chief of operations of the 50th Light Tank Brigade. Before the war itself, in April 1940, he was transferred to the same position in the 57th Tank Division, which was located in Mongolia. Within two weeks of the start of the Great Patriotic War, Captain Puzyrev arrived in the Western Front together with the 57th Tank Division.

For the next six months, Viacheslav Alekseevich had to carry out three completely different duties, from staff to command, and moreover in three different places. In September 1941, he received an assignment to the staff of the 112th Motorized Rifle Division, which was fighting under the control of Western Front. Just a month later, however, he was in reserve in Briansk Front's personnel department. He was not there long;

in December he was assigned to the Voronezh Front to serve as the deputy commander of an anti-tank rifle battalion. Incidentally, at this time the 40th Army, in which Puzyrev's battalion was serving, was occupying a defensive position in Prokhorovka district, not far from that station itself, where six months later, now as a lieutenant colonel, Puzyrev would be leading the 181st Tank Brigade in its attack on the SS Panzer Corps.

Puzyrev joined the 18th Tank Corps in July 1942 when it was near Voronezh. At that time the corps, becoming part of the Voronezh Front, was fighting together with elements of the 40th Army to liberate a part of that city that had been seized by the enemy. In the middle of July, Viacheslav Puzyrev became the deputy commander of the 170th Tank Brigade, but from the end of August to the end of the year, he served as the brigade's chief of staff. In November 1942, he was lightly wounded. On 21 January 1943, he became the acting commander of the 181st Tank Brigade, and was confirmed in this post on 24 June. For his skillful leadership of the formation and his personal courage, in May 1943 Lieutenant Colonel Puzyrev was awarded the Order of the Red Banner.

In December 1943, Puzyrev was sent to the Red Army's Academy of Motorization and Mechanization for a short-term course of instruction. Upon completing it in August 1944, he became commander of the 24th Guards Tank Brigade, a position he retained until the end of the war.

In addition to the tank brigades discussed above, at the time of the Prokhorovka engagement the 18th Tank Corps also had the **110th Tank Brigade** under its operational control. Unfortunately, I was unable to find any information about its origins or combat record prior to July 1943. It is only known that as of 2 April 1943, Colonel I. M. Kolesnikov was commanding this formation. Ivan Mikhailovich was born on 15 January 1905 in the city of Akhtyrka in Sumy Oblast. Prior to his summons into the Red Army in 1920, he had only managed to complete two years of primary schooling. After graduating in 1922 from the 6th Khar'kov Infantry School, he commanded in turn a platoon, a company, a battalion, and then served as a regimental chief of staff. Between 1932 and 1934, Ivan Mikhailovich taught tactics at the Ul'ianovsk Armor School. Between 1935 and 1939, he served as the chief of staff, then the commander of a tank battalion, and then as the chief of staff of the 4th Separate Tank Brigade in the Belorussian Military District. Before the war, he graduated from the M. V. Frunze Military Academy. After 19 July 1941, Kolesnikov served on the staff of the 32nd Army as the chief of the department of fuel and lubricants. At the beginning of October 1941, he was appointed chief of staff, and as of May 1942, deputy commander of Western Front's 2nd Separate Guards Tank Brigade. On 26 July 1942, he became commander of the 186th Tank Brigade of the very same *front*. In February 1943, Colonel Kolesnikov was reassigned to the Southwestern Front and appointed chief of staff of the 18th Tank Corps.

The **32nd Motorized Rifle Brigade** was formed between 5 May and 24 June 1942 in the Volga Military District in the city of Vol'sk in Saratov Oblast. It was equipped as a fully self-sufficient combat unit, with artillery fire support provided by an inherent artillery battalion. At the end of June, the brigade transferred to the Stalingrad Front in the region of Kalach, where it became part of the 28th Tank Corps. As part of this corps, it conducted heavy defensive fighting until the beginning of August, when on 8 August it was reassigned to 64th Army command. It operated in the region of the small villages of Nizhnii, Verkhnii-Gnilovskoi, and Vertiachii, and suffered heavy losses in men and equipment in the bitter fighting. Therefore, on 28 August, the brigade moved by rail to Saratov for rest and refitting.

At the time of the Prokhorovka battle, Colonel M.E. Khvatov, who had been assigned to this post back in November 1942, was commanding the 32nd Motorized Rifle Brigade. However, Khvatov had been severely wounded at the beginning of 1943. His deputy, Lieutenant Colonel I. A. Stukov, took over as acting commander of the brigade during Khvatov's extended absence between 10 February and 28 June 1943. However, because of a mistake in all the reports concerning the period of fighting at Prokhorovka (28 **June** was mistakenly entered as 28 **July**), Khvatov was not listed as the brigade commander at Prokhorovka. I was able to establish the truth by examining the brigade's few surviving operational documents.

Khvatov's life was very hard and full of sharp turning points and major events. Mikhail Emel'ianovich was born in Volgograd Oblast on 5 December 1896. He received four years of education in a village school, and worked as a carpenter. Then he was called into active service with the Tsarist army as a private. He participated in the First World War in 1915-1916 as a non-commissioned officer. After 1918, he sided with the Soviets on the battlefields of the Russian Civil War. In the 1920s, he rose from platoon commander to assistant battalion commander. In 1931 he was discharged from the Red Army, after which he worked as a military instructor at a technical college. In 1936, Khvatov was called back into the Red Army from the reserves. For more than a year, Captain Khvatov fought in Spain. After his return from this mission, in September 1938 he was appointed commander of a rifle regiment in the 72nd Rifle Division in Vinnitsa. He remained in this post until the outbreak of the Great Patriotic War. Between 1938 and 1940, he was awarded the Order of the Red Banner three times.

Mikhail Emel'ianovich took part in fighting from the first days of the war, and he was wounded. In August 1941, while trying to flee encirclement in the sector of the Southwestern Front, he was taken prisoner, but he managed to escape after a week of captivity. In the period of September to December 1941, he was again serving as a regimental commander, this time in the 295th Rifle Division of the 21st Army. The second year was particularly hard one for Khvatov. At the beginning of 1942, he was continuing to command a regiment, but then became deputy commander of Stalingrad Front's 199th Rifle Division, then subsequently the deputy commander and commander of a motorized rifle brigade. He was wounded in action twice during this time, for a total of three wounds throughout the war.

Khvatov was a successful commander. At the Prokhorovka engagement, the 32nd Motorized Rifle Brigade was at the epicenter of the fighting, but the brigade commander led his formation confidently and skillfully. He began the war as a major in charge of a regiment, and ended it as a major general and deputy commander of a rifle corps. Khvatov was honored with the Orders of Lenin, Bogdan-Khmel'nitsky, and Aleksandr Nevsky.

The 32nd Motorized Rifle Brigade joined the 18th Tank Corps on 1 December 1942 in the region of Nizhnii Mamon after a period of reorganization. After 15 December, as part of this corps, the brigade became subordinated the 1st Guards Army in the Southwestern Front, which was commanded by Colonel General N. F. Vatutin. The brigade took part in Operation Little Saturn, the goal of which was to crush the forces of Army Group Don, which was trying to relieve von Paulus's Sixth Army trapped in

Stalingrad. The brigade liberated Millerovo. Then at the end of January 1943, it spent a week in Southwestern Front's reserve. On 30 January, the 18th Tank Corps (together with the 32nd Motorized Rifle Brigade) became part of the Southwestern Front's mobile group under the command of Major General M. M. Popov. This operationally mixed command became the shock force during Operation Gallop in the Donbas and the Ukraine. Unfortunately, the possibilities for Popov's Mobile Group were overestimated during the operation's planning, and the operation ended unsuccessfully. Between 10 and 23 March, the brigade, now as part of the 18th Tank Corps, was caught in heavy, bloody fighting near Khar'kov, together with elements of the 3rd Guards Army. After 23 March, the brigade together with other units of the 18th Tank Corps went into the reserve of the Steppe Military District in the vicinity of Rossosh', where it remained until 7 July 1943.

From the autumn of 1942, Colonel (as of 14 October 1942 – Major General) B.S. Bakharov commanded the 18th Tank Corps. Boris Sergeevich was a native of the village of Demiansk in Novgorod Oblast. He began serving in the Red Army in 1918, but didn't take part in the Russian Civil War. He graduated from the Unified International Military School in 1926, and from the M.V. Frunze Military Academy in 1932. Later, he completed the Leningrad Armor Course for the Improvement of Command Personnel. After leaving the Frunze Academy, Bakharov continued to serve in the Belorussian Military District as the 4th Motorized Brigade's chief of operations. Between May 1936 and October 1938, Bakharov commanded training battalions in the 10th and 18th Mechanized Brigades.

The whirlwinds of political terror, which swept the entire country in the middle of the 1930s, didn't leave the 33-year-old battalion commander untouched. In 1937, he was formally rebuked for "lack of party vigilance".

Despite this black mark on his record, because of the shortage of mid-level and high-ranking commanders, which arose as a result of the repressions in the Red Army, at the end of 1938 Bakharov was appointed to a position that required considerably more experience and knowledge than he had as a battalion commander. He was required to fulfill the duties of the chief of auto-armored forces of the Khar'kov Military District. Nevertheless, Boris Sergeevich successfully coped with the new responsibilities, demonstrating exceptional organizational skills.

Within a year, on 29 November 1939, Bakharov assumed command of the 52nd Separate Light Tank Brigade. In May 1941, he became commander of the 50th Tank Division in the 25th Mechanized Corps. From the first days of the war, his division participated in heavy defensive fighting along the Dnepr and Sozh rivers as part of the Southwestern Front's 13th and 21st Armies. At that time, Boris Sergeevich didn't have sufficient experience in leading such a large formation in combat conditions, which became one of the main reasons for the division's less than bold handling and high losses in the first months of the Great Patriotic War.

The chief of staff of the 21st Army, Major General V. N. Gordov, wrote about Bakharov in a report dated 18 August 1941:

> Comrade Bakharov handles combat operations clumsily. He commits his tanks in a piecemeal fashion, as a result of which the division suffers high material losses and lacks due success. Comrade Bakharov is personally brave. In the fighting for

> Vovka he served as an example, advancing his own tank rapidly upon a detected enemy column, and destroyed 12 vehicles, 7 machine guns, and 1 anti-tank gun. Afterwards, his tank was knocked out by the enemy. Under hostile submachine gun fire, Comrade Bakharov crawled over to another tank and continued to destroy the enemy.[9]

Despite this criticism, there were successes. At the beginning of August 1941, the division fought successfully in the Central Front during the breakout from encirclement by elements of the 13th Army's 45th Rifle Corps, under the command of Major General E. Ia. Magon, in the region of Miloslavich and the Lozhbniak River.

In September 1941, the remnants of the 50th Tank Division were reorganized into the 150th Tank Brigade and sent to the Briansk Front to join Major General A. I. Ermakov's operational group, which distinguished itself in the autumn of 1941 in fighting against General Guderian's formations. B. S. Bakharov's tankers also operated successfully during the Elets offensive at the beginning of December 1941. As part of 13th Army's northern group, the 150th Tank Brigade was the first to break into Elets.

Nevertheless, during the formation of the first wave of tank corps, Bakharov was not promoted to lead one of the new formations. Likely, his not quite successful operations in the border battles played the primary role in this decision. Despite this disappointment, Bakharov's combat experience did not go unnoticed. On 20 June 1942, Boris Sergeevich was appointed chief of staff of the 17th Tank Corps. Then on 25 July he transferred to the same position in the Voronezh Front's 18th Tank Corps, which at the time was involved in counterattacks on the advancing enemy, primarily in the sector of the 60th Army. On 7 September 1942, Bakharov assumed command of the 18th Tank Corps.

In February-March 1943, the 18th Tank Corps as part of the Southwestern Front actively participated in the fighting in the Donbas. This was a very difficult period for General Bakharov. At the beginning of March, the corps was withdrawn from Popov's Mobile Group, after its brigades had suffered between 40% and 80% losses in personnel and equipment. On 9 March, German panzer and motorized formations launched a powerful blow at the junction between the Voronezh and Southwestern Fronts, and having broken through the defenses, they emerged in the region of Liubotin and Peresechnoe, striving to outflank Khar'kov from the north. On 10 March, Bakharov received an order from the commander of the Southwestern Front, General N. F. Vatutin: the 18th Tank Corps would have to conduct a 150-kilometer march from its current positions around Izium to the eastern outskirts of Khar'kov, where it was come under the command of the Voronezh Front.

The corps commander combined the remnants of his corps (4 T-34 and 15 T-70 tanks) into the 170th Tank Brigade, added to its limited fuel supplies with fuel from the corps' remaining vehicles, and according to his orders, sent the brigade on its way. Bakharov himself, with his headquarters and the corps' remaining units went to Velikii Burluk. The 170th Tank Brigade didn't have enough fuel for the entire march to Khar'kov, so it halted in Chuguev. For the next two days, the poor brigade commander was bombarded with orders from the headquarters of the Southwestern Front, Voronezh Front, and from the commander of Khar'kov's city defenses. The brigade tried to implement the orders, but eventually returned to Chuguev, without having completed the remaining 80-kilometer march to Khar'kov, and without having entered the fighting for the city. At this time, the corps commander drove off in his Willys jeep in pursuit of the 170th Tank Brigade, but his vehicle came under fire, and he was forced to return to Velikii Burluk.

Thus, in the conditions of a rapidly changing situation and dwindling supplies, when our weakened units began to reel in retreat from the enemy's blows, General Bakharov was "caught between the hammer and the anvil" – between the headquarters of two *fronts,* which were both using Bakharov's worn-out tank corps to attempt to resolve their pressing problems. As a result, on 25 March 1943, N. F. Vatutin and Lieutenant General A. S. Zheltov, a member of the Southwestern Front's Military Council, sent the following report to Stalin:

> The commander of the 18th Tank Corps, Major General of Tank Forces Bakharov, while conducting operations on the Southwestern Front, demonstrated his inability to command a corps. He seeks to evade battle, and when in combat he tries to leave it prematurely. He personally lacks the elements of courage, bravery and necessary willpower. He is inclined toward deception and eyewash. He is far from honest. He is a large demagogue.
>
> In the period of the December operation, he was removed from command and arrested. In the January and subsequent fighting, Comrade Bakharov was given the opportunity to redeem himself – he was given command of a corps. However, he didn't draw the correct conclusions and failed to measure up. During the defense of Khar'kov, he was given an order to insert his corps by a forced march through Chuguev to Khar'kov. He sent a brigade through Chuguev, while he himself with his headquarters staff set off through Velikii Burluk, avoided battle, and for several days he lost control of his corps. He failed to justify the title of "general". He cannot command a corps. I ask your permission:
>
> a) To remove Major General Bakharov from his post.
>
> b) To appoint Major General Bakharov as a brigade commander.

The *Front* command plainly rushed to make such proposals. The written accusations were an echo of the conflict, which had arisen back in January, and in Moscow after a short investigation they understood this. The Supreme Commander decided that it wasn't worth letting go of another commander – at the time, he didn't have enough of them – and Bakharov remained in his post as corps commander. One can imagine what an emotional toll this episode took on Boris Sergeevich, but the trouble for the corps commander didn't stop here.

Before the beginning of June 1943, the 18th Tank Corps was located in the Steppe District. But on 6 July, it was subordinated to the command of the 5th Guards Tank Army under Lieutenant General P. A. Rotmistrov, and transferred together with the Army to the Voronezh Front, which at that moment was commanded by General of the Army N. F. Vatutin. The situation once again became strained. As documents testify, on the march to the battlefield and then during the Prokhorovka battle itself, Bakharov's corps performed no worse than the 5th Tank Army's other formations. Its losses in the course of the counterattack were less, for example, than those of the neighboring 29th Tank Corps, while the 18th Tank Corps managed to make a greater advance. Likely, the past had caught up with the general. Immediately after the conclusion of the defensive phase of the Kursk battle, Bakharov was nonetheless removed from his post as corps commander, but the story of this will come later.

I have lingered on this story from the life of one corps commander, but this was done only to show how capricious are the turns in fate for people, and how subjective evaluations and unforeseen situations meant a lot in those difficult times. Similar cases, when not only corps commanders, but also army commanders and even *front* commanders were trapped by fate, were not few.

The Artillery of the 5th Guards Tank Army

The 5th Guards Tank Army headquarters had only two artillery regiments under its direct command: the 678th Howitzer Regiment and the 689th Destroyer Anti-tank Regiment. In addition, each of the three corps had one destroyer anti-tank regiment (20 45mm and 76mm guns), and one mortar regiment, one mixed composition self-propelled artillery regiment, with 21 SU-76M and SU-122 self-propelled guns (the 18th Tank Corps had a regiment of Churchill tanks, armed with 57mm main guns), as well as one Guards mortar battalion with 8 BM-13 *Katiusha* rocket launchers. During an offensive, the rocket battalions were usually combined with the army-level 76mm Guards mortar regiment into one group, in order to launch more powerful strikes on targets.

For conducting fire upon enemy fortifications, enemy reserves in the depth of the defenses, and for counter-battery fire, this quantity of artillery available to the 5th Guards Tank Army was plainly insufficient, particularly in howitzers. The calculation that the *front* would provide the army with necessary support units as it went into battle did not justify itself in the very first operation – in the fighting for Prokhorovka. Not all the assigned artillery regiments managed to arrive in time for the start of the attack, while the *front* command was compelled to redirect an anti-tank brigade to a different sector.

The organization and material means of controlling the army's artillery were also inadequate. The artillery commander's staff did not have adequate communications with the artillery units of the army and corps, nor did the army's artillery command include a command, control and communications team. The headquarters had only one vehicle attached to it – a one-and-a-half-ton truck.

The army also had noticeably limited means for anti-aircraft defense. Each corps only had one anti-aircraft artillery regiment (each with 16 37mm anti-aircraft guns, and 16 12mm and 17mm DShK anti-aircraft machine guns). Such a regiment could reliably protect only the corps headquarters. In addition, the army was strengthened by the 6th Anti-aircraft Artillery Division under the command of Colonel G. P. Mezhinsky. This formation had 64 DShK-39 machine guns and 64 anti-aircraft guns, including 16 85mm guns, and was capable of covering 63 square kilometers of territory (9 kilometers wide and 7 kilometers deep) with a density of one and a half guns per kilometer. Wrote A. I. Radzievsky:

> Regarding the anti-aircraft artillery regiments of the corps, they were capable of covering the major grouping of the forces when it was not in motion. But with the start of the attack, and also during regroupings, the effectiveness of the anti-aircraft artillery cover sharply declined as a consequence of the insufficient cross-country capabilities of the anti-aircraft artillery's wheeled vehicles. Therefore, fighter aircraft carried out the basic assignments for protecting the tank armies from aerial attack,

> especially during combat operations. The quantity of fighter aircraft formations assigned for this purpose constantly grew.[10]

While preparing for the counterattack of 12 July 1943, the 5th Guards Tank Army received in addition the 26th Anti-aircraft Artillery Division, since the army by that time had increased by one and a half times, having been temporarily assigned two additional tank corps. Despite this, the available anti-aircraft fire was not able to offer adequate protection to the ground forces from the air. The anti-aircraft artillerymen, like all artillerymen of the army, experienced significant difficulties in securing an adequate number of vehicles.

From the "Report on the combat operations of the artillery of the 5th Guards Tank Army during the Prokhorovka engagement, 12-25 July 1943" that was prepared by the chief of staff of the Army's artillery Colonel Koliaskin:

> The experience of combat operations showed the high maneuverability of tank and motorized units on the attack, which created great difficulties for the anti-aircraft artillery and for securing the anti-aircraft defense of the forces given the low number and poor [quality] of vehicles and prime movers in the division's units. As a rule, anti-aircraft batteries were moved in two ways. The ZIS-42 turned out to be an unsuitable prime mover for the 85mm guns because of its slow speed (only 6 to 8 kilometers per hour), poor cross-country performance in uneven terrain; in rainy weather it was practically worthless. It would be more useful to provide Studebaker trucks to the division's units, which are operating together with the tank formations.[11]

Unfortunately, this was not the only problem that the 5th Guards Tank Army's artillerymen encountered. We'll turn again to the "Report", prepared by Colonel Koliaskin, in which he in more detail describes and objectively evaluates both the general condition of the Army's artillery units, and the experience of their use in the Prokhorovka engagement:

> The officer staff of the artillery for the most part began service in the tank army first, young in age and low in rank, and had a shaky familiarity with the rules of gunnery, a poor grasp of the types of artillery fire patterns, and insufficient knowledge of equipment, ammunition, and instruments. Moreover, because of their youth, they had little experience in organizational questions. The entire command and personnel staff of the artillery had been put fully through training in artillery gunnery. However, fuel limits, the effort to conserve most of the artillery transport, and the strict effort to conserve tanks, had a negative influence on artillery training, particularly in rehearsing maneuvers and practicing cooperation with other types of forces. The scarcity of vehicles was the greatest weakness in the combat readiness of the units. The 271st and 285th Mortar Regiments, the 6th Anti-aircraft Artillery Regiment, and the 1446th Self-propelled Artillery Regiment had the fewest number of vehicles. This deficit in transport reduced combat readiness, and the lack of all-terrain tow vehicles all the more hampered the maneuverability of the tank army's artillery. The lack of sufficient fuel did not allow the opportunity to work

> out more fully the concerted action of the artillery with the tanks and motorized infantry, and complicated the preparation and training of the command staff for the performance of their duties in observation vehicles and in directing fire from radio-equipped tanks.
>
> Headquarters at all levels, because of the absence of authorized communication and control detachments, were not tested in their ability to control artillery fire in battle, while the absence of communication and control detachments themselves weighed heavily upon the work of knitting together the units, which adversely affected the results of the first battles.[12]

A separate problem was the preparation and training of personnel in the self-propelled artillery units. This was a new type of force for the Red Army. The first self-propelled artillery vehicles became available only in January 1943. There was no experience in using them at the front, which meant that self-propelled artillery units lacked trained and seasoned personnel. The recruits for these units came primarily from tank and artillery units. But operating a tank is considerably different from operating a self-propelled gun. Self-propelled guns had their main guns positioned in fixed, covered (SU-122, SU-152) or open (SU-76) crew compartments. Therefore, self-propelled guns could fire only in the direction that the entire vehicle was pointing. This detail created extra difficulties for the driver-mechanic, since he not only had to select the optimal route and control the vehicle, but also adjust its movement at the direction of the gun layer. Self-propelled guns on the attack typically followed the first line of tanks, about 400 meters behind them, with the task of destroying detected enemy anti-tank threats.

The driver-mechanics of tanks were trained differently. The successful operations of our tanks depended much upon high speed and skillful maneuver. Thus they rehearsed the technique of driving a tank until the motions became automatic (their life depended upon this), and it was not easy to adjust the psychology of the tank driver from the tank's headlong dash to the assault gun's methodical "bringing up the rear" of the attacking forces. As the first experience of combat at Prokhorovka later showed, self-propelled gun crews often rushed ahead, placing their lightly armored vehicles under direct hostile anti-tank fire – which resulted in heavy losses.

"All the [self-propelled artillery] regiments went through lengthy training as part of the corps," wrote Colonel Koliaskin. "Combat gunnery training and tactical exercises with tanks were conducted, [but] in connection with the shortage of fuel, they were few. In general, the regiments were in sufficient shape, with the exception of the driver-mechanics, whose preparation was unsatisfactory."[13]

Such a problem arose not only in the 5th Guards Tank Army. Order No. 1130714c from the deputy commander of the Red Army's Armored and Tank Forces, Lieutenant General Vol'sky, to the Voronezh Front command contained the following language:

> From the experience of operations at the front it has become clear that a significant number of SU-76 self-propelled guns in the self-propelled artillery regiments frequently break down due to mechanical problems not only in combat operations, but even during the stage of assembling the units prior to battle. The basic cause of this situation is the driver-mechanics' poor grasp of the particulars of driving the

SU-76 and their shaky knowledge of the self-propelled gun's mechanics. In order to eliminate the noted deficits

I hereby order:

The immediate inspection of all SU-76 driver-mechanics on their knowledge of mechanics and the particulars of driving the SU-76.

Immediately replace weak driver-mechanics ... devote 10 hours to the practice of driving ... report on the execution of this order by 15.07.43.[14]

The situation with self-propelled guns for the Germans was somewhat different. The first self-propelled guns appeared in the *Wehrmacht* even before the attack on the Soviet Union. Having encountered an unexpected surprise with the Red Army's new models of armored vehicles in the summer of 1941, the Germans at the end of September 1941 began to implement the modernization of their own tanks and assault guns (self-propelled guns). In the years 1942-1943, they significantly increased the production of self-propelled guns and increased their quality, having greatly improved their armament: the main gun caliber ranged from 75mm up to 150mm. As a rule, these assault guns were used as part of anti-tank battalions, or as part of the artillery units of panzer, motorized and infantry divisions. The large number of these mobile and powerful guns greatly strengthened the enemy's anti-tank defenses.

Despite the disagreement of certain generals, by Hitler's orders the number of self-propelled guns and their variants in the *Wehrmacht* continued to grow. It is true that in connection with the diversity of models and gun modifications, problems increased with logistics and finding spare parts for repairs, but this didn't seriously affect their use, at least in the summer of 1943. By the start of Operation Citadel, the German army had rather well-developed tactics for using self-propelled guns, and well-trained officers and crews to man them, especially in the SS Panzergrenadier divisions. Thus, the Soviet tankers faced a very difficult situation.

For reconnaissance purposes, the tank army had a motorcycle regiment. For the same purpose, corps and brigades had reconnaissance battalions (or armored car battalions) and reconnaissance companies respectively. They were capable of reconnoitering the enemy to a depth of 30 kilometers in the army's sector of attack. The limited range of the radios in their possession did not permit them to increase the range of their scouting.

Long-range reconnaissance – to a depth of up to 300 kilometers – was a serious problem. *Front* aviation conducted this reconnaissance at the request of army headquarters. Thus *front* headquarters should have provided the army with the results of long-range reconnaissance before the army went into battle. However, for a number of reasons, the information that arrived wasn't always of sufficient quality or in requisite volume. Thus, during the Prokhorovka engagement, the 5th Guards Tank Army's command was forced to resort to using the PO-2 airplanes of the 994th Army Aviation Regiment of night bombers for reconnaissance purposes. However, these slow-moving planes were not adapted for conducting reconnaissance during daylight hours – they were quickly shot down.

The 4th Separate Signals Regiment and two overhead line companies (responsible for constructing and maintaining overhead telephone lines) provided communications for the 5th Guards Tank Army. In addition, each corps also had a separate signals battalion and an aviation signals unit. While the army was located in the reserve, it made wide use of communication wires and mobile radio stations, but upon going into battle, radio communications played a much greater role. Given this, the TO&E's authorized number of signals regiments for the army plainly did not meet the requirements of battle. The entire 5th Guards Tank Army had only 800 radio sets, including those in command tanks. The army's command and control unit possessed only 26 or 27 radio receivers and one *Sever* ("North") radio set [a small, portable radio 1.2 W radio set, popular with agents and partisans, with a communications range of up to 400 kilometers], three or four RAF wireless sets, and 16 RSB high-frequency wireless sets; each corps had seven or eight radio receivers and radio sets, including one or two RAF radio sets, and four RSB radio sets. There was an acute deficit of radios capable of long-range transmission and reception. Right up until 1944, only one or two types of powerful radio sets with a reliable range of reception and transmission of more than 50 kilometers ever reached the troops.

The situation with radio communications at the brigade level was particularly difficult. For both controlling its subordinate units and maintaining communications with the corps, brigade headquarters had only two weak 12-RP sets with an effective range of only 8 kilometers. In combat conditions, they were frequently knocked out at the start of the battle by artillery fire and bombing attacks, which forced the brigade commander to pull radio-equipped tanks (as a rule, a T-34 or KV tank) out of the combat line in order to reestablish reliable communications with his battalions – thereby at the same time weakening the fighting strength of the battalions.

The RB radio set, which equipped the corps' reconnaissance units, secured communications over a range of less than 20 kilometers, and would not operate while in motion. Moreover, it must be noted that the majority of the line T-34 tanks, not to mention the light T-70 tanks, were not equipped with two-way radios at all, and only a few of them even had radio receivers.

The dynamic nature of tank combat, the large number of critical situations, and the adversary's high combat-readiness demanded an increased tempo in receiving, analyzing, and transmitting information to the troops, and in communicating orders and instructions. The deficit and low quality of the means of communication, as well as the limited number of officers connected with this work – all this told negatively on the work of the command and control units, the staff of which was largely inexperienced and untested in battle. There was also a large disparity between the numbers of officers who worked directly under fire, and those who served in the rear support units – of course, in favor of the latter.

The training of the command cadre was an acute problem. As P. A. Rotmistrov later wrote:

> In the second half of March the army was relocated to the vicinity of Ostrogozhsk, where it began to prepare for combat operations. The units and formations of the army embarked upon planned exercises. … The officers learned to control subordinate units on the offensive, to conduct meeting tank engagements, to deploy

> from the march into combat formations, to coordinate with other types of forces in battle, and to organize and conduct constant reconnaissance and surveillance of the enemy. Headquarters prepared to direct subordinate units in combat capably and clearly. Staff officers underwent exercises and attended a theoretical meeting on the subject, 'The Use of the Tank Corps as Part of the Tank Army in an Offensive Operation'. Training exercises with live fire were conducted on the theme, 'The Attack on a Hastily Prepared Enemy Defensive Position by a Tank Brigade, Supported by Artillery, a Self-Propelled Artillery Regiment, and Means of Communication.'[15]

However, the results of this training were not fully satisfactory. In a letter, Lieutenant General Vol'sky stressed:

> ... the combat training plans lack purposefulness and specificity with respect to times and assignments (2nd Tank Corps, 1st Guards Mechanized Corps). [Despite] daily functional training, the commanders of headquarters, services, and the rear, and of formations and units are still not developing the necessary habits (brevity, precision, clarity) in preparing documents and speeding work. The quality of functional training is low. Chiefs of staff, and of formations and units, are excusing themselves from participating in these training exercises (19th Tank Corps, 5th Guards Tank Army). The staging of training [exercises] for the signals officers has been poor. They are not being taught what will be expected of them in battle, [which] in the first place are an excellent knowledge of topography, the ability to depict a situation on a map accurately and quickly, and to give verbal reports.[16]

There was a catastrophic shortage of staff officers. Indicative in this respect was the situation in the operations department of the 5th Guards Tank Army's headquarters. Because of a lack of educated officers with work experience in a headquarters on that level, by the middle of March 1943, it had only 65 to 70% of the staff authorized by the TO&E. Only one officer – the chief of the department Lieutenant Colonel F. M. Belozerov – had a higher education. A similar situation had developed in other of the army's command and control units. For example, of the 20 commanders of the tank, mechanized, and motorized rifle brigades, only three had graduated from a military academy: Colonel N. K. Volodin of the 25th Tank Brigade, Colonel A. K. Brazhnikov of the 4th Guards Tank Brigade, and Lieutenant Colonel N. P. Lipichev of the 53rd Motorized Rifle Brigade. The majority of the remaining commanders had completed seven to ten years of education and various courses for improving commanders or chiefs of staff.

However, despite the shortcomings in organizing professional training, officers quickly gained combat experience on the battlefield and, as a rule, handled their subordinate units in battle no worse than, and sometimes even better than, those officers who had graduated from military specialist schools or academies, but still lacked combat experience.

In connection with the deployment of the tank armies, as well as the analysis of the experience in the preceding battles, the Red Army high command adopted a series of measures to increase the level of training of tankers. At the beginning of 1943, a large number of officers were sent to courses for improving the command staff. The period of training was reduced to three months, but the training day was lengthened to up to twelve hours. With the aim of increasing the status of these courses, they were called Higher Officer Courses. A significant number of senior officers and generals were accepted into the I.V. Stalin Military Academy of Motorization and Mechanization of the Red Army. The period of study in this academy was also reduced: for the command faculty, to one year, for the engineering faculty, to three years.

On 3 January 1943, Stalin signed an order of the People's Commissariat of Defense, which fundamentally changed the system of training at the lowest element of the tank units – the tank crews. By this order, the entire process of combat training was concentrated in one unit – the training tank brigade. Seven such brigades were created; they consisted of two to three training and one reserve regiments. The training regiments prepared specialists, while the reserve regiments formed crews and march companies. In such a way, the entire responsibility for the quality of training fell upon the command of the training brigade. The structure of units at the tank factories changed as well. Battalions and companies were converted into reserve tank regiments, which not only formed the march subunits, but also led their training and brought together the crews. In May 1943, self-propelled artillery units were transferred to the armored forces. In connection with this, in addition to the already available training center for self-propelled artillery and two training artillery regiments, two training tank brigades were converted to train self-propelled artillery crews.

They also worked on the preparation of tank crew specialists in the acting army. Experience showed that in order to preserve the combat efficiency of the corps, it was extremely important to have a reserve of combat-ready tank crews. At the start of the Kursk battle, the new system of training was fully in place, but the acting army felt the results of the new system's work only by autumn, when it began to operate at full power.

However, because of the high combat losses, which the high command often tolerated, it proved impossible to restore fully the cadre staff of specialists in the tank formations and to raise their level of training. Here is one example of the, at the very least, irrational use of specialists with combat experience, who had received months of training. As General of the Army A. I. Gribkov recalled:

> ... In the winter of 1942 and the spring of 1943, I was a representative of the General Staff with the 19th Tank Corps, which was conducting an offensive in the direction of Kursk, Dmitriev-L'govskii and Sevsk as part of Briansk Front, when the Kursk bulge was formed. Ivan Dmitrievich Vasil'ev was commanding the corps – an experienced, competent and brave general. At the outbreak of the war, he was commanding the 14th Tank Division, which became part of General Vasilii Ivanovich Vinogradov's 7th Mechanized Corps.
>
> The 19th Tank Corps in the course of the winter offensive suffered heavy losses in tanks and vehicles, while the rear support units lagged behind because of the deep snow drifts. Vasil'ev had been forced to use bulls and cows harnessed to sleighs to deliver fuel and ammunition to his units.
>
> The corps continued to attack, but in those conditions the Front command did something that, in my view, was utterly inexcusable. Striving at any cost to continue to advance, it ordered that tank crews, which had lost their tanks in battle,

to be sent into the infantry. The tankers, operating as regular infantrymen, suffered heavy losses.

'We're overseeing the destruction of the tankers,' General Vasil'ev declared indignantly one day. 'They'll send us another batch of replacement tanks, but who will I have to put in them? What do you have to say to this as a representative of the General Staff?'

What could I say, when I myself had witnessed tankers in black uniforms and sheepskin coats darkened by diesel fuel stains, who were marching with tank machine guns in their hands among the thin ranks of the infantry.

'I feel sorry for the lads,' an aged infantry battalion commander told me, when we were lying together in a snowdrift before the next attack on a nearby little hamlet, half hidden by the falling snow. 'They don't know our infantry business and are throwing away their lives for nothing.'

Taking stock of the situation that had developed, I sent a coded message to the General Staff, and a copy of it to our senior representative of the General Staff with the Front, Colonel V. T. Fomin. I described the circumstances, the true situation with the units of the corps, and offered the conclusion that it was necessary to withdraw the corps into the reserve for refitting, or more accurately, for reforming. The Front commander, Colonel General M. A. Reiter, found out about my report. He wrote the following upon it:

'1. Withdraw the corps into reserve.

2. Re-assign Gribkov to a post outside the *Front*.'[17]

The mobility of the tank army depended to a great extent on the mobility of its rear support elements. By the middle of 1943, the weight of one day's ammunition load for the army was 1,200 tons, while it required 600 tons of fuel daily. A tank army of typical composition should have had: 4,380-5,000 cargo trucks, 467-740 special vehicles, and 163-236 light vehicles. At the beginning of July 1943, the 142nd and 144th Separate Autotransport Battalions were serving the 5th Guards Tank Army's need for transportation, while the subordinate corps were supported by separate fuel and lubricant supply companies. When at full strength, the supply units were able to satisfy fully the requirements of the army, bringing up everything necessary for battle. However, the supply units in the army and the formations were usually missing up to 25% of their authorized number of vehicles. There were also serious problems with the quality of the available supply trucks, and with finding spare parts to keep them running.

Despite these problems, the situation with the forming of the units of the 5th Guards Tank Army and their material supply was significantly better than in the other homogenous composition tank armies that formed at the same time. Lieutenant General M. E. Katukov's 1st Tank Army serves as one example. Here is an excerpt from the "Operational-tactical description of the defensive operation of the 1st Tank Army on the Belgorod axis in the period 5-15 July 1943," where there is a discussion of the condition of the Army's units prior to the start of the summer fighting:

The corps-level artillery units were wanting in the following:

a) Self-propelled artillery regiments were absent in all the corps;

b) The 31st Tank Corps was missing a destroyer anti-tank regiment, a regiment of anti-aircraft defense, and a heavy mortar regiment;

c) The [6th] Tank Corps was missing a regiment of anti-aircraft defense. Anti-aircraft machine gun companies were deficit in all the corps.

By the start of the operation, other units had not yet been organized and were missing:

a) The Army's motorcycle regiment;

b) In the 31st Tank Corps, the motorized rifle brigade had not yet been formed, nor the motorcycle regiment. The aviation signals detachment had not yet arrived;

c) The Army's 385th Bomber Aviation Regiment was lacking 12 U-2 bombers.

In addition, the 1st Tank Army's light tanks were T-60 tanks, which had been produced in 1941. They had thin armor (25 to 35mm) and a weak 20mm gun. The 5th Guards Tank Army also received light tanks, but the more powerful T-70 tanks, which had a larger caliber gun (45mm) and an armor thickness of 35 to 45mm. However, neither tank was capable of taking on the German medium tanks in open battle, much less the German heavy tanks.

4

Fighting on Voronezh Front's Sector 5–9 July 1943

On 1 July 1943, a meeting took place at Hitler's Headquarters in East Prussia. The list of participants was small: the *Führer* himself, Field Marshal E. von Manstein, the commander of Army Group South, H. von Klüge, the commander of Army Group Center, and the commanders of the armies and corps of the ground forces and *Luftwaffe* due to take part in Operation Citadel. It was fated for these men to play an important role not only in the *Wehrmacht's* summer offensive on the Eastern Front, but also, as it turned out, to participate in the decisive battle, which proved tragic for German fascism and inspirational for the peoples of occupied Europe.

"At this meeting," recalled E. von Manstein, "where Hitler was the only one to present a report, he announced his final decision to launch Operation Citadel. The offensive was to begin on 5 July."[1]

Hitler's decision initiated the deployment of forces and the final stage of preparations for the offensive. On 3 July, Field Marshal von Manstein arrived in Bucharest. In the presence of a retinue and specially invited journalists, he delivered a gold medallion to Marshal I. Antonescu, Romania's dictator, for that country's participation in the Crimean campaign. This was a diversion, designed to mislead Stalin about Germany's plans. Unquestionably, Soviet intelligence had already informed the Supreme High Commander that the Field Marshal was one of the key figures in the anticipated offensive in the region of Kursk. Field Marshal von Manstein's absence from the front was supposed to provide another argument in support of the idea that Germany had no plans to undertake active combat operations in the East. However, that very evening, the commander of Army Group South secretly boarded his headquarters train, which was sitting in a forest on a reserve rail branch, and prepared to depart the next day for a point closer to the front, where he could respond more quickly to issues in the sector of the armies that were preparing for the operation.

Lieutenant General Chistiakov's 6th Guards Army was defending along the axis of Army Group South's main attack.[2] The immediate plan for breaking through its first line of defenses with the forces of the Fourth Panzer Army was relatively simple and thus sufficiently predictable. Colonel General H. Hoth was placing his main hope on his panzers, the attack of which in the first stage of the offensive was going to be directly accompanied by various types of self-propelled artillery and self-propelled guns. It was namely these forces that had the task of breaching the Soviet defenses, with the powerful support of artillery and the *Luftwaffe*'s dive bombers and bombers.

The terrain, which the forces of the 6th Guards Army had occupied at the end of March, was rather difficult – a plain cut by a large number of deep ravines and gullies, dotted with numerous villages and farms. Moreover, in front of the II SS Panzer Corps and the right flank of the XXXXVIII Panzer Corps lay the swampy valley of the Vorskla

River and its tributary the Vorsklitsa, while tributaries of the Pena River confronted the XXXXVIII Panzer Corps' left wing and the LII Army Corps on its left. About 12 kilometers behind the forward zone of defenses, a significant portion of the 6th Guards Army's second line of defenses had been constructed behind a bend in the Pena River (the "Pena bulge"). Thus, the valleys of these rivers alone presented a serious obstacle to enemy forces attacking from the south. As archival documents of the 6th Guards Army reveal, of the 64 kilometers in its sector, the 6th Guards Army's headquarters considered 28 kilometers to be difficult for tanks to navigate, while the remaining 36 kilometers were accessible to armored vehicles. Of the 13 potential routes of advance suitable for tanks, four ran along the primary roads leading to the north and northeast (towards the village of Iakovlevo, Oboian', and so forth). Each of the 13 possible routes of advance had a width of 0.5 to 20 kilometers, and altogether they spanned 38 kilometers across 6th Guards Army's front.

It is no secret that natural barriers, like gullies, flood lands, and swampy branches of rivers significantly strengthen a defensive position, and with proper, often not even very extensive fortifications laid out by engineers, they can become powerful anti-tank barriers. There were enough such natural barriers along the likely lines of tank advance in the 6th Guards Army's sector. The Germans for their part very carefully studied the information gleaned from observation posts and aerial reconnaissance photographs, and therefore knew that the Soviet side had conducted extensive work throughout the length and depth of their defenses to prepare for the offensive.

Taking these considerations into account, H. Hoth decided to take no chances, and chose, just as the Voronezh Front anticipated, a well-tested approach – a breakthrough along the major roads. However, he planned to strike the main blow not from one area, as had been the previous practice, but from two areas simultaneously: the II SS Panzer Corps, along both sides of the Tomarovka – Bykovka – Iakovlevo road; and the XXXXVIII Panzer Corps, from the Bytovo-Cherkasskoe area along another good road leading to Iakovlevo. Both formations had the task to link up as quickly as possible in the vicinity of Iakovlevo. Thrusts along these graded roads would allow the panzers to avoid the boggy and well-fortified flood lands of the Vorskla and Vorsklitsa Rivers, and a successful development of events would enable them to avoid getting tied up in heavy fighting, and lead to the encirclement of the Soviet forces in this region. Hoth formulated this task in his order to his subordinate corps in the following fashion. The third point in his Order No. 6 to his corps stated:

> 3. The II SS Panzer Corps, supported by tanks, after strong artillery preparation, developing a systematic offensive, breaks through the forward zone of the enemy's defenses in the sector Berezov, Zadel'noe. The heights, necessary for artillery observation, must be occupied at night. One division, echeloned to the right, attacks toward the vicinity of Zhuravlinyi and takes control of the Belgorod – Iakovlevo road. After finishing the battle for the enemy's first position, the Corps must immediately continue the offensive toward the second position – between Luchki and Iakovlevo. The left flank along the Vorskla River will be covered by 1/3 [one regiment] of the 167th Infantry Division.
>
> After breaking through the second position, the Corps will pause to regroup and make itself ready, so that, after adopting a formation echeloned to the right, it

> can attack with its main forces to the northeast – south of the Psel sector, and with its right flank – through Prokhorovka.[3]

Thus, the II SS Panzer Corps had to carry out three tasks: first, to break through the first line of defense to its entire depth. Secondly, parallel with the breakthrough operation, its left flank formations had to maintain pressure on the Soviet forces defending along the Vorsklitsa River (the 153rd Guards Rifle Regiment of the 52nd Guards Rifle Division), and cooperate with the XXXXVIII Panzer Corps in encircling them. Finally, two of its divisions on the latter half of the first day of the offensive (according to the plan) had to overcome the second army-level defensive line and emerge on the Prokhorovka axis, toward the bend in the Psel River. In addition, the commanders of the *Leibstandarte* and *Das Reich* Panzergrenadier Divisions had an additional order: if things went well, to force a crossing of the Psel River and create a bridgehead on its northern bank, to support a further offensive to the northeast, and at the same time to attack Prokhorovka Station.

Consequently, the advance of the XXXXVIII Panzer Corps to the north, towards Oboian', depended directly on how quickly the SS troops would be able to overcome the line of the 6th Guards Army in the Dubrova – Iakovlevo area and to move out on the Prokhorovka axis. Headquarters, Fourth Panzer Army expressed the XXXXVIII Panzer Corps orders this way:

> 4. … on day "X" (5 July), the Corps continues its offensive through the main belt of the enemy's defenses from the lines it has already obtained. After a strong artillery preparation and with the support of panzers, the Corps advances at first west of Cherkasskoe, and then seizes the enemy's line of defenses along both sides of the Butovo – Dubrova road. After turning to the north-east, it will deploy its panzers to the front and strike in the direction of Dubrovka, having the task to block the retreat of the enemy to the north, south of Ol'khovatka, and to support the offensive of the II SS Panzer Corps east of the Vorskla River. Make decisive use of any possibility to penetrate the enemy's second echelon of defenses …
>
> After seizing the Belgorod – Oboian' road, the corps must be ready to advance against the sector of the Psel River lying between Ol'khovskii and Shipy.[4]

Thus, in the first stage of Army Group South's offensive, the II SS Panzer Corps was given the leadership role, and it both had to clear the XXXXVIII Panzer Corps' starting positions along the Belgorod – Kursk highway for the breakthrough toward Oboian' and to cover the right flank of General Otto von Knobelsdorff's XXXXVIII Panzer Corps. The SS Panzer Corps' three Panzergrenadier divisions had to split the enemy's most heavily-fortified defensive sector – the main band of defenses west of the Belgorod – Kursk highway and to clear a corridor to Iakovlevo, and then subsequently pivot to the right, in the Prokhorovka direction, leaving Iakovlevo for its stronger neighbor. After completing the breakthrough of the main line by both panzer corps and the II SS Panzer Corps' turn to the northeast, it would fall to General von Knobelsdorff's XXXXVIII Panzer Corps to accomplish the Fourth Panzer Army's, indeed the entire Army Group South's, main assignment. In order to cover the flank and secure the captured territory, von Knobelsdorff's panzer corps was strengthened by Lieutenant General Trierenberg's 167th Infantry Division (minus one infantry regiment and an artillery battalion) and

Lieutenant General Schaefer's full-strength 332nd Infantry Division from LII Army Corps. General Eugen Ott's LII Army Corps was to cover the left flank of Fourth Panzer Army as it advanced, and General Werner Kempf's Army Detachment would cover the right.

The German command paid particular attention to increasing the combat worthiness of the forces that were to take part in the Kursk offensive. In order to conduct Operation Citadel, they assigned some of the best panzer and motorized formations in the German Army to the offensive. Their strengths lay in the fact that they had been brought back up to almost full strength with personnel and had been equipped with upgraded and new medium and heavy tanks, self-propelled guns and artillery, and anti-tank guns. In addition, these were all veteran units with extensive combat experience. Their commanders at all levels of command were seasoned professionals.

The German panzer corps was a numerically strong and very powerful combat formation. It is difficult to compare it to any Soviet formation. In numbers it was roughly comparable to a Soviet combined arms army, which had been strengthened by three tanks corps.

Thus, on 1 July 1943, the XXXXVIII Panzer Corps, which consisted of the 3rd and 11th Panzer Divisions and the *Grossdeutschland* Panzergrenadier Division, numbered a total of 61,692 men, of which 59,729 were soldiers and officers, and 1,963 were civilians. At full strength, the 167th Infantry Division had a total of 17,837 men. Notably, the XXXXVIII Panzer Corps' 3rd Panzer Division had 1,106 former Red Army prisoners, who had gone over to the German side. On 4 July, the XXXXVIII Panzer Corps had 674 armored vehicles (464 tanks and 147 assault guns and self-propelled artillery vehicles). At the start of Operation Citadel, this formation was strengthened by the 10th Panzer Brigade, which contained two battalions of Panther tanks in its 39th Panzer Regiment with a total of nearly 200 Panthers. The brigade had specifically been assigned to the XXXXVIII Panzer Corps to serve as a shock formation in the anticipated struggle with the 1st Tank Army, which the command of the Fourth Panzer Army assumed would enter the battle in the XXXXVIII Panzer Corps' sector of operations already at some point in the first stage of Citadel.

By number of armored vehicles, the II SS Panzer Corps yielded to the XXXXVIII Panzer Corps among the formations of the Fourth Panzer Army. On 4 July 1943, its three SS Panzergrenadier divisions had a combined total of 390 tanks, but also 104 anti-tank StuG assault guns, and 98 self-propelled guns of the Marder, Hummel, and Wespe types. According to data presented by the American scholar David Glantz, the II SS Panzer Corps had an operational strength of 356 tanks on 4 July 1943.[5] At the start of the operation, the SS Panzer Corps was also given the 315th Infantry Regiment and a battalion of the 238th Artillery Regiment from the 167th Infantry Division. In addition, the SS Panzer Corps received Colonel Grewen's 3rd Division of *Nebelwerfer* Troops, which consisted of two powerful rocket artillery regiments, the 55th *Werfer* and the 1st *Werfer Lehr* (Training), with a mixture of light (150-210mm) and one heavy (280-320mm) battalions of the German rocket launcher, the *Nebelwerfer*. Each of these regiments had approximately 1,500 men, 54 rocket launchers, and up to 10 captured Soviet 76mm anti-tank guns.

At the start of Operation Citadel, the II SS Panzer Corps mustered 73,380 men, with a combat effective strength of 39,106. Of its divisions, the SS *Leibstandarte Adolf*

Hitler had a ration strength of 20,933 men, of which 12,893 were combat effectives; SS *Das Reich* had respectively 19,812 and 10,441 men; and SS *Totenkopf* had respectively 19,176 and 10,214 men. Units directly subordinate to corps headquarters had a ration strength of 8,800 men, and 5,558 combat effectives.[6]

On the left flank of Voronezh Front's 6th Guards Army, the SS men would first encounter two divisions of Major General P.P. Vakhrameev's 23rd Guards Rifle Corps. At 0300 July 5, the enemy began a general artillery preparation and bombardment of our forward zone. But even a few hours before this moment, advancing enemy assault groups had encountered forward outposts of Colonel I. M. Nekrasov's 52nd Guards Rifle Division and Colonel P. D. Govorunenko's 375th Rifle Division, and triggered the initial fighting. The 52nd Guards Rifle Division was positioned in the Army's first echelon, and was covering one of the likely major panzer routes of advance – the graded rode between Tomarovka and Iakovlevo. Its regiments had dug in on the line (excl.) Trirechnoe – Gremuchii – Nepkhaevo – Koz'mo-Dem'ianovka, with a forward zone running along the line: southern edge of the Lapin grove – southern outskirts of Zadel'noe – southern outskirts of Berezov – southern outskirts of Gremuchii.

The SS Panzer Corps went on the offensive immediately with all three formations from the Stepnoi ravine, the wooded slopes of Sukhoi Verkh, and Rakovo (north) on the front: Hill 227.4 – Hill 218.0 – Iakhontov – Hill 228.6 – Streletskoe. The SS Divisions *Leibstandarte* and *Das Reich* fell heavily on the sector of the 52nd Guards Rifle Division's line, which was approximately 6 kilometers wide between Hill 228.6 and Hill 218.0, running through Iakhontov. The axis of the offensive first lay along the graded main road running from Tomarovka to Iakovlevo. This route was most suitable for tank operations, so it was also heavily fortified under the supervision of engineers. The 52nd Guards Rifle Division's command concentrated most of its attached destroyer anti-tank regiments here. The SS Panzergrenadier Division *Leibstandarte* with the attached 315th Infantry Regiment on its left (from the 167th Infantry Division) struck the right flank of the 52nd Guards Rifle Division, while the SS Panzergrenadier Divisions *Das Reich* and *Totenkopf*, echeloned to the right of *Leibstandarte*, struck the 52nd Guards Rifle Division's center and left regiments. Thus, at the main point of Hoth's attack, each Guards regiment from the 52nd Guards Rifle Division faced one SS Panzergrenadier Division.

From the first minutes of the offensive, the bitterest fighting erupted for Hills 220.5 and 217.1 (in the sector of the 151st Guards Rifle Regiment) and in the region of the farming village Berezov (held by the 155th Guards and 156th Guards Rifle Regiments, 51st Guards Rifle Division). The 3rd Rifle Battalion of the 51st Guards Rifle Division's 156th Rifle Regiment, which was under the 52nd Guards Rifle Division's operational control and had been reinforced with special combat engineer and flamethrower companies, was defending the village of Berezov itself. It had prepared an all-round defense of the village. Its 9th Company had dug in on the western outskirts, the 8th Company on the southern outskirts, and the 7th Company on the the northern and northeastern outskirts. Unfortunately, it is difficult to reconstruct the events of this unequal battle, because none of the defenders survived it, and the combat operations of such small elements as a rifle company received scant coverage in the reports of higher headquarters. I have been able to gather only a few fragmentary lines on the fighting at Berezov, but even they bear witness to the unparalleled courage and dedication to duty of our troops. From the combat diary of the 51st Guards Rifle Division:

> ... 3/156 Gds RR [Guards Rifle Regiment], defending in the vicinity of Berezov, was under the operational control of the 52nd Gds RD [Guards Rifle Division].
>
> At dawn on 5.07.1943, the enemy knocked aside the security outpost of this division in the region of Iakhontov and launched an attack on Berezov. ... The 9th Rifle Company did not abandon its positions, and in the initial stubborn fighting, the entire company was wiped out together with its equipment; remnants of the 7th and 8th Companies – 41 men – fell back under the enemy's onslaught to the main defensive line of their regiment, and by the morning of 6.07.1943, set up a defense in the area of Hill 246.3.[7]

At 0720, Voronezh Front's deputy chief of staff, Major General S. Teteshkin, while informing the commander of the 5th Guards Tank Corps about the unfolding situation, stressed that the fighting on this sector had reached the point of hand-to-hand combat in the trenches.

Berezov was the first populated location in the main belt of defense of General I. M. Chistiakov's army that the SS troops had to take. As II SS Panzer Corps documents testify, it had sufficiently accurate information on the condition of the Soviet formations opposing it, the extent of fortifications in the village, and the layout of their lines. However, the initial attacks disheartened the enemy, indicating that even the corps command, not to mention the subordinate regiment commands, were not prepared to encounter such stubborn resistance from the Soviet forces.

Hausser, personally observing the attack on Berezov from the Panzergrenadier Regiment *Der Führer*'s command post in the SS *Das Reich* sector of the attack, watched as lines of grenadiers fell like freshly-mown grass under the fire from Soviet artillery and the *Katiusha* rockets. Black mushroom clouds of smoke and flashes of flame erupted here and there along the entire front of Panzergrenadier Regiment *Deutschland*'s attacking wedges. Over the radio, casualty reports began to arrive: many killed, even more wounded. It had become clear: the artillery preparation and air strikes had done relatively little damage to the enemy's minefields, fortifications and artillery. The calculation that the Soviet troops would be stunned by the powerful air attack and unable to resist was not realized. The first assault on the lines of the 52nd Guards Rifle Division confirmed the worst of the *Obergruppenführer*'s assumptions – there would be no clean, swift penetration of the enemy's positions; they would have to gnaw their way through them meter by meter.

This was indeed the focus of his first orders after temporarily halting the offensive. SS *Das Reich*'s artillery regiments were given the assignment to conduct intensive counter-battery fire on identified targets. The attached batteries of six-barreled rocket launchers of the 55th *Werfer* and 1st *Werfer Lehr* Regiments received instructions to destroy the Soviet troops sheltering in the trenches and in foxholes. In order to destroy the Soviet artillery grouping in the region of the Zhuravlinyi woods, which was pounding Berezov and Gremuchii with its fire and was particularly vexing the attackers, Junkers Ju 87 *Stuka* dive-bombers from the VIII Air Corps were urgently requested through the *Luftwaffe*'s liaison officer with the ground forces.

Around 0600, under covering fire provided by the panzers, the Germans advanced sappers into the minefields. A special group of combat engineers was detached to collapse the walls of an anti-tank ditch in front of Berezov, in order to fill it in and create a crossing for the combat vehicles.

An account of the action by Voronezh Front's headquarters notes:

> The working over of our defenses from the air, in combination with artillery fire, was supposed to secure a breakthrough for their tanks by means of the suppression of our fire systems, the destruction of a significant portion of our troop strength, and the demolition of the fortifications and weapons of our defenses at the intended breakthrough sector. Just for this reason, the Germans conducted a systematic, uninterrupted aerial bombardment of the ground in and around the breakthrough sectors by large numbers of airplanes, with the use of large incendiary bombs, small fragmentation bombs, and small cluster bombs.
>
> However, the extensive system of trenches and shelters in our defense prevented the enemy from realizing his optimistic expectations regarding the effect [of the bombing]; our losses in men from the [enemy] aviation were insignificant.[8]

The main forces of the *Luftwaffe*'s VIII Air Corps supported the II SS Panzer Corps. According to some data, over the course of the entire day on 5 July, the VIII Air Corps supported the offensive with 400 airplanes, primarily bombers and dive-bombers.[9]

Dawn, 5 July 1943; sappers from one of the Fourth Panzer Army's divisions prepare a passage through a belt of the Soviet defenses. (RGAKFD)

At some time between 0930 and 1000, the Germans broke through the forward defenses of the 52nd Guards Rifle Division and advanced into its depths, where troops of the 151st and 155th Guards Rifle Regiments joined battle against enemy tanks and assault guns. Trying to destroy all resistance, the crews of the enemy vehicles crushed the trenches beneath their tracks in a rage. Striving to grind everything living into the earth, the tanks turned "figure eights" over the dugouts, bunkers, and foxholes.

Despite the heavy attack, the command staff of the 52nd Guards Rifle Division maintained its composure, never lost control over its units, and skillfully held its lines practically until the end of the day. The formation made effective use of the advantages of the defensive line, obstacles like wire and minefields, concealed weapon emplacements, and all types of weapons and means of struggle, especially in the region of Berezov and Gremuchii.

It should be noted that despite the enemy's significant numerical superiority, the fact that the rifle division's company sectors had three, and in places four lines of trenches connected by communication trenches contributed to the stubborn and prolonged resistance. This enabled regiment commanders to maneuver their battalions and companies quickly and with minimal losses, containing the attackers and averting a full breakthrough in the sector.

According to the testimony of Voronezh Front's artillery commander, General S. Varentsov, it was in the sector of the 6th Guards Army where gun crews of Major V. I. Barkovsky's 538th Destroyer Anti-tank Artillery and Major I. K. Kotenko's 1008th Destroyer Anti-tank Artillery Regiments, together with the 151st Guards Rifle Regiment's artillery under Colonel I. M. Nekrasovai, first encountered SS Panzergrenadier Division *Leibstandarte*'s 13th Company of Tiger tanks and the StuG battalion that was covering it. Both anti-tank artillery regiments had been transferred from the 1st Tank Army's 6th Tank Corps and placed under the operational control of the 52nd Guards Rifle Division even before the start of the operation. Their main forces were echeloned in depth on the most dangerous axis, and straddled the road running from Tomarovka to Iakovlevo. The 538th Destroyer Anti-tank Artillery Regiment deployed in the first echelon. Its guns were not concentrated in one region, but had been scattered by battery throughout the 151st Guards and 155th Guards Rifle Regiments' sectors of defense. The crews of the 1008th Destroyer Anti-tank Artillery Regiment had dug in on Hill 217.1 in the second echelon, though part of this regiment remained in the division commander's anti-tank reserve.

On the line Zadel'nyi ravine – Hill 220.5 – Hill 217.1, on the morning of 5 July occurred the first major battle between our artillery units and the enemy's tanks. Member of the 1st Tank Army's Military Council, Lieutenant General N. K. Popel', an eyewitness to the repulse of one of the enemy's attack by the anti-tank artillery regiments, recalled:

> The gun emplacements of the artillery were closer than one could suppose. The guns were standing in low fields of wheat, concealed from observation by the short stalks of grain.
>
> There is no need for binoculars. The German tanks are plainly visible without them. They are rolling forward in a wide ribbon, broken here and there by gaps. Their spearhead is striving to gobble up more and more ground. The left flank of the column crushed a dense grove of nut trees, and the leading vehicles, as if in

a moment of indecision, came to a stop in open ground. Black shell bursts coil tight plaits of smoke around them. The barrels of the anti-tank guns were lying horizontally, just above ground level. The spurts of flame from their barrels barely avoid the bent ears of wheat.

The regiment fires for less than an hour and one-third of the guns have already been put out of action. The gun crew members are dwindling in number. The losses are not so much from the tanks, as from enemy air attack.

German dive-bombers rule the skies. Now and then, they form into a closed ring formation, or shake out into a file. Then once again they are whirling in a round dance, releasing their bombs one after the other. Dozens of such round dances are revolving in the sky. And below them, columns of earth and flames are rising, and pieces of gun carriages and logs are sent flying …

Just a bit ago, Major Kotenko, the commander of an artillery regiment, tried to slip through to the gun emplacements in his jeep. The smoldering frame of his vehicle is now in the field. It is unknown how the surviving major still managed to reach the guns and is now serving a gun as part of the crew. There is nobody left at the observation posts – there is nothing for them to do there, if the regiment is firing over open sights. Many battery and platoon commanders are also manning guns in place of gun layers and loaders who have been knocked out of action.

Smoke, dust, cinders … A torrent of anti-tank fire and metal is directed against a torrent of fire and metal, discharged by German tanks and German artillery. A roaring blaze and whistling shell fragments are inundating everyone around like a boundless sea. In it, a person seems as fragile and short-lived, as a moth near a burning candle …

The bitterness of the fighting is unparalleled. After several hours, nothing remained of two of our destroyer anti-tank artillery regiments but, as they say, their unit number.[10]

The losses of the artillerymen were indeed high; from the 44 guns in the two regiments, only 12 remained by the end of the day.[11] Men died alongside their weapons and equipment.

The commander of the 6th Tank Corps, Major General A. L. Getman, reported:

The 538th Destroyer Anti-tank Artillery Regiment, in action against the enemy, has losses: 45mm guns – 18, Willys jeeps – 18, 12 men are wounded, 145 men have been killed or are missing in action; the loss of personnel is being determined more precisely. The regiment commander has been badly wounded, and has been sent to a hospital. The remaining officers and men of the regiment and its rear services have been attached to the headquarters of the 52nd Guards Rifle Division's artillery.[12]

In the latter half of the day, there was a turning point in the combat operations in the sector of the 52nd Guards Rifle Division. Headquarters, Voronezh Front reported:

At 1200, an enemy force of up to an infantry regiment together with 60 tanks launched an attack along the road to Bykovka, and a small group reached Hill 217.1 (1.5 kilometers northwest of Berezov); a battalion of infantry with 30 tanks entered

Berezov, and a tank unit has broken into Gremuchii.[13]

Thus, SS Panzergrenadier Division *Leibstandarte* by midday had already penetrated to the crest of Hill 217.1 (500 meters northeast of Hill 220.5), and a little later, by around 1330 – 1400, the SS Panzergrenadier Division *Das Reich* had fully seized the village of Berezov. At the same time, SS Panzergrenadier Division *Totenkopf* was engaged in fighting for Gremuchii and trying to expand the breakthrough in the direction of the Belgorod – Kursk highway.

From the 52nd Guards Rifle Division's combat diary:

> [In] the 155th Guards Rifle Regiment's sector ... after taking control of Berezov, the adversary set up a defensive position on the northern outskirts of the village, and brought up as much as a regiment of infantry and tanks. At 1430 on the northwest outskirts of Berezov, 85 tanks and a battalion of infantry moved out in the direction of Zhuravlinyi, and simultaneously – toward Gremuchii. Companies of the 2nd Rifle Battalion beat off this attack. Under the onslaught of the adversary's superior forces, the remnants of the 1st and 3rd Rifle Battalions began to withdraw in the direction of Zhuravlinyi. The 2nd Rifle Battalion was occupying its former region of defense in the area of Gremuchii. Over the course of the entire battle, the adversary's air force bombed the combat positions and the depth of the regiment's defenses. As a result of the bombing, many artillery pieces, weapons and men were knocked out of action. At 1600, the adversary took control of the Zhuravlinyi woods, thereby blocking the 2nd Rifle Battalion, which was still holding its previous lines, from its path of retreat.[14]

The retreat of the 155th Guards Rifle Regiment's battalions was disorderly; confusion reigned, which the constant German bombing only increased. Soldiers left the battlefield in groups and in ones and twos; part of the regiment was trapped in the village [Gremuchii]. The daily summary of the II SS Panzer Corps notes:

> After bitter fighting the enemy, beginning in the middle of the day, is retreating to the north. Despite the fact that the initial resistance has been overcome, we should expect the enemy to consolidate on the second line. The activity of our air force is energetic and is successfully supporting the fighting troops.[15]

By this time, units of the 52nd Guards Rifle Division were running low on ammunition. Enemy air attacks had set fire to several stockpiles of shells, which had been brought up in 13 trucks. However, the Guardsmen, who remained encircled, were continuing to inflict casualties on the enemy by fire and in hand-to-hand fighting. The division commander's last remaining anti-tank reserve was the 230th Tank Regiment, under the command of Colonel D. A. Shcherbakov. It was equipped with M3 Stuart and M3 Lee tanks. According to the defensive plan, three of the regiment's four companies had been concentrated in the area of Bykovka.

The M3 Stuart light tank and the "two-story" M3 Lee medium tank (so-called because it had a 37mm gun in the turret, and a 75mm howitzer mounted in a sponson on the right-hand side) had weak armor; therefore, they could only be used effectively from ambush positions and against infantry targets that didn't have the support of tank or a well-organized anti-tank defense. However, the situation gave no choice in the matter, for the enemy was breaking into the depth of the division's lines. At this moment it was imperative to give the retreating battalions a chance to break free from the pursuit and to consolidate in the positions in the region of Bykovka. Therefore Colonel I.M. Nekrasov at approximately 1400 hurled one tank company against a *kampfgruppe* [combat group] from the SS Panzergrenadier Division *Das Reich*, with the task of stopping its advance. According to German records, our tanks joined battle in the sector approximately 6 kilometers north of Berezov, on the rear slopes of Hill 233.3. At the same time, two more tank companies from the 230th Tank Regiment attacked the vanguard of *Leibstandarte* about 1.5 kilometers south of Bykovka. This was the first case of the Soviet side's use of tanks against the SS Panzer Corps in the Kursk battle. An officer of the General Staff with the 6th Guards Army, Lieutenant Colonel Shamov, reported on it to Moscow:

> ... A company of the 230th Tank Regiment was thrown into the fighting by the division commander. Units of the division, with the support of tanks, were offering stubborn resistance. Gun salvos, the roar of engines, the explosion of bombs, and the chatter of machine guns and submachine guns merged into a general roar. One after another, German tanks were blazing up in flames.[16]

This quotation from the report contains a lot of emotions and very little truth; the information is far from what really happened in that battle, including the assertion about the enemy's tank losses. Unfortunately, everything that happened was quite the opposite.

A German Marder self-propelled anti-tank gun in battle. On the left is the smoking wreckage of a Soviet M3 tank obtained through Lend-Lease. (RGAKFD)

In essence, this was a sacrificial attack for our tankers. In little more than a half an hour, the company ceased to exist as a combat unit. The crews of the enemy armored vehicles, taking advantage of their qualitative superiority of their guns at longer ranges, did not give our tanks even a chance to approach to within direct fire range, and simply shot them to pieces.

The results of the 230th Tank Regiment's counterattack are reported dryly in the daily report of the SS Panzergrenadier Division *Das Reich*'s chief of operations:

> 1445 [1645 Moscow time]. An enemy tank counterattack from the direction of Hill 233.3 has been repulsed. 7 tanks were knocked out. [There is] stubborn enemy resistance on Hill 233.3 and in the direction of Bykovka.[17]

After 1500, the enemy's bombing of our positions in the sector Kamennyi Log – Hill 215.4 – Hill 233.3 grew heavier. Especially intensive air strikes were inflicted upon the 52nd Guards Rifle Division's command post in the vicinity of Koz'mo-Dem'ianovka and Bykovka. Significant portions of two rifle regiments of the 52nd Guards Rifle Division were encircled and destroyed, while its remaining forces were on the move for Bykovka and weren't able to occupy the new line of defense in time. More than half of the guns of the 538th and 1008th Destroyer Anti-tank Artillery Regiments and the division's artillery had been smashed, all observation and command posts of the 151st and 155th Rifle Regiments had been overrun, and communications and control had been lost.

The region of Bykovka had important tactical significance. Together with Koz'mo-Dem'ianovka, this settlement was the last well-fortified strongpoint before the 6th Guards Army's second defensive belt. To the east of the village ran three deep, swampy ravines; to the west lay the flood lands of the Vorskla River. Thus, the only route open to tank movement from this region toward Oboian', was the Tomarovka – Iakovlevo main road, which ran through the center of Bykovka. Further on this highway entered Koz'mo-Dem'ianovka, which lay just north of Bykovka, across a bridge. However, Colonel I. M. Nekrasov by this time had practically nothing left with which to defend the twin villages.

According to the plan of maneuver for the 6th Guards Army's anti-tank reserve, Major Kosachev's 28th Separate Anti-tank Artillery Brigade should have been covering the routes of advance vulnerable to tanks in the sector of the 52nd Guards Rifle Division. At midday on 5 July, its regiments were still in their initial positions, in the vicinity of Pokrovka and Hill 254.2 (approximately 10 kilometers north of Bykovka). By its TO&E, the Brigade should have had three fully-equipped anti-tank artillery regiments: two with 76mm guns, one with 45mm anti-tank guns and, what is most important, a vehicle to tow each gun. In actual fact, this brigade had only two regiments, which had 76mm and 45mm anti-tank guns, as well as only 50% of the vehicles necessary to move the guns, the ammunition, and the personnel. However, the command of the 6th Guards Army did not have exactly this moment in mind when selecting and positioning the reserve formations, and choosing the times of their commitment in order to localize the breakthrough by the II SS Panzer Corps. The brigade commander received the order for moving his regiments to the vicinity of Bykovka too late, and the regimental columns set off on their way only after fighting for the village had already begun. Therefore,

Colonel Nekrasov's Guardsmen never received the expected assistance on this day. From the report of the 28th Separate Anti-tank Artillery Brigade:

> ... 5.07.43 The brigade received an order from the Army's artillery commander to throw forward one of the better 76mm gun batteries to the region of the *Smelo k trudu* [Stout-heartedly for labor] Collective Farm in order to destroy 13 enemy tanks that have broken through there. At 1445, the 4th Battery of the 1838th Destroyer Anti-tank Artillery Regiment moved out to fulfill this honorable task.
>
> At 1500, the remaining portion of the brigade that had tow vehicles was given an order: three batteries of the 1838th Destroyer and three batteries of the 1842nd Destroyer Anti-tank Artillery Regiments, and one battery from the 1840th Anti-tank Artillery Regiment, the brigade commander's mobile reserve, were to move forward to the region of Bykovka with the assignment to block the primary roads leading to that village: the roads from Pushkarnoe, from Tomarovka and the *Smelo k trudu* Collective Farm.
>
> At 1600, the remaining portion of the brigade that had tow vehicles moved out with the brigade commander to carry out the assignment. The 1838th Destroyer Anti-tank Artillery Regiment moved along the route Pokrovka – Iakovlevo – Hill 218.3 – Bykovka. The 1842nd Destroyer Anti-tank Artillery Regiment, together with brigade headquarters and its mobile anti-tank reserve, took the route Hill 254.4 – Dubrova – Ol'khovka – Vorskla – Bykovka.
>
> At 1700, the units of the brigade, under strong enemy air attack and uninterrupted bombing, suffering minor losses, reached the line Ol'khovatka – Hill 234.8, where the forward reconnaissance and the commander's personal observation established that the village Bykovka and the southern edge of Koz'mo-Dem'ianovka were already in enemy possession. In the area of Bykovka and Hill 224.2, a crowd of up to 150 enemy tanks was observed.
>
> Having determined that the primary mass of enemy tanks and motorized infantry were skirting Bykovka and Koz'mo-Dem'ianovka and moving in the direction of Iakovlevo, the brigade commander decided to fall back to the previous lines of defense, in order to repulse the enemy tank attack. At 2200 5.07.43, the units of the brigade reoccupied their former fighting positions and made everything ready to repulse the enemy attack.[18]

The enemy divisional *kampfgruppen* (combat groups) were superior to our units in mobility and maneuverability. The German fully exploited this superiority and already by 1630, forward detachments of *Leibstandarte* had seized the southern part of Bykovka, and a little earlier, at 1600, *Das Reich*'s Panzergrenadier Regiment *Deutschland* had overrun the defenses on Hill 233.3. At 1700, the 52nd Guards Rifle Division abandoned Bykovka, and two hours later, the SS troops seized Koz'mo-Dem'ianovka. Lieutenant Colonel Shamov reported:

> ... units of the division, fighting stubbornly in semi-encirclement as separate, uncoordinated battalions and companies, dying in complete companies, by the end of the day of 5.07.43 had fallen back to the line: the 153rd Guards Rifle Regiment – Lapin ravine, Voznesenovskii; the 151st Guards Rifle Regiment –

> (excl.) Voznesenovskii, Vorskla, (excl.) Solonets; the 155th Guards Rifle Regiment – (excl.) Gonki, the grove west of Nepkhaevo, and are exchanging fire with the adversary. A significant portion of the battalions have continued to fight stubbornly in encirclement ...[19]

Primarily the battalion and company commanders, and in some sectors, regimental command staff officers, organized the retreat of the troops. Headquarters, 52nd Guards Rifle Division, which was located in the region of Koz'mo-Dem'ianovka, having lost communications with its retreating units and under heavy *Luftwaffe* attack, hastily abandoned this region. At 1800, its communications link with 6th Guards Army was broken, and remained lost until the end of the day. Thus, army command didn't know the position of its own units or the situation in its own formation, and most importantly – it had been deprived of its primary source of information about the operational situation in such a dangerous sector.

From the day's summary report by II SS Panzer Corps headquarters:

> On the enemy side, which at first fought extraordinarily stubbornly, we are observing by the measure of our offensive's advance, apart from the weakening of resistance, also retrograde movements.
>
> In order to prevent the enemy from consolidating in the second line of defense, the divisions *Leibstandarte* and *Das Reich* will be given the order, despite the late hour, around 1700 [1900 Moscow time] to move up their panzer regiments and to break through the second defensive belt while there is still daylight. The *Totenkopf* Division is receiving the order to dispatch a strong reconnaissance unit into the Zhuravlinyi woods to establish a connection with the right wing of *Das Reich* and to mop-up the woods.
>
> ... Around 1840 [2040], *Leibstandarte* is attacking the second line of defense and at 1900 [2100], it stands 500 meters south of the second line in front of a defile, which runs in a southeasterly direction to the southern outskirts of Iakovlevo. Since *Das Reich* has poor roads, and traffic jams on its route of advance are significantly delaying the moving up of the panzer regiment, the offensive was halted by order of the Corps. The second line must be just as systematically attacked after concentrating [our forces] on the following morning. During the night, if it is possible, the fortified outposts should be taken, and infantry should advance to Hill 214.5."[20]

According to the records of 6th Guards Army's headquarters, already by 1630 SS troops had joined battle against elements of the 51st Guards Rifle Division in the vicinity of Hill 218.3, and subsequently had taken the village of Vorskla on the west bank of the river and closed in on the village of Solonets. Thus, according to the daily summary for 6 July from *Leibstandarte*'s headquarters, by the end of 5 July its units had reached the line: Hill 234.8 (1 kilometer north of Koz'mo-Dem'ianovka) – northern outskirts of Koz'mo-Dem'ianovka, approximately 0.5 to 1 kilometer from the 6th Guards Army's second defensive belt.

The bulk of the 52nd Guards Rifle Division's remaining forces, the 153rd and 151st Guards Rifle Regiments, retreated behind the Vorskla River and consolidated on the line

Major General N. T. Tavartkiladze, commander of the 51st Guards Rifle Division (1945 photo). (TsAMO, Central Archives of the Russian Federation's Ministry of Defense)

Hill 233.6 – Hill 238.4 – ravine 1.5 kilometers west of Solonets. However, the remnants of the 155th Guards Rifle Regiment drifted the opposite direction into the neighboring 375th Rifle Division's sector of defense and rallied in the region of Nepkhaevo.

The offensive on the flanks of the II SS Panzer Corps developed with many more complications and with less success. Despite strenuous efforts, although the *Totenkopf* troops had managed to place some pressure on the right flank of the 375th Rifle Division, they had not succeeded in achieving their assigned goal – to "crush" its defenses, seize crossings over the Lipovyi Donets and to gain a foothold on its eastern bank. The right flank of the 375th Rifle Division stubbornly held its ground, and all the battalions of the right-flank 1243rd Rifle Regiment remained combat-capable and continued to hold their positions. This day turned out to be successful as well for the other units of Colonel P. D. Govorunenko's division.

In the course of fighting on the left flank of the II SS Panzer Corps, by midnight *Leibstandarte*'s attached and reinforced 315th Infantry Regiment [from the 167th Infantry Division] and a *kampfgruppe* had managed to force a crossing over the Vorskla River in the sector Zadel'noe – Kamennyi Log – Veselyi – Vorskla. Pushing back elements of the 52nd Guards Rifle Division's 153rd Guards Rifle Regiment, it had created a bridgehead across the Vorskla River about 3 to 3.5 kilometers wide.

Thus, after approximately seventeen hours of fighting since the start of the offensive, the SS Panzer Corps had entirely broken through the 6th Guards Army's first defensive belt in the area of the Belgorod – Kursk highway, and had reached the second defensive belt, the forward zone of the 154th and 156th Guards Rifle Regiments of Major General N. T. Tavartkiladze's 51st Guards Rifle Division on a front of 6 to 6.5 kilometers.

★ ★ ★

Events unfolded more successfully for the Soviet side on the right wing of I. M. Chistiakov's 6th Guards Army in the sector held by two Guards divisions from General N. B. Ibiansky's 22nd Guards Rifle Corps. It was against their sector of the front where Fourth Panzer Army's numerically more powerful formation, von Knobelsdorff's XXXXVIII Panzer Corps, launched its offensive. Even before the start of the attack, the enemy encountered very serious problems due to minefields and the difficulties with assembling such a significant number of troops and equipment on such a narrow sector. During the approach march to the forward area, a unit of the new Panther tanks from the attached 10th Panzer Brigade stumbled into a minefield and became stuck there, and then blocked the way forward for *Grossdeutschland*'s panzer regiment. Thus, the initial attack by *Grossdeutschland*'s grenadiers went in without panzer support. Then the situation became even more complicated, as the panzers spent a lot of time searching for some way across a natural barrier, a marshy gully, to which the command of the 67th Guards Rifle Division had skillfully added a system of anti-tank obstacles in front of its 196th Guards Rifle Regiment.

Kampgruppen of Lieutenant General F. Westhoven's 3rd Panzer Division and the *Grossdeutschland* Panzergrenadier Division struck the boundary between Colonel A. I. Baksov's 67th Guards Rifle Division and Colonel I. S. Sibakov's 71st Guards Rifle Division, trying to overrun two powerful strongpoints in their forward zone, the villages of Cherkasskoe and Korovino. Having created a lodgment in the defensive fortifications between the two villages, von Knobelsdorff's forces bogged down there for the course

Germans assault a burning Russian village. (RGAKFD)

of the entire day, and by the end of the day, despite repeated efforts, they had not been able to carry out even half of their first-day assignments. They were tied up in heavy, bloody fighting in the web of the Army's first defensive belt. Only by midnight did they manage to take rather tenuous possession of Cherkasskoe and Korovino, which meant the Germans had only managed an advance of 5 to 7 kilometers, if you include the 67th Guards Rifle Division's line of fortified outposts. Therefore, there could not be even any talk of a clean breakthrough of the first defensive lines of Ibiansky's 22nd Guards Rifle Corps.

The main instrument of the planned breakthrough – the Tiger and new Panther tanks – had failed to work. Already the initial hours of combat had indicated that the high hopes placed on the Panthers had not been justified. Guderian's apprehensions had been fully realized; the contribution of the brigade of Panthers to the *Grossdeutschland* Panzergrenadier Division was not as substantial as Hitler had calculated when he had repeatedly postponed the date for Operation Citadel, in order to ensure the participation of the Panthers. *Grossdeutschland* together with 200 of the new Panthers became stuck in the very first line of defenses. If the weak influence of the Tigers on the course of the offensive can be excused by their insignificant numbers in the divisions, in contrast the command and personnel of the Panther brigade demonstrated an inability to cooperate with the troops of Hörnlein's division and were incapable of overcoming the Russians' deeply-echeloned defenses quickly, while the Panther tanks themselves were plagued with mechanical problems.

At the same time, the command of the Fourth Panzer Army, the XXXXVIII Panzer Corps, and the *Grossdeutschland* Division committed a number of errors and oversights when planning for the use of this powerful battering ram in real frontline conditions. Thus, H. Hoth rashly concentrated the entire 10th Brigade in the hands of only one division commander. In addition, their point of attack was poorly chosen. On a narrow sector of the front, the XXXXVIII Corps had to deploy not only the 10th Panzer Brigade's two battalions of Panthers, but also the shock forces of the *Grossdeutschland* Panzergrenadier Division. The area had not been fully swept of minefields left behind by the Soviet forces. The German command jammed several hundred armored vehicles, four battalions of infantry mounted on halftracks and trucks, and towed artillery pieces onto just 3 kilometers of road. Given the poor conditions of the roads, this concentration could lead to nothing but traffic jams along the main routes, and losses from minefields and attacks by Il-2 *Shturmovik* ground attack planes of the 2nd Air Army; in fact, these were the results. The unexpectedly strong and stable system of defense of the 6th Guards Army's 22nd Guards Rifle Corps aggravated the situation facing the XXXXVIII Panzer Corps.

The penetration of Voronezh Front's main line of resistance by the II SS Panzer Corps and its threatened rupture of the second line of defense near Iakovlevo caused Vatutin in the late afternoon of 5 July to mobilize his armored reserves and take other steps to forestall a further German advance. Voronezh Front chief of staff Lieutenant General S. P. Ivanov phoned Major General A. G. Kravchenko, commander of the 5th Guards 'Stalingrad' Tank Corps, and informed him that he was about to receive an order. The teletype machine in Kravchenko's headquarters spat out a narrow ribbon of paper:

> Ivanov here. Greetings. I'm passing along a combat order. The text: To the commander of the 2nd Guards Tank Corps and the 5th Guards Tank Corps. Copy: to the Chief of the General Staff.
>
> Combat Private Order No. 005/OP from Headquarters, Voronezh Front, 5.07.43; 1635.
>
> The enemy at 1430 5 July 1943 seized Gremuchii and with a force of up to two tank divisions is trying to reach the Belgorod-Oboian' highway, in order to further the offensive on Kursk.
>
> I am ordering:
>
> 1. The commander of the 2nd Guards 'Tatsinskaia' Tank Corps by 2400 5 July 1943 to advance to the region: MTS [Machine Tractor Station], Sazhnoe, Lozy, Sazhnoe.
>
> Shtakor [Corps headquarters] – Sazhnoe.
>
> The assignment:
>
> Stubbornly defend the indicated region. Prevent the enemy's expansion to the north and northeast. Be ready at dawn 6.07.43, in concert with the 5th Guards Tank Corps, to go on the counterattack in the direction: Kriukovo, Krapivenskie Dvory and further on Gremuchii, Belgorod.
>
> 2. The commander of the 5th Guards Tank Corps by 2400 5 July 1943 to move forward to the region: Lunino, Teterevino, Malinovka.
>
> Shtakor – Kalinin (2 km south of Belenikhino). The assignment:
>
> a) Take up a defense on the line: Lunino, Teterevino, Petrovka and under no circumstances permit an enemy breakthrough in the direction of Prokhorovka.
>
> b) Be ready at dawn 6.07.43 in concert with the 2nd Guards Tank Corps to go on the counteroffensive in the direction: Teterevino, Bykovo and further Rakovo.
>
> 3. Dig in the tanks on the defense. Demand rapid and decisive actions from the troops.
>
> 4. Keep in mind that in the course of the night, the 1st Tank Army will be moving up to the line Melovaia, Syrtsevo, Iakovlevo.
>
> 5. Report on the fulfillment of these orders.[21]

Once in position, both the 2nd Guards and 5th Guards Tank Corps passed to the operational control of the 6th Guards Army. Chistiakov now seemed to have ample armor for the next day under his direction, but as we shall see, he mishandled them with rather serious consequences.

About an hour later, at 1740 5 July, Lieutenant General M. E. Katukov, commander of the main component of Voronezh Front's armored reserve, the 1st Tank Army, received similar orders:

> 1. The commander of the 1 TA General-Lieutenant t. [comrade] Katukov is to advance two of his corps into the 6th Guards Army's second line of defense by 2200 5.7.43 and to take up a firm defense: the 6th Guards Tank Corps [as in the order, but the 6th Tank Corps was not a Guards unit] on the line Melovoe, Rakovo, Shepelevka; the 3 Mechanized Corps on the line Alekseevka, Syrtsev, Iakovlevo; the

> 31st Tank Corps is to deploy on the defensive at the 3rd Mechanized Corps' current position on the line Studenok, Stalinskii State Farm, Vladimirovka, Orlovka. Army headquarters – in the area of Zorinskie Dvory.
>
> The assignment: Under no circumstances permit an enemy breakthrough in the direction of Oboian'.
>
> Be ready from the dawn of 6.7.1943 to shift to a counteroffensive in the direction of Tomarovka.
>
> 2. Dig in and thoroughly camouflage the tanks on the defense.
>
> 3. Demand from the troops the maximum effort in carrying out the assigned combat mission.[22]

One of the variants of the plan for the defensive phase of the battle was for Vatutin to employ his armored reserves in a coordinated counteroffensive on the second day of the fighting. We can see by the wording of the orders that Vatutin wanted to preserve this option, but he wasn't yet fully committed to the idea. Nevertheless, his orders must have put the tank corps commanders in something of a conundrum, as they were being told to prepare for a counteroffensive while at the same time to prepare a solid defense with dug-in and camouflaged tanks. The latter point in the order – to occupy and defend a sector of the front – placed the tank corps in an unusual role. The intent behind the design and structure of these formations was to give the Red Army an offensive weapon, capable of sustaining operations deep in the enemy rear. They were not intended to hold a static line of defense.

All through the night of 5/6 July 1943, the tankers moved into position, labored to dig emplacements for their tanks, and set up ambush positions. Since the 1st Tank Army had actually been ordered to move into the second line of defense, its tankers particularly took to the work of digging in their tanks, especially those in the Army's second-echelon 31st Tank Corps. The terrain to the northeast of the village Iakovlevo – in the direction of Prokhorovka Station right up to Komsomolets State Farm (in the army's third line of defenses) – was an expanse of relatively open and level terrain.

It is important to note that a continuous line of trenches and engineered obstacles had not been laid out on the ground lying between the second and third defensive lines. Moreover, in the spring, when the defenses were being planned and erected, the distance between the second and third defensive belts had been deliberately increased in order to make maximum use of a natural barrier, the Psel River, within the third line of defense. The swampy river basin and the high northern bank of the river were themselves a serious obstacle to the advance of the enemy's tanks and, in addition, gave the defenders a sweeping field of fire over the approaches to the Psel out to a distance of 3 kilometers [1.8 miles] to the south.

In the relatively open terrain between the second and third defensive belts, the Soviet tankers had to dig their vehicles in up to their turrets and use them as anti-tank guns. This defensive system, which combined tank ambush positions and anti-tank strongpoints, created by the tank and motorized rifle brigades and supporting artillery, plus a mobile tank reserve for launching sharp counterattacks, allowed the repulse of the battering attacks from the enemy's significantly superior forces.

The 1st Tank Army, in order to cover the Oboian' axis, moved into a 30-kilometer sector of the line running between Melovoe and Iakovlevo and assumed a doubleecheloned formation. Major General A. L. Getman's 6th Tank Corps occupied strong positions behind the swampy basin of the Pena River, buttressing the left and center of the 90th Guards Rifle Division. To its left in the Army's first echelon, the 3rd Mechanized Corps occupied a more vulnerable sector extending from the Pena River valley to Iakovlevo. The ground in this area was much more suitable for tank movement, and hence was more likely to be the focus of the German attack. Here, the 3rd Mechanized Corps backed the 90th Guards Rifle Division's left flank and the right flank of the 51st Guards Rifle Division. Major General D. Kh. Chernienko's 31st Tank Corps remained in reserve about 18 kilometers behind the first echelon. The 1st Tank Army was also reinforced by the 38th Army's 180th Tank Brigade, the battalions of which were instructed to deploy behind 1st Tank Army's second echelon, south of Oboian' in the Semenovka – Afanas'evka sector. The 1st Tank Army's arrival on the 6th Guards Army's second line of defense increased the quantity of artillery (including the tank guns and all the 1st Tank Army's artillery) available to the latter army by 85%.

Incidentally, there is the opinion that the arrangement of Katukov's formation was mistaken, that a more mobile tank corps should have been placed where the 3rd Mechanized Corps was positioned. However, Krivoshein's mechanized corps was better suited to the role of defending this sector. Chernienko's reserve 31st Tank Corps was lacking an anti-tank regiment and a motorized rifle brigade at the start of the battle, while the 6th Tank Corps' 536th Destroyer Anti-tank Artillery Regiment, together with the 1st Tank Army's 1008th Destroyer Anti-tank Artillery Regiment and 316th Separate Guards Mortar Regiment had already been transferred to the command of the 6th Guards Army. Thus, the 3rd Mechanized Corps had more anti-tank artillery and – significantly – motorized infantry than either of the tank corps.

This was an important decision, because the 3rd Mechanized Corps was facing two full-strength divisions of the XXXXVIII Panzer Corps and part of the II SS Panzer Corps. Vatutin and Katukov realized that it was probably unwise to rely upon the thin rifle divisions of the 6th Guards Army to protect the dug-in tanks and guns, so decided to use Krivoshein's motorized infantry to cover them.

Major General A. G. Kravchenko's 5th Guards Tank Corps assembled behind the 51st Guards Rifle Division's positions on a 12-kilometer sector between Iakovlevo and the Lipovyi Donets River, straddling two important roads, the Butovo-Dobrovo road and the Belgorod-Kursk highway. Its deployment here, behind the lines of the defending rifle infantry in front of it and with access to two serviceable roads, seems to reflect Vatutin's intention to counterattack on the morning of 6 July. Finally, Major General Burdeiny's 2nd Guards Tank Corps deployed on a 10-kilometer wide sector in the area of Gostishchevo, behind the Lipovyi Donets River, where it could strike the extended right flank of the advancing II SS Panzer Corps.

Vatutin's armored reserve represented a powerful force. Altogether on 6 July, Voronezh Front command would be committing 1,051 tanks into the battle, of which 754 (71%) were T-34s (see Tables 7 and 8).

Vatutin's preparations for 6 July did not stop with his armored reserve. He issued further orders to his remaining infantry reserve to strengthen the Voronezh Front's defenses on likely avenues of German advance. Major General S. G. Goriachev, commander of the reserve 35th Guards Rifle Corps, received the order to move Major General V. V. Tikhomirov's 93rd Guards Rifle Division to the region of Prokhorovka by 0300 on 6 July and position it behind Major General's A. S. Kostitsyn's 183rd Rifle Division.

Two more divisions of this rifle corps – the 94th Guards, under the command of Colonel I. G. Russkikh, and the 92nd Guards, under the command of Colonel V. F. Trunin – were subordinated to the commander of the 7th Guards Army, Lieutenant General M. S. Shumilov. These formations were assigned to block the Korocha axis. In addition, Shumilov received operational control of the 69th Army's 111th and 270th Rifle Divisions, which were occupying the rear line of defense.

Additional steps were taken within Voronezh Front on the night of 5/6 July in the sector of the 7th Guards Army, which was confronting Army Detachment Kempf. In order to liquidate the bridgeheads that the enemy had created across the Northern Donets River, the command of the 7th Guards Army planned at 0330 on 6 July to launch a counterattack with the forces of the army's second echelon. Two groups were created for this purpose. The first group was placed under the control of the commander of the 25th Guards Rifle Corps Major General G. B. Safiullin, and included the 73rd Guards Rifle Division, the 31st Destroyer Anti-tank Artillery Brigade, the 167th Tank Regiment, the 1438th Self-propelled Artillery Regiment, the 262nd Destroyer Anti-tank Artillery Regiment, the 309th and 97th Guards Mortar Regiments, and the 329th Engineer Battalion. Major General N. A. Vasil'ev, commander of the 24th Guards Rifle Corps, commanded the second group. It included the 213th Rifle Division and the 27th Tank Brigade. These formations were to attack in the direction of the village Maslova Pristan', while the corps' mobile group – the 201st Tank Brigade, the 1529th Heavy Self-propelled Artillery Regiment, and the 1669th Destroyer Anti-tank Artillery Regiment – was to strike from the region of Gremuchii and the Poliana State Farm toward Krutoi Log. After the 15th Guards Rifle Division replaced the 111th Rifle Division, the latter was pulled back into the army's second echelon, where it was to take up defensive positions along the eastern bank of the Koren' River in the Nekliudovo – Churaevo sector.[23]

Despite these reinforcements and the reshuffling of forces, Lieutenant General I. M. Chistiakov, whose 6th Guards Army had been fated to receive the main German blow on the southern shoulder of the Kursk bulge, still had to be concerned about the strength of the forward edge of his defenses for the second day of combat. While ample, fresh armor reserves were now assembling behind his forward line of battle, this line was occupied by three rifle divisions of his former second echelon: the 51st Guards, 89th Guards and 90th Guards Rifle Divisions. These rifle divisions were all below authorized strength even before the battle started, and N. T. Tavartkiladze's 51st Guards Rifle Division and V. P. Chernov's 90th Guards Rifle Division had already yielded several rifle battalions and part of their artillery to the first echelon. They were thus much weaker than the first echelon rifle formations that had buckled the previous day. Chistiakov knew that these thin rifle divisions would have to withstand another powerful blow from the XXXXVIII and II SS Panzer Corps. Significant anti-tank resources were urgently necessary. Though I. M. Chistiakov received all he needed on the evening of 5 July when he obtained operational control of the 2nd Guards and 5th Guards Tank Corps, further events will show that he failed to handle them as he ought to have.

★ ★ ★

Major General A. S. Kostitsyn, commander of the 183rd Rifle Division (February 1943 photo). (Author's personal archive)

The general results of the combat operations for 5 July of the forces of Army Group South on the axis of the main attack by Fourth Panzer Army were as follows. According to the plan for Citadel, by the end of 5 July the panzer divisions of XXXXVIII Panzer Corps – the strongest formation in General Hoth's formation – were supposed to have broken through the first and second defensive belts, and to have penetrated approximately 45 kilometers (taking into account the screen of outposts) into the depth of 6th Guards Army's defenses, to crossing locations on the Psel River. At the same time, the neighboring II SS Panzer Corps had the task to overcome two defensive belts of the 23rd Guards Rifle Corps and to emerge on the Prokhorovka axis of advance. As a result, a salient in the Soviet defenses 30 kilometers deep and 15 kilometers wide was supposed to have been created. Thus, on the first day of Fourth Panzer Army's offensive, 6th Guards Army's two primary belts of defenses were to have been fully ruptured, and the Soviet forces should have been forced by 6 July to be defending the third (rear) line of defense. However, this did not happen. General von Knobelsdorff's panzer corps did not even manage to advance even a fourth of the planned distance on the first day.

Despite a certain measure of success, the II SS Panzer Corps also faced genuine problems as the first day of the offensive came to a close. The shock grouping's strength had already begun to dissipate rather quickly. It had already become apparent that the Panzergrenadier divisions did not have nearly enough infantry, as, incidentally, was true of the other formations as well. The calculation that the resistance of Russian units in the Vorsklitsa River valley (on the inner flanks of II SS Panzer Corps and XXXXVIII Panzer Corps) would weaken after a breakthrough along the graded Tomarovka – Iakovlevo road and in the vicinity of Cherkasskoe was not realized. The Soviet forces continued to fight stubbornly. The XXXXVIII Panzer Corps had become enmeshed almost immediately

Formation	Medium T-34 tanks			Light T-70 tanks			Mk-IV Churchill Tanks			Total
	Total	Operational	Under repair	Total	Operational	Under Repair	Total	Operational	Under Repair	
2 Gds Tank Corps	**131**	**121**	**10**	**75**	**75**	**-**	**21**	**21**	**-**	**227**
4 Gds Tank Bde	32	32	-	21	21	-	-	-	-	53
25 Gds Tank Bde	32	22	10	21	21	-	-	-	-	53
26 Gds Tank Bde	32	32	-	21	21	-	-	-	-	53
47 Gds Hvy Tank Regt	-	-	-	-	-	-	21	21	-	21
Corps Reserve	35	35	-	12	12	-	-	-	-	47
5 Gds Tank Corps	**131**	**127**	**4**	**70**	**63**	**7**	**21**	**21**	**-**	**222**
4 Gds Sep Signal Bn	2	2	-	-	-	-	-	-	-	2
20 Gds Tank Bde	32	32	-	28	21	7	-	-	-	60
21 Gds Tank Bde	48	44	4	21	21	-	-	-	-	69
22 Gds Tank Bde	49	49	-	21	21	-	-	-	-	70
48 Gds Hvy Tank Regt	-	-	-	-	-	-	21	21	-	21
Total tanks in both corps	**262**	**248**	**14**	**145**	**138**	**7**	**42**	**42**	**-**	**449**

Sources: TsAMO RF, f. 3400, op. 1, d. 23, l. 86; TsAMO RF, f. 203, op. 2843, d. 438, l. 252, 253.

Table 7. Tank Strength in the 2nd Guards 'Tatsinskaia' and 5th Guards 'Stalingrad' Tank Corps, 5 July 1943

in the lines of the 71st and 67th Guards Rifle Divisions, and could not expect any great results from the sole attack of the 167th Infantry Division's 315th Infantry Regiment against the 52nd Guards Rifle Division's 153rd Guards Rifle Regiment on the west bank of the Vorsklitsa River in the region of Streletskoe, Zadel'noe, and Kamennyi Log.

At the same time, an even more difficult situation had formed on II SS Panzer Corps' right flank. There, the lines of the defending Soviet 375th Rifle Division turned out to be so strongly fortified that the full-strength SS Panzergrenadier Division *Totenkopf*, which had been hurled against those positions in anticipation of a breakthrough, could do nothing. In this situation, the complete failure of the launch of Army Detachment Kempf's offensive, which was supposed to cover Fourth Panzer Army's right flank, but

Formation and units	T-34	T-60	T-70	Total tanks	BA armored cars	Total Armor
3rd Mechanized Corps (a)						
1 Mechanized Bde	30	-	10	40	6	46
3 Mechanized Bde	36	-	3	39	-	39
10 Mechanized Bde	31	-	8	39	1	40
1 Gds Tank Bde	40 (b)	-	-	40(b)	5	45
49 Tank Bde	44	2	7	53	-	53
34 Sep Recon Bn	10(b)	-	7	17	?	17
346 Sep Signals Bn	10	-	-	10	-	10
Corps Total:	201	2	35	238	12	250
6th Tank Corps (c)						
22 Tank Bde	45	6	3	54	-	54
112 Tank Bde	44	-	9	53	2	55
200 Tank Bde	45	3	5	53	-	53
6 Mot Rifle Bde	-	-	-	-	3	3
Corps Total:	134	9	17	160	5	165
31st Tank Corps (d)						
100 Tank Bde	43	2	8	53		53
237 Tank Bde	43	-	10	53	4 (e)	53
242 Tank Bde	43	-	10	53		53
Corps Total:	129	2	28	159	4	163
1st Tank Army, Total	**464**	**13**	**80**	**557**	**21**	**578**

(a) Sources: TsAMO RF, f. 3427, op. 1, d. 58, l. 6, 6 obr.

(b) Note that 10 T-34 tanks of the 1st Guards Tank Brigade had been operationally attached to the 34th Separate Reconnaissance Battalion.

(c) TsAMO RF, f. 3412, op. 1, d. 26, l. 152, 152 obr.

(d) TsAMO RF, f. 203, op. 2843, d. 341, l. 6, 6 obr.

(e) Subordinate assignment unknown.

Table 8: Operational Armor in the 1st Tank Army at 2400 on 3 July 1943

spent the entire day making little headway against the Soviet defenses, was another blow to General Hoth's plans.

Thus, although II SS Panzer Corps did in fact manage to break through the first line of defenses in its sector, the corridor it had carved through the 6th Guards Army's positions was rather narrow, and immediately the need arose for strengthening the security of its flanks. Therefore in the first stage of the offensive, it fell to Hausser to break through the defense AND to protect his own flanks AND to consolidate the territory gained, all with only the units of the Panzergrenadier divisions, which were plainly insufficient to fulfill all of these basic tasks.

The timetable for Operation Citadel had thus collapsed in the first hours of its implementation. The results of the first twenty-four hours of the grandiose battle were disquieting; the formations of the Fourth Panzer Army had broken through the 6th Guards Army's main defensive belt only in one place, expending a large amount of strength and resources just to achieve this. In the given circumstances, this was a limited tactical success, but in order to achieve the aims set forth in the plan for Citadel, it was extremely important to develop this success to an operational (and then even strategic) level, and for this it was necessary to break through at least the first three defensive belts of the Soviet forces in the first two or three days of the operation.

Another important result of the first day's fighting was that it forced the enemy to take a more sober view of the tasks in front of them. The Russians, with surprising resolve and tenacity, fighting to the last man in complete platoons and companies, were grinding down the German forces. Everyone who participated in this battle maintains in one voice that after just the first several hours of the offensive, the Germans understood that they had collided with a new Red Army. Instead of the demoralized Russian soldier, fleeing under the blows of the *Wehrmacht*, they had encountered steadfast and courageous fighting men, well-prepared positions, and a well-designed system of artillery fire, minefields, and anti-tank obstacles. All this shocked the antagonist, who now understood that even if victory in this operation was achieved, he would have to pay dearly for it.

Nevertheless, despite all the aforementioned problems and difficulties, which arose in the course of the first day of the offensive, the forces of Army Group South did manage to achieve one very real result. Thanks to the excellently developed cooperation between the different types of forces and the persistence of the formations, first of all the Fourth Panzer Army, the command of the Voronezh Front had been forced to commit practically all of its operational reserves by the end of 5 July. As already mentioned above, the destruction of the Red Army's reserves was second in significance to the capture of Kursk among the goals for Field Marshal von Manstein's Army Group South. In reality, however, the luring in and destruction of the Red Army's operational, as well as strategic reserves, in the course of Operation Citadel on the southern face of the Kursk bulge had emerged for the Germans as the top priority, and this objective was growing in significance. If on 5 July, Hoth's forces had battled against the 6th Guards Army's first echelon and reserves (the struggle had forced Chistiakov to commit more than 90% of his army's artillery, including its anti-tank reserve, as well as part of his second echelon rifle divisions), then on 6 July, the command of the Voronezh Front already had to commit to the Fourth Panzer Army's sector of attack all of its remaining tank reserves and a significant part of its artillery, as well as its single reserve rifle corps – the 35th Guards Rifle Corps.

Having advanced General Katukov's tank army and two tank corps into the first echelon, the Voronezh Front commander was now practically without operational reserves. By the second day of fighting, Vatutin no longer had any fresh, still inactive forces. This was a serious success for the enemy.

German intelligence quickly detected the arrival of fresh units (Katukov's 1st Tank Army and the two tank corps), and already by the evening of 6 July, it was reporting to the *Wehrmacht* General Staff:

> The attempt by the enemy – before ascertaining the scale and goals of our operation – to hold back the German offensive with forces in position and *front* reserves has basically failed. He has prematurely committed the operational reserves ... The enemy, apparently, is trying to keep the German offensive as far as possible from Kursk, and with this aim he is throwing all available forces into the fighting.[24]

That is an accurate and precise understanding of the logic behind Voronezh Front command's actions.

However, this was now 1943, and the situation on the Soviet-German front had changed qualitatively. The *Stavka* had created a powerful strategic reserve – Steppe Front. It was directed to support the defending forces in the Kursk bulge. Therefore, if needed, Vatutin could count upon its support. This was in fact the basic miscalculation by the Nazi leadership. Having correctly evaluated the actions of the Soviet side, it did not consider the reserves of the Soviet Supreme High Command, upon which the Voronezh Front began to lean starting from 9 July.

Summing up the results of 5 July, one can assert with complete confidence that the day proved more successful for the forces of Voronezh Front than for the enemy. The main aim – to contain von Manstein's panzer wedges within the army-level defensive lines while wearing down his forces – had been accomplished, although with great difficulty.

5

The II SS Panzer Corps Reaches the Prokhorovka Axis

Fighting resumed before dawn on 6 July, when the XXXXVIII Panzer Corps launched fresh attacks against the 6th Guards Army's sector. Thus, the Germans beat Vatutin to the punch, and in fact, his contemplated general counteroffensive with his armored reserves never materialized. At some point in the pre-dawn or early morning hours of 6 July, Vatutin had canceled the coordinated counterattack.

There were likely several factors behind this decision. General Katukov, commander of the 1st Tank Army, had argued against the idea of a counterattack, fearing the consequences if his tankers took on the German Tigers and Panther in open combat. The superior firepower, optics and gunnery of the German panzers would have given them a decisive advantage. As Katukov penned in his memoirs:

> Wouldn't it be better in these circumstances to put off the counterattack, and as before place our bets on our carefully prepared, deeply echeloned defenses?
>
> Let the fascists come crawling forward in the hope that at any moment, they'll succeed in breaking out into operational space. Let the Hitlerites get enmeshed in our defenses and die. We in the meantime will be grinding down the enemy's material and manpower. Once we bleed their units white and smash the fascists' armored fist, then the suitable moment will ripen for launching a mighty counterattack. But such a moment had not yet arrived.[1]

Katukov already had information about the effectiveness of the German panzers' powerful guns by late evening of 5 July. The leading tank brigades of the 3rd Mechanized Corps – the 1st Guards Tank Brigade and the 49th Tank Brigade – had bumped into the SS Panzer Corps south of Pokrovka and had quickly suffered losses at the hands of the long-range guns of the Tigers. As his memoirs reveal, the point about the counteroffensive in Vatutin's orders for the 1st Tank Army had made Katukov increasingly worried as the dawn of 6 July approached.

Vatutin also had to consider the readiness of the tank corps to go on the attack. Indeed, as the sun came up on 6 July, while the 1st Tank Army had deployed behind the 6th Army's second echelon of rifle divisions, the main forces of the 2nd Guards and 5th Guards Tank Corps were still not in position to attack; they only began to arrive in their designated sectors between 0500 and 1200. By this time, of course, the fighting for the second defensive belt had already started.

The Voronezh Front command was thus not able to use the armor of the 1st Tank Army as a single, unified formation. Its tanks and assault guns were primarily used in static positions, serving as anti-tank guns to support the infantry on defense. Accordingly, the army lost its striking power; its armored fist became dispersed. However, in those circumstances it was impossible to operate any other way. The Soviet tanks had no superiority over the German tanks. If you consider that on his chosen lines of attack the enemy threw more than a hundred tanks simultaneously at the defenses, then tank engagements in the open terrain would have turned into the foreordained destruction of our tank army.

It should be noted here that the Voronezh Front commander N. F. Vatutin was inherently disposed towards active defense. He didn't like to wait passively for the adversary to strike the first blow, and always tried to impose his will on the enemy. Unfortunately, his decisions here, as further events would show, were not always based on a comprehensive evaluation of the situation and adequate foresight, and not supported by precise operational-tactical calculations.

On 6 July the Fourth Panzer Army command had to solve a very important and complex problem. After heavy fighting as it ground its way through Voronezh Front's first defensive belt, it needed to regroup its formations in order to undertake combat operations in a new direction. The II SS Panzer Corps, which had broken through to the 6th Guards Army's second line in the Iakovlevo – Luchki (south) sector, had to shift to the Prokhorovka axis of advance, while leaving its position in the region of Syrtsevo and Iakovlevo to the XXXXVIII Panzer Corps. After accomplishing this regrouping, General O. von Knobelsdorff's divisions would assume the main task of the first stage of Operation Citadel– a northward advance against the 1st Tank Army toward Oboian'. Meanwhile, the divisions of the II SS Panzer Corps would break through toward the northeast and destroy the Soviet reserve armor formations hurled against it on the Prokhorovka axis.

By the end of the first day of the offensive, the SS corps of *Obergruppenführer* P. Hausser had managed to break through to the forward zone of Major General N. T. Tavartkiladze's 51st Guards Rifle Division, which was occupying a sector of the second defensive line south of Iakovlevo. Therefore, by the morning of 6 July, the SS troops were already in position for a lunge toward Prokhorovka. The situation in XXXXVIIII Panzer Corps' sector was more difficult. Its divisions had been unable to penetrate the 6th Guards Army's first defensive belt on 5 July. It was nearly at a standstill, locked in savage fighting with the 71st and 67th Guards Rifle Divisions along the front Korovino – Cherkasskoe – Hill 246.0.

Attempting to make up for lost time, the XXXXVIII kicked-off the resumption of Fourth Panzer Army's drive at 0300 on 6 July with a powerful attack on the left wing of General I. M. Chistiakov's army. The 11th Panzer Division and the *Grossdeutschland* Panzergrenadier Division received the order to make every effort to break through along the Butovo – Iakovlevo road in the region of Ol'khovka and Dubrova, in order to link up with the 167th Infantry Division's 315th Grenadier Regiment that was guarding the II SS Panzer Corps' left flank. This move would result in the encirclement of the main forces of the 67th Guards Rifle Division and the 52nd Guards Rifle Division's 153rd Rifle Regiment in the region of Novo-Cherkasskoe, Trirechnoe, Dragunskoe, and Veselyi (Ol'khovskii). It was assumed that by this time, the *Leibstandarte* and *Das Reich* divisions would already have overcome the line of the 51st Guards Rifle Division and be emerging on the Prokhorovka axis, while *Totenkopf* would be pressuring the 375th Rifle Division in the region of Visloe, Shopino and Erik, with the aim of driving it back across the Lipovyi Donets River, thereby expanding the breakthrough corridor of the entire army.

The Germans attacked from the vicinity of Cherkasskoe toward Podimovka, Zavidovka, and Alekseevka; and toward Ol'khovka, Dmitrievka and Syrtsevo. However, despite all efforts, in these regions the enemy failed to achieve noticeable results: the forces of the XXXXVIII Panzer Corps were only able to make a few lodgments in the second defensive belt in several locations, but could make no further headway, much less break free into operational space. Units of the 71st Guards Rifle Division, under attack simultaneously from 300 tanks and two regiments of infantry, held its sector of the defenses for around two and a half hours, after which it abandoned Krasnyi Pochinok and fell back to a new line. The XXXXVIII Panzer Corps' 3rd Panzer Division reached Rakovo and seized control of Zavidovka on the southern bank of the Pena River, but could advance no further.

Again, the enemy relied upon massed armor employed on a narrow sector of the front, exploiting the tactical-technical advantages of their Tiger tanks. Heavy and more ponderous than our T-34s, they possessed qualities that were important for that time – thick armor and powerful guns with excellent optical sights and long range direct fire capabilities. All this, in combination with the active support of the *Luftwaffe*, enabled them to achieve results. In some cases, German Tigers that had broken into the depth of the defenses remained almost impervious to fire, and overran infantry and artillery positions.

The Germans also evidently employed various stratagems in the first days of Operation Citadel, designed to augment the intimidating factor of these heavy tanks and to shake the resolve of the defenders. An officer of the General Staff with the 1st Tank Army, Major Petukhov, reported on one of these curious ploys:

> Through observations from the 10th Motorized Brigade it has been established that on 6 July 1943 the enemy hitched wooden dummy Panzer VI tanks (2-3) behind their real Panzer VI tanks to give the appearance of a larger number of tanks. Under a barrage from our artillery, splinters and boards flew from [these wooden dummies]. Subsequently the enemy dropped such methods. Artillerymen of the 1212th Destroyer Anti-tank Artillery Regiment RGK [*reserv glavnogo komandovaniya*, or the *Stavka* Reserve] reported this.[2]

Of course, the Soviet side countered with its own unusual combat methods. The 6th Guards Army had on its roster a 27th Battalion, which trained and handled 76 tank-hunting dogs. The following report appears in the Ministry of Defense's Central Archive:

> ... The military use of tank-hunting dogs on the Voronezh Front was first put into operation between 4 July and 18 July 1943. Experience indicates this is a very effective means for the struggle against enemy tanks. In the first days of fighting, a company of tank-hunting dogs operated in the forward zone of the defense, distributed by platoon to the 375th Rifle Division, the 52nd Guards Rifle Division, and the 67th Guards Rifle Division. Of the three platoons located in combat positions, two platoons (those with the 375th and 52nd Guards Rifle Divisions)

> had no opportunity to employ their dogs, because no German tanks were in the vicinity. Lieutenant Lisitsin's platoon, which was operating in the sector of the 67th Guards Rifle Division's 169th Guards Rifle Regiment (Berezov), blew up 12 tanks with its dogs, for which 16 dogs were expended (4 dogs were killed as they approached the enemy tanks).
>
> Lieutenant Lisitsin's platoon, having blown up the enemy tanks, stubbornly defended their position, driving back repeated German attacks, and fell back only after receiving an order. In addition to the 12 tanks blown up by dogs, Lisitsin's platoon destroyed 3 enemy tanks through anti-tank rifle fire, and with their personal weapons an additional 150 enemy soldiers and officers. After 11.07.43 the company of tank-hunting dogs carried out its duties as a mobile anti-tank reserve of the 6th Guards Army's commander.[3]

The most savage fighting went on in the sector of Colonel A. I. Baksov's 67th Guards Rifle Division and Colonel I. M. Nekrasov's 52nd Guards Rifle Division. Between 1500 and 1700 *kampfgruppen* from the *Grossdeutschland* Panzergrenadier Division and the 11th Panzer Division managed to overrun the line of these formations, and battered their way into four well-fortified villages: Novo-Cherkasskoe, Trirechnoe, Dmitrievka, and Ol'khovka.

After abandoning Dmitrievka and Ol'khovka, the command of the 6th Guards Army was forced to instruct the 67th Guards and 52nd Guards Rifle Divisions to fall back beyond the second line, because of the heavy losses each had suffered. However, the divisions were unable to execute this order fully. The inner flank units of von Knobelsdorff's and Hausser's corps were able to cut off significant portions of these formations in the valleys of the Vorskla and Vorsklitsa Rivers. The artillery regiment and two rifle regiments of Baksov's 67th Guards Rifle Division, as well as a rifle regiment and part of the artillery regiment of Nekrasov's 52nd Guards Rifle Division, were ensnared by nightfall on 6 July. Despite the fact that overnight, more than half of these trapped troops managed to slip out of the pocket through gaps in the German lines, the loss of Guardsmen was substantial. The enemy's attempt to continue the attack by ousting Soviet forces from Zavidovka, Lukhanino, and Syrtsevo, all of which lay in the basin of the Pena River, was frustrated by the stubborn resistance from elements of 6th Guards Army's 90th Guards Rifle Division, as well as the 6th Tank Corps and 3rd Mechanized Corps.

Tankers of Major General A. L. Getman's 6th Tank Corps were the first of M. E. Katukov's 1st Tank Army to clash with the Germans. Getman's corps, reinforced with the 270th Mortar Regiment from the *Stavka* Reserve and the 79th Separate Guards Mortar Regiment, spent the rest of the day repulsing four tank attacks in the Podimovka – Alekseevka sector, preventing a German breakthrough here, while inflicting significant damage on a panzer group from the 3rd Panzer Division in Zavidovka, forcing it to abandon the village and retreat.

To the left of the 6th Tank Corps' defenses, Major General S. M. Krivoshein's 3rd Mechanized Corps was holding the line in the Lukhanino – Dubrova – Iakovlevo sector, straddling both the Butovo – Dubrova road and the Belgorod – Kursk highway. In addition to defending against the XXXXVIII Panzer Corps' thrust toward Syrtsevo, the 3rd Mechanized Corps also had to counter the II SS Panzer Corps' attacks in the

Iakovlevo sector. 1st Tank Army commander Katukov recalls a visit to this sector and describes what he found there in his memoir:

> After the conversation with General Vatutin, I set off for Krivoshein's [3rd Mechanized] corps, where at that time the adversary was undertaking his next attack. On a narrow front, attacking along the Oboian' highway, he hurled up to 200 tanks into the battle. A muffled, uninterrupted rumble carried from the direction of Iakovlevo. A dense curtain of dust hung on the horizon.
>
> I found Krivoshein in a wooded ravine. His van, in which the corps commander roamed along the frontline roads together with his wife, was parked next to his slit trench. The general was shouting something over the telephone. Catching sight of me, he concluded the conversation, laid down the phone, and raised his hand in salute:
>
> 'Comrade Commander, the enemy is attacking.'
>
> 'I can see that for myself: in what force?'
>
> 'On the corps' sector, up to 400 tanks!'
>
> 'Aren't you exaggerating, Semen Moiseevich?'
>
> 'What exaggeration? On Gorelov's [V. M. Gorelov – commander of the 1st Guards Tank Brigade in the 1st Tank Army's 3rd Mechanized Corps – *Author*] position alone – 100 tanks. On Babadzhanian's [A. Kh. Babadzhanian – commander of the 3rd Mechanized Brigade in the 1st Tank Army's 3rd Mechanized Corps – *Author*] position – 70!'
>
> We climbed up to the observation post, which had been set up in a loft of a barn adjacent to the ravine. Although it was the middle of the day, it seemed twilight had arrived: the sun was covered by dust and smoke. The log barn was trembling as if nervous. In the sky, airplanes were beginning to howl, and machine-gun bursts crackled. Our fighters were trying to chase away the enemy's bombers, which were dropping their deadly loads on our positions. The observation post was located about 4 kilometers from the front lines. But what was happening in that hellish smoke, in that sea of fire and smoke, it was impossible to make out.
>
> At last the field telephone began to ring. Gorelov, then Iakovlev [I. Ia. Iakovlev – commander of the 10th Mechanized Brigade in 1st Tank Army's 3rd Mechanized Corps – *Author*] and Babadzhanian were reporting that the enemy's first attack had been beaten back. I sighed with relief and congratulated Krivoshein on the good start.[4]

On the morning of 6 July, Hausser and his II SS Panzer Corps had waited for the results of the fighting in the XXXXVIII Panzer Corps' sector. At 0600, only the SS *Totenkopf* initiated active combat operations, launching an attack on the positions of Colonel P. D. Govorunenko's 375th Rifle Division. Meanwhile, the SS Panzergrenadier Divisions *Leibstandarte* and *Das Reich* were busily preparing to resume the offensive. For the time being, after an intensive bombardment and artillery barrage, these two SS divisions limited themselves to a reconnaissance-in-force in the region of the villages Solonets, Iakovlevo, and Luchki (south), where units of the 51st Guards Rifle Division were defending.

N. T. Tavartkiladze's division faced a tall order, holding a sector of the second army-level defensive belt along the line Hill 229.4 – Hill 226.0 – southern outskirts of Solonets – Hill 243.2 – Hill 246.3 – Nechaevka – southern outskirts of Teterevino – (excl.) Malinovka. This line stretched for 16.5 kilometers, which was 4.5 kilometers longer than the norm established for a full-strength rifle division on the defense.[5] According to its TO&E, a full-strength rifle division in the Red Army was supposed to have 10,595 men.[6] Yet on 1 July 1943, the 51st Guards Rifle Division had only 8,405 men, not including officers.[7] In addition, before the start of the German offensive, two rifle battalions had been withdrawn from the division in order to strengthen the first-echelon 52nd Guards Rifle Division.

Almost half of the 51st Guards Rifle Division's sector, a span of 7 kilometers, offered good tank country. The terrain here allowed the enemy to assemble almost 220 tanks for the attack on the Guardsmen's positions – almost all the tanks that Wisch's *Leibstandarte* and Krüger's *Das Reich* SS Panzergrenadier Divisions possessed that dawn. In order to block the three most likely avenues of tank attack, the 51st Guards Rifle Division prepared three anti-tank regions.

Lieutenant Colonel F. T. Sushkov's 154th Guards Rifle Regiment occupied the most vulnerable sector: the line Hill 229.4 – Hill 246.3 – southern outskirts of Solonets – Iakovlevo, with a length of almost 5.5 kilometers (of which 4 kilometers were vulnerable to tank attack).[8] On 1 July 1943, it had numbered only 2,734 men.[9] This number includes the personnel of the 3rd Rifle Battalion, which had been transferred to the operational control of the 52nd Guards Rifle Division before the start of the offensive.

The gun crew of a German 105mm field howitzer conducting fire on the positions of Soviet forces. A captured photo. (RGAKFD)

As partial compensation, the 51st Rifle Division's Separate Guards Training Battalion, numbering 394 men, also held a section of the 154th Guards Rifle Regiment's line.[10] The regiment was also buttressed by the attached 2nd and 3rd Battalions of the 122nd Guards Artillery Regiment. Altogether the 154th Rifle Regiment had 26 guns, including 4 45mm anti-tank guns, 16 76mm anti-tank guns, and 6 122mm howitzers, as well as 46 mortars, of which 17 were 50mm mortars. The division had also set up one of its anti-tank regions, No. 1, in the 154th Guards Rifle Regiment's sector of the defense. Its commander was the chief of the Regiment's artillery, Guards Captain S. K. Klimchuk.

Two rifle companies of Captain Chernikov's 2nd Rifle Battalion and Captain Kiiko's Separate Guards Training Battalion were holding the two commanding heights, Hills 243.2 and 246.3. A powerful barrage on these two hills from the "screechers" of the II SS Panzer Corps' 55th *Werfer* Regiment (as our fighters called the German six-barreled rocket launchers) announced the start of *Leibstandarte*'s effort to break through the lines of the 51st Guards Rifle Division. The place selected for the attack was not accidental – it was the most suitable sector for a breakthrough by tanks. In the first place, the terrain was relatively flat, and up to 180 armored vehicles could cross it at the same time. Secondly, Hill 246.3 marked the boundary between the 154th and 156th Guards Rifle Regiments. At the same time, in front of the 156th Guards Rifle Regiment, where *Das Reich* was supposed to attack, only a limited amount of armor could be deployed, and even then, only against that regiment's right flank, which extended to that same Hill 246.3. Only here was there passable terrain for tanks, and at that only about a 1 kilometer wide section of it. To top it off, the Germans didn't have any real choice in selecting the ground of the attack; this narrow land bridge ran between the strongly fortified village of Iakovlevo and the Vorskla River which flowed beside it, and the gullies and swampy basin of the Lipovyi Donets River.

What were the forces that the opponent possessed before its lunge toward Prokhorovka? On the evening of 5 July, 334 tanks remained under the II SS Panzer Corps.[11] The number of remaining assaults guns is known only for *Leibstandarte* and *Das Reich*, which had 23 and 21 remaining assault guns respectively. The panzer regiments of these two divisions, which were concentrated on the axis of the SS Panzer Corps' main attack, numbered a total of 213 armored fighting vehicles, of which *Leibstandarte* had 99, while *Das Reich* had 121. In Wisch's *Leibstandarte,* 85% of the tank pool consisted of Tigers and the latest versions of the Panzer IV. Krüger's *Das Reich*'s situation was somewhat less favorable; Panzer IV and Panzer VI tanks made up only 31% of the total number of serviceable armored vehicles, while upgraded Panzer III tanks with the long 50mm gun barrel comprised 44%. In addition, *Das Reich* had 16 captured T-34 tanks that it had converted for its own use.

Up until 1030, the SS troops made three unsuccessful attempts to break through the lines held by the 154th and 156th Guards Rifle Regiments, after which they resumed pounding the Soviet line with the almost simultaneous fire of *Leibstandarte*'s and *Das Reich*'s artillery regiments, as well as the 55th *Werfer* Regiment. At the same time, up to 150 German airplanes appeared in the sky over the 51st Guards Rifle Division's sector. A half hour later, the main formations of the II SS Panzer Corps went on the attack from the region of Koz'mo-Dem'ianovka. The two SS Panzergrenadier divisions struck Major General N. T. Tavartkiladze's division simultaneously. The fighting raged for about two hours, as the 51st Guards Rifle Division's defense doggedly held on despite the enemy's superiority in tanks and infantry. From the report of Lieutenant Colonel Shamov, an officer of the General Staff attached to 6th Guards Army's headquarters:

> The 51st Guards Rifle Division continued to fight on its chosen line. At 1120, the enemy went on the attack with a force of up to two infantry regiments and 100 tanks in the direction of Iakovlevo and Luchki, after first working over the positions of the division with groups of up to 50 planes. For a long time, the tanks of the 230th and 245th Tank Regiments, together with artillery fire, repelled the fierce attacks of the savage fascists. The enemy, strengthening the force of his attack with fresh forces, at 1300 assembled up to two infantry regiments and 200 tanks in a grove 5 kilometers southeast of Iakovlevo and made another attack upon Luchki. Breaking through the defenses in the sector of the 156th Guards Rifle Regiment, by 1500 the enemy had seized Luchki and Nechaevka. Unable to withstand the enemy's intense pressure, the 154th and 156th Guards Rifle Regiments abandoned Iakovlevo, Luchki and Nechaevka, and began a disorderly retreat to the northwest. The 158th Guards Rifle Regiment, swinging back its right flank to Hill 210.7, continued to defend the line: Hill 210.7 – Teterevino – (excl.) Volobuevka.
>
> At 0400 7.07, the army commander, having learned of the disorganized retreat of the 51st Guards Rifle Division, gave an order – restore the division to full order and immediately consolidate on the line: southern outskirts of Sukh. [Sukho] Solotino – southern outskirts of Mal. [Malye] Maiachki.[12]

The SS attacked on a sector only 2 kilometers wide. A *kampfgruppe* of the SS Panzergrenadier Division *Das Reich* attacked the right flank of the 156th Guards Rifle Division, and after breaking through at Hill 246.3 shortly after noon, turned its advance in the direction of Luchki (south) – Sobachevskii – Kalinin – Ozerovskii. At practically the same time, the SS Panzergrenadier Division *Leibstandarte* overran the left flank of the 154th Guards Rifle Division on Hill 243.2 and took possession of the southern part of Iakovlevo, then resumed its attack with its primary forces on Iablochki – Luchki (north) – Ozerovskii.

Earlier on 6 July, by 0500, the bulk of the 5th Guards 'Stalingrad' Tank Corps had arrived at its assigned region, Teterevino – Ozerovskii – Kozinka ravine (3 kilometers) northeast of the village of Luchki (south), in order to backstop the thin infantry lines. Its 6th Guards Motorized Rifle Brigade, however, arrived in the vicinity of Luchki with only its artillery battalion, mortar battalion and an anti-tank rifle company.

The corps adopted the following combat formation: In the first echelon, the 22nd Guards Tank Brigade under the command of Colonel F. A. Zhilin, the 20th Guards Tank Brigade under the command of Lieutenant Colonel P. F. Okhrimenko, and part of the 6th Guards Motorized Rifle Brigade deployed on the line Kozinka ravine – Hill 232.0 – Luchki (south) – Teterevino. The second echelon – Colonel K. I. Ovcharenko's 21st Guards Tank Brigade and the 48th Heavy Tank Regiment – deployed to block the enemy tanks' most likely routes of advance in the vicinity of Ozerovskii and the grove north of Sobachevskii. The central positioning of the heavy tank regiment gave it the possibility to maneuver freely to either of the corps' flanks.

The corps had no connection with the 1st Tank Army's 3rd Mechanized Corps on its right flank. The II SS Panzer Corps' attack had torn a gap 4 kilometers wide

Colonel K. I. Ovcharenko, commander of the 5th Guards 'Stalingrad' Tank Corps' 21st Guards Tank Brigade (May 1943 photo). (TsAMO)

in the defenses in the direction of Prokhorovka. Realizing the consequences that this threatened, the corps commander advanced a tank detachment, reinforced by a rifle company, to the line Hill 243.2 – Hill 246.3 as a stopgap measure to fill the gap, and in order to secure a link with its left-hand neighbor (units of the 2nd Guards 'Tatsinskaia' Tank Corps), sent a tank company and a reinforced motorized rifle company to the line Petrovskii – Nechaevka.[13] This arrangement of his forces allowed him the possibility to offer stubborn resistance on the occupied line of defense, while at the same time giving the corps commander an impressive mobile tank reserve.

Immediately after penetrating the positions of the 51st Guards Rifle Division, the *kampfgruppe* from *Das Reich* ran into stubborn resistance from elements of Colonel A. M. Shchekal's 6th Guards Motorized Rifle Brigade from the 5th Guards 'Stalingrad' Tank Corps in the village of Luchki, but the forces were unequal. The enemy crushed the defenses and continued to advance in the direction of Kalinin, where the headquarters of A. G. Kravchenko's 5th Guards Tank Corps and his major forces had already deployed. The attack of panzers and motorized infantry was accompanied by heavy air attacks on the retreating Red Army troops. As surviving participants in those events remember, the *Luftwaffe*'s airplanes literally hovered over this region, not giving them even a chance to raise their heads. The powerful air cover for the SS divisions was an important reason for their success on this day.

Receiving a report by telephone from General I. M. Chistiakov about the breakthrough, Voronezh Front commander N. F. Vatutin gave the order for the 1st Tank Army and the separate tank corps of A. G. Kravchenko and A. S. Burdeiny to counterattack in order to localize the breakthrough. However, due to a number of reasons, these armored formations were unable to carry out Vatutin's plan fully, as further discussion will show.

The left flank of the 6th Guards Army had been smashed, the forces of three divisions simultaneously (the 51st Guards, 52nd Guards, and 67th Guards Rifle Divisions) had been encircled or scattered, and now the tank brigades of M. E. Katukov's 1st Tank Army had to bear the brunt of the fighting against the SS Corps. Striving to block the enemy in the village of Iakovlevo, and prevent his advance through Bol'shie Maiachki and Greznoe toward the village of Kochetovka, where the headquarters of the 6th Guards Army was currently situated, Mikhail Efimovich [Katukov] gave an order at 1330 to the commander of the 3rd Mechanized Corps, Major General S. M. Krivoshein, to support the operations of Colonel V. M. Gorelov's 1st Guards Tank Brigade in the region of Iakovlevo with one battalion from the 49th Tank Brigade. He simultaneously ordered the commander of the 31st Tank Corps, Major General D. Kh. Chernienko,[14] to advance Colonel N. I. Ivanov's 100th Tank Brigade to the north of Iakovlevo, to the region of the *Krasnyi Pakhar'* [Red Plowman] Collective Farm at Mikhailovka, with the order to plug the gap between the flanks of the 3rd Mechanized Corps and the 5th Guards 'Stalingrad' Tank Corps. However, it was already too late – as Colonel N. I. Ivanov's brigade was moving out for Mikhailovka, SS troops were already approaching Luchki (north), and Ivanov's tank battalions were forced to deploy and go into battle in the region of Ul'ianov, Bol'shie Maiachki, and Iablochki.

At this time, the SS Panzergrenadier Division *Das Reich*, closely pursuing the units of the 51st Guards Rifle Division and the 5th Guards 'Stalingrad' Tank Corps which had been driven out of Luchki, launched two attacks: the first in the direction of Ozerovskii, the second in the direction of Sobachevskii and Kalinin. Clearly, P. Hausser was trying to encircle the units of the 5th Guards Tank Corps. The isolated counterattack by F. A. Zhilin's 22nd Tank Brigade from the Kozinka woods in the direction of Hill 232.0 and Luchki (south) met with no success. General A. G. Kravchenko sent the 21st Tank Brigade and the 48th Guards Heavy Tank Regiment to the 22nd Tank Brigade's help, but the combined forces could not stop the SS panzers and Panzergrenadiers. Moreover, the decision to commit the corps' mobile reserve, which had no qualitative superiority in tanks and lacked the necessary artillery support, practically into the teeth of the attacking SS *Das Reich*, only aggravated the situation. The adversary crushed the 22nd Tank Brigade near the villages of Ozerovskii and Kalinin, and by 1630 it had encircled both tank brigades and the heavy tank regiment in the vicinity of the Kozinka woods, after which it attempted to seize Belenikhino Station and strike in the direction of Storozhevoe. The 5th Guards Tank Corps commander no longer had sufficient reserves to prevent the encirclement of his main forces.

Here's how A.G. Kravchenko reported to the Voronezh Front commander about the circumstances of his [Kravchenko's] 5th Guards Tank Corps' encirclement:

> On 6 July 1943, at 1200 the enemy began to move out in two columns from the region of Smorodino, Koz'mo-Dem'ianovka and the woods east of that place, with a major tank force, no less than two tank divisions, plus motorized infantry [Panzergrenadiers], advancing in the north and northeast directions. As has by now been precisely determined, the enemy launched his main attack against the units of the corps. The spearhead of the attack, numbering up to 300 tanks and a

Burning armor of the 5th Guards 'Stalingrad' Tank Corps in the area of the Kozinka wooded ravine (a captured photo, 6 July 1943). (RGAKFD)

> mechanized [Panzergrenadier] division, was right here. From the beginning of this advance, the enemy's air force was systematically working over the positions and assembly areas of the corps' units. Through the course of the day, no less than 1500 sorties were counted.
>
> As the enemy tank grouping was moving out, the commander of the 23rd Rifle Corps handed me a demand in your name about mobilizing two tank brigades and a regiment of Churchill tanks for a counterattack in the region of Hills 246.3, 243.2 and the woods northeast of there. Right after I received this directive, given in your name, a Colonel Nikiforov arrived at my headquarters with the full authority of the 6th Guards Army's commander, who threatened the use of his sidearm if the corps wouldn't launch the counterattack. I carried out this instruction. Despite the fact that the corps' sector of defense was weakened, units of the corps until 2300 6.07.43 continued to hold back the enemy's primary forces until they were fully encircled. Fighting their way out of encirclement, the corps took up a defensive line along the railroad in the sector Ivanovskii Vyselok – Belenikhino – (excl.) Teterevino, leaving outposts 1 km west of the railroad. In savage fighting with the enemy's major tank forces and not supported by operations of our neighbor on the right (units of the 1st Tank Army) or on the left (elements of the 2nd Guards Tank Corps), the corps in the course of 6.07.43 lost 110 tanks.[15]

At 1700 Kravchenko issued an order to Lieutenant Colonel P. F. Okhrimenko, whose 20th Guards Tank Brigade remained outside the encirclement, to leave one tank company in Teterevino, and with the rest of his forces to advance immediately to the woods north of Sobachevskii, in order to prevent the enemy's expansion in the direction of Belenikhino Station, but it was already too late. At 1900, as the brigade was moving to carry out the order, Okhrimenko was forced to halt his units and take up a hasty defense 500 meters south of the Belenikhino Station, since by this time the SS forces had taken control of Kalinin and had continued their attack on Belenikhino.[16]

While defending the farming village of Kalinin, the men of the 1698th Anti-aircraft Artillery Regiment of the 5th Guards 'Stalingrad' Tank Corps displayed tenacity and courage. From the report of the regiment's headquarters:

> 6.07.43 at 0600 at your orders, the regiment took up defensive positions in the region of Kalinin with the assignment of protecting the headquarters and the corps' tank groups from enemy air attack. … At 1700, under massive enemy dive-bombing attacks on the corps' tank groups and on the gun crews of the batteries, despite the nearby explosion of bombs, 5 enemy planes were shot down and destroyed with precision fire. During this attack, several Red Army men and junior commanders, despite their wounds, continued to carry out their duties, remaining at their guns and continuing to fire.
>
> At 1800, under attack from enemy tanks and submachine gunners, by order of the commander all batteries went over to anti-tank defense, during which many fighters and commanders died a hero's death. The regimental commander Major Savchenko and the regiment's deputy political commander Gumanovsky continued to command the batteries and to direct the fighting from their command post, killing the attacking submachine gunners, until the final moments of their lives.
>
> Lieutenant Biriukov, carrying out the order of the regiment commander by communications with the battery, directed the defense of his battery and led by his personal example, using his submachine gun to shoot a German assault team off the tank they were riding while shouting 'For the Motherland! For Stalin!' Having led his men into battle against the tanks and enemy submachine gunners, he died a hero's death.
>
> During the fight with the tanks, having knocked out and destroyed 3 Panzer VI tanks and up to a platoon of submachine gunners, the Red Army trooper Bogdanov revealed himself to be a steadfast son of the Motherland; as two Panzer VI tanks approached to within 15 – 25 meters and began to fire at point blank range at the battery, he courageously, at risk of his life, abandoned cover to take them on, and with three anti-tank shells, he put one tank out of action, and set fire to and destroyed the second.
>
> Senior Lieutenant Korotkov, Guards Sergeant Dudko, and Red Army trooper Dodonov by the massed fire of their guns and battery, put one Panzer VI tank out of action and wiped out up to a platoon of submachine gunners, after which at the order of their gun commander, they withdrew the guns and personnel of the battery to safety while under enemy fire …[17]

Communications with the 5th Guards Tank Corps headquarters in Kalinin were lost. Units defending this village began to retreat toward Iasnaia Poliana. The after-action report from the command of the 23rd Separate Reconnaissance Battalion of the 5th Guards Tank Corps describes the scene:

> The battalion commander dispatched a separate reconnaissance team consisting of one platoon of armored cars on a mission to reestablish communications with the corps and to clarify the situation. The platoon of Lieutenant Stepanov left along the route Kalinin – Ozerovskii – Bol'shie Maiachki. The reconnaissance platoon didn't return. No orders of any sort arrived from corps headquarters prior to 1800. Meanwhile the bombing only intensified, and the situation was unclear … the corps' chief of intelligence Guards Major Efremov and other staff officers decided to reposition the battalion. By an order of the battalion commander Captain Chuev, the battalion took up defensive positions at Belenikhino Station. Soon the 80th Motorcycle Battalion arrived at this place, and joined the 23rd Separate Reconnaissance Battalion's defense of the station. After 2000, tanks from the corps' 20th Guards and 21st Guards Tank Brigades in ones and twos began to break out of the encirclement to Belenikhino Station, and bolstered the 23rd Separate Reconnaissance Battalion's defense of the place. In a little while, much of the 20th Tank Brigade had assembled here, and they began an intensive fire on the enemy. Tanks continued to arrive at this place throughout the night, and in this way, the Belenikhino Station became a strongpoint of resistance and the grave for dozens of enemy tanks …[18]

Gathering all available forces – the 23rd Separate Reconnaissance Battalion, the 80th Motorcycle Battalion, as well as 60 men from the 6th Guards Motorized Rifle Brigade's 3rd Rifle Battalion, the commander of the 20th Tank Brigade in the shortest time created a stiff defense, digging the tanks into the ground. Thanks to this he succeeded in driving back an attack of SS troops, which not only failed to take the station, but also fell back to Kalinin.

As already mentioned, after the headquarters of the 5th Guards 'Stalingrad' Tank Corps abandoned Kalinin, communications with the encircled units (the 21st and 22nd Tank Brigades and the 48th Heavy Tank Regiment) had been lost. With no orders from above, the tankers in the pocket continued to fight. At 2300, gathering together all the remaining tanks into one group (by this time, the 22nd Guards Tank Brigade had only 8 T-34s and 16 T-70 tanks left), the commanders of the brigades and the regiment decided to fight their way out of encirclement in the direction of Belenikhino Station.[19] The surrounding ring turned out to be thin, and by 0800 7 July, units of the corps had fully escaped the pocket, losing 11 more T-70 tanks in the process. They reassembled in the woods about 1.5 kilometers to the east.

As one participant in the fighting at Prokhorovka, I. S. Vakhrameev, recalled:

> Unfortunately, not all the soldiers and officers fighting at Iakovlevo and near Luchki managed to escape the encirclement. A portion of them, mainly the wounded and those with concussions, wound up as prisoners of the fascists. After the fighting at Veselyi a private named Semon Lychkov, a native of Kursk, joined our platoon as a replacement. I became friends with him, and he informed me that he had been captured by the Germans in the fighting for Iakovlevo, and had been placed in

a prisoner camp, located just behind the German lines. There were a little more than 100 prisoners in the camp. The Hitlerites treated them cruelly: early the next morning, they led the prisoners out into the steppe, to a gully, where they lined them up and shot them down with machine guns that had been set up on the edge of the gully, and then to make sure that no one had survived, they crushed their bodies with tanks. As the tanks approached, Semon and two other lightly wounded soldiers leaped up and started running for the opposite side of the gully away from the machine guns. The machine gunners fired at them, but thank God, no bullets struck them. The escapees hid in a grain field for the rest of the day, and that night they crossed the front line and reached our forces.[20]

As already noted above, the SS Panzergrenadier Division *Totenkopf* began active operations prior to its neighbors that were near the village of Iakovlevo. Early in the morning, two of its regimental groups launched an attack on the villages of Nepkhaevo and Sashenkovo, trying to force a crossing of the Lipovyi Donets River. The goal of these attacks was to destroy the Soviet forces in this area, and at the same time secure the right flank of the rest of the II SS Panzer Corps, which was preparing to attack in the Prokhorovka direction. At 0900, the troops of *Brigadeführer* Priess managed to dislodge the 52nd Guards Rifle Division's 155th Guards Rifle Regiment after inflicting heavy losses on it, and seized the villages of Nepkhaevo and Sashenkovo. However, elements of Colonel A. S. Burdeiny's 2nd Guards 'Tatsinskaia' Tank Corps, which N. F. Vatutin was planning to transfer to the 6th Guards Army, were already approaching this area on the morning of 6 July.

Thus, Hoth's plan began to yield its first substantial results on that afternoon of 6 July. Hausser had managed to implement the first stage of the Fourth Panzer Army commander's plan. His divisions had in the shortest time emerged on the Prokhorovka axis, where the terrain was relatively flat, and thus it would be possible to make full use of the qualitative superiority of the German panzers over the T-34s and T-70s.

The Germans' lunge to the north and northeast had serious consequences for the Soviet side. Of all the formations of the Voronezh Front that took part in the fighting on the southern side of the Kursk bulge between 5 July and 23 July 1943, the divisions and corps that resisted the German advance toward Prokhorovka, or participated in the counterattack there suffered the heaviest losses. The 51st Guards Rifle Division opened this mournful account: of the 8,405 men who reported for duty on the morning of 1 July 1943, there remained only 3,354 men on 7 July.[21] I'll remind the reader that its primary forces only became engaged in the fighting on 6 July.

The SS Panzergrenadier Division *Das Reich* attained particularly substantial results on 6 July. By 1400, it had overrun the defenses of the 51st Guards Rifle Division, and having emerged on the Prokhorovka axis, it had begun the process of destroying the Soviet operational tank reserves. Kravchenko's 5th Guards Tank Corps, as we have seen, because of the ill-considered actions of the commander of the 6th Guards Army and the *front* leadership, which led to the piecemeal commitment of the Corps' brigades, became its first victim. SS Panzergrenadier Division *Leibstandarte*'s attack developed less

Colonel A. S. Burdeiny, commander of the 2nd Guards 'Tatsinskaia' Tank Corps (1944 photo). (Author's personal archive)

successfully. Although by 1330 one of its *kampfgruppen* had in fact taken control of Hill 230.5, about 4 kilometers northeast of Iakovlevo, the bulk of the division, including its panzer regiment, was still enmeshed in street fighting in Iakovlevo.

Three primary factors played a role in *Leibstandarte*'s difficulties. First, a significantly greater number of Soviet artillery, including anti-tank artillery, was located on its front. Second, shortly after noon, the battalions of two tank brigades had attacked the armored group of Wisch's division. Finally, Iakovlevo had been thoroughly tied into the second line of defenses and was well prepared for defense, while to assault a populated area is always more difficult than to assault a hill.

Striving to block the rapidly developing breakthrough, Lieutenant General I. M. Chistiakov had decided to launch a synchronized attack on the front and right flank of the SS Panzergrenadier Division *Das Reich* with the forces of Kravchenko's and Burdeiny's two tank corps. At midday, the army commander informed Vatutin of the breakthrough in the sector of the 51st Guards Rifle Division, and having obtained the *Front* commander's support, he ordered the 2nd Guards 'Tatsinskaia' Tank Corps commander Colonel A. S. Burdeiny to launch an attack at the base of the II SS Panzer Corps' salient, by crossing the Lipovyi Donets River and attacking in the region of Sashenkovo and Nepkhaevo toward the village of Krapivenskie Dvory and the *Smelo k trudu* Collective Farm with the aim of cutting the Belgorod – Kursk highway. At the same time, as we have seen, Major General A. G. Kravchenko's 5th Guards 'Stalingrad' Tank Corps from the vicinity of Ozerovskii and Kalinin was to launch a frontal attack on the *kampfgruppe* from SS Panzergrenadier Division *Das Reich*, and throw it back to the line Iakovlevo – Luchki (south). It was planned for both tank corps to go on the attack simultaneously. A communication from Colonel Burdeiny, commander of the 2nd Guards 'Tatsinskaia' Tank Corps, to the commander of the 5th Guards Tank Corps:

> Kravchenko
> I have received the order. It [the attack] will start at 1600 6.07.43.
> I am attacking in the direction of Krapivenskie Dvory and the *Smelo k trudu* Collective Farm. Keep me informed of your operations.[22]

This was the first attempt by the Soviet command to use tank formations to try to stop the enemy and drive him from the Prokhorovka axis of advance. Unfortunately, it did not yield the desired result, though it did have a certain positive effect. Even as the 2nd Guards 'Tatsinskaia' Tank Corps launched its attack, the SS Panzergrenadier Division *Das Reich* was enveloping the flanks of the 5th Guards 'Stalingrad' Tank Corps, striving to snare Kravchenko's formations in its pincers. Despite the fact that Colonel A. S. Burdeiny's corps had significant strength (his corps numbered 165 tanks), the counterattack of the 2nd Guards 'Tatsinskaia' Tank Corps did not go smoothly – the *Luftwaffe* literally swarmed over the combat formations of the units. Nevertheless, by 2000, the 26th Guards Tank Brigade had managed to reach the Kursk – Belgorod highway, and having seized the *Smelo k trudu* Collective Farm, it was blocking that main supply artery. To eliminate this threat, Hausser had to divert some of *Totenkopf*, including its panzer regiment, as well as part of *Leibstandarte*'s right-flank forces. This somewhat weakened the pressure on Kravchenko's embattled tank corps. However, further advance of the 2nd Guards 'Tatsinskaia' Tank Corps placed it in a precarious position. Because of the encirclement of the 5th Guards 'Stalingrad' Tank Corps, the 2nd Guards 'Tatsinskaia' Tank Corps' right flank became exposed; therefore, on 7 July at 0030, the Voronezh Front command issued the order for it to withdraw to the eastern bank of the Lipovyi Donets River.

The enemy's breakthrough of the 51st Guards Rifle Division's defenses and encirclement of the 5th Guards Tank Corps meant that the second army-level line of defenses had been breached. Moreover, taking advantage of the confusion during the retreat of the rifle units, SS forces managed to penetrate to the third and final defensive belt in the sector of the Komsomolets State Farm and Teterevino, which lay approximately 9 kilometers southwest of Prokhorovka. The defenses of the 183rd Rifle Division's 285th Rifle Regiment were situated here.

From the 285th Rifle Regiment headquarters' Combat Report No. 8 of 8 July 1943, issued after occurrence of the events in this report:

> 1. The enemy with up to 130 tanks and air support at 1800 6.07.43 approached our forward edge of the main defensive belt. At 1630, a group of 10 tanks had managed to infiltrate in the sector of the 4th Rifle Company along the road leading from Teterevino to Ivanovskii Vyselok. The cause of the enemy tank breakthrough was as follows: the enemy was closely following the retreating vehicles and tanks of the 6th Guards Army's 51st and 52nd Guards Rifle Divisions, which prevented the possibility to block the road leading from Teterevino to Ivanovskii Vyselok with anti-tank mines.
>
> The 10 tanks approached the edge of the woods south of the Komsomolets State Farm. Our anti-tank artillery knocked out 2 tanks; the remaining returned to the region of Hill 258.2 and fought their way down the communication trenches of the 4th Rifle Company, as a result of which part of the 4th Rifle Company

> was crushed or shot up by the tanks, and part retreated to the 1st and 3rd Rifle Battalions. Up to 70 tanks with groups of submachine gunners engaged our 3rd and 5th Rifle Companies. On the night of 6 to 7.07.43, the enemy shelled and placed rifle and machine-gun fire [on our positions], simultaneously conducting a reconnaissance of the 3rd Rifle Company's right flank, which was repulsed.
>
> As a result, from 1800 6.07.43 until the dawn of 7.07.43, 6 enemy tanks were destroyed and up to 30 of their infantry.[23]

The struggle in the trenches in Lieutenant Vakulov's 4th Rifle Company's sector of the final defensive belt was assessed by the command of the 183rd Rifle Division as an extraordinary occurrence [a "ChP" in Russian parlance, which can mean a disaster, an accident, or an unanticipated event]. Essentially, that is indeed what is was, because when constructing the defenses, the planners had anticipated that defensive fire would first meet the enemy's tanks and infantry at a range of 200 – 400 meters from the first line of entrenchments. For this purpose, the engineers had laid out an array of obstructions on the approaches to the trenches: minefields, anti-tank ditches, barbed wire, and finally, combat outposts. The latter were supposed to provide the command early warning of the enemy's approach and as far as possible reveal the enemy's numbers and resist the attack until receiving other orders.

The defenses of the 285th Rifle Regiment had been also constructed according to this scheme. However, the enemy from the march, with a relatively small force (10 tanks) had reached the first line of trenches and begun to overrun the fighters of the 4th Rifle Company in their trenches. What had happened; why hadn't the obstacles worked? From the Combat Report No. 3 of the 183rd Rifle Division's headquarters:

> Supply wagons, vehicles, and a unit of tanks, pursued by German tanks and hounded from the air, were retreating along the road to Hill 258.2 … the forward edge of the 285th Rifle Regiment's 4th Rifle Company ran along the southwestern slopes of Hill 258.2; an anti-tank ditch had been placed in front of the forward edge, with removable road blocks on the road itself. Both sides of the road had been mined and obstructed. An obstacle removal team had been positioned by the road obstacles with the task of blocking the road after the passage of the units of the 51st and 52nd Guards Rifle Divisions, but failed to do this job; as a result, the enemy tanks penetrated to Hill 258.2.
>
> According to a report by the 285th Rifle Regiment command, the following people are responsible for permitting enemy tanks to break through the forward edge of the defensive belt in the 4th Rifle Company's sector: the commander of 2/285 Rifle Regiment Senior Lieutenant Sedov, the commander of the 4th Rifle Company Lieutenant Vakulov, the commander of the artillery support group Senior Lieutenant Orzheshko, the commander of the 5th Battery of the 623rd Artillery Regiment Junior Lieutenant Krutov, and the commander of the 285th Rifle Regiment's sapper platoon, Junior Lieutenant Mikhailov.
>
> An investigation is underway.[24]

Back on 5 July, the commander of the 48th Rifle Corps, Major General Z. Z. Rogozny had inspected the corps' defensive lines and had issued instructions to the commanders of the 107th, 183rd and 305th Rifle Divisions to eliminate shortcomings in guarding passages through the defenses and in the arrangement of positions:

> The inspection of the corps' defensive readiness has indicated a number of genuine shortcomings.
>
> I am ordering:
>
> 1. Construct positions on the parapets of the anti-tank ditches and man them with infantry.
>
> 2. Replace the mines in cleared areas of the minefields.
>
> 3. Have teams ready to mine the roads and to remove barriers from anti-tank and anti-infantry obstacles.
>
> 4. Clear away obstacles to lines of sight and lines of fire by removing shrubs, weeds and standing grain.
>
> ...
>
> 6. By the morning of 6.07.43 fully complete the camouflaging of the defensive lines, having removed telephone lines from poles.
>
> 7. Take measures to guard headquarters reliably. Have teams ready to destroy paratrooper landings and isolated tank breakthroughs.
>
> 8. Organize the service of divisional blocking detachments, put together a scheme of outposts, and present it by 0600 6.07.43.
>
> 9. Report on the fulfillment [of this order] by 1400 6.07.43.[25]

As we can see, commanders were well aware of the basic defects, which contributed to the breakthrough of the defenses at Hill 258.2, even twenty-four hours prior to its occurrence, but nonetheless, the 4th Rifle Company's position was overrun. In general, there were many such instances of this type during the period of the Voronezh Front's defensive operation, and it is important to remember that they had serious consequences. Similar examples were noted at all levels of command; however, the day of 6 July in this respect was special, simply because there were more such tragic occurrences on this day.

The enemy's attack south of Iakovlevo had been expected. The 5th Guards Tank Corps had moved out to counter this blow. However, enemy intelligence had ascertained the concentration of our reserves on the right flank of his shock grouping. General Hoth assessed the threat and took measures to eliminate it. It must be acknowledged that the enemy command, which had greater combat experience in employing tank formations, skillfully exposed the weak spots in the defenses of the Soviet forces and delivered his attacks in a timely fashion primarily at the junctions of Soviet formations and units.

The adversary took advantage of the confusion and disagreement between the headquarters of the 6th Guards Army and the 5th Guards Tank Corps over the handling of the corps' forces. As a result, the enemy surrounded the main forces of the corps on the very day of its commitment to the fighting and inflicted serious damage upon them.

Over two days of bitter fighting, the Fourth Panzer Army's shock grouping, at the cost of heavy losses, had managed to break through the 6th Guards Army's main defensive belt and in the sector Iakovlevo – Luchki, the second defensive line as well. On the Prokhorovka axis, the enemy had advanced to a depth of 18 to 20 kilometers by the end of the second day of operations.

After the battle, Voronezh Front command, in a report to Stalin dated 24 July 1943, tried to present the events in such a way so as to make the enemy's penetration on the second day of the offensive to our third and final defensive belt look like just an unpleasant moment:

> ... In the course of 6.07.43, the enemy suffered enormous losses and had almost no success. We however over the course of the day lost only 50 tanks.
>
> *Only toward evening did the enemy succeed in shoving back the 5th Guards Tank Corps, and the enemy began to infiltrate between Iakovlevo and Luchki at the boundary between Katukov and Kravchenko* [Author's emphasis]. In order to liquidate this infiltration, it was necessary to hurl the 1st Tank Army's 31st Tank Corps into a counterattack in the direction of Luchki, and this corps successfully carried out this order.
>
> ... Not a single unit perished *or fell into encirclement* [Author's emphasis].[26]

That's how the history of the Kursk battle was written, while events were still fresh! In just a few days' time, the *Front* headquarters had put together a report on the combat operations which erased all the events that might interfere with the "victory parade". It was as if there had been no breakthrough of the 51st Guards Rifle Division's lines on 6 July; no encirclement of the 5th Guards Tank Corps; the loss of more than half the corps' combat vehicles had never happened; the tragic combat in the trenches of the 285th Rifle Regiment of the 183rd Rifle Division against enemy tanks had never occurred; and there were never any commissions that investigated what had happened.

Incidentally, the only person who received punishment for this breakthrough was the commander of the 6th Guards Army's 23rd Guards Rifle Corps, Major General P. P. Vakhrameev.[27] Already on 7 July, he was temporarily relieved of corps command,[28] and replaced by the commander of the 51st Guards Rifle Division, Major General N. T. Tavartkiladze. On 19 July, by decision of the *Front*'s Military Council, Pavel Prokop'evich was formally relieved of his duties "for non-accordance, since he could not handle the work."[29]

The appearance of the II SS Panzer Corps at the rear defensive belt was convincing evidence of what serious capabilities and resources that the enemy possessed, and of how skillfully he used them. The breakthrough on 6 July is especially impressive: in just eight hours of time, the SS divisions had managed to advance approximately 20 kilometers into the defenses of a *front* that had been several months in preparation. However, one shouldn't overdramatize the situation that had developed. The emergence of the SS Panzergrenadier Divisions *Leibstandarte* and *Das Reich* on the Prokhorovka axis was unarguably a success for the enemy, but the breach was quite narrow – only 15 kilometers wide. Their forces, like a sharp, but narrow blade, had seemingly found a small crack in the second line of defense and had slipped their way through, but there still remained the task of expanding the breakthrough: *Das Reich*, toward the Lipovyi Donets, and *Leibstandarte*, towards the villages Iakovlevo, Malye Maiachki, Bol'shie Maiachki, and Greznoe. This caused the two diversions to diverge from each other, and in the meantime, they hadn't been able to connect their inner flanks. Thus, *Das Reich*'s left flank and *Leibstandarte*'s right flank, which had both advanced the furthest, were exposed and consequently required serious strengthening, primarily with tanks and anti-tank guns.

Taking stock of the entire situation, Hoth passed an order to Hausser to reorganize his forces after the two days of most brutal fighting, in order to consolidate the gains they had made, and to close the gap that had arisen between *Das Reich* and *Leibstandarte*, thereby creating a solid front for the corps. At the same time, the divisions of General von Knobelsdorff's XXXXVIII Panzer Corps received the orders to continue their attack. It had two objectives: the main one was to reach the vicinity of the Psel River, after having broken through the second defensive belt along the Belgorod – Kursk highway; the secondary goal was to crush the defense along the Pena River and throw the defending Soviet formations back to a line 5 kilometers west of Berezovka. Already that morning of 6 July, when it had become clear that the Soviet command had brought up fresh tank reserves, Hoth during a telephone conversation with von Knobelsdorff had defined the goal more precisely: the main thing was to close the gap between the right flank of the 11th Panzer Division and the left flank of the II SS Panzer Corps and to block all attempts by the Russians to attack from the northwest.

The forces of the Voronezh Front that were defending in this region were also in a difficult situation. The 6th Guards Army had been split into pieces, its 23rd Guards Rifle Corps, which had been guarding the Prokhorovka axis, had been practically shattered, the headquarters had lost control over its divisions and the army commander had exhausted all his reserves, as incidentally had the Voronezh Front itself. Considering this circumstance, N. F. Vatutin placed the responsibility for defending this sector on M. E. Katukov's 1st Tank Army.

Katukov did make an attempt to exploit the vulnerable configuration of the enemy's lines. He decided to try to smash the II SS Panzer Corps' thin wedge between the "anvil" of the firm and active defense along the Lipovyi Donets River and the armored "hammer" of heavy blows from the five tank brigades of the 3rd Mechanized Corps and the 31st Tank Corps from the north and northeast. The role of the "hammer" was played by: the 1st Guards Tank Brigade, in the region of Iakovlevo; the 49th Tank Brigade, in the Stanovaia woods, directed at the region of Pokrovka; the 100th Tank Brigade, in the Bol'shie Maiachki – Iablochki sector; the 242nd Tank Brigade, situated in the area of Ryl'skii with the task of striking towards Luchki (south); and the 237th Tank Brigade, which was preparing to deploy along the Greznoe – Teterevino line. The front of the "anvil", which was not only supposed to hold on, but also to fix the enemy in position by active measures, was to be held by the forces of the 5th Guards 'Stalingrad' Tank Corps, the 2nd Guards 'Tatsinskaia' Tank Corps, and the 375th Rifle and 93rd Guards Rifle Divisions. This plan of the 1st Tank Army commander fully responded to the demands of the Voronezh Front leadership, which at the end of the day of 6 July made the following report to the *Stavka*:

> The Military Council has resolved: to defeat the enemy in defensive fighting on previously prepared lines, having reinforced the vulnerable Iakovlevo and Prokhorovka directions by means of advancing two brigades of the 31st Tank Corps and one destroyer anti-tank artillery brigade to the junction between the 1st Tank Army and the 5th Guards Tank Corps. *Front* aviation is to come down with all its might upon enemy tanks and troops on the Oboian' axis for their destruction.[30]

In the five brigades, which were deployed in the first echelon of the 1st Tank Army, there were a total of 256 tanks (in the 31st Tank Corps – by TO&E; in the 3rd Mechanized Corps – operational). In addition, there were two more brigades in the second echelon: Colonel M. Z. Kiselev's 180th Tank Brigade and Lieutenant Colonel A. F. Karavan's 192nd Tank Brigade, which had a combined total of 127 combat vehicles (by TO&E).

In addition to their tanks, in the fighting on 7 July these brigades could employ their own destroyer anti-tank artillery batteries, which counted a combined total of 19 76mm anti-tank guns in the 100th, 237th, 242nd, 49th and 1st Guards Tank Brigades (one gun had been lost in previous fighting), with an additional 8 guns in the 180th and 192nd Tank Brigades. In addition to these weapons, Major General D. Kh. Chernienko's 31st Tank Corps had 24 85mm anti-tank guns in two separate anti-tank battalions, and 59 45mm and 76mm guns in the attached destroyer anti-tank artillery regiment and Colonel E. F. Petrunin's 29th Separate Destroyer Anti-tank Artillery Brigade. Consequently, if you also take into account the 13 guns in the 51st Guards Rifle Division's 122nd Guards Artillery Regiment, the crews of which were also manning positions in the sector of the 31st Tank Corps, then a total of 123 anti-tank guns could be deployed against the II SS Panzer Corps, of which 99 were 76mm and 85mm anti-tank guns.

Despite the fact that M. E. Katukov's 1st Tank Army was strengthened by a significant amount of tanks and artillery, one must not view them as reinforcements. The *Front* was merely supplying the remainder of that, which the army had not yet received prior to the start of the fighting. For example, the 6th and 31st Tank Corps were missing, according to their TO&Es, destroyer anti-tank artillery regiments, rocket-launching regiments, motorcycle regiments, self-propelled artillery regiments (or separate tank regiments), anti-aircraft artillery regiments, separate destroyer anti-tank artillery battalions, as well as a motorized rifle brigade and a mortar regiment (in the 31st Tank Corps). The 3rd Mechanized Corps, which was located on the axis of the main attack, was also missing its authorized anti-aircraft and self-propelled artillery regiments. This did not allow Katukov as army commander to create a deeply echeloned anti-tank and anti-aircraft artillery defense on the important lines of attack and limited the tank brigades' and tank regiments' possibilities of maneuver. He was compelled to compensate for this with an insufficient number of anti-tank guns. Thus, Mikhail Efimovich had, in essence, to hold back two powerful enemy groupings with only the units and formations that had been authorized for his army. We must therefore pay the army commander his due: he carried out this difficult combat assignment under complicated conditions both successfully and very professionally.

In the course of 7 July, there were no serious changes in the operational situation on the Prokhorovka axis. Throughout the day, Katukov's 1st Tank Army mixed stubborn defense with sharp counterattacks by its tank brigades to resist the Germans. The heaviest fighting continued in SS Panzergrenadier Division *Leibstandarte*'s sector of attack. Its forces launched an attack from the vicinity of Pokrovka in the direction of Bol'shie Maiachki, Malye Maiachki, and Greznoe, trying to fight its way through to Kochetovka and the bend in the Psel River at Krasnyi Oktiabr'. The formations of the 31st Tank

Corps repulsed *Leibstandarte*'s main assault here. An account of an episode from this fighting testifies to the intensity of the combat and the resolve of our tankers.

For over five hours without pause, the tankers of the 100th Tank Brigade resisted attacks on the outskirts of Bol'shie Maiachki. At times, fighting reached the point of hand-to-hand combat. During one of the attacks, the T-34 of Lieutenant Gustov was the first to take a hit. The tank began to smoke, and some of the crew was injured, others were unconscious. While those who could still move began to exit the damaged tank through the emergency hatch, the tankers of Lieutenant Bondarenko and Lieutenant Alafirenko kept the approaches to the stricken tank under fire, trying to prevent enemy infantry from approaching it. The brigade chief of staff Colonel Pimenov described what happened next in the brigade's after-action report:

> Nevertheless, German submachine gunners approached Lieutenant Gustov's tank, just as members of the crew regained consciousness. Seeing that they were surrounded, they engaged the enemy in hand-to-hand combat. The struggle boiled down to a genuine fistfight … Gustov and the members of his crew … drove back the German submachine gunners ….[31]

Even though the brigade put up stubborn resistance, that evening it was compelled to yield Bol'shie Maiachki by an order from higher command. That afternoon, the enemy had also seized control of Greznoe. However, despite applying heavy pressure, the SS troops were unable to advance any further to the northwest.

One of the brigades of the 1st Tank Army attacks a hamlet on the Prokhorovka axis that had been seized by the enemy, July 1943. (RGAKFD)

SS officers examine several knocked out T-34s. (RGAKFD)

The antagonist's attempts to seize Krasnyi Oktiabr' with a subsequent emergence directly on the Psel River were also beaten back. The SS Panzergrenadier *Das Reich* Division, attacking on the right of *Leibstandarte*, unsuccessfully attacked Belenikhino Station and the Komsomolets State Farm. Battalions from Colonel P. F. Okhrimenko's 20th Tank Brigade and the 6th Guards Motorized Rifle Brigade from General Kravcheko's 5th Guards Tank Corps were dug in at Belenikhino and stubbornly held their positions. The fighters of these two formations resisted 11 attacks over the course of 7 July. In the second half of the day, the enemy halted the attacks and began to dig in his armor in the region of Kalinin and Ozerovskii.

The strong pressure on the defenses of the 31st Tank Corps from the line Pokrovka, Bol'shie Maiachki, Malye Maiachki, Greznoe, the appearance of a portion of the SS Panzer Corps in the vicinity of Krasnyi Oktiabr', as well as the attacks of the SS Panzergrenadier Division *Das Reich* seriously concerned N. F. Vatutin. On the night of 7 July, Katukov additionally received the 29th Separate Destroyer Anti-tank Artillery Brigade. Reinforcements also arrived to strengthen this line from the more quiet sectors of the 40th and 38th Armies, including the 309th Rifle Division and several anti-tank artillery regiments. On this same day (7 July), Lieutenant Colonel G. G. Pantiukhov's[32] 52nd Guards Rifle Division, without a single reconstituted rifle regiment, moved back into positions on the north bank of the bend in the Psel River. After the first day's fighting against superior enemy forces on the main defensive belt and the subsequent retreat, this division's command had spent the next two days gathering up disorganized elements in the vicinity of Teterevino; then it had moved to continue its reorganization at Skorovka and Svino-Pogorelovka.

In addition, Major General A. F. Popov's 2nd Tank Corps, which was being transferred from the Southwestern Front, was already moving toward Pokrovka. Its tank brigades were due to arrive on the afternoon of 8 July.

The battle plan of the 1st Tank Army commander for 7 July had been crowned with success; the enemy forces on the Prokhorovka axis had been contained, and P. Hausser acknowledged this. In the II SS Panzer Corps' daily journal of combat operations, it was noted: "*The day's main situational feature became the advance of all units in order to close up the combat formations and to repulse strong attacks on both flanks.*" [Author's emphasis][33] I think it is likely that if the SS divisions had succeeded in breaking through the fronts of the 100th Tank Brigade at Iablochki or the 237th Tank Brigade east of Greznoe, they would not have suspended the offensive to wait for the next day, and would have continued to press their attacks to the north.

With every passing day, the Fourth Panzer Army's commander's optimism was diminishing. He still believed in the correctness of the operational plan that had been worked out for his army and remained focused on the intended goal – an engagement at Prokhorovka. However, now even the slender hopes of success for the entire Operation Citadel were gradually melting away. The tank attacks of the Soviet forces, even such intensive ones, had not been a surprise for Hoth. He had assumed the presence of significant operational reserves available to the Soviet command. With a qualitative superiority in armor, though, he had hoped to destroy them on the Prokhorovka axis with the SS Corps; for the time being, it seemed his calculations were being realized. Only one thing troubled him – whether or not he had miscalculated the size of the Soviet reserve. When, finally, would this deep river of Red Army tanks run dry? Intelligence was reporting that the Russians were continuing to bring up more and more forces. From the II SS Panzer Corps journal of combat operations:

> 2400. Results of aerial reconnaissance on the enemy's movement in front of the Fourth Panzer Army (130 tanks confirmed):
>
> Aerial reconnaissance reports [on] 7.7 heavy traffic on the roads: Korocha – Belgorod, 90 vehicles moving to the northeast, 60 vehicles to the southwest; Skorodnoe – Prokhorovka – Oboian', 400 vehicles moving to the east, 150 vehicles to the west; on the roads 6 kilometers west of Prokhorovka, 100 vehicles moving to the northeast. Oboian', Iakovlevo and the route west of them – a total of 110 tanks were spotted, and another 30 tanks on the march from the north. In the area that lies 18 kilometers east of Belgorod, 20 tanks …
>
> Evaluation of the enemy on 7.7.1943. General impression.
>
> The information obtained by aerial reconnaissance creates the impression that major enemy forces, first of all infantry, are retreating from regions threatened by the II SS Panzer Corps' offensive to the northeast, in the direction of Prokhorovka, and to the north, in the direction of Oboian'. The enemy has assembled major tank and motorized forces in the region of Mar'ino, as well as south and north of the Psel River near Oboian' as an operational reserve, which are defending in an aggressive style. The enemy counterattacks were on 7.7 less organized than the attempted tank breakthrough on 6.7 from Smorodino to the west and from Iakovlevo to the east. These counterattacks were directed against our attacking spearheads, which were

> attacked frontally, in the flanks and from the rear. In the attempt the enemy lost many tanks.[34]

If one compares the results of the third day of the defensive operation with the preceding two days, then the command of the Voronezh Front had accomplished a lot. Most importantly, despite the strong attack by the XXXXLVIII Panzer Corps against the center of the 1st Tank Army's defenses, the *Front* had managed to keep the situation on the main axis of the attack under control. Despite the fact that the enemy had been able to drive a rather deep wedge into the army-level system of defensive belts, the configuration of the front lines allowed the *Front* to contain the hostile forces by the method of active defense and to keep the enemy from breaking into operational space. At the same time, the losses of the 1st Tank Army on this day were not very significant. It is particularly noteworthy that there, where the tankers of the 31st Tank Corps had employed the "Katukov method" of mobile defense, the enemy had been able to inflict only minimal damage.

The breakthrough operations in the first stage of the operation, in the regions that had been planned by Hoth, were proceeding with great difficulty. The Russian lines turned out to be significantly stronger and more resistant to tank attacks than had been anticipated. In addition, by bringing its operational tank reserves into the battle, the Soviet side had created conditions where even having split the front of the 6th Guards Army in two and having penetrated the second defensive belt, the Fourth Panzer Army was still tied up in heavy fighting across the entire sector of attack. Wisch's and Krüger's SS divisions had not even been able to close the gap between them, not to mention the gaps between the Fourth Panzer Army's corps. In the separate corridors that each had punched through the defenses, Hausser's Panzergrenadier divisions were experiencing strong pressure not only at the tip of the attacking spearhead, but also on the flanks. Army Detachment Kempf had failed to crack the defenses of the 7th Guards Army and was now badly lagging behind Hoth's Fourth Panzer Army, leaving the II SS Panzer Corps' right flank exposed. Thus Hausser was forced to divert substantial forces to cover those exposed flanks. This led to the dissipation of force and weakened the strength of the main effort. The absence of a solid, unified breakthrough front and the constant concern with the flanks were the most important problems that the commands of the Fourth Panzer Army and Army Group South had to solve in the nearest days.

In addition, another important factor had emerged, which would have a negative influence on the operations of von Manstein's formations: the failures of General W. Model's Ninth Army of Army Group Center on the northern side of the Kursk bulge. It had become fully bogged down in the defenses of General K. K. Rokossovsky's Central Front. The OKW already had to take a number of steps on the evening of 7 July to try to break the impasse on this sector, and whatever reinforcements von Klüge's Army Group Center might receive, Berlin had to take from von Manstein's Army Group South.

Nonetheless, N. F. Vatutin had still not succeeded in bringing a complete halt to the advances of Army Group South into the depth of his *front*'s defenses and had not yet compelled the adversary to terminate his plan for breaking through to the north. He hoped to achieve this in the next few days by launching strong flank attacks with the tank formations that the *Stavka* had already allotted to him. With these attacks, Vatutin hoped to relieve the pressure on center of the 1st Tank Army by compelling the enemy to shift forces to counter the Soviet flank attacks. It was a calculated gamble, because the enemy still had superiority in tanks.

On the night of 7 July, Vatutin issued an order to Lieutenant General I. M. Chistiakov, commander of the battered 6th Guards Army, to try to divert part of the adversary's forces from the Oboian' axis and to dislodge him from the Prokhorovka axis, by means of a counterattack in the region of Iasnaia Poliana, Pokrovka, and Iakovlevo together with elements of Lieutenant General V. D. Kriuchenkin's 69th Army. Vatutin was by now plainly losing his grip on the situation. The daily phone calls from Moscow also contributed to the strained, nerve-wracking conditions in Vatutin's headquarters.

I'll discuss these conversations between Vatutin and members of the *Stavka* a bit later, but for now let's turn to the memoirs of a member of the *Front*'s Military Council, N. S. Khrushchev:

> The battle was intensifying. Anxiety was beginning to appear on all our faces, including Vatutin's. The news that the enemy now had some sort of new tanks, with armor that could not be penetrated by our anti-tank shells, extremely concerned us. Sweat was pouring down our bodies. What could be done? We gave instructions that artillery of all calibers should fire at the tracks. A tank's tracks are always a weak spot. Even if you can't penetrate the armor, the tracks are always vulnerable. And once you've broken the tracks, it is no longer a tank: [it is] more like immobile artillery. Things will become easier. Our men began to do just what we had instructed, and rather successfully. Simultaneously, we began to bomb the tanks from the air. On the spot, we reported to Moscow that we had encountered new tanks. The Germans called them 'Tigers' … Soon they sent us new anti-tank shells, which could penetrate the thick hide of the 'Tigers,' – shaped charge anti-tank shells, which could burn through the metal.[35] However, the 'Tigers' had managed to shake the confidence of our anti-tank artillerymen. We, on the other hand, had been thinking that it was going to be no problem, and that we would smash the German tanks.
>
> In general, very important events were happening then. The fate of the war and the fate of the nation were being decided. It is now unpleasant to think back on a lot of what happened. Both the circumstances and the times are different today …
>
> … The enemy had driven us back to the third line of defense. Our defenses' three belts, including the final one, had anti-tank ditches, a variety of ground and field fortifications, and firing positions for the infantry, artillery and tanks. Yet within the span of a week, he [the enemy] had overcome almost all of these, until he was now butting up against the rear belt of army-level defenses. The situation had become particularly acute at Prokhorovka Station, in the direction of Kursk.[36]

Vatutin assembled significant forces for the counterattack on 8 July: four tank corps (the 2nd, 2nd Guards, 5th Guards, and 10th Tank Corps) and two rifle divisions (the 89th Guards Rifle and 375th Rifle Divisions). The deputy commander of the 6th Guards Army, Major General P. F. Lagutin, was placed in charge of this operation. This was already the second time that Pavel Filippovich found himself fighting on the ground around Prokhorovka. Between February and April 1942, the 293rd Rifle Division, which he was commanding at that time, had participated in an assault on Prokhorovka Station and the several farms and villages connected with it. After the failed spring 1942 offensive at Khar'kov, his division had fallen back to the Don River and together with the 5th Guards Tank Corps it had covered the withdrawal of our units from the pocket in the region of Staryi Oskol.

The aim of Voronezh Front's 8 July ambitious counterattack was through the simultaneous attack of four tank corps and supporting rifle formations to cleave the II SS Panzer Corps' divisions on the Prokhorovka axis and to encircle them. The 2nd Guards Tank Corps with the support of infantry from the 89th Guards Rifle Division was to attack Luchki, and thereby cut off part of the opposing force from the enemy's main forces in the vicinity of Iakovlevo, while the 10th, 2nd and 5th Guards Tank Corps were to attack from the region of Vasil'evka, Komsomolets State Farm, and Belenikhino in order to drive a wedge between the SS Panzergrenadier Division *Das Reich* and the SS Panzergrenadier Division *Leibstandarte Adolf Hitler*. Units of the 6th Guards Army and brigades of the 31st Tank Corps, which were defending on the line Psel River bend – Greznoe – Malye and Bol'shie Maiachki, were to form the northwest part of the anticipated ring of encirclement.

During the 8 July 1943 counterattack. Deputy commander of the 6th Guards Army Major General P. F. Lagutin (extreme left) and commander of the 5th Guards Tank Corps Major General A. G. Kravchenko (second from the left) report on the operational situation to a member of the Voronezh Front's Military Council, Lieutenant General N. S. Khrushchev (second from the right). (RGAKFD)

The very idea of this counterattack, when the enemy had not yet expended its strength, was mistaken. The correlation in armor strengths did not allow the Soviet side to count upon substantial results. In addition, our troops were ill-prepared for the attack. Several units that were to take part in it had not managed to arrive by its designated start time. There was not even time to regroup the forces prior to the attack. Thus, the commander of the 6th Guards Army issued the order to prepare for the attack to his units at 0200 on 8 July, while the attack itself was planned to begin at 1000. This amount of time was simply not realistic: within eight hours, the order had to reach all the subordinate headquarters (in fact, the commander of the 2nd Guards Tank Corps didn't receive it until 0530), the plan of action for all the formations and units had to be completed, the combat assignments had to go out to all the units and elements, cooperation had to be worked out, and forces regrouped. At the same time, it was necessary to reorganize the troops after three days of fighting, feed the soldiers, and give them their ammunition, after having first brought up the cartridges, shells and mines from the rear areas. Naturally, it was simply impossible to carry out all these tasks in such a short period of time.

The situation was even worse in the tank formations. The brigades of the 2nd Tank Corps were still on their way and were running three or four hours behind schedule for the start of the counterattack. Everyone was aware of this even before dawn. After the lengthy march, the crews were exhausted, and their tanks needed inspection and service. The Corps' motorized riflemen would not arrive for two more days. The forces of A.G. Kravchenko's 5th Guards Tank Corps had only just escaped encirclement on the morning of 7 July, having lost about half its tanks, while a third of the remaining tanks required repairs. There had been serious losses in personnel, especially among the company and battalion commanders. Colonel Burdeiny's 2nd Guards Tank Corps had also been involved in two days of fighting without stop, but the situation with its tank complement was a bit better.

Accordingly, it was impossible to create a united armored fist by the indicated time, and whatever force available at jumping-off time would still be plainly lacking in strength. In a situation like this, it was extremely important not to rush things, not to disperse the available strength, but instead to gather all the tanks into a single strike force, to supply them with everything necessary, and to arrange for artillery support. If you consider that some tank brigades would reach Prokhorovka only by around 1300, then it would be possible to attack no sooner than 1500 to 1600. By this time, it might have been possible to gather the forces and define assignments more precisely. Unfortunately, it was precisely time that the *Front* command lacked.

The commander of the 5th Guards Tank Corps, General A. G. Kravchenko wrote:

> At 0400 on 8.07.43, I personally received a combat assignment from the *Front* chief of staff, Lieutenant General Ivanov, to switch the corps over to the attack at 1030 on 8.07.43 in cooperation with neighbors on the right and left. Units of the corps launched the attack at 1030 8.07.43 in the designated direction, and by 1500 on 8.07.43 they had seized the village of Kalinin and reached the line Ozerovskii – Sobachevskii – unnamed hill south of Sobachevskii.
>
> The 2nd and 10th Tank Corps (on the right) and the 2nd Guards Tank Corps (on the left) did not attack. Thus, our neighbors did not exploit the initial success of

> the corps, although we maintained constant communications with them, and they had received timely information about the corps attack.
>
> The poor organization of cooperation between the tank formations by Voronezh Front's staff and their insufficient control over the execution of a combat order should be noted, which led to the undisciplined and criminal actions of a number of tank formations (2nd, 10th, and 2nd Guards Tank Corps) that never joined the attack.
>
> The adversary, sensing that the assault from our side was on a relatively narrow sector of the front, quickly regrouped and hurled 130 tanks, including 30 'Tigers', up to a division of motorized infantry, 4 six-barreled rocket launchers, and up to 30 guns of various caliber against the corps in the direction Luchki (north) – Teterevino (north) – Iasnaia Poliana from the direction of Luchki (south). Simultaneously, a large number of aircraft appeared over the battlefield, which for several hours without interruption bombed the combat formations of the corps. First in this operation from 1600 to 1930, the enemy used a large group of Me 110s, which strafed the tanks of the 20th Guards and 21st Guards Tank Brigades.
>
> As the result of the enemy's strong attack on the flanks and the rear from the direction of Teterevino (north), and with no support from our neighbors on the right and left, by the end of the day on 8.07.43 the units of the corps, suffering heavy losses, retreated to its previously occupied positions along the line of the railroad. As a result of the fighting, 46 enemy tanks, several self-propelled guns and mortars, 55 vehicles, and up to a battalion of infantry were destroyed. Our losses – 31 tanks.
>
> ... In the course of these days of fighting, the corps lost a large number of battle-tested commanders, participants in the destruction of the enemy at Stalingrad.
>
> Two regiment commanders were killed, two brigade chiefs of staff were seriously wounded, and the commander of the 48th Guards Tank Breakthrough Regiment was seriously wounded. 75% of the battalion commanders and 70% of the company commanders were killed or wounded.
>
> The entire command staff and fighting men demonstrated exceptional bravery in the fighting, a desire to destroy the enemy by any means. There were dozens of cases, when a crew refused to abandon a burning tank.[37]

It is possible to understand Kravchenko's rebuke toward his neighbors: over three days of fighting, his full-strength corps, which bore the honorific title 'Stalingrad', had suffered significant losses in men and equipment. On 5 July, the formation had 216 tanks; by the end of 8 July, only 41 tanks remained, and 17 of those were under repair.

Somehow, the failure to carry out orders and the large losses had to be explained. It was impossible for Kravchenko to state that it was indeed the *Front* leadership that had failed to organize a coordinated attack and had permitted the tank corps' piecemeal commitment, and was therefore largely responsible for the disaster. That is why he shifted blame to the neighboring formations. However, the fact is that the neighboring corps faced precisely the same unenviable situation.

Let's examine some of the other cases. Early on the morning of 8 July, the 2nd Guards Tank Corps received the following order:

A combat instruction from the commander of Voronezh Front to the commander of the 2nd Guards Tank Corps, 8 July 1943 00 hr 50 min.

1. I have decided 8.07.43 to counterattack the enemy in the general direction of the Prokhorovka – Tomarovka axis.

2. The 2nd Guards Tank Corps will attack from the region of Petrovskii, Kriukovo, Chursino in the direction of Luchki, in order to link up with a corps that is attacking Luchki from the northeast. Encircle and destroy the enemy, after which attack in the direction of Luchki, Gonki, and Bolkhovets.

The immediate assignment: take control of the Gonki region, having in view the further occupation of Bolkhovets and Streletskoe. The 5th Guards Tank Corps will be attacking on the right of you with the task to emerge in the Krapivenskie Dvory – Gremuchii – *Smelo k trudu* Collective Farm region and further to attack toward Rakovo. The 89th Guards Rifle Division will be attacking on your left, in the direction of Visloe and Erik, to emerge on the Erik – Shopino front, having in view a further offensive toward Belgorod.

Take the 47th [Tank] Breakthrough Regiment with you; as soon as the corps has success, the 93rd Guards Rifle Division will attack in the direction of Kriukovo and Krapivenskie Dvory and will emerge on the front Koz'mo-Dem'ianovka – (excl.) Erik.

Be ready for the attack at 1000 8.07.43.

The attack will begin at 1030 8.07.43

Artillery preparation will continue for not more than 30 minutes. Confirm the receipt [of this order] and report on its fulfillment.[38]

The 2nd Guards 'Tatsinskaia' Tank Corps, as it had been ordered, went on the attack at 1030 in two directions at the signal "555". Colonel A. K. Brazhnikov's 4th Guards Tank Brigade tried to attack Nechaevka, but a storm of fire from the Germans in Luchki and Nechaevka prevented it from crossing the Lipovyi Donets River. Somehow the infantry managed to make its way over the river, but the tanks were unable to force a crossing. Without tank support and under unceasing bombardment, the infantry could not take Nechaevka.

The second group – a tank battalion of the 26th Guards Tank Brigade, a motorized rifle battalion of the 4th Guards Motorized Rifle Brigade, and elements of the 89th Guards Rifle Division under the command of Colonel M. P. Seriugin – forced a crossing of the river in the region of Visloe and from the march conducted an attack in the direction of the *Smelo k trudu* Collective Farm and took Hill 209.5, but there it met with a storm of fire and counterattacks by up to 50 panzers. Bitter fighting continued in the area of this hill for the entire day, but the group was unable to advance further. At day's end, the battalions fought off another enemy counterattack.

The attack of General A. F. Popov's 2nd Tank Corps began much later, at 1600. Three tank brigades consisting of 145 T-34 and T-70 tanks took up the jumping-off line for the attack (the 26th Tank Brigade: 34 T-34 and 19 T-70; the 99th Tank Brigade: 34 T-34 and 19 T-70; and the 169th Tank Brigade: 19 T-34 and 20 T-70),[39] while 11 Mk IV Churchill tanks of the 15th Guards Separate Tank Breakthrough Regiment stood ready under cover in the Storozhevoe woods. The following citation from an account of the 99th Tank Brigade's participation eloquently testifies to how the attack went:

A crew manning a 50mm anti-tank gun from a grenadier regiment of the 167th Infantry Division repels a Soviet tank attack, 8 July 1943. (RGAKFD)

This offensive operation had a number of features, which determined the outcome of the battle:

1. The lack of time for preparation.

2. The lack of information about the enemy and about the layout of the forward edge of defense of our units that were operating in front of us.

3. The receipt of maps for the attack order at 1200 8.07.43, which depicted only the direction of the planned attack at 1000 8.07.43 and did not allow us to organize an attack in the proper fashion.

Having been notified by telephone to begin extending the units [as written in text – Author], the brigade's command and headquarters left for the units to implement the order, and to oversee and assist the column's deployment.

At 1235, the head of the brigade's column had passed the point of departure – the northeast outskirts of Priznachnoe, and in sequence had completed a march along the route Priznachnoe – Mordovka – Grushki and further along the gully, and had assembled on the eastern edge of a grove standing on the Stalinskoe Branch of the [Oktiabr'skii] State Farm.

... A reconnaissance of the march route, the attack's point of departure, and the line of deployment for the attack (the railroad crossing 600 meters north of Ivanovskii Vyselok) was conducted. Meanwhile, the tanks were unloading their extra ammunition and spare fuel drums, and removing spare containers from the rear part of the tanks.

Commander of the 2nd Tank Corps Major General A. F. Popov directing the fighting of his tank brigades over the radio. (RGAKFD)

All of this work was done hastily, under pressure from higher command, which was accusing the brigade of dawdling.

Instead of at 1000, the attack went in at 1400 8 July 1943. The 99th Tank Brigade attacked in the second echelon, behind the 169th and 26th Tank Brigades, with a combat formation also in two echelons: in the first – the T-34 tanks, in the second – the T-70 tanks. A motorized rifle battalion and an anti-tank rifle company rode into battle aboard the tanks. Thus, practically without preparation, without any notion about the enemy and his forces that were operating in front and on the flanks, the brigade went into battle in the designated direction Hill 258.2 – Teterevino – Luchki.

As the 169th Tank Brigade advancing in front of us reached the line of the Komsomolets State Farm, the adversary opened up on the tanks with artillery, heavy mortars, and the guns of dug-in Panzer VI tanks, and began to execute massed attacks by Ju 88 and anti-tank Ju 87 planes, the latter mounting three 37mm automatic cannons [the Ju 87G only had two such cannons]. The aerial attacks increased in step with the brigades' advance, and approximately by 1800 of 8 July 1943, these raids had become an uninterrupted attack from the sky. ... As a rule, the Ju 87s, when attacking our tanks, struck the engine compartment with their cannon fire.

In the period between 1400 and 1900 on 8 July, around 425 enemy sorties had been counted. Our aviation showed no activity.

Colonel I. Ia. Stepanov, commander of the 2nd Tank Corps' 169th Tank Brigade. (TsAMO)

The commander of the 1st Tank Battalion, which was to attack in the brigade's first echelon behind the 169th Tank Brigade, even as he was deploying the battalion at the jumping-off line for the attack (the railroad hut 500 meters north of Ivanovskii Vyselok), took a wrong turn and wound up 2 kilometers south of Ivanovskii Vyselok. Taking immediate corrective measures, the brigade command directed the 2nd Tank Battalion to attack in the first echelon in place of the 1st Tank Battalion. The 1st Tank Battalion was halted, and it was assigned a different direction – to attack the southwestern edge of the grove on the Komsomolets State Farm. Thus, the 1st Tank Battalion wound up in the second echelon.

In the vicinity of the highway, the 1st Tank Battalion bumped into the 26th Tank Brigade's column, although the battalion commander knew that the 26th Tank Brigade was supposed to be operating on his right. Then the 1st Tank Battalion commander turned his column and began to attack along the shoulder of the highway in the direction of Teterevino. On the approach to Hill 258.2, the battalion came under fire from two Panzer VI enemy tanks. An exchange of fire erupted, and the 1st Tank Battalion, suffering tank losses, fell back to the western edge of the woods on the Komsomolets State Farm and fired from its position there.

The 2nd Tank Battalion, moving behind the 169th Tank Brigade, reached the southwestern slopes of Hill 258.2, but having encountered heavy fire from Hills 224.5 and 258.2 and having lost two T-70 tanks, it fell back to the eastern part of Iar Zaslonnyi, where it took up suitable positions together with 10 tanks of the 169th Tank Brigade and the 15th Guards Heavy Tank Breakthrough Regiment (some of the remaining tanks of these units had been immobilized or destroyed, while the rest had become lost).

An Il-2 squadron of the 1st Storm Aviation Corps prepares for a sortie, 8 July 1943. (RGAKFD)

The motorized rifle battalion and the anti-tank rifle company, riding aboard the tanks of the 1st and 2nd Tank Battalions, under the attack of enemy aircraft, leaped from burning, knocked-out, and then even from still operational tanks, and having fragmented into small groups (6 to 10 men), together with infantry from other units, they took cover from the bombing and strafing. The commander of the motorized rifle battalion, having a mortar company with him, lost control of his battalion, and together with his headquarters staff he tried to rally his men. In essence, the brigade headquarters was busy with the same thing.

The destroyer anti-tank artillery brigade, coming under enemy artillery shelling and ceaseless attacks by enemy planes, retreated and took up a position on a nameless hill a half kilometer to the southwest of the grove on the Stalinskoe Branch of the State Farm, where it prepared to repulse enemy tank attack from the direction of Teterevino and Iasnaia Poliana.

The firefight between our tanks and artillery and the enemy's tanks and artillery, while under fierce enemy air attack, continued until late in the night. By this time, through the efforts of the battalion commanders and the brigade headquarters, the infantry had been reassembled and brought back into order.

Over the course of the night leading into 9 July 1943, by order of the Corps chief of staff, the brigade took up a firm defense on the southeastern slopes of Hill 258.2, in readiness with the coming of dawn to carry out the assignment of the preceding day. The infantry were well entrenched, and the tanks had been dug in deeply into the earth.

> In the conditions of rigid defense, communications between the brigade headquarters and the units and elements were established. During the fighting of the preceding day, headquarters staff, acting as messengers, had been the chief means of maintaining communications.
>
> In this severe battle, the 99th Tank Brigade lost: 21 T-34 tanks, knocked out or burned-out and 2 T-70 tanks. 21 commanders and fighting men were killed, wounded – 53 men.
>
> The losses of the enemy amounted to 13 medium tanks, 8 anti-tank guns, and 6 machine guns. Around 300 soldiers and officers were killed.[40]

The above excerpt from the document, in essence, requires no additional commentary, but the report didn't reveal all the problems and confusion of that day. Here's the Extraordinary Combat Report No. 05 from the 183rd Rifle Division's headquarters at 0500 9 July:

> At 1600 8.07.43, the command post of the 285th Rifle Regiment heard the noise of engines from Prokhorovka Station in the direction of Point 241.6. Tanks were moving, which deployed into combat formation and opened heavy cannon fire on our combat positions; the anti-tank rifle company; the guns, standing in their firing positions; and on the observation post. Advancing in the direction of Vasil'evka, the tanks set alight several buildings with their fire and left one tank of the 10th Tank Corps (our neighbor to the right, Vasil'evka) burning. Later these same tanks poured fire on the positions of the 1st Rifle Battalion of the 285th Rifle Regiment and began to crush the fighting men in their trenches beneath their tracks, especially in the 3rd and 5th Rifle Companies, as a result of which in the critical period of the attack to regain our former lines, our combat formations of the 3rd Rifle Company, as well as of the 4th and 5th Rifle Companies, were disrupted.
>
> The tanks were moving without any oversight, and failing to observe a combat formation and order. The command of the 285th Rifle Regiment tried to explain the situation to the tankers, but they continued to fire upon our combat positions. Regiment command sent people with the task to explain the combat situation to the tankers and to demand that they immediately cease their fire.
>
> The tank company commanders replied that they had been given the order to attack in the direction of Andreevka, Vasil'evka, with a supplementary order to attack toward Greznoe, and continued to fire upon and attack the elements of the 285th Rifle Regiment and the 11th [Guards Tank] Brigade, which were positioned in Vasil'evka.
>
> The attacking tanks were from the 99th Tank Brigade of the 2nd Tanks Corps. The corps commander is Major General Popov.
>
> As Captain Piniuk, chief of staff of the 99th Tank Brigade informed us, the commander of the 2nd Tank Corps, Major General Popov, personally gave the order for the brigade's attack: ' … the enemy is located in the region of Andreevka, Vasil'evka, Kozlovka, and Greznoe.' And they were acting in accordance with their assigned order.
>
> According to incomplete information, elements of the regiment have losses from the fire of their own tanks: 25 men killed, 37 wounded.

> The loss of personnel in the regiment's companies, primarily in the 3rd and 5th Rifle Companies, was primarily caused by the 99th Tank Brigade, the command of which did not seek clarification of the situation and did not notify me of the coming offensive. The command of the brigade went on the attack against positions of the 285th Rifle Regiment. As a result of which, they shot the fighting men, crushed them in their trenches under their tanks' tracks, and blew up their own tanks on our minefields.
>
> Reporting to you about this, I ask your permission to take severe measures against the individuals who permitted this criminal carelessness, who bear responsibility for the shooting and crushing of the fighting men of our companies, as well as the explosion of their own tanks on our minefields.[41]

At this time, the situation was becoming very serious in the sector of the 1st Tank Army, so at 1420, N. F. Vatutin signed the following order to the commanders of the 10th and 2nd Tank, and the 2nd and 5th Guards Tank Corps:

> 1. I categorically demand the most resolute and bold actions and the complete fulfillment of the assigned orders. Stop all dawdling and attack impetuously.
>
> The enemy's main grouping, up to 300 tanks, is moving against Katukov from the region of Gremuchii toward Verkhopen'e.
>
> Swiftly fall upon the rear of this grouping.

The 2nd Tank Corps attacks in the area of the hamlets Storozhevoe and Iasnaia Poliana. (RGAKFD)

A Soviet aerial reconnaissance photo of the battlefield in the area of Luchki and Teterevino. In the foreground is a knocked-out German Pz IV tank, July 1943. (RGAKFD)

2. Signal me by radio about the measures you have taken.[42]

Despite the poor organization of the belated introduction of the 2nd Tank Corps into the battle and the absence of air cover, the attack of almost 150 tanks immediately alarmed the commander of the II SS Panzer Corps. Hausser considered it a more serious threat than all the other tank attacks in the course of the entire day, and made a fundamental decision. That evening, the *kampfgruppen* of Wisch's and Krüger's divisions, which had been attacking the left wing of the 1st Tank Army in the 31st Tank Corps sector, trying to establish a connection between the flanks of the II SS Panzer Corps and the XXXXVIII Panzer Corps, fell back to positions southeast of Malye Maiachki – Greznoe, abandoning positions they had already taken earlier that day: the eastern part of Kochetovka (by the SS *Das Reich*'s reconnaissance battalion), Greznoe (by a *kampfgruppe* of *Das Reich*), and Veselyi, Ryl'skii, and Malye Maiachki (by *Leibstandarte*). The II SS Panzer Corps was now squeezed together into a tightly balled fist in the Iakovlevo – Luchki (south) – Luchki (north) – Ozerovskii – Teterevino region, having also yielded a 5-kilometer projection of territory to the northwest and north that had been taken by *Leibstandarte* that day.

The 31st Tank Corps' ability to hold its line was a success, which in large part had been facilitated by the attacks of the 5th Guards and 2nd Guards Tank Corps, but primarily by that of the 2nd Tank Corps. However, N. F. Vatutin's hope that the counterattacks would force Hoth to transfer part of his forces from the Oboian' axis to the Prokhorovka axis had not been realized. Although II SS Panzer Corps' U-turn in front of the 31st Tank Corps was extremely important, Chernienko's 31st Tank Corps had fought to the limit of its strength.

We can find interesting evidence in the memoirs of the former commander of the 6th Guards Army, I. M. Chistiakov:

On the night before 8 July, our intelligence had established that 500-600 tanks and self-propelled guns, and a large quantity of infantry, had been concentrated in the region of Iakovlevo, Pokrovka and Krasnaia Poliana.

I gave a report on the situation to *Front* Commander N. F. Vatutin, who in turn gave me an order:

'Assemble the units of the 71st Guards Rifle Division in the area of Berezovka and Noven'koe. Take the 6th Tank Corps and attack the enemy in the left flank in the general direction of Krasnaia Poliana, and I will support you with aviation.'

Then he immediately informed me:

'At the same time, the 5th and 2nd Tank Corps will strike the right flank of the enemy from the region of Teterevino and Belenikhino, in the general direction of Malye Maiachki and Greznoe.'

I wanted to leave immediately for the area where preparations for the attack were underway and carry out the *Front* commander's order, but the commander proposed to entrust this operation to my deputy, General P. F. Lagutin, and for me to remain where I was.

After several hours, P. F. Lagutin had managed with great difficulty to assemble the units for the counterattack, and at 10 o'clock on 8 July he began the artillery and aviation preparation. However, our attacks on the flanks of the Fourth Panzer Army did not bring the desired result, and we were stopped by a strong enemy grouping of tanks, artillery, and aviation before we could reach Krasnaia Poliana. In order to avoid needless losses, the *Front* commander ordered us to dig in on the lines we had obtained. He asked me reproachfully:

'Why did your highly-praised Lagutin fail to carry out the assignment?'

'Comrade Commander, the enemy is strong.'

He himself understood this and concluded in a softer voice:

'Yes ... Don't attack, but keep a grip on the enemy, so he can't divert tank units away from your front ...'[43]

If we assess the day's fighting from a strictly conventional standpoint, then the counterattack didn't yield any real results – it failed to force the adversary to shift at least some of his force from the Oboian' axis to the Prokhorovka axis, as N. F. Vatutin had planned. The lines here had managed to hold out only thanks to the skillful actions of M. E. Katukov and the courage of his troops. Facing a real shortage of forces and means, he was still able to devise a balanced system of defense. However, when you acquaint yourself with German documents, the situation looks differently.

As is known, the counterattack is one defensive method, which can help the defenders not necessarily to rout the enemy (this is a very large task!), but to disrupt his plans – primarily by causing the enemy to disperse his shock grouping to various points along the front and at the same time, preventing him from concentrating his forces for a breakthrough on a narrow sector and not permitting his further advance.

Reasoning thusly, can one consider the counterattack unsuccessful, even considering the way it unfolded, if the Germans not only failed to achieve their assigned order (the encirclement and destruction of enemy forces on the adjacent flanks of the II SS Panzer Corps and the XXXXVIII Panzer Corps), but even abandoned the ground it had won with great difficulty, falling back to its starting positions under the threat of a penetration by a Soviet tank corps into its rear area? This is exactly what the II SS Panzer Corps had been compelled to do. Late on the evening of 8 July, its command withdrew the *kampfgruppen* of the SS Panzergrenadier Divisions *Leibstandarte* and *Das Reich* from the region of Veselyi, Ryl'skii, Malye Maiachki and Greznoe to their previous jumping-off line.

Moreover, the attack by the Soviet tank formations had even more substantial consequences. They forced not only Hausser, but also Hoth, to reexamine their short-term plans. At 1435 8 July the II SS Panzer Corps received its order-mission for 9 July from Fourth Panzer Army headquarters. It was formulated in the following fashion:

> The II SS Panzer Corps destroys the hostile tank forces between the stream along both sides of the Greznoe and the Solotinka sector. *Afterwards, the corps makes preparations and attacks south of the Psel sector with its right flank through Prokhorovka, in order to outflank [the enemy] and seize the elevated ground east of Oboian'* [Author's emphasis].
>
> The XXXXVIII Panzer Corps breaks through north of the Solotinka sector to the Psel at the Il'inskii – Shipy sector, keeping its northern flank covered, in order to prevent the retreat of the enemy positioned in front of II SS Panzer Corps to Oboian'. It is essential to prepare a crossing over the Psel.[44]

However, after reports of the Soviet counterattacks had reached Fourth Panzer Army headquarters, at 2120 8 July the II SS Panzer Corps received a new order:

> ... 3) The II SS Panzer Corps destroys the enemy in the region northeast of Beregovoe and seizes the eastern bank of the Solotinka on both sides of Kochetovka. For this, the corps will concentrate all available forces on 9.7 against the enemy attacking from the direction of Prokhorovka and will remain on defense on 9.7. *Then the corps will prepare on 10.7 to move out in the direction of Prokhorovka* [Author's emphasis]. The battalion of assault guns from the SS Division *Totenkopf* remains subordinated to the 167th Infantry Division.
>
> 4) The XXXXVIII attacks north along both sides of the Iakovlevo – Oboian' road, with its weight on its right flank, hurls back the hostile tank forces opposing it toward the Psel, and seizes the ridge of heights between Kochetovka and north of Novoselovka. Then the corps will hold itself ready to rout the 6th Guards [sic] Tank Corps, positioned behind the west bank of the Pena, by an outflanking maneuver. An advance beyond the Pena to the west is currently prohibited.[45]

It would seem that the formulations of the orders have remained the same, but an important point is missing from the second order. The situation had plainly changed; therefore the ambitious plans for seizing the "elevated ground east of Oboian'", to which the SS Corps was previously supposed to break through with its major forces, have been postponed. Its main task was now to concentrate all efforts on Prokhorovka, for it was precisely to this place, as indeed had been anticipated, where the Russians were moving their major mobile reserves.

However, Hoth's forces, which had been designated to participate in this long-planned clash at Prokhorovka, were currently in a difficult situation. Their losses in armor as they had churned their way through the skillfully constructed lines of Russian defenses had been so significant, that the Fourth Panzer Army was now compelled to set more modest goals – to launch an attack on Prokhorovka with an entire panzer corps. Under the influence of the Soviet tank corps' counterattacks that day, it was precisely on 8 July that Hoth decided it was time to pivot the entire II SS Panzer Corps in the direction of Prokhorovka Station.

On the evening of 8 July, reassuring intelligence began to arrive at Voronezh Front headquarters. In a combat dispatch from the headquarters of the 48th Rifle Corps at 1900 it was noted: " … From the second half of the day the enemy began entrenching in the region of Hill 258.2."[46] At the same time, the placing of wire obstacles in the region of Nechaevka and Luchki was observed.

These reports could be interpreted in two ways: as evidence that the enemy forces were spent and no longer able to attack, or as an indication of Hoth's constant regard and concern for Fourth Panzer Army's flanks, by fortifying them. Given the intended breakthrough to Kursk and the possible pocketing of our forces, it would be necessary to create a solid defense for the external ring of the encirclement. So the adversary was showing timely concern over this, while simultaneously protecting itself from the repeated, though not fully organized, strong counterattacks.

Nevertheless, N. F. Vatutin himself was rather critical in his assessment of the counterattack on 8 July. In the course of conversations with the corps commanders, he justifiably observed:

> Today, in view of a whole series of mistakes that were committed by the corps, my plan was not realized. However, even the modest advance of the corps has forced the enemy to tether part of his force on this axis. Only the failure to fulfill my plan permitted the enemy in the second half of the day to bring down his full weight once again on Katukov. As a result of this, the enemy succeeded in obtaining a small success and to advance to Kochetovka – Verkhopen'e. On the other side, in the Shumilov sector, despite enormous losses, the enemy [Army Detachment Kempf] managed to seize Melikhovo. On this axis the enemy is striving to attack northwards from Melikhovo. This will create an extremely unfavorable situation for us.[47]

With the appearance of the SS units directly on the Prokhorovka axis, another possibility opened up for the Army Group South commander – an attack at the junction between the 6th Guards and 69th Armies (a favorite and well-tested tactic of the Germans), not only to emerge at Oboian', but also to launch an attack from the Prokhorovka direction to link-up with Army Detachment Kempf. This group from the first day of Operation Citadel had been trying from the vicinity of Belgorod to drive through the defenses at the boundary between Lieutenant General V. D. Kriuchenkin's 69th Army and Major General M. S. Shumilov's 7th Guards Army in the direction of Melikhovo. Thus, Field Marshal von Manstein was striving to close the iron jaws of the II SS Panzer Corps and Army Detachment Kempf around 69th Army's 48th Rifle Corps. However, the opportunity to realize this scheme would appear only a bit later, beginning on 11 July, but until then, Army Group South was forced literally to gnaw its way through the defense of the 6th and 7th Guards Armies.

A gun crew manning a 152mm howitzer fires on the attacking enemy. (RGAKFD)

In the 7th Guards Army's sector, from the morning of 8 July savage fighting had involved its 92nd Guards and 94th Guards Rifle Divisions. Having concentrated more than 100 tanks on a sector of the front just 3 to 4 kilometers wide, Army Detachment Kempf attacked in the direction of Blizhniaia Igumenka and Sevriukovo with the aim of seizing Melikhovo. After several attacks, by 1900 the enemy had only partially succeeded in his design; the further advance of Kempf's forces on this sector was brought to a halt. The Soviet artillerymen and combat engineers knew their business. As early as 7 July in the diary of one of the OKW's representatives, there appears the note: " … our losses in tanks because of mines are significant, first of all in Army Detachment 'Kempf'."[48]

After four days of heavy fighting, results for the Voronezh Front were mixed. On the one hand, the stubborn defense of the Soviet forces had seriously jeopardized the plan's timetable for Operation Citadel. According to the plan, the Germans were to have reached Kursk on the fourth day of the offensive. By 6 July, the enemy had only managed to seize the second line of defenses in the region of Iakovlevo. On the other hand, since that date, the Fourth Panzer Army had continued to develop the offensive toward Oboian' – along the highway and in the direction of the bend in Psel River. If one considers that Voronezh Front's main hope rested upon the first three lines of defense (because of their particular strength), then indeed this German advance may be considered rather rapid and worrisome. What allowed Army Group South to operate so successfully?

The Germans selected armor to be their main instrument in the conducting of Operation Citadel. From the first days of the offensive, the command of Army Group South had managed to create a more than six-fold superiority in armored forces in the 6th Guards Army's tactical zone of defense. The attacks of the tank formations were closely supported by the operations of the *Luftwaffe*. All this allowed the enemy to launch a very powerful initial assault. Neither before nor after Kursk did the *Wehrmacht* ever employ such a massive force of armor, especially on such a narrow sector of front.

However, our defenses proved to be sufficiently strong as well. The Fourth Panzer Army's armored battering ram had only enough strength to break through the first two army-level defensive belts and reach the third, but difficulties arose for it beyond that. No matter how complete the belts of defensive fortifications were, though, the soldiers of the Red Army were the foundation of the defense. That the *Wehrmacht* command on the fourth day of fighting began to recognize the hopelessness of the further implementation of Operation Citadel can be explained by the stubborn resistance and courageous actions of the Red Army's soldiers and officers.

The day of 9 July became decisive for the further development of combat operations in the region of the southern shoulder of the Kursk bulge. A basic task still stood before Army Group South on the axis of its main attack: to rout the Soviet mobile formations on the boundary between the XXXXVIII Panzer Corps and the II SS Panzer Corps and to establish contact between their flanks, thus creating a solid breakthrough front. At the same time it was important to shove the Russians away from the Prokhorovka axis as far as possible to the north. Failing to accomplish these goals, it would be difficult either to count upon a further advance to the northeast or to execute the plan of taking Prokhorovka and destroying the mobile Red Army formations approaching it.

Hoth's first attempt to resolve the problem of linking the corps' flanks had come to nothing on 8 July. The Russians had brought up additional and significant mobile reserves on Hausser's deep right flank, and using them to launch strong attacks they had not permitted Hausser to obtain notable success on any one of the sectors of his front. Moreover, the adversary had suffered significant damage (the II SS Panzer Corps alone reported the loss of 121 tanks), and the Russians had been able to prevent either a breakthrough in their defenses, or the destruction of their forces. The territory gained by two of the II SS Panzer Corps' divisions had to be abandoned by the end of the day. Only Knobelsdorff's XXXXVIII Panzer Corps had managed to advance, albeit slowly. However, he alone was incapable of fundamentally altering the situation.

Thus, the shock wedge of the Fourth Panzer Army, although it had deeply penetrated the defensive system of Voronezh Front, was now in essence marking time in a fiery cul-de-sac, and its prospects, especially when you consider the failure of the Ninth Army's offensive in the north, were plainly not comforting. In documents from the headquarters of Hoth's Fourth Panzer Army for 9 July it is noted that, considering the great activity of the Russian tank formations and the systematic strengthening of their lines, it was necessary to ponder the real possibility that the Soviet side was trying to encircle its attacking spearheads. The Fourth Panzer Army's relatively slender projection into the Soviet lines was quite vulnerable to such an attempt.

With the aim of preparing for the looming fight for Prokhorovka, Hausser took a number of important steps on 9 July. At about 0200 on 9 July, the panzer regiment from the SS Panzergrenadier Division *Leibstandarte Adolf Hitler* finally established contact with elements of the SS Panzergrenadier Division *Das Reich*, thereby liquidating the dangerous gap between *Das Reich*'s left flank north of Teterevino and *Leibstandarte*'s right flank north of Luchki (south). From the moment they had reached the Prokhorovka axis, Wisch and Krüger had been compelled to keep significant forces on these flanks, in order to keep the situation under control.

At the same time, the commander of the II SS Panzer Corps undertook a regrouping of the forces within the corps and consolidated its combat formations, trying to gather them into a solid fist southwest of Prokhorovka and to reduce the divisions' attack sectors in half. *Das Reich*, having turned over its sector up to Luchki (south) inclusively to the 167th Infantry Division, concentrated on the line Teterevino – Kalinin – Iasnaia Poliana. Meanwhile, *Totenkopf* was sent from the right of the II SS Panzer Corps in the Sazhnoe – Gostishchevo region to the left in the sector Teterevino – Luchki (north). It was now to operate on the main axis of the corps' attack, moving in the direction of the bend in the Psel River. For this purpose on the morning of 9 July, two of its *kampfgruppen* launched an attack: the first, in the direction of Malye Maiachki – Veselyi – Kochetovka, with the aim of shoving elements of the 31st Tank Corps as far as possible to the west; the second, in the Krasnyi Oktiabr' – Il'inskii and Kozlovka – Vasil'evka direction, trying to drive Soviet forces out of the villages on the south bank of the Psel, and thereby create the conditions for a river crossing.

By 1225, a *Totenkopf kampfgruppe* under the command of O. Baum had seized the hamlet of Veselyi (north of Malye Maiachki) and had advanced toward Hill 224.5 (1.5 kilometers south of Kochetovka), where the fighting intensified. At 1300, *Kampfgruppe* Becker struck out from Ozerovskii toward the north, in the direction of Krasnyi Oktiabr', with the aim of seizing a bridgehead on the right (northern) bank of the Psel River. Toward the end of the day, the 10th Tank Corps' 11th Motorized Rifle Brigade had to abandon Krasnyi Oktiabr' under heavy pressure from *Kampfgruppe* Becker and fell back to Kozlovka. The SS men tried to break through to the north, but they were stopped 2.5 – 3 kilometers from Il'inskii. They then switched their attack toward the village of Kozlovka and captured it at 1845, but their further advance toward Vasil'evka was halted.

As a result, by the end of 9 July, a 5- to 6-kilometer stretch of the left (southern) bank of the Psel River was now in enemy hands. This was enough to attempt a river crossing and to consolidate a grip on the right bank. The commander of the 680th Pioneer Regiment was instructed to bring up the bridging column to Luchki and to be prepared to construct a bridge over the Psel River, so that the main forces of *Totenkopf* could make a crossing after the establishment of a bridgehead. Only one little task remained – to force a crossing and create the bridgehead on the opposite bank, but from the march, this didn't happen. Artillerymen and infantrymen of Lieutenant Colonel Pantiukhov's 52nd Guards Rifle Division, which were dug in on the northern bank, began to put up strong resistance even as the SS troops approached the river. Hausser was forced to reinforce *Oberführer* Priess's division. A battalion of 150mm six-barreled rocket launchers and a battalion of assault guns were returned to *Totenkopf*. It was decided to form an assault party and send it across the river that night.

Meanwhile, von Knobelsdorff's XXXXVIII Panzer Corps continued to hammer at the lines of the 1st Tank Army along and north of the Pena River, striving to secure the II SS Panzer Corps' left flank and to turn the 6th Tank Corps' position along the Pena. The 11th Panzer Division, attacking up the Oboian' road, finally managed to penetrate the lines of the 3rd Mechanized Corps and seized Hill 260.8, and also managed to link-up with *Leibstandarte* north of Sukho-Solotino. However, late in the day its advance was halted just south of Novoselovka by the 309th Rifle Division and the fire of numerous supporting anti-tank and artillery units. *Grossdeutschland*, with active Stuka support, finally cleared Verkhopen'e, though it continued to be plagued by flanking fire from across the Pena River to the west due to 3rd Panzer Division's lagging advance. Critically, with its focus still fixed on the 6th and 10th Tank Corps and concerned about its own left flank, *Grossdeutschland* would be unable to assist the II SS Panzer Corps in its push across the Psel River and toward Prokhorovka as Hoth had hoped.

Thus, on 9 July both of Hoth's panzer corps operated very energetically, which permitted them to obtain relatively greater results than previously. To a significant extent, their divisions fulfilled the tactical assignments that were given to them for the day. The XXXXVIII Panzer Corps managed to seize almost complete control over three key points in the defenses of 1st Tank Army and 6th Guards Army on the second line of defense – the major villages of Verkhopen'e, Sukho-Solotino, and Greznoe, which were located in swampy river basins that presented very difficult terrain for armor operations. The II SS Panzer Corps created the conditions for a strike toward Prokhorovka: in heavy fighting, the stubborn 31st Tank Corps was driven back to the north beyond the Solotinka River, and *Totenkopf*'s 6th SS Panzergrenadier Regiment seized the left (southern) bank of the

Armor of the German XXXXVIII Panzer Corps in the vicinity of the main road to Oboian'. (RGAKFD)

Psel River in the sector of Krasnyi Oktiabr' and (partially) Vasil'evka. At the same time, however, the SS Panzergrenadier Division *Totenkopf* proved unable to complete one very important task – the forcing of the Psel River and the creation of a bridgehead on its northern bank of sufficient size to develop the attack in the east and northeast directions.

The forces of the XXXXVIII Panzer Corps made noticeable gains to the north on 9 July, and although it had not fully broken through the second line of defenses by the end of the day, it had overcome its most strongly fortified section. Only a few kilometers remained to reach the third (and final) army-level line of defenses.

Despite Fourth Panzer Army's accomplishments, the Voronezh Front on this day still managed to retain a tenuous hold on the situation and prevented any clean breakthrough. Despite the fact that Hoth's and Kempf's corps fought stubbornly to carry out the tactical assignments of their own command, the entire enormous machine of Army Group South, which had been counted upon for a rapid lunge to Kursk, was as before still essentially grinding away in place, still enmeshed in the *Front*'s second army-level belt of defenses. It still remained for Field Marshal von Manstein to search out the weakest point in Vatutin's skillfully prepared defense, create the prospects to penetrate it in the nearest days, and break into operational space.

However, it is difficult to call these prospects anything other than utopian, since by the end of 9 July, only 132 tanks remained in the panzer regiments of XXXXVIII Panzer Corps' divisions. What von Manstein could count upon to give fresh impetus to the offensive isn't clear. Only General Nehring's reserve XXIV Panzer Corps remained available. On 9 July, Hitler finally yielded to von Manstein's repeated requests and agreed to commit this formation into the battle, but the hopes for it were too optimistic. According to information, marked on one of Army Group South headquarters' operational maps that I found among the captured German documents in the collection of the U.S. National Archives, on 9 July 1943 this corps only counted 147 tanks; that is, just a little bit more than a full-strength panzer division. Army Group South faced a most critical and very complex task – the struggle with Soviet forces on the flanks of Fourth Panzer Army and Army Detachment Kempf, which would require very substantial forces. In this situation, the XXIV Panzer Corps might be able to inflict significant damage to the Soviet side, but it was not a force upon which the Germans could seriously rely for a breakthrough to Kursk, especially after the Voronezh Front had already ground down formations that were significantly stronger than the XXIV Panzer Corps.

6

The Advance of the *Stavka*'s Reserves to Prokhorovka

The question about reinforcing the Voronezh Front arose as early as the second day of the German offensive. On 6 July, N. F. Vatutin had ordered all his *Front*'s reserves to advance to the second line of defense. On 7 July, forces from the sectors of the 38th and 40th Armies, which were not involved in repulsing the main attack of Army Group South, were shifted to the 6th Guards Army and 1st Tank Army. Thus, by the third day of the defensive operation, the Voronezh Front had practically exhausted its possibilities to reinforce its forces on threatened directions.

On 6 July the commander of Voronezh Front, reporting on the developing situation, requested the *Stavka* to transfer four tank corps and two air corps to him. His report, which was transmitted by telegraph, received a supplementary comment from A. M. Vasilevsky, Chief of the General Staff:

> On my part, I consider it advisable for further active operations to reinforce [Vatutin's] *Front* with two tank corps, sending one of them to the region of Prokhorovka (30 kilometers [18 miles] southeast of Oboian') and the other – to the region of Korocha; for this purpose, it is possible to use the 10th Tank Corps from Zhadov and the 2nd Tank Corps from Malinovsky near Valuika. In addition, I would consider it expedient for Rotmistrov to advance to the Oskol River, to the area south of Staryi Oskol.[1]

Stalin agreed with Vasilevsky's proposal. By 1900 on 7 July 1943, the 10th Tank Corps under the command of Major General V. G. Burkov had concentrated near Prokhorovka. Major General A. F. Popov's 2nd Tank Corps was on the move from the Southwestern Front. At 0040 7 July, the Chief of the General Staff gave instructions for the Southwestern Front's entire air fleet (the 17th Air Army) to be diverted to fly combat missions on Voronezh Front's sector.

On 8 July at 1540, N. F. Vatutin and N. S. Khrushchev reported:

> The two newly arrived tank corps (the 10th and the 2nd), which have been strengthened with two anti-tank artillery battalions of 85mm guns and two motorized rifle regiments from *Front* reserve, have been deployed on the Prokhorovka axis.
>
> The enemy is persistently trying to break through our front on the Oboian' axis, despite enormous losses.
>
> It is not excluded that he will continue to reinforce his efforts on the Oboian' axis with forces drawn from other sectors of the front, chiefly from the sectors in front of Southwestern Front and Southern Front.

Marshal of the Soviet Union A. M. Vasilevsky. His report spared the commander of the 5th Guards Tank Army from execution after the heavy losses at Prokhorovka. (RGAKFD)

> In order to strengthen the screening of the Oboian'-Kursk axis, and more importantly, to ensure the timely shift of our forces to the counteroffensive at the most suitable moment, we consider it necessary at this time to begin the rapid advance:
>
> A) of Zhadov's [5th Guards] army – to the region of Oboian', Prokhorovka and Mar'ino;
>
> B) of Rotmistrov's [5th Guards Tank] army – to the region of Priznachnoe (10 kilometers east of Prokhorovka), Korocha and Skorodnoe.
>
> In addition, we request the reinforcement of Voronezh Front's aviation with two fighter and one ground attack air corps.[2]

The *Stavka*, having determined that the strongest enemy grouping was attacking from the south, took measures to reinforce the threatened axis. Orders went out to activate A. S. Zhadov's 5th Guards Army with the task of occupying the rear belt of defenses in the sector Oboian' – Prokhorovka. The 2nd Tank Corps was temporarily attached to Voronezh Front. Finally, the 5th Guards Tank Army was directed to move out onto the same axis with the order to concentrate behind Voronezh Front – southwest of Staryi Oskol – in readiness to operate in the direction of Kursk or Oboian'.

P. A. Rotmistrov wrote about the advance of his tank army:

> … On 5 July 1943 the chief of staff of Steppe Front, Lieutenant General M. V. Zakharov, informed me by telephone that savage fighting had erupted on the Central and Voronezh Fronts.
>
> He ordered, 'General B. S. Bakharov's 18th Tank Corps is being added to your

army. Get in touch with him. Bring all your army's forces to full combat readiness and wait for instructions.'

… On the next day (6 July), Colonel General I. S. Konev, commander of Steppe Front, flew to my headquarters to meet with me. He then informed me in more detail about the combat situation:

'The enemy's strongest blow is along the Kursk axis from the region of Belgorod. In connection with this,' said Ivan Stepanovich, 'the *Stavka* has made the decision to transfer the 5th Guards Tank Army and the 5th Guards Army to Voronezh Front. You are to concentrate right here in a very short period of time.' The commander marked a region southwest of Staryi Oskol with a red pencil.

About an hour after I.S. Konev flew off, Stalin called.

'Have you received the directive to shift your army to Voronezh Front?' he asked.

'No, Comrade Ivanov [Stalin's code name], but I was informed of this by Comrade Stepiny [another code name, but unclear whether it refers to Konev or Zakharov].'

'How do you think you'll implement your move?'

'Under our own power.'

'But Comrade Fedorenko is saying that when tanks move a great distance, they break down, so he is proposing instead to move them by rail.'

'That can't be done, Comrade Ivanov. The enemy's air force can destroy the trains or railroad bridges by bombing, and then we won't be able to gather the army quickly. Moreover, infantry moving alone aboard trucks to the assembly area will quickly wind up in a difficult situation if they encounter enemy tanks.'

'Do you plan to march only by night?'

'No. Night lasts only for seven hours, and if I move only during the hours of darkness, during the day I'll have to direct the tank column into forests, then in the evening bring them back out of the woods, which, incidentally, are scarce along the route.'

'What are you proposing?'

'I request your permission to move the army by day and night …'

'But you just said they'll be bombing you in daylight.' Stalin interrupted me.

'Yes, it is possible. Therefore I ask you to give a directive to the air force to give the army reliable air cover.'

'Fine,' the Supreme [Commander] agreed. 'Your request for covering your army's march from the air will be carried out. Inform the commanders of the Steppe and Voronezh Fronts about the start of your march.'

He wished me success and hung up the phone.

We immediately outlined the army's route of movement. For the march, we determined a total column width of 30 to 35 kilometers, with the corps moving along three routes. The two tank corps [the 29th and 18th Tank Corps] would be moving in the first echelon, while the 5th Guards 'Zimovniki' Mechanized Corps, other combat units, and the tail of the army would be moving in the second echelon.

The 6th of July – my birthday. Naturally, I wanted to observe it among the circle of my combat friends. Previously, invitations to a comradely dinner had gone

Major General (at the time of the Kursk battle Colonel) S. A. Solovoi, assistant commander of the 5th Guards Tank Army for maintenance and supply (1944 photo). (TsAMO)

> out to the different corps commands, to the field officers and field generals that controlled the army. With the change in the situation, I decided not to cancel the invitations, but to use the gathering of commanders as an opportunity to issue the preliminary instructions for the march.
>
> How surprised the gathering was, when instead of a festively decorated table they saw me standing behind an operational map! I informed them of the upcoming army move and issued orders. Nevertheless, after discussing all the questions connected with the march, I was given a captured bottle of champagne, and my combat friends congratulated me on my birthday and expressed their best wishes. Afterwards, the commanders returned to their headquarters to carry out the instructions they had received.[3]

The army command was no less concerned with the technical capabilities of its combat equipment and the preparation of its personnel than it was with the air cover. After all, this was the first experience with moving more than 800 armored vehicles under their own power for several hundred kilometers by forced march. What percentage of the armor would eventually reach the destination, and what condition would they be in when they arrived? P. A. Rotmistrov's corps commanders asked themselves these two questions every day, for it was their efforts and their painstaking labor that largely determined the army's combat capability.

A great responsibility lay on the on the army commander's assistant for maintenance and supply Colonel S. A. Solovoi, and the service under his command in the corps and brigades. They were responsible for the formation's logistics support. The precisely calculated work of bringing up the formation's rear units and carefully organized service of the repair units played the leading role in this.

Medical officers of the 5th Guards Tank Army pose for a photograph before moving out toward Prokhorovka, July 1943. (Author's personal archive)

The march was a serious test as well for the army's engineering units, which were headed by Colonel B. D. Isupov. Reconnoitering the movement routes, repairing and reinforcing bridges, checking the roads for the presence of mines – his units carried out all this work in the shortest period of time. As further events demonstrated, both the logistics services and engineering services were not able to solve their assigned tasks fully and with the necessary quality. However, there were also no major problems, which might have caused a lot of trouble during the movement.

The account of the 5th Guards Tank Army's command states, "On 6 July at 2330, Army Headquarters received a written order from Steppe Front command for the army's units to assemble on the western bank of the Oskol River in the region Saltykov – Melovoe – Konysheno – Orlik – Korostovo – Verkhne-Atamanskoe by a forced march, in readiness for further operations in the direction of Kursk and Oboian'."[4]

The march would occur in two stages. At the end of the first stage, all three corps should close on the Oskol River, force a crossing of it, and assemble, while waiting for their rear services and remaining equipment to move up to the designated areas. By its scale, by the technical possibilities of an army of that time, and most importantly, by its results, this was a movement unparalleled by any other in the war to that point.

The march to Prokhorovka was difficult. The army was supposed to arrive at a specific time and be combat-ready, but neither the army command nor the leadership of the Armored and Mechanized forces of the Red Army had any experience in moving such a major tank formation under its own power for a distance of 230 to 280 kilometers. Many problems arose, but only two major ones. The first was covering the moving column from enemy air attack. In order to reach the designated area in time, it was necessary to keep the column moving day and night, with short intervals for refueling. It was practically impossible to conceal this movement from prowling enemy aerial reconnaissance: the column of the 29th Tank Corps alone stretched for nearly 15 kilometers. With the aim of covering the column from the air, our pilots actively tried to keep the enemy's air force tied up over the battlefield, and significant efforts were also made to provide direct air cover for the columns.

The tanks' technical capabilities presented the second major problem. Armored vehicles had not been expected to move over such large distances under their own power, especially in such a short amount of time. What percentage of the tanks and self-propelled guns would break down, and how quickly could they be repaired? These questions troubled all the officers and generals concerned with this move. Rotmistrov had an even more complex problem looming in the near future – to lead his newly formed army into battle for the first time in his role as its commander. Success would depend directly upon the condition of his corps upon arrival at their destination.

Colonel General Ia. N. Fedorenko, the commander of the Red Army's Armored and Motorized Forces, sent a group of specialists to the 5th Guards Tank Army under the leadership of N. I. Gruzdev. The group was supposed to analyze the causes of combat vehicular breakdowns (whether they were due to improper handling by the tankers themselves or to a manufacturing defect).

The primary burden on the road fell upon the driver-mechanics of the combat vehicles. The working conditions for the entire crew inside a tank were always difficult. The space in the vehicle was tightly cramped, and the constant rumble of the running engine made it impossible to catch the words spoken by a fellow crewmate sitting just

Motorcyclists of a reconnaissance battalion of one of the tank corps of the 5th Guards Tank Army on the march to Prokhorovka Station. (RGAKFD)

Table 9: Data on the Strength and Equipment of the Divisions of the 5th Guards Army as of 10 July 1943[1]

	6 Gds Airborne	9 Gds Airborne	13 Gds Rifle	42 Gds Rifle	66 Gds Rifle	95 Gds Rifle	97 Gds Rifle	29 AA Artillery
Command staff	866	856	926	889	863	862	885	224
Junior command staff	2561	2586	2545	2167	2348	2433	1911	483
Rank and file	5467	5576	5096	4990	5626	5476	6041	1123
Divisional total:	8894	9018	8567	8046	8837	8771	8837	1832
Total for Army (in divisions):	**62802**							

Rifles	5410	4985	4197	4622	4350	4720	4884	1273
PPSh-41 SMG	2433	2652	2588	2676	2506	2644	2581	414
Light machine guns	570	489	499	473	501	489	473	-
Heavy Machine guns	166	166	161	157	133	165	163	-
Anti-tank Rifles	256	258	236	216	219	218	263	2
Guns of all calibers	94	76	92	94	96	96	96	-
Mortars of all calibers	157	170	163	137	163	170	140	-
Anti-aircraft machine guns	-	-	-	-	-	-	-	48
Anti-aircraft guns	-	-	-	-	-	-	-	64
Trucks and cars	121	125	131	74	89	188	84	112
Tractors	-	-	1	2	7	7	18	-
Towers	50	44	44	51	48	28	37	67
Horses:								
Riding	72	81	200	74	62	78	95	-
Artillery	176	168	133	150	115	271	121	-
Supply	554	554	614	618	651	574	557	-
Total horses:	802	803	947	842	828	923	773	-

Note: According to Glantz and House, the 5th Guards Army numbered 80,000 officers and men, including the separate regiments and battalions not listed in the above table.

Source: TsAMO RF, f. 5 gv. A, op. 4852, d. 38, l. 53.

a half-meter away. To all these "delights", the driver-mechanic had to add the physical burden of driving the tank. The hydraulic system for controlling the movement of the tank did not fully obviate these physical labors – after all, the combat mass of the T-34 and T-70 tanks reached up to 30 tons.

A veteran tanker once told me:

> If in battle one must keep watch in every direction, so a shell doesn't strike the tank, then on the march it is even worse: You must keep your speed and space interval in the column constant, and constantly watch the road. There is a tank in front of you and a tank behind you; the dust is dense, and you must keep constant, strained watch, so that because of the poor visibility you don't run into the vehicle in front of you or the tanks behind you don't run into you. After a full day of tugging on the levers, you can't lift your arms, you can't straighten your back, and there's nothing but a continuous roar in your head.[5]

At 0130 on 7 July, the army moved out. The forward detachment under the command of Major General K. G. Trufanov took to the roads first, followed by the first echelon – the 29th and 18th Tank Corps. Each corps was assigned two routes. The 5th Guards Mechanized Corps was in the second echelon. The commander of Steppe Front, General Konev, observed the movement of the Guards tanks from the air, aboard a U-2 plane. Ivan Stepanovich was personally against the commitment of the *Front* in this way. He considered it more advisable to hold it in reserve; otherwise there would be nothing left for the counteroffensive that was to follow immediately upon the completion of the defensive operation. However, the *Stavka* had decided that it was first necessary to stop the enemy, and only then think about the decisive crushing blow.

According to the order, the 29th Tank Corps was supposed to reach its assembly area at 1400, but it was late. Its units were moving behind the forward detachment, which even at the start of the march in the region of Lesnoe Ukolovo (8 kilometers from Ostrogozhsk) had delayed its movement by almost three hours. At the same time, there were no bridges across the Oskol River that could support 50 to 60 tons of weight. Therefore, General I. F. Kirichenko's brigades didn't reach their assembly areas until 2030 on 7 July.

The formations and units of the army spent 8 July checking their combat equipment and transportation, bringing up lagging vehicles, and doing ongoing repairs and refueling. The men rested from the exhausting march. However, the arrival in the region south of Staryi Oskol was only the first stage of the formations' movement. In connection with the enemy shock grouping's breakthrough on 9 July to the third and final defensive belt of the 6th Guards Army, Rotmistrov's tank army was ordered to move out directly on the Prokhorovka axis. At 2340 [8 July], the order was received, which directed the formations of the 5th Guards Tank Army to reach the region Bobryshevo – Bol'shaia Psinka – Prelestnoe –Aleksandrovka (Prokhorovka Station) – Bol'shie Seti, approximately 100 kilometers from where it had spent the day resting, by the end of 9 July.

As a whole, the almost 350-400 kilometer movement of the tank army over the course of 6 to 9 July proceeded in an organized fashion. The enemy air force had almost no influence over the march.

By the quantity of tanks, Kirichenko's 29th Tank Corps was the largest, and moreover its preparation of the technical services and handling of the march was better organized than the others. After the first 150-kilometer leap, out of the formation's more than 220 combat vehicles, only 12 tanks and one Su-76 self-propelled gun broke down. According to the 29th Tank Corps headquarters' Operational Summary No. 88, at 1200 of 10 July, its units had operational: 123 T-34 tanks, 8 Su-76 self-propelled guns, 81 T-70 tanks, and 12 122mm howitzers. For its successful fulfillment of a difficult assignment with a minimal number of accidents, 5th Guards Tank Army command expressed its gratitude to Major General I. F. Kirichenko and the entire personnel staff of the 29th Tank Corps.

In the other formations, the percentage of disabled vehicles was significantly higher, especially in the 5th Guards Mechanized Corps. Thus, by 1600 of 10 July, only 62 T-34 and T-70 tanks in total remained in the 11th and 12th Guards Mechanized Brigades and the 24th Guards Tank Brigade.

Altogether on the road from Ostrogozhsk to Prokhorovka Station, in the three corps, two self-propelled artillery regiments, the 53rd Guards Tank Regiment, and the 1st Guards Separate Motorcycle Regiment, from a combined total of 721 armored vehicles, 198 tanks and self-propelled guns lagged behind, or 27.5% of the total number. In addition, by the evening of 11 July, another 24 tanks had caught up, but they were sent immediately for repairs. Thus, altogether in the course of the transfer of the 5th Guards Tank Army, 227 tanks and self-propelled guns broke down and went out of service, or nearly a third (31.5%) of the army. However, thanks to the intense work of the repair services, at the moment when the army went into battle, about 50% of the disabled vehicles had been returned to service. According to information from army headquarters, at 1700 11 July, a total number of 101 of these vehicles were on their way back to the army.

The army's artillery units conducted the march as part of the corps' mobile columns. By the end of the day on 9 July, they had assembled in their designated area and were occupying firing positions on the line of Rzhavets, 4 kilometers west of Mar'ino. The three-day march of 250 kilometers had also had an effect on the condition of the motor transport. The lagging vehicles and their towed artillery pieces arrived over the course of the next half-day. Vehicles lagged behind also because of the insufficient training of the drivers.

By noon on 9 July, the 29th Tank Corps had concentrated in the region Bol'shie Seti – Pristennoe – Svino-Pogorelovka – Glafirovka (approximately 20-25 kilometers north of Prokhorovka), and had begun preparing a line of defenses. The 18th Tank Corps received an order to advance to Prokhorovka and from the march take up a defense in the second echelon of our forces on that axis – on the line Veselyi – Polezhaev – Oktiabr'skii State Farm – Storozhevoe. On 11 July, the 2nd Guards 'Tatsinskaia' Tank Corps and the 2nd Tank Corp were transferred to 5th Guards Tank Army command.

The 5th Guards Army was also transferred out of the Steppe Front and subordinated to Voronezh Front. The 5th Guards Army commander, General Zhadov, talked about his army's advance into the Voronezh Front's defensive belt:

> On 8 July, Colonel General I. S. Konev arrived at the army's command post by plane, and informed me that by *Stavka* order, the 5th Guards Army was being

placed under Voronezh Front command, and immediately gave me an additional order: by the morning of 11 July to appear on the line of the Psel River, take up a defense there, and prevent the further advance of the enemy to the north and northeast. Konev alerted me that by the end of 9 July, Lieutenant General of Tank Forces Rotmistrov's 5th Guards Tank Army would be assembling east of Prokhorovka.

We quickly and in an organized fashion carried out the advance of the army to the indicated line; previously conducted reconnoitering assisted us in this. In agreement with my decision, the army's headquarters staff, headed by Major General N. I. Liamin, planned the march in just a few hours: they marked out the sectors and movement routes for the corps, the boundary lines, and the areas of halt. Four routes were marked for each corps, with two routes for each division in the leading echelon. Army headquarters and the units subordinate to it were given a separate route. At this time, I assigned march orders to the commanders of the corps, units and formations subordinate to the army. Having completed the organization of the march, I together with member of the Military Council Major General A. M. Krivulin; the commanders of the artillery and the armored forces; the Army's chief engineer; a group of officers from the headquarters' operational and intelligence departments; and signals detachments drove ahead, to the area of the Army's new command post – a forest 1.5 km southwest of Iarigino. My first deputy, Major General M. I. Kozlov, took control over the execution of the march together with my chief of staff, who both monitored the march from the headquarters' column on the Army's central route.[6]

The army completed the march at full strength without any sort of interference from the *Luftwaffe*. Information about the combat and personnel strength of the formations of the 5th Guards Army as of 10 July 1943 is shown in Table 9.

Zhadov continues:

On the morning of 11 July, the divisions of the 32nd Guards Rifle Corps began moving into defensive positions along the northern bank of the Psel River in the Oboian' – Ol'khovatka sector. In front of us, units of 1st Tank Army's 31st and 10th Tank Corps together with elements of 6th Guards Army's 51st Guards Rifle Division were repulsing the attacks of small groups of enemy tanks.

The formations of the 33rd Guards Rifle Corps were taking up a defense on the line Semenovka – Veselyi. In their front, the 6th Guards Army's 52nd Guards Rifle Division was involved in heavy fighting with enemy tanks. There was no continuous front line.[7]

Unfortunately, while making the march, the army's formations did not put out a strong advance guard of forward detachments. This complicated their process of taking up a defensive line.

In addition, the *Stavka*, in order to exclude the possibility of any type of surprise, advanced two more combined-arms armies to the Belgorod – Kursk axis: the 27th Army, to the region of Kursk, to take up the defense in the Kursk fortified district; and the 53rd Army – to the first *Front*-level line on the Seim River, with an order with its three divisions to take up the defense on the Bunino – Solntsevo – Nechaevo sector, in order to create a strong barrier on the Prokhorovka – Kursk axis. By the morning of 12 July, the army had occupied the indicated line.

7

Combat Operations on 10 and 11 July – The Beginning of the Prokhorovka Engagement

The heavy, but unsuccessful fighting on the Oboian' axis and the intelligence reports about the concentration of major Soviet mobile formations near Prokhorovka prompted Field Marshal von Manstein to initiate Hoth's alternative to the original plan for the operation: The Fourth Panzer Army, without halting XXXXVIII Panzer Corps' attacks against the 1st Tank Army and the 6th Guards Army would pivot the II SS Panzer Corps for a strike directly at Prokhorovka, with the aim of destroying the next, even larger wave of Soviet reserves. Once that was accomplished, the II SS Panzer Corps would then be in position either to drive north toward Oboian', or to strike to the south, into the rear of the 69th Army. On the evening of 9 July, Colonel General H. Hoth, commander of the Fourth Panzer Army, signed Order No. 5, which spelled out the tasks for the army on 10 July:

> 1) The enemy 9.07.43 undertook no attacks against the eastern flank of the Panzer Army. In front of II SS Panzer Corps and XXXXVIII Panzer Corps, he conducted a fighting withdrawal to the north. He is trying to hold the western bank of the Pena R. The retreat on the Rakovo sector in a northerly heading was halted on the afternoon of 9.07. The enemy ceased his attacks on LII Army Corps' western flank. The village of Voskhod has been taken once again. Fresh hostile motorized units are advancing from the direction of Novyi and Staryi Oskol in a westerly direction.
> 2) Fourth Panzer Army is to expand its attacking wedge through an attack to the northeast and with the envelopment of the enemy forces in the bend of the Pena River, and will thereby create the conditions for a further attack to the northeast.
> 3) The 167th Infantry Division will take up the positions presently occupied by the *Totenkopf* Division.
> 4) The II SS Panzer Corps is to attack the enemy southwest of Prokhorovka and press him back to the east. It is to seize the heights on both sides of the Psel River northwest of Prokhorovka.
> 5) Keeping its flank covered from the direction of Oboian', the XXXXVIII Panzer Corps will destroy the 6th Guards [sic] Tank Corps on the western bank of the Pena River. For this it will continue its maneuver with the aim of outflanking the enemy from the direction of Novoselovka in a southwesterly heading. It is necessary to push reconnaissance operations to the Psel River in the Il'inskii – Shipy sector. One-third of the 167th Infantry Division will remain subordinated to the Panzer Army in its current area. The arrival of needed reserves on the 167th Infantry Division's northern flank is expected on 11 July.

Type of Tank or Self-propelled gun	6th Panzer Division	7th Panzer Division	19th Panzer Division	503rd Heavy Panzer Battalion	228th Assault Gun Battalion	Total
Pz II	7	4	-	-	-	11
Pz III with 5cm L/42	-	-	2	-	-	2
Pz III with 5cm L/60	24	16	5	-	-	45
Pz III with 7.5cm	12	1	4	-	-	17
Pz IV with 7.5cm /L24	-	3	1	-	-	4
Pz IV with /L43 and 48	14	12	23	-	-	49
Pz VI	-	-	-	33	-	33
StuG assault gun	-	-	-	-	23	23
Command tanks	3	3	1	-	-	7
FlammPz flamethrower tanks	10	-	-	-	-	10
Total:	70	39	36	33	23	201

Source: N. Zetterling and A. Frankson, *Kursk 1943: A Statistical Analysis* (London: Frank Cass, 2000), Tables A 6.7, A 6.8, A 6.9, A 6.10.

Table 10: Amount and Types of Armor in the Divisions of the III Panzer Corps on the evening of 9 July, 1943

6) LII Army Corps will hold its current positions in readiness, on the order of the Panzer Army, to force a crossing of the Pena R. in the Alekseevka – Zavidovka sector. It is necessary to utilize any opportunity to implement the crossing by 10.07.
7) Maintain current communication methods.
8) Army headquarters: Aleksandrovka Train Station.[1]

In the vicinity of Melikhovo, Kempf's forces were also preparing to launch an attack toward Prokhorovka from the south across the flood lands of the Northern Donets River. The III Panzer Corps' 7th Panzer Division had been concentrated here behind the 6th and 19th Panzer Divisions. The types and quantity of armored vehicles available to the divisions of the II SS Panzer Corps and the III Panzer Corps on the evening of 9 July 1943 are reflected in Tables 10 and 11.

The II SS Panzer Corps commander elaborated on Fourth Panzer Army's Order No. 5 in an order to his subordinate divisions that he signed at 2200 on 9 July, which spelled out their own specific assignments:

1) The enemy in front of II SS Panzer Corps, which had been greatly weakened on 8.07, continues active defensive fighting with the support of tanks. The strongest tank grouping is southeast of Oboian'. One should anticipate the arrival of fresh hostile tank and motorized reserves in the region of Prokhorovka and to the west of it.
2) The II SS Panzer Corps, after regrouping its forces to ensure the security of both flanks, launches an attack to the northeast to the line Prokhorovka – the hill 5 kilometers to the east of Kartashevka, and destroys the enemy in this region.
3) Tasks:

The right flank of **SS Division "R"** [*Das Reich*] remains on its former lines and regroups, so that the "*Deutschland*" Regiment can attack *en echelon* behind the Division "*AH*" and cover its right flank. If no stronger enemy forces are detected on the flank, then it should take up a security line by means of creating strongpoints.

The **SS Division "AH"** [*Leibstandarte Adolf Hitler*], after preparations, launches an attack from the region southwest of Teterevino with concentrated panzer forces along the main road to the northeast and seizes Prokhorovka.

The **SS Division "TK"** [*Totenkopf*] overnight creates a bridgehead in the designated region, regroups its panzers across the Psel River, and launches an attack up the Psel River valley and to the north of it in order to take Beregovoe and the heights northwest of it. The panzers should reach the hills north of the Psel River undetected. Security of the left flank should run along the southeastern bank of the Solotinka – Psel – Ol'shanka Rivers. Make a junction with the 11th Panzer Division, which is covering the area north of the Solotinka from the north. If no stronger enemy forces approach, secure the flank by creating a strongpoint.

4) Reconnaissance: Conducts a reconnaissance in the region Ivanovka – Pravorot' – Krasnoe – Iamki – Pogorelovka (including its environs) – Nizhniaia Gusynka – southern bank of the Seimitsy River – Khimichev (incl.) … Ol'shanka – the settlements closely adjoining Ol'shanka to the west … Krasnyi Oktiabr'.

Boundary lines: Division "*R*" on the right, division "*AH*" on the left – the woods west of Ivanovskii Vyselok – Storozhevoe – Leski (held by the flank "*AH*") – Khlamov – Priznachnoe (held by Division "*R*").

Boundary Line: Division "*AH*" on the right, Division "*TK*" on the left: the populated points on the eastern bank of the Psel River (held by Division "*TK*") … to Ol'shanka (held by Division "*TK*").

5) The air force in good weather is to support the attacking units of the divisions "*AH*" and "*R*" with tactical aerial reconnaissance and bombers.

6) The commander of the 680th Pioneer Regiment is to lead the bridging column to Luchki by dawn. The bridging column is to follow a *kampfgruppe* of the *Totenkopf* Division, in order to build a crossing over the [Psel] river at a proper time.

7) Three batteries of the Corps' *werfer* regiment will be attached to the *Totenkopf* Division. The batteries are to be on the move tonight for Luchki. The commander of the Corps' *werfer* regiment will be located with the combat formations of *Das Reich* Division.

8) II SS Panzer Corps is to regulate traffic to the line Kalinin – Luchki (and the adjoining populated points inclusively), starting at 0400 on 10.07.

9) The attack will begin: for the "*AH*" Division – 0600; the "*TK*" Division is to report on its progress in creating the bridgehead throughout the night.

10) Communication means: Telephone and radio. Given breaks in the communications lines, radio use is preferable.

11) The Corps' command point will remain in its previous position.[2]

The essence of the cited documents is that the enemy command was not formally rejecting the basic plan of Operation Citadel – the breakthrough to Kursk, bypassing Oboian' to the northeast. However, now the immediate aim was to secure the extended flanks and to liquidate the threat presented by the 6th Tank Corps and elements of the

6th Guards Army on the Pena River on one side, and the 69th Army's 48th Rifle Corps on the other. It was clear that the mobile formations that had entered the fighting on 8 July on the Prokhorovka axis presented only the first wave of Russian reserves. Consequently, after five days of the offensive, the forces of Hoth and Kempf had still not achieved the goal of the first stage of Operation Citadel. Moreover, the II SS Panzer Corps was now in a very difficult situation. Its divisions had suffered painful losses, and it could no longer count upon the assistance of the brigade of Panthers, as had been previously planned. Meanwhile, judging from arriving intelligence information, the Russians were moving up very significant forces. In Hoth's Order No. 5, the commander of the Fourth Panzer Army's great concern over the intelligence reports about the approach of fresh Soviet tank and mechanized corps from the east (from the region of Novyi and Staryi Oskol) toward Prokhorovka is evident. The first lines of the order directly indicate this. Therefore, he was hurrying to seize the region of Prokhorovka, in order to take up suitable positions on the commanding heights in the area, in the supposition that savage fighting with the Russian reserves would develop here in the nearest future. These two orders, together with the yet to be discussed Soviet operational documents by the commanders of the Voronezh Front and the 69th Army on 9 July on the subject of strengthening the defenses southwest of Prokhorovka, set the stage for what I will call the Prokhorovka engagement (see Appendix I).

As is known, primary reconnaissance efforts are concentrated on those places where major events are being prepared or where they are already occurring. Prior to 10 July, the Oboian' axis had been the important one, not the Ozerovskii region. Now, Fourth Panzer Army's reconnaissance forces were being instructed to scout thoroughly in the Prokhorovka direction even a day before the order went out that shifted the main attack from Oboian' toward Prokhorovka. Headquarters, Fourth Panzer Army, was trying to protect itself from any surprises and keeping close watch over the operations of the Soviet forces, so in case of necessity it could reach a timely and well-founded decision.

Tank and Assault Gun Types	***SS Leibstandarte Adolf Hitler***	***SS Das Reich***	***SS Totenkopf***	**Total**
Pz II	4	-	-	4
Pz III with 5cm/L42 gun	-	-	47	47
Pz III with 5cm/L60	4	31	-	35
Pz IV with 7.5cm/L43 or L48	32	13	20	65
Pz IV with 7.5cm/L24	-	-	7	7
Pz VI	4	1	2	7
Captured T-34/76	-	7	-	7
Command Tanks	5	7	5	17
StuG Assault Guns	22	26	12	60
Total:	71	85	93	249

Source: N. Zetterling and A. Frankson, *Kursk 1943: A Statistical Analysis* (London: Frank Cass, 2000), Tables A 6.4, A 6.5, A 6.6.

Table 11. Amount and Types of Armor in the Divisions of the II SS Panzer Corps at 1905 Hours on 9 July 1943

Judging from contemporary German maps, in the course of Operation Citadel the German intelligence performed well in detecting and identifying the Soviet armies that were opposing them. Doubtlessly, enemy intelligence had noticed that the positions in the Psel River bend and in the region of Prokhorovka Station had not been fully and thoroughly prepared (the local population had been mobilized to build railroad branch lines, while the troops didn't have sufficient time), and that until 9 July, relatively weak forces had been concentrated on this line, and at that only on scattered sectors. The command of Army Group South indeed sought to take advantage of these relatively favorable circumstances when it selected the time to change the direction of its main attack from Oboian' toward Prokhorovka.

It must be acknowledged that the enemy's combat reconnaissance operated quite successfully: reconnaissance detachments, strengthened by tanks, rather quickly exposed the weaknesses in our defenses and uncovered the system of fire. Combat documents of the II SS Panzer Corps formations testify to the well-organized aerial reconnaissance that operated on behalf of the ground forces. As a result, the enemy was very aware of the changing situation in the tactical depth of our defenses and took timely measures to repel counterattacks.

For a long time, it has been considered that the appearance of the Soviet tank reserve in the region of Prokhorovka on 9 July had surprised the Germans. The orders cited above show quite the opposite: the Fourth Panzer Army command not only knew of the arrival of formations of the 5th Guards Tank Army's 18th Tank Corps, but was also anticipating the approach of additional forces.

At the very same time, judging from archival documents, our own intelligence, while noting the presence of three SS panzer divisions on the Oboian' axis, was never able to establish that they were formations of the II SS Panzer Corps throughout the entire course of the defensive operation. Even after the battle had ended, on 24 July 1943 Voronezh Front command sent a report to Stalin, which stated that on 11 July on the Prokhorovka axis, the adversary had regrouped forces of the V SS Panzer Corps and the 17th Panzer Division! As we see, Soviet intelligence was unable to establish the precise identity of the corps, which had attacked on this axis between 6 and 17 July, and moreover included a panzer division as part of the hostile grouping, which wasn't even present. This gives evidence of the low professional training of the *Front*'s intelligence officers.

In order to understand the logic behind the further progress of combat operations on the southern face of the Kursk bulge, it is extremely important to draw up a chronology of events. Thus, from 5 to 9 July 1943, the main forces of Army Group South, following the plan for Operation Citadel, launched the main attack to the north – along the Belgorod – Kursk highway – and to the northeast in the direction of the Psel. For Voronezh Front, this was the first, initial phase of the defensive operation. Despite all of the enemy's efforts, our defenses had held. The soldiers and officers of the 6th Guards and 7th Guards Armies, and the 1st Tank Army, played the main and decisive role in this. Eternal glory to them! They did everything possible and impossible to prevent a breakthrough of the defense, inflicted significant damage to the enemy's shock grouping, and ground down his forces.

Failing to obtain success, the adversary regrouped the formations of the II SS Panzer Corps for a strike in the eastern and northeastern directions. It was exactly on this day that Colonel General H. Hoth for the first time gave *Obergruppenführer* P. Hausser the specific tasks to seize Prokhorovka Station and the heights near it, to force a crossing of the Psel River, and thereby create the conditions for the development of the offensive toward Kursk while bypassing Oboian'.

In my view, it is more correct to consider that the second stage of the defensive operation on the southern face of the Kursk bulge began on 10 July 1943. The basic events of this stage unfolded in the area of a major point of resistance of our forces – the Prokhorovka railroad station (which was an integral part of the district center, the village of Aleksandrovka). Therefore it was logical to give this stage of the battle its own name, one with a connection to this point –Prokhorovka.

Voronezh Front's operational objective in this period consisted of preventing a German breakthrough of the third and final army-level line of defenses on the Prokhorovka axis. At the same time, they were to inflict further damage to the enemy and create conditions for his complete destruction, if possible.

Troops of the 5th Guards and 5th Guards Tank Army, as well as the 69th Army, were fated to play the major role in the second stage of the operation. The formations of the 6th and 7th Guards Armies and the 1st Tank Army continued to participate actively in the fighting until the end of the operation, but this was no longer the main axis. The second defensive stage came to an end on 17 July, when the command of Army Group South, unable to complete the tasks set for it in Operation Citadel, began to withdraw its forces (including from the sector of the front in the region of Prokhorovka), which meant it had switched to carrying out a different operational task. Correspondingly, the assignments of our own forces changed as well – from the defense, they went over to the pursuit of the enemy. This allows us to confirm that the battle for Prokhorovka ended on 16 July.

The third, concluding stage of Voronezh Front's defensive operation was the pursuit (in some sectors, the pushing back) of the enemy. It ended on 23 July, when in most places our forces reached the lines they had been occupying back on 5 July.

For 10 July, P. Hausser placed before the II SS Panzer Corps the task of breaking through our rear belt of defenses to its entire depth, and to emerge on the line Prokhorovka Station – Hill 252.4 (2.5 kilometers to the northeast) – Beregovoe – Hill 243.5 (2 kilometers to the southwest of Korytnoe) – Kartashevka. Thus, each division of the II SS Panzer Corps would have to make a 12 to 13 kilometer advance in order to reach the mission objective. Judging by the pace of their offensive in the first forty-eight hours of Operation Citadel, this task seemed feasible. However, after five days of brutal fighting, the II SS Panzer Corps no longer had sufficient strength to overcome yet another belt of fortifications in the course of only the daylight hours of 10 July.

In addition, the terrain in front of the station was very difficult, full of deep ravines and gorges, impassable for armor, together with the swampy basin of a river. Therefore, Hoth could not employ two or three panzer divisions abreast in one sector in order to smash through the now third defensive position of the Russians, as had been done on 5 July to penetrate the first defensive belt. Hoth was compelled to consider this circumstance when making the concrete assignments for the II SS Panzer Corps.

The task of seizing Prokhorovka Station had been mentioned more than once in the orders of the German command, but the station itself had never been an independent objective of an "order of the day", as the enemy plans labeled certain points or lines, which were required to be seized by the end of the specified day. Prokhorovka Station was for the first time designated as such in Hausser's orders for 10 July. The SS Panzergrenadier Division *Leibstandarte* was placed in the center of the corps' attacking wedge. It was this division that was supposed to seize Prokhorovka Station, and thereby lay the groundwork for solving the corps' main task – the passage of the SS Panzergrenadier Division *Totenkopf* over the Psel River to Kartashevka and beyond in a northeasterly direction. Moreover, the seizure of the ground around Prokhorovka Station would create the opportunity to launch an attack into the rear of 69th Army's 48th Rifle Corps, which was opposing Army Detachment Kempf.

Considering such a significant role which the SS Panzergrenadier Division *Leibstandarte* had to play from the first day of the Prokhorovka engagement, I will cite excerpts from Operational Order No. 17 to the division for the fighting on 10 July, which was signed by its commander SS *Oberführer* T. Wisch at 2215 on 9 July:

> 1. *Enemy forces prepared for defense* are equipped with anti-tank weapons and tanks and are standing in a line from the western edge of the forest at Svkh. [State Farm] Komsomolets to the railway line at Ivanovskii Vyselok.
>
> 2. *The II SS Panzer Corps* is to move out on 10.7.1943 with the *LSSAH to the right* and SS Panzergrenadier Division *Totenkopf to the left* on both sides of the Psel and head northeast.
>
> *Attack objective*: Prokhorovka/East – Hill 252.4 (2.5 kilometers northeast of there) – Beregovoe – Hill 243.5 (two kilometers northwest of Korytnoe) – Kartashevka.
>
> 3. *The reinforced LSSAH* is to move out at 0600 on 10.7.1943 after the barrage by the entire Artillery-Regiment/*LSSAH* and *Werfer* Regiment 55. After the Luftwaffe's preparation, the *LSSAH* is to move along the road from Teterevino to Prokhorovka, capture the latter town, and hold it.
>
> *First attack objective*: Prokhorovka – Hill 252.4
>
> *SS Panzergrenadier Division Das Reich* is to set out with the *LSSAH* and to capture the high ground two kilometers southeast of Ivanovskii Vyselok.
>
> *SS Panzergrenadier Division Totenkopf* is to move forward from the Kliuchi bridgehead to the northeast.
>
> 4. *Boundary lines*: *To the right* between the *LSSAH* and Division *DR*: Teterevino (held by the *LSSAH*) – forest just east of Ivanovskii Vyselok (held by the *LSSAH*) – Storozhevoe (held by the *LSSAH*) – Iamki (held by the *LSSAH*) – Hill 230.5 (south of Prokhorovka and held by the *LSSAH* – road from Prokhorovka to Priznachnoe (held by the *LSSAH*).
>
> *To the left* between the *LSSAH* and Panzergrenadier Division *T*: Hill 254.5 (five hundred meters north of Teterevino and held by the *LSSAH*) – Vasil'evka

(held by *T*) – the towns in the Psel basin (held by *T*) – rail line to the northwest (held by the *LSSAH*).

Between the reinforced 2. Panzergrenadier Regiment and the reinforced Reconnaissance Battalion LSSAH: northern tip of the forest at Svkh. Komsomolets – Svkh. Oktiabr'skii (held by the Reconnaissance Battalion) – Hill 252.4 (held by the Reconnaissance Battalion) – Dumnoe (held by the Reconnaissance Battalion).

5. *To accomplish this, I order the following:*

a) *The reinforced 2. Panzergrenadier Regiment LSSAH* (the assault gun battalion, the Tiger Company, one Company of the Pioneer Battalion, and the 5th Flak Battalion) is to attack at 0600 hours on 10.7.1943 after the barrage from the entire Artillery Regiment *LSSAH* and *Werfer* Regiment 55 (minus one battalion). It is to attack the enemy's installations, penetrate them, and then continue the attack immediately on Prokhorovka.

Attack objective: Eastern edge of Prokhorovka.

b) *The reinforced Reconnaissance Battalion LSSAH* (one company of the anti-tank battalion deployed to cover the left flank) is to start out on 10.7.1943 after the 2. Panzergrenadier Regiment's successful breakthrough. It is to bypass the northern tip of the Svkh. [State Farm] Komsomolets forest and it is then to move through the Svkh. Oktiabr'skii to Hill 252.4 There it is to halt.

c) *The Panzer Regiment LSSAH* (minus the Tiger company) is to stand ready in the area south of the road from Teterevino to Luchki (excluding the towns) in order to be moved up behind the reinforced 2. Panzergrenadier Regiment *LSSAH.*

The subordination of the Tiger company is to end after the successful breakthrough.

The 6./Flak Battalion *LSSAH* is to be moved up to the Artillery Regiment *LSSAH* and to be subordinated to it.[3]

At 1905 on 9 July, the II SS Panzer Corps numbered 49 tanks and assault guns. SS *Leibstandarte* had 71 operational tanks and assault guns (see Table 11).

How was the defense of the Soviet forces set up at Prokhorovka prior to the engagement? What forces and resources were activated on 9 July?

Prior to 10 July, all of the actions of Voronezh Front's command had been directed at strengthening the Oboian' axis. On the evening of 8 July by the personal order of N. F. Vatutin, Lieutenant General V. G. Burkov's 10th Tank Corps was shifted from Prokhorovka to the 1st Tank Army's sector of the defenses. On 8 July at 2200, by his order the 5th Guards Tank Corps was supposed to give up its line of defense in the sector Komsomolets State Farm – Iasnaia Poliana – Teterevino and also be placed under the operational subordination of the 1st Tank Army. At this moment, Vatutin's main concern was to stop the German advance in the sector of the 6th Guards Army. It must be said that the *Front* commander did consider that von Manstein might alter the direction of his attack. But in this event, the two Guards armies were already on the move in the direction of Prokhorovka.

On 10 July, A. M. Vasilevsky let the commander of one of these two Guards armies, Lieutenant General A. S Zhadov, know about this possibility:

> On 10 July, I encountered the *Stavka* representative and Marshal of the Soviet Union A. M. Vasilevsky in the vicinity of the Army's command post. This was my first meeting with Aleksandr Mikhailovich. I reported to him on the army's condition and on the assignment it had received. Aleksandr Mikhailovich was very concerned. He told me:
>
> 'The situation in the sector of the 6th Guards Army and the 1st Tank Army is very difficult. The enemy is straining toward Oboian'. Although so far our troops have stopped his advance, there is the possibility that he will regroup his main forces, and try to attack through Prokhorovka and beyond it make a turn to the north, in order to bypass Oboian' to the east. Therefore you must quickly reach the indicated line, organize a defense, and not allow an enemy breakthrough across the Psel River.'[4]

Some scholars accuse Nikolai Fedorovich [Vatutin] of incorrectly assessing the situation on the Prokhorovka axis that had developed by 10 July. The Germans were concentrating their best panzer formations here, but at the same time, the *front* commander was transferring two tank corps [the 5th Guards and 10th Tank Corps] from this axis to General Katukov's 1st Tank Army, plainly weakening the defense of the 69th Army. At the same time, the area of the Psel River bend held the boundary line between two armies, the 6th Guards and the 69th, and such boundaries, as is well known, are always the weakest spot in the layout of any defense.

However, appearances are deceiving. N. F. Vatutin understood quite well what von Manstein was trying to achieve. He had watched as day after day von Manstein's assault groupings, grinding their way through the Voronezh Front's defenses, headed toward the same location – the region of Prokhorovka, and he fully recognized the real possibility of the 69th Army's encirclement if Prokhorovka Station fell into enemy hands. However, at the time he made these decisions, the Oboian' axis was still his main concern, and the Prokhorovka axis was a subsidiary one – the *front*'s resources were not limitless. So N. F. Vatutin was compelled to use only those forces that had already been already been committed into the fighting, and to draw more actively upon the 7th Guards Army's forces to assist the 69th Army. His communications with Lieutenant General Shumilov, commander of the 7th Guards Army, on 9 July at 2220 reveal his thinking:

> Act according to your decisions, and absolutely be prepared for active operations on 11 July. Report your considerations to me. Keep in view that the enemy has concentrated major tank forces on Kriuchenkin's flanks, and it is not beyond possibilities that on 10 July, the enemy will be pressing on Kriuchenkin's flank. I have great apprehensions for Kriuchenkin, therefore for tomorrow you must have your right flank be very strong, so you can help Kriuchenkin with heavy fire from your positions, if necessary, or by counterattacks and maneuvering with your anti-tank means.

Closely coordinate the actions of your right flank with Kriuchenkin's left wing, and under no circumstances allow the enemy to breakthrough at your junction with Kriuchenkin.[5]

Front headquarters intently followed the developing operational situation both on the Prokhorovka and the Korocha directions, and took necessary measures as far as was possible. The following document gives evidence of this:

Combat Order No. 0015/OP, Headquarters, Voronezh Front, 09.07.43, 1130.

With the aim of best fulfilling the assigned task and [for] the more suitable direction of the forces

I hereby order:

1. To place responsibility for the defense of the Korocha axis on the commander of the 69th Army Lieutenant General Comrade Kriuchenkin. The task of 69th Army – firmly to defend the front occupied by its forces, Vasil'evka – Belenikhino – Visloe – Shopino – Chernaia Poliana – Staryi Gorod – Blizhniaia Igumenka – Miasoedovo, to prevent an enemy breakthrough of the indicated front from the direction of Melikhovo and his further advance. Destroy the enemy in the region of Melikhovo. Pay particular attention to blocking the Prokhorovka axis and to securing your left flank.

1. [sic.] To subordinate the following forces to the 69th Army:

The 48th Rifle Corps with the 183rd, 305th and 107th Divisions;

The 35th Rifle Corps with the 92nd Guards, 93rd Guards, and 94th Guards Divisions;

The 375th Rifle Division and the 89th Guards Rifle Division from the 6th Guards Army; the 81st Guards Rifle Division from the 7th Guards Army; the 96th Tank Brigade and the 148th Tank Regiment.

Artillery – the 30th Destroyer Brigade, the 27th Anti-tank Artillery Brigade, two destroyer anti-tank artillery regiments, one regiment of rocket launchers, and all other means of reinforcement, presently located within the boundary limits of the 69th Army, except the tank corps.

2. From 1800 9.07.43 to establish the following boundaries:

From 6th Guards Army on the right: Greznoe – Vasil'evka – Malaia Psinka – Petrovka – Chuguevo – Iushkovo.

From 7th Guards Army on the left: Razumnaia River – Miasoedovo – Arkad'eevka – Novoselovka – Nechaevka – Velikomikhailovka.

...

4. To transfer the 49th Rifle Corps with the 11th and 270th Rifle Divisions from the 69th Army to the 7th [Guards] Army.

5. The commanders of the 6th and 7th Guards Armies are to turn over the forces withdrawn from you to the operational control of 69th Army before 1800 9.07.43.

Report on the completion of this order.[6]

Rifle Division	Manpower	Rifles	Machine guns	Guns, all calibers	PPSh-41 submachine guns	Anti-tank Rifles	Mortars
183rd	7,981	4,908	71	75	1,579	205	146
305th	7,803	4,626	68	76	242	212	159
107th	7,920	3,876	71	75	1,211	208	158
92nd Guards	9,574	5,312	472	37	1,852	225	94
93rd Guards	9,426	6,189	676	91	2,482	282	175
94th Guards	9,385	5,889	595	96	2,394	201	149
375th	8,715	5,696	500	88	2,123	206	147
Total	60,804	36,496	2,453	538	11,883	1,539	1,028

Source: TsAMO RF, f. 203, op. 2843, d. 426, l. 165.

Table 12: Strength and Equipment of the Divisions of the 69th Army on 5 July 1943

This document clearly demonstrates that the leadership of Voronezh Front not only anticipated the adversary's looming operations, but also took timely measures to improve the control of the forces that were defending the rear army-level line of defense. It concentrated the handling of the forces on the Prokhorovka and Korocha directions in one set of hands, and greatly reinforced the defense on these directions. Already by the end of 9 July, the main forces of the 5th Guards Tank Army were assembling in the Bobryshevo – Sredniaia Ol'shanka – Mar'ino – Prokhorovka region. The Army had received the order to reinforce the defense of the rifle units. Since the troops of the 69th Army took a most active participation in the fighting for Prokhorovka, its rifle formations and their strengths as of 5 July 1943 are shown in Table 12.

At 2300 on 9 July, Rotmistrov signed Combat Order No. 4. Having received it, the 18th Tank Corps was supposed to take up a defense on the northern bank of the Psel River along the line: Veselyi – Polezhaev – southern edge of Prelestnoe – southern edge of Aleksandrovskii.[7]

The tanks and the artillery guns were ordered to dig in. In reserve, the corps commander was supposed to have not less than one tank brigade on his left flank, that is, in the direction of Storozhevoe, ready to repulse the enemy's attack and to undertake active offensive operations from dawn on 10 July.

This same order gave Major General B. M. Skvortsov, commander of the 5th Guards Mechanized Corps, the task to advance two mechanized brigades to the northern bank of the Psel – to the sector of the Zapselets River, excluding Veselyi, and to take up the defense on the right flank of the 18th Tank Corps. In this fashion, on the night before 10 July on the Prokhorovka axis and in the bend of the Psel River, a strong second echelon had been created in the rear of the forces already occupying the prepared rear defensive belt.

The authors of some publications accuse the 5th Guards Tank Army commander, and together with him the *front* headquarters, of not fully considering their decisions when deploying the tank army on the line of defense in the Psel River bend and at Prokhorovka Station. Thus, G. A. Oleinikov, a veteran of the Kursk fighting with the 5th Guards Tank Army, asserts that two armies – the 5th Guards Army and the 5th Guards

Colonel General (at the time of the battle Major General) B. M. Skvortsov, commander of the 5th Guards 'Zimovniki' Mechanized Corps (1941 photo). (TsAMO)

Tank Army – were deployed at the same time on the same sectors of defense. Moreover, Oleinikov maintains that Rotmistrov's order to the corps commands contained a number of omissions: it failed to indicate the units that were already occupying those sectors, with which it would be necessary to cooperate when taking over those positions; it did not assign responsibility for the sectors' defense during the process of relieving those units presently holding the positions; and it did not identify who was responsible for the boundaries between adjacent units. If this was so, then the commander of the tank army failed to perform the elementary duties of command: to require that his staff and subordinates organize cooperation both within their own formations and with their neighbors.[8] Oleinikov, in my view, has it all backwards, and without immersing himself in all the details of the situation, he accuses the higher commands of all sorts of sins. In reality it was all completely opposite to what he asserts.

The order for the defense was issued to the forces of the 5th Guards Tank Army on the evening of 9 July, when they had already reached Prokhorovka. Meanwhile, the commander of the 5th Guards Army issued his order – for the troops of the 32nd Guards and 33rd Guards Rifle Corps to occupy the same sector as the 5th Guards Tank Army – at 0430 on 9 July, when those two rifle corps were still only preparing to march and were still a day's march away from Prokhorovka.

Only with Combat Order No. 16/OP of 10 July at 1430 did the command of the 5th Guards Army require:

> 1. Under the personal responsibility of commanders of the corps and divisions, the units of the army are to move into the indicated line by 0400 11.07.43, where they are fully to take up the defense.
> 2. Pay special attention to anti-tank defense, for which you are to deploy your artillery on the line of defense as the first order of business.[9]

And just who was supposed to be defending these lines for twenty-four hours, while the 5th Guards Army was moving up to Prokhorovka Station? For the time being, there was nothing else available to place on the indicated line than the tankers of the 5th Guards Tank Army. They were digging in behind the forward units of the 52nd Guards Rifle Division, the 11th Motorized Rifle Brigade, and the 2nd Tank Corps' 26th and 99th Tank Brigades (between Vasil'evka and the rail line), and the 169th Tank Brigade (at Storozhevoe), but within twenty-four hours they had turned over their defensive sectors to the arriving formations of the 5th Guards Army. As concerns the level of cooperation during this process, this scholar simply inattentively read the documents – the army commander precisely assigned the responsibility for the boundaries between the subordinate formations. Thus, for example, Major General B. M. Skvortsov bore responsibility for the boundary between the left flank of his 5th Guards Mechanized Corps and the right flank of the 18th Tank Corps. It was so written in the order itself.

The 5th Guards Tank Corps, despite the order transferring it to the 1st Tank Army, was not able to give up its sector of the line southwest of Prokhorovka within the established time period, and moreover it was in a pretty tattered condition. Its 20th Guards Tank Brigade, having turned over its sector of defense and all its material (10 T-34s, of which two were in good order; nine T-70s, of which three were in good order) to the 21st Guards Tank Brigade, pulled out and moved to the area of Krasnoe only on the evening of 9 July.[10] But its motorized rifle battalion continued to man the defenses in the brigade's former position until it was replaced on the night of 10 July. The 22nd Guards Tank Brigade (with only eight T-34 tanks and five T-70 tanks)[11] together with the 21st Guards Tank Brigade also went nowhere until 0600 10 July, while the 6th Guards Motorized Rifle Brigade was pulled out of this area only on the evening of 14 July. The 10th Tank Corps also did not move to the 1st Tank Army with all its units. Its 11th Motorized Rifle Brigade remained on the Prokhorovka axis until the evening of 12 July.

We've already discussed which forces were used for building the second echelon of defense southwest of Prokhorovka. Now we'll take a look at the combat deployment of the formations of the first echelon. Units of the 52nd Guards Rifle were dug-in along the northern bank of the bend in the Psel River: its 151st Guards Rifle Regiment was holding the sector stretching from a knoll 500 meters north of Kliuchi to a point 1.5 kilometers southwest of Hill 226.6; its 155th Guards Rifle Regiment lay ready on the sector running between Hill 226.6 and the grove southeast of Kliuchi; its 153rd Guards Rifle Regiment was holding the sector between a path lying 1.5 kilometers east of Hill 226.6 and the village of Polezhaev. The artillery battalions of the 124th Guards Artillery Regiment were positioned behind the trenches of the rifle battalions in two locations: 1 kilometer southwest of Polezhaev and 400 meters southeast of Veselyi. The 11th Motorized Rifle Brigade's 3rd Motorized Rifle Battalion was dug in on the crest of Hill 226.6.

Lieutenant Colonel L. I. Malov, commander of the 2nd Tank Corps' 99th Tank Brigade (1941 photo). (TsAMO)

Lieutenant Colonel L. I. Malov's 99th Tank Brigade of the 2nd Tank Corps was defending the left (southern) bank of the Psel, in the villages of Vasil'evka and Andreevka. Its defenses were buttressed by two batteries from the 2nd Tank Corps' 1502nd Destroyer Anti-tank Artillery Regiment, as well as the 11th Motorized Rifle Brigade's 1st and 2nd Motorized Rifle Battalions.

The most suitable ground for the enemy to employ tanks lay in the sector between the two villages on the left bank of the river (Vasil'evka and Andreevka) and the Storozhevoe woods. The 183rd Rifle Division's 285th Rifle Regiment, which as we have seen experienced the fratricidal attack from the 99th Tank Brigade on 8 July, was holding this key portion of the line.[12] According to the 183rd Rifle Division's defensive plan, adopted by divisional commander Major General A. S. Kostitsyn on 20 May 1943, this regiment had been withdrawn to the sector of the rear defensive belt Vasil'evka – Vinogradovka – Hill 258.2 (excl.) – Oktiabr'skii State Farm, which extended along 11 kilometers of the front. The 285th Rifle Regiment's 1st and 2nd Rifle Battalions, reinforced by the 2nd Battalion of the 183rd Rifle Division's 623rd Artillery Regiment, were defending the sector Vasil'evka – Komsomolets State Farm – Hill 258.2 (north of Teterevino) – Ivanovskii Vyselok. As of 30 June, the 285th Rifle Regiment had a strength of 1,748 men,[13] equipped with the following weapons: 878 rifles, 41 PPSh submachine guns, 43 light machine guns, 17 heavy machine guns, eight 50mm mortars, 23 82mm mortars, five 120mm mortars, six 45mm anti-tank guns, four 76mm anti-tank guns, and 54 anti-tank rifles.[14]

The 35-year-old Lieutenant Colonel A. K. Karpov commanded the 285th Rifle Regiment. Aleksandr Karpovich was born in Leningrad, and finished five years of general education schooling. He was drafted into the ranks of the Red Army in

Positions of the 183rd Rifle Division southwest of Prokhorovka Station shown in a photo taken by a Soviet Po-2 reconnaissance plane, June 1943. (RGAKFD)

January 1930, and served in Leningrad Military District's 16th Rifle Division. There he graduated from a regimental school, and in 1937 – a course of instruction for those senior adjutants (chiefs of staff) of rifle battalions that were located in reserve. His formal military education stopped at this point, but Aleksandr Karpovich managed to master the military profession well. By the end of the war, he was still commanding a regiment, but had been honored with five Orders, including three commanders' Orders: the Order of Suvorov, 3rd Degree (1943), the Order of Aleksandr Nevsky (1944), and the Order of Kutuzov, 3rd Degree (1945). It was rare even for a *front* commander to earn such honors during the war years, and for the commander of a rifle regiment even more so.

Karpov took command of the 183rd Rifle Division's 285th Rifle Regiment at the beginning of 1943. Back on the morning of 6 February 1943, a composite detachment of the regiment's 1st Rifle Battalion, under the command of deputy battalion commander Captain A. Tkachev, having completed a 40-kilometer march, had launched an assault on the Prokhorovka Station, and had seized it after some fighting. Five months later, Aleksandr Karpovich had to endure in these same places one of the most difficult tests of his military life – two weeks of heavy defensive fighting.

The regiment had already done some fighting since 6 July, but on 10 July it found itself facing the sharp point of the II SS Panzer Corps' spearhead. Jumping ahead, I will say here that the commander and his warriors demonstrated courage and professionalism in their struggle against superior enemy forces, and played an important role in the defense of Prokhorovka. After the war, A. K. Karpov visited the old battlefield more than once, where he always spent time on the ground his regiment had defended in front of Prokhorovka. As one eyewitness later told me, it was very emotional to watch the old soldier, standing in an empty field with a bouquet of flowers in his hands, as he silently remembered his fallen comrades, not bothering to hide his tears.

Lieutenant Colonel I. Ia. Stepanov's 169th Tank Brigade of the 2nd Tank Corps defended the village of Storozhevoe, together with the 285th Rifle Regiment's 3rd Rifle Battalion. Colonel P. V. Piskarev's 26th Tank Brigade of the same tank corps was holding the line Andreevka – rail line – Storozhevoe. The combat vehicles of all three tank brigades, the 99th, the 169th and the 26th, were dug-in (except for the brigade commanders' reserves), essentially serving as anti-tank guns. At the same, each formation had the assignment to be prepared to counterattack. Thus, for example, Lieutenant Colonel Malov's 99th Tank Brigade had the order to be ready to attack with its tank group in two directions: the Greznoe – Mikhailovka direction, and toward Hill 255.9.

Prior to 10 July, the SS forces had with great persistence tried to penetrate the defense in two locations: at the Psel River bend, and in the direction of Teterevino, Ivanovskii Vyselok, and Storozhevoe. For four days, starting from 6 July, when Hausser's forces had reached the approaches to Belenikhino Station, *kampfgruppen* of the II SS Panzer Corps' divisions had repeatedly attacked on the line Iasnaia Poliana – Ivanovskii Vyselok. Striking from the region of Teterevino in the direction of Storozhevoe, Belenikhino, and Leski, the Germans had tried to find weak spots in the Red Army's defense.

The tank brigades of the 5th Guards Tank Corps had given enormous assistance to the rifle units during these days. As we have seen, on the morning of 10 July, it was supposed to pull out of the line from the Belenikhino region after V. G. Burkov's 10th Tank Corps departed. Given this, the Ivanovskii Vyselok – Teterevino sector was particularly vulnerable to attack on the morning of 10 July. Back on 6 July, the Nazis had managed to drive a wedge into these defenses at Hill 258.2, and over the next few days they had shown great activity there. In addition, intelligence had reported a concentration of more than 100 enemy tanks in Teterevino. Considering these circumstances, the commander of the 69th Army decided to regroup his forces on the night before 10 July.

As far back as 0150 on 9 July, General V. D. Kriuchenkin had warned Major General Z. Z. Rogozny, commander of the 48th Rifle Corps, by Private Combat Order No. 00950/OP:

> … 2. The 48th Rifle Corps (183rd, 93rd, 89th Rifle Divisions, 121st and 123rd Anti-tank Rifle Battalions) is to defend the line Vasil'evka – Teterevino – (excl.) Gostishchevo – Khokhlovo and to prevent an enemy tank breakthrough.
>
> Pay special attention to the directions: a) Krasnyi Oktiabr' – Prokhorovka – Priznachnoe; b) Shopino – Sabynino – Bol'shie Pod'iarugi.[15]

Only one mobile formation remained in the sector of the 69th Army guarding Prokhorovka after the departure of the 10th and 5th Guards Tank Corps – the 2nd Tank Corps. The corps was directly subordinate to N. F. Vatutin as Voronezh Front commander, who advised the corps' commander A. F. Popov in a telephone conversation: "The enemy has assembled no less than 250 tanks on the Vasil'evka – Belenikhino front, and it must be assumed that on 10 July, he will go on the offensive in this sector."[16] However, in such a tense situation, the corps' direct subordination to *front* command did not permit its timely use in case of any sort of complications. Therefore, 2nd Tank

Corps was transferred to 69th Army command. At 0300 10 July, V. D. Kriuchenkin signed the order:

> To the Commander of the 2nd Tank Corps.
> Private Combat Order No. 00967/OP 69th Army Headquarters 10.07.43, 0300.
> 1. The enemy has assembled a major tank grouping on the front Vasil'evka – Belenikhino. From the morning of 10.07.43, you must expect his attack in the eastern and southeastern directions.
> The *Front* commander has ordered the 2nd Tank Corps at 0000 10.07.43 to be subordinated to me.
> I hereby order:
> The 2nd Tank Corps, remaining in its current region, to prepare counterattacks:
> - To the northwest, in the general direction of Greznoe and Kochetovka;
> - To the southwest, in the general direction of Belenikhino and Iakovlevo;
> - To the south;
> - To the southeast, together with the 2nd Guards Tank Corps.
>
> 2. Confirm the receipt of this order. Report on the execution of this order by 0800 10.07.43.[17]

A note is written on the order: "Received 0700 10.07.43 NO-1" and the inscription: "To the chief of staff. For execution 10.07.43. Popov."

At the same time, another private combat order of the 69th Army headquarters, No. 00969/OP, was issued for regrouping the forces:

> To the Commanders of the 2nd Guards 'Tatsinskaia' Tank Corps and the 48th Rifle Corps:
> 1. The enemy has concentrated a major tank grouping on the front: Vasil'evka, Belenikhino. From the morning of 10.07.43, one must anticipate his offensive in the eastern direction and with part of his forces in the southeastern direction.
> I order:
> 1. To organize a strong defense on the front Vasil'evka, Belenikhino and to repel the enemy's offensive, not permitting his breakthrough under any circumstances, for which:
> - by 0500 10.07.43, the 93rd Guards Rifle Division is to replace the 2nd Guards Tank Corps, and the 2nd Guards Tank Corps is to be brought to the region Belenikhino – Leski – Shakhovo – Dal'nii Dolzhik. The 2nd Guards Tank Corps' headquarters – Plota.
>
> 2. The 89th Guards Rifle Division firmly is to defend the sector:
> Kalinin, skirting the woods along the Lipovyi Donets River, Hill 187.7 and further along the western bank.
> 3. Report on the execution [of this order] by 0800 10.07.43[18]

Thus, the Voronezh Front command undertook real measures to strengthen the defense on the Prokhorovka axis, even at the expense of the just arrived forces, which had been transferred from *Stavka* Reserve.

Thus, on the morning of 10 July, a combination of two Soviet armies – the 6th Guards Army and the 69th Army – were confronting the three divisions of the SS Panzer Corps. The boundary between the 6th Guards Army and the 69th Army ran along the Psel River. In *Totenkopf*'s sector of attack, the 51st Guards Rifle Division of the 6th Guards Army was defending the sector Hill 211.9 – Hill 207.8 – Il'inskii; 6th Guards Army's 52nd Guards Rifle Division was holding the sector Hill 226.6 – Polezhaev (along the northern bank of the Psel River). The positions of the 285th Rifle Regiment of the 183rd Rifle Division and the 11th Motorized Rifle Brigade of the 10th Tank Corps lay in front of *Leibstandarte* and *Das Reich*, on the sector Vasil'evka – Molozhavaia gully – Komsomolets State Farm – Ivanovskii Vyselok – Storozhevoe.

The 2nd Guards 'Tatsinskaia' Tank Corps and the 6th Guards Motorized Rifle Brigade of the 5th Guards 'Stalingrad' Tank Corps occupied defensive positions on a line running 1 kilometer northwest of Belenikhino through a landmark hut 1 kilometer north of Teterevino to Zhimolostnoe. Behind the 183rd Rifle Division's 285th Rifle Regiment, in the second echelon, the brigades of Major General A. F. Popov's 2nd Tank Corps were dug-in.

According to the conception of the command, A. F. Popov's and A. S. Burdeiny's corps were to strengthen the line of the rifle units "by fire and maneuver" and to create a unique armored hoop binding the rear belt on the axis of the II SS Panzer Corp's likely attack. However, it was not easy to realize this plan. By the start of the Prokhorovka engagement, the 2nd Tank Corps and the 2nd Guards 'Tatsinskaia' Tank Corps had suffered appreciable losses. At 0800 10 July, they had a combined force of 257 operational tanks of three types: T-34, T-70 and Lend-Lease MK IV Churchill. Of this total of 257 operational tanks, the 2nd Tank Corps had 116 tanks, and the 2nd Guards 'Tatsinskaia' Tank Corps had 141.

The 2nd Tank Corps was in particularly bad shape. Thus, while the 2nd Guards 'Tatsinskaia' Tank Corps' brigades were on average at 88-89% of authorized strength, in the 2nd Tank Corps, the 26th Tank Brigade had only 58% of its authorized strength still operational, the 99th Tank Brigade 55%, and the 169th Tank Brigade 55%. The 15th Separate Guards Breakthrough Tank Regiment had only 57% of its authorized strength still operational. Moreover, of the 89 tanks located in the three tank brigades of the 2nd Tank Corps, 43 were light T-70 tanks. Considering that this corps was situated directly in the path of the main attack of the II SS Panzer Corps, which still had significant forces (on July 10, units of all three of Hausser's divisions operated against the 2nd Tank Corps), then the qualitative aspect of its tank complement significantly affected its prospects and the ensuing combat results.

Let us examine the course of combat operations on the Prokhorovka axis. As uncovered documents testify, *Leibstandarte*'s neighbor, the SS Panzergrenadier Division *Totenkopf*, was the first to launch active operations.

The Psel River was the primary natural obstacle to the Germans' offensive to the northeast. The river channel was relatively narrow – from 20 to 30 meters in width. However, its wide – up to 200 meters – swampy basin presented a serious obstacle to tanks. In the predawn hours of 10 July, *Totenkopf* Panzergrenadiers, who had crossed the river under the cover of darkness, attempted to establish a bridgehead on the northern bank, in order to secure the laying of a pontoon bridge for the tanks to cross. This attempt was repulsed by units of the 52nd Guards Rifle Division and artillery fire from the vicinities of Vasil'evka and Andreevka.

It should be noted that the enemy's plan for the crossing attempt precisely here, in the bend of the Psel River, was correct. It is well known that a loop in a river, in the direction of the attacker, is the most suitable place for a forced crossing, since it precludes flank fire from the defenders. At the same time, the defensive forces on the other side of the river in the river bend are subjected to destructive fire not only from the front, but also from both flanks.

The 2nd Tank Corps command anticipated this development in events. On the night before 10 July, reconnaissance scouts had detected a concentration of enemy combat vehicles and equipment in the vicinity of the Molozhavaia gully, while a prisoner from a *Totenkopf* Panzergrenadier regiment captured near the Komsomolets State Farm had provided information about the forthcoming morning assault on Vasil'evka. The 99th Tank Brigade was sent to strengthen the 11th Motorized Rifle Brigade's 2nd Motorized Rifle Battalion, which was defending the village. The 99th Tank Brigade's motorized rifle battalion with two batteries of the 1502nd Destroyer Anti-tank Artillery Regiment took up defensive positions on the northeastern outskirts of Vasil'evka, while the third destroyer anti-tank battery deployed on the eastern outskirts. The 99th Tank Brigade's 2nd Tank Battalion was dug in on the northwestern edge of Andreevka, while the brigade commander's reserve, the 1st Tank Battalion, was positioned on the northwestern outskirts of Mikhailovka.

At 0530, units of *Totenkopf* conducted a reconnaissance-in-force with up to one Panzergrenadier battalion and ten panzers in the direction of these villages – their task to probe the defenses and disclose the firing positions. After a two-hour battle, the enemy fell back. This episode can be considered the start of the Prokhorovka engagement.

Parallel with this reconnaissance-in-force, *Leibstandarte* began to show activity. From the Operational Summary No. 7 from 183rd Rifle Division's headquarters:

> At 0700 up to a company of enemy infantry with the support of five tanks launched an attack on the 1st and 2nd Rifle Companies of the 285th Rifle Regiment. The attack was beaten back.
>
> From 0600 to 0930, groups of enemy aircraft, numbering between 20 and 25 Ju 88 bombers escorted by 10 to 15 Me 109 fighters, constantly worked over the areas of the 1st and 2nd Battalions of the 285th Rifle Regiment, through both dive bombing and even more so by level bombing from altitude. The hostile aviation didn't show any particular activity over other areas, with the exception of solitary reconnaissance planes.[19]

At 0800, the commander of the 2nd Tank Corps, Major General A. F. Popov, reported to Lieutenant General V. D. Kriuchenkin about the assembly in the Molozhavaia gully (north of the Komsomolets State Farm) of up to a battalion of infantry, up to two artillery batteries, batteries of six-barreled rocket launchers [*Nebelwerfer*] and ten enemy tanks. Going upon the intelligence reports, pointing to the concentration of enemy units between the river and the rail road (primarily at Teterevino), and observing the enemy's behavior that morning, the 69th Army drew the conclusion that the SS divisions were preparing for a lunge at Prokhorovka Station. Therefore, Private Order No. 00967/op, from the night before, directing a counterattack by brigades of the 2nd Tank Corps in the direction of Greznoe and Kochetovka with the aim of pinning the Germans in place, remained in effect.

The sharp counterattack of Lieutenant Colonel L. I. Malov's 99th Tank Brigade in cooperation with Colonel P. G. Borodkin's 11th Motorized Rifle Brigade had some success. By 1100, panzers and Panzergrenadiers from the SS Panzergrenadier Division *Totenkopf* had been driven from the village of Prokhorovka (10 kilometers west of Prokhorovka Station), Kozlovka, and the western outskirts of Vasil'evka. This spoiling attack somewhat delayed the timetable for the enemy's assault upon Prokhorovka Station, but the enemy refused to abandon his plan.

The attack of *SS Oberführer* Wisch's *Leibstandarte* Division began at 1045. Simultaneously, an assault group from SS Panzergrenadier Division *Totenkopf* attacked in the region of Kozlovka and Vasil'evka. As noted in documents of the II SS Panzer Corps, this was done intentionally with the aim of dispersing the strong fire of our artillery in front of the Panzer Corps. Two battalions of *SS Obersturmbannführer* H. Krass's 2nd Panzergrenadier Regiment immediately attacked the positions of the 285th Rifle Regiment.[20] SS *Hauptsturmführer* Becker's I Battalion attacked towards the southwestern outskirts of the Komsomolets State Farm, while SS *Sturmbannführer* Sandig's II Battalion thrust along the Teterevino – Ivanovskii Vyselok road toward the bend in the rail road; the III Battalion remained assembled in Teterevino aboard armored halftracks in reserve, ready to be thrown into the breakthrough toward Prokhorovka Station. The key to the defenses here was the Komsomolets State Farm, which lay on a line between Vasil'evka and Ivanovskii Vyselok. From Vasil'evka to the Komsomolets State Farm, the defenses were fronted by deep gullies, which came to an end about 300-400 meters from the railroad embankment; therefore any advance to Prokhorovka Station was possible only after first seizing the State Farm.

The 2nd Rifle Battalion of the 183rd Rifle Division, with the support of the 2nd Battalion of the 623rd Artillery Regiment, was directly defending the State Farm. Making use of the well-prepared line of defense, the companies of the 1st Rifle Battalion of the 285th Rifle Regiment managed to repel the attack and hang on to the sector Vasil'evka – Komsomolets State Farm. Meanwhile, *Leibstandarte*'s *kampfgruppe* was able to penetrate the first line of defense of the 2nd Rifle Battalion, defending the sector Komsomolets State Farm – Ivanovskii Vyselok, after approximately an hour of fighting. However, the SS troops could not exploit the success here. Their path forward was blocked by the dense and well-organized fire from forces of the second echelon – the 2nd Tank Corps' 169th Tank Brigade, 1502nd Destroyer Anti-tank Artillery Regiment, and 269th Mortar Regiment. The line from the bend in the rail line through Ivanovskii Vyselok to Storozhevoe had been most strongly fortified. In a grove near Ivanovskii Vyselok, tanks of the 370th Tank Battalion had been dug-in, together with the 1st and 2nd Batteries of the 1502nd Destroyer Anti-tank Artillery Regiment, and also the 1st Battalion of the 269th Mortar Regiment. After the enemy's breakthrough of its defenses near the rail line, a significant portion of the 2nd Rifle Battalion consolidated again near Ivanovskii Vyselok, where the Battalion's command post was located.

Major S. I. Orzhezhko (who at the time of the Kursk battle was a senior lieutenant), commander of the 5th Battery of the 183rd Rifle Division's 623rd Artillery Regiment (1945 photo). (Author's personal archive)

A "Devil's wheel" whirled over our positions – that's how Red Army soldiers christened the special tactic that the Germans dive bombers used. Having arranged themselves into a circle, from 30 to 70 bombers, one after another, would launch their individual strikes. They would continue this operation without interruption, as a rule, from thirty minutes to up to two hours. Several minutes before the completion of the bombing, a large group of armor, usually with heavy Tiger tanks moving in front, would advance. At the moment the bombing ceased, the tanks would be just several hundred meters from our rifle entrenchments. The infantry, still not fully recovered from the bombing, were now compelled to repel a tank attack. It was very difficult to withstand such an attack, lacking a second line of trenches, as was the case in the vicinity of Komsomolets State Farm. The Germans first used this method of breaking through combat positions at Kursk, with the aim of overcoming our well-engineered and deeply-echeloned defenses.

Having overcome the railroad embankment, the Panzergrenadiers of *Leibstandarte*'s I/2nd SS Panzergrenadier Regiment made no additional headway against the stubborn resistance of the defending forces before 1400. The enemy operated more effectively at the State Farm. After the II/2nd SS Panzergrenadier Regiment had driven the 285th Rifle Regiment from the line of trenches southwest of Komsomolets State Farm, the *Leibstandarte* command introduced its reconnaissance battalion into the gap. It had the order to augment the assault and to cover the left flank of the II/2nd SS Panzergrenadier Regiment.

By 1300 these two SS Panzergrenadier battalions with the support of *Leibstandarte*'s full artillery regiment, the company of Tigers and the assault gun battalion, reached the approaches to Hill 241.6, whereupon the reconnaissance battalion pivoted and struck into the rear of the companies of the 285th Rifle Regiment defending the Komsomolets State Farm and the 169th Tank Brigade's 371st Tank Battalion, which was positioned in a patch of woods north of the State Farm. From a II SS Panzer Corps report: "… At 1420, the *Leibstandarte* Division overran the bend in the rail line to the northeast and took Hill 241.6, despite fierce resistance and after hostile counterattacks, primarily by tanks from the area of the Stalinsk [Stalinskoe Branch of the Oktiabr'skii] State Farm." At the time indicated in the report, the SS forces had only reached the crest of the hill, and the fighting for it continued for approximately another two hours.

As a result of the four-hour battle, the battalions of the 285th Rifle Regiment were forced to abandon their positions. "The well dug-in enemy," – the headquarters of SS Panzergrenadier Division *Leibstandarte* reported, – "defended desperately, but after the capture of their positions, the resistance weakened. Numerous Russians began fleeing the field."[21]

The fighters of the 1st Rifle Battalion one by one and in small groups fell back to the 99th Tank Brigade's area of defense in Vasil'evka under pressure from superior enemy forces. The 2nd Rifle Battalion, which received the enemy's main blow at the State Farm, was scattered. Headquarters staff officers were busy rallying and assembling soldiers,

Chief of the Red Army General Staff Marshal of the Soviet Union A. M. Vasilevsky (seated second from the right) and member of Voronezh Front's Military Council Lieutenant General N. S. Khrushchev (seated on right) interrogate a prisoner at the Front command post in the area of Rzhava Station, 10 July 1943. (RGAKFD)

who were retreating towards Prokhorovka Station. The SS troops crushed the line of the 3rd Rifle Battalion as well. It, together with the tankers of the 169th Tank Brigade, abandoned Ivanovskii Vyselok and was forced to retreat toward Storozhevoe. The loss of the Komsomolets State Farm and Ivanovskii Vyselok seriously disrupted the system of defense on the approaches to Prokhorovka. Enemy units exploited the retreat of our units: a group of tanks from *Leibstandarte*, with Panzergrenadiers on board, using the railroad embankment to cover their left flank from the fire of our artillery in the villages along the southern bank of the Psel River, tried to push the attack to the northeast along the rail line toward Prokhorovka Station. At the same time, SS Panzergrenadier Division *Das Reich* tried to penetrate the defense in the vicinity of the Storozhevoe forest and break through to Iamki.

The commands of the 69th Army and the 48th Rifle Corps, which controlled the 183rd Rifle Division, took emergency measures. At 1440, the chief of staff of the 48th Rifle Corps headquarters sent a signals officer with a letter to Major General A. F. Popov:

> 1. The enemy with a force of up to a regiment of infantry and the support of 50 tanks, which deployed in the region of Hill 258.2, attacked and broke through the forward edge of the 183rd Rifle Division's 285th Rifle Regiment, and is developing this success in the direction of Ivanovskii Vyselok and Storozhevoe.
>
> 2. I request the assistance of a counterattack with one tank brigade. I ask you to arrange the tank brigade's jumping-off position and the time of the attack with the commander of the 183rd Rifle Division, the command post of which is situated on the southern outskirts of Krasnoe.[22]

There is a note on the document, indicating that it was received at 1620. The nearest tank formation to the crisis point was the 26th Tank Brigade. Its tanks had been dug in since 8 July on the line Mikhailovka – Stalinskoe Branch of the Oktiabr'skii State Farm, which lies a half kilometer from the railroad embankment. Having received the request from its neighbor, Major General A. F. Popov issued an order to brigade commander Piskarev to advance his brigade to Hill 241.6 – the key terrain feature in the area of the breakthrough.

Thanks to measures that had been taken, the enemy was stopped on the eastern and northeastern fringes of Komsomolets State Farm by the flanking fire of the 99th Tank Brigade, the 11th Motorized Rifle Brigade, and the 1502nd Destroyer Anti-tank Artillery Regiment from the villages situated along the left bank of the Psel River, and the 26th Tank Brigade from the vicinity of Hill 241.6. In addition, sapper battalions of the *front*'s anti-tank reserve, which was based in Prokhorovka, had mined this axis. Batteries of the Colonel V. A. Malyshkov's 27th Destroyer Anti-tank Artillery Brigade conducted fire from the region of Prokhorovka Station, Iamki, Grushki, and Storozhevoe. Units of the 169th Tank Brigade and the 15th Guards Separate Heavy Tank Breakthrough Regiment of the same 2nd Tank Corps defended Storozhevoe itself.

The tankers and motorized riflemen fought stubbornly and did not permit the SS troops to penetrate into the depths of the defense. The fighters and commanders of the 15th Guards Separate Heavy Tank Breakthrough Regiment served as an example of steadfastness and self-sacrifice. At 1330, the regiment launched a counterattack on the right flank of *Leibstandarte*'s 2nd Panzergrenadier Regiment, elements of which were advancing from Ivanovskii Vyselok toward Storozhevoe. The combat was savage and bloody. The regiment attacked repeatedly with its still operational MK IV Churchills, but Tigers were spotted at the head of the SS column. The Churchill tanks' 57mm guns were helpless against the Tigers' armor and the power of their 88mm guns. Moreover, the attacking wedge of the SS regiment had just been detected, when enemy planes appeared in the sky above it. The superiority of the enemy force was apparent.

The 15th Guards Separate Heavy Tank Breakthrough Regiment managed to delay the enemy's advance, but in doing so it suffered serious losses. It practically ceased to exist as a tank unit. Out of 12 tanks that had started the attack, only one remained operational, while five tanks had been knocked out and left abandoned on enemy-occupied territory; an additional tank went missing together with its crew. Senior Lieutenant Korol'ko, commander of the 1st Tank Battalion, was killed; 12 men were wounded, including the commander of the 2nd Tank Battalion Captain Ivanin, who received a severe concussion while riding in the tank of the acting commander of the regiment, Lieutenant Colonel Frankov.

In the process of rescuing the commander, Senior Mechanic-Lieutenant Naumov displayed courage and resourcefulness. The officer while under heavy artillery fire single-handedly managed to repair the disabled vehicle and refuel it. He drove the tank off the field of battle, and then evacuated the lieutenant colonel to the rear. For his demonstration of courage he was awarded the Order of the Red Star.[23]

Events developed less successfully for us in the bend of the Psel River – in the sector of defense of Lieutenant Colonel G. G. Pantiukhov's 52nd Guards Rifle Division. The SS Panzergrenadier Division *Totenkopf*, despite the dogged resistance of our troops, forced a crossing of the river and, after an airstrike by 80 bombers, at 1600 launched a powerful attack. The acting chief of staff of the 52nd Guards Rifle Division, Major K. N. Turiansky, reported:

> At 1800 a group of enemy submachine gunners up to a platoon in strength infiltrated the 155th Guards Regiment's forward edge of defense and broke into the trenches in a region 1.5 kilometers southeast of Kliuchi. As a result of the ensuing fighting, the group was almost completely destroyed; the remnants retreated in the direction of the woods northeast of the Oktiabr'skii State Farm.
>
> At 1830 up to one and half battalions of enemy infantry and submachine gunners conducted an attack in the direction of Kliuchi from the grove north of Prokhorovka. Crushing the defense of the 151st Guards Rifle Regiment, the adversary burst into the trenches, driving the elements of the 151st Guards Rifle Regiment's battalions to the north, and began to exploit in the direction of Veselyi.[24]

From a dispatch forwarded by the SS Panzergrenadier Division *Totenkopf*'s headquarters at 2000:

> *Gruppe* Becker after bitter fighting seized an 800-meter sector north of the branch [Author's note: A tributary flowing into the Psel River] before 1700 [1900 Moscow time]. It is advancing on Hill 226.6. *Gruppe* Baum is attacking across the branch into the woods near Kliuchi. The Russians are fleeing the bombing. The 1st Company of the Reconnaissance Battalion has blocked a retreat to the north – at

a location 1.5 kilometers south of Veselyi, and is conducting a reconnaissance of Veselyi.[25]

Fourth Panzer Army's headquarters reported in its diary, at 2030 [2230 Moscow time]:

> … In the after dinner hours, units of the SS Division *Totenkopf*, under heavy enemy artillery and mortar fire, managed to create a bridgehead 1 kilometer northwest of Pelo at Krasnyi Oktiabr'. Units of the division established contact with the 11th Panzer Division at Kochetovka."[26]

The German command made the decision to exploit this tactical success and during the night of 10 July sought to cross tanks and assault guns over the river, so that a *Totenkopf kampfgruppe*, reinforced with armor, could in the morning breakthrough the position of the 52nd Guards Rifle Division to its full depth. For this purpose it hastily reinforced the Panzergrenadiers in the bridgehead, and called up the bridging column of the II SS Panzer Corps' 680th Pioneer Regiment. Due to the Guardsmen of the 6th Guards Army, these plans were condemned to failure.

	287th Rifle Regiment	109th Separate Penal Company
Personnel	1,896 (authorized 2,244)	247 (authorized 230)
Rifles (1898-1930 models)	917	119
Carbines	84	14
Sniper's rifles	56	3
Semi-automatic Tokarev rifles	251	6
PPSh-41 SMG	260	39
Degtiarev LMG	163	12
HMG	53	-
DShK-39 12.7mm HMG	2	-
Anti-tank rifles	52	7
45mm guns	12	-
76mm guns	4	-
50mm mortars	18	3
82mm mortars	26	-
120mm mortars	8	-
Radio sets	3	-
Vehicles	6	-
Horses	209	4
Sabers	3	-

Source: TsAMO RF, f. 5 gv. A, op. 4852, d. 38, l. 72, l. 72 obr.

Table 13: Strength and Equipment of the 287th Rifle Regiment and the 109th Separate Penal Company on 24 June 1943

By 2100, a counterattack by the 151st Guards Rifle Regiment, the 52nd Guards Rifle Division's training battalion, and a company of tanks from the 245th Separate Tank Regiment had driven the SS men from the second line of trenches. Through the night, fighting continued for possession of the first line of trenches. By 0400 11 July, units of the 52nd Guards Rifle Division had managed to oust the Germans from the first trenches in the area of Kliuchi, but did not succeed in sweeping clean the river bend. SS troops stubbornly clung to the bridgehead in the area of Krasnyi Oktiabr', Kliuchi, and the southern slopes of Hill 226.6.

In some sources it is claimed that on this day, tank elements of the 5th Guards Tank Army supported the efforts of Lieutenant Colonel G. G. Pantiukhov's rifle units. Here's an excerpt from the book *Bitva pod Kurskom. Oboronitel'noe srazheniye (iul' 1943)* [*The Battle of Kursk. The defensive engagement (July 1943)*], which was prepared by a group of officers and generals of the Red Army's General Staff in 1946:

> ... An enemy group in a strength of up to an infantry regiment and 50 tanks from the area of Kliuchi (1 kilometer northeast of Krasnyi Oktiabr') crossed over the Psel River and broke through to the western slopes of Hill 226.6 (northeast of Bogoroditskoe). However, a counterattack by the [52nd Guards Rifle] division's second echelon, supported by tanks of the leading units of the 5th Guards Tank Army, which had arrived in this area on the morning of 10 July, repelled the enemy that had broken through.[27]

From the given quote it would seem that formations of General P. A. Rotmistrov's tank army had already entered the fighting at Prokhorovka on 10 July. This assertion does not correspond with the actual facts. The 5th Guards Tank Army's 18th Tank Corps, which had moved into defensive positions in the bend of the Psel River in the second echelon, was in fact prepared to render assistance to the units of the 52nd Guards Rifle Division that was defending in front of it. At 1700 10 July, Lieutenant Colonel M. K. Sinitsyn, commander of the corps' artillery group, and Colonel M. E. Khvatov, commander of the 32nd Motorized Rifle Brigade, received an order to render fire support to the infantry, in case of an enemy breakthrough, and just a half hour later, the tank brigades of the 18th Tank Corps were alerted for battle by an order of the corps' chief of staff, but the 52nd Guards Rifle Division managed to hold with its own forces. The single tank unit that took immediate part in the fighting in the bend of the Psel River at that time was the 4th Tank Company of the 6th Guards Army's 245th Separate Tank Regiment. Under the command of Lieutenant Colonel M. K. Akopov, this regiment had been subordinated to the commander of the 52nd Guards Rifle Division on the night of 9 July, and at 0600 on 10 July, it was occupying defensive positions on the northern slopes of Hill 226.6. By this time, the 245th Separate Tank Regiment had only eight American Lend-Lease tanks still operational: three M3 Stuart light tanks and five M3 Lee tanks. These tanks had all been consolidated into the 4th Tank Company. The tank regiment operated in the Psel River bend for four days,[28] including 12 July, but this fact is not noted in the 52nd Guards Rifle Division's operational documents. The tank regiment's participation in the fighting together with the 52nd Guards Rifle Division is only mentioned in an appendix to the Voronezh Front Headquarters' Operational

Summary No. 00182 at 1000 on 11.07.43 and in the regiment's own report. Probably, this is the source of the later confusion.

The command of the II SS Panzer Corps summed up the results of the day at 1925 [2125 Moscow time], when it sent a summary report to Fourth Panzer Army headquarters. Here is an extract from this document:

> The enemy is bitterly resisting on the northeastern and northern fronts (sectors), [there is] the threat of arrival of tanks and motorized infantry in the Leski – Vinogradovka – Belenikhino sector (the right flank of the corps).
>
> The SS Division 'Adolf Hitler' started the attack at 1000 [1200] from the region (sector) of Teterevino in a northeasterly direction, and at 1130 [1330] it reached the bend [in the rail line] northeast of Teterevino. At 1420 [1620] this bend was overcome, and Hill 241.6 was taken, despite fierce enemy counterattacks, primarily by tanks from the Stalinskii State Farm [a reference to the Stalinskoe Branch of the Oktiabr'skii]. Strong flanking artillery fire from the northern bank of the Psel River delayed the division's advance.
>
> The SS Division '*Totenkopf*' moved out at 1000 [1200], but failed to force a crossing of the Psel River because of heavy enemy artillery and mortar fire. At 1515 [1715] *Kampfgruppe* Becker advanced across the Psel north of Kozlovka and at 1540 [1740], it broke into the first hostile trenches. The attack is continuing with the support of ground attack aviation.
>
> The continuation of the attack is as has been foreseen [by order] on 10.07.43.
>
> It is cloudy, with scattered rain, the overall condition of the roads is satisfactory, but in places poor.[29]

By 2100 on 10 July, the intensity of fighting along the Prokhorovka axis was subsiding, but fighting in the region of Storozhevoe continued until midnight. The first day of the Prokhorovka engagement was coming to a close. What were its results? Most importantly, the forces of Voronezh Front had disrupted Hausser's plans by preventing his divisions from reaching Kartashevka and seizing Prokhorovka Station. The adversary, despite every effort, was only able to advance 2.5 to 3.5 kilometers. Nevertheless, the capture of one of the key points of the defense on the Prokhorovka axis – the Komsomolets State Farm – and the creation of a bridgehead on the northern bank of the Psel River (which permitted the start of construction of a crossing for heavy equipment) demonstrated that the enemy was still strong and had no intention to retreat from his designated objective.

It should be noted that the SS on this day did not manage to play its ace in full measure – a panzer battering ram with the support of dive bombers. SS Panzergrenadier Division *Leibstandarte* did not commit its panzer regiment into the breakthrough; only Tigers of the 13th Company and the battalion of assault guns went into action on this day. The reason for this was the narrowness of the breakthrough sector, which was further restricted by Soviet minefields – there was simply insufficient room for the tanks to deploy in the cramped space. Yet even if the tanks of the panzer regiment had been committed into the fighting, then the heavy fire of our dug-in tanks and assault guns, in combination with the engineered obstacles, would have inflicted heavy losses

	Divisions								
	6 Gds Airborne	9 Gds Airborne	13 Gds Rifle	42 Gds Rifle	66 Gds Rifle	95 Gds Rifle	97 Gds Rifle	29 AA	Total
Manpower									
Command staff	866	856	926	889	863	862	885	224	6,371
Junior command staff	2,561	2,586	2,545	2,167	2,348	2,433	1,911	483	17,034
Rank and file	5,467	5,576	5,096	4,990	5,626	5,476	6,041	1,123	39,395
Total	8,894	9,018	8,567	8,046	8,837	8,771	8,837	1,830	62,800
Equipment									
Rifles	5,410	4,985	4,197	4,622	4,350	4,720	4,884	1,273	34,441
PPSh-41	2,433	2,652	2,588	2,676	2,506	2,644	2,581	414	18,494
Light MGs	570	489	499	473	501	489	473	-	3,494
Heavy MGs	166	166	161	157	133	165	163	-	1,111
Anti-tank Rifles	256	258	236	216	219	218	263	2	1,668
Guns, all calibers	94	76	92	94	96	96	96	-	644
Mortars, all calibers	157	170	163	137	163	170	140	-	1,100
Anti-aircraft MGs	-	-	-	-	-	-	-	48	48
Anti-aircraft Guns	-	-	-	-	-	-	-	64	64
Vehicles	121	125	131	74	89	188	84	112	924
Prime movers	-	-	1	2	7	7	18	-	35
Tow vehicles	50	44	44	51	48	28	37	67	369
Horses, all	802	803	947	842	828	923	773	-	5,918

Source: TsAMO RF, f. 5 gv. A, op. 4852, l. 38, l. 53.

Table 14: Strength and Equipment of the Divisions of the 5th Guards Army on 10 July 1943

on them. SS *Totenkopf* had faced the same problems, and it had not been able to cross its armor over to the northern bank of the river. Only artillerymen and *Nebelwerfer* crews assisted the assault groups of *Totenkopf* grenadiers during the process of consolidating the bridgehead.

Fighting in the area of Ivanovskii Vyselok and in the bend of the River Psel continued beyond midnight. The commander of the 69th Army, General V. D. Kriuchenkin, was already taking urgent measures to strengthen the defenses southwest of Prokhorovka. Due to the lack of reserves, he was forced to shuffle and regroup already committed units and formations.

At 1715 10 July, Kriuchenkin passed operational control over Major General I. K. Morozov's 81st Guards Rifle Division to the 48th Rifle Corps. The division moved into positions in the second echelon along the line Hill 147.0 – Volobuevka – Sazhnoe – Krivtsovo – Shcholokovo with the assignment, while firmly holding this line, to be ready to counterattack together with the 2nd Guards Tank Corps in the direction of Belenikhino and Malye Maiachki – into the extended right flank of the II SS Panzer Corps's divisions. The 81st Guards Rifle Division was in poor condition after spending four days of the most difficult combat while encircled in the region of Staryi Gorod and Blizhniaia Igumenka (northeast of Belgorod). By the morning of 10 July, it had just fought its way out of encirclement, leaving behind all its divisional, regimental and anti-tank artillery. At 0300 on 11 July, the division numbered around 3,500 to 4,000 men.[30]

In order to strengthen the immediate approaches to Prokhorovka, the 183rd Rifle Division's 227th Rifle Regiment moved into positions on the line Storozhevoe – Vinogradovka – Zhimolostnoe with the order to cover the southern outskirts of the village and station. Major V. E. Sazhinov, commander of the 227th Rifle Regiment, remembered:

> On the afternoon of 10 July, I received an order from the division commander to withdraw the regiment with the onset of darkness to a previous sector of defense (in the Novoselovka – Kireev – L'vov – Shcholokovo area). Approximately 0200 in the morning on 11 July, having completed a 20-kilometer march, the regiment's battalions had already begun to settle into their defensive positions, when suddenly a new order arrived: to continue the march and by morning take up the defensive sector of the 285th Rifle Regiment southwest of Prokhorovka.
>
> Very little time remained, and we were compelled to move at a forced march in order to reach the position before dawn. Exerting all efforts, the regiment hastened to carry out its assigned order. Nonetheless, dawn caught us as we were approaching the 285th Rifle Regiment's sector of defense, but fortunately, there was a dense fog that morning, and a light drizzle began to fall. By 0500 on the morning of 11 July, the 227th Rifle Regiment, having completed a 28- to 30-kilometer forced march at night from the region of Sazhnoe through Shakhovo, Plota, and Novoselovka, took up a defensive position straddling the Belgorod – Prokhorovka rail line in the vicinity of the First of May State Farm, or the Stalinskoe Branch of the [Oktiabr'skii] State Farm, to the right of a projection of woods and further – the highway.[31]
>
> For support of the regiment, the division commander had created a powerful regimental artillery group (RAG), comprised of 2 *Katiusha* battalions, the division's artillery regiment, and 2 Army-level 120mm mortars. Major Sadovnikov,

> commander of the division's artillery regiment, was appointed commander of the RAG. He was a modest, intelligent, exceptional artilleryman. Even before the approach of our regiment, the artillery group had already occupied prepared firing positions, and the surrounding terrain had been well registered. [The RAG] had tremendous firepower. In addition to this support, the regiment possessed a full complement of artillery and mortars, as well as several attached anti-tank guns.[32]

However, it was extremely important to strengthen the first echelon of defense on the main axis – the Komsomolets State Farm, Hill 241.6, the Oktiabr'skii State Farm, and the northern bank of the Psel River. On the night of 10 July, this indeed became the main concern of the commanders of the 69th Army and the 2nd Tank Corps. General A. F. Popov's tank formation would have to carry out functions to which it was unaccustomed – to create a firm defense, and moreover, in the shortest time, over the course of one night. A tank corps was not adapted to carrying out the tasks of rifle divisions, but there was no other alternative. Firstly, the 2nd Tank Corps was the closest formation to this threatened area; and secondly, the 69th Army simply had no other reserves – just as the commander of Voronezh Front had exhausted all his reserves as early as 6 July. The catastrophically short amount of available time and the insufficiency of reserves – these were the determining factors in Soviet decision-making during the fighting for Prokhorovka. They were most noticeable on the night before 11 July.

The significance of the events of 11 July for the defense of Prokhorovka Station has still not been fully appreciated by military historians, because as it happens, no one

	Actual	By TO&E
Manpower	2,025	2,708
Rifles	940	1,794
PPSh-41 or PPD-40 SMG	519	344
Light MG	126	162
Heavy MG	44	54
Anti-tank rifles	43	75
45mm guns	4	12
76mm guns	3	4
50mm mortars	18	18
82mm mortars	27	27
120mm mortars	7	8
Radio sets	5	9
Vehicles	1	-
Horses	230	363

Source: TsAMO RF, f. 5 gv. A, op. 4852, d. 38, l. 70, 70 obr.

Table 15: Strength and Equipment of the 26th Guards Airborne Regiment on 24 June 1943

has undertaken a serious study of the Prokhorovka engagement. By the intensity of the fighting, its results, the quantity of troops involved, and the importance of the decisions made by the command of Voronezh Front on 11 July, this day stands out among all the days of the engagement, and only 12 July rivals it in intensity and significance.

These were very difficult hours for the Voronezh Front's leadership. Overnight, by the early dawn of 11 July it had virtually recreated two lines of defense in front of Prokhorovka Station. However, the adversary's powerful pressure compelled Vatutin and Rotmistrov to decide upon a frontal counterattack at Prokhorovka on 12 July. Preliminary steps for this counterattack were taken in the course of the evening and night of 11 July (how this was done is a separate topic of discussion), forces were regrouped, and by the end of the day through incredible efforts, Prokhorovka Station was held. All of this became the basis for continuing a successful defense and the foundation for future victory.

After yielding the Komsomolets State Farm, the defense southwest of Prokhorovka lost its previous stability. Now the tank brigades of Popov and Burdeiny had to provide the basis of the new defensive line. These combat formations from the very beginning had not been intended for holding sectors of a front; their strength lay in the main gun, speed, and maneuverability of their armored vehicles. They had a limited amount of infantry, but when constructing a defense, the rifleman is the very "brick" from which the defense is built. In addition, after the fighting of the previous days, these brigades were much diminished in tank strength.

The single fresh formation, which had a sufficient quantity of infantry, was the 2nd Tank Corps' 58th Motorized Rifle Brigade. In numbers, it was equivalent to a full-strength rifle regiment and during an attack by the corps, it fulfilled the functions of infantry – consolidating ground seized by the tanks, destroying local pockets of resistance, and protecting the tanks from infantry close assault. The weakness of the motorized rifle brigade lay in its insufficient quantity of artillery. During a corps offensive, after the initial breakthrough, the absence of sufficient artillery was scarcely felt; the tanks' own fire was often adequate. But when defending an axis vulnerable to tank attack, artillery is extremely necessary.[33]

This brigade was still on its way to Prokhorovka, and the corps commander was waiting for it impatiently. At last at 2120 10 July, the headquarters of the 2nd Tank Corps received a coded telegram from Major M. S. Sekutorov, the 58th Motorized Rifle Brigade's chief of staff: "To Koshelev. The units and elements [of the brigade] at 2100 10.07.43 have assembled in Krasnoe. The infantry needs rest after completing the march."[34]

But within forty minutes, the 2nd Tank Corps Chief of Staff Colonel V. V. Koshelev was sending Combat Order No. 136 to the subordinate brigades, and first of all to the commander of the 58th Motorized Rifle Brigade, Lieutenant Colonel E. A. Boldyrev:

> The Corps commander has ordered:
>
> 1. The commander of the 58th Motorized Rifle Brigade upon receipt of this order shall by rapid march lead the brigade to the region of Mikhailovka,

Colonel A. M. Sazonov, commander of the 9th Guards Airborne Division. (TsAMO)

Andreevka, the woods north of Storozhevoe, and Hill 245.8 and take up a defense on the lines:

a) With two battalions and two batteries of the artillery battalion on the line Vasil'evka (excl.) – Hill 241.6 – rail line;

b) With one battalion and one battery of the artillery battalion on the line railroad (excl.) – southern edge of the woods north of Storozhevoe.

Command Post – at Oktiabr'skii State Farm

2. 99th Tank Brigade on its existing line of defense – Vasil'evka – northern spur of the ravine south of Vasil'evka.

26th Tank Brigade, defending its existing line of defense: northern spur of the ravine south of Vasil'evka – Hill 241.6 – rail line.

169th Tank Brigade, defending the southern edge of the woods north of Storozhevoe, is to secure the arrival and deployment of the 58th Motorized Rifle Brigade on its indicated line of defense.

Once the 58th Motorized Rifle Brigade has taken up its line of defense, the 99th, 26th and 169th Tank Brigades are to organize strongpoints of resistance within the defensive zones of the 58th Motorized Rifle Brigade's battalions, as indicated by its commander.

3. The commander of the 58th Motorized Rifle Brigade, making full use of all available transport, is first to move the artillery, mortars, and anti-tank rifles to the line of defense, guarding them through combat security measures..

4. The defenses shall be ready by 0400 11.07.43.

5. Send reports upon the departure from the region of Krasnoe, upon arrival in the region of defense, and upon completion of occupying the defenses.

6. Command Post – western outskirts of Pravorot'.[35]

The order contains a note by Major M. S. Sekutorov: "Received at 0016 11.07.43." Thus, on the night before 11 July, the first echelon of defense southwest of Prokhorovka Station was to be headed by the commander of the 58th Motorized Rifle Brigade, Lieutenant Colonel E. A. Boldyrev. In alarm, the brigade set out at 0130 for the indicated region, which lay 15 to 17 kilometers from Krasnoe. The soldiers, exhausted from the day's march, and burdened by their weapons, ammunition and supplies, could barely shuffle their feet. They had already been on the march for three days. There was not enough transport; the available vehicles were loaded with shells and mines, and were towing artillery and mortars. All this slowed the movement. The formation had not managed to arrive fully, bring up their heavy weapons, and to dig in before the Germans launched their attack.

According to the *front* commander's order, an additional two rifle divisions of Major General I. I. Popov's 33rd Guards Rifle Corps [5th Guards Army] were committed to this area to form a second line of defense in the Psel River bend and in front of Prokhorovka. Colonel A. N. Liakhov's 95th Guards Rifle Division was to move into positions in the bend of the Psel River on the line Veselyi – Polezhaev, while Colonel A. M. Sazonov's 9th Guards Airborne Division was assigned the line Vasil'evka – Prelestnoe – Iamki. These two formations were to play a most important role on 11 and 12 July in keeping possession of Prokhorovka Station.

The first units of the 95th Guards Rifle Division began moving into their positions at dawn on 11 July and immediately began throwing up fortifications under the cover of the 52nd Guards Rifle Division and the 11th Motorized Rifle Brigade, which were

Regiment commanders of the 33rd Guards Rifle Corps of the 5th Guards Army and its command. Front row, center is Corps commander Major General I. I. Popov. To his right is the commander of the 42nd Guards Rifle Division's 136th Guards Rifle Regiment, Lieutenant Colonel M. A. Shkunov (1944 photo). (Author's personal archive)

Lieutenant Colonel V. I. Solov'ev, commander of the 95th Guards Rifle Division's 287th Rifle Regiment. (TsAMO)

positioned in front of it. From headquarters' Operational Summary No. 2 of the 287th Rifle Regiment of the 95th Guards Rifle Division at 1500 on 11 July 1943:

> 1. At 1800 [10 July] the 287th Rifle Regiment set out on the route:
>
> 1st Rifle Battalion – Krasnoe, Prokhorovka and by 0600 11.07 occupied defensive lines along the road leading from Petrovka to Prokhorovka Station. The battalion's line of defense: Petrovka – northern branch of the gully lying north of the Oktiabr'skii State Farm.
>
> 2nd Rifle Battalion – Dranyi – Mordovka – Prokhorovka – Oktiabr'skii State Farm and by 0530 11.07.43 occupied a defensive line along the road toward Mikhailovka and approaching [elevation] contour line 240.
>
> 109th [Penal] Rifle Company – Bakhteevka – Mordovka – Prokhorovka – Oktiabr'skii State Farm and occupied a defense in the region of Mikhailovka and [elevation] contour line 30.
>
> 3rd Rifle Battalion – Zeleny – Mordovka – Prokhorovka and concentrated in the area of Prelestnoe's two mills. It did not manage to assume a line of defense by dawn. Regiment headquarters and specialist subunits took position in the branches of the gully, leading from Petrovka and Prokhorovka Station. The regiment's rear has assembled in Vyshniaia Ol'shanka.[36]

As indicated in the report, the regiment had been reinforced with the 109th Separate Army Penal Company (see Table 13).

Colonel G. M. Kashpersky, commander of the 9th Guards Airborne Division's 26th Guards Airborne Regiment (1945 photo). (Author's personal archive)

The 287th Guards Rifle Regiment under the command of Lieutenant Colonel V. I. Solov'ev[37] was destined to operate in isolation from the division's main forces. According to an order from the commander of the 33rd Guards Rifle Corps, the rest of the 95th Guards Rifle Division was soon withdrawn from this sector of the defense and moved across the Psel River to the northern bank. The 287th Guards Rifle Regiment, however, took up defensive positions on the southern bank of the river – on the outskirts of the villages Andreevka, Mikhailovka, and Prelestnoe, and on the northeast outskirts of the Oktiabr'skii State Farm. To its left – on the line Oktiabr'skii State Farm to Lutovo – units of the 9th Guards Airborne Division were positioned.

The 9th Guards Airborne Division played a key role in the defense of Prokhorovka Station on 11 July. This division was the strongest formation of the 5th Guards Army (see Table 14).

Of the seven divisions in the 5th Guards Army, the 9th Guards Airborne had the most men – 9,018, and the maximum number of authorized machine guns – 170.[38] But at the same time, it had the least number of anti-tank guns – 76 (the other divisions had between 94 and 96 guns each). Therefore, in order to beef up the 9th Guards Airborne's anti-tank strength, the commander of the 33rd Guards Rifle Corps, Major General I. I. Popov attached the 301st Destroyer Anti-tank Artillery Regiment to it.

All the tank brigades of the 2nd Tank Corps had been committed to the defense, strengthening with their own tanks' main guns the fire of the anti-tank artillery. The 5th Guards Tank Army was held back for the counterattack; in connection with this decision was the growing role of artillery as the main and most effective means of struggle with the enemy's tanks. The system of artillery fire was arranged in such a way that the entire line – from the river to Lutovo – could be swept by artillery fire. On the most dangerous sector, stretching from the Oktiabr'skii State Farm to the railroad embankment, several lines of artillery were positioned.

The 9th Guards Airborne Division deployed into two echelons. In the division's first echelon, Lieutenant Colonel G. M. Kashpersky's 26th Guards Airborne Regiment dug in on a line extending from the southwest outskirts of Oktiabr'skii State Farm to Lutovo. Behind it along the road between Kartashevka and Prokhorovka Station, covering its southwestern outskirts and the slopes of Hill 252.4, was the 23rd Guards Airborne Regiment. Lieutenant Colonel Ponomarev's 28th Guards Airborne Regiment was positioned immediately to the southwest of the station itself.

The first echelon 26th Guards Rifle Regiment's line straddled the rail line and the graded road, which passed through the center of its defenses. Guards Captain D. I. Boriskin's 3rd Rifle Battalion was dug into positions on the Oktiabr'skii State Farm itself, and its sector extended across the railroad to the crest of Hill 252.2 (100 meters from the road that ran through the Stalinskoe Branch of the Oktiabr'skii State Farm), and from there down to the southwest outskirts of Lutovo. Guards Major Anikin's 1st Rifle Battalion was defending positions behind a gully running toward the road in the rear of the Oktiabr'skii State Farm. In the village of Lutovo itself, with its front facing to the south, was Guards Captain Sabirov's 2nd Rifle Battalion.[39]

The gun positions of the 9th Guards Airborne Division's artillery were positioned along the railway. The 301st Destroyer Anti-tank Artillery Regiment's 3rd and 4th Batteries stood at the fork of the roads leading to Oktiabr'skii State Farm and to its Stalinskoe Branch. The guns of the 3rd Battalion of the 7th Guards Airborne Artillery

A battalion of 122mm howitzers at Prokhorovka Station deploying to fire. (RGAKFD)

Regiment were deployed among the combat positions of the 26th Guards Airborne Rifle Regiment's 1st and 3rd Rifle Battalions. The artillery battalion's command post was set up on the eastern border of Oktiabr'skii State Farm. To the left of the 26th Guards Airborne Rifle Regiment's 3rd Battalion, among the combat positions of the 26th Guards Airborne Rifle Regiment's 2nd Battalion, was the 1st Battalion of the 7th Guards Airborne Artillery Regiment. Within the defensive belt of the 287th Guards Rifle Regiment on the sector Mikhailovka – Prelestnoe, crews of the 1st and 5th Batteries of the 301st Destroyer Anti-tank Artillery Regiment, each with four 45mm guns, were dug-in.[40]

Thus, on the 7-kilometer sector running from Prelestnoe through Oktiabr'skii State Farm to Lutovo, the 287th Guards Rifle Regiment and the 9th Guards Airborne Division had approximately 100 guns of all calibers (almost half of which were 76mm and 122mm), and more than 170 mortars. This concentration of artillery was deliberate. The Soviet command was expecting the main blow of the German attack toward Prokhorovka to fall precisely here – and they were not mistaken. However, as further events demonstrated, even this number of guns was not enough to withstand II SS Panzer Corps' panzer assault. The main attack on the immediate approaches to Prokhorovka Station on 11 July fell upon the 26th Guards Airborne Regiment (see Table 15).

As the data in the table indicates, the regiment was short of its authorized strength in combat personnel by 683 men (25%). Of the 162 light machine guns authorized by TO&E, only 126 were present on 24 June 1943, and it had only 44 of its authorized 54 heavy machine guns. Incidentally, the 45mm anti-tank gun platoon in all three rifle battalions had been reformed by this time, but had not yet received their equipment. The guns arrived at the start of the battle.

The second echelon of the defenses in front of Prokhorovka consisted of the 287th Guards Rifle Regiment, the 26th Guards Airborne Regiment, and the 227th Rifle Regiment, as well as the tank brigades of Popov's tank corps, which were positioned practically in the immediate rear of these rifle regiments. At dawn on 11 July, the headquarters of the 2nd Tank Corps received a couple of coded telegrams from the commander of the 58th Motorized Rifle Brigade:

> To Koshelev:
> Units have reached the line of defense by 0500. Heavy equipment is still being brought up. 11.07.43 Boldyrev.
>
> To Koshelev:
> The 26th Regiment of the 9th Airborne Division is digging in on the sector of the 26th Tank Brigade. I request permission to defend with one battalion in reserve. Boldyrev.[41]

The last message indicates confusion in unit deployments on the Soviet side on the morning of 11 July. It is speaking of the 9th Guards Airborne Division's 26th Guards Airborne Regiment's sector of the defense. By this time, the units of the 26th Guards Airborne Regiment were already supposed to be occupying their positions in the second echelon of the defense, some 3 to 4 kilometers closer to Prokhorovka Station – *behind* (author's emphasis) the positions of the 26th Tank Brigade on Hill 241.6. The message also suggests that the 2nd Tank Corps' 58th Motorized Rifle Brigade had not managed to reach its designated Vasil'evka – Hill 241.6 – Storozhevoe sector in time, but had dug in somewhat to the east of that line. They now occupied a defense together with the 26th Tank Brigade along the eastern spurs of the gully that runs from Andreevka to the railway, approximately 1 kilometer southwest of the road running between Mikhailovka and the railroad hut. The Germans, whose scouts were working very intensively, likely sniffed out that the defenses were still not fully ready, so they started their attack not at the customary 0400, but an hour earlier – at 0300.

The 26th Tank Brigade in the preceding days had suffered serious losses. On 8 July alone, of the 53 tanks in the brigade, 27 had been knocked out; in the course of 8 and 9 July, 150 men of the brigade had gone missing. On 10 July, the brigade had only three T-34 tanks and nine T-70 tanks still operational. At 0400 on 11 July, by order of the 2nd Tank Corps commander, the commander of the 15th Guards Separate Heavy Tank Breakthrough Regiment turned over the four remaining Churchill tanks still operational in the regiment to the 26th Tank Brigade. The crews of these tanks set up an ambush position on the Stalinskoe Branch of the Oktiabr'skii State Farm.

Thus, the first line of defense took shape somewhat further to the east than had been proposed. The 58th Motorized Rifle Brigade's 3rd Motorized Rifle Battalion was occupying positions south of Vasil'evka, on the eastern slopes of Hill 241.6, while the 2nd Motorized Rifle Battalion had dug in on the eastern slopes of the same hill closer to the highway. Tankers of the 26th Tank Brigade had dug in their tanks behind these battalions. The line of defense of the aforementioned units didn't quite extend right up to the main road leading to Prokhorovka Station; a heavily-mined anti-tank ditch filled the gap here. On its eastern side, incorporating both roads in the vicinity of the railroad hut, the 26th Guards Airborne Rifle Regiment's 3rd Battalion was dug-in, tied in with the left flank of the 287th Guards Rifle Regiment's 2nd Rifle Battalion.

These units were destined to receive the initial blow from SS Panzergrenadier Division *Leibstandarte* on the morning of 11 July, since Hausser had decided to attack precisely in the Vasil'evka – Storozhevoe sector. Wisch's *Leibstandarte* led off, because SS Panzergrenadier Division *Totenkopf* wasn't yet ready to attack; the II SS Panzer Corps' engineering units had not managed by the morning to bring up and deploy the pontoon bridge across the Psel River for *Totenkopf*'s heavy tanks to cross due to the poor road conditions and the concentrated Soviet artillery fire. Hausser declined to resume the attack north of the Psel without panzer support after the savage resistance *Totenkopf* had encountered the night before from the 52nd Guards Rifle Division.

The attacking formation of Wisch's *Leibstandarte* resembled a trident: the central and right *panzerkiel* [armored wedge] formations – battalions of the 2nd Panzergrenadier Regiment, strengthened by assault guns and a company of Tigers – were directed along the rail line across Hill 252.2 toward Prokhorovka and the Storozhevoe forest; while the left *panzerkiel* – the reinforced reconnaissance battalion – was directed against the defenses of Vasil'evka and Andreevka. *SS Oberführer* Priess was supposed to have crossed his tanks to the northern bank of the Psel River and to have seized Kartashevka by this time, thereby liquidating the threat to *Leibstandarte*'s left flank. As before, the right flank of *Leibstandarte* was being covered by *Das Reich*, which was attacking in the direction of Belenikhino Station and Storozhevoe.

★ ★ ★

Dawn arrived on the morning of 11 July. Only twenty-four hours remained until the start of the planned counterattack. However, the main question was yet to be answered: Would the forces defending Prokhorovka be able to hold the approaches to Prokhorovka Station until the next morning, and by doing so, retain a jumping-off line for Voronezh Front's main shock force, the 5th Guards Tank Army? The day before, the SS divisions, by driving back the units of the 183rd Rifle Division and the brigades of the 2nd Tank Corps had already overrun the intended jumping-off positions for the 5th Guards Tank Army's commitment into the battle. Where would our forces stop the adversary today? With just these thoughts nagging his mind, Chief of the General Staff Marshal A. M. Vasilevsky arrived at the 2nd Tank Corps' observation post at dawn.

The Corps' chief of reconnaissance E. F. Ivanovsky recalled:

> The morning of 11 July broke in relative tranquility: From time to time, guns were firing, and you could hear in the distance the rumble of an engine. The dawn was cool. An orange tint was coloring the eastern horizon.
>
> A few commanders and I had gathered at the Corps' observation post, which was situated in a trench on the outskirts of the village Pravorot'. I remember that I glanced at my watch: it was 4: 15 in the morning. I began to examine the enemy lines through the stereoscope, trying to determine what had happened on his side during the night. I took my eyes away from the scope; someone was persistently tugging at my elbow. The commander of a reconnaissance platoon, Sergeant Storozhuk, was saying something to me, falling into his native Ukrainian tongue in his excitement: 'Comrade Lieutenant Colonel! Some sort of high command has just pulled up. Look, they're coming this way ...'
>
> Two vehicles had rolled up, and several generals had stepped out of them. The one in front was a tall man, with gray hairs slipping out from beneath his field cap at his temples. He was wearing large, unfamiliar stars on his shoulder boards. I was seeing a marshal for the first time, and I didn't respond immediately. But once he had stepped up to a point in front of me, I grasped the situation, straightened up, and reported properly:
>
> 'Comrade Marshal of the Soviet Union, chief of reconnaissance of the 2nd Tank Corps Lieutenant Colonel Ivanovsky reporting.'
>
> Marshal A. M Vasilevsky shook my hand, and then asked:
>
> 'What's the situation, Comrade Ivanovsky? What's the enemy doing?'
>
> I gave him the latest information on the enemy, and then started showing him the terrain and the position of our units on a map. I imperceptibly gave a wink to Storozhuk; he understood me, and hurried off to get the corps commander.
>
> General Popov, who had laid down for a couple of hours of sleep, appeared quickly. The Marshal wanted to hear a report, so Popov began to give a formal map talk, with what seemed like academic precision. He directed the sharp tip of a pencil over the map, not touching its surface, while pointing out the directions to the north and to the south, and established that our observation post was located on the outskirts of Pravorot'.

A grin flashed across the face of the Marshal. Interrupting the general's speech with a soft gesture, he said simply:

'Your assignment, Comrade, is to hold your present line for twenty-four hours, at whatever the cost. It is anticipated that the Germans will throw his select divisions, *'Adolf Hitler'*, *'Das Reich'* and *'Totenkopf'*, into battle on this direction ... You must, I repeat, hold on. Just for twenty-four hours ... Tomorrow, things will be easier.'

Marshal Vasilevsky summoned the corps commander to one side. They took a seat amidst the rows of corn and spoke alone together for about ten minutes. General Popov later told us, 'Tomorrow Rotmistrov's 5th Guards Tank Army will attack here.'

We had already been fighting for several days, but one more blow here ... with the forces of an entire tank army! The Soviet command did have reserves – it lifted our spirits to realize this.

Marshal A. M. Vasilevsky spent about a half hour at our observation post. But no sooner had he left, when it seemed that the reigning calm literally exploded. Dive bombers attacked with their howling sirens and their death-dealing loads, and a massive artillery barrage began. That same hell, which had been raging here already in the preceding several days, unfolded across the field of Prokhorovka ... We fought over this obscure little village as if it was a major city.[42]

From the 183rd Rifle Division's Operational Summary No. 9 at 1300 on 11 July 1943:

... at 0700 in the region of Storozhevoe and the Stalinskoe Branch of the [Oktiabr'skii] State Farm, 20 to 25 enemy Ju 88 bombers escorted by a small group of fighters made a level bombing run. The same areas have continued to be attacked by groups of 10-13 Ju 88 bombers throughout the morning and early afternoon. Altogether by 1300, 250 sorties have been registered.

According to reconnaissance reports, the adversary has set up a screen on the line Kalinin, Petrovskii with units of the *'Reich'* and *'Adolf Hitler'* divisions, facing east, and is trying to break through with his main forces in the direction of Prokhorovka. The operation of up to 130 enemy tanks has been established in the region of Teterevino, Ivanovskii Vyselok, and the Komsomolets State Farm.

For the purpose of blocking the further advance of enemy infantry and tanks, the entire 227th Artillery Regiment has been deployed behind and within the defensive areas of the 2nd and 3rd Rifle Battalions of the 285th Rifle Regiment. With the exception of one battalion, which remained in the previous position, the 285th Rifle Regiment has moved into the area of Vinogradovka's outskirts and taken up defensive positions there.[43]

The offensive began before dawn. The commander of the 3rd Artillery Battalion of the 183rd Rifle Division's 623rd Artillery Regiment, then Captain S. I. Chernyshev[44] recalled:

Early on the morning of 11 July, bitter fighting erupted on the division's front, especially on the approaches to Prokhorovka. It was just beginning to get light. The observer on duty at the stereoscope came running into the dug-out and reported:

'Comrade Captain, on enemy territory between the village of Teterevino and the Komsomolets State Farm, some sort of new settlement has sprung up.'

I quickly hurried to the stereoscope. I didn't believe that the Germans overnight could have built a settlement. In 1942, taking part in the fighting for Rzhev, I knew of one case when a large church on the German side of the lines, which had been serving as a registration point for our artillerymen, had disappeared. On that same night, we hadn't heard a single explosion. What was going on now?

In reality, northeast of the village Teterevino at a distance of some 6 to 7 kilometers from our observation post, the vague outlines of some sort of structures were faintly visible through the thick shroud of morning mist. Making a quick triangulation and having pinpointed the location on the map, we established that this new settlement had appeared in an empty field – in the vicinity of a road intersection [a road running from Greznoe joins the main road to Prokhorovka in this location]. Yesterday, some fierce fighting with German tanks, trying to breakthrough to Prokhorovka, had occurred in that area.

The sun began to warm up. The mist quickly dissipated, and with it, so did our bewilderment. The contours of dozens of tanks, armored personnel carriers, and other vehicles, which stretched across the field for a whole kilometer, were now clearly revealed in the stereoscope …[45]

The enemy's main forces fell upon the flanks of the defensive position – on our left, in the region of the woods near Storozhevoe and the Stalinskoe Branch of the Oktiabr'skii State Farm, where tankers of the 169th Tank Brigade were defending together with the 3rd Battalion of the 2nd Tank Corps' 58th Motorized Rifle Brigade and the 227th Rifle Regiment of the 183rd Rifle Division; and on our right as well, in the direction of Vasil'evka and Andreevka. It was precisely the flanking fire of our artillery from Storozhevoe and the villages in the Psel River valley the day before that had created a zone of fire through which the Germans had not been able to break through to Prokhorovka, after seizing the Komsomolets State Farm. From reports of the II SS Panzer Corps:

11 July 0450 [06.50 local time]. The reinforced 2. Panzergrenadier-Regiment of the SS Panzergrenadier Division *LSSAH* under [air] cover has attacked the large forest tract lying 1.5 kilometers southwest of Iamki for the breakthrough to Prokhorovka.

… Under heavy artillery fire from hill 252.4, Prelestnoe, and Petrovka, our offensive has been stopped. [There has been] a tank counterattack from the woods 10 kilometers southwest of Prokhorovka, and an anti-tank ditch has been discovered south of the Oktiabr'skii State Farm.[46]

Major V. E. Sazhinov, commander of the 227th Rifle Regiment, later said:

The enemy didn't detect our approach and continued to lay down the usual methodical, harassing artillery and mortar fire. At approximately 7:00 in the morning, the fog dissipated and drizzling rain stopped. The enemy began to work over the front line and combat positions of our regiment with mortar and artillery fire, and at the same time, on both sides of the rail line, enemy tanks crested a hill to our front and began to crawl down its slope in our direction. I remember clearly how the tanks moved slowly, often halted, and from time to time fired their main guns. Clearly, they had not detected our well-camouflaged firing positions. Tiger tanks, which were distinctive by their size and their long gun barrels, led the attack, rolling slowly forward in a loose wedge formation, while other tanks began to appear in the intervals between them or behind them. From our observation post, Major Sadovnikov and I counted more than 140 armored vehicles, but still they were continuing to emerge from behind the hill. We still couldn't see any enemy infantry.

The regiment was frozen in anticipation and in a high state of nervous tension, but held its fire. It had been established – we would open fire only after a *Katiusha* salvo. These minutes were very tense, since although we had already taken part in many battles, none of us had ever seen with our own eyes such a large number of enemy tanks. The fact that they were not rushing forward like an avalanche, but crawling slowly – this was reassuring to us.

Soon and somehow right behind the tanks, dense lines of enemy infantry appeared. I gave the order to open fire, and Major Sadovnikov issued the order by telephone to the corresponding artillery commanders. A salvo of *Katiusha* rockets soared overhead with a howl, and immediately a hurricane of artillery and mortar fire fell upon the enemy, and raged at a maximum tempo for about five minutes from the rapid-firing of all tubes. Almost the entire slope of the hill in our front began to seethe in a thunder of explosions, which raised an enormous black cloud of dust that covered the field of battle. Here and there through this dense haze of pulverized earth, one could see the dark crimson, scattered pyres of burning tanks and the flare of *Katiusha* thermite rocket warheads [actually, the eyewitness was seeing fires caused by the massive blasts of the *Katiusha* high-explosive warheads; the *Katiusha* rockets were not equipped with thermite warheads – Author].

But now the intense concentration of fire stopped, the churning earth quickly settled, and the cloud of black and gray smoke being carried away by the breeze from our positions began to disappear. The firing from our front line started to subside. Only scattered firing points, guns and mortars continued to conduct aimed, methodical fire. The enemy infantry in this attack was literally swept away by our fire, and only pitiful, broken and stunned fragments of it disappeared over the crest of the hill together with the retreating cloud of dust.

In front of our lines, about ten tanks were burning brightly or being licked by dying flames, including several Tigers, probably after taking a direct hit from one of the shells. More than two dozen vehicles had been knocked out. The remaining tanks halted their advance and, covering each other with fire, began to back up, before retreating to their starting positions. Thus the first enemy attack had been thrown back. The regiment suffered insignificant losses, but the enemy had been dealt a serious blow. The successful repulse of this attack, which had at first seemed so menacing and frightening, gave us a serious advantage, lifted our men's spirits, and instilled a firm confidence in our own forces. For the rest of the day, the

> regiment stubbornly held on to its ground, successfully repelling another six attacks that were even heavier than the first.
>
> Two hours after the failure of the first attack, the enemy launched a second attack over the same ground on both sides of the railroad embankment. It began with an air strike and a strong barrage from mortars and heavy artillery. Around 9:00 [A.M.], up to 80 Ju 88 dive bombers attacked the large finger of woods to the left of the regiment's defensive sector and in front of the command post. In the tract of woods to our left, scattered blazes were already sending plumes of smoke into the air, and periodically a shell from an old ammo dump exploded – but there were no men or equipment there. I don't know how or by whom this sector of the forest had been set afire, but now the scattered blazes and plumes of smoke, perhaps taken as a sign of an aggregation of troops, caught the enemy's attention. The fascist planes went into their dives and furiously bombed this ruined forest, which over the span of ten to fifteen minutes received the full strike of the bombers, but did no damage to our defenses. Having dropped their bombs, the bombers flew away, but, to our regret, with no losses of their own, and on this day they didn't appear above us again. The enemy went on the attack, but was beaten back again with losses in front of our lines, though our own losses were beginning to mount.[47]

Fierce fighting developed as well on the southern bank of the Psel River. Battalions of the 11th Motorized Rifle Brigade, reinforced by the remaining tanks of the 99th Tank Brigade and two batteries of the 2nd Tank Corps' 1502nd Destroyer Anti-tank Artillery Regiment were fighting here.

A coded message from the commander of the 58th Motorized Rifle Brigade to the commander of the 2nd Tank Corps:

> To Popov. The enemy is not on Hill 252.2. [My] battalions are at sector 99 along the southern outskirts of Andreevka, Mikhailovka, the slopes of the nameless height

	Present	By TO&E
Personnel	484	667
Rifles	217	475
PPSh-41 or PPD-40 SMG	103	44
Light MG	41	51
Heavy MG	16	18
Anti-tank Rifles	5	16
50mm mortars	6	6
82mm mortars	9	9
Gas masks	361	667
Horses	31	55

Source: TsAMO RF, f. 5 gv. A, op. 4852, d. 38, l. 70, 70 obr.

Table 16: Strength and Equipment of the 26th Guards Airborne Rifle Regiment's 3rd Rifle Battalion on 24 June 1943

1.5 km southwest of the Oktiabr'skii State Farm, and sector 169. I am engaged in fighting – heavy artillery fire and a large number of [enemy] airplanes.[48]

Howitzer batteries of the 7th Guards Airborne Artillery Regiment rendered great assistance to our forward units around Storozhevoe. Their powerful blocking fire from concealed positions separated the attacking enemy infantry from the tanks. However, our rifle units plainly lacked sufficient air support. The *Luftwaffe*'s bombers swarmed over the battlefield. Sometimes groups of five to ten Soviet fighters appeared in the sky, where they would become entangled in dogfights with the covering fighters of the VIII Air Corps, but they had no real influence over the general course of events on the ground.

At 0625, the commander of I/2nd Panzergrenadier Regiment SS *Hauptsturmführer* Becker reported to regiment headquarters that his battalion had stumbled upon an anti-tank ditch, which the Russians were keeping under intense fire, and requested suppressing fire on the hostile artillery. The anti-tank ditch in front of Hill 252.2 had not been completely finished. Civilian residents of the Prokhorovka and Belenikhino districts had been assisting soldiers of the 183rd Rifle Division's 285th Rifle Regiment to construct it. However, in the middle of June, construction had started on a section of the rail line Staryi Oskol – Rzhava, and the local workforce had been transferred there. The field in front of the ditch and the defenses of the 9th Guards Airborne Division had been mined on the night of 10 July, but all these obstacles had been placed hastily, so therefore they alone were incapable of stopping the *kampfgruppe* from SS Panzergrenadier Division *Leibstandarte*. However, the anti-tank ditch and mines did slow the German advance and gave the airborne troops behind the obstacles time to prepare to receive the

Pilots of one of the fighter squadrons of the Luftwaffe's VIII Air Corps prepare for a sortie. (RGAKFD)

attack. By 0700, Colonel A. M. Sazonov's division was basically ready for battle in its combat positions.

Leibstandarte's commander, *Oberführer* T. Wisch, decided to halt the attack almost right out of the gate and to secure his flanks thoroughly. The artillery fire from Iamki and the northern bank of the Psel River had tormented his division the day before, and had prevented its further advance to Prokhorovka. Tank counterattacks, especially from the vicinities of Storozhevoe and Ivanovka, also concerned the SS division commander. Reconnaissance was reporting that the Russians had concentrated significant armored forces in this area. Therefore at 0630, the commander of *Leibstandarte*'s 1st SS Panzergrenadier Regiment, which was situated in the region of Bol'shie Maiachki, received an order: to advance toward Luchki (north) and to prepare for an attack through the woods north of Storozhevoe. Fifteen minutes later, at 0645, the commander of the 1st SS Panzergrenadier Division's reconnaissance battalion was given the assignment to cover the left flank of the division and the 2nd Panzergrenadier Regiment. The division's artillery regiment and the 55th *Werfer* Regiment received the order to concentrate their fire on the revealed firing positions of the Soviet artillery along the northern bank of the Psel.

Between 0730 and 0900, the enemy intensively worked over our positions with artillery fire and bombers. At 0905, *Obersturmbannführer* Krass' 2nd SS Panzergrenadier Regiment launched its attack on the right in concert with the reconnaissance battalion's attack on the left. Krass concentrated a company of Tigers and the bulk of his assault guns on his regiment's left flank. They were given the order to support the attack of *Sturmbannführer* Sandig's II Battalion. Companies of the regiment's I Battalion also joined the attack on the positions of the 227th Rifle Regiment.

Around 1000, Panzergrenadiers of the I SS Battalion, having shoved back the right flank of the 227th Rifle Regiment at the railroad embankment, ran into the combat outposts of the 9th Guards Airborne Division – the positions of the 26th Guards Airborne Regiment's 3rd Rifle Battalion on the approaches to Hill 252.2 and the Oktiabr'skii State Farm (3 kilometers southwest of Prokhorovka Station). The most intense and difficult moment of the defense of Prokhorovka on 11 July had begun. Just 4 kilometers lay between the forward edge of Colonel A. M. Sazonov's division and the outskirts of the station.

Aleksandr Vasil'evich Selianin, who in 1943 was a sergeant major with a signals platoon, recalls:

> After joining the division, I was sent to the 3rd Rifle Battalion of the 26th Guards Airborne Regiment as the assistant commander of the signals platoon. When I arrived, I found that there was no platoon commander, so I had to carry out his duties.
>
> We marched into Prokhorovka at 2210 [10 July] and stopped there for a short halt. Commanders were given their defensive assignments.
>
> At this time, an officer to take over the signal platoon's command showed up in the battalion from somewhere. The commander of the 3rd Rifle Battalion Guards Major D. I. Boriskin ordered me to turn over command of the signals platoon immediately and to take command of a platoon of submachine gunners in the 9th Rifle Company. Without waiting for me to reach the platoon and formally take

command of it, Boriskin told me that he was assigning my new platoon to join the regiment's forward outposts, and took me to the regiment commander, Lieutenant Colonel G. M. Kashpersky to receive the assignment.

After getting the orders, we returned to the battalion, where Boriskin began to form a platoon for me from among the men of the 9th Rifle Company. He knew the men well and personally called out the names of the experienced and reliable soldiers and sergeants. My platoon was strengthened with two anti-tank rifles, a Maxim heavy machine gun, and a light machine gun. Altogether, I had 32 men under my command.

Boriskin gave us our order:

'Comrades! You have been assigned to combat security. Your task is to prevent German scouts from infiltrating the forward edge of our defenses. Remember Order No. 227. Not a step back! Do not pull back without an order!'

We took up our positions. I placed one of the anti-tank rifles and the Maxim heavy machine gun on the right flank, the other anti-tank rifle and the light machine gun on the left flank, and in the center – the submachine gunners and the platoon's own light machine gun. They connected me with the battalion command post. The night was quiet. In the distance, gleaming illumination rockets soared into the night sky, and [there were] the rare distant reports of artillery firing. By dawn we were fully entrenched, and had carefully camouflaged our positions.

The bright, sunny morning of 11 July arrived. We had excellent visibility of the terrain in front of us out to a considerable distance.

At 7 o'clock (I was wearing a watch), I spotted a group of calmly walking German submachine gunners, about 40 men. Plainly, it was a reconnaissance party. They were heading toward us, but because of the bushes they didn't see us. I decided not to give our position away prematurely, but to let them approach a little closer, before wiping them out in our ambush. I gave the order to get ready for battle. I reported the situation to the battalion commander. As the Germans moved closer, D. I. Boriskin and even G. M. Kashpersky called me several times and asked me why I hadn't opened fire yet. But I waited until the Germans had passed the bushes concealing our position, and barked the order: 'Fire!'

The Germans immediately returned fire and charged us. Not a single German tried to turn around and run or to surrender. The Germans were completely wiped out. I reported about this to the battalion commander.

At 0930 I saw a second group of German submachine gunners, about company strength, also moving forward calmly, but about 400-500 meters to our right. The Germans were heading toward the right flank of our battalion. I contacted the battalion commander about this. As soon as the Germans had reached the line of our trenches, I ordered the Maxim heavy machine gun to open fire. The Germans dropped to the ground. Pinned down by the machine gun, they were plastered by the fire of our artillerymen and mortar men. The entire group was destroyed. During this battle, for the first time the Germans opened return fire from guns and mortars on our positions, but their fire missed us. I phoned the battalion commander and reported the results of this action.

At 1030, I spotted German tanks and several armored personnel carriers with infantry aboard moving toward us, followed by a line of submachine gunners. The tanks were moving in two groups. One group (up to 10 tanks), to our left, was moving toward the Oktiabr'skii State Farm, while the second group (more than 10 tanks) to our right was advancing upon the boundary between our battalion and our neighbor to the right. I reported on my observations to the battalion commander. The German tank attack was accompanied by artillery and mortar fire. German planes appeared in the sky above us, and in one group after another they bombed the forward edge of our defenses. We could watch as the bombs were released from the planes above us and flew in the direction of the battalion's trenches and the workers' settlement of the Oktiabr'skii State Farm. They didn't bomb us. Our artillery and mortars opened fire on the German tanks and motorized infantry. Two tanks were knocked out in the left-hand group, in the right group – four tanks, and several of the armored personnel carriers. We also fired at the tanks and infantry. They reported to me that the tank-hunting team with the anti-tank rifle on the right flank knocked out one of the tanks. The Germans retreated. We remained in place.

After this, the Germans sent out another reconnaissance party, approximately a platoon of submachine gunners. Now the Germans were advancing in short rushes, making use of available cover. They were moving directly toward my position. I signaled the battalion commander about this, and asked for a mortar barrage on the Germans, so as not to reveal our own positions. The mortar men were on target and killed many of the Germans, but the survivors able to do so continued to advance stubbornly and were wiped out by machine gun and submachine gun fire literally

An anti-tank rifle team of the 9th Guards Airborne Division's 26th Guards Airborne Regiment in action southwest of Prokhorovka Station, 11 July 1943. (RGAKFD)

within 40 meters of our trenches. I reported to the battalion commander about the results of the fighting. He inquired about our losses. I reported that we had no losses. He congratulated me, and then informed me that there were heavy losses in the rifle companies of the battalion from the German bombing and the artillery and mortar fire from the area of Hill 252.2.[49]

At about 1030, *Leibstandarte*'s I/2nd Panzergrenadier Regiment seized part of the anti-tank ditch south of Hill 252.2 and began to assault the height. Sappers of its 1st Company began to clear passages through the minefield for the following armored vehicles. Observing the course of the battle, *Oberführer* Wisch decided that the turning point was at hand, and gave the order to the commander of the division's panzer group, *Sturmbannführer* J. Peiper[50] to advance to the front in the sector of I Battalion. Peiper's group was the shock force of Wisch's formation; it consisted of III/2nd Panzergrenadier Regiment mounted in armored personnel carriers, and II/1st Panzer Regiment under the command of *Sturmbannführer* M. Gross.[51]Around noon, this armored group moved up to the anti-tank ditch and began passing over it on a crossing laid by the sappers. As the armored group crossed the ditch, Hill 252.2 and the Oktiabr'skii State Farm were undergoing intense bombing.

From the 2nd Tank Corps commander's Combat Report No. 103 at 1300 on 11 July to the commander of the 69th Army:

Between 1225 and 1250, enemy aviation, up to 80 planes, bombed the combat formations of the Corps' units.

... 2. Units of the Corps are stubbornly defending their current line, experiencing heavy losses from enemy tanks and aviation.

...4. I request the immediate assistance of fighter and bomber aviation, and the tanks of the 2nd Guards Tank Corps.[52]

The air strike, requested in the above report, was instead delivered by the VIII Air Corps at the request of *Leibstandarte*'s command. It worked over the positions on Hill 252.2 and around the Oktiabr'skii State Farm methodically and intensively. It was clear – a new attack was being prepared. The bombing was very heavy. But as soon as the Junkers and Messerschmitts flew off, the Soviet artillery guns came to life again.

W. Roes, a *Sturmmann* (Lance-Corporal) in SS Panzergrenadier Division *Leibstandarte*'s 1st Panzer Regiment and a participant in the engagement recalled:

As concerns the defensive works ... They were ... powerful ... Our Stukas could only destroy the dug-in tanks from the rear. This was completely unexpected for us. We had never encountered such defensive works before, but we faced them here.

There were real professionals there. They behaved sensibly, but there were also those who simply lacked training, who ran around chaotically among our tanks. We simply shot them down like rabbits. That's why you had such losses. We didn't count up the enemy's losses; everywhere, we saw a multitude of wounded and dead infantry, and the burned bodies of tankers. These were good tankers ... in a leather uniform. This was the single drawback, because when the tank burned,

> their uniforms caught fire as well. Burning tankers leaped from their tanks, rolled around on the grass and died all the same. The things we saw – it was terrible.[53]

The next attack began at 1300. The SS commanders not only pushed their armor forward by 1.5 – 2 kilometers, but also their moved up their field artillery. Airborne veterans recalled that at this time, they could watch from their positions as the Germans unloaded artillery shells and mortar shells directly on the ground, preparing to give direct support to their tanks from exposed positions within the panzer formations. Such insolence on the part of the enemy didn't go unpunished. The commander of the 3rd Airborne Rifle Battalion, D. I. Boriskin, having obtained the coordinates of the enemy's batteries from the combat outposts, passed them along to divisional headquarters. The artillery regiment's howitzer batteries did not delay with their response, and accurately blanketed the enemy positions with fire.

Major V. E. Sazhinov remembered:

> It seems around the fifth attack (I don't remember clearly), but it was already in the afternoon, the enemy put great pressure on the left flank of our regiment, which was defended by Captain Katantsev's 2nd Rifle Battalion. Seven enemy tanks with submachine gunners penetrated in the area of the 5th (or 4th) Company's defense. Their path was blocked by Junior Lieutenant Ukhnalev's tank-hunters. Artillerymen laid down a dense wall of blocking fire. A company of submachine gunners from the reserve launched a counterattack. Junior Lieutenant Ukhnalev was an example of real courage and valor in this fight. He leaped aboard one enemy tank and tossed two grenades into an open hatch, leaped off, but didn't have time to run away before the powerful explosion. The tank's crew was wiped out by the grenades and the tank's onboard ammunition exploded, but Ukhnalev was seriously wounded. The assault detachment of enemy submachine gunners was destroyed by the fire of the 2nd Rifle Battalion and the counterattack of the submachine gun company, and the situation in the sector was restored.
>
> We managed to take no prisoners, but the enemy left behind more than 50 dead on this narrow sector. In the majority of soldiers' booklets, taken from the dead, were notes indicating that they belonged to the *Das Reich* Panzer Division, but a few of the booklets showed membership in the *Adolf Hitler* Panzer Division. It was now clear that the *Das Reich* and *Adolf Hitler* Panzer Divisions were in front of the regiment's sector of defense. This conclusion was later confirmed by prisoners' statements and other documents.[54]

At approximately 1330, Peiper's panzer group with the support of grenadiers from the I Battalion reached the crest of Hill 252.2 along the railroad embankment and hurled the defending battalions of the 26th Guards Airborne Regiment back to the elevation's eastern slopes. After seizing the crest of Hill 252.2, the SS force pivoted to the north and attacked the Oktiabr'skii State Farm. Almost simultaneously, the line of the 287th Guards Rifle Regiment's 2nd Battalion buckled under the attack of *Leibstandarte*'s reconnaissance battalion. Because of the inept leadership of this rifle battalion's commander, it began a disorderly retreat to the village of Prelestnoe, opening a path to the swampy basin of the Psel River around the villages of Prelestnoe and Petrovka. Panzergrenadiers of the reconnaissance battalion and Tigers of the 13th Company advanced through the crumpled right-flank of the disintegrating 2nd Battalion in the direction of the Oktiab'rskii State Farm and the two villages beyond it. The boundary between the 287th Guards Rifle Regiment and the 26th Guards Airborne Regiment disappeared into a quickly expanding gap, and the 3rd Battalion of Kashpersky's 26th Guards Airborne Regiment was caught in the closing pincers of Peiper's panzer group and *Leibstandarte*'s reconnaissance battalion. From Combat Dispatch No. 49 from the Headquarters of the 9th Guards Airborne Division at 1500:

> 1. Enemy aviation in groups of 15-20 planes at 20-30 minute intervals is bombing the division's defenses. The main attack is falling upon Hill 252.4, Barchevka, Oktiabr'skii State Farm, and Hill 252.2.
> 2. The enemy has attacked the forward edge of the 3/26th Airborne Rifle Regiment [the strength and equipment of the 3rd Rifle Battalion of the 26th Guards Airborne Rifle Regiment are shown in Table 16] three times in up to battalion strength with the support of 6-7 tanks. All the attacks were repelled, and 6 tanks were knocked out. At 1400 up to 30 tanks and up to a regiment of infantry attacked for the fourth time in the direction of 3/26th Airborne Rifle Regiment (Oktiabr'skii State Farm). Taking advantage of superiority in force, the enemy seized the Oktiabr'skii State Farm.
>
> The division commander has decided to concentrate all of the division's artillery fire on the attacking enemy units, and restore the situation with a counterattack by 2/26th Airborne Rifle Regiment and the 23rd Airborne Rifle Regiment. The 28th Airborne Rifle Regiment is to be ready to support the attack of the 23rd Airborne Rifle Regiment in the direction of the Machine Tractor Station, Lutovo, and Hill 252.2.
> 3. The 26th Airborne Rifle Regiment is experiencing an ammunition shortage, and resupply is being delayed. Ammunition is being gathered from the fallen. I have issued an order to reduce the 28th Airborne Rifle Regiment's ammunition allotment and transfer it to the 26th Airborne Rifle Regiment.[55]

It should be noted that a most important factor, which contributed to the SS troops' rapid overcoming of the anti-tank ditch and their tanks' breakthrough to the Oktiabr'skii State Farm was a number of mistakes made by the 9th Guards Airborne Division commander A. M. Sazonov in setting up the anti-tank defenses as his forces hastily moved into position in the hours before the SS attack. Firstly, in contradiction to army commander A. S. Zhadov's orders, Sazonov did not throw out an outpost screen or bring up the division's artillery to Prokhorovka as the first order of business, so as to create an operational, strong anti-tank barrier even before the arrival of his division's main forces. The artillery of the 9th Guards Airborne Division began moving into position at the same time as the rifle units, after midnight, even though significantly more time is required to organize the fire of artillery battalions, than, for example, for a rifle battalion. Secondly, the headquarters of the division and the division commander himself failed to look into the operational situation, did not recognize all the danger of the German build-up in front of his line of deployment, and gave Colonel V. K. Valuev, commander of the Division's 7th Guards Airborne Artillery Regiment, an order that would be difficult to call anything other than nonsensical.

Instead of an echeloned artillery position on a tank-vulnerable sector between the Oktiabr'skii State Farm and the rail line, two battalions (the 2nd Battalion of the 7th Guards Airborne Artillery Regiment and the 10th Guards Separate Destroyer Anti-tank Artillery Battalion) were placed in reserve in the region of the village of Kusty. Instead, only Senior Lieutenant Svinukhin's 3rd Battalion of the 7th Guards Airborne Artillery Regiment was deployed on this line, in the direct path of the main attack of Wisch's division, and it was given the following assignment: to set up both batteries with their guns facing the railroad (in the opposite direction from the anti-tank ditch), and in case of the appearance of an enemy armored train, to destroy it. I will stress that not once during the entire period of the enemy's offensive did the Germans even try to use this archaic form of armor. To this it must be added that the 3rd Artillery Battalion deployed at night, in unfamiliar terrain, without any reconnaissance, and the crews selected a poor position – on the reverse slopes of Hill 252.2 approximately 400-500 meters in the rear of the infantry trenches. Therefore when the SS began to cross the ditch and their tanks began to overrun the infantry's trenches, Svinukhin's artillerymen simply didn't see them. The barrels of their guns were pointed in the opposite direction. Meanwhile the first three hostile attacks were driven back only by the 26th Airborne Regiment's own battalion and regimental artillery. A battalion of the 9th Airborne Division's artillery regiment – that is to say, the 3rd Battalion of the 7th Guards Airborne Artillery Regiment – fully engaged Peiper's panzer group only after it had overrun the first line of the paratroopers' trenches and was moving toward the Oktiabr'skii State Farm.

The State Farm changed hands several times. Its defense, consisting of the 3rd Rifle Battalion of the 26th Guards Airborne Rifle Regiment together with the 3rd Artillery Battalion of Senior Lieutenant Svinukhin (who was killed later in October 1943 on the Dnepr River) and Major Bugaev's 1st Artillery Battalion of the 95th Guards Rifle Division's 233rd Guards Artillery Regiment, which had been brought up to localize the breakthrough, received the enemy's main assault. The airborne artillerymen repelled several extremely strong tank attacks, during which many of the crew members were killed. The 3rd Artillery Battalion's observation post was set up on the eastern outskirts of the State Farm together with the command post of the 3rd Battalion of the 26th Guards Airborne Rifle Regiment, while its headquarters was on the State Farm's northern edge. Guards Senior Lieutenant I. Ustinov's 7th Battery was set up for firing over direct sights to the left of the State Farm; Guards Senior Lieutenant's I. Dmitrievsky's 8th Battery – to the left of and behind the 7th Battery; and the 9th Battery – to the right of and behind the 7th Battery, in a concealed position in a ravine north of the State Farm.

Here is how Guards Lieutenant A. A. Obisov, the chief of reconnaissance for the 3rd Airborne Artillery Battalion, described the fight (at that moment he was in the 7th Battery's firing position):

> A wedge formation of more than 100 armored vehicles attacked the battery, slowly emerging from behind a hillock to the right of the designated direction of fire. Heavy Tiger tanks and self-propelled guns were moving in front, behind them were medium tanks and armored personnel carriers.

> Suddenly a wall of blocking artillery fire erupted in front of the armored armada. It was the 9th Battery beginning to support us from its concealed firing position. The commander of the 8th Battery's fire direction platoon, Senior Lieutenant Vladimir Romashin (who was killed on the Dnestr in April 1944) adjusted the fire from the forward observation post. The 7th Battery allowed the tanks to approach a little closer, in order to shoot with certainty of scoring a hit, and opened fire. The hollow became clouded with dust and smoke.
>
> The tanks halted 300 meters from our battery, while the Panzergrenadiers withdrew behind the hillock. The cruel duel in the hollow lasted for more than two hours. In this combat, the 7th Battery, which fired more than 200 shells at the enemy, heroically died almost to the last man. Only a few men, who remained alive, continued to defend the ground of their smashed guns with anti-tank grenades. Twelve to fifteen tanks and self-propelled guns were burning on the field of battle.
>
> Much later, already after the liberation of Poltava, I learned that the commander of the 9th Battery, Guards Senior Lieutenant Kronin and the fire direction platoon with several wounded men were taken prisoner at the Oktiabr'skii State Farm. The fascists shot Kronin. The commander of the 9th Battery's fire direction platoon, Lieutenant Dmitrii Lobazov, who was wounded when he was captured, told me about this – we found him [Lobazov] in a hospital after the liberation of Poltava.[56]

According to the Operational Summary No. 45 from the artillery headquarters of the 9th Guards Airborne Division, on 11 July 50 men among the junior officers and the rank and file went missing in action, four 76mm guns and seven vehicles were destroyed, and two horses were killed. The document also states that among the missing were the commander of the 9th Battery, Guards Senior Lieutenant Dubravny, and the commander of the fire direction platoon of this battery, Guards Lieutenant Lobazov. But the Operational Summary No. 48 for 12 July informs us that a Red Army man Stepanov, from the 3rd Battalion's fire direction platoon, who went missing in action on 11 July, managed to escape his captors.[57]

Unfortunately, I have not been able to establish clearly who actually was in command of the 9th Battery – whether Guards Senior Lieutenant Kronin or Guards Senior Lieutenant Dubravny. Meetings and discussions with many veterans of the war persuade me that in such matters they are rarely mistaken. Obisov testified that Guards Senior Lieutenant Kronin was in command of the 9th Battery. At the same time, however, one shouldn't ignore official documents, and the just cited operational summaries maintain that Senior Lieutenant Dubravny was commanding the battery. As the participants in this action have said, the artillerymen fought stubbornly and courageously. Let the names of these people remain as part of the history of the Prokhorovka engagement. The precise post they were occupying then is much less important.

The 9th Battery, which was equipped with Model 1931-1937 122mm howitzers, fired from concealed positions, laying down a so-called blocking fire pattern in front of the forward edge of the defense. It was impossible to pass through this zone of fire without losses. One of the howitzer's 25-kilogram fragmentation shells was capable of destroying everything living within a 40-meter wide, 8-meter deep area. The 9th Battery lent great assistance to the other two batteries of the battalion, which were destroying tanks over open sights at a distance of several hundred meters from their 76mm guns.

Trying again and again to break through to Prokhorovka, the SS troops were no longer using such massed panzer attacks, as they had while breaking through the *front*'s main defensive belt. The adversary was seeking out weaknesses in our defense and was attacking in groups of 25 – 60 tanks, supported by Panzergrenadiers. These attacks were being repulsed by resisting units and battalions, supported by artillery.

Unfortunately, no centralized direction over the attached artillery units was set up on the approaches to Prokhorovka. This prevented the flexible adjustment of fire in accordance with the changing situation: to concentrate it on a dangerous axis in time; to shift it in a timely fashion to a different target; or when necessary, to change the position of the artillery itself.

This shortcoming undoubtedly affected the durability of the defense in the region of Prokhorovka. In addition, the important sector between the river and the rail line was being defended by the 287th Guards Rifle Regiment (and the attached 109th Separate Penal Company) of the 95th Guards Rifle Division, the major portion of which was concentrated on the other side of the river, and the 26th Guards Airborne Rifle Regiment of Colonel A. M. Sazonov's 9th Guards Airborne Division, the bulk of which was located on the other side of the railroad. In essence, no one was responsible for the boundary between the two divisions. This flaw in the defenses, as further events would demonstrate, would lead to grave consequences.

Thus, for example, a detached artillery battalion of the 2nd Tank Corps' 58th Motorized Rifle Brigade, which by happenstance found itself southeast of the Oktiabr'skii State Farm, helped the airborne troops repel one of the strong enemy tank attacks (made by an element of Peiper's *kampfgruppe*) along the rail line to Prokhorovka. Lieutenant Colonel Boldyrev's 58th Motorized Rifle Brigade had been the first to meet the attacking units of the SS Panzergrenadier Division *Leibstandarte* at dawn that morning. The motorized riflemen played an important role on this day, and many of them fell in the severe fighting.

From a dispatch from the chief of the political department of the 58th Motorized Rifle Brigade, dated 12 July:

> After completing a 200-km march, the brigade went into action at 0600 on 11.07.43. Over the twenty-four hours of combat operations, the brigade, according to preliminary data, has the [following] losses in dead, wounded, and missing in action: in the 1st Battalion – 300 men; in the 2nd Battalion – 150 men; and in the 3rd Battalion – 24 dead, 53 wounded, and 39 missing in action, for a total of 116 men. In the artillery battalion, 31 men are dead, wounded, or missing in action. Altogether, the brigade has lost 597 men.
>
> Losses in equipment: 76mm guns – 3; GAZ trucks – 3; personal weapons – 200.
>
> The brigade's forces have knocked out or destroyed approximately 40 tanks, of which 16 were Tigers, 2 vehicles, a company of infantry, and approximately 50 submachine gunners of the enemy.
>
> In this combat, the artillery battalion's Komsomol organizer, Party member and gun layer Sergeant Borisov particularly distinguished himself, knocking out 7 tanks of the Tiger type from his own gun.[58]

The artillerymen of the brigade's separate destroyer anti-tank artillery battalion of 76mm guns was late in reaching its indicated line, and was hurrying along the road from Prokhorovka Station in the direction of the Komsomolets State Farm (through the lines of the 1st Battalion of the 26th Guards Airborne Rifle Regiment), when it collided with almost 20 German tanks that had already overrun the line of the 26th Guards Airborne Rifle Regiment's 3rd Battalion and were advancing on the positions of the 1st Battalion. The 19-year-old Komsomol organizer Mikhail Borisov on this day found himself in the 3rd Battery, which was commanded by Senior Lieutenant Pavel Azhippo. The artillery battalion had the order to advance to the region of the Komsomolets State Farm, but it was behind schedule, when suddenly at the head of the column they spotted the tanks – the command rang out: "Prepare for battle!"

Nineteen tanks were advancing on the battery. During the ensuing fighting, the crew of one of the guns, which was standing beside the graded road, was killed. M. Borisov rushed to the gun. The sergeant was a gun layer by training, so therefore he could handle aiming the gun without any difficulty. The first tank erupted in flames at medium range, the second and third – quite near the gun's firing position.

The combat of artillerymen and anti-tank gunners was always marked by particular desperation. The gun crew and the tank crew, when entering into a close engagement, recognized that one of them was fated to perish. Either you destroy the tank, or it will crush you together with your gun into the earth. Not infrequently, the first tank shell plastered the entire gun crew – the German optical sights, which equipped the tanks,

A gun layer fires a ZIS-3 76mm anti-tank gun at the enemy in the area of Prokhorovka Station. (RGAKFD)

Hero of the Soviet Union Lieutenant (at the time of the battle a sergeant) M. F. Borisov, who in one action on 11 July 1943 knocked out seven German tanks (1945 photo). (Author's personal archive)

were distinguished by their high quality. In this case, a single artilleryman managed alone to stand out in a most desperate struggle and to knock out seven tanks!

During the repulse of this attack, the entire battery under the command of Senior Lieutenant Pavel Azhippo distinguished itself. Of the 19 advancing tanks, 16 were knocked out – a very high result. After M. Borisov knocked out his seventh tank, the enemy tankers concentrated all their fire on his gun. After several minutes, one shell demolished the gun and knocked the sergeant unconscious. From the observation post of the 1st Battalion of the 58th Motorized Rifle Brigade, which was located in the village of Iamki, corps commander Major General A. F. Popov was observing the duel. At his order, Mikhail Borisov was picked up by a vehicle and brought to a hospital in the village of Chernianka. His concussion was light, and after several days he was already back in action. For this feat, Senior Sergeant M. F. Borisov was awarded the title Hero of the Soviet Union.

Parallel with Peiper's *kampfgruppe*, which was storming the Oktiabr'skii State Farm from the rail line through its western and southwestern outskirts, *Leibstandarte*'s II/2nd Panzergrenadier Regiment broke into the northern part of the State Farm together with a company of Tigers and a battalion of self-propelled guns. Several hundred grenadiers with the support of the heavy tanks attacked the left flank of the 287th Guards Rifle Regiment, crushed it, and burst into Petrovka. The 2nd Battalion of the 287th Guards Rifle Regiment fell directly under this attack. In a dispatch from Lieutenant Colonel Solov'ev it is indicated that the battalion was driven from its line during an attack by 80 enemy tanks and communications with it were lost. In other words, the battalion

The Victory Memorial on the Prokhorovka Field erected on Hill 252.2, 2 kilometers southwest of Prokhorovka. The memorial opened on 3 May 1995.

The location of the SS Division *Totenkopf's* crossing over the Psel River in the vicinity of the hamlet of Kliuchi. The photograph was taken from the right, Soviet-held bank of the river.

The bend in the Psel River. The photograph shows the opposite, higher bank of the river, which was being defended by Soviet troops and below it the swampy river basin across which the SS troops attacked.

A panoramic view of Hill 252.2 from the right bank of the Psel River at Polezhaev, where elements of the SS Division *Totenkopf* attempted to recross the river and attack the flank of the 18th Tank Corps on 12 July 1943.

A memorial marker in honor of the troops of the 95th Guards Rifle Division, which fought in the bend of the Psel River, on the eastern slopes of Hill 226.6. Erected by veterans of the division in May 1985.

A panoramic view from the Komsomolets State Farm of the positions held by the 183rd Rifle Division's 285th Rifle Regiment. In the distance Hill 258.2 is visible; below it to the right is an overgrown branch of the Molozhovaia ravine. The line of trees climbing the slope to the left marks the right-of-way of the Iakovlevo – Prokhorovka road.

The view of the Vasil'evka and Andreevka area, marked by the buildings in the mid-ground, from the Komsomolets State Farm.

A German artilleryman's panoramic view of the Oktiabr'skii State Farm on the high ground in the distance from the eastern slopes of Hill 241.6, where firing emplacements of SS Division *Leibstandarte Adolf Hitler*'s artillery regiment were located.

The view from the same vantage point on Hill 241.6, now looking to the left toward the bend in the Psel River and the higher ground beyond, where Soviet forces were defending.

All that remains of the Soviet anti-tank ditch, 500 meters southwest of Hill 252.2, which SS Division *Leibstandarte Adolf Hitler*'s 2nd Panzergrenadier Regiment struggled to cross on 11 July 1943. In the distance is the upper portion of the Victory Memorial on Prokhorovka Field, which marks the summit of Hill 252.2.

Another view from Hill 241.6, where on 12 July 1943 the observation post for SS Division *Leibstandarte Adolf Hitler* was located. In the background on the right is the monument marking Hill 252.2, and on the left are buildings of the Oktiabr'skii State Farm.

The area of Storozhevoe: the hamlet itself is out of view on the left. The road in the foreground leads through Storozhevoe to the railroad crossing on Hill 252.2. In the background is the balka that runs through the Storozhevoe woods and extends toward the southern outskirts of Prokhorovka.

An echo of the past war: A Soviet anti-personnel RDG-33 grenade, found in the Storozhevoe woods on 17 April 2010.

A fraternal grave of Soviet troops in Storozhevoe.

The "corridor" between the Storozhevoe woods (on the left) and the belt of woods along the railroad, which a group of tanks from the 32nd Tank Brigade under the command of Major S. P. Ivanov used to break through to the Komsomolets State Farm on 12 July 1943.

A panoramic view of Hill 252.2 from the Stalinskoe Branch of the Oktiabr'skii State Farm.

First of a small group of photographs, taken by author Valeriy Zamulin from the top of the Victory Memorial on Hill 252,2, which rises 47 meters above the ground. This view is looking to the southwest across the lower slopes of Hill 252.2.

Another view from the top of the Victory Memorial. In the foreground is the railroad bed in the area of Hill 252.2. Beyond the field behind the wooded belt along the railroad are the Storozhevoe woods. The field is the "corridor" used by elements of the 32nd Tank Brigade to slip through the German defenses to the Komsomolets State Farm on 12 July 1943. Remember, this photo was taken from the top of the Victory Memorial, so the wooded belt along the railroad would have obscured the view of the corridor from Hill 252.2.

A third view from the top of the Victory Memorial, looking generally to the southwest from Hill 252.2: In the mid-ground, offset to the left, is the railroad crossing; the road running from it to the right leads to Prelestnoe. The road angling from it to the left into the trees in the distance leads to the Stalinskoe Branch of the Oktiabr'skii State Farm and the village of Storozhevoe. In the background, running parallel to the road to Prelestnoe, is a belt of trees marking the former anti-tank ditch. It connected with the Prokhorovka-Iakovlevo road, which ran alongside the railroad.

Panoramic view of the Oktiabr'skii State Farm from the top of the Victory Memorial on Hill 252.2.

In the center of the photo is the deep ravine on the eastern edge of the Oktiabr'skii State Farm (out of view to the left) that drains toward the Psel River. In the distance is the village of Beregovoe.

The main road to Prokhorovka: view from Hill 252.2 in the direction of the Komsomolets State Farm and Iakovlevo. Prokhorovka is in the opposite direction.

The author, V. N. Zamulin, with an RDG-33 anti-personnel grenade found on 29 September 2009 in a rifle pit together with the remains of a soldier of the 9th Guards Airborne Division during archeological excavations on Hill 252.2.

Members of search teams from Belgorod and Staropol'skii, pictured extracting a portion of a T-34/76 tank turret from the earth of Hill 252.2 on 29 September 2009.

Ammunition found during archaeological diggings on Hill 252.2 in September 2009. In the foreground is a shell from a German 158mm six-barreled rocket launcher.

A monument to Soviet tankers and artillerymen – the first monument erected on the Prokhorovka tank field, 12 July 1973.

The armor display field on Hill 252.2, adjacent to the Victory Memorial, as seen from the top of the memorial. The outskirts of Prokhorovka are visible in the distance.

A view from the eastern base of Hill 252.2, showing the field crossed by the brigades of the 5th Guards Tank Army's 29th Tank Corps in their attack on 12 July 1943. Among the trees in the distant background are buildings on the outskirts of Prokhorovka and the 29th Tank Corps' jumping-off positions.

The southwestern outskirts of Prokhorovka: in the foreground is the elevated roadway at the brick factory, over which on the morning of 12 July 1943 the brigades of the 29th Tank Corps rolled into their jumping-off positions.

View toward the hamlet of Shipy from the village of Rzhavets. In the foreground is the overgrown channel of the Northern Donets. In the background is the hill held by defending troops of the 69th Army and 5th Guards Tank Army.

Panoramic view of the heights overlooking the overgrown channel of the Northern Donets River, as seen from the center of Rzhavets.

The road leading toward Prokhorovka from Rzhavets. In the distance is the area of the 6th Panzer Division's staging area on the morning of 12 July 1943.

In the center of the photo are remnants of the wooden bridge in the village of Rzhavets, over which *kampfgruppen* of the III Panzer Corps crossed to the right bank of the Northern Donets River.

View of the vicinity of the German crossing of the Northern Donets River in the village of Rzhavets and the heights rising above the opposite bank.

The monument in the center of Shakhovo to the Soviet troops who fell in the Battle of Kursk.

A T-34/76 is being moved into a new wing of the Prokhorovka Battlefield State Museum, where it is now on display, 30 July 2009.

The Military Museum in Prokhorovka.

The Church of the Holy Apostles Peter and Paul, built in memory of the Soviet soldiers who fell at Prokhorovka. Consecrated on 3 May 1995 by the Patriarch of Moscow and All Russia Aleksii II.

was scattered by superior German forces, and its companies fell back to the northern outskirts of Prelestnoe, while the enemy's main forces lunged toward Petrovka.

At this time, a topographical platoon and the remnants of the 3rd Battalion of the 7th Guards Artillery Regiment were leaving the Oktiabr'skii State Farm, heading toward Prelestnoe. The assistant commander of the topographical platoon, V. Utkin recalls:

> We were moving along a ravine toward the village of Prelestnoe. It was under random machine gun fire. A bullet passed cleanly through Private L. Ioffe's puttee without harming his leg. There were a lot of infantrymen in the village, crouched behind the buildings. Southeast of the village, where from time to time you could hear the explosion of heavy shells, some senior officer in a rain cape with a pistol in his hand was rushing around the field, stopping retreating individual soldiers and returning them to the trenches.[59]

The breakthrough to Petrovka was not only due to the enemy's numerical superiority. The 287th Guards Rifle Regiment's headquarters had planned to erect a defense in two echelons. In the first echelon: from the southwest outskirts of Mikhailovka (from the bridge leading to Andreevka) to the northeast outskirts of Prelestnoe – the 109th Separate Penal Company under the command of Senior Lieutenant Chudotvorov; from the southern outskirts of Mikhailovka (marked Point "30" on the map) along a ravine to a bend in the ravine 1 kilometer southwest of Oktiabr'skii State Farm – Guards Senior Lieutenant Polunsky's 3rd Rifle Battalion; and from the bend in the ravine to elevation level 240 on Hill 252.2 – the 2nd Rifle Battalion. Guards Captain K. Askhakov's 1st Rifle Battalion was supposed to back up the boundary between the 3rd and 2nd Rifle Battalions together with batteries of 45mm and 76mm guns. A battery of 120mm mortars, according to this plan, was supposed to take position in the ravine east of Petrovka and offer fire support to the forward battalions.

However, the actual defense was laid out somewhat differently. This had a tragic effect on the course of events for the entire 287th Guards Rifle Regiment. The 3rd Rifle Battalion did not manage to reach its designated position by dawn and assembled instead in Prelestnoe, around the two mills, so the 2nd Rifle Battalion dug in on the 3rd Rifle Battalion's intended sector. In connection with this, the regimental commander reduced the penal company's sector of defense and ordered it to hold only Mikhailovka (the southern and southwestern outskirts of the village), and decided to strengthen the defense of Prelestnoe with the late arriving 3rd Battalion – in case the enemy managed to reach the Oktiabr'skii State Farm. The decision of the regiment commander was a responsible one, but something unforeseen happened. Let's turn to the documentation. From a report of the 287th Guards Rifle Regiment's commander to the commander of the 95th Guards Rifle Division:

> … On 11.07.43 Senior Lieutenant Polunsky was given the order to take up defensive positions on a line: macadam road in Mikhailovka – railroad booth – letter 'o' in the inscription 'Prelestnoe', but Comrade Polunsky did not occupy the indicated line, instead choosing to concentrate his entire [3rd] battalion in the ravine lying southwest of the Voroshilovskii State Farm.

> During the course of fighting from 11 July to 19 July 1943, Comrade Polunsky always directed his battalion from a dug-out – at a distance of 2 or more kilometers.
>
> I consider the actions of the 3rd Battalion commander as a failure to carry out an order, and I request that Guards Senior Lieutenant Polunsky be removed from his current command, and turned over to face a military tribunal.
>
> I ask that Guards Senior Lieutenant Blinov assume the duties of temporarily acting commander of the 3rd Rifle Battalion.[60]

The report was signed on 19 July, already after the event, but on 11 July, as indeed the regiment commander had assumed, the forces of the 2nd Rifle Battalion were insufficient to repel the attack of *Leibstandarte*'s 2nd Panzergrenadier Regiment.[61] The SS forces struck the 2nd Rifle Battalion in two locations: *Leibstandarte*'s reconnaissance battalion attacked the battalion's right flank, while Peiper's *kampfgruppe* on its left crossed the anti-tank ditch next to the railroad near the forward trenches of Kashpersky's 287th Guards Rifle Regiment's 3rd Rifle Battalion. This regiment's dedicated artillery and two attached batteries of the 301st Destroyer Anti-tank Artillery Regiment became engaged in the fighting. The right-hand SS force, having turned the left flank of the 2nd Rifle Battalion, crushed the defenses of the 26th Guards Airborne Rifle Regiment's 3rd Battalion, and through the gap torn in the boundary between the two regiments, advanced to the Oktiabr'skii State Farm, and from there – toward Petrovka. There was no one to stop the SS troops on the previously prepared line at Prelestnoe, and the German tanks burst into Petrovka. From a daily report of the SS Panzergrenadier Division *Leibstandarte* (between 1640 and 1700):

> 11 July at 0450 [0650 local time], the 2nd Panzergrenadier Regiment (reinforced) of the SS Panzergrenadier Division *Adolf Hitler* moved out from under the cover of the large forested tract 1.5 km southwest of Iamki for the offensive toward Prokhorovka. At 0830 [1030], an anti-tank ditch south of the Oktiabr'skii State Farm was overcome, and at 1030 [1230], an assault was launched on the northwest portion of Hill 252.2, southeast of the State Farm … which, at 1410 [1610] with the introduction of the division's 2nd Panzer Battalion and the 2nd Panzergrenadier Regiment's 3rd Battalion, was taken.
>
> Flank attacks from the village of Iamki and the heights north of the River Psel had a decisive effect on the results of the general offensive. The offensive on Prokhorovka on 11.07.43 was brought to a halt as a result of the lagging positions of both neighbors [Author's note: SS Panzergrenadier Divisions *Totenkopf* and *Das Reich*]. The frontal attack on Prokhorovka, because of the strong anti-tank and artillery fire from the southeast outskirts [of the Oktiabr'skii State Farm – author's note] and the commanding elevation 252.4 is possible only with great losses.
>
> Proposal. After the capture of Hill 252.4 by the left-hand neighbor, conduct an artillery preparation and bombing of Prokhorovka.
>
> In order to exclude an immediate danger to the flanks, at 1215 [1415] the 1st Panzergrenadier Regiment was introduced through the woods north of Storozhevoe, while the division's main forces were to take Hill 245.8 and the Stalinskoe Branch of the [Oktiabr'skii] State Farm still on 11 July.

> The reinforced reconnaissance battalion of Division *Adolf Hitler* since 10 July has been in combat south of Andreevka in order to cover the northern flank of the division.
>
> The activity of enemy aviation, first of all ground attack planes, has become lively. The activity of our air force has been measured. Eleven bombs have fallen on the assault gun battalion, there have been losses.
>
> Attained lines: up to 1630 [1830] the western part of Storozhevoe and the woods north of it along the direction of the road, 500 meters northwest of Hill 252.2, eastern outskirts of the Oktiabr'skii State Farm.
>
> The 1st Panzer Regiment has been subordinated to the reinforced 2nd Panzergrenadier Regiment.
>
> The 1st Panzergrenadier Regiment (reinforced) of the Division *Adolf Hitler* – Teterevino. The 2nd Panzergrenadier Regiment – south of the Oktiabr'skii State Farm. The artillery regiment – Teterevino. The 55th *Werfer* Regiment – Komsomolets State Farm.[62]

Brigadeführer Wisch proposed concentrating the fire of all available artillery on SS Panzergrenadier Division *Totenkopf*'s sector of attack, with the aim of giving its units the possibility of at least seizing Hill 226.6 and the area surrounding it. Only after this was accomplished, likely, in the early morning hours of 12 July, would his division be ready together with the neighboring divisions of the corps to resume the offensive on Prokhorovka.

As the daily log above noted, at this moment (1830), the units of *Leibstandarte* had reached a line running from the western portion of Storozhevoe and the woods north of it to a point along the rail line about 500 meters northwest of Hill 252.2, over to the eastern outskirts of the Oktiabr'skii State Farm. The reinforced 2nd Panzergrenadier Regiment was south of the State Farm, with its attached 1st Panzer Regiment in the vicinity of Hill 252.2. The reinforced 1st Panzergrenadier Regiment was at Teterevino, together with the division's artillery, while the 55th *Werfer* was at the Komsomolets State Farm.

Paul Hausser got in touch by telephone with the corps' chief of staff, *Oberführer* W. Ostendorff,[63] and set forth the situation and the *Leibstandarte* command's proposal. After a short discussion, the following decision was taken for 12 July:

> The reinforced 1st Panzergrenadier Regiment with the attached Panzerjäger Battalion is to set out at 0450 and capture the Stalinskii State Farm [Stalinskoe Branch of the Oktiabr'skii State Farm] and Iamki. It is to establish a position adjacent to I/2nd Panzergrenadier Regiment at the road beside Hill 252.2.
>
> The reinforced 2nd Panzergrenadier Regiment, the panzer group and the reinforced reconnaissance battalion are to stand ready to move in conjunction with the elements of the *Totenkopf* Division as soon as that Division has neutralized the enemy's attacks on our flank along the Psel and to capture Prokhorovka and Hill 252.4.
>
> The Artillery Regiment *Leibstandarte* is to send an artillery liaison Kommando [team] to the *Totenkopf* Division in order to support the attack by that Division on Hill 226.6.[64]

That the enemy had broken through the forward edge of the last line of defense at Prokhorovka and that his panzer group had penetrated to the vicinity of Hill 252.2, Chief of the General Staff Marshal of the Soviet Union A. M. Vasilevsky only learned about while on a reconnoitering trip together with the commander of the 5th Guards Tank Army, Lieutenant General P. A. Rotmistrov. The Army commander remembered:

> Around 1900 hours on 11 July, Marshal Vasilevsky arrived at my KP [command post]. I reported to him on the army's combat formation and the assignments given to the corps and the attached artillery. He approved my decisions, and informed me that he had a conversation with the Supreme Commander I. V. Stalin, who had ordered him to remain continually with the 5th Guards Tank and 5th Guards Armies, to coordinate their operations during the course of the engagement and to render needed assistance. Stalin had ordered the *front* commander, N. F. Vatutin, to remain at his KP in Oboian'. The *front* chief of staff, Lieutenant General S. P. Ivanov, had moved to the Korocha axis.
>
> There still remained sufficient daylight, so the Marshal proposed to survey the jumping-off positions that I had designated for the 29th and 18th Tank Corps. Our path took us through Prokhorovka toward Belenikhino. The nimble Willys jeep, bouncing up and down on the pits and bumps in the road, passed vehicles loaded with ammunition and fuel moving toward the front. Transports with the wounded were slowly passing in the opposite direction. Here and there, damaged trucks and broken wagons were standing on the side of the road.
>
> The road ran through broad fields of yellowed wheat. Beyond them, a forest began, which adjoined the village of Storozhevoe.
>
> 'There, along the northern edge of the woods, are the start positions for the 29th Tank Corps. To the right, the 18th Tank Corps will be attacking,' I was explaining to Vasilevsky.
>
> He was gazing intently into the distance and listening to the ever-growing rumble of the fighting. From the puffs of smoke and the explosions of aerial bombs and shells, he was trying to divine the front lines of our combined arms armies. To the right, about 2 kilometers away, agricultural structures of the Komsomolets State Farm were visible.
>
> Suddenly, Vasilevsky ordered the driver to stop. The vehicle turned off the road and sharply braked amid some dust-covered, roadside brush. We opened the jeep's little doors and stepped off to the side for several paces. The rumble of tank engines was plainly audible. Then the tanks came into view.
>
> Abruptly turning to me, Aleksandr Mikhailovich asked me with annoyance in his voice, 'General! What's going on? You've been forewarned that the enemy must not know about the arrival of our tanks. But here they are in the light of day under the Germans' eyes …'
>
> I instantly raised my binoculars. Indeed, across the field, stirring up the ripened grain, dozens of tanks were moving in combat formation, firing on the move from short-barreled guns.
>
> 'But these are not our tanks, Comrade General. They are German.'
>
> 'So, the enemy has broken through somewhere. He wants to forestall us and seize Prokhorovka.'

> 'This cannot be permitted,' I said to Vasilevsky and by radio I gave a command to General Kirichenko to advance immediately two tank brigades to meet the German tanks and to stop their advance.
>
> Having returned to my KP, we learned that the Germans were undertaking active operations against almost all our armies.[65]

In the course of the fighting for Oktiabr'skii State Farm, several dozens of armored vehicles from *Leibstandarte*'s panzer regiment tried to breakthrough along the rail line to the outskirts of Prokhorovka Station. Having overrun the 3rd Rifle Battalion of the 26th Guards Airborne Regiment, they advanced upon the combat positions of the 23rd Guards Airborne Regiment. Things would have been very tough for its fighters, if there had been no help from our aviation. However, at that critical moment, pilots of Lieutenant General V. G. Riazanov's 1st Ground Attack Aviation Corps struck.

Here are the impressions of an eyewitness to that aerial attack, I. S. Vakhrameev, a soldier in the 1st Rifle Battalion of the 287th Guards Rifle Regiment, who at that moment was watching from his battalion's position on Hill 254.2:

> ... A group of yellowish-brown fascist light bombers were attacking the artillerymen's positions, which were laid out in front of us. They were Italian Caproni. Flying at low altitude, they dove vertically on the positions, very precisely releasing their bombs almost at ground level. The bomb explosions were rising in close proximity to the guns.

A commander of one of the aviation regiments congratulates an Il-2 crew upon the successful fulfillment of a combat mission. (RGAKFD)

Replenishing the ammunition on an airplane on one of the airbases of the Soviet 2nd Air Army. (RGAKFD)

At the first moment of the bombing, the artillerymen sought to take cover in foxholes. But apparently, at this same moment the German attack began, and there followed the command to lay down a blocking fire pattern. The battery members rushed to their guns and opened fire.

... After several minutes the fascist planes flew away to the south. When the smoke and dust settled, we saw overturned guns in blackened positions, around which only a few human figures were moving about; plainly, they were the few who remained alive from among the brave gun crews, who had been fighting to the limits of possibility.

This time, the attack of the Germans was successful, and the forward units of the Soviet forces fell back to the line of Prokhorovka. Around and among the State Farm's installations along the road leading to Prokhorovka appear the 'little boxes' of the fascist tanks, kicking up dust. They are in their dozens, now nearly a hundred of them, and more and more armored vehicles are emerging from behind the crest of the hill, adding to the enemy tank column which stretched almost one and a half kilometers along the road. At the head of the column, the distinct enormous hulks of Tiger tanks are now plainly visible.

The wind is blowing away from us and carrying away the rumbling of the tank engines. The tank column, which was rushing toward Prokhorovka, is moving without firing and, it seems, almost noiselessly, which increases the impression of its irresistible onslaught.

The Soviet forces have also halted fire along the entire front, and it seems that our battalion with its rifles and machine guns, and the three squat anti-tank guns of support behind its positions are confronting the fascist armada alone. At this tense moment, the racing imagination involuntarily leads to thoughts of the unequal possibilities of the contending forces and the hopelessness of the infantrymen's situation. Pressing themselves to their weapons, the fighters were ready to take on the desperate fight, the start of which was only a few minutes away.

Suddenly behind us we hear the rising howl of airplane engines. We turn around in our slit trenches and see in the distance a compact group of our planes, skimming above the earth, quickly approaching the front. They cross the front a little to the right of our positions. From close range, the distinctly characteristic silhouette of our famous Il-2 ground-attack aircraft – the menace to fascist tanks – is plainly visible. There are a lot of them. At almost treetop height, the 'Ils' masterfully carry out a maneuver as they reach the target that is most difficult for a large group of airplanes to perform – a shift into a line across the front. Then, plainly upon command, they immediately tip their noses downward, aiming the entire plane at the enemy tanks. A moment later, plumes of smoke from their launching rockets appear from beneath their wings and the rockets streak ahead. Simultaneously, some of the ground attack planes open fire from machine guns positioned in the nose of the planes – one can see the rapid gun flashes.

Having launched a salvo of rockets, the 'Ils' leveled out, and flying over the length of the column, they plaster it with a large number of anti-tank bombs.[66] Afterwards the planes sharply climbed skywards, hastily fleeing the anticipated blast wave.

The deafening clap of thunder from the simultaneous explosion of thousands of bombs and rockets rolled all through the immediate area. Where the German tank column had been, along its entire length a storm of fire, black smoke, and erupting earth began to rage. I remember how one of the telegraph poles was snapped like a matchstick by one powerful blast, and tossed several dozen meters into the air.

... When about a quarter of an hour later the wind had dissipated the dense clouds of dust and smoke, in front of us was an extended strip of field, blackened by flames and churned soil, over which the column of fascist tanks had recently been moving toward Prokhorovka. On this strip, approximately 20 knocked-out enemy armored vehicles were smoking, while the undamaged German tanks were crawling away back toward the Oktiabr'skii State Farm.[67]

At 1700 on 11 July, the SS split the defenses of the 99th Tank Brigade and burst into Vasil'evka. Brigade commander Lieutenant Colonel L. I. Malov's tank was knocked out, and he himself was wounded and sent to a *medsanbat* [medical sanitation battalion]. The chief of staff Major Osipov took over direction of the battle. In order to restore the situation, it was decided to launch a counterattack by the reserve tank battalion. The attack was so impetuous and audacious that the Germans fell back with little resistance.

After a spell, the attack was resumed on the left-hand neighbor, the 287th Guards Rifle Regiment. As we have seen, its battalions were driven from their positions after a fierce struggle; the resulting German advance to Petrovka encircled the 99th Tank Brigade in Andreevka, where it continued to fight in the pocket until the next morning.

★ ★ ★

It should be recognized that in the most difficult moment of fighting at Prokhorovka, when the enemy was trying to rupture the final army-level defensive line and to turn the right flank of the 69th Army, that Army's command was not fully in control of the situation – its direction over its subordinate forces was wretched. The acting chief of staff Colonel S. M. Protas not only failed to keep the *front* headquarters informed of the operational situation in a timely fashion, but he himself plainly knew little about it. Here is one obvious case. At 1240, N. F. Vatutin was compelled to request information about the situation by telegraph:

1. Has the rifle division from Zhadov arrived at the sector Vasil'evka, Komsomolets State Farm? If not, then where is it?
2. Where is the 96th Tank Brigade, what mission is it conducting?
3. Where is your attached 148th Tank Regiment?
4. What is Burdeiny doing?
5. What do you know about the situation in the area of Bogoroditskoe?
6. Do you have communications with Rogozny? How many tanks does the 148th Tank Regiment have?[68]

The commander could not receive an intelligible answer to his questions. The 69th Army headquarters didn't know the situation on the Prokhorovka axis, and it had no communications link with the divisions of the 5th Guards Army, which at this time was embroiled in heavy fighting in that area. The *front* commander was himself forced to explain the situation on the right flank of the 69th Army to its chief of staff, and to inform him of the number of operational combat vehicles remaining in the tank units and formations assigned to his army. N. F. Vatutin directed Protas:

1. Quickly eliminate the shortcomings in the work of the headquarters. To your own shame, you know nothing about the situation at such a serious moment … Organize an uninterrupted channel of communications.
2. Don't unnecessarily involve Burdeiny in the fighting, considering the prospect known to you [Author's Note: the commander of the 48th Rifle Corps General Rogozny had been inquiring about possible assistance from the 2nd Guards Tank Corps, which Vatutin wanted withheld for the upcoming counteroffensive]. Rogozny must repulse the attack on the Prokhorovka axis by his own means, and Rogozny will personally answer for this.
3. … On the Prokhorovka axis, one division from your neighbor on the right should be arriving. Immediately organize cooperation with it.
4. I am ordering the 148th Tank Regiment to set off immediately on the route … The regiment is to arrive in Bol. Psinka and is to be placed under Zhadov's operational control. Zhadov's headquarters – Sokrovo (3 km west of Bol. Psinka). The regiment is to arrive at the designated point by 2000 11 July. Supply it with fuel and ammunition. The regiment commander or his chief of staff is to drive to Zhadov immediately and is to appear before him no later than 1800 after receiving this order …[69]

The cited conversation testifies not only to the weak executive discipline in the command of the 69th Army and the low level of the chief of staff's training, but also to the very difficult situation, in which the commander of the Voronezh Front was forced to work in those tense days.[70] After 6 July, when I. V. Stalin personally directed the Voronezh Front's chief of staff S. P. Ivanov to go to Korocha – to the commander of the 69th Army "as a reinforcement", the burden on Vatutin grew significantly. He was forced to occupy himself not only with planning the operations of the forces of the entire *front*, but also, as is apparent from the above conversation, to resolve ongoing questions on behalf of the now absent chief of staff: to put right the work of his lower armies' headquarters; to lecture negligent officers; and to gather together the remaining tanks of fragmented units in case of a breakthrough at Prokhorovka. Without a doubt, N. F. Vatutin was a talented, well-educated commander. In addition, during his service in the General Staff he had acquired a broad mental outlook, and had brilliantly acclimated to the staff environment. Nikolai Fedorovich gained practical experience in 1941, as the chief of staff of the Northwestern Front, and in 1942, as commander of the Voronezh Front. However, the situation that had developed in the *front* headquarters could not but affect the work of the commander, the quality of his decisions, and importantly – their execution by subordinate headquarters at all levels.

At 1945 on 11 July, the Voronezh Front commander signed a combat order to the commander of the 69th Army and the commander of the 2nd Tank Corps:

> As a consequence of your carelessness and poor direction, the enemy has broken through to Petrovka and toward Prokhorovka. I order you, under your personal responsibility, together with the units of Rotmistrov and Zhadov to destroy the enemy that has broken through and this very day to reach the line Vasil'evka, Belenikhino.[71]

Subsequently, the commander of the 5th Guards Army remembered this dramatic moment in this way: "… [I] must confess that we didn't anticipate that events at the front would develop so swiftly and that we wouldn't succeed in taking up the defense on the line Oboian', Prokhorovka in good time."[72]

It is possible to understand Vatutin's emotions. The breakthrough of the Germans toward Prokhorovka Station had no catastrophic consequences in the strategic sense, but it promised a lot of unpleasantness. The Station was located as if on the edge of the rear belt of defense of the 6th Guards Army; beyond it were the army-level switch lines, and then – at a distance of 20 to 23 kilometers – the initial line of the final *front*-level defensive belt. When planning the defensive operation, the *front* command had based its main calculations on containing the opponent within the tactical zone of the defense – within its first two army-level belts. Consequently, their planning and construction were much more careful and thorough, and the density of engineered obstacles reflected their importance to the planning. Thus, the first two belts had been built by the troops of the armies of the first and second echelons that would be occupying them: the 6th Guards, the 7th Guards, and the 69th Armies. The soldiers and commanders of these formations knew without any explanations that their lives to a great extent would depend upon the level of preparation of the defenses, so they labored conscientiously. The higher army-level leadership systematically made on-site inspections of the readiness of the fortifications. For three months the troops studied the terrain, the landmarks and the lines, and registered their guns on them – in a word, they were preparing the positions for themselves.

The army (rear) belt was on the other hand built by field engineers and the local population. Much of this band of fortifications was still unfinished by the time of the German offensive. Thus, on the line Vasil'evka – Komsomolets State Farm – Hill 258.2, civilians and soldiers of the 285th Rifle Regiment had constructed only one line of trenches, and on the sector Prelestnoe – Oktiabr'skii State Farm – Hill 252.2 – Iamki – Storozhevoe, work on the trenches had only just begun. The units of the 9th Guards Airborne Division that had arrived here on the night of 10 July got busy with digging positions for themselves and hastily laying mines, but not until the Germans had already reached the Prokhorovka axis.

Today it is possible to speculate what might have happened, if the enemy had taken Prokhorovka – that is to say, if the Germans had overcome the final army line of defense. Doubtlessly, the Germans would have been stopped: the main forces of the 5th Guards Tank Army were now standing just 10 kilometers away and the 5th Guards Army was approaching, but during the withdrawal to the new lines of defense, the Soviet forces would have suffered great losses.

In addition, upon seizing the Prokhorovka Station, a real possibility would have opened up for the enemy to drive into the rear of the 6th Guards Army across the bend in the Psel River and further – on to Oboian'. Fortunately, nothing like this happened on 11 July, nor did the enemy manage to accomplish this even on the following days.

The capture of the Oktiabr'skii State Farm and the adversary's further advance toward Prokhorovka did disrupt the preparations for the counterattack on 12 July, which had already begun on Vatutin's orders. The 5th Guards Tank Army's line of deployment had to change, and the work already done to prepare the artillery positions went to waste.

In order to liquidate the breakthrough, the hasty gathering of available nearby forces began. The ground attack aviation was the first to land a blow (as has already been discussed), but this turned out to be insufficient. The SS panzers continued persistently to attack the positions of the airborne troops. The 69th Army headquarters' Operational Information No. 00260 at 1930 on 11.7.43 reveals:

> At 1920 up to 100 enemy tanks broke through from the area of Mikhailovka and reached Hill 252.2. The infantry has been separated [from the tanks], combat against the tanks that have broken through continues.
>
> The commander of the 69th Army has ordered:
>
> The 48th Rifle Corps in concert with the 2nd Tank Corps and the 2nd Guards 'Tatsinskaia' Tank Corps to destroy the enemy's grouping that has broken through. The 48th Rifle Corps commander has driven to the area of the fighting in the vicinity of the 2nd Tank Corps.[73]

At 1700, the 2nd Guards 'Tatsinskaia' Tank Corps moved under the operational control of the 5th Guards Tank Army commander. Coded telegram No. 00117 at 2235 on 11 July 1943, from A. S. Burdeiny to P. A. Rotmistrov:

> I received the mission from the commander of the Voronezh Front through the commander of the 48th Rifle Corps, Rogozny, to counterattack the enemy tanks in the direction of Storozhevoe, Prokhorovka at 2000 11.07.43:
>
> The 4th Guards Tank Brigade has moved out along the rail line north of Belenikhino and has become engaged in fighting in this region.
>
> The 25th Guards Tank Brigade is attacking in the direction of Storozhevoe and the Stalinskii State Farm [Stalinskoe Branch of the Oktiabr'skii State Farm].
>
> I am moving the 26th Guards Tank Brigade from the region of Shakhovo into the woods east of Vinogradovka.
>
> With the approach of darkness, the brigades will hold in their places in accordance with your instruction.
>
> From the morning of 1207.43 the corps will be ready to operate according to your orders.[74]

As the situation dictated, the 95th Guards Rifle Division commander Colonel A. N. Liakhov was the first to react. The defense in the area of the breakthrough began to be strengthened with artillery. Two batteries of Major P. D. Boiko's 103rd Destroyer Anti-tank Artillery Regiment were hastily shifted to Hill 252.4 from beyond the Psel River. In order to block the enemy's attempts to force a crossing of the Psel at Petrovka, the 5th Battery of the 233rd Guards Artillery Regiment's 2nd Battalion deployed southeast of Petrovka, joined by the 284th Guards Rifle Regiment's 3rd Battalion. The division commander's reserve – a company of submachine gunners – was moved up into the 287th Guards Rifle Regiment's sector of defense north of the Oktiabr'skii State Farm. The chief of staff of the 95th Guards Rifle Division's artillery Major F. I. Terekhov arrived in order to centralize direction over all the artillery in this sector.[75] As the commander of the division's artillery Colonel N. D. Sebezhko subsequently noted, the chief of staff managed this task in a difficult combat situation with honor. Terekhov took operational control over all the artillery in the breakthrough area into his hands and organized uninterrupted, concentrated fire on the advancing enemy tanks. This yielded results; the Germans abandoned Petrovka and even briefly withdrew from the Oktiabr'skii State Farm. However, by the end of the day the State Farm was again taken by the 2nd Panzergrenadier Regiment with fire support from panzers of *Leibstandarte*'s II/1st SS Panzer Regiment.

As the SS tanks were breaking through to Petrovka, around 1730 a company of the *Totenkopf* Division with twelve tanks tried to force a crossing of the Psel River at Krasnyi Oktiabr', in order to divert some of the defending forces from the main axis of the attack. But this attempt failed – the 290th Guards Rifle Division hurled the adversary back with a counterattack.

From Operational Report No. 00262 of the 69th Army headquarters at 2300 on 11 July 1943:

> By 2200, on the right flank of the 183rd Rifle Division the offensive had been stopped, 10 tanks were breaking through in the direction of Prokhorovka from the area of Hill 252.2 …
>
> … At 2000 46 tanks were attacking from Shliakhovoe toward Lomovo, while enemy aviation in two groups of 70-75 aircraft subjected a column of vehicles and the rear of the 35th Rifle Corps to a heavy bombardment in the area of Kazach'e, Verkhnii Ol'shanets and Novo-Oskochnoe. According to unverified information, at 2200 the enemy broke into Verkhnii Ol'shanets with a force of up to 30 tanks.[76]

The situation at Prokhorovka managed to be stabilized only between 2200 and 2300 through the combined efforts of the defending units and the arriving reserves.

One piece of the enemy's plan begins to emerge from the above cited documents. The commander of the Fourth Panzer Army was planning on 11 July to use part of his forces to encircle the 69th Army's 48th Rifle Corps *after* [author's emphasis] the breakthrough to Prokhorovka. The jaws of this pincer operation were plainly visible: the SS Panzer Corps southwest of Prokhorovka, and Army Detachment Kempf, from the south. Thanks to the stubborn and firm resistance of the Guardsmen, the enemy was not able to implement this scheme out of hand. However, the plan remained active with only a postponement in time. While the SS Panzergrenadier Division *Leibstandarte*, the advance of which had finally been blunted on the evening of 11 July near Prokhorovka Station, delayed a decisive storming of the station until 12 July, the III Panzer Corps on the evening of 11 July began to break through in the direction of Prokhorovka from the south, taking advantage of the confusion and partial loss of control in the 69th Army after penetrating the boundary between the 48th Rifle Corps and the 35th Guards Rifle Corps. As a result, a 6th Panzer Division *kampfgruppe* at dawn on 12 July seized the villages of Rzhavets, Vypolzovka and Ryndinka, thereby creating a most serious threat to the rear of the counterattack grouping of the 5th Guards Tank Army and the 5th Guards Army.

By midnight of 11 July, the bitter fighting had subsided. SS *Brigadeführer* Wisch withdrew part of the panzer regiment to a position behind the anti-tank ditch southwest of Hill 252.2. As German veterans of the fighting recall, combat vehicles of the advance-guard 7th Panzer Company under the command of *Hauptsturmführer* Tiemann were positioned about 150 meters from the eastern outskirts of the Oktiabr'skii State Farm. Altogether, as the chief of staff of *Leibstandarte* Lehmann wrote, there remained approximately 33 panzers on Hill 252.2. In the vicinity of the hill and on the State Farm, men of II/2nd SS Grenadier Regiment were laboring intensively to dig positions for themselves and the anti-tank guns, while I/2nd SS Grenadier Regiment was on the other side of the railroad with the division's assault guns. On the left flank of the division, the reconnaissance battalion and anti-tank battalion were digging in around the villages of Prelestnoe, Mikhailovka and Andreevka. These units of the II SS Panzer Corps would be the first to engage the leading brigades of the 29th and 18th Tank Corps of General P. A. Rotmistrov's army on 12 July.

But where had the enemy been stopped on the evening of 11 July? This is a complex and important question. The answer to this question permits us to establish the line, from which the 5th Guards Tank Army launched its attack, which in turn will allow us to assess the territorial gains made during the Army's counterattack.

As has been mentioned previously, a detailed and, more importantly, complex analysis of the fighting at Prokhorovka has not been done. In the meantime, now and then research and the memoirs of participants of those events have appeared. They indeed have become the primary sources of information on the battle, but no one has evaluated them for accuracy, while the information in them at times is not reliable. As a result, a distorted image has emerged not only of certain facts and events, but also of the battle as a whole. One of the clearest examples of this is the widely-held conviction that the enemy did in fact reach the outskirts of Prokhorovka on the evening of 11 July. The first to write about this was the chief of staff of the 32nd Guards Rifle Corps I. A. Samchuk and the assistant chief of staff of the 26th Guards Airborne Rifle Regiment P. G. Skachko in their book, *Atakuiut desantniki* [*The Paratroopers Attack*]:

> The tanks, which were breaking through along the rail line to the western outskirts of the settlement, ran into the fire of the 7th Guards Artillery Regiment and the 23rd and 28th Guards Airborne Rifle Regiments. The artillerymen of Guards Major V. K. Valuev were firing at them over open sights. The first to receive the attack of the enemy's tank avalanche was the battery under the command of Guards Lieutenant N. N. Troitsky. The gun platoon of Guards Lieutenant B. S. Nikulin particularly distinguished itself. The guns were firing at point-blank range at the attacking tanks. Gun commanders stepped in to replace the wounded and dead gun layers.
>
> Troitsky's men knocked out seven medium tanks and one heavy tank, and were firing canister shells at point-blank range at up to two companies of motorized infantry. But the adversary's onslaught didn't slacken. Bypassing Troitsky's battery, the fascist tanks near the graded road attacked Guards Senior Lieutenant's P. S. Gruzinsky's battery. The artillerymen allowed the tanks to approach so closely that their vision slits were visible. Two medium tanks and a self-propelled gun burst into flames. A Tiger, covering one of the burning vehicles with its hull, destroyed the left-flank gun with a well-placed shot from close range. Then the battery commander, who was with the right-flank gun, turned it to target the Tiger, and together with the crew of a second gun shot up the Tiger from the flank. Disregarding their losses, the fascists continued to attack. The battery destroyed two more medium tanks, two vehicles, and up to two platoons of infantry, before the enemy at last halted the attack.
>
> But at the brick factory the struggle didn't diminish. This was the position of Guards Lieutenant V. Ia. Korobko's 5th Battery. The crew of Gun Number One, where Korobko was situated, knocked out a hostile medium tank. The steel colossus, rocked by the hit, came to a stop. The tank crew in black uniforms leaped from the opened hatches. They tried to find cover in a depression, but artillerymen using carbines shot them down. A burst of machine-gun fire from another tank riddled the gun crew, wounding the battery commander. But the courageous officer himself stood up behind the panoramic sight [*panorama*], and together with the remaining able crew members, continued to fire. The artillerymen, inspired by the

> example of their commander, knocked out two more enemy tanks and one vehicle. Having destroyed three tanks and the vehicle, Guards Lieutenant Korobko's battery did not let the enemy gain entry into the brick factory.
>
> With the coming of darkness, the enemy withdrew his tanks to the area of the Oktiabr'skii State Farm, leaving behind some infantry and anti-tank artillery on the northeast slopes of the hill north of the State Farm.[77]

From the cited extract it would seem that Guards Lieutenant Troitsky's 1st Battery and Guards Senior Lieutenant Gruzinsky's 2nd Battery from the 1st Artillery Battalion dueled against the enemy tanks from positions in front of the brick factory (named the Bolshevik Cooperative), while Lieutenant Korobko's battery from the 2nd Battalion was positioned at the brick factory itself. On the map accompanying the text in Samchuk's and Skachko's book, the positions of both artillery battalions are generally depicted behind the brick factory. This cooperative was located several hundred meters from the western outskirts of Prokhorovka Station. If you accept this map as an accurate depiction of the events, then it seems that the SS troops on 11 July had practically entered Prokhorovka. Moreover, the authors of this version of events purport to be relying upon documents in the Central Archive of the Ministry of Defense of the Russian Federation. However, if one relies upon archival documents that are accessible to scholars today, one can see that the events of 11 July did not unfold in this way in this sector.

Despite all its efforts, the enemy never reached Prokhorovka. In Operational Summary No. 1 for 2000 11 July 1943, the chief of staff of the 33rd Guards Rifle Corps (in which, incidentally, one of the authors of this book P. G. Skachko served) Guards Colonel Strazhevsky reported: " … 2. The enemy tank and infantry offensive has been stopped on the line running from the southern side of the ravine lying east of Petrovka to the western outskirts of Prokhorovka."

The result of a direct hit by a heavy artillery shell on a German Pz IV tank. (RGAKFD)

This line runs approximately 2 kilometers from the brick factory. The batteries of the 7th Guards Airborne Artillery Regiment's 1st Battalion were never in this area throughout the entire day. Their positions had been established on the other side of the railway and were covering the southwestern and southern outskirts of Prokhorovka. Here is an excerpt from the memoirs of the commander of the 1st Artillery Battalion of the 7th Guards Airborne Artillery Regiment, K. V. Kazakov:

> At the beginning of July 1943, I held the rank 'Guards Captain' and was in command of the 7th Guards Airborne Artillery Regiment's 1st Battalion. The regiment was part of the 9th Airborne Division, which at that time was situated in the area of Staryi Oskol.
>
> My battalion had three batteries: the 1st (ZIS-3 76mm guns) under the command of Guards Lieutenant Nikolai Nikolaevich Troitsky, the 2nd (ZIS-3 76mm guns) under the command of Guards Senior Lieutenant Pavel Semenovich Gruzinsky, and the 3rd (122mm howitzers) under the command of Vasilii Dmitrievich Troshkin. The battalion was fully staffed and equipped. We had Studebaker trucks to tow the guns.
>
> The night before 11 July 1943 the regiment received the order to conduct a march of approximately 120 kilometers and to reassemble in the area of Prokhorovka by 0400 on 11 July. The battalion arrived at the designated place at approximately 0330. I was given the order to occupy a position on the southwestern outskirts of Prokhorovka (to the left of the railroad), and to be ready to fire over open sights by 0700.
>
> After reconnoitering the terrain, I made the decision to place the 1st Battery on the southwestern edge of Prokhorovka (with its front to the west); the 2nd Battery echeloned to the front and right (along the railroad embankment), east of Hill 252.2; and the 3rd Battery to the front and left. Our orders were to protect Prokhorovka with flank fire against an enemy tank breakthrough, and to give fire support to the 2nd Battalion of the 26th Guards Airborne Rifle Regiment, which was in position to the left of the railway, and to the 28th Guards Airborne Rifle Regiment on the division's left flank.
>
> After receiving the orders, the men of my battalion took to digging in their guns, preparing observation posts, and laying communications lines. In the batteries' firing positions, an area was cleared around each gun, niches for the ammunition and slit trenches for the gun crews were dug, and the firing positions and towing equipment were camouflaged. The battalion's signals platoon prepared a command post, linked by telephone lines to the battery commanders in their firing positions. All the ammunition was brought up, unloaded and laid out in the firing positions, while the Studebaker trucks were parked under cover about 250-400 meters behind the batteries' firing positions.
>
> By 0700 the battalion was fully prepared for battle. At around 1000, approximately 20 German tanks emerged from a depression southwest of Hill 252.2. Pushing back the rifle companies and continuing to advance on Prokhorovka, the tanks reached a line 700-800 meters from the 1st Battery. A self-propelled gun was moving in front. Having evaluated the situation, I ordered the commander of the 1st Battery Guards Lieutenant Troitsky to open fire on the self-propelled gun with

> one gun. The first shot was a direct hit! However, the armor-piercing shell, striking the front armor, ricocheted harmlessly away. The self-propelled gun stopped and with an answering shot knocked out the anti-tank gun that had fired upon it (the round penetrated the gun shield and smashed the panoramic sight).
>
> At just this moment, the tactical decision I had made to deploy the 2nd Battery in a staggered position in front of the 1st Battery was justified. I gave the order to Guards Senior Lieutenant Gruzinsky to open fire with one gun on the self-propelled gun, which was still standing where it had stopped to fire, and was only 450-500 meters away from the 2nd Battery. The first shot penetrated the side armor of the self-propelled gun, and with the second shot it began to blaze (to my great regret, Pavel Semenovich Gruzinsky, who had exhibited great courage in this battle, was later struck down by an enemy bullet while visiting a forward infantry unit on 14 or 15 July). Inspired by this success, the 1st and 2nd Batteries (the 3rd Battery took no part in this action) opened fire on the enemy's tanks with armor-piercing shells, and with case-shot at the infantry. Having lost still another Tiger, seven medium tanks and up to two companies of infantry, the Germans were forced to retreat.
>
> After some time had passed, the enemy launched a second attack, this time taking into consideration the location of the 1st and 2nd Batteries, and came under the flank fire of Guards Lieutenant Troshkin's 3rd Battery. The pernicious fire on the sides and tracks of the tanks from the howitzer battery was a major, if not decisive contribution to the repulse of this German tank attack. Leaving behind another Tiger, five more medium tanks, two vehicles and up to a platoon of infantry on the battlefield, the enemy on our sector was once again forced to withdraw to his starting positions and ceased his attacks.
>
> Despite the furious tank attacks, the artillery and mortar fire, and the bombing, our losses in men and equipment were minimal: one gun had been knocked out (the one that had first opened fire on the self-propelled gun), and approximately ten men from the gun crews had been wounded. Another three men from the signals platoon had been wounded while repairing broken communications lines. Almost all the wounded remained in the ranks, while the gun was repaired and ready for battle again later that night.
>
> Under enemy pressure, the 2nd and 3rd Battalions of the 28th Guards Airborne Rifle Regiment fell back toward Prokhorovka, leaving the 3rd Battery virtually without cover. From my battalion command post, I watched as our regiment commander Guards Major V. K. Valuev with a pistol in his hand tried to stop the retreating riflemen.
>
> At the time, I didn't know that the situation to the right of the rail line was even more threatening and difficult than in our sector. Considering the successful arrangement of the battalion's firing positions, I decided not to change them.[78]

Here is another piece of testimony from the deputy commander of the 1st Rifle Battalion Guards Senior Lieutenant F. A. Galaganov:

> The night before 11 July the battalion arrived at Prokhorovka and occupied a temporary defensive position in the regiment's second echelon. The defenses extended to the hill to the right of the rail line and west of Prokhorovka Station. The

> left flank of the battalion was located 100-150 meters from the railroad; the right flank was anchored in a gully. The anti-tank gun (45mm) platoon took up a firing position approximately 100 meters behind the positions of the rifle companies and closer to the right flank.
>
> From the morning of 11 July, the companies in the first echelon were engaged in battle with the enemy. At some point that morning, a group of five or six soldiers were placed under my command, with the order to carry ammunition to the rifle companies of the first echelon. Picking up the ammunition, they set off along a depression from behind the battalion's right flank.
>
> That afternoon, around ten German tanks broke through the forward defenses and emerged on the right flank of the 1st Battalion. In connection with the preparations for the forthcoming offensive, the battalion's defenses were not set-up for anti-tank defense. These circumstances demanded endurance, willpower, courage and self-control from the men in the ranks. The German tanks approached quite closely. No one moved. At a single command, the anti-tank guns, anti-tank rifles and infantry weapons opened fire simultaneously. The Germans were caught by surprise. The fighting lasted for about an hour. Three German tanks were knocked out; the remainder withdrew to their starting positions and made no more appearances.
>
> We had losses; both 45mm guns were smashed. There were injured and dead among the crews. In the rifle companies there were no losses.[79]

The map of the artillery commander of the 95th Guards Rifle Division Colonel N. D. Sebezhko, which he used over these days, also bears witness to the fact that the enemy was never in Prokhorovka on 11 July.[80] The front lines as of 2000 on 11 July are precisely marked on it – they run approximately 500 meters from the outskirts of Prokhorovka and about 1.5 kilometers from the brick factory, as indeed was reported by the chief of staff of the 33rd Guards Rifle Corps.

Around 1900 on the evening of 11 July, A. M. Vasilevsky arrived in Prokhorovka. After evaluating the situation, the Chief of the General Staff ordered P. A. Rotmistrov to advance the 18th Tank Corps in order to ease the situation of the 9th Guards Airborne Division in the area of Petrovka, and to use it to counterattack the Germans at 2100 in case the enemy tried to advance further. But the Germans showed no more activity that evening.

At 2000 11 July, the commander of the 33rd Guards Rifle Corps Major General I. I. Popov reported to General A. S. Zhadov: "I have instructed the commander of the 95th Guards Rifle Division Colonel Liakhov and the commander of the 9th Guards Airborne Division Colonel Sazonov to drive the enemy out of their occupied positions with a night attack, and to restore the situation."[81]

The fighting resumed before dawn, but it yielded no real results. The SS troops had quickly constructed a powerful system of fire with the use of anti-tank guns and self-propelled guns. Our units drove back the enemy's security outposts, but were unable to return to Oktiabr'skii State Farm or even approach to within direct fire range of it.

Under cover of this night attack, with the sounds of their movements masked by the noise of the fighting, the brigades of the 5th Guards Tank Army and units of the 42nd Guards Rifle Division began to move into their lines of departure, prepared to enter the battle the next morning.

How did events unfold on 11 July southwest of Prokhorovka, east of the rail line? Throughout the day, bloody fighting had gone on east of the woods near Storozhevoe and on the approaches to the Stalinskoe Branch of the Oktiabr'skii State Farm, which was located just to the northeast of the Storozhevoe woods. In the area of the Stalinskoe Branch, which straddled the rail line, battalions of the first echelon 183rd Rifle Division's 227th Rifle Regiment fought. Remembered Major V. E. Sazhinov, the commander of this regiment:

> Toward the end of the day, after the eighth attack, enemy tanks had driven a deep wedge into the regiment's defenses along the railroad embankment. But after the ninth attack, German tanks had reached the regiment command post, which the regiment chief of staff Captain A. P. Sokolov reported to me at the last minute. There were no longer any communications with the headquarters or any of the companies, and we had been forced to abandon the observation post. Twilight quickly gathered and night was approaching. However as a result of the energetic actions of Captain Sokolov, deputy commanders Paramoshkin and Bobkov, staff officers of the regiment and the battalion commanders, we managed quickly to restore control over the regiment, withdraw it, and bring it back into order. After several hours, it was combat-capable again, although it had suffered significant losses, and was badly worn out by the night march and the day's heavy combat.
>
> Although the outcome of the fighting was unsatisfactory, given the unequal correlation of forces between the opposing sides it was something like a victory. As a result of our resistance, we had gained entire days for the command, which received the possibility to concentrate its forces for a counterattack.[82]

Throughout the day, with brief interruptions, bitter fighting had gone on in the woods near Storozhevoe. Taking advantage of the folds in the forested terrain, the 169th Tank Brigade, strengthened by a battalion from the 58th Motorized Rifle Brigade, and units of the 183rd Rifle Division successfully defended their positions. The sector Ivanovskii Vyselok – Storozhevoe – Pravorot' and Hill 241.6 – woods north of Storozhevoe – Stalinskoe Branch of the [Oktiabr'skii] State Farm – Iamki, was a second, more dangerous axis of advance, where the enemy could break through to Prokhorovka. All day long, units of *Das Reich* (from Ivanovskii Vyselok) and *Leibstandarte* (through the Stalinskoe Branch of the [Oktiabr'skii] State Farm) persistently tried to break through along these two lines of advance.

Together, the two SS Panzergrenadier divisions managed to edge their way into the grove northeast of Storozhevoe and to seize the Stalinskoe Branch. The 169th Tank Brigade in Storozhevoe was threatened by encirclement, if *Das Reich* managed to drive through Ivanovskii Vyselok into the woods south of the small village. The enemy might be able to close these jaws around the 169th Tank Brigade under the cover of darkness. Therefore, the commander of the 2nd Guards Tank Corps Colonel A. S. Burdeiny, who arrived at the command post of the 25th Guards Tank Brigade in the small village of Dal'nii Dolzhik at 2030, ordered Lieutenant Colonel S. M. Bulygin to deploy his brigade on the northwestern, western and southern outskirts of Storozhevoe in order to repulse a potential German attack from the direction of the Stalinskoe Branch. At 2130, the brigade's battalions reached their assigned areas and took up defensive positions, but took no part in combat that evening. Other units had driven the Germans from Petrovka, and the enemy undertook no further attempts to attack Storozhevoe. Even before midnight, the 25th Guards Tank Brigade left their positions around Storozhevoe and moved back toward Vinogradovka, in order to prepare for the morning counterattack.

From the morning of 11 July, the 2nd Guards Tank Corps' 755th Separate Destroyer Anti-tank Battalion under the command of Captain Terekhov had been involved in especially heavy fighting. This battalion prior to 10 July had been under the operational control of the commander of the 26th Guards Tank Brigade, and had been located in an anti-tank strongpoint in Shakhovo, guarding the road leading from Leski to Ryndinka. After the enemy had seized the Komsomolets State Farm and Ivanovskii Vyselok, Colonel Burdeiny, fearing the enemy's further advance to Vinogradovka and Storozhevoe, ordered the battalion to move to the area of Vinogradovka, to a nameless height 2 kilometers east of the village.

The battalion, which was equipped with Model 1939 85mm anti-aircraft guns, was a particularly powerful force. This gun was a high-velocity weapon, capable of sending an armor-piercing shell at a flat trajectory through up to 100 mm of armor out to a range of 1000 meters. This meant that the crew serving this weapon could take on any enemy tank. Moreover, this gun was capable of 360° of fire from its fixed position. Its automatic breech mechanism enabled the crew to maintain a high rate of fire – up to 20 rounds a minute. Its only serious shortcoming while using the weapon in an anti-tank role was its tall profile (higher than two meters). Because of this, it was difficult to camouflage, and therefore the gun crews suffered heavy losses when defending against tank attacks.

On the morning of 11 July, units of *Das Reich* had launched an attack from Teterevino in the direction of Storozhevoe through Ivanovskii Vyselok. Fifteen German tanks had reached the southern edge of the woods lying southwest of Storozhevoe, and three heavy armored vehicles had even managed to break through to some outlying buildings of the village. Simultaneously with the attack from Teterevino, 15 more tanks accompanied by Panzergrenadiers moved out along the railway. The enemy had probably identified the position of the 755th Separate Destroyer Anti-tank Battalion even prior to the attack, and had blanketed it with concentrated *Nebelwerfer* rocket artillery fire. However, the artillerymen withstood this strike, and when the German tanks moved out onto the attack, the crews made full use of the power of their anti-aircraft guns. Unable to endure the heavy and accurate fire, the enemy halted the attack. Enemy vehicles were left smoking on the battlefield. The artillerymen also had losses: 6 men were killed and 31 were wounded, while four of the 85mm anti-aircraft guns and three Studebaker trucks were destroyed.[83]

The decisive repulse inflicted by the 755th Separate Destroyer Anti-tank Battalion forced the enemy to change his plans. This was the only attack along this axis in the course of the day. The SS troops directed their main efforts toward Prokhorovka, along the rail line and through the woods east of Storozhevoe.

In the bend of the Psel River, the operational situation also didn't substantially change from what it had been on 10 July. Hausser's plans to force a crossing of the river with units from *Totenkopf* and to break through in a northeasterly direction were completely disrupted. From the morning report:

> The planned crossing of the [Psel] river on the night of July 10 by the *Totenkopf* division in order to continue the attack out of the bridgehead in the early morning has been delayed, because the bridging column had to take cover in a gully due to enemy artillery fire, and only arrived at the designated place for erecting a crossing early in the morning. Therefore, the start time for the attack has been postponed, and is now planned to begin after completing the construction of the bridge.
>
> … Although two bridges across the Psel River were discovered at 1420 [16.20] north of Bogoroditskoe, the division's offensive out of the bridgehead on 11 July is now impossible. So much rain has dissolved the roads and terrain, as well as the stream embankments, so that even the tanks are bogging down in places. Thus, the transfer of heavy weapons to the very steep eastern bank [of the Psel] has been ruled out. Moreover, air support is impossible due to the weather conditions. These circumstances compel the postponement of the start of the offensive to 12 July. Considering the enemy's growing possibilities, this is the last possible moment to conduct an offensive on the northern bank.
>
> Given any further delay of the attack it will be impossible to hold the relatively small bridgehead against the repeated enemy attacks in the course of 11 July, the number and strength of which are growing.[84]

Thus, despite the fact that the defenders had managed to avert an enemy breakthrough of the rear defensive belt and had kept possession of Prokhorovka Station, by day's end on 11 July, the operational situation here remained extremely complicated and fluid. Over two days of fighting, the Germans had advanced 5 kilometers and had taken possession of key strongpoints in the defense – the Komsomolets and Oktiabr'skii State Farms and Hill 252.2 – and were pushing back our units in the area of Storozhevoe. A portion of the 2nd Tank Corps, defending Vasil'evka, Andreevka and Mikhailovka, had been encircled. The SS had managed to create a bridgehead on the northern bank of the Psel River and were preparing crossings to transfer their panzers, including Tigers, into the river bend. All this was accomplished despite the fact that the command of Voronezh Front had managed to concentrate significant forces in this 10-kilometer sector at Prokhorovka.

One and a half kilometers remained to Prokhorovka Station, but importantly, units that had hastily taken up the defense were still blocking the adversary. However, it was clear that the enemy was preparing for a decisive breakthrough at this location.

In this difficult situation, the main hope of the *front* command was pinned on General Rotmistrov's tank army. According to Vatutin's plan, it was this formation that was to change fundamentally the situation on the next day and to seize the initiative from the enemy.

At 2100 on 11 July, A. M. Vasilevsky arrived at the headquarters of the 5th Guards Tank Army. Having listened to a report on the army's combat readiness, he announced that in connection with the complex operational situation, it was possible that they would have to move up the counterattack to 0300. That meant the army command had to be ready for such a turn of events.

8

Combat Actions on the Sector of 69th Army's 35th Guards Rifle Corps, 9-11 July 1943

From the first hours of Operation Citadel, the attack of General Kempf's forces had not at all gone according to his headquarters' plans. Importantly, Army Detachment Kempf had not been able to keep pace with the advance of II SS Panzer Corps, leaving the latter's right flank dangerously exposed. Serious problems with the defense of his right flank immediately arose for Hausser, since as early as 6 July the command of Voronezh Front had brought tank formations into this area to launch heavy counterattacks. Because of the stubborn resistance of Soviet forces on the boundary between the Fourth Panzer Army and Army Detachment Kempf, their attacking spearheads had diverged. The SS Panzer Corps had advanced significantly further on the Prokhorovka axis and had already reached the bend of the Psel River, while Army Detachment Kempf's divisions had yet to reach the Northern Donets. Gradually, a bulge in the lines, similar to a pouch, had emerged between the Northern and Lipovyi Donets Rivers, where the 69th Army was continuing to hold out. Considering the danger that this Soviet grouping between the rivers presented to the flank of the offensive, by 11 July the point of view had developed in Army Group South's command that if they failed to drive out the Soviet forces defending here, and the Soviet troops continued to struggle with the same stubbornness, then this bulge would have to be eliminated at whatever the cost, even if that required diverting the II SS Panzer Corps to the assistance of the III Panzer Corps. This thought was expressed without any ambiguities at the conference, which Field Marshal Manstein conducted with Hoth and Kempf at the headquarters of Army Detachment Kempf in Dolbino Station on the morning of 11 July.

Army Detachment Kempf had begun Operation Citadel noticeably weaker in strength than the Fourth Panzer Army, and over the past several days of bitter fighting, it had suffered serious losses. However, von Manstein persistently demanded the continuation of the offensive in the direction of Prokhorovka. Between 5 July and 8 July, Kempf's shock formation, Lieutenant General Hermann Breith's III Panzer Corps had managed to drive a wedge into the defenses of Lieutenant General M. S. Shumilov's 7th Guards Army and to reach the sector of the second army-level defensive line occupied by Lieutenant General V. D. Kriuchenkin's 69th Army. General Hünersdorff's 6th Panzer Division, General von Funck's 7th Panzer Division, and General Schmidt's 19th Panzer Division, stubbornly chewing their way through the *front*'s defenses, were slowly advancing between the valleys of the Northern Donets and Razumnaia Rivers.

Notes the III Panzer Corps combat diary:

> Our losses reflect the severity of the fighting. We constantly have to remove thousands of mines. Aerial reconnaissance has still not been able to ascertain the approach of the enemy's operational reserves to the corps' front and flank. But two new divisions [Author's note: the 92nd and 94th Guards Rifle Divisions] reinforced with tanks [Author's note: the 96th Tank Brigade] and anti-tank artillery regiments have been introduced in the sector of the 7th Panzer Division.
>
> For the continuation of the offensive on 8 July, the 7th Panzer Division must secure its greatly extended right flank. With panzers leading, the 6th and 19th Panzer Divisions must attack in a concentrated combat formation along the ridge of heights northeast of Blizhniaia Igumenka to Melikhovo and, correspondingly, to Dal'niaia Igumenka.[1]

By the evening of 8 July, by dint of great exertions, the III Panzer Corps succeeded in seizing a significant part of the villages Melikhovo and Blizhniaia Igumenka, which were major strongpoints in the Soviet defenses. Nevertheless, this tactical success didn't substantially change the situation in Army Detachment Kempf's sector, nor did it affect the situation in the II SS Panzer Corps sector.

For 9 July, Breith gave the 6th and 19th Panzer Divisions the assignment to attack through Bol'shaia Igumenka in the direction of Postnikov, and having broken through the defenses of the 69th Army, to reach the Northern Donets River. At this moment the forward formations of the III Panzer Corps were acutely lacking infantry and armor. Therefore Breith, in the effort to create a strong armored fist to lead the attack, decided to create a *kampfgruppe* consisting of the 19th Panzer Division's 27th Panzer Regiment and the 74th Panzergrenadier Regiment (*Kampfgruppe* Westhofen) and attach it to Major General Hünersdorff's 6th Panzer Division. The commander of the 19th Panzer Division, Lieutenant General Schmidt, in turn received the 168th Infantry Division's 442nd Infantry Regiment and was ordered with it and the rest of his own division to gain full control over the area around Blizhniaia Igumenka.

The troops of Lieutenant General S. G. Goriachev's 35th Guards Rifle Corps of the 69th Army would receive the III Panzer Corps' attack on 9 July.[2] On 9 July, Goriachev's headquarters was also controlling Colonel P. D. Govorunenko's 375th Rifle Division from the 6th Guards Army, which was defending the line Petropavlovka (excl.) – 1 kilometer northeast of Chernaia Poliana; and Major General I. K. Morozov's 81st Guards Rifle Division from the 7th Guards Army. This division together with the 92nd Guards Rifle Division's 276th Guards Rifle Regiment occupied positions along the line: Staryi Gorod – village Machine Tractor Station – Blizhniaia Igumenka – Postnikov. The rest of Colonel V. F. Trunin's 92nd Guards Rifle Division was arranged as follows: the 282nd Guards Rifle Regiment was occupying a line running from a small ravine at Belyi Kolodets to the northeast edge of the woods north of Postnikov; the 280th Guards Rifle Regiment was defending a line running from the Shliakhovoe Machine Tractor Station to Iar Orlov. In addition, Colonel I. G. Russkikh's 94th Guards Rifle Division had been returned to the 35th Guards Rifle Corps by 9 July; its positions extended from the Razumnaia River at Iar Orlov through the northern half of Miasoedovo to the woods lying 2 kilometers east of Miasoedovo.

The heaviest fighting on 9 July developed in the sector of the 81st Guards and 92nd Guards Rifle Divisions. During the third assault of the day at 1400, the enemy crushed the 1st and 3rd Battalions of Lieutenant Colonel I. I. Somoilenko's 282nd Guards Rifle Regiment; 50 tanks with submachine gunners, outflanking the regiment to the right, reached Hill 185.7 on the road running from Staryi Gorod to Dal'niaia Igumenka. From the 35th Guards Rifle Corps' summary of combat operations:

> Remnants of the 1st Company of the 3rd Rifle Battalion, conducting an unequal battle, at 1900 fell back to the area of Andreevka, where together with the 2nd Rifle Battalion they continued to resist the enemy's attacks ... Commanders and soldiers of the 197th Guards Artillery Regiment together with the 282nd Guards Rifle Regiment clung courageously to their defensive line, firing at tanks and infantry at point-blank range. Being surrounded by tanks and submachine gunners, the fighters of the 3rd Artillery Battalion took up an all-round defense; firing in turn from their artillery pieces and their submachine guns, they launched counterattacks. Many gun crews fired at tanks from ranges of 20-30 meters; refusing to abandon their guns, they were crushed beneath the tracks of overrunning tanks.
>
> As the result of bitter fighting, units of the 92nd Guards Rifle Division destroyed up to 60 enemy tanks, while suffering heavy losses in men and equipment in return (16 guns alone were lost). In the fighting for the small village of Postnikov, the courageous commanders of the 197th Guards Artillery Regiment Lieutenant Colonel Shapovalov and its 3rd Artillery Battalion Guards Captain S. S. Smorzh were killed.[3]

The German attack from the area of Melikhovo in the direction of Khokhlovo failed to achieve any results. The 6th Panzer Division ran into extremely heavy opposition, especially in the vicinity of the grove on Hill 217.4. Here, tanks of the 228th Tank Battalion from Major General V. G. Lebedev's 96th Tank Brigade had been dug-in. For four hours, the 13 T-34 tanks of the battalion held their position and offered stubborn resistance. By 1800, having lost six tanks and having expended all their ammunition, the battalion was forced to withdraw. The six remaining tanks (one was lost during the retreat) took up a defensive position on the eastern outskirts of Kiselevo. The enemy took control of the wooded hill, but could advance no further.

Despite all their efforts, the 6th and 19th Panzer Divisions on this day were unable to break through to the Northern Donets River. The enemy continued to be stuck between the first and second defensive belts.

From the "Description of Combat Operations of the 19th Panzer Division between 5 July and 18 July 1943":

> The available forces here were hardly sufficient. We succeeded in taking Blizhniaia Igumenka only after an anti-tank ditch and dense minefields had been overcome, and after the resistance of an enemy vastly superior in numbers had been broken. The powerful minefields in the areas of Postnikov and Shishino, as well as the reduced numbers in the grenadier motorized regiment (up to 400 men with extra weapons and the headquarters company) did not give *Kampfgruppe* Westhofen the possibility to achieve its objective of Shishino on 9 July. The enemy devoted every effort to holding on to the heights east of Shishino. Elements of two Guards rifle divisions (the 92nd and the 81st) were in action here.[4]

Nevertheless, the enemy had managed to begin closing a ring around the 81st Guards and 375th Rifle Divisions, plus two regiments of the 92nd Guards Rifle Division (the 276th Guards and 282nd Guards Rifle Regiments); the 69th Army command was forced at 2200 to begin withdrawing these forces to new lines. At 0145 on 10 July, General S. G. Goriachev sent a coded telegram to the commander of the 375th Rifle Division:

> 1. Around 1430, the enemy in strength of up to 250 tanks attacked units of the 81st Guards Rifle Division in the area of Blizhniaia Igumenka and Postnikov and by day's end had taken Dal'niaia Igumenka and Shishino.
>
> 2. I order: to withdraw rapidly in the direction of Kiselevo and by 0600 10.07.43 to take a defense [on the line]: Kiselevo to the southwest slopes of Hill 211.5 (excl.), Machine Tractor Station, west of Shliakhovoe, Sabynino.
>
> Task: to prevent a breakthrough of enemy infantry tanks in the direction of the sugar factory.
>
> KP [command post] of the division headquarters – the region of woods 2 kilometers southeast of Sabynino. Until your arrival, remnants of the 92nd Guards Rifle Division and the 96th Tank Brigade will defend the designated line.[5]

The Division's chief of operations received this order at 0435; from this moment indeed began the regrouping of the forces on the most important sector of the 69th Army's defenses. After the 375th Rifle Division occupied its new line, the 81st Guards Rifle Division was transferred to the 48th Rifle Corps and assembled on the right bank of the Northern Donets River, on the line: Hill 147.0 – Hill 213.4 – Sazhnoe – Krivtsovo – Novo-Oskochnoe – Shcholokovo. Meanwhile, the 92nd Guards Rifle Division headquarters, pulling back into the woods southwest of Verkhnii Ol'shanets, began to rally its troops that were withdrawing from the fighting.

The sector which Colonel P. D. Govorunenko's 375th Rifle Division now occupied was part of the system of fortifications in the second Army-level defensive belt. Holding it was important not only for keeping the 69th Army's entire defense intact, but also psychologically, for maintaining the troops' high combat morale. The 69th Army command further juggled its forces, trying to strengthen the 35th Guards Rifle Corps and to simplify the task of its commander, Lieutenant General Goriachev, with handling the forces on this axis. On the night before 10 July, Goriachev was given Colonel A. V. Seriugin's 305th Rifle Division. This division occupied positions behind the 375th Rifle Division, on the sector Sabynino – Shliakhovoe – Iar Orlov – Mazikino – Sheino – Ushakovo. On its right flank, the Lieutenant Colonel N. I. Novikov's 280th Guards Rifle Regiment of the 92nd Guards Rifle Division continued to defend together with remnants of Major General V. G. Lebedev's 96th Tank Brigade. The 35th Rifle Corps commander also received Colonel P. M. Bezhko's 107th Rifle Division. This formation dug in along the line Novo-Oskochnoe – Verkhnii Ol'shanets – *Ob'edinenie* [Union] Collective Farm – Komintern – the woods 1 kilometer northeast of Shukhtsovo – the lake lying 1.5 kilometers northeast of Shukhtsovo – Hill 221.0 – southern outskirts of Gremuchii – Popovka, thereby creating a second echelon of defense.

★ ★ ★

The plans of the antagonist became more obvious to the Soviet side with each passing day: Army Detachment Kempf was not only trying to divert forces of the Voronezh Front from the Oboian' axis, but it also had the same task as the II SS Panzer Corps on the Prokhorovka axis: to penetrate our defenses as deeply as possible and to encircle the 69th Army's 48th Rifle Corps. There was no doubt that the headquarters of both German groupings were coordinating their actions. Therefore it was important for Kriuchenkin's forces to wear down and bleed both enemy corps as much as possible, until the moment arrived when the Red Army could launch its offensive.

For its part, the command of Army Group South understood that its plans were no secret for the Soviet side, and therefore it anticipated that the Soviet command would take further steps to strengthen the defense and reinforce the forces on these directions. From the "Description of Combat Operations of the 19th Panzer Division between 5 July and 18 July 1943":

> The adversary sensed the encirclement that was threatening him in the region northeast of Belgorod and therefore on the night before 10 July withdrew his forces to the north along the valley of the Donets River, leaving behind a large quantity of weapons, ammunition and other military supplies. This was done in order to hold the crossings over the Donets River in the vicinities of Kiselevo and Rzhavets with all available withdrawn and arriving forces; in sum, to hold the line Verkhnii Ol'shanets – Sabynino.
>
> Judging by the forces that the enemy has brought up to the line Kiselevo – Rzhavets, the advance of German forces along the Donets River was particularly unsettling for him. The adversary hadn't withdrawn all his forces located between the Donets and the SS Panzer Corps. For this he needed to hold the threatened crossings. In any case, he had to prevent the link-up between the III Panzer Corps units attacking toward the Donets from the southeast and units of the SS Panzer Corps, since this eventuality would mean the encirclement of his divisions operating on the Donets.
>
> The Russians made all sorts of regroupings in order to hold onto the line Kiselevo – Hill 211.5 – Ol'shanets. They committed into the fighting: remnants of the 81st and 73rd Guards Rifle Divisions, units of the 375th Rifle Division, the 89th Guards Rifle Division, two regiments of the 107th Rifle Division, one regiment of the 305th Rifle Division, remnants of the 92nd Guards Rifle Division, remnants of the 4th [Guards] Motorized Rifle Brigade (of the 2nd [Guards] Tank Corps) and, given the presence of the SS Panzer Corps, one anti-tank rifle battalion with 112 weapons. Against them stood the 19th Panzer Division with two groups of motorized infantry (altogether around 400 bayonets), a weakened reconnaissance battalion, and 17 combat-ready tanks.[6]

The staff officers of the 19th Panzer Division were exaggerating the situation. Actually, the situation forced the Soviet command to conduct the regrouping. In the 69th Army sector, rifle divisions, strengthened with artillery, comprised the basis of the defense. With the exception of the shattered remnants of the 47th Guards Separate Heavy Breakthrough Regiment, the 148th Separate Tank Regiment and the 96th Tank Brigade, the 69th Army had no armor. The *front*'s Military Council had decided that it wasn't useful to employ major tank formations on secondary sectors, recognizing that the II SS Panzer Corps and XXXXVIII Panzer Corps represented the main threats. Because of this decision, the main burden of the struggle against Army Detachment Kempf's panzers lay upon the infantry. After five days of the bitterest fighting, the rifle regiments had been weakened and could no longer offer effective resistance, but it was precisely the officers and men of these divisions who had reduced the divisions of Army Detachment Kempf to exhaustion, including the 19th Panzer Division.

The analysis of combat operations in the sector of the II SS Panzer Corps and the III Panzer Corps indicates that the headquarters of these formations used 10 July – the first day of the Prokhorovka engagement – to prepare for a decisive lunge. In carrying out the assignment of encircling our forces between the Northern and Lipovyi Donets, the command of Army Group South gave the leading role to Hausser's II SS Panzer Corps, since it was the more powerful and mobile formation. Its most immediate task was to seize Prokhorovka and thereby create suitable conditions for an attack to the north, toward Oboian', and to the south, toward Pravorot' and Rzhavets. Breith's III Panzer Corps was playing a secondary role, diverting the forces of the 69th Army onto itself. Therefore the II SS Panzer Corps on 10 July was the first to initiate active operations, trying to create a bridgehead on the right bank of the Psel River, to gain possession of Komsomolets State Farm (one of the key points of the defense at Prokhorovka), and to drive our units back toward Storozhevoe.

After the heavy fighting on 9 July, the III Panzer Corps was not ready to resume active operations on 10 July. It spent the day resting and resupplying its forces, bringing up the heavy mortars and artillery to the lines it had gained, conducting a partial regrouping, and directing intense reconnaissance of the Soviet lines, including some strong probes. Parallel with this, as is noted in the documents of the 35th Guards Rifle Corps, the enemy never ceased an intensive shelling of the forward zone of our defenses throughout the day.

On the evening of 10 July, V. D. Kriuchenkin again reshuffled his forces. The 69th Army headquarters tried to make full use of all available means and at the same time to create at least a small reserve. At 2330 35th Rifle Corps commander Lieutenant General Goriachev signed Combat Order No. 8:

> 1. The 92nd Guards Rifle Division is to defend strongly the line: Kiselevo – Hill 211.5 – Machine Tractor Station – west of Shliakhovoe – Sabynino. Division command post: Sabynino.
> 2. The 375th Rifle Division is to be withdrawn into the 69th Army reserve. By dawn on 11 July, the division is to occupy a line of defense: Zhimolostnoe – Mal. Iablonovo – Shakhovo, having the assignment to defend the designated line firmly and not to allow an enemy breakthrough to the east.
>
> Division command post: Plota
>
> Basis: Combat Order No. 00978 of 10.07.43 from the 69th Army headquarters[7]

The lack of reserves was a major problem for the 69th Army command. Therefore, on the night of 10 July, Colonel V. F. Trunin's 92nd Guards Rifle Division, which just the day before had been withdrawn out of encirclement, once again had to move into the front line. Its units were to create a solid defense together with the 305th Rifle

Division. At 0330 11 July, Major M. E. Simonov's 276th Guards Rifle Regiment replaced Lieutenant Colonel N. I. Novikov's 280th Guards Rifle Regiment in the front lines, and together with the 305th Rifle Division's 1002nd Rifle Regiment it occupied the line: (excl.) Hill 122.5 – (excl.) Shliakhovoe Machine Tractor Station. The 92nd Guards Rifle Division's 280th Guards Rifle Regiment took over the sector on the right of the 276th Guards Rifle Regiment, and occupied the line: Kiselevo – Hill 211.5. The 96th Tank Brigade was positioned on the 280th Guards Rifle Regiment's right flank.

In the second echelon of the 92nd Guards Rifle Division, the division commander deployed Lieutenant Colonel I. I. Samoilenko's 282nd Guards Rifle Regiment. It occupied a line running from the bend in the Sabynino-Znamenka road to Hill 224.4, and from there to the edge of the woods at Iar Dubravo (excl.). The battalions of the 197th Guards Artillery Regiment and the 99th Guards Destroyer Anti-tank Artillery Regiment deployed among the combat positions of the infantry. As before, units of the 107th Rifle Division were occupying the 35th Guards Rifle Corps' second echelon.

These were the Soviet formations that waited to receive the III Panzer Corps' next attack between the valleys of the Northern Donets and Razumnaia Rivers. It would come the next morning.

Before making this decisive assault, the III Panzer Corps returned *Kampfgruppe* Westhofen to the 19th Panzer Division. In the corridor between the two rivers, the III Panzer Corps arranged its divisions for the attack. On the far left was the 168th Infantry Division. It was to protect the left flank of the 19th Panzer Division to its right, which was to attack along the valley of the Northern Donets River toward its objectives of Khokhlovo and Kiselevo, with the ultimate goal of seizing crossings over the river. As before, the 6th Panzer Division occupied the center of the III Panzer Corps' combat formation and was preparing to attack from the area of Melikhovo in the direction of Kazach'e and Rzhavets. Next to it on the right, the 7th Panzer Division was assembled at Miasoedovo. It had the order to break through the lines of the 94th Guards Rifle Division and if necessary to reinforce the 6th Panzer Division's attack. The 198th Infantry Division was covering the 7th Panzer Division's right flank, and thus the right flank of the III Panzer Corps as a whole.

In this fashion, Breith's forces entered the Prokhorovka engagement on 11 July from the line Shishino – Khokhlovo – Kiselevo – Hill 211.5 – Shliakhovoe Machine Tractor Station – Sheino – eastern part of Miasoedovo. Around 0500, after a three-hour preparatory artillery bombardment and a massed air attack (in which, according to the data of the 35th Guards Rifle Corps more than 200 aircraft participated) the enemy simultaneously went on the attack in two areas. One prong of the attack struck at Kiselevo and Khokhlovo, while the other was directed at the northern outskirts of Miasoedovo. Let's take a look at the savage fighting that erupted in the villages of Khokhlovo and Kiselevo through the eyes of officers of the 19th Panzer Division and the 35th Guards Rifle Corps. From the "Description of Combat Operations of the 19th Panzer Division between 5 July and 18 July 1943":

> At night, the concentration of artillery in the area southeast of Dal'niaia Igumenka was completed. Stuka support during the attack was also arranged. On 11 July, the division commander personally for the first time would direct the attack of the re-assembled division. The offensive was implemented by two assault groups from

the area northwest of Hill 217.4 (north of Dal'niaia Igumenka) in the direction of Khokhlovo and Kiselevo through valleys leading to the north. The panzer regiment was located with the group attacking on the right.

The resistance in Kiselevo was most serious. The flanking Hill 211.5, behind which strong Russian artillery was positioned, was again a genuine fortress in its elaborate system of trenches.

Because of their low general numbers, only small forces could be committed to the attack on this hill. The dive bombers completed their strike on the hill and reported that they could see nothing on it. In actual fact, a reinforced regiment was firmly entrenched there; the trenches were impossible to spot even from five meters. In addition, the majority of defenders were Asians, against whom psychological effects were useless; moreover, in their narrow trenches, they had almost suffered no losses from our dive bombers. To our great misfortune, all the ravines and the eastern outskirts of Kiselevo were still mined, so the panzers tried to bypass the minefield barriers to the left, southeast of Kiselevo. In doing so, they wound up in a swamp and bogged down 1 kilometer northeast of the outskirts of Khokhlovo.[8]

From the account of the 35th Guards Rifle Corps:

The 92nd Guards Rifle Division was involved in intensive combat with the enemy's tanks and motorized infantry [Panzergrenadiers]. By 1200, the 280th and 276th Guards Rifle Regiments had repulsed enemy attacks in strength of up to two battalions and 30 tanks each. At 1400, the enemy in strength of up to 25 tanks again launched an attack on Kiselevo from the area of Khokhlovo, but suffering heavy losses from the fire of the 96th Tank Brigade's tanks, he was forced to retreat.

Having reinforced his grouping in the vicinity of Hill 217.4, the enemy hurled up to a regiment of infantry and 60 tanks at Kiselevo. At 1525 the enemy managed at the cost of heavy losses to penetrate with tanks into the combat positions of the 280th Guards Rifle Regiment, break into Kiselevo, and take possession of the village.[9]

Again from the "Description of Combat Operations of the 19th Panzer Division between 5 July and 18 July 1943":

During this offensive, more than 800 mines have been cleared from the battlefield. They are reporting that the enemy west of the Donets is retreating to the north.

Despite the heavy fire from at least 100 anti-tank guns brought up to this place on 10.07, the 122nd Anti-tank Rifle Battalion and the heavy tanks of the 4th Motorized Rifle Brigade, our assault group is attacking and seizing Kiselevo at almost the same time that the left group is taking Khokhlovo. At this minute, two British Churchill tanks suddenly appear on the outskirts of Khokhlovo, plainly with the intention to get behind our panzers in Kiselevo. They had no concerns about the two bogged down panzers, before which they now presented themselves as if on an open palm. One Tiger immediately dealt with both of them. The Donets has been reached, and the crossing over which the enemy had hurried units of the 375th Rifle Division (which had been operating northwest of Khar'kov) for the defense of Kiselevo, is now in our hands.

Just before evening the 74th Panzergrenadier Regiment broke into the superbly laid out flanking system of trenches east of Kiselevo. However, they did not manage to consolidate their gains, since the companies were down to only 20 active bayonets each. In order to repulse night-time attacks and the operations of assault groups, the regiments took up circular defenses on the hills they had gained that day, since it was impossible to create a solid line of defense. Throughout the entire night, the forward attacking detachments were subjected to strong artillery and mortar fire.[10]

The enemy's 6th Panzer Division managed to achieve significantly more. From the "Description of Combat Operations of the 35th Guards Rifle Corps over the period 7 to 18.07.43":

> Attacking from the direction of Dal'niaia Igumenka and Melikhovo toward Shliakhovoe, the enemy in strength of up to a regiment of infantry with the support of 80 tanks broke through the defenses on the boundary between the 276th Guards Rifle Regiment and the 1004th Rifle Regiment and began to exploit the success in the direction of Hill 230.3 and Ol'khovatka, seizing Kazach'e by the end of the day.
>
> After the enemy breakthrough, the 276th Guards Rifle Regiment withdrew its left flank to the western slopes of Hill 230.3, where it took up an all-round defensive posture and repulsed enemy attacks.
>
> At 1530, the 282nd Guards Rifle Regiment was thrown into a counterattack in the direction of Sabynino and Kiselevo, but the counterattack was broken up by a concentrated air attack and the attack of a large group of enemy tanks. The regiment, suffering large losses, went over to the defense with its remnants on a line running from the Sabynino Machine Tractor Station to some woods lying two kilometers to the east, where it in fact continued to operate.
>
> At 2300, according to an order, the division began to withdraw to the northeast with the task to occupy a new defensive line between Vypolzovka and the southern outskirts of Aleksandrovka, and to delay the enemy's further advance. By morning on 12.07.43, the indicated line was occupied by the reconnaissance company and the division's training battalion, the 2nd Battalion of the 280th Guards Rifle Regiment and remnants of the 96th Tank Brigade.[11]

The 96th Tank Brigade's summary report for the period 5 July to 14 July 1943 offers this description of the battle:

> At 1200 11.07.43, the enemy in strength of up to 40 tanks and two battalions of infantry began to attack in the direction of Kiselevo. The 228th Tank Battalion firmly clung to its occupied line, not permitting the enemy tanks entry into Kiselevo. Meanwhile, the destroyer anti-tank artillery battalion and the 1st Battalion of the Motorized Rifle Regiment were decimating the following [enemy] infantry.
>
> At 1600 11.07.43, 25 enemy tanks broke through the front lines west of Shliakhovoe and advanced in the direction of Verkhnii Ol'shanets and Rzhavets, threatening the brigade with encirclement. The 228th Tank Battalion with its six

> remaining tanks emerged from the closing ring to the right of Kazach'e and took up a defensive position in Sviridovo. The brigade's remaining battalions fought their way through the encircling German forces between Rzhavets and Kazach'e, and by morning of 12.07.43, had reassembled in the area of Aleksandrovka at the order of the brigade commander.[12]

Parallel with the attack of the 19th and 6th Panzer Divisions, a 7th Panzer Division *kampfgruppe* struck positions of the 15th Guards and 94th Guards Rifle Divisions of the 35th Guards Rifle Corps. Between 1000 and 1500, units of Colonel I. G. Russkikh's 94th Guards Rifle Division beat back several panzer attacks on the northern outskirts of Miasoedovo. Having determined the boundary between the 94th Guards and 15th Guards Rifle Divisions, at 1500 the Germans hurled up to a regiment of infantry with the support of 50 tanks against that point and simultaneously attacked the line of one of the rifle regiments of the 94th Guards Rifle Division along the road running to Sheino from Miasoedovo. The attack had heavy artillery and air support. Having penetrated the defenses of the flank battalions on the boundary between the Guards divisions, by 1700 German tanks had emerged in the rear of the 94th Guards Rifle Division's 283rd Guards and 288th Guards Rifle Regiments. Simultaneously, a group of up to 40 armored vehicles, operating along the road to Sheino, crushed the resistance of Lieutenant Colonel M. P. Aglitsky's 288th Guards Rifle Regiment and advanced to a position northeast of Sheino. This development left the 283rd Guards and 288th Guards Rifle Regiments encircled. Division commander Colonel I. G. Russkikh ordered the commander of the 286th Guards Rifle Regiment Major D. S. Chuev to make a diversionary counterattack from Sheino with two rifle battalions. At the same time, the 283rd Guards Rifle Regiment, attacking in the direction of Miasoedovo, linked up with elements of the 288th Guards Rifle Regiment. By midnight, both regiments had fully withdrawn from the pocket.

In this manner, in the course of 11 July units of the 6th Panzer Division had practically overcome the second army-level defensive belt in the sector of the 35th Guards Rifle Corps. In addition, that night it penetrated the rear defensive line by seizing Rzhavets. The 19th Panzer Division had also made some gains during the day. It had fully pushed Soviet forces out of the villages of Khokhlovo and Kiselevo, and had rolled forward to the channel of the Northern Donets River. As a result, the Germans had pinned the 81st Guards Rifle Division against the river in the sector Rzhavets – Strel'nikov – Krivtsovo – Sabynino, and were continuing to compress the pocket. In this situation, the 35th Guards Rifle Corps command issued an order for a withdrawal to a new line of defense: Vypolzovka – Aleksandrovka – Sviridovo – western bank of the Razumnaia River – Mazikino – Sheino – Ushakovo.

The II SS Panzer Corps' attack on 11 July had progressed with great difficulties. Only the *Leibstandarte* succeeded in making clear gains, reaching the outskirts of Prokhorovka Station. Nevertheless, albeit slowly, Army Group South's armored spearheads were driving ever more deeply into the defenses of the 69th Army. The enemy command was persistently and deliberately implementing its plan to encircle and destroy our 48th Rifle Corps.

For N. F. Vatutin, this day became one of the most stressful moments of the defensive operation. In the course of one day, the adversary had fully seized the intended start lines for the 5th Guards Tank Army's counterattack by shoving the rifle units of the 5th Guards Army back to the prepared trenches on the outskirts of Prokhorovka Station. All the preparatory work of the artillerymen and reconnaissance troops for introducing the 18th and 29th Tank Corps into the battle went to waste. At the same time, the penetration of the lines of the 35th Rifle Corps 18 kilometers south of the station threatened the rear of Rotmistrov's and Zhadov's forces, which were preparing for the counterattack. Considering the pace of advance of Army Detachment Kempf's panzer divisions on 11 July and the battered condition of the 69th Army's forces, these concerns were real.

In these circumstances, Vatutin, lacking his own reserves, was personally forced to gather whatever bits and pieces of units or detachments that he could find in order to cover the Prokhorovka axis. The situation, which had developed in the 69th Army's sector, forced the diversion of significant forces from the formations of the shock grouping, which was then concentrating southwest of Prokhorovka. One must acknowledge that the enemy managed to compel serious changes in the plans of the Voronezh Front command for 12 July, forcing it to adjust the counterattack's intended

Formation	Pz II	Pz III 50/ L42	Pz III 50/ L60	Pz III 75mm	Pz IV L24	Pz IV L43 or L48	Pz VI	T-34	StuG	Hummel	Total
II SS Panzer Corps											
1st SS *LAH*	4	-	5	-	-	47	4	-	10	7	77
2nd SS *DR*	-	-	34	-	-	18	1	8	27	7	95
3rd SS *T*	-	54	-	-	4	26	10	-	21	7	122
Total	4	54	39	-	4	91	15	8	58	21	294
III Panzer Corps											
6th Pz	2	2	11	7	-	6	-	-	-	2	30
7th Pz	-	-	24	2	1	9	-	-	-	3	39
19th Pz	-	-	7	4	-	3	-	-	-	1	15
503rd Heavy Pz Bn	-	-	-	-	-	-	23	-	-	-	23
228th Sep Assault Gun Bn	-	-	-	-	-	-	-	-	19	-	19
Total	2	2	42	13	1	18	23	-	19	6	126

Note: Records for the II SS Panzer Corps are for 1835 11 July. Those for the 6th Panzer Division and the 503rd Heavy Panzer Battalion are for the morning of 11 July, while those for the 7th Panzer and 19th Panzer Divisions, and the 228th Separate Assault Gun Battalion are for the morning of 12 July. Note that the number of operational tanks was often at its lowest in the evening, while vehicles were still in the repair workshops. Morning records would usually show a higher total as repaired vehicles returned to action.

Source: Niklas Zetterling and Anders Frankson, *Kursk 1943: A Statistical Analysis* (London: Frank Cass, 2000), Tables A6.4 – A6.10.

Table 17: Operational Tanks Remaining in the II SS Panzer Corps and III Panzer Corps 11 July 1943

start line, weaken its shock grouping substantially and to pay attention not only to the main axis southwest of Prokhorovka, but also to the south, in the area of Shcholokovo, Rzhavets and Vypolzovka.

The status of the II SS Panzer Corps and the III Panzer Corps for 11 July 1943 is shown in Table 17.

9

Preparations for Voronezh Front's Counterstroke

The idea of conducting a counterattack with the *Front*'s forces, including the 5th Guards Tank Army and the 5th Guards Army from the *Stavka* Reserve, developed in N. F. Vatutin's mind on 9 July, when the enemy was still located 10 kilometers from Prokhorovka. What was that particular circumstance, which prompted Vatutin's decision to launch a counterstroke? Probably, it was the result of a comparative analysis of the different tactical approaches and means previously used while conducting the defensive operation, as well as the information on the condition of the enemy's forces obtained by reconnaissance and intelligence.

On 9 July, the XXXXVIII Panzer Corps had at last been able to penetrate the second army-level defensive line to its full depth, having advanced approximately 12-13 kilometers that day. Thus, both of Hoth's panzer corps had overcome two-thirds of Voronezh Front's most heavily fortified belts on both sides of the Oboian' highway and to the east, on the Prokhorovka axis. The results obtained by von Knobelsdorff's divisions on the fifth day of Operation Citadel were greater than any previous day's results, and were comparable to the results gained by II SS Panzer Corps' attack on the first day of the operation. If however one looks at what the adversary had managed to achieve on 7 and 8 July, then it appears that the work of Voronezh Front's forces had been almost twice as effective as it was on subsequent days. The Germans' advance on 7 and 8 July comprised all of only 5 to 7 kilometers, and they still seemed bogged down in the second defensive belt. By 9 July, accordingly, it would have been logical to assume that the enemy's capabilities must have diminished due to losses.

Then what was the reason for the XXXXVIII Corps' surprising success after four days of the bloodiest combat? Of course, N. F. Vatutin was asking himself this same question. Let's try to ponder his line of thinking as he sought to answer this question.

One can assume that after the first two days of the offensive, the German groupings on the Oboian' and Prokhorovka directions had suffered painful losses. The German command must have considered this possibility during the planning of Citadel; therefore it must have brought up its operational reserves on 7 and 8 July, and it was likely their introduction into the fighting on 9 July that had yielded such a noticeable effect. This is a sufficiently realistic line of thinking and the Voronezh Front commander might have agreed fully with it, especially if you consider that the *front*'s reconnaissance had been constantly reporting on the approach of enemy reserves. According to its information, by 8 July the Germans had committed three fresh divisions on the axis of the Fourth Panzer Army's main attack, though as it later turned out, this information was incorrect.

N. F. Vatutin had no precise information on the composition of Army Group South, nor of course could he know about the daily losses in von Manstein's combat formations. Therefore he had to make estimates based upon the losses in his own armies and corps, and they had been significant. To a certain extent, Vatutin could draw upon the information from prisoner interrogations, but so far they had primarily been able to grab only ordinary soldiers or *unteroffiziers,* very rarely junior officers, who primarily answered on the losses in even their own units based only on what they had seen with their own eyes. In this situation, it was not sensible to trust such a source of information. It was difficult to extrapolate general losses from such scanty data.

On the first morning of the offensive on 5 July, in the sector of the 6th Guards Army the enemy had encountered four rifle divisions, two destroyer anti-tank artillery brigades, a tank brigade, and two separate tank regiments. Over the four next days on the sector of Chistiakov's 6th Guards Army alone, six tank and one mechanized corps; two rifle divisions; three tank and two destroyer anti-tank artillery brigades; three separate tank and three destroyer anti-tank artillery regiments; three separate destroyer anti-tank artillery battalions; and a regiment of *Katiusha* rocket-launchers and a howitzer regiment had been brought up, and they all had been committed into the fighting. Logic suggests that the Germans *must* have reinforced their forces, if it had been able to achieve such noticeable results while attacking against such powerful forces. With this in mind, the *front* commander must have taken seriously the intelligence warnings about the arrival of fresh enemy divisions.

In any event, Vatutin could not have failed to see that the adversary was behaving very actively and had driven into the depths of the *front*'s lines on just those days, when the defense had been conducted passively. After all, on 7 July M. E. Katukov had managed to delay the enemy with the short, but sharp counterattacks of his tank brigades, supported by artillery, even though he hadn't been able to prepare any solid line of defense, and the 6th Guards Army had been simply shattered. On 8 July, thanks to the activity of only one brigade from the [2nd Guards] 'Tatsinskaia' Tank Corps, one and a half brigades from the [5th Guards] 'Stalingrad' Tank Corps, and the combined actions of three brigades from the 2nd Tank Corps, the enemy grouping on the Prokhorovka axis had not only been stopped, but had even been forced to yield some of the ground it had gained previously. In contrast on 9 July, when all four tank corps of the *front* had remained inactive on the first half of the day (excluding combat reconnaissance probes), the Germans had made a 13-kilometer advance, and had been stopped finally only after 10th Tank Corps' counterattack. From all this evidence it followed that only an active defense with the application of significant tank forces yielded substantial, positive results.

N. F. Vatutin had to have noticed these facts, especially if one considers that the *front*'s artillery was dwindling due to significant losses. Already more than ten destroyer anti-tank artillery regiments had lost all their equipment and had been withdrawn for refitting, while more than 20 had lost more than 50% of their guns. In return, only one mortar brigade had arrived as reinforcements for Voronezh Front, and it was still awaiting the arrival of one destroyer anti-tank artillery brigade.

At the same time, there were several intelligence reports that seemed to indicate that the enemy's strength was becoming exhausted and he was running out of reserves.

1. Voronezh Front's chief of intelligence General Vinogradov's intelligence summary for 0700 on 8 July reported: 'Trench construction has been observed in the region of Mikhailovka and Hill 210.3 north of Cherkasskoe.'[1]
2. From Voronezh Front headquarters' intelligence summary for 1200 8 July: 'On the night of July 7, a reconnaissance party captured a prisoner from the 255th

Infantry Division's veterinarian company. During preliminary interrogation, the prisoner revealed that on 5 July, up to 30 men were transferred as a group to the vicinity of Hill 219.8, where a machine gun company of the 465th Infantry Regiment was positioned after replacing the 332nd Infantry Division's 676th Infantry Regiment on this sector of the front.'[2]

3. From the intelligence summary of the 1st Tank Army for 2200 9 July: 'The enemy is laying mines in the area of Hills 210.3 and 210.7/north of the northern part of Cherkasskoe, west of Syrtsevo, and on the eastern bank of the Pena River in the region of Verkhopen'e. According to information from our neighbor on the right [the 40th Army – *author*], seven prisoners from the 332nd Infantry Division were seized. The division has suffered heavy losses, 120-130 men remained in the battalions, and the division has the orders to defend on the lines it has obtained. The defense is weak – one battalion per 3 kilometers of front.'[3]

4. From information of Voronezh Front headquarters' intelligence branch for 9 July: '… on the sector Luchki/south of Luchki/*Smelo k trudu* Collective Farm, the enemy has been constructing trenches. In addition, information has begun to arrive that the enemy on several sectors in the flood lands along the Lipovyi Donets is strengthening positions with two or three rows of barbed wire.'[4]

All the indicated hills and sectors indicated in the reports were on the flanks of the Fourth Panzer Army. The ongoing engineering work of this nature on the flanks of the shock grouping after five days of the offensive, and the commitment of personnel from the rear units (veterinarians) into the front lines seemed to point to one thing: the enemy's strength was dwindling, his reserves were running out, but there was the strict order to keep attacking at whatever the cost. Therefore, scraping up forces and weapons, the Germans were removing panzer and motorized formations from the flanks and hurling them into the main axis of the attack, while strengthening the weakened sectors with obstacles and fortifications.

One more fact supports this conclusion. It was something the enemy command had to know: tank forces of the 40th Army, although indeed not significant, were nevertheless operating on LII Army Corps' front. Considering the experience of the recent days of fighting, there was the likelihood that the Soviet side might bring up even larger formations here. A similar situation was forming on II SS Panzer Corps' right flank, on the Donets. A strong tank formation, the 2nd Guards 'Tatsinskaia' Tank Corps, was located here. Despite these armor threats, in both areas primarily only German infantry and artillery were defending, and moreover some of them were rear-area personnel. All this taken together indicated one thing: the adversary was in no condition to augment his forces further and was exhausting his strength. In the next couple of days, it was necessary to anticipate a final, decisive effort to break through the third defensive belt.

The conclusion about the lack of reserves and the concentration of the most capable and mobile formations at the focal points of the attack at the expense of stripping bare the flanks suggested itself, and in essence, it was correct. At this moment, the Fourth Panzer Army's flanks, especially the western flank, were the weakest spots in its combat formation. Let's recall the regrouping of *Totenkopf* to the Psel River, and the order to transfer units of *Das Reich* and the 167th Infantry Division to the sector along the Lipovyi Donets River in order to take over the positions of units shifted to reinforce the main attack. There was intelligence information that in front of the 1st Tank Army on the Oboian' axis, documents had been removed from a dead German soldier of the 255th Infantry Division, which had previously been operating in the 40th Army's sector.

However, where should the decisive assault be launched? Here, command talent would play a role in making this determination, alongside rational analysis. N. F. Vatutin possessed this talent, and he had the gift of foresight, which he successfully demonstrated in the course of the Kursk battle.

Despite the fact that on all preceding days, the enemy's main forces had been applied against M. E. Katukov's [1st Tank] and M. Chistiakov's [6th Guards] armies in the attempt to break through their lines, already by the afternoon of 9 July Vatutin sensed that the enemy was changing the direction of attack, and was preparing on 10 July to eliminate the threat to his extended flanks by encircling both the 6th Tank Corps with its attached forces behind the Pena River, and the 48th Rifle Corps between the Lipovyi Donets and Northern Donets River. That the Fourth Panzer Army was attempting to liquidate A. L. Getman's 6th Tank Corps in the bend of the Pena River had become clear, when the pressure on the 309th Rifle Division and the 3rd Tank Corps north of Novoselovka eased, and the enemy began to probe the area west of the village in the direction of Hill 232.8 and the left flank of the 6th Tank Corps (north of Verkhopen'e). At the same time, attacks on the lines of the 90th Guards Rifle Division and the 10th Motorized Brigade at Lukhanino and Shepelevka were intensifying. The pincers that von Knobelsdorff was forming from the 3rd Panzer Division in the south and *Grossdeutschland* in the north were obvious to N. F. Vatutin. The concentration of the 10th Tank Corps in the Kruglik – Kalinovka – south of Malinovoe area also gives evidence that the Soviet command understood the enemy's plan. The deployment of a major mobile formation in this area blocked the northern axis of advance on this sector, and in case of a turn to the west or southwest by *Grossdeutschland*, it would present the opportunity of an attack on its flanks.

Two developments strongly hinted at von Manstein's immediate plans on the Prokhorovka axis. The first was the SS formations' persistent effort to force a crossing of the Psel River and to break through the defenses in the river bend. The second was arriving intelligence about the concentration of several hundred armored vehicles in this area. Aerial reconnaissance was the first to provide information on this massive assembly of armor, and then evidence began to arrive from the commands of the 6th Guards Army and 1st Tank Army. The SS Panzergrenadier Division *Totenkopf*'s appearance in the area of Kochetovka was the first sign that the adversary was gathering significant forces here. This was an important indication of the enemy's intention to seize the area around Prokhorovka, especially if one takes into account that a boundary line between two Soviet armies ran through this area.

Thus, considering firstly that the enemy had suffered substantial losses and was strengthening the attacking spearheads at the expense of his flank protection, and secondly that the enemy had a powerful grouping of 100,000 men and more than 900 armored vehicles in the area bounded by the Pena, Psel and Lipovyi Donets Rivers, *front* command believed that it would be ineffective to scatter its accumulated forces across the entire front. Five days of combat had indicated that an active defense would yield better results than passive restraint. Therefore, Vatutin concluded that the best way to continue the defensive operation would be a powerful, decisive counterstroke from Prokhorovka in the direction of the Oboian' highway. Simultaneously, it would be necessary for the 1st Tank Army and the Sixth Guards Army to launch holding attacks on the Syrtsevo – Verkhopen'e – Novoselovka sector to pin down the German forces there.

The counterattack would finally bring the enemy to a halt and force him to abandon further offensive operations. According to intelligence, the enemy had up to 250 tanks in the Vasil'evka – Belenikhino sector, while Voronezh Front had assembled almost four times that amount of armor and infantry at Prokhorovka. Such a correlation of forces promised success.

The selection of the Prokhorovka area for the counterattack was not accidental. In the opinion of N. F. Vatutin, it was exactly here at Prokhorovka that the main events must unfold in the immediate future, since the Germans were clearly aiming to encircle the 48th Rifle Corps, and it was here where the stronger of the two enemy formations – the II SS Panzer Corps, which was to carry out this plan – was operating. If the enemy managed to execute its plans, this would substantially weaken the *front*, and noticeably ease Fourth Panzer Army's task of withdrawing its forces in case that became necessary. It was also already becoming clear that the Germans were running out of strength, and a major counterstroke might quickly prompt them to begin a withdrawal.

There is one more important factor that must be considered while exploring Vatutin's thought processes about the given problem. On 9 July in Central Front's sector on the northern face of the Kursk bulge, the advance of the German Ninth Army had ground to a halt. On 12 July, the neighboring Briansk Front was to launch an attack on the enemy's Orel grouping. On 15 July, Central Front itself was to go on the offensive. However, in the south, in Voronezh Front's sector, the situation was much less clear. Not only had Army Group South not been stopped, but it was even continuing to advance, driving our units back toward Prokhorovka. The real threat of Prokhorovka Station's capture had arisen on 11 July.

I. V. Stalin had spoken repeatedly about whose responsibility it would be, if the enemy "began to roam around the rear areas" of Voronezh Front. To all that this implied, one had also to add the daily psychological pressure applied by the *Stavka*. In such a difficult situation, it was rather hard to expect equanimity, focus and cool thinking from N. F. Vatutin, on whose shoulders rested such an enormous burden, while making decisions.

It is also no secret that there also existed an unspoken rivalry between the *front* commanders, which Stalin encouraged and exploited in his own interests. In this unique competition, the peculiarities of combat operations, the terrain, the enemy strength or the relative losses did not matter – only results counted. Combat honors and the Supreme Leader's opinion of the capabilities of a general or marshal depended precisely on results. In the ongoing defensive operation, the Voronezh Front was plainly lagging behind the Central Front, despite the fact that Vatutin's *front* had more forces; thus it was vital for Vatutin to stop the Germans at Prokhorovka.

★ ★ ★

It is very difficult to establish a chronology of the decisions regarding Voronezh Front's counterattack and the implementation of measures for its preparation. Unfortunately, my research was unable to uncover any sort of schematic map or written plan for the operation. Perhaps future researchers will be more fortunate. However, in the course of searching through the documentary materials, I began to form the impression that a single document, laying out the operational situation for 12 July, and our command's conclusions and plans based upon that, simply does not exist. On the other hand, the details of the plan for Voronezh Front's counterattack have been spelled out in sufficient detail in certain publications since the war. It is difficult to assert with any confidence that the documentary files of the Voronezh Front's headquarters is the source of these publications, but the analysis of this information allows one to regard it with some confidence. Therefore we will try to recreate the picture of events on the basis of these secondary sources.

In order to prepare the Voronezh Front's forces for the counterattack, a number of things had to be accomplished: first the commands of the subordinate armies, which were to participate in attack, had to be informed of the plan; concrete tasks had to be delivered to the headquarters in the form of distributed orders; units temporarily subordinated to the *front* for purposes of strengthening the attacking divisions and corps had to receive their instructions (on their movement to new locations and their assignments) and the execution of these instructions had to be monitored; the troops needed to be provided with at least the most essential things (ammunition, fuel, rations); and the instructions going out from the headquarters of forward formations to their subordinate units had to be reconciled with the general plan. This list of only the most necessary measures had to be completed within at most twenty-four hours! Of course, it is completely obvious that to complete all of this work within this period of time without oversights or errors is virtually impossible.

Voronezh Front's headquarters immersed itself in planning the counterattack, but according to the established routine, its Military Council was obliged to report to Moscow on its proposal and supply the *Stavka* a rationale for it. The official History of the Great Patriotic War, published in 1962, contains the following statement:

> On the night of 10 July, the Military Council of the Voronezh Front reported to the *Stavka* that in six days of fighting on the Oboian' axis, the enemy had suffered enormous losses and had no more reserves. Therefore it [the enemy] had concentrated its remaining strength in the shock grouping on the Prokhorovka axis at the expense of weakening its flanks. Pursuant to an agreement with the *Stavka*, the Voronezh Front command took the decision to launch a powerful counterstroke on the morning of 12 July ...[5]

As uncovered documents disclose, the bulk of Voronezh Front's main forces were preparing to take part in the counterattack: six of its eight armies, including the two armies from the *Stavka* Reserve – the full 5th Guards Tank Army and the 5th Guards Army, plus the temporarily attached 2nd Tank Corps and 2nd Guards 'Tatsinskaia' Tank Corps. The two exceptions were the 40th and 38th Armies, which in the preceding days had transferred significant forces to the operational control of the 6th Guards Army and 1st Tank Army and by 12 July had been substantially weakened. Even so, General K. S. Moskalenko's 40th Army was instructed to launch demonstration attacks on its front.

The *front* command's primary hopes for success were pinned on the two fresh armies from the *Stavka* Reserve. Yet although the counterstroke of 12 July was due to N. F.

On 10 July 1943, N. S. Khrushchev reports over the telephone to I. V. Stalin on the arrival of the 5th Guards Tank Army in the area of Prokhorovka Station. Seated next to him is the commander of the Voronezh Front's Armored and Mechanized Forces Lieutenant General A. D. Shtevnev. Standing to Shtevnev's immediate right is 5th Guards Tank Army commander Lieutenant General P. A. Rotmistrov, and standing on Rotmistrov's right is the deputy commander of the Voronezh Front General of the Army I. P. Apanasenko. (RGAKFD)

Vatutin's initiative, he doubtlessly had received the approval of the *Stavka* of the Supreme High Command for just such a use of the strategic reserves that had been placed under his control. Rotmistrov's 5th Guards Tank Army was fully staffed and equipped. By the evening of 11 July, all three of its tank corps and its mechanized corps had assembled 30 kilometers from the front lines. The amount of armor in the units and formations of the 5th Guards Tank Army for 11 July 1943 is shown in Table 18. The Army had more than 40,000 soldiers and officers on its roster, and more than 700 tanks and self-propelled guns. In the 5th Guards Army, the rifle divisions alone had more than 62,000 men. With the introduction of these two armies into the fighting, the correlation of strength and means on the threatened axis sharply changed in favor of the Voronezh Front.

Two shock groupings were formed from the armies committed to the counterattack:

The first, the main grouping, was deploying in the areas of Novye Lozy, Belenikhino Station, Prokhorovka Station, Polezhaev, Veselyi, and Kochetovka (excl.). It consisted of one rifle corps from the 69th Army, two rifle corps from the 5th Guards Army, and four tank and one mechanized corps from the 5th Guards Tank Army.

The second, auxiliary grouping consisted of two rifle corps from the 6th Guards Army, two tank corps, and brigade-level units of the 3rd Mechanized Corps from the

No.	Units and Formations	T-34			T-70			Mk-IV Churchill			KV-1	Su-76	Su-122	Su-152	Total Tanks/ SP Guns	Armored Cars		
																M3A-1	BA-64	M-2
		Runners	En Route	In Repair	Runners	En Route	In Repair	Runners	En Route	In Repair						Runner/ In repair	Runner/ In repair	Runners
1	1 Gds MC Reg	6	2	2	-	-	-	-	-	-	-	-	-	-	10	12	2	5
2	53 Gds Sep Tank Reg	39	3	-	1	-	-	-	-	-	-	-	-	-	43	-	-	-
3	18 Tank Corps (a)	68	26	5	58	5	-	18	2	1	-	-	-	-	183	-	31	-
4	Corps HQ	5	-	-	-	-	-	-	-	-	-	-	-	-	5	-	-	-
5	419 Sep Signals Bn	2	-	-	-	-	-	-	-	-	-	-	-	-	2	-	10	-
6	110 Tank Bde	22	-	2	21	-	-	-	-	-	-	-	-	-	45	-	3 (BA-20)	-
7	170 Tank Bde	22	-	-	17	-	-	-	-	-	-	-	-	-	39	-	-	-
8	181 Tank Bde	24	-	-	20	-	-	-	-	-	-	-	-	-	44	-	3	-
9	36 Gds Sep Hvy Reg	-	-	-	-	-	-	18	2	-	-	-	-	-	20	-	3	-
10	29 Tank Corps (b)	123	8	7	81	4	4	-	-	-	2	10	11	12	229/37	(2 Su on way/repair)		
11	363 Sep Signals Bn	3	-	-	-	-	-	-	-	-	-	-	-	-	3	-	10	
12	38 Sep AC Bn	-	-	-	7	-	-	-	-	-	-	-	-	-	7	12 (BA-10)	10	-
13	25 Tank Bde (c)	31	-	1	36	-	3	-	-	-	1	-	-	-	73	-	3	-
14	31 Tank Bde	29	-	3	38	-	1	-	-	-	-	-	-	-	71	-	3	-
15	32 Tank Bde	63	-	1	-	-	-	-	-	-	-	-	-	-	64	-	3	-
16	1446 SP Gun Reg	-	-	-	-	-	-	-	-	-	-	10	11	-	21	-	-	-
17	1529 SP Gun Reg	-	-	-	-	-	-	-	-	-	1	-	-	11	13	(1 Su in repair)		

Table 18: Number of Tanks and Self-propelled Guns in the Units and Formations of the 5th Guards Tank Army, 11 July 1943

Continuation of Table 18

No.	Units and Formations	T-34			T-70			Mk-IV Churchill			KV-1	Su-76	Su-122	Su-152	Total Tanks/SP Guns	Armored Cars		
		Runners	On way	In Repair	Runners	On way	In Repair	Runners	On way	In Repair						M3A-1 Runner/In repair	BA-64 Runner/In repair	M-2 Runners
18	5 Gds Mech Corps (d)	120	43	1	56	4	1	-	-	-	-	10	11	-	225/21	-	-	-
19	10 Gds Mech Bde	30	-	-	14	-	-	-	-	-	-	-	-	-	44	-	-	-
20	11 Gds Mech Bde	16	-	-	15	-	-	-	-	-	-	-	-	-	31	9	8	-
21	12 Gds Mech Bde	20	-	-	15	-	-	-	-	-	-	-	-	-	35	-	-	-
22	24 Gds Tank Bde	48	13	-	-	-	-	-	-	-	-	-	-	-	61	-	-	-
23	1447 SP Gun Reg	-	-	-	-	-	-	-	-	-	-	4	7	-	21	(10 Su on way/in repair)		
24	2 Gds Tank Corps	86	-	-	52	-	-	3	-	-	-	-	-	-	141	-	-	-
25	4 Gds Tank Bde	28	-	-	19	-	-	-	-	-	-	-	-	-	47	-	-	-
26	25 Gds Tank Bde	28	-	-	19	-	-	-	-	-	-	-	-	-	47	-	-	-
27	26 Gds Tank Bde	30	-	-	14	-	-	-	-	-	-	-	-	-	44	-	-	-
28	47 Gds Hvy Tank Reg	-	-	-	-	-	-	3	-	-	-	-	-	-	3	-	-	-
29	2 Tank Corps	35	-	7	46	-	2	3	-	7	-	-	-	-	100	-	-	-
30	15 Gds Sep Hvy Tank Reg	-	-	-	-	-	-	3	-	7	-	-	-	-	10	-	-	-
31	26 Tank Bde	6	-	9	8	-	7	-	-	-	-	-	-	-	30	-	-	-
32	99 Tank Bde	10	-	4	10	-	-	-	-	-	-	-	-	-	24	-	-	-
33	169 Tank Bde	14	-	-	4	-	-	-	-	-	-	-	-	-	18	-	-	-
34	894 Sep Signals Bn	4	-	-	-	-	-	-	-	-	-	-	-	-	4	-	-	-
35	12 Sep AC Bn	-	-	-	11	-	-	-	-	-	-	-	-	-	11	-	-	-

Continuation of Table 18

Notes

(a) Data for the 18th Tank Corps comes from the document "On the condition of equipment and provisioning of the 5th Guards Tank Army at 1700 11.07.43", signed by the 5th Guards Tank Army's deputy chief of staff Lieutenant Torgalo. However, the 18th Tank Corps' own combat dispatch No. 36 at 1600 11 July 1943 reports different figures: 159 tanks, including those under repair in the 110th Tank Brigade and those *en route* to the 36th Guards Separate Heavy Breakthrough Regiment (TsAMO RF, f. 3415, op. 1, d. 26, l. 8, 8 obr.).

(b) Again, slightly different figures for the 29th Tank Corps are given in the document "On the condition of equipment and provisioning of the 5th Guards Tank Army at 1700 11.07.43": 120 T-34, 81 T-70, 12 Su-122, 8 Su-76 operational; 8 T-34, 4 T-70, 1 Su-76 *en route*; and 2 T-34 in repair (TsAMO RF, f. 5 gv. TA, op. 4948, d. 67, l. 12). However, Combat Dispatch No. 73 from the headquarters of the 29th Tank Corps at 1600 provides data for the tank brigades and the total number of tanks of all types in the Corps. Both documents indicate that the Corps had a total of 81 T-70 tanks. However, it is impossible to establish the precise number of T-70s, since while the total number of T-70 tanks reported in Combat Dispatch No. 73 is 81 it also states that 74 T-70 tanks were operational, while 4 were in the repair shop. It is unknown where the other three T-70 tanks were. Nevertheless, the document from the 5th Guards Tank Army's headquarters reports 81 T-70 tanks were operational, none were in the repair shop, and 4 were *en route*. In Table 18's column "Total Tanks/SP Guns", we have given a figure of 81 T-70 tanks.

(c) There was one captured Czech Pz-38(t) tank in the 29th Tank Corps' 25th Tank Brigade (TsAMO RF, f. 29tk, op. 1, d. 7, l. 101)

(d) According to the Operational Summary No. 110 from the headquarters of the 5th Guards Mechanized Corps at 0200 12.07.43, it was anticipating the arrival within the Corps from the march 2 T-34 tanks, 4 T-70 tanks, and 4 Su-76 self-propelled guns by sunrise on 12 July 1943.

The following sources for the data according to the units and formations are given in the order of their number in the first column of the table. I have supplied the time and date for each source report within the notes. Note that the corps-level data may not equal the totals for the subordinate brigades because of differing report times, tanks in the repair shop and the exclusion of tanks in the corps located in support units.

1. (1500 11 July 1943) TsAMO RF, f. 332, op. 4948, d. 70, l. 129.
2. (1500 11 July 1943) Ibid., l. 128.
3. (1700 11 July 1943) TsAMO RF, f. 332, op. 4948, d. 67, l. 12.
4. (5 July 1943) TsAMO RF, f. 18 tk, op. 1, d. 93, l. 122.
5. (5 July 1943) Ibid.
6. (1700 11 July 1943) TsAMO RF, f. 3415, op. 1, d. 26, l. 8, 8 obr; f. 18 tk, op. 1, d. 93, l. 226 obr (for armored cars)
7. (1700 11 July 1943) Ibid.
8. (1700 11 July 1943) TsAMO RF, f. 18tk, op. 1, d. 93, l. 122.
9. (1700 11 July 1943) TsAMO RF, f. 36 gv. otpp, op. 119565, d. 5, l. 94; f. 5 gv. TA, op. 4948, d. 67, l. 12; f. 18 tk, op. 1, d. 93, l. 84 (for armored cars).
10. (1600 11 July 1943) TsAMO RF, f. 5 gv. TA, op. 4948, d. 70, l. 124; f. 29 tk, op. 1, d. 36, l. 28 (for armored cars).
11. (9 July 1943) TsAMO RF, f. 29 tk, op. 1, d. 36, l. 28.
12. (9 July 1943) Ibid.
13. (9 July 1943) Ibid.
14. (9 July 1943) Ibid.
15. (9 July 1943) Ibid.
16. (9 July 1943) TsAMO RF, f. 5 gv. TA, op. 4948, d. 67, l. 1; f. 3420, op. 1, d. 8, l. 65.
17. (1800 10 July 1943) TsAMO RF, f. 333 gv. tsap, op. 27736, d. 3.
18. (1700 11 July 1943) TsAMO RF, f. 5 gv. TA, op. 4948, d. 67, l. 12.
19. (0200 12 July 1943) TsAMO RF, f. 5 gv. TA, op. 4848, d. 75, l. 10 a.
20. (0200 12 July 1943) Ibid.
21. (0200 12 July 1943) TsAMO Rf, f. 5 gv. TA, op. 4948, d. 75.
22. (0200 12 July 1943) Ibid.
23. (0200 12 July 1943) Ibid.
24. (1700 11 July 1943) Ibid., l. 29 obr.
25. (1700 11 July 1943) Ibid.
26. (1700 11 July 1943) Ibid.
27. (0600 12 July 1943) Ibid.
28. (1700 11 July 1943) Ibid.
29. (1700 11 July 1943) TsAMO RF, f. 332, op. 4948, d. 67, l. 12.
30. (12 July 1943) TsAMO RF, f. 8 gv. tk, op. 1, d. 233, l. 41, 41 obr.
31. (0700 12 July 1943) TsAMO RF, f. 332, op. 4948, d. 70, l. 203, 203 obr; f. 58 gv. tbr, op. 1, d. 7, l. 108.
32. (0700 12 July 1943) TsAMO RF, f. 332, op. 4948, d. 70, l. 203, 203 obr.
33. (0700 12 July 1943) Ibid.
34. (10 July 1943) Ibid., l. 130 obr.
35. (10 July 1943) Ibid.
36. Author's calculations: the first number (the numerator) is the total for the corps plus the 1st Guards Separate Motorcycle Regiment and the 53rd Guards Separate Tank Regiment; the second number (the denominator) is the total for the 1st Guards Separate Motorcycle Regiment and the 53rd Guards Separate Tank Regiment and the regiments and brigades. The number of self-propelled guns is displayed within parentheses.

1st Tank Army. It was to be deployed in the areas of Melovoe, Noven'koe, Kruglik, Kalinovka (excl.), and Hill 244.8.

The 7th Guards Army's 49th Rifle Corps was also preparing to conduct a holding attack from the Hill 209.6 – Gremiachii – Machine Tractor Station – Hill 202.8 area.

Judging from the *front* command's plan, the committed forces, and the directions of the attacks, the counterattack was pursuing a decisive goal – the encirclement of the main forces of the enemy grouping on the Prokhorovka axis, their complete destruction, the re-establishment of former lines, and the creation of conditions for a subsequent going over to a general counteroffensive.

P. A. Rotmistrov personally received the order and his army's assignments for 12 July from N. F. Vatutin in the presence of Military Council member N. S. Khrushchev. According to Rotmistrov's memoirs, Vatutin knew that one-third of the 5th Guards Tank Army consisted of light T-70 tanks, which were inferior to German medium tanks in open combat. That meant that even before the attack, the possibility of large losses had been taken into account. Pavel Alekseevich recalled:

> On 10 July the 5th Guards Tank Army joined the Voronezh Front. I was immediately summoned to the *front* commander General of the Army N. F. Vatutin's command post, located in the vicinity of Oboian'. *Stavka* representative Marshal A. M. Vasilevsky, who was coordinating the operations of Voronezh Front and Southwestern Front, and the *front*'s chief of staff Lieutenant General S. P. Ivanov were also here. They greeted me warmly, and then thoroughly briefed me on the situation that was facing the Voronezh Front.
>
> The *front* commander invited me closer to the map, and pointing with a pencil at the Prokhorovka region, said: 'Having failed to penetrate to Kursk through Oboian', clearly the Hitlerites have decided to shift the axis of their main blow eastward along the railway toward Prokhorovka. There, the forces of the II SS Panzer Corps have assembled, which must attack along the Prokhorovka axis in cooperation with XXXXVIII Panzer Corps and tank formations of Group Kempf.'
>
> N. F. Vatutin glanced at A. M. Vasilevsky and then, turning to me, he continued: 'Thus, Pavel Alekseevich, we have decided to oppose the SS tank divisions with your tank Guardsmen – to deliver a counterstroke against the enemy with the 5th Guards Tank Army, reinforced by a further two tank corps.'
>
> 'Incidentally,' said A. M. Vasilevsky, 'the German tank divisions possess new heavy Tiger tanks and Ferdinand self-propelled guns [the new tanks, of course, were the Panthers, and Fourth Panzer Army had no Ferdinands – author's note]. Katukov's 1st Tank Army has suffered considerably from their fire. Do you know anything about this equipment and how do you feel about fighting them?'
>
> 'We know, Comrade Marshal. We received tactical-technical information about them from the Steppe Front staff. We have also thought about means for combating them.'
>
> 'Interesting!' added Vatutin, and nodding to me, said, 'Please, continue.'
>
> 'The fact is that the Tigers and Ferdinands not only have strong frontal armor, but also a powerful, long-range direct fire 88mm gun. In that regard they are superior to our tanks, which are armed with 76mm guns. Successful struggle with them is possible only in circumstances of close-in combat, with exploitation of the

T-34's greater maneuverability and by flanking fire against the side armor of the heavy German machines.'

'In other words, engage in hand-to-hand fighting and take them by boarding,' said the *front* commander, and again he turned to conversation about the forthcoming counterstroke, in which 1st Tank Army, 6th, 7th and 5th Guards Armies were to take part.

N. F. Vatutin expressed the concern that the German tanks might break through to Oboian', and was pleasantly surprised when at my own initiative I proposed to protect his command post with part of my reserve task force. Immediately I got in touch with K. G. Trufanov [5th Guards Tank Army's deputy commander] via the radio in my vehicle, and issued the corresponding order. Within two hours, the forward detachment of the task force took up a defense along a large brook, in front of the *front* commander's command post, and established a connection with General I. M. Chistiakov's 6th Guards Army.

That afternoon I returned to my command post with my combat orders. They required the army to go on a decisive offensive on the morning of 12 July together with the 1st Tank and 5th Guards Armies, to destroy the enemy southwest of Prokhorovka, and to reach the line Krasnaia Dubrova – Iakovlevo by day's end.[6]

The organization of the counterstroke had its own unique feature. The command not only had to prepare a counterattack, but simultaneously had to direct a defense. Typically counterstrokes occur at the moment when the enemy has penetrated deeply into the defense, and there is the threat of a breakthrough and his emergence into the rear. Exactly just such a picture had developed by 12 July for the forces of Voronezh Front in the region of Prokhorovka. Therefore it was so important to halt the enemy's advance, and to hold the line, intended for the introduction of the strategic reserves into the engagement.

Recalled the deputy chief of operations of the 5th Guards Tank Army Lieutenant Colonel I. A. Dokukin:

Front commander General of the Army N. F. Vatutin and member of the Military Council N. S. Khrushchev arrived at the army's command post on the evening of 10 July. They gathered the corps commanders and their deputies for political affairs. General Vatutin described the situation of the *front*'s forces in detail, gave a description of the enemy, and gave the army its orders. In conclusion he said:

'The jumping-off line must be held at whatever the cost. From here we will go on the offensive. Don't count upon an easy success. Consider that in front of you is a strong, active, and embittered foe. You must achieve success through stubbornness, decisive actions and skillful maneuvering.' The *front* commander looked at the map spread out before him, and then shifted his gaze to everyone present with the words: 'I repeat: the line must be held!'

Nikita Sergeevich Khrushchev spoke after Vatutin.

'I want to add a few words to what the commander said,' he said. 'Get your men ready for fighting. Explain to them the goals of our war. Remind them of those

Chief of intelligence of the 5th Guards Tank Army Colonel L. G. Grechannikov (1942 photo). (Author's personal archive)

> deprivations that the Soviet people are suffering under fascist occupation. Tell the warriors and officers that the end is near, that our victory is close, and that the origin of this victory will be forged here, at the Kursk bulge. The troops of our Guards army will not be fighting for the first time. In honor of our Motherland, in the name of a rapid and conclusive victory over the Hitlerite aggressors!'[7]

The success of the counterstroke depended upon the thoroughness of its preparation. In the course of the night of 10 July and the morning of 11 July, the *front*'s staff prepared a plan for the operation. The army commanders learned about the operation by the evening of 10 July. Order No. 001/OP of the 69th Army's 48th Rifle Corps headquarters regarding the offensive was signed at 1445 on 11 July.[8] Probably, the order reached the commands of the 5th Guards Tank Army and the 5th Guards Army later, since Rotmistrov signed his Order No. 003 to the army only at 1800 on 11 July.[9] At the same time, Combat Instruction No. 63 of the 5th Guards Army headquarters to the commander of the 42nd Guards Rifle Division regarding that division's transfer to the operational control of the 33rd Guards Rifle Corps commander and its tasks for 12 July was signed.[10] Thus, the specific tasks were delivered to the armies' headquarters on 11 July between 0900 and 1700. All preliminary measures for the counterattack were designated to be taken on 11 July and the overnight hours before dawn on 12 July. However, even before receiving the main planning documents, the 5th Guards Tank Army commander and his corps commanders strived to make maximum use of remaining daylight hours of 11 July to prepare the troops for the coming offensive.

First of all, it was necessary to select the most suitable jumping-off line for the tank army's attack. As former chief of staff of the 5th Guards Tank Army General V.

N. Baskakov recalled in 1987, initially the *front* headquarters proposed to launch the tank attack from the region of the bend in the Psel River in the direction of Iakovlevo. However, due to the difficult terrain, the steep bank of the river, the swampy flood lands and the lack of a sufficient number of crossing points, as well as concerns over a frontal attack against the *Totenkopf* Panzergrenadier Division operating here, rather than against its flanks, this proposal was unacceptable.

There existed another alternative to deploy the army south of Prokhorovka and to strike the right flank of the II SS Panzer Corps in the direction of Shakhovo and Iakovlevo. Carrying out the order of the army commander, 29th Tank Corps commander I. F. Kirichenko with a group of staff officers and subordinate brigade commanders departed at 0300 11 July on a reconnaissance of the area Leski – railroad booth 2 kilometers west of Leski – barracks (on the northern outskirts of Teterevino Station) – Shakhovo, with several tasks:

a) to choose jumping-off positions for the corps;

b) to determine if tanks and artillery could move across the branches of the Sazhnovskii Donets, the railroad (the embankment of which had been mined) and the Sukhaia Plota ravine;

c) to determine approach routes to the jumping-off positions;

d) to determine the possibility of massing infantry for the attack in the Sukhaia Plota ravine;

e) to select locations for the command post and observation post, as well as the artillery's firing positions.

At 0600 11 July 1943, the reconnaissance party returned and reported its findings to General Rotmistrov in the region of Shakhovo.[11]

The axis Shakhovo – Iakovlevo seemed to offer better prospects: a relatively weak adversary, the 167th Infantry Division, was opposing our forces here. A strike here with the strongest corps of the tank army on a front of only 4 to 5 kilometers would lead directly into the rear of the II SS Panzer Corps. Having cut the main road between Belgorod and Oboian', our forces would create a genuine threat of encircling the main elements of the enemy's Fourth Panzer Army. And after Stalingrad, the Germans were quite sensitive to the threat of being "pocketed"!

Unfortunately, this alternative was also rejected. Apparently, not just because of the difficulties in overcoming the natural obstacles and the mined railroad embankment. After all, the 2nd Tank Corps attacked on this axis on 12 July anyway, though on a broader front. However, it had lacked the forces to exploit its initial success.

The sector of terrain between the Psel River and Storozhevoe was viewed as the only satisfactory place for employing major tank formations. After conducting a reconnaissance of the area with the corps commanders, it was exactly here that Rotmistrov proposed to strike with the army's main forces. This idea was approved by the *front* headquarters, and already at 1100 11 July, the 29th Tank Corps commander was signing Combat Order

No. 3, which spelled out the corps' tasks on 12 July, and indicated the line of departure for the attack – 2.5 kilometers southwest of Prokhorovka Station:

> 1. The adversary – up to four tank divisions and one mechanized division – continues to push our units in a northeasterly and easterly direction, trying to link up with the northern grouping on the Orel-Kursk axis.
>
> By 11.07.43, the forward units have reached a line: Kochetovka – Krasnyi Oktiabr' – Vasil'evka – Komsomolets State Farm – Ivanovskii Vyselok – Iasnaia Poliana – Belenikhino, and further to the south, along the rail line to Gostishchevo.
>
> 2. The 29th Tank Corps with the 366th Light Anti-aircraft Artillery Regiment, the 76th Rocket Artillery Regiment, and a destroyer anti-tank artillery regiment of the 10th Tank Brigade have the task at 0300 12.07.43 to attack the enemy in the sector to the right of Hill 252.4 – the woods 1 kilometer north of Komsomolets State Farm – northern outskirts of Bol'shie Maiachki – Hill 251.2.
>
> To the left, Grushki, Storozhevoe, Hill 223.4, northwest outskirts of Pogorelovka; destroy the enemy in the region of Hill 255.9 – woods 1 kilometer northeast of Teterevino – Hill 258.9. Subsequently operate in the direction of Bol'shie Maiachki and Pokrovka.
>
> 3. I have decided to attack with the 32nd Tank Brigade as one echelon in front, and behind it – the 31st, 25th Tank Brigades and the 53rd Motorized Rifle Brigade.
>
> 4. The 32nd Tank Brigade with three batteries of the 1446th Self-propelled Artillery Regiment is the corps' forward brigade. The task – to attack in the direction: Komsomolets State Farm – Teterevino – northern outskirts of Luchki – Bol'shie Maiachki; to destroy the enemy in the area of Teterevino and the woods 2 kilometers northwest of Iasnaia Poliana, and to operate subsequently toward Bol'shie Maiachki.
>
> The departure line for the attack is the depression 2.5 kilometers west of Prokhorovka – which is to be occupied by 2400 11.07.43. The attack will begin at 0200 12.07.43.
>
> 5. The 31st Tank Brigade is to attack behind the 32nd Tank Brigade to the right of the highway in the direction of Komsomolets State Farm – Hill 255.9 – Hill 251.2, to destroy the enemy in the area of Komsomolets State Farm and the woods to the west, and subsequently to operate in the direction of Bol'shie Maiachki. The line of departure for the attack is the depression 1 kilometer northwest of Prokhorovka, which is to be occupied by 0100 12.07.43. The attack will begin at 0300 12.07.43.
>
> 6. The 25th Tank Brigade with two batteries of the 1446th Self-propelled Artillery Regiment has the task to attack in the direction of Ivanovskii Vyselok – edge of the woods 1 kilometer northwest of Iasnaia Poliana – Luchki – Bol'shie Maiachki, to destroy the enemy in the area of Teterevino and the woods to the southeast, subsequently to operate in the direction of Luchki. The line of departure for the attack is Iamki, which is to be occupied by 2400 11.07.43. The attack will begin at 0300 12.07.43.
>
> 7. The 53rd Motorized Rifle Brigade with the 271st Mortar Regiment and a regiment of the 10th Destroyer Anti-tank Artillery Brigade has the task to attack behind the 31st and 25th Tank Brigades to destroy the enemy in the areas of Hill

258.2, Teterevino, fork of the road 1 kilometers north of Iasnaia Poliana, and to operate subsequently in the direction of Luchki and Bol'shie Maiachki.

The line of departure for the attack is Oktiabr'skii State Farm – Hill 258.8 – Storozhevoe, which is to be occupied by 2300 11.07.43. Ensure the assembly of formations and units of the corps in the jumping-off region. The attack will start at 0300 12.07.43.

8. The 108th Destroyer Anti-tank Artillery Regiment and the 76th Rocket Artillery Regiment will be my reserve, and are to concentrate in the region of the brick factory, 1 kilometer northwest of Prokhorovka, and be ready to operate in the direction of Komsomolets State Farm and Luchki. They are to support the attack of 32nd, 25th and 53rd Brigades.

9. The 366th Light Anti-aircraft Artillery Regiment is to cover the area of the corps' jumping-off positions, and is subsequently to accompany the combat formations of the 53rd Motorized Rifle Brigade in the direction of Komsomolets State Farm and Luchki.

It is to occupy its firing positions by 2000 11.07.43.

10. I will be with the operations group of the corps headquarters until 0800 12.07.43 – at the brick factory 1 kilometer northwest of Prokhorovka. Subsequently, behind the combat formations of the 31st Tank Brigade.[12]

All day long, preparations for the counterstroke were underway in the forces of the 5th Guards Tank Army. An interesting document has been preserved in the files of the 18th Tank Corps' Operations Department. It is Major General B. S. Bakharov's Order No. 0011/72 to the command staff of the corps, issued on 11 July 1943 at 1400. Familiarizing ourselves with its contents, we get an idea of the "hurry-up" atmosphere that reigned in the corps as its units prepared for combat and moved into their jumping-off positions:

For the commander alone.
In his absence, the deputy commander or the chief of staff is to carry it out.
I order:

By 1800 11.07.43, the first combat echelon of your corps is to assemble in the region indicated on the map, moving in separate groups and observing the strictest measures to mask the movement.

All vehicles, not needed for movement into the breakthrough, and all personnel, not assigned to the first echelon, are to be sent away to the area of Viazovoe by the morning of 12.07.

By 2200 11.07.43, the 1st combat echelon should be provided with 3 allotments of fuel, 3 combat loads for the tanks and 2 combat loads per ground gun, while the men should have 8 days of rations.

The 1st combat echelon is to be divided into an active breakthrough echelon and a support echelon, for which a firm chief should be designated.

Until special instructions otherwise, the support echelon will be positioned together with the combat echelon, but with the initiation of implementing the combat task, it will follow [the combat echelon] upon special orders under the protection of the 110th Tank Brigade and the 36th Guards Tank Regiment.

In the new area, indicated on the map, take all camouflage and security measures and be ready to go into battle from the region you have occupied.

Notify the battalion commanders and company commanders that at 1800 11.07.43, they will be summoned to the vicinity of the crossroads on the Voroshilovskii State Farm for a study of the terrain.

From 2100 11.07.43 all units should be ready for movement to the jumping-off area for introduction into the breakthrough.

The chiefs of staff, the chiefs of communications and those individuals who are in charge of the supply process are to finish all preparatory measures by 2200 11.07.43, in order to give the personnel a chance to rest before conducting a difficult combat assignment.

During movement to the new area, increase vigilance in view of the enemy's heightened activity.

Take up the telephone lines between 1600 and 1800 11.07.43 and simultaneously re-lay them again.

Strive to keep the tanks and motor vehicles in ravines.

Routes to the vicinities of Prelestnoe (excl.) and Oktiabr'skii State Farm for a night march to the jumping-off position should be checked ahead of time.

I categorically forbid the occupation of areas east of the places indicated on the map, since a major formation is arriving there.

The commander of the 1694th Anti-aircraft Artillery Regiment is to set up firing positions on the eastern bank of the Psel River in the area of Vyshniaia Ol'shanka.

The 419th Separate Signals Battalion and the 115th Separate Sapper Battalion is to prepare to move out to the new area.

Enclosure: one map copy.[13]

The cited document is very interesting. The corps commander precisely expressed in it the formation's task for 12 July: "From 2100 11.07.43 all units must be ready for movement to the jumping-off area for *introduction into the breakthrough* [author's emphasis]." As is known, the breakthrough is an important stage in an offensive, and not a way of handling a defensive operation, like a counterattack. Yet there is not a single mention of a counterattack in the order. So what was the Soviet command planning on 12 July: to halt an adversary that had penetrated deeply into the *front*'s defenses with a counterattack, or to go over to an offensive?

An analysis of the documents indicates that, formally speaking (after all, the enemy was still attacking), this was a frontal counterstroke – but in essence, southwest of Prokhorovka the Soviet forces were going over to an offensive, for which General Rotmistrov's army was being planned to introduce into a breakthrough. Yet in so doing, the tank army was given tasks for which it was not intended, and the effort to carry out these tasks did not receive the proper support.

As is known, the success of an offensive is determined primarily by its initial stage, and depends accordingly upon how quickly the forces manage to break through the tactical zone and into the depth of the enemy's rear. Typically, two echelons are created for a breakthrough. The first echelon consists of combined-arms formations, strengthened by a powerful artillery grouping. They must shatter the enemy's front lines,

Equipment	29 Tank Corps	18 Tank Corps	2 Tank Corps	2 Gds Tank Corps	5 Gds Mech Corps	Army-level units	Total
1. Operational							
T-34	120	68	35	84	120	36	463
T-70	81	58	46	52	56	8	301
Mk-IV Churchill	-	18	4	3	-	-	25
Total Tanks	201	144	85	139	176	44	789
Su-76	8	-	-	-	7	-	15
Su-122	12	-	-	-	10	-	22
Total SP Guns	20	-	-	-	17	-	37
Total, Tanks and SP Guns	221	144	85	139	193	44	826
AT Guns: 122mm	-	-	-	-	-	20	20
85mm	-	-	-	12 (a)	-	-	12
76mm	12	12	18	-	43	-	85
45mm	20	12	26	19	23	12	112
2. En Route to Prokhorovka Station							
T-34	8	26	-	-	43	3	80
T-70	4	5	-	-	4	1	14
Mk-IV Churchill	-	2	-	-	-	-	2
Total tanks	12	33	-	-	47	4	96
Su-76	1	-	-	-	2	-	3
Su-122	-	-	-	-	2	-	2
Total SP Guns	1	-	-	-	4	-	5
Total, Tanks and SP Guns	13	33	-	-	51	4	101
AT Guns: 76mm	-	-	-	20	-	-	-
3. In repair shop							
T-34	2	5	7	-	1	5	20
T-70	-	-	2	-	-	1	3
Mk-IV Churchill	-	1	-	-	-	-	1
Total tanks	2	6	9	-	1	6	24
Total Armor							
Total tanks on roster	215	183	94	139	224	54	909
Total SP Guns on roster	21	0	0	0	21	0	42
Total, all armor	236	183	94	139	245	54	951

(a) Other than anti-aircraft guns.

Table 19: Report on the Equipment and Supplies of the 5th Guards Tank Army at 1700 11 July 1943

Table 19 continued

Equipment	29 Tank Corps	18 Tank Corps	2 Tank Corps	2 Gds Tank Corps	5 Gds Mech Corps	Army-level units	Total
4. Supplies (in daily loads)							
Fuel and lubricants:							
For tanks	1.5	1.5	-	1	1.5	-	-
For vehicles	0.5	1	-	1.5	0.3	-	-
Ammunition							
For tanks	1.5	1.5	-	1	1.4	-	-
For AT Guns	1	1	-	1	1	-	-

Source: TsAMO RF, f. 5 gv. TA, op. 4948, d. 67, l.12.

destroy his anti-tank defenses, and create conditions for introducing the second echelon into the breakthrough – the mobile formations of the tank army, which are to develop the tactical success of the first stage into an operational success.

Factually speaking, at Prokhorovka, the 5th Guards Tank Army was expected to carry out the tasks of both the first and second echelons; that is, it had to both break through the defense and to develop the success. However, in front of the tankers were the rifle divisions of the 5th Guards Army, which were containing the attacking enemy only with great difficulty, and as for a powerful artillery grouping, there was nothing of which to speak. Discussion of how muddled the organization of the artillery preparation was on the morning of 12 July still lies ahead. However, even at that the tank army itself didn't have the necessary amount of artillery to ensure the destruction of the enemy's defenses, so the entire burden of the combat task would fall upon the tanks and motorized infantry. In such conditions, excessive losses of combat vehicles were predetermined.

Out of fairness, it should be noted that the very same miscalculations were also made, for example, when employing the 3rd Guards Tank Army during the Orel offensive following Kursk. Its losses over the period of that operation comprised 60.3% of its T-34s and 72.9% of its T-70s.[14]

Voronezh Front command was seemingly trying to carry out two assignments at once: both to stop the enemy offensive, and at the same time to split up and to destroy his shock group with an armor battering ram. Such an unsupportable burden was placed on the tank army, probably because of the *front* command's lack of experience in using this type of formation, and also because of the heightened demands that the *Stavka* was bringing to bear on the command of the Voronezh Front, after the Central Front had practically concluded its defensive operation by this time.

I will note that the problem of the "pre-breakthrough," as it was often called in Soviet military documents, or more simply speaking the creation of a stable corridor for the introduction of tank corps and tank armies, was characteristic for the entire Red Army and was directly connected with the inability of its senior and higher command to organize tight cooperation among different types of forces in battle. Alas, a significant number of our generals indeed never developed this ability before the end of the war.

Major General B. S. Bakharov, commander of the 18th Tank Corps (1942 photo). (TsAMO)

Lieutenant General (at the time of the battle Major General) I. F. Kirichenko, commander of the 29th Tank Corps (1945 photo). (Author's personal archive)

As the initiator of the counterattack, N. F. Vatutin placed his major hope on the tanks under his command. On the axis of the main assault, he succeeded in creating an unprecedented density of armor per kilometer of front. At 1700 on 11 July, P. A. Rotmistrov received the 2nd Tank Corps and the 2nd Guards 'Tatsinskaia' Tank Corps under his operational control. As a result, the number of tank corps in his army increased to four, while the amount of armor rose by more than 200 vehicles to a total number of 931 tanks, 42 SU-76 and SU-122 self-propelled guns, as well as 12 SU-152,[15] including 581 T-34 (62.4%) and 314 T-70 (33.7%). Of this number, 797 tanks and 43 self-propelled guns were located in the area of the main force concentration (east of Prokhorovka); the remainder was either under repair or still *en route*. At dawn on 12 July, a few more tanks and self-propelled guns came up, bringing the operational total in the army before the attack to 808 tanks and 32 SU-76 and SU-122. Data on the available armor in the 5th Guards Tank Army on 11 July 1943 are shown in Table 19.

The three tank corps – the 18th, 29th and 2nd Guards 'Tatsinskaia' – that comprised the first echelon of 5th Guards Tank Army – had 538 tanks and 20 self-propelled guns in formation. Under the original plan, General B. S. Bakharov's 18th Tank Corps and General I. F. Kirichenko's 29th Tank Corps were to lead the main attack from the line Prelestnoe – southern outskirts of Storozhevoe. Their entire sector would have extended along a frontage of only 7 kilometers. The 18th Tank Corps' sector ran from the Psel River basin through Prelestnoe to map contour line 240 (3 kilometers), while the 29th Tank Corps' front ran from Hill 241.6 to the southern outskirts of Storozhevoe (4 kilometers). After the SS troops seized this area on 11 July, the line of deployment had to be pulled back to a line east of Oktiabr'skii State Farm. Here, because of a deep ravine north of the State Farm that ran for almost 2 kilometers to the river, the 18th Tank Corps' breakthrough sector was actually reduced to approximately 1.5 – 2 kilometers. This in turn shrank the combined frontage for the counterstroke to 5.5 – 6 kilometers. On the morning before the attack, these two tank corps had a combined 368 tanks and 20 self-propelled guns. Consequently, the density of armor in the breakthrough sector under the original plan was to have reached almost 56 armored vehicles per kilometer of front. In reality, after the change in the attack's line of departure the assault formations were able to achieve even more than that – 60 tanks per kilometer of front, not including self-propelled guns.

Therefore, the hopes of the Soviet command to split the II SS Panzer Corps seemed fully justified. Moreover if one considers that another 217 tanks of the second echelon (the 5th Guards Mechanized Corps' 158 tanks and the 2nd Tank Corps' 59 tanks) were to enter the battle together with the infantry of the 5th Guards Army, then a breakthrough to a depth of 30 kilometers seemed to be a fully obtainable, though difficult objective. However, in making this calculation, two most important factors were not considered: the technical capabilities of the Soviet armored vehicles, and the terrain in the sector where 5th Guards Tank Army would attack.

After *Leibstandarte* had seized Oktiabr'skii State Farm and Hill 252.2 on 11 July and thus had overrun the counterattack's designated line of departure, the original plans for the counterattack were thrown into disarray. Rotmistrov later wrote:

> The situation for launching the counterattack had become acutely more complicated; its planned preparation had been disrupted. In connection with the altered situation, we revised the corps' assignments the night before the attack. Leaving the operational formation unchanged, we moved the line of deployment of the army's main forces immediately to the west of Prokhorovka.
>
> Ten to twelve hours remained for preparing for action, half of which would be under conditions of darkness. This situation led to the corps commanders making decisions and assigning orders to brigades by map. But the orders for the offensive reached the brigades and separate regiments by midnight, 11 July.[16]

The combat assignment to the army's corps was spelled out in Combat Order No. 3 of 11 July at 1800:

> 1. The enemy on the Belgorod axis, introducing major tank forces into the fighting, is trying to exploit the success in a northerly direction, toward Oboian' and Kursk (200 tanks), and in the easterly direction, toward Aleksandrovskii, Skorodnoe and Staryi Oskol (up to 300 tanks). Up to 100 enemy tanks have been spotted in the area Pokrovka – Iakovlevo – Bol. Maiachki.
> 2. The 5th Guards Tank Army with the 2nd Tank Corps, the 2nd Guards 'Tatsinskaia' Tank Corps, the 10th Destroyer Anti-tank Artillery Brigade, the 27th Artillery Brigade, the 522nd and 1148th Howitzer Artillery Regiments, the 26th Anti-aircraft Battalion, the 16th and 80th Guards Mortar [*Katiusha*] Regiments, and the 1329th Self-propelled Artillery Regiment will launch an attack at 1000 12.07.43 in the sector: to the right – Beregovoe, Andreevka (excl.), Krasnaia Poliana,

Krasnaia Dubrova; to the left – Pravorot', Belenikhino, Point 232.0, barrow with the mark +1,1 (3 kilometers southeast of Iakovlevo), and together in concert with the 5th Guards Army and the 1st Guards Tank Army, it will eliminate the enemy breakthrough grouping in the area Pokrovka, Greznoe, Kochetovka, preventing its withdrawal to the south.

By the end of day it will reach the line: Krasnaia Dubrova – Point 254.5 – Iakovlevo, having in view a subsequent attack to the southwest.

The jumping-off line: Prelestnoe – Storozhevoe – Mal. Iablonovo will be occupied by 2400 11.07.43.

Preparations for the attack will be completed by 0300 12.07.43.

Attack start – by following order.

3. The 18th Tank Corps with the 80th Guards Mortar Regiment, and one 76mm anti-tank regiment and one 57mm anti-tank regiment of the 10th Destroyer Anti-tank Artillery Brigade, is to break the enemy's resistance on the line: Andreevka – woods lying northwest of the Komsomolets State Farm, to destroy the enemy in the area Krasnaia Dubrova – Bol. Maiachki – Krasnaia Poliana, and having turned its front to the north, it is subsequently to secure the attacking operation of the army to the south.

Boundary on the left: Point 252.4 (excl.) – northwest edge of the woods lying 1 kilometer northwest of the Komsomolets State Farm (excl.) – Machine Tractor Station on the northern outskirts of Bol'shie Maiachki.

4. The 29th Tank Corps with the 76th Guards Mortar Regiment and the 1529th Self-propelled Artillery Regiment is to break the enemy resistance on the line: woods lying 1 kilometer north of the Komsomolets State Farm – Komsomolets State Farm. Destroy his grouping in the regions of Luchki, Bol'shie Maiachki and Pokrovka. By the end of the day on 12.07.43, reach the area of Pokrovka and the groves lying west and south of Pokrovka, and be ready for subsequent actions to the south.

Boundary to the left: Grushki, Storozhevoe, Iasnaia Poliana, Point 228.4, mill on the northern outskirts of Pogorelovka.

Prior to the start of the attack, the 378th Howitzer Artillery Regiment is to support the corps.

5. The 2nd Guards 'Tatsinskaia' Tank Corps with one 76mm anti-tank regiment from the 10th Destroyer Anti-tank Artillery Brigade is to break the enemy resistance on the line Iasnaia Poliana – Belenikhino, to destroy his grouping in the area of Iakovlevo and the woods to the east, and subsequently to be ready for an offensive to the south.

6. The 2nd Tank Corps, holding its current line, is to cover the concentration of the army in the jumping-off area, and to prevent an enemy breakthrough to the east.

With the start of the attack, support the offensive of the 18th, 29th and 2nd Guards 'Tatsinskaia' Tank Corps with your means of fire, and then allow them to pass through the corps' combat formations – and be ready to attack the enemy in the direction of Sukh. Solotino.

7. The 5th Guards [Mechanized] 'Zimovniki' Corps is to assemble in the Sokolovka – Dranyi – Krasnoe – Vysypnoi – Sagaidachnoe – Kamyshevka area and

be prepared to exploit the success of the 29th and 2nd Guards 'Tatsinskaia' Tank Corps in the general direction of Prokhorovka, Luchki and Smorodino.

With the start of operations, the 678th Howitzer Artillery Regiment will come under corps control.

8. The artillery:

A) The support group [*gruppa usileniia*]: chief – deputy commander of the 38th Army's artillery Colonel Davydov. Complement: 27th Gun Artillery Brigade, 522nd and 1148th High-power Howitzer Artillery Regiments [equipped with 203mm howitzers]

B) The rocket artillery group: chief – Colonel Iofa.[17] Complement: 76th Guards, 16th Guards and 80th Guards Mortar Regiments [equipped with *Katiusha* rocket launchers].

C) Assignments: For the support group

a) A ten-minute barrage on the front lines in the sector Vasil'evka – Komsomolets State Farm – Ivanovskii Vyselok – Belenikhino;

b) A five-minute methodical fire on the enemy's rear area;

c) A five-minute barrage on the enemy's front lines and rear area (open fire on targets according to the corps commanders' requests and needs).

For the rocket artillery group:

a) a salvo on the forward zone of the enemy's defense at the moment the artillery preparatory fire on the enemy begins;

b) a second salvo on targets in the forward zone at the conclusion of the artillery preparatory fire;

c) At the start of the tank attack the artillery support group will, at the requests and directions of the corps commanders, shift its fire into the enemy's depths, right up to the Oboian's – Belgorod highway at Hill 251.2 and Hill 254.5, with up to 2/3 of the artillery on the right flank firing on the area to the right: Krasnyi Oktiabr' – Veselyi – Greznoe – Kozlovka, and further – Kochetovka – Sukho-Solomino – Ryl'skii. One-third of the artillery will fire on the area to the left: Kalinin – Sobachevskii – grove at Kozinka – Teterevino, and further in the area Luchki – Hill 246.3 – copses of woods west of Petrovskii;

d) The artillery subordinate to the corps will accompany the tank attack by fire and wheel maneuver, according to the corps commanders' plans.

9. Major General Trufanov's task force consisting of the 1st Separate Guards Motorcycle Regiment, the 53rd Guards Tank Regiment, the 689th Destroyer Anti-tank Artillery Regiment and a battery of the 678th Howitzer Artillery Regiment will be my reserve.

Be prepared to concentrate in the area of Petrovka with the aim of securing the army's left flank.

10. The forward army headquarters team will be at Skorovka (7 kilometers northeast of Prokhorovka) from 1700 11.07.43.

Observation post: Point 252.4 (2 kilometers northwest of Prokhorovka).

11. Report:

A) Upon setting out for the departure area;

B) Upon assembling in the departure area;

A group of German servicemen, who had crossed over to the side of the Red Army during the fighting for Prokhorovka Station. In the background is the cottage that housed the headquarters of the 5th Guards Tank Army in the village of Skorovka (a 14 July 1943 photo). (Author's personal archive)

C) Upon readiness for the offensive;
D) Upon starting the offensive;
E) Subsequently every two hours according to the fixed timetable of reports.[18]

The 5th Guards Tank Army command was well-aware of the danger to the army that a frontal attack presented. Of the 177 tanks in the 18th Tank Corps either in formation or *en route* on 11 July, 35.5% were T-70 tanks; the remaining were T-34 and Churchill Mk-IV tanks. The "shock" 29th Tank Corps had an even greater percentage of T-70s (38.8%). The T-70 was a light tank and unable to fight on equal terms with a single German tank type at Kursk or the enemy's primary anti-tank guns. The only exception was when the T-70s' ammo load included armor-piercing discarding sabot shells or high-explosive anti-tank projectiles, but at that time, the 18th and 29th Tank Corps did not have such special ammunition.

Rotmistrov attempted to address this situation. During the days before the intended operation, the army and corps headquarters had prepared their troops for heavy fighting, trying to find the optimal arrangement of the corps' combat formations, so as to be able to carry out the order it had received in light of the developing situation. Thus, four brigades had been assigned to the first echelon, 30% of which consisted of T-70 light tanks. However, the brigade commanders were given an order to move one battalion of T-34s into the first echelon, and place one of the T-70 battalions in the second echelon. To enhance the firepower up front, a self-propelled artillery regiment was attached to each brigade of the first echelon in the 29th Tank Corps. In this fashion, P. A. Rotmistrov did everything within his power to strengthen the impact of his lead echelon while planning his army's commitment into battle – the sharp edge of its assault wedge consisted of his strongest formations.

The start time for the attack was changed several times. At first it was planned to launch the counterstroke on 12 July at 1000. When Marshal of the Soviet Union A. M. Vasilevsky arrived at the 29th Tank Corps headquarters on the late afternoon of 11 July, he gave an order in case of a further advance by the enemy to be ready to attack at 2100 that same day. However, by evening the enemy's activity was diminishing and the order was canceled. The time for the corps' counterattack was now set for 0300 12 July. In the 29th Tank Corps journal of combat operations, however, there is the following entry:

> At 0300 12.07.43, the signal [for the attack] did not arrive. At 0400, an order from the commander of the 5th Guards Tank Army was received regarding the postponement of the attack start:
>
> 'To the commander of the 29th Tank Corps Lieutenant General Kirichenko.
>
> 1. The corps' task remains as before, that is, operating with the 76th Guards Mortar Regiment and the 1529th Self-propelled Artillery Regiment to break the enemy resistance on the line of the grove 1 km north of Komsomolets State Farm, to destroy his grouping in the region Luchki – Bol'shie Maiachki – Pokrovka, to reach the region of Pokrovka by the end of day 12 July, preparing subsequently for operations to the south.
> 2. The start of the attack: 0830 12.07.43. The artillery preparation will begin at 0800.
>
> I authorize the use of a radio from 0700 12.07.43. Commander of the 5th Guards Tank Army Lieutenant General P. A. Rotmistrov.'[19]

Other corps commanders also received similar confirmations of the new time for the attack to begin. This was the final change in the time set for the attack start.

On the morning of 12 July, the 18th Tank Corps commander conducted a supplementary reconnaissance from a point near the Kartashevka – Beregovoe road, 3 to 4 kilometers from the line of departure for the brigades of the first echelon. His Order No. 67 for the offensive was signed just an hour and a half before the attack was to begin – at 0700 12 July. Here is the text of the order:

> 1. The enemy in major formations is striving to seize Oboian'.
>
> In front of the corps, separate tank groups are pressuring our units.
>
> 2. The corps and its artillery group have the task to destroy the enemy in the region Andreevka – grove north of the Komsomolets State Farm – Krasnaia Dubrovka – Bol'shie Maiachki – Krasnaia Poliana in concert with the 29th Tank Corps and with impetuous actions it is to cut the Belgorod – Oboian' highway by the end of day 12.07.43 and reach the line Krasnaia Dubrovka – Hill 254.5. Subsequently with a turn to the north, it is to cover the offensive operations of the army to the south.
>
> Sector on the right – Psel River, center of Vasil'evka, bridge in the center, Greznoe, Krasnaia Poliana (excl.), Krasnaia Dubrovka.

On the left – Hill 254.5 (excl.), northern edge of the grove northwest of Komsomolets State Farm (excl.), Machine Tractor Station (northern outskirts of Bol'shie Maiachki) (excl.).

3. I have decided with an attack in the direction of the southern outskirts of Vasil'evka and the height with Points 220.4, 252.5, and 251.2 to destroy the resisting enemy with a combat formation of the corps in three echelons.

On our right – units of the 5th Guards Army are defending along the Psel River. On the left, the 29th Tank Corps is attacking.

4. In the first echelon, the 181st and 170th Tank Brigades will attack in line the enemy in the corps sector with the immediate task of seizing Malye Maiachki, subsequently to reach the following lines: 181st Tank Brigade – Hill 251.5 – Krasnaia Poliana; the 170th Tank Brigade – Krasnaia Poliana (excl.) – Krasnaia Dubrovka.

The second echelon, the 32nd Motorized Rifle Brigade with the artillery group consisting of the 292nd Mortar Regiment and a 76mm destroyer anti-tank regiment will attack behind the first echelon, in order by day's end to take over the defense of the 181st and 170th Tank Brigades on the line Krasnaia Poliana – Krasnaia Dubrovka.

The third echelon, the 110th Tank Brigade and the reconnaissance battalion, is to reach the region of Hill 251.2 by day's end.

The corps headquarters will be in the third echelon, between the 110th Tank Brigade and the reconnaissance battalion.

By day's end, the command post will be in the grove east of Hill 251.2.

The 36th Guards Tank Regiment will attack behind the 170th Tank Brigade in the second echelon, and secure the right flank of the combat formation. Assemble at the Sukhaia River.

5. My reserve will be the 110th Tank Brigade.

6. The line of deployment is Mikhailovka – Oktiabr'skii State Farm.

7. The infantry's artillery support group will be the 292nd Mortar Regiment and the 58th Regiment of rocket artillery; the tanks' support group will consist of the 1000th Destroyer Anti-tank Artillery Regiment and the 36th Guards Tank Regiment.

Task: Secure the infantry and tank attack in the sector of the corps' offensive.

8. The brigade rear services will follow in the third echelon under the protection of the 110th Tank Brigade. The corps medical-sanitation battalion will be in Viazovoe.

9. The second echelon of the corps' and brigades' rears will be in Bobrovo-Dvorskii.

Command post: Beregovoe; switch axis: southern outskirts of Andreevka – Hill 224.5 – Hill 220.4 – southern outskirts of Malye Maiachki – grove at Dolgii Verkh.

10. Reports are to be sent at the start of the offensive and subsequently every two hours thereafter.

11. The start of the artillery preparation: 0800

12. The start of the attack: 0830 upon the signal 'Storm'.[20]

★ ★ ★

A most important factor for the successful introduction of a tank army into the engagement is its artillery support, especially in the first hours of fighting, which is to say during the first 5 to 10 kilometers of advance. A great deal of organizational work must be carried out when preparing the artillery's role in the tank attack. First, the artillery of the tank army and its subordinate corps, as well as the artillery of the rifle divisions and regiments, must all be prepared to cooperate with the tankers. In turn, precise cooperation between the headquarters of the tank corps and those of the defending rifle formations through which the armor must advance as it enters into battle must be arranged. Secondly, firing positions must be selected, fire plans worked out, communications established and ammunition must be brought up. Finally, the effectiveness of the artillery preparatory fire depends upon the thorough and deep reconnaissance of the adversary's defenses, and the establishment of suitable observation posts for assessing the effectiveness of the fire and for making corrections to the fire. All of this takes time, which is precisely what the Voronezh Front lacked at Prokhorovka.

Because of the deficit of motorized transportation, the main forces of the artillery began to arrive only on the evening of 10 July and the following morning. During all this time, bitter fighting against a hard-pressing adversary was going on; reconnaissance and scouting was practically impossible due to the rapid pace of the battle and the density of fire. The artillery units deployed their guns under intensive bombing. The majority of the artillery didn't reach their firing positions until the evening and night of 11 July.

There were a large number of gaps in the staff work and some problems of a purely technical nature. Little attention was given to working out the questions of cooperation between the tank formations and the artillery units of the rifle divisions operating in front of them.

The readying of the attached artillery units, with which the *front* had strengthened the 5th Tank Guards Army, created a particular difficulty. It was quite difficult to connect them with the offensive's general plan for the artillery. Because of the lack of motorized transport, they were late in reaching their designated areas and unable to set up communications with the headquarters of the formations participating in the counterstroke, and did not have time to conduct fully all the necessary fire preparation measures. To a great extent, the difficulties in assembling the artillery were explained by the enemy's seizure of the line, which had been originally designated for the introduction of the tank army into the engagement.

The 5th Guards Tank Army was reinforced by the following artillery units from Voronezh Front:

The 1529th Self-propelled Artillery Regiment (11 152mm guns) arrived without its rear support, which had been cut off by the enemy in the region of Ryndinka; this adversely affected the regiment's performance in the first hours of combat.

The Long-range Artillery Group:

The 522nd High-power Guards Artillery Regiment – 12 203mm guns;

The 1148th Guards Artillery Regiment – 18 152mm guns;

The 142nd Gun Artillery Regiment – 18 122mm guns;

The 93rd Gun Artillery Regiment – 18 122mm guns.

The *Front*'s group of Guards mortar units:

The 16th Guards Mortar Regiment – 24 M-13 (132mm) rocket launchers;
The 80th Guards Mortar Regiment – 24 M-13 (132mm) rocket launchers.

This group, under the command of Guards Colonel Iofa, also had the Army's Guards mortar units – the 76th Guards Mortar Regiment, and the 409th and 307th Guards Mortar Battalions.[21]

While preparing for the counterstroke, the psychological factor also played a negative role. After all, the greatest responsibility was now lying upon the *front*'s leadership. Too much was now hinging on the success (or failure) of the plan. This gave rise to nervous stress, to shortcomings in the preparation and organization of the 12 July counterattack. N. S. Khrushchev recalled how the psychological pressure from Moscow affected the Voronezh Front command:

> By that time our situation had deteriorated. We were running out of reserves. The situation was becoming serious, and Moscow was displaying nervousness. I remember how before my departure to join Katukov, Vatutin and I were speaking with Stalin. Then Molotov called. In such situations he always spoke more crudely than Stalin, uttered a few insulting expressions, and lost all verbal control. But anything concrete, other than swearing, we didn't hear from him. He couldn't help us in any way, because he was a zero in military questions, but Stalin used him as a lash or truncheon. He spoke with the commander [Vatutin] in an insulting tone, then with me. I don't want to permit myself, in return, any disrespectful expressions toward him, because even with all his negative qualities, Molotov was an honest man in his own way, and his dedication to Soviet power doesn't give me the right to speak badly about him, when the conversation is on the war. In moments of crisis, he displayed rudeness, but not in a calm situation, and I understood that in those hours he could only curse. The situation had turned threatening, to say the least: the enemy had chewed his way through three belts of defense, which had been almost completely filled with tanks.[22]

However, Vatutin's self-control and concentration were extremely necessary. The adversary had already penetrated 35 kilometers into the *front*'s defense, many formations had already suffered heavy losses, and after a week of uninterrupted fighting, fatigue was beginning to manifest itself in the troops – all of this was weighing on their combat spirit.[23] The absence of precision in the *front* command's orders and directions, the uncertainty in the higher command, rattled the staffs of the armies' headquarters, and in the final account had an effect on the results of their work. It was not possible to acknowledge this at the time, but a person is a living being, and he or she cannot toss aside emotions, especially in critical minutes.

Moreover, it is necessary to take into account the enormous scale of the engagement. The strong enemy pressure explained the difficulties in assembling the artillery and other units in the area of the tank army's introduction into the battle. They first had to be withdrawn from the fighting, that is to say removed from one commander or another, for subsequent regrouping. This was very difficult to do under the intense enemy pressure.

This also contributed to the uncoordinated actions, the haste and confusion, and the contradictory orders and directions.

The situation that developed on 10 July while transferring the 10th Destroyer Anti-tank Artillery Brigade to Prokhorovka can serve as one example. From the Southwestern Front, the brigade had been put under the operational control of the 69th Army's artillery commander. It was a powerful artillery formation, equipped with 60 of the highly reputable 76mm artillery guns and 57mm anti-tank guns. Under the counterattack's plan, all three regiments of this brigade were subordinated to the 18th and 29th Tank Corps. They were to operate between the Psel River and Storozhevoe. Until the evening of 11 July, the 10th Destroyer Anti-tank Artillery Brigade was located in an anti-tank strongpoint in the Lomovo – Korocha region.

Between 1800 and 2200 on 11 July, the brigade command received four contradictory orders from higher headquarters regarding the routes the formation should take for its movement. Thus, at 1800 the brigade commander set off for the headquarters of the *front*'s artillery in order to receive orders. He hadn't yet managed to arrive at Rzhava Station, when already within two hours of his departure, at the direction of the 69th Army's headquarters, his assistant chief of staff Captain Seriuk was heading to General Rotmistrov's headquarters in order to receive the order on the brigade's participation in the counterstroke. At 2100, when the units of the brigade were ready to march, the commander of the 69th Army's artillery issued an order that sent the brigade in the opposite direction, to the Novo-Oskochnoe – Kazach'e region. The brigade quickly set off toward the designated area. Two hours later, through a report to the Military Council of the 69th Army, the brigade's chief of staff received a new combat order from General Vatutin: to move in on the line Vypolzovka – Aleksandrovka – Sviridovka – Podsumki – Zaiach'e. At 0200 on 12 July, while on the march toward the indicated line, the brigade was turned around and redirected to deal with a new threat, since at that time the panzers of Army Detachment Kempf were already fighting for Rzhavets and breaking through toward Vypolzovka. Thus, in this way Rotmistrov's tankers never received the vitally important support of this anti-tank formation.

Army Detachment Kempf's heavy pressure on the Rzhavets – Vypolzovka sector also interfered with the movement of the 1529th Self-propelled Artillery Regiment, which was equipped with the heavy SU-152. This massive assault gun had been designed as a "bunker buster", but it was also quite effective against the enemy's heavy tanks (among the troops, the SU-152 carried the nickname "Beast-killer" [*zveroboi*]. It had been planned to use the regiment to reinforce the 29th Tank Corps, operating on the axis of the main attack. However, it didn't arrive in the vicinity of Prokhorovka until 1800 12 July, and with only a limited supply of shells (its rear elements had been held up *en route* due to the enemy's appearance at Rzhavets); thus, the regiment took no part in the fighting on this day.

Rotmistrov recalled:

> As a result of the limited withdrawal of the *front*'s forces [on 11 July], the conditions for the artillery's support of the 5th Guards Tank Army's counterstroke had deteriorated, since part of the artillery was destroyed by enemy tanks while moving into their firing positions.

> In order to forestall the enemy's offensive west of Prokhorovka, with insufficient time for assembling the artillery, I designated the start time for the attack at 0830 12 July and restricted the duration of the artillery preparation from thirty to fifteen minutes.
>
> We were fully aware that in these circumstances, it was impossible to expect great results from the artillery fire. But considering that the adversary had managed to obtain certain successes on a number of sectors of Voronezh Front's defense, we hurried with the start of the offensive, in order to take the initiative away from the enemy on the Prokhorovka axis.
>
> ... Moreover it should be noted that there was almost no artillery reconnaissance because of the lack of time; the artillery was moving up together with the tank and motorized rifle brigades of the corps. This led to the situation where by the start of the attack, there were almost no artillery observation posts among the combat formations.[24]

Significant aviation forces were pulled together with the aim of providing air cover for the counterstroke. The 2nd Air Army conducted aerial reconnaissance on behalf of the ground forces, and launched bombing and ground attack strikes on enemy tanks, artillery and motorized infantry in the areas of Sukho-Solotino, Pokrovka, Ozerovskii and Malye Maiachki.[25] Voronezh Front also brought in Southwestern Front's 17th Air Army to support its ground forces; this air army primarily operated in the sector of 7th Guards Army to block the approach of enemy reserves to the Prokhorovka axis.

Counterstrokes with the use of several tank corps had already occurred in the battle, but the experience with their organization was not fully taken into account for the 12 July counterattack, first of all in the matter of providing air cover for the attacking echelon. Despite its seeming power, the tank army at that time was particularly vulnerable to air strikes. The enormous accumulation of armor on a narrow sector of the front presented easy booty to the enemy's bombers and dive-bombers.

The adversary in the course of Operation Citadel made wide use of air power in the struggle with our tanks. A new and powerful Junkers Ju 87 G-1 Stuka had been created and put into production for this purpose. Though relatively slow and vulnerable to our fighters, these "tank busters", firing 37mm armor-piercing shells at the thin armor on the top of the turret or the engine compartment, caused a lot of problems for our tankers.

Thus, the Soviet command tried to provide adequate fighter cover of the counterattack grouping. Fighters of the 5th Fighter Aviation Corps, patrolling the skies above the Prokhorovka – Vasil'evka – Belenikhino – Maloe Iablonovo region, valiantly attempted to protect the armor and troops of the 5th Guards Tank Army's main assault grouping. In the course of 12 July, the fighter divisions of the 5th Fighter Aviation Corps conducted a total of 320 individual sorties, during which they engaged in 14 air battles and downed approximately 20 enemy aircraft, while losing 14 of their own. Unfortunately, they were unable to secure our ground forces from enemy air strikes.

The archive of the 69th Army's documents contains one particularly telling comment regarding a key problem in providing air support to the Red Army:

> The Air Force's surveillance over [enemy] lines and notification of enemy movements was not organized, and limited to using the radio network of the divisions and corps on the ground, which even without this was overburdened with the work to secure control over the ground forces. The system to give recognition of our own ground forces to aircraft overhead was also weakly organized.
>
> Battalion and regiment commanders, *because of fear of their own aviation* [author's emphasis], did not always mark their forward positions.[26]

The primary shortcomings in the use of air power was the absence of a direct line of communications between the headquarters of the *front*'s subordinate formations and the command post of the air army and the military airfields; the lack of air force liaison teams with communication means among the staff of corps headquarters; and the absence of forward air controllers with the units of the counterattack grouping. In these circumstances, a request for an air strike on an enemy grouping during the battle had to travel a lengthy process up the chain of command to the *front* command, which alone could decide upon the request. While the call traveled through all the intervening levels of command, the situation on the ground was changing, and the air strike when it came was frequently delivered either on an empty patch of ground, or against their own forces – something that happened all too often. Miscalculations of this type doubtlessly affected the results of the counterstroke.

The noted deficiencies frequently led to interference in the cooperation between the ground forces and the air force, often with tragic consequences. For example, on 9 July at 0258, the 69th Army's chief of staff Colonel S. M. Protas was sending the following coded message to *front* headquarters, with a copy to the commander of the 2nd Air Army:

> I request:
> 1. 9.07.43 a bombing of the enemy's tanks and infantry on the axis:
>   a) Prokhorovka,
>   b) Belenikhino and Korocha *with preliminary thorough reconnaissance* [author's emphasis] and at a call from the command post of the army commander.
> 2. Air cover over the army's combat formations.
> 3. An air force liaison team with communications means at the command post of the army commander.[27]

How this request was carried out is reflected in another coded message from the very same S. M. Protas on 10 July 1943 at 1230:

> From 0700 to 0900 9.07.43, up to 60 Il-2 bombed the combat positions of the 183rd Rifle Division's 285th and 295th Rifle Regiments in the vicinities of Vasil'evka, Komsomolets State Farm and Hill 241.6. We are ascertaining the losses.
>
> I am asking you to inform me, at whose request were the specified points bombed.[28]

The villages and hill indicated in the document were located in the 285th Rifle Regiment's sector; elements of the 295th Rifle Regiment were positioned to the south. Thus, the main strike of the Il-2 *Shturmoviki* ground attack aircraft was delivered against the line of defense of Major A. K. Karpov's 285th Rifle Regiment, which on the following day had to repulse the attack of SS Panzergrenadier Division *Leibstandarte*. Even someone who is not a military specialist can imagine what became of the trenches, minefields, and other elements of the regiment's fortifications over the two hours of the Il-2 strike. I was unable to find precise data on the losses caused by this instance of fratricide or the results of the subsequent investigation in the files of the Russian Ministry of Defense's Central Archives.

With respect to the ground anti-aircraft defenses, the *front* organized the anti-aircraft artillery cover for its main attack grouping in the following manner: the 29th Anti-aircraft Artillery Division from the *Stavka* Reserve, under the command of Colonel Ia. V. Liubimov, was covering the forces of the 5th Guards Army with three regiments of small-caliber anti-aircraft artillery and one regiment of medium anti-aircraft artillery. Colonel G. P. Mezhinsky's 6th Anti-aircraft Artillery Division from 2300 11 July was providing anti-aircraft defense for the 5th Guards Tank Army in the following areas: the 1062nd Anti-aircraft Regiment – Iamki, Machine Tractor Station (southwest of Prokhorovka Station); the 516th Anti-aircraft Regiment – south and southwest of Prokhorovka Station; the 366th Anti-aircraft Regiment – with the 29th Tank Corps; the 146th Anti-aircraft Regiment – in the area of the 5th Guards Mechanized Corps; and the 1694th Anti-aircraft Regiment – with the combat formations of the 2nd Guards Tank Corps. Units of Colonel A. E. Frolov's 26th Anti-aircraft Artillery Division prior to 8 July had been subordinate to the 6th Guards Army, and was concentrated in the following areas: the 1357th Anti-aircraft Artillery Regiment – Prokhorovka Station; the 363rd Anti-aircraft Artillery Regiment – Oktiabr'skii State Farm; the 1369th Anti-aircraft Artillery Regiment – Storozhevoe and the woods north of it; and the 1352nd Anti-aircraft Regiment – Grushki, Iamki and Pravorot'.[29] Note that the 1062nd and 1352nd Anti-aircraft Regiments were both equipped with medium anti-aircraft guns; the remaining regiments were all equipped with small-caliber anti-aircraft weapons.

The 18th Tank Corps did not receive any anti-aircraft units. It was planned that the 6th and 26th Anti-aircraft Artillery Divisions would cover it on its line of departure; once the 18th Tank Corps' attack was underway, the 1062nd and 516th Anti-aircraft Artillery Regiments would escort it to protect its combat formations from air strikes. However, these units never left the positions they occupied prior to the attack, and the 18th Tank Corps was subjected to air attacks throughout the day as it attacked toward Vasil'evka.

Considering the highly dynamic nature of tank combat, the anti-aircraft artillery regiments could not physically keep up with the tank and mechanized formations, especially when moving out on the attack and when closing on the enemy. It was precisely during this period that the armored formations suffered their greatest losses at the hands of enemy aircraft. If however the anti-aircraft units had moved out together with the combat formations, they would have immediately suffered serious losses from both the shell fragments of exploding bombs and the machine-gun fire from strafing aircraft (the vast majority of Soviet anti-aircraft guns were either towed or mounted on trucks). Therefore the tankers sought to close with the enemy as quickly as possible, so their combat formations would become intermingled with the Germans', but this tactic didn't always prove successful.

There was a whole series of other miscalculations that affected the results of the anti-aircraft gun crews. Here is just one short citation from Voronezh Front's artillery commander's Order No. 18, concerning the actions of the anti-aircraft artillery divisions between 5 July and 20 July 1943:

> The unit commanders' control over the combat readiness and combat work of the batteries and machine gun companies (1366th Anti-aircraft Regiment, 6th Anti-aircraft Division, 26th Anti-aircraft Division) was weak, as a consequence of which the fire of some batteries didn't have the desired effect. There were numerous cases of senseless, ineffective fire. The command posts of regiments and divisions lack any control over the batteries' fire or their execution of directions regarding target selection and when to open fire, and there is no coordination with [our] fighter aviation; there were instances of firing at our own aircraft (6th Anti-aircraft Division).[30]

As subsequent events demonstrated, the anti-aircraft regiment commanders poorly handled the fire and movement of their batteries. Unfortunately, the anti-aircraft units, particularly the medium anti-aircraft guns, were relatively immobile: it required a rather large amount of time to shift a battery or regiment to a different location and to prepare it to defend against an air attack. It was impossible to fire the anti-aircraft guns while they were being transported, leaving the covered ground units and even the anti-aircraft units themselves defenseless against air attack. Moreover, as events showed, the shifting of firing positions and the maneuver of the regiments were poorly considered.

Preparations for the counterattack occurred in even more difficult conditions for the 5th Guards Army, the main forces of which had already been committed into the fighting on 11 July. The 5th Guards Army commander recalled:

> That evening [11 July] I received an order from the *front* commander, which ordered the army to launch a counterattack on the morning of 12 July with the left-flank 33rd Rifle Corps in conjunction with the 5th Guards Tank Army in the direction of Bol'shie Maiachki; with the right-flank 32nd Rifle Corps jointly with the 6th Guards Army in the direction of Krasnaia Poliana and Gremiachii. The 5th Guards Army's immediate task was to reach the Greznoe – Malye Maiachki – Teterevino – Komsomolets State Farm area, and subsequently the region of Pogorelovka and Iakovlevo.
>
> Only several hours of daylight and a short summer night remained to organize the counterstroke. There was a lot to do in this period of time: decisions had to be reached, assignments had to be delivered to the formations, necessary regrouping

had to be conducted, and the army's own artillery and attached artillery had to be allocated and deployed (that evening, the army had received a lot of mortar and howitzer artillery brigades as reinforcements). Unfortunately, the artillery had an extremely limited quantity of ammunition – less than half the standard combat load.

... All the organizational work took place at the army's observation post. The final decisions were reached in the presence of the army's leading command and operations staff. Here the chief of operations marked the plan on his map with the individual objectives for the corps and divisions. Simultaneously these tasks were converted into combat orders, which were then sent off to their designations with signals officers. Next the tasks of the artillery and engineering troops were determined, as well as the resolution of other questions connected with the forthcoming offensive. After the completion of all this work, the majority of staff officers and officers of the political department set off to the formations and units, in order to assist their commanders in preparing their subordinates to carry out the given tasks.[31]

The final Combat Order No. 064/OP for the 5th Guards Army was signed by Lieutenant General A. S. Zhadov at 0115 on 12 July:

1. In connection with 5th [Guards] Tank Army's attack on the morning of 12.07.43 to the left of the army in the general direction of Dumnoe and Pokrovka, as a partial change to the previously issued order, the army will attack in the pending offensive on 12.07.43 not by the right flank, but the left flank.
2. The 33rd Guards Rifle Corps, exploiting the tank attack, is to destroy the opposing enemy with a decisive offensive in the general direction of Bol'shie Maiachki in conjunction with the 32nd Guards Rifle Corps and the tanks.

The corps main blow will be inflicted with the forces of the 97th Guards, 95th Guards and 42nd Guards Rifle Divisions, and the 9th Guards Airborne Division and 52nd Guards Rifle Division arranged in one echelon, having its greatest strength on its left flank. The immediate and subsequent tasks are as before.
3. The 6th Guards Airborne Division, as the army reserve, will assemble in the region of Sredniaia Ol'shanka – Hill 243.5 – Ostren'kii. If necessary, it has the task to develop the success in the general direction of Petrovka, Vasil'evka and Greznoe.

Some scholars, critically evaluating the planning and organization of the 12 July counterstroke have placed a lot of blame on N. F. Vatutin. However, it seems improper to lay all the responsibility for such an important matter on one person, even if he occupies such a high post. In any sphere, the questions of "who" and "how" the orders and directions are being carried out are no less important to achieving success. In the given case, the staff of Voronezh Front bears most of the blame for the flaws committed in organizing the counterattack.

There were a lot of gaps and purely technical problems in the work of the *front* staff and the headquarters of subordinate formations. Little attention was given to the questions of working out collaboration between the artillery units, the tank formations,

Chief of staff of the Voronezh Front, Lieutenant General S. P. Ivanov working with a map in the headquarters of the 69th Army. Korocha, 11 July 1943. (Personal archive of M. S. Dutova, daughter of S. P. Ivanov)

and the rifle divisions operating in front; communications between the cooperating branches were particularly weak.

It is paradoxical, but true: Voronezh Front's chief of staff from 6 July was located in Korocha! General S. P. Ivanov recalls:

> The Supreme Commander placed great significance on the presence of leadership directly on site. On 6 July, speaking with N. F. Vatutin over a direct line, Stalin ordered one commander to remain at the command post. He assigned the other commanders to different army headquarters to oversee their operations as follows: Marshal A. M Vasilevsky was to meet the reserves – the 5th Guards and 5th Guards Tank Armies – and lead them into the battle; N. S. Khrushchev was to travel to the Oboian' axis to General I. M. Chistiakov's 6th Guards Army; I was assigned to Lieutenant General Kriuchenkin's 69th Army on the Korocha axis; and General I. P. Apanasenko, deputy *front* commander, to General M. S. Shumilov's 7th Guards Army on the boundary with Southwestern Front.
>
> I immediately set off for Korocha, where I remained until the end of the engagement at Prokhorovka.
>
> This had no effect on the work of the staff, since thanks to the well-organized and uninterrupted flow of information from the [Voronezh Front] commander, his deputies, the members of Military Council and I were constantly informed of all the events happening on the [Voronezh] *front*.[32]

Lieutenant General P. A. Rotmistrov, commander of the 5th Guards Tank Army (on the left) and Lieutenant General A. S. Zhadov, commander of the 5th Guards Army, presumably at the command post of the 5th Guards Tank Army at Skorovka, July 1943. (RGAKFD)

The absence from his post of such an important figure as the *front* chief of staff doubtlessly adversely affected the quality of the headquarters' work in handling its forces, especially at such a difficult moment as the introduction of two fresh armies into the engagement. Here are the opinions of two army commanders, who took part in the operation, on the effectiveness of Ivanov's work regarding only one aspect of the preparations – keeping lower headquarters informed. A. S. Zhadov, commander of the 5th Guards Army, recalled: "The army was committed into the fighting, but we knew little about the situation, which on this sector was extremely complex and intense. Information from the *front* command … on movements of the enemy and of our own forces was irregular." P. A. Rotmistrov, commander of the 5th Guards Tank Army, seconds Zhadov's opinion: "… Without complete information on the enemy's grouping and his intentions, on 12 July the forces of Voronezh Front launched the counterstroke." As the reader will later be able to convince himself, there was no attempt by these army commanders in these utterances to shift blame onto the shoulders of others.

For the sake of justice it must be said that a significant portion of the blame for the poor organization of the intelligence on behalf of the tank units and formations (including those assigned to the *front* in the course of the engagement) should go to the chief and staff of the *front*'s Armored and Mechanized Forces. In the archive, there is a report by the chief of intelligence for the Armored and Mechanized Forces of Voronezh Front Lieutenant Colonel P. I. Shul'gin to the Red Army's Commander of Armored and Mechanized Forces (with a copy to the Chief of Voronezh Front's Armored and Mechanized forces[33]), written on 14 July 1943.

A number of facts are laid out in this document, testifying to the extremely poor, bordering on irresponsible, intelligence work of the staff of the Armored and Mechanized Forces, and its undemanding attitude toward the staff of subordinate headquarters with respect to implementing the demands of State Defense Committee Order No. 0072 from 19 April 1943 on measures to improve the reconnaissance activities of Red Army forces. The primary shortcomings, as noted in this report, include the following:

> Troops and headquarters, including those located in the depth of the defense, do not strive in all possible ways to supplement the available information on the enemy, and make no effort at all to study his defenses, especially the anti-tank defenses. As a result, the tank units and formations go into battle blindly and suffer unnecessary losses;
>
> Commanders and chiefs of staff do not involve themselves with the selection and strengthening of the cadre of reconnaissance commanders, and do not create the necessary conditions for the intelligence departments and reconnaissance detachments to carry out their important responsibilities to obtain additional information on the enemy, the identification of his units, and his combat possibilities and intentions;
>
> Reconnaissance commanders are often used outside their assigned roles at the most important moments of combat operations.[34]

Subsequently, the Red Army's Chief of Armored and Mechanized Forces Colonel General Ia. N. Fedorenko demanded:

> … 3. Don't allow attacks by units without thorough scouting of the terrain, the artificial obstacles, the anti-tank defenses, and the enemy's system of fire. Commanders who neglect to conduct reconnaissance and operate blindly will be called to account.
>
> … 7. Thoroughly analyze the causes of your own losses. On the basis of this analysis, announce the strict responsibility of commanders at all levels to avoid unjustified losses.[35]

10

Combat Operations on the Main Axis of Attack – The 5th Guards Tank Army

One of the most widely discussed questions regarding the Prokhorovka engagement is whether or not the German command knew about the Soviet preparations for a strong counterattack. Those who consider this operation as indisputably successful rely primarily on P. A. Rotmistrov's memoirs, in which he clearly wrote that the operation was unexpected for the enemy, and in the first minutes of the fighting, came as a shock to the II SS Panzer Corps. In Rotmistrov's opinion, this was one of the factors that helped our forces. However, there are large doubts about the accuracy of this point of view.

When conducting any offensive operation, the attacking side pays particular attention to reconnaissance. Without this, it is impossible to uncover the enemy's intentions, which makes it impossible to plan further operations of one's forces with any reliability or accuracy. In the fighting at Prokhorovka, the adversary made wide use of all types of reconnaissance, from small probes by scout parties to aerial observation. All night and into the early morning of 12 July, the Germans kept careful watch, keeping track of all movements on our side.

The tank brigades of the 5th Guards Tank Army moved into their jumping-off positions between 2300 and 2400 11 July, which means more than 400 tanks and assault guns were assembling on a sector just 5 to 6 kilometers wide just 1.5 to 2 kilometers from the enemy's forward positions. After moving into their start line, more than eight hours were to pass before the start of the attack. Judge for yourselves: is it really possible to conceal such a concentration of armor right under the enemy's nose for such a long time?

At 0030 on 12 July, units of the SS Panzergrenadier Division *Leibstandarte* conducted a reconnaissance-in-force. Up to a battalion of infantry with the support of a panzer company emerged from the woods northwest of Storozhevoe and attacked in the direction of Lutovo. By this time, the 29th Tank Corps' 25th Tank Brigade was already in its jumping-off positions around Lutovo. The 1st Company of the 362nd Tank Battalion and a company of submachine gunners from the 25th Motorized Rifle Battalion emerged from the southern outskirts of Lutovo and counterattacked the SS troops. The combat didn't last long, and at 0100 the enemy fell back to Storozhevoe.[1]

The reconnaissance-in-force indicated that south of Prokhorovka (on the main axis), fresh Soviet tank units had appeared where throughout the previous day the Soviet side had practically made no use of tanks, and in strength sufficient to throw back an attack by a panzer company and a battalion of infantry within thirty minutes. To a professional, this was enough information to draw conclusions about the adversary's immediate plans.

Captain Z. P. Grigorenko, commander of the motorized rifle battalion in the 29th Tank Corps' 25th Tank Brigade (1941 photo). (TsAMO)

The Germans had no doubts that these tank units were going to be used at dawn. Direct confirmation of this comes from recently published documents of the II SS Panzer Corps. They reveal that its command had already known for at least two days before the counterattack about the assembly of fresh Soviet mobile corps formations in front of its attack sector. For example, at 2030 on 9 July, the II SS Panzer Corps headquarters received information from the Fourth Panzer Army headquarters: "New motorized formations are on the move to the west from the direction of Novyi and Staryi Oskol." An hour earlier, P. Hausser himself had signed a combat report, in which it was noted: "According to intelligence from aerial reconnaissance, the distant approach of operational tank and motorized reserves toward the region of Prokhorovka (railroad) is being observed. Part of the revealed forces might be hurled against our neighbor, advancing on the right."[2]

On the following day, 10 July, Hausser's headquarters announced, "A new adversary is in the bend of the Psel River, presumably units of the 5th Guards Army, which until now has been located in the Ostrogozhsk region: the enemy is bringing up operational reserves from distant sectors of the front. The appearance of 1-2 tank or motorized corps in front of the attacking group of the corps should be expected."[3]

The opponent must be given his due. As is obvious from the cited quotes, well before the counterattack, the II SS Panzer Corps command was not only expecting a strengthening of the defense in the region southwest of Prokhorovka with two corps, but also assumed that part of these forces could be used in the sector of the 69th Army against its right-hand "neighbor" – Army Detachment Kempf. That indeed occurred on the morning of 12 July.

On the basis of this intelligence, the II SS Panzer Corps headquarters at 2250 11 July issued the following assignments to its formations:

> The II SS Panzer Corps smashes the enemy south of Prokhorovka, and will create by this the preconditions for a further advance through Prokhorovka. The assignments for the divisions:
>
> Division-*TK* [*Totenkopf*] launches an attack from the bridgehead at dawn, to capture the hills to the northeast and first of all to reach the Prokhorovka – Kartashevka road. It is to take possession of the Psel River valley by an attack from the southwest, securing the left flank of Division-*AH* [*Adolf Hitler*].
>
> Division-*AH*, holding its occupied line on the left flank, on the right flank seizes Storozhevoe and the woods north of it, the Stalinskii [Stalinskoe Branch of the Oktiabr'skii] State Farm and Iamki, as well as the heights 2 kilometers to the east. With the neutralization of threats on the left flank along the Psel, it is to seize Prokhorovka and Hill 252.4 in conjunction with elements of the *T*-Division.
>
> *R*-Division [*Das Reich*], holding the line it has achieved on the right flank, seizes Vinogradovka and Ivanovka. After right-flank elements of *AH*-Division have seized Storozhevoe and the woods to the north, taking advantage of their success, it is to shift its primary efforts in the direction of the hills southwest of Pravorot'. It will hold the new line Ivanovka – hills southwest of Pravorot' – hill 2 km east of Storozhevoe (excl.).[4]

The fact calls attention to itself that with the dawn, only *Totenkopf* was to go on the attack with all its forces, in a sector where there were no Soviet tank formations. At the same time, *Leibstandarte*, which the day before had been most active in front of Prokhorovka, and which was destined to receive the main blow of the 5th Guards Tank Army, was supposed only to hold its "occupied line" and wait for the results of the offensive of its neighbor on the left. This document is evidence of Hausser's decision to assume a defensive posture on the Soviet tank grouping's probable axis of attack. In the given situation, this was the most sensible decision.

The night-time reconnaissance-in-force toward Lutovo confirmed the previous calculations and clarified the concrete assembly locations of Soviet tank units. The command of SS Panzergrenadier Division *Leibstandarte* knew that in its assigned sector, major Soviet tank reserves had assembled, and it was anticipating a strong attack with the coming of dawn.

The SS commanders tried to take full advantage of all this information and implemented measures to repulse the likely attack of the *front*'s forces. The results of the fighting on 12 July exquisitely confirm this supposition. I will cite two more facts. Precisely on the operational axis of the revealed 25th Tank Brigade, the adversary placed several self-propelled guns from the 1st SS Panzerjäger Battalion in ambush positions on the Stalinskoe Branch of the [Oktiabr'skii] State Farm; during the very first attack on 12 July, the guns of these hidden tank destroyers would render the 25th Tank Brigade combat incapable as a tank formation.

In addition, at dawn before the start of the counterattack, scouts of the 9th Guards Airborne Division revealed an enemy trap – a tank ambush 2 kilometers south of Prokhorovka's outskirts (to the right of the railroad embankment). The commander of the 7th Guards Artillery Regiment's 1st Battalion K. V. Kazakov recalls:

> Early on the morning of 12 July, a scout named Balabanov from the command platoon (a Buriat by nationality) reported to me that overnight he had heard the rumble of engines and the clatter of tracks, and at dawn he had discovered that at a place where knocked-out German tanks had been on 11 July, there were now an even greater number of operational tanks. I immediately reported to regiment commander Comrade Valuev. There were no doubts that the Germans had been preparing for a sudden offensive on our sector and were intending to attack our positions from close range. At 0800 that morning, the German tank positions were given a salvo of Guards rocket artillery fire and an artillery barrage. Our battalion also fired. The majority of the German tanks were knocked-out; the remaining (not more than 10) retreated into the ravine south of Hill 252.2 and to the villages of Lutovo and Iamki. In those conditions, it was difficult to determine how many tanks were knocked out by the 1st Battalion.[5]

Today only documents from the political command of the 5th Guards Tank Army can tell us what occurred in the pre-dawn hours of 12 July in the units and formations of the tank army. Here's what the chief of the political department of the 29th Tank Corps' 31st Tank Brigade Colonel Povolotsky reported:

> We assembled at the start line by 0100 12.07.43 in full strength, with the exception of one T-34 tank (the tank of the 277th Tank Battalion's commander, driven by mechanic-driver Shcherbin, was disabled).
>
> At the jumping-off line, discussions were conducted with the crews on the subjects of the military oath, their knowledge of the *Stavka* directives, hidden sabotage, the approach of the hour of revenge, the situation on the other *fronts*, and the operations of tanks in combat. Applications for Party membership were written up. Seven applications for the Party were distributed, and nine for Komsomol membership. The political awareness and morale was high. In their jumping-off positions, the men received a hot meal.[6]

At sun-up on 12 July, of the Voronezh Front leadership, only the *front* commander N. F. Vatutin remained at his headquarters. His chief of staff Ivanov was now with Kriuchenkin's 69th Army; deputy *front* commander Apanasenko was with Shumilov's 7th Guards Army. *Stavka* representative and Chief of the General Staff Marshal Vasilevsky was together with Rotmistrov at the observation post of the 29th Tank Corps. From this vantage point, the region of the Oktiabr'skii State Farm – the field of the looming engagement – lay spread out before the commanders as if on an open palm. In agreement with Rotmistrov's decisions, the 5th Guards Tank Army's main blow would be directed at Luchki and Iakovlevo. The army was arranged in two echelons, with the 18th, 29th and 2nd Guards 'Tatsinskaia' Tank Corps in the first echelon, and the 5th Guards Mechanized Corps in the second echelon to exploit any success. Rotmistrov kept General K. G. Trufanov's mixed detachment of the 53rd Guards Tank Regiment, the 1st Guards Motorcycle Regiment, the 689th Destroyer Anti-tank Artillery Regiment and the 678th Howitzer Artillery Regiment as his reserve.

Brigades of the 29th Tank Corps in their jumping-off positions southwest of Prokhorovka, in the area of the brick factory, 12 July 1943. (RGAKFD)

With the first rays of dawn on 12 July, the army commander drove with his operations group to General I. F. Kirichenko's 29th Tank Corps. The command post had been set up on a low rise southwest of Prokhorovka, in an orchard. The trunks of the apple trees displayed the lacerations of shell fragments; wrinkled apples were visible among the withered leaves. Radio antennas protruded above the sandy breastworks of the trenches, which were sparkling with the morning dew, and the mingled speech of the phone operators, who were checking the connections, was audible.

From the dugout, a broad view opened to the southwest, toward there, where the concealed enemy was waiting. The bright rays of the morning sun bathed the expansive fields of grain, which were gently waving in the light morning breeze, in a golden light.

Beyond the fields, here and there columns of smoke rose above half-destroyed villages. Long shadows fell from the chimneys of torched homes. Patches of woods fringed with golden-yellow light extended above the horizon.

Slowly turning the cold knob of the stereoscope, General Rotmistrov was closely examining the German positions. It was quiet.

But exactly at 5:30 AM muffled, heavy explosions could be heard. The characteristic strained whine of airplane engines carried to our position. To the right and left in the sky above, several groups of Junkers appeared. They were flying calmly, in large waves … and only in one location, high above the clouds, could be seen the rapid motions of fighter combat. Having selected a target, the Junkers

> reformed into a large circle. With a flash of the sun on the glass of their cockpit canopies, they in sequence rolled over and plunged into a dive with a howl. Dense smoke and dust, frequently interrupted by crimson explosions, rose above the woods.[7]

Soon the army commander received a report: a new order from *front* headquarters had arrived. It made serious alterations to the counterattack plan. Vatutin announced that the enemy had broken through the defenses of the 69th Army in the area of Rzhavets, was forcing a crossing of the Northern Donets River, and in doing so was trying to emerge in the rear of the 5th Guards Tank Army. In addition, units of the 81st Guards Rifle Division were repelling German attempts to make a crossing in the region of Shcholokovo as well. Vatutin ordered the creation of a composite detachment, consisting of the army's forward detachment, two mechanized brigades of the 5th Guards Mechanized Corps and one tank brigade from the 2nd Guards 'Tatsinskaia' Tank Corps, and to send them to the area of the breakthrough. Moreover, in case of an enemy breakthrough from the south, P. A. Rotmistrov created an anti-tank barrier on the army's left flank: in the region of Hill 243.8 and Hill 242.7 west of Podol'khi, batteries of the 104th Guards Destroyer Anti-tank Artillery Regiment and the 1447th Self-propelled Artillery Regiment (as of 0200 12.07, with a combined strength of eight 76mm and eleven 45mm guns, and seven Su-122 and four Su-76 self-propelled guns)[8] deployed and dug in.

Thus, the counterstroke hadn't even yet started, but to parry the breakthrough threats on the Army's left flank, it was forced to detach a considerable force: 161 tanks (almost one-fifth of the 5th Guards Tank Army's total number of tanks), 11 self-propelled guns, 36 armored cars, two artillery regiments, and two anti-tank batteries. All this substantially affected the army's assault formation on the Prokhorovka axis: first, the Army's first echelon had been weakened with the detachment of one tank brigade from the 2nd Guards 'Tatsinskaia' Tank Corps; second, the second echelon had been reduced by half with the removal of two mechanized brigades from the 5th Guards 'Zimovniki' Mechanized Corps. As a reserve, Rotmistrov now only had two brigades (the 10th Guards Mechanized Brigade and the 24th Guards Tank Brigade) of the 5th Guards Mechanized Corps, which had a combined 92 tanks (by morning, an additional two T-34 tanks, two T-70 tanks and four Su-76 self-propelled guns should have arrived).[9] The 1529th Self-propelled Artillery Regiment was still on its way, and had assembled at Prokhorovka Station only by day's end, with only one combat load of shells and without its support services.

The dispersal of the army's forces, the delayed arrival of artillery units allocated by the *front* to reinforce the army, the insufficiently effective artillery barrage and the weak air cover for the counterattack grouping – all these things adversely told on the results of the attack by the 18th and 29th Tank Corps.

On 12 July at 0515, Rotmistrov signed Combat Report No. 8 to the headquarters of Voronezh Front:

1. The army's forces have taken their start lines for the offensive: Prelestnoe – Storozhevoe – Maloe Iablonovo, and are ready to execute the assigned combat tasks.
2. Artillery preparation from 0800. The attack – at 0830.[10]

According to the plan, the first *Katiusha* salvo from the Guards mortar regiments on the morning of 12 July was to serve as the signal for the initiation of the artillery preparation. Its aim was to disrupt the command and control in the enemy's forward units; to smash, as it seemed then, the hastily-prepared defenses (which had been thrown up over the course of one night); to suppress the enemy's anti-tank means; and by all of this to create the basis for a successful attack by the tank brigades of the first echelon. However, in connection with the changes inserted into the plan, only a fifteen-minute artillery barrage was conducted, which failed to damage the enemy's system of fire seriously and to suppress his anti-tank means. From an after-action account by the 5th Guards Tank Army's artillery staff, compiled after the operation:

1. Reconnoitering of the enemy did not precede the start of the artillery preparation; it was not possible to establish fully the location of his firing means; aerial reconnaissance intelligence did not arrive, and there were no communications with aviation. The latter point prevented the possibility of fully using the long-range artillery group against the approaching enemy tanks to further disorganize their command and control from a distance.
2. There were also no communications links with the headquarters of the artillery units, previously positioned on this sector. Communications were further hindered by the fact that the commanders of the army's artillery and corps artillery had no artillery reconnaissance means or means of communication.
3. … Information on the readiness of artillery units was late in arriving from the corps and the army's attached artillery units. Because of the lack of communications, coordination with neighbors was lost, while the divisions' artillery commanders often paid little regard to this matter. Thus, for example, the artillery commander of the 42nd Guards Rifle Division Colonel Kholodny on 12.07.43, in the face of intensifying combat, only took questions of cooperation with the artillery commander of the 29th Tank Corps under study and rejected any mutual assistance and exchange of information. The primary connections with the units were conducted … through runners and staff officers, which retarded the delivery of supplementary assignments and the passing of any type of intelligence or orders.

Fire direction, the issuing of new tasks, or the clarification of the conditions and the situation in the units were conducted exclusively by means of travel to the unit's position and by signal wire.

… The launching of the army's offensive on 12.07.43 was preceded by a short artillery preparation, in which the supplemental artillery and the corps artillery took part. The supplemental artillery was directed by artillery staff of the Voronezh Front, [but] was working in essence on behalf of the 5th Guards Tank Army, though it had no communications with the army headquarters or the army's artillery staff.

The firing plan and the schedule for the artillery attack were compiled without regard for intelligence; therefore the effectiveness of the fire was low. Moreover, the inadequate amount of daylight hours did not permit the selection of suitable

No.	Artillery Units		Area of Combat Operations	Caliber and Gun Type	Number of Guns	
					Authorized	Available
Bend of Psel River						
1	52 Gds Rifle Div	124 Gds Artillery Reg	Division sector (1/124 with the 153 Gds Rifle Reg in area of Veselyi, 2/124 in the area of Hill 226.6 with the 155 Gds Rifle Reg)	76mm Guns; 122mm Howitzers	24 76mm 12 122mm	Had losses
2		57 Gds AT Artillery Bn	With the rifle regiments of the 52nd Gds Rifle Div	45mm Guns	?	Had losses
3		649 AT Artillery Reg (attached)	In the sector of the 52nd Gds Rifle Div	45mm Guns	?	?
4	95 Gds Rifle Div (33 Gds Rifle Corps, 5 Gds Army)	233 Gds Artillery Reg	In the sector of the 95 Gds Rifle Div	76mm Guns; 122mm Howitzers	24 76mm 12 122mm	24 76mm/ 11 122mm
5		103 Gds AT Artillery Bn	In the sector of the 95 Gds Rifle Div	45mm Guns		12 45mm
6		301 Gds AT Artillery Bn (*Stavka* Reserve)	In the sector of the 95 Gds Rifle Div	76mm Guns	20 76mm	20 76mm
7		1322 AT Artillery Bn (*Stavka* Reserve)	In the course of the day supported the 66 Gds Rifle Div (32 Gds Rifle Corps); after 1800 shifted to the area of Nizhniaia Ol'shanka to cover the line on the Ol'shanka River	76mm Guns	20 76mm	20 76mm
8	6 Gds Airborne Div (5 Gds Army reserve)	8 Gds Artillery Reg	From 1300 in combat in the area of Hill 226.6	76mm Guns; 122mm Howitzers	24 76mm 12 122mm	Prior to 1207 did not take part in combat
9		5 Gds AT Artillery Bn	From 1300 in combat in the area of Hill 236.7	45mm Guns	?	Prior to 1207 did not take part in combat
SW of Prokhorovka Station (the sector between the Psel River and the Stalinskoe Branch of the Oktiabr'skii State Farm)						
10	42 Gds Rifle Div (33 Gds Rifle Corps, 5th Gds Army)	91 Gds Artillery Reg	In the sector of the 42 Gds Rifle between the Psel River and the railroad embankment. One battalion in sector of 127 Gds Rifle Reg, two battalions in reserve	76mm Guns/ 122 mm Howitzers	24 76mm 12 122mm	Prior to 1207 did not participate in combat
11		45 Gds AT Artillery Bn	2 batteries in area of Voroshilov State Farm; 1 battery and company of AT rifles – area of Beregevoe in reserve. (Battalion likely never fired)	45mm Guns	?	Prior to 1207 did not participate in combat
12	18 Tank Corps (5 Gds Tank Army)	1000 AT Artillery Reg	1 km southeast of Petrovka	45mm Guns 76mm Guns	8 45mm 12 76mm	8 45mm 12 76mm (10.07.43)

Table 20: Combat composition of the Artillery Units of the Rifle Divisions and Tank Corps, which took part in the 12 July 1943 counterattack in the sector of the 5th Guards Army's 33rd Rifle Corps and the 5th Guards Tank Army South and Southwest of Prokhorovka Station

No.	Artillery Units		Area of Combat Operations	Caliber and Gun Type	Number of Guns	
					Authorized	Available
13		Motorized Rifle and Tank Bde AT batteries	In brigade sectors of attack	37mm Guns 45mm Guns 76mm Guns	4 37mm 24 45mm 12 76mm	4 37mm 24 45mm 12 76mm
14	678 Howitzer Artillery Reg (5 Gds Tank Army)	2/678 11.07.43 with 18 Tank Corps in Dranyi; 1,3/678 in reserve; 4/178 area of Oboian' in Trufanov's detachment	1/678 fired upon enemy personnel and equipment (southeast outskirts of Pravorot'), 2/678 in sector of 2 Gds Tank Corps (north of Maloe Iablonovo); batteries (or entire battalion) 4/678 with Trufanov's detachment	122mm Howitzers	?	20 122mm
15	9 Gds Airborne Division (33 Gds Rifle Corps)	7 Gds Airborne Artillery Reg	In sector of 9 Gds Airborne Div	76mm Guns/ 122mm Howitzers	24 76mm 12 122mm	Had losses
16		10 Gds AT Artillery Bn	In sector of 9 Gds Airborne Div; 1 Bn – reserve in area of Kusty (did not fire)	45mm Guns	12 45mm	11 45mm
17	29 Tank Corps (5 Gds Tank Army)	108 AT Artillery Reg	Brick factory, 1 km northwest of Prokhorovka (Corps reserve)	45mm Guns 76mm Guns	8 45mm 12 76mm	Had losses
18		1446 Self-propelled Artillery Reg	1 and 6 Batteries supported 25 Tank Bde; 2, 3 and 5 Batteries operated with 32 Tank Bde	Su-76M Su-76122M	9 Su-76 12 Su-122	9 Su-76 11 Su-122
19		Motorized Rifle and Tank Bde AT batteries	In brigade sectors of attack	45mm Guns	24 45mm	
Between Storozhevoe and Teterevino						
20	2 Tank Corps (5 Gds Tank Army)	1502 AT Artillery Reg	In area of Grushki	45mm Guns	20 45mm	19 45mm
21		Motorized Rifle and Tank Bde AT batteries	In brigade sectors	45mm Guns 76mm Guns	12 45mm 20 76mm	?
In the attack sector of the 2nd Guards 'Tatsinskaia' Tank Corps						
22	2nd Gds Tank Corps (5 Gds Tank Army)	1500 AT Artillery Reg	Southern outskirts of Vinogradovka	45mm Guns	20 45mm	19 45mm
23		755 AT Artillery Bn	Northeast outskirts of Vinogradovka	85mm AA Guns	12 85mm	12 85mm
24		Motorized Rifle and Tank Bde batteries	In brigade attack sectors	?	?	?
25	183 Rifle Div (69 Army's 48 Rifle Corps)	623 Artillery Reg	In 183 Rifle Div's sector	76mm Guns 122mm Howitzers	?	?

Table 20 continued

No	Artillery Units			Area of Combat Operations	Caliber and Gun Type	Number of Guns	
						Authorized	Available
26		18 AT Artillery Bn		In 183 Rifle Div's sector	45mm Guns	?	?
27	Front Long-range Artillery Group	522 Hvy Howitzer Reg		1/522 – east of Prokhorovka St.; 2/522 –north of Tikhaia Padina (on the Prokhorovka-Dumnoe road)	203mm Howitzers	?	12 203mm
28		1148 Howitzer Artillery Reg		Southern outskirts of Aleksandrovskii (Prokhorovka Station)	152mm Gun-Howitzers	?	18 152mm
29		27 Sep Hvy Gun Artillery Bde	142 Gun Artillery Reg	Area of Krasnoe	122mm Gun-Howitzers	?	18 122mm
30			93 Gun Artillery Reg	Hill 247.7 (North of Plota, on the Shakhovo-Pravorot' road)	122mm Gun-Howitzers	?	18 122mm
31	Front Group of Gds Mortar Units	16 Gds Mortar Reg (Col. I. S. Iufa's Army Operational Group)		216/16 – 1 km west of Zhimolostnoe, fired on Kalinin 217/16 – 1 km west of Zhimolostnoe, fired on Kalinin 218/16 – 1 km west of Zhimolostnoe, fired on Ozerovskii	132mm BM-13 rocket-launchers: BM-13	24 rocket-launchers	23 BM-13
32		80 Gds Mortar Reg (Col. I. S. Iufa's Army Operational Group)		360/80 – Malaia Psinka, fired on Komsomolets State Farm 361/80 – Beregovoe, fired on Bogoroditskoe, Vasil'evka, Andreevka, area 1 km SE of Mikhailovka	132mm BM-13 rocket-launchers	24 rocket-launchers	18 BM-13
33		76 Gds Mortar Reg (Col. I. S. Iufa's Army Operational Group)		345/76 – northern outskirts of Prokhorovka St., fired at the grove north of Storozhevoe; 346/76 – Tikhaia Padina, fired at the grove north of Storozhevoe.	132mm BM-13 rocket-launchers		
34		66 Red Banner Gds Mortar Reg (Col. Tereshonok's Army Operational Group)		8/66 – grove 2 km east of Kartashevka, fired on areas 1km southeast and 2 km south of Veselyi; 312/66 and 314/66 – grove 1.5 km east of Karteshovka, fired on area of Kochetovka	132mm BM-13; 312 and 314/66: BM-8 rocket-launchers	24 rocket-launchers	16 BM-8 8 BM-13

Table 20 continued

Table 20 continued

No.	Artillery Units		Area of Combat Operations	Caliber and Gun Type	Number of Guns	
					Authorized	Available
35	Front Group of Gds Mortar Units	316 Gds Mortar Reg (Col. Tereshonok's Army Operational Group)	444/316 – 1.5 km east of Karteshovka, fired on area of Kliuchi 445/316 – 600 meters southeast of Karteshovka, fired on area of Kliuchi; 446/316 – Peresyp', did not fire	132mm BM-13 rocket-launchers	24 BM-13	15 BM-13
36		Separate Gds Mortar Bn (Col. I.S. Iufa's Army Operational Group)	Pravorot', did not fire	82mm BM-8 rocket-launchers	8 BM-8	8 BM-8
37		Separate Gds Mortar Bn (Col. I. S. Iufa's Army Operational Group	Zelenyi, did not fire	132mm BM-13 rocket-launchers	8 BM-13	6 BM-13
38	1529 Sep Hvy Self-propelled Artillery Reg	Withdrawn from the Voronezh Front for reinforcing the 5th Gds Tank Army	Was assembling in the course of 1207 and by the end of the day concentrated in the area 1 km northwest of Mordovka. Did not fire.	Su-152	12 Su-152	11 Su-152
39	5 Gds 'Zimovniki' Mech Corps (5 Gds Tank Army)	104 Gds AT Artillery Reg	Hill 242.7 (3.5 km south of Krasnoe. Did not fire	45mm Guns 76mm Guns	12 45mm 8 76mm	11 45mm 8 76mm
40		1447 SP Artillery Reg	In area of Hill 243.8, did not fire. However, according to other documents, participated in the fighting in the area of Rzhavets	Su-76 Su-122	9 Su-76 12 Su-122	4 Su-76 (a) 8 Su-122
41	Forward Detachment of 5 Gds Tank Army	689 AT Artillery Reg	Spent the day until 1700 on the march. From 1700 to 2200 fought against enemy panzers together with the 53rd Guards Tank Regiment for the village of Aleksandrovka	45mm Guns		20 45mm Guns

(a) Data for the 1447th Self-Propelled Artillery Regiment comes from Operational Summary No. 110 of the 5th Guards 'Zimovniki' Mechanized Corps at 0200 12.07.43; headquarters expected the arrival of four more Su-76 self-propelled guns by the morning (TsAMO RF, f. 5 gv. TA, op. 4948, d. 75, l. 10, 10 obr.).

Source: The table has been composed on the basis of dispatches from corps' headquarters, from the artillery headquarters of the 5th Guards Tank Army, and from the headquarters of Voronezh Front's Group of Guards Mortar Units.

> observation posts, as a result of which the observation posts could not support targeted fire at revealed positions in the process of the offensive itself.
>
> ... Area fire was the practice; the concentration of artillery means on one axis was insufficient; there was a lot of firing, but it was uncoordinated. The enemy however managed to organize his fire by 12.07.43, especially on the main sector of his offensive, which was expended on the road junction and important point of Prokhorovka.
>
> The enemy conducted especially strong fire from the vicinities of the grove 1 kilometer southeast of Oktiabr'skii State Farm, the Oktiabr'skii State Farm itself, the woods southwest of the Stalinskii [Stalinskoe Branch of the Oktiabr'skii] State Farm, Storozhevoe, and the Komsomolets State Farm.[11]

The situation, in essence, was absurd: the artillery was firing with the aim of securing the 5th Guards Tank Army's introduction into the battle, while it was being commanded from *front* headquarters, which had no reliable communications with the Army's artillery staff. This was, however, the reality with which Rotmistrov had to deal.

Given all the inadequacies and failures of the army-level artillery, the entire burden of supporting the offensive was laid on the corps artillery, which had not been configured to resolve large-scale fire missions. Elements of the self-propelled artillery and destroyer anti-tank regiments were used to reinforce and support the attacking tank brigades. The combat strength and composition of the Soviet artillery units, which took part in the 12 July counterattack, are shown in Table 20.

Rotmistrov was fully aware of all these problems, but had no power to alter anything. In a combat dispatch from the 5th Guards Tank Army's headquarters at 1000 on 12.07.43, Rotmistrov reported that the artillery preparation was weak, pointing to the low density of artillery and the absence of the 10th Destroyer Anti-tank Artillery Brigade and the 1529th Self-propelled Artillery Regiment.[12]

Observing the artillery's work from his observation post, the army commander could easily envision the conditions in the corps. A professional tanker with great combat experience, he understood better than anyone else the situation of the corps and brigade commanders in the situation that was taking shape. They were forced, as they say, to attack from scratch against an adversary that was plainly strong, judging from the course of combat operations over the preceding days.

Even Lieutenant General P. A. Rotmistrov himself was not in an enviable position. He had no possibility (because of terrain conditions) to employ the full potential of his combat equipment. He had been deprived of a reserve (Trufanov's detachment), a unit of the first echelon, and half the second echelon (two mechanized brigades of the 5th Guards Mechanized Corps and one tank brigade of the 2nd Guards Tank Corps). He had also not received the necessary support from the *front's* artillery and aviation (having at his disposal only one howitzer regiment). In spite of all this, the commander was supposed to strike the strongest formation of the Fourth Panzer Army (which was fully-prepared to receive the attack), split it, and drive 30 kilometers deep into enemy-held territory. All this, while periodically repelling attacks from his own air force (about this, a little later).

A significant number of problems arose within the corps themselves. For example, the 29th Tank Corps commander Major General I. F. Kirichenko was not a novice in military affairs; as a brigade commander he had taken part in the fighting for Moscow, demonstrating not only personal courage, but also professionalism in a difficult situation. However, Kirichenko had never commanded such a major formation as a corps before, and the battle at Prokhorovka would be his first in his role as corps commander. In addition, the headquarters of the 29th Tank Corps had just been organized. While the staff had passed through an intensive four-month training course, the main test of the quality of combat training remained genuine battle itself. It is precisely combat that developed the professionalism of commanders and staff, initiated and honed the work routines in headquarters, and forged the ability to work together smoothly in the midst of battle.

The 18th Tank Corps had been added to the 5th Guards Tank Army just before the march to Prokhorovka. P. A. Rotmistrov had been previously acquainted with the 18th Tank Corps commander, General B. S. Bakharov, but this would be the first time they would be working together in a combat situation. The army commander had been dissatisfied with how Boris Sergeevich Bakharov had handled the corps march from Ostrogozhsk. His formation had lost a lot of vehicles *en route*; the corps commander and headquarters staff had plainly underestimated the difficulty of the assignment. Although by the morning of 12 July the brigades' repair teams and crews had managed to restore most of the disabled vehicles to good working order and the corps was fully combat-ready, Rotmistrov decided to send his chief of staff Major General V. N. Baskakov to the 18th Tank Corps, in order to assess the corps commander, to prevent mistakes on his part in the extremely complex situation, and to assist him in coordinating the work of his staff with the army units.

Tank combat is characterized by its highly dynamic nature and by sharp changes in the situation. Therefore, strict control over the tank formations, stable and efficient communications with the brigades, and the rapid processing of orders and instructions are extremely important. However, there were no conditions for fulfilling these demands, and problems arose in securing communications between the corps and the brigades, and especially between the brigades and their subordinate battalions. Furthermore, the command and control in several of the brigades were as yet untested by combat.

In short, the 5th Guards Tank Army was entering its first battle. Therefore, the army commander and the subordinate commanders at all levels strove to spend time in the forward units before the start of the battle. On the evening of 11 July General I. F. Kirichenko, leaving behind his chief of staff Colonel E. I. Fominykh at the command post, journeyed to Colonel S. F. Moiseev's 31st Tank Brigade; his deputy Colonel A. V. Egorov went to A. A. Linev's 32nd Tank Brigade.

At 0830, the *Katiushas* of the 76th Guards Mortar Regiment fired its final volley from their position southwest of Prokhorovka. At the instant the explosions died away, a relative calm fell over the field. As eyewitnesses later recalled, for the next several minutes, a rustling wave passed across the field, like a heavy, but short summer squall. The dust raised by the explosions settled to the earth. For a few brief moments, everything fell silent. They were only seconds, followed immediately by the sound of a powerful, rising

The 5th Guards Tank Army attacks! (RGAKFD)

rumble. The tanks of the 5th Guards Tank Army were moving out of their jumping-off positions and accelerating into the attack.

The army commander attentively watched the departure of the tank brigades. He had been waiting for this moment for several months. Pavel Alekseevich Rotmistrov had been appointed to command an army that did not yet exist at the time. He had spent four months forming it, equipping it, and organizing the training of its staff and combat troops. Now the moment of its first trial by fire had arrived. For us, who did not travel that hard path, it is difficult today to understand the thoughts and feelings of a man, who was witnessing the combat baptism of his progeny.

Rotmistrov recalled after the war:

> Our artillery's squall of fire had not yet subsided, when the volleys of our Guards mortar regiments rang out. This signified the start of the attack, which my radio set duplicated. 'Steel,' 'Steel,' 'Steel' – the chief of my radio apparatus Junior Technician-Lieutenant V. P. Konstantinov sent out over the radio. Immediately there followed the signals to attack from the commanders of the tank corps, the brigades, the battalions, the companies and the platoons.
>
> I look through my binoculars and watch, as our glorious 'Thirty-fours' move out from under their cover and, accelerating, rush ahead. At the same instant, I spot a mass of enemy armor. It turned out that both we and the Germans went on the attack simultaneously. I'm surprised by how quickly our tanks and the hostile tanks are closing the distance to each other. Two enormous avalanches of tanks were moving towards a collision. The morning sun rising in the east blinded the

> eyes of the German tankers and brightly illuminated the contours of the fascist tanks for us.
>
> Within several minutes, the tanks of the first echelon of our 29th and 18th Tank Corps, firing on the move, sliced head-on into the combat formations of the German fascist forces, having literally pierced the enemy's formation with an impetuous, penetrating attack. The Hitlerites, apparently, had not expected to encounter such a large mass of our combat vehicles and such a decisive attack by them.[13]

Unfortunately, Rotmistrov's account is highly misleading. The actual course of the battle, as set forth in the documents of the brigades of the tank army's first echelon, does not correspond with the army commander's words. Incidentally, the sunrise on 12 July was at 0502. Therefore at 0830 it could not have blinded the eyes of the German tankers. However, the morning sun's rays might have illuminated the contours of their tanks – if they had moved out on the attack, and were not staying concealed behind the positions of their anti-tank guns. At 0920, N. F. Vatutin reported to I. V. Stalin:

> After a 30-minute artillery preparation, at 0830 the forces of Voronezh Front's center (6th Guards Army, 1st Tank Army, 5th Guards Army, 5th Guards Tank Army) went on the offensive according to plan. The forces of the 7th Guards Army are completing preparations to go over onto the offensive – the artillery preparation from 0900, the offensive at 0940.[14]

The 5th Guards Tank Army command rested its plans on an impetuous lunge into the depth of the enemy's from the first minutes of the attack. The area of Oktiabr'skii State Farm – the main fulcrum of the German positions, which indeed Zhadov's Guardsmen proved unable to crack in the morning – was supposed to be enveloped on two sides: on one side, by the 18th Tank Corps' 181st Tank Brigade, 170th Tank Brigade and the 36th Guards Separate Heavy Tank Regiment; on the other side, by the 29th Tank Corps' 32nd Tank Brigade with three batteries of the 1446th Self-propelled Artillery Regiment. Infantry of the 5th Guards Army's 33rd Guards Rifle Corps would follow behind the armor. It was assumed that the 181st Tank Brigade, attacking through the villages along the river would not encounter any heavy enemy resistance, since they (Andreevka and Vasil'evka) had only been abandoned by the tankers of the 2nd Tank Corps that morning; thus, its advance would be more rapid. Along the railway, the shock 32nd Tank Brigade was to clear a path for the main forces of the 29th Tank Corps. The 9th Guards Airborne Division and two regiments of the 42nd Guards Rifle Division were to consolidate the success of the 32nd, 170th and 181st Tank Brigades by mopping up the areas of Hill 252.2 and the villages along the river of any remaining enemy.

The second echelon of Kirichenko's 29th and Bakharov's 18th Tank Corps (the 31st Tank Brigade and the 32nd Motorized Rifle Brigade with an artillery group) had the assignment to bolster the strength of the assault and to replenish the tank losses of the first echelon, suffered during the breakthrough of the defenses on Oktiabr'skii State Farm and Hill 252.2. However, this plan collapsed in the first minutes of the attack.

The 29th Tank Corps went on the offensive in the sector Oktiabr'skii State Farm (incl.) – Iamki – Sazhinskii ravine (1.5 kilometers south of Iamki). Its attack formation

Colonel S. F. Moiseev, commander of the 29th Tank Corps' 31st Tank Brigade. (TsAMO)

Colonel A. A. Linev, commander of the 29th Tank Corps' 32nd Tank Brigade, posing with his family (1942 photo). (Author's personal archive)

had the 32nd Tank Brigade (63 tanks) and the 25th Tank Brigade (69 tanks) in the first echelon, and the 31st Tank Brigade (67 tanks) in the second echelon. To the right, between Oktiabr'skii State Farm and the Psel River, the 18th Tank Corps was to advance. Its combat formation was arranged in three echelons: in the first – the 181st Tank Brigade (44 tanks) and the 170th Tank Brigade (39 tanks), supported by the 36th Guards Separate Heavy Tank Regiment (19 Churchill tanks); in the second – the 32nd Motorized Rifle Brigade (which had no tanks); in the third – the tank brigade of the corps' forward detachment (38 tanks). Thus, in the first attacking echelon of the two corps in a sector approximately 7 kilometers wide, four tank brigades and one tank regiment were attacking with a total of 234 tanks.

Immediately after the attack start, the field was covered by dozens of mushroom clouds of erupting earth from exploding bombs and shells, and dozens of tanks blazed up like torches. The battlefield became enveloped in a bluish-gray shroud of smoke and the exhaust gases of hundreds of armored vehicles, lit up by the fiery discharges from tank guns. The guide brigade in the 29th Tank Corps was Colonel A. A. Linev's 32nd Tank Brigade. Colonel S. F. Moiseev's 31st Tank Brigade was supposed to follow it, but Moiseev's battalions were slow in moving into their jumping-off positions, so Linev's tanks in the first minutes of the attack were greeted by a hurricane of anti-tank fire from Oktiabr'skii State Farm and Hill 252.2. Quickly, more than twenty tanks (almost one-third of the brigade's complement) blazed up like torches or began to emit thick plumes of dark smoke. The brigade's combat formation was shattered, and the surviving tanks began to maneuver on the battlefield and to crawl away in different directions, trying to use any folds in the terrain in order to escape the ruinous fire. However, the sector was narrow, and approximately 100 armored vehicles had crowded into it, not including the self-propelled artillery, the artillery and the infantry of the 42nd Guards Rifle Division.

The commander of *Leibstandarte*'s 1st SS Panzer Regiment's 6th Company, *Obersturmführer* R. von Ribbentrop, described the scene from the German lines:

... I spotted the section leader of the company headquarters personnel, whom I had left at the infantry battalion's command post. Shrouded in a gigantic cloud of dust, he was racing down the slope on his motorcycle, all the while extending his fist into the air: Move out at once!"

With that the company set itself in motion and deployed on the slope as if on the exercise field. It deployed with a precision that made my twenty-two-year-old heart beat faster. It was an especially uplifting feeling for me to lead these young but experienced soldiers into battle.

On reaching the crest of the slope we saw another low rise about 200 meters away on the other side of a small valley, on which our infantry positions were obviously located.

By radio I ordered my company to move into position on the slope ahead of us and take up the battle from there.

The small valley extended to our left and, as we moved down the forward slope, we spotted the first T-34s. They were attempting to outflank us from the left.

We halted on the slope and opened fire, hitting several of the enemy. A number of Russian tanks were left burning. For a good gunner, 800 meters was the ideal range.

As we waited to see if further enemy tanks were going to appear, I looked all around, as was my habit. What I saw left me speechless. From beyond the shallow rise about 150 to 200 meters in front of me appeared fifteen, then thirty, then forty tanks. Finally there was too many to count. The T-34s were rolling toward us at high speed, carrying mounted infantry.

Red Army tank riders dismount. (RGAKFD)

My driver, Schueler, called over the intercom: 'Sir, to the right, right! They're coming! Do you see them?'

I saw them only too well. At that second I said to myself: 'It's all over now!' My driver thought I had said 'Get out!' and began to open his hatch. I grabbed him rather roughly and hauled him back into the tank. Meanwhile, I had poked the gunner in the right side with my foot. This was the signal for him to traverse right.

Soon the first round was on its way and, with its impact the T-34 began to burn. It was only fifty to seventy meters from us. At the same instant the tank next to me took a direct hit and went up in flames. I saw SS Sergeant Papke jump clear, but that was the last we ever saw of him. His neighbor to the right was also hit and soon it was also in flames.

The avalanche of enemy tanks rolled straight towards us: Tank after tank! Wave after wave! It was a simply unimaginable assembly, and it was moving at very high speed.

We had no time to take up defensive positions. All we could do was fire. From this range every round was a hit, but when would a direct hit end it for us? Somewhere in my subconscious I realized that there was no chance to escape. As always in such hopeless situations, all we could do was take care of what was at hand. So we knocked out a third, then a fourth T-34, from distances of less than thirty meters.

The Panzer IV we were using carried about eighteen to twenty rounds of ammunition within immediate reach of the loader, of which the majority was high-explosive. The rest were armor-piercing.

Soon my loader shouted: 'No AP left!'

All of our immediately available armor-piercing ammunition had been expended. Further ammunition had to be passed to the loader by the gunner, radio operator and driver. At this point remaining stationary was the surest means of being spotted and destroyed by the Russian tanks. Our only hope was to get back behind the slope again, even though the Russians had already crossed it. Our chances of escaping there were better than in our present exposed position.

We turned in the midst of a mass of Russian tanks, rolled back about fifty meters and reached the reverse slope of the first rise. There we turned to face the enemy again, now in somewhat better cover.

Just then a T-34 halted about thirty meters off to our right. I saw the tank rock slightly on its suspension and traverse its turret in our direction. I was looking right down the muzzle of its gun. We were unable to fire immediately, as the gunner had just passed the loader a fresh round.

'Step on it, now!' I shouted into the microphone. My driver Schueler was the best driver in the battalion. He had already put the tank in gear, and the lumbering Panzer IV set itself in motion. We moved past the T-34 at a distance of about five meters. The Russian tried to turn his turret to follow us, but was unable to do so. We halted ten meters behind the stationary T-34 and turned. My gunner scored a direct hit on the Russian's turret. The T-34 exploded, and its turret flew about three meters through the air, almost striking my tank's gun. While all this was going on, other T-34s with mounted infantry were rolling past us.

Captain (Major at the time of the Kursk battle) P. S. Ivanov, commander of the 1st Tank Battalion of the 29th Tank Corps' 32nd Tank Brigade (1941 photo). (Archive of A. V. Skidachenko, P. S. Ivanov's granddaughter)

In the meantime, I tried to pull in the Swastika flag that was lying across the box on the rear of the tank. The flag's purpose was to let our pilots know where we were. I only half succeeded in this, with the result that the flag then fluttered in the wind. One of the Russian commanders or gunners would have to notice it sometime. It was only a question of time until we received the fatal hit.

We had only slim chance: We had to remain constantly in motion. A stationary tank would immediately be recognized by the foe as an enemy and fired upon, because all the Russian tanks were rolling at high speed across the terrain.

We then faced the additional challenge of being destroyed by one of our own tanks, which were sitting below at the anti-tank ditch by the railway embankment in a wide line. They had begun firing at the approaching enemy tanks. On the smoke- and dust-shrouded battlefield, looking into the sun, it would be impossible for our crews to distinguish us from a Russian tank. I repeatedly broadcast our code-name: 'All stations: This is Kunibert! We are in the middle of the Russian tanks! Don't fire at us!'

I received no answer. In the meantime, the Russians had set several vehicles on fire as they rolled through Peiper's battalion and our artillery battalion. But by then the fire of our two remaining tank companies was beginning to have an effect. The artillery's battalion of self-propelled guns and Peiper's Panzergrenadiers – the latter with close-range weapons – were also taking a toll of the Russian tanks and pinning down the Russian infantry, which had jumped down from the T-34s and were attempting to advance on foot.

> The entire battlefield lay under a thick pall of smoke and dust. Fresh groups of Russian tanks continued to roll out of this inferno. They were knocked out on the broad slope by our tanks.
>
> It was an indescribable jumble of wrecked tanks and vehicles. This undoubtedly contributed to our salvation, in that the Russians did not recognize us.[15]

The first to encounter the Germans' anti-tank defenses on the outskirts of the Oktiabr'skii State Farm and on Hill 252.2 were two companies from the 32nd Tank Brigade's 2nd Tank Battalion, commanded by Captain A. E. Vakulenko. Under their covering fire, the commander of this tank brigade's 1st Tank Battalion, Major P. S. Ivanov, directed his tanks across the railway embankment, in order to bypass the State Farm. The 15 T-34s, concealed by a belt of woods, found a seam in the German line, dashed at full speed past the most dangerous points of Hills 242.5 and Hill 241.6, where German anti-tank gun batteries and self-propelled guns were positioned, and broke into the southern outskirts of the Komsomolets State Farm from the rear, some 5 kilometers into the depth of the enemy's defenses. Motorized riflemen of the 53rd Motorized Rifle Brigade, which managed to slip through the enemy's defenses in the wake of the tanks, reinforced the tankers' sudden and unexpected advance. However, this local breakthrough had no effect on the tenacity of the defense at the Oktiabr'skii State Farm, which was SS *Leibstandarte's* focal point of resistance. Even an hour after the start of the 5th Guards Army's follow-on attack, the State Farm remained in the hands of *Obersturmbannführer* H. Krass' 2nd Panzergrenadier Regiment, although individual T-34 tanks, having broken through to the crest of Hill 252.2, were already battling its anti-tank defenses and the tanks of SS *Sturmbannführer* M. Gross' II/1st SS Panzer Regiment, positioned behind the anti-tank ditch.

It was becoming clear that the offensive was not going according to plan. Observing the battlefield and listening over the radio to the transmissions and reports from the corps commanders, Rotmistrov understood that his army had collided with a strong, well-organized enemy anti-tank defense, bristling with a significant quantity of artillery.

It is impossible for one person to see the entire course of such a massive event as this clash between two powerful groupings, the Prokhorovka tank engagement. Each person views it as he saw it from the place where he was at that time. However, the recollections of eyewitnesses are invaluable, since this is a piece of the events, refracted through the consciousness and disposition of a real person. The greater the number of such pieces, the more clear and distinct is the resulting picture of what occurred. The excerpt of the army commander's [Rotmistrov's] memoirs, cited above, is the impression of a man who was standing on the pinnacle of an army's pyramid and observing everything as if from this summit. But what was happening inside the battle? Here are the stories of two participants, who were directly located in the first ranks of the attackers. All the events that they describe occurred in the epicenter of the engagement – in the vicinity of Hill 252.2 –within the first hour of the attack.

Gunner-radio operator Sergeant Savelii Baase of the 29th Tank Corps' 32nd Tank Brigade remembers:

> I recall that from our jumping-off positions, which were in a shallow depression in the area of the brick factory, we drove onto a hillock, from which point a level

field spread before us, covered with either ripened wheat or barley. On our left were a railroad and a planted forest; on the right, in the distance beyond the field, was a cluster of buildings. I was told that the Oktiabr'skii State Farm was over there. Soon shells exploded nearby, and in front of us there were flashes, tanks and dust. Even though our tank was not in the first line, we were also firing our main guns at clusters of tanks and individual targets, which were moving toward us. The range closed quickly. Soon tanks began to burn, both ours and the Germans'. I remember how we were firing at a Tiger, but our shells were ricocheting off its thick armor, until someone managed first to knock off a track, and then to plant a shell in its flank. But the tank didn't blaze up, and its crew began to leap out of opened hatches. We shot them up with our machine gun. The combat formations of the two sides became intermingled ...[16]

Lieutenant I. M. Fomichev, the commander of the 1st Rifle Company's 1st Rifle Platoon in the 23rd Guards Airborne Rifle Regiment's 1st Battalion, remembers:

At dawn on 12 July, we rose and went into the attack without artillery preparation. My platoon and I were moving to the right of the railway. Two Messerschmitts appeared from the enemy's direction, which flew along the combat formation of our regiment, strafing as they went, before disappearing in the distance. We emerged onto an open field, and the Germans immediately blanketed us with artillery fire. Killed and wounded appeared. Without much understanding of what was going on amid the continuous crash of explosions and the cries of the wounded, I crawled along the platoon's line and bandaged the wounded. The fingers of my hands were sticky with blood.

After some time (I wasn't wearing a watch), I watched as a wave of our tanks passed through the regiment's positions. I prepared to move out after them, but the order 'Forward!' never came. A second wave of our tanks passed through our lines, and still there was no order to advance. A third wave of tanks passed through, carrying mounted submachine gunners, and only after this did they give the order: 'Forward!'

Later I learned that before our tank attack, there had been an artillery barrage and a salvo of Guards' mortars [*Katiusha* rockets] on the enemy positions, but I didn't see or hear them. Perhaps they coincided with an enemy artillery barrage on our forces.

My platoon and I were running behind the tanks. We reached a trench and leaped into it. At the entrance to a bunker, I saw the body of a senior lieutenant, whose uniform had been mostly burned off (only the collar with three bars on the shoulder boards remained), lying on top of an anti-tank rifle. I glanced into the bunker and spotted an ammunition drum for a PPSh submachine gun, so I grabbed it. It was fully loaded with cartridges.

We ran on ahead. In the dense smoke and dust, we could not see our neighbors on the right or the left ... As they had trained us in the specialist school, we tried to take cover from enemy fire behind the hulls of the tanks. Moving along the platoon's line, I took cover behind one of the knocked-out tanks, and when I raised my head to take a look around, I saw crosses on the armor. I realized that my

Captain G. I. Penezhko, deputy chief of staff of the 29th Tank Corps' 31st Tank Brigade (1944 photo). (Author's personal archive)

platoon and I were in the thick of a tank battle. This was between the railroad and the Oktiabr'skii State Farm.

Moving on, we ran up to another trench. I hopped into it and almost collided with a German. His hand were upraised. I was stunned by the surprise and lost my head, because this was the first living German soldier I'd ever seen. One of the men from my platoon, who leaped into the trench right behind me, shouted: 'Lieutenant, shoot him, what are you looking at!' At that moment, a burning tank nearby suddenly exploded; the German flinched and turned his head, and in my fright I squeezed my trigger and fired a long burst into the back of his head.

Just beyond the trench, I met a colonel who had been wounded in the shoulder. He said he was the deputy commander of our division, Grachev, and ordered me to escort him to the nearest aid station. While we moved toward an aid station, Messerschmitts dove on us three times and strafed us with their machine guns. On the third pass, the plane flew so low that I couldn't stand it and I fired at it with my submachine gun; of course, I didn't do it any damage. Colonel Grachev, apparently from the loss of blood, seemed indifferent to what was happening all around him, and leaned on me heavily. I supported him with difficulty.

My platoon was accompanying us. We crossed the rail line in the area of Hill 252.2, and found ourselves in the middle of the 26th Regiment's offensive.

Here, to the left of the railway, we spotted a group of soldiers lying in the field, apparently without any commanding officers. Grachev told me he could reach the aid station by himself, and ordered me to take command of these soldiers and get them moving forward. The soldiers responded to my order and started moving, but once we had passed through a wheat field and emerged into an open area, I saw that

> a few of the soldiers had lagged behind. Apparently, they didn't want to follow an unknown commander.
>
> Reaching the trench line where I had bumped into the colonel, I first saw a senior lieutenant, who said he was the commander of a machine gun company. He had nine Maxim heavy machine guns. I decided to reinforce the machine gun company's defensive position. Here in the trench I ran into Junior Lieutenant Gerasimenko, with whom I had trained together back at the specialist school. We exchanged impressions. The Germans began to outflank our position on both sides. The company commander made the decision to fall back through the wheat field. My platoon and I pulled back together with him. While retreating, my messenger Private Odintsov was wounded. The bullet entered his shoulder from behind and buried itself there. We pulled back beyond the wheat field and occupied the first trench line we had passed, where we dug-in again.[17]

The combat that took place on Hill 252.2 had no equal in its drama and intensity. Immediately after 1000, at the moment when the second echelon of Kirichenko's 29th Tank Corps (the 31st Tank Brigade) entered the battle, the Germans began an intensified bombardment of the assault wedges of both our tank corps east of the Oktiabr'skii State Farm. The VIII Air Corps headquarters sent the following message to the II SS Panzer Corps: "Two *gruppen* of dive bombers have been assigned to operate against the enemy group, [and are] moving from Petrovka to the southwest."[18]

The situation in the 31st Tank Brigade at the start of the attack received only a brief description in combat documents: "The pace of the offensive has slackened; the brigade

A Nebelwerfer battery of the SS *Leibstandarte Adolf Hitler* Division on Hill 241.6 conducting fire on the combat formations of the 18th Tank Corps, 12 July 1943. (RGAKFD)

has begun to mark time in place." The tankers didn't succeed in giving fresh impetus to the attack. Chronologically, the start of the attack began as follows.

The movement of the 32nd Tank Brigade from its line of deployment (in the area of the brick factory) began at approximately 0840-0845; approximately an hour later, the battalions of the 31st Tank Brigade moved out, and tanks from both brigades neared the borders of the Oktiabr'skii State Farm at approximately 1030. I repeat: they didn't break into the State Farm at that time – this didn't occur until 1300 – but they closed to within firing range of the State Farm, approximately 500 meters from its outskirts, where anti-tank guns of *Leibstandarte's* 2nd SS Panzergrenadier Regiment were dug-in. Moreover, this division's panzer regiment had already deployed at a distance approximately 0.5 to 1 kilometer from the State Farm, and behind it – east of Hill 241.6 – its artillery regiment, consisting of 105mm and 155mm howitzers, *Nebelwerfers*, and *Hummel*, *Wespe* and *Brummbär* self-propelled artillery vehicles. Thus, the first echelon of the 18th and 29th Tank Corps ran into a wall of fire. For the next two hours of the attack, the 31st and 32nd Tank Brigades advanced approximately 1.2 to 1.5 kilometers. How can one speak of any "pace of the offensive" here!

The foe's artillerymen took advantage of the moment, and fired their guns both intensively and with deadly accuracy. This beaten zone east of Hill 252.2 and Oktiabr'skii State Farm, bordered on the north and east with gullies, and on the south by the railroad embankment, became a genuine graveyard for the tank battalions of these brigades. They suffered their greatest losses here, at the start of the attack.

Reports from the corps headquarters and the brigades of the 29th Tank Corps speak to the nature and intensity of the fighting:

> ... Despite the heavy fire put up by the enemy, the 32nd Tank Brigade, maintaining the organization in its combat formations in cooperation with the 25th Tank Brigade, moved forward, while opening a concentrated fire from its tanks. Upon the approach to the borders of the Oktiabr'skii State Farm and the Stalinskoe Branch of the [Oktiabr'skii] State Farm, they came under artillery and mortar fire and were compelled to dig in on the line they had reached, gather strength for a resumption of the offensive, and prepare to repulse enemy attacks.
>
> Separate elements, penetrating even as far as the Komsomolets State Farm and suffering heavy losses from artillery fire and fire from tanks in ambush positions, fell back to the line occupied by the fire support forces [author's note: as stated in the text].
>
> ... a) The 32nd Tank Brigade: At 0830 12.07.43 *without working over the enemy's forward edge of defense with artillery and aviation* [author's emphasis], lacking accurate information about the enemy's fire means, the brigade in two echelons attacked the enemy in the direction ... along the railroad line in a sector up to 900 meters wide. On this (main) axis, the enemy concentrated a large number of Panzer VI tanks, Ferdinand self-propelled guns [there were no Ferdinands with the Fourth Panzer Army], and other anti-tank means.
>
> ... The attack of the 32nd Tank Brigade flowed at an exclusively rapid pace. All the tanks went into the attack, and there was not a single case of indecisiveness or refusal to fight. By 1200 12.07.43 the tank battalions reached the area of the enemy's artillery positions. [Enemy] Infantry began to run away in panic. ... The

> enemy hurled up to 150 aircraft at the forward edge of defense, which suppressed the infantry of the 53rd Motorized Rifle Brigade (following behind the tanks) and knocked out several tanks. The 32nd Tank Brigade began to falter .... The adversary noticed that the pace of the attack had slackened, and brought up fresh tank reserves and infantry. By this time the brigade had lost up to 40 tanks and 350 men and was compelled to stop.
>
> b) The 31st Tank Brigade: At 0830 following the signal (the rocket artillery salvo), the attack of the tanks and infantry *began without artillery preparation or air cover* [author's emphasis]. Groups of 8 to 37 Me 110 and Ju 87 were conducting attacks.
>
> The tanks suffered heavy losses from the enemy's artillery fire and aviation. ... At 1030 the tanks reached the border of the Oktiabr'skii State Farm. Further advance was stopped by the ceaseless influence [author: as in text] of the enemy's aviation.
>
> Air cover for the attacking tanks was absent until 1300. At 1300, cover was provided by groups of 2 to 10 fighters.[19]

The 31st Tank Brigade's chief of the political department Colonel Povolotsky reported:

> The large losses, especially in equipment, and the insufficiently active advance of our brigade are explained by the strong influence of the enemy's aviation given our aviation's lack of support for the offensive, and the enemy's strong artillery and mortar fire, in contrast to our very weak artillery preparation at the moment of attack. The long presence of the tanks and personnel in their starting positions (eight hours) *allowed the enemy to reorganize his defense in order to repulse* the attack [author's emphasis].

As we see, there is little resemblance here to a meeting engagement involving hundreds of tanks. Moreover, there is also nothing that corroborates the assertion that "on 12 July of this year occurred the greatest tank battle in the history of the Great Patriotic War, in which up to 1500 tanks of both sides met in a head-on attack" (from the 5th Guards Tank Army's summary of combat operations at Prokhorovka).[20]

In the 29th Tank Corps, 199 tanks took part in the attack, in the 18th Tank Corps – 149 tanks; altogether 348 tanks, which moreover were echeloned in depth. On the enemy's side (SS Panzergrenadier Division *Leibstandarte*'s 1st Panzer Regiment, and elements of *Totenkopf*'s and *Das Reich*'s panzer regiments), approximately 140 to 150 tanks participated in this battle. Altogether on 12 July 1943, a combined maximum of up to 500 tanks from both sides could have participated in the battle southwest of Prokhorovka.

The battle of several hundred armored vehicles disintegrated into separate duels between groups of tanks, over which unified command and control was lost. The combat formations of the two sides became intermingled. Radio became the only possible means of communication in the companies and platoons. However, while all the German tanks were equipped with two-way radios, the Soviet T-34 tanks, not to mention the T-70 tanks, lacked radio communications in all but the commanders' tanks.

According to the testimony of veteran tankers, the 5th Guards Tank Army, which from the beginning had been formed as a Guards army, was in a more advantageous situation in this respect than other formations. Down to the platoon level, commanders' tanks were equipped with radios, while even some non-command tanks had radio receivers, in order to receive orders from the commander. In other formations, even these were entirely lacking. Only commanders at the company level and higher had full communications in their tanks. All other tanks operated following the example of the commander's tank, according to the principle "Do whatever I'm doing." Under the conditions of limited visibility and given the concentration of a large number of armored vehicles on a relatively narrow sector, this left the crews practically without any communications.

Knowing this detail, the Germans took advantage of it in full measure. German tanks, assault guns and anti-tank guns concentrated all their fire first of all on those Red Army tanks with antennas. In addition, our radio sets were not reliable. As M. Dovbysh, a veteran of the 18th Tank Corps told me that only one or two solid hits on a tank that failed to penetrate were enough to cause the radio to quit working due to the concussive impact. The summary report of the 29th Tank Corps command also testifies to this; in it there is a statement that radios on the Su-152 would stop operating after five to eight shots from its own gun. All of this prevented the company or platoon commander from smoothly directing the tanks under his command in battle, concentrating their fire or strength in a certain direction (or on specific targets).

In such circumstances, the training and experience of the crew commander and the driver-mechanic played a special role. In the battle on the fields of Prokhorovka, the "birth defect" of the T-34 manifested itself in full measure. In the years before the war, trying to decrease the size of the tank, designers had removed the position of the fifth crew member, the gun layer, and turned his functions over to the commander. This meant that with the start of a battle, the tank crew was practically left without a commander, since he could not physically carry out two duties at the same time. All his attention was concentrated on gunnery. That is why the actions of the crew were fettered, and its attention focused more on self-preservation than common action. These problems substantially increased tank losses.

The 5th Guards Tank Army's summary of the battle points to the critical problems caused by the failures in intelligence, information and communication: "The enemy aviation reigned supreme in the sky – up to 200 individual sorties. The absence of reconnaissance, as well as the lack of fire direction, had an immediate effect on the process of the fighting, and choked the attack."[21]

On the Oktiabr'skii State Farm and in the region of Hill 252.2, even before the start of the summer fighting, the soldiers of the 14th Separate Destroyer Anti-tank Artillery Brigade and the 183rd Rifle Division had set up a battalion strongpoint and gun positions for one anti-tank regiment. On the night of 10 July and the morning of 11 July, the elements of the 9th Guards Airborne Division that moved into these positions significantly expanded them. After taking control of the State Farm, the SS troops took advantage of these fortifications. Overnight they strengthened them, digging in anti-tank guns and immobile tanks on the eastern outskirts of the Oktiabr'skii State Farm and on Hills 241.6, 242.5 and 231.3, and partially mining the approaches to their defenses. Judging from archival documents, SS Panzergrenadier Division *Leibstandarte*'s sector, which extended for approximately 6.5 kilometers, had more than 300 guns and mortars of all types, or more than 46 gun barrels per kilometer of front. The vast majority of the German anti-tank means and tanks had guns with a caliber from 50mm to 105mm, while the guns of the field artillery ranged from 105mm to 155mm. Thanks to the high density of guns on the lines of defense, as well as the intelligent use of the suitable terrain for repulsing an enemy armored attack, the enemy already within the span of two and a half hours from the start of the attack had managed to halt the first echelon of two corps from Rotmistrov's army. From a dispatch from the headquarters of the SS Panzergrenadier Division *Leibstandarte*:

> At 0915 [11.15 Moscow time], the attacks of 40 tanks from the village of Iamki on the Stalinskoe Branch of the [Oktiabr'skii] State Farm, 40 tanks from Petrovka in the direction of the crossroads 1 km southeast of Oktiabr'skii State Farm were conducted with the strongest artillery support. The tanks moved at high speed. A local breakthrough at Hill 252.2 was liquidated by a panzer counterattack at 1115 [13.15]. More than 40 tanks have been destroyed, some in close combat.[22]

Colonel A. A. Linev tried to rectify the situation, despite the enemy's artillery fire, the bombing and the psychological shock, which the tank crews and the company commanders experienced from the loss of so many tanks in just a few minutes. The brigade commander moved up into the first echelon, bringing with him the 277th and 278th Battalions of the 31st Tank Brigade and directing the remnants of that brigade toward the State Farm at top speed. At that same time, the neighboring 18th Tank Corps on the right was also attacking the Oktiabr'skii State Farm. In the situation that had developed, this leap from the frying pan into the fire appeared to be the only correct decision. There was simply no other choice, other than a retreat, and no one even gave a thought about that.

Major General A. V. Egorov, the deputy commander of the 29th Tank Corps who was at the start of the battle situated with the 32nd Tank Brigade, later remembered:

> We were met by a storm of artillery fire. Aircraft of both sides were bombing the same area of battle. East of the Oktiabr'skii State Farm, the uninterrupted roar of battle drifted from the direction of Storozhevoe, where Colonel Volodin's 25th Tank Brigade was attacking. A shroud of black dust was covering everything around. It was a tank column moving at full speed onto our flank. Shaking out into a combat formation on the move, it opened fire at our tanks. I watched as Linev, adjusting his helmet, dropped down into his turret. Instantly the field, which had seemed barren of life, sprang to life. Crushing shrubs in their way and churning up the crops with their tracks, the tanks rushed forward, firing on the move. Gradually all the battalions became drawn into the fighting. The commanders understood that the 'Tigers' would take advantage of every halt, slightest hesitation in motion, or moment of indecision.

Major General F. A. Bobrov, commander of the 42nd Guards Rifle Division. (TsAMO)

> Fascist aviation again appeared overhead, and the barrier artillery fire strengthened. German shells exploded to our tanks' front, sending up large columns of dirt. I wanted to press the button on my microphone, but delayed a little. On the airwaves, one could overhear how the crews were operating. 'Three o'clock, target -- gun, fragmentation shell. Load … Fire, fire!' 'Gun layer – at the infantry; good man, Vania, that's the way! Driver, give it more gas …' – the commands of the battalion commanders flew through the air. There were requests of information regarding the advance. Company commanders were reporting.
>
> 'Ivanov! Reduce the range! Vakulenko, speed up! Everyone! Everyone! Everyone! More fire!' – Linev's voice rang out in my headset.
>
> The brigade at full speed sliced into the combat formations of enemy tanks. The foe's desperate counterattacks could not overcome the steadfastness of our tankers, their resolve, and their will for victory. The first knocked-out German tanks began to smoke. I watched as the dismounted crew of one of our damaged tanks continued to struggle in hand-to-hand combat … Tanks were ramming into each other, firing at one another at point-blank range, or were burning around us. Soviet troops, when the guns of their damaged vehicle no longer worked, leaped out of their burning tank and rushed at the Germans.[23]

At the start of the attack, the tankers of the 18th and 29th Tank Corps were being supported by the mounted infantry companies of their tank brigades, the motorized infantry of the 32nd and 53rd Motorized Rifle Brigades, and the infantry of the 127th and 136th Guards Rifle Regiments of Major General A. F. Bobrov's 42nd Guards Rifle Division. By 1000, the regiments were approaching the Oktiabr'skii State Farm. But unfortunately, they were poorly supplied with ammunition. For example, at 1000 on 12 July, here is what the 127th Guards Rifle Regiment was reporting on its levels of ammunition:

> … 3. Ammunition supplies. Available at the OP: rifle cartridges – 1 ammunition load; 76mm shells – 0.5 ammunition load; 45mm shells – 0.5 ammunition load; 120mm mortar shells – 0.4 ammunition load; 82mm mortar shells – 0.7 ammunition load; the 91st Artillery Regiment and the 45th Separate Guards Destroyer Anti-tank Artillery Battalion each have 1 ammunition load.[24]

The situation was further complicated by the fact that as the 42nd Guards Rifle Division was moving into its jumping-off positions on the evening and night of 11 July, the 9th Guards Airborne Division and the 287th Guards Rifle Regiment of the 95th Guards Rifle Division were still fighting in the area of the Oktiabr'skii State Farm in front of them until 0600 12 July. Because of this, the battalion commanders could not conduct any reconnaissance prior to the attack start or determine the front lines accurately; consequently, they were unable to generate clear and firm assignments for the day. As a result, from the first minutes of fighting under the heavy enemy fire, the companies became mixed up, command and control collapsed, confusion and chaos began, and the shock power of the rifle units dissipated. The division commanders began to alter the attack plans on the fly, while the regiment commanders, in order to mobilize all possible strength to support the tank brigades and complete their assignments, were being forced to assemble scattered battalions. From the combat dispatch of the chief of staff of the 9th Guards Airborne Division Major Goriachev at 1800 12 July:

> 2. The 23rd Guards Airborne Rifle Regiment with its 1st Battalion moved into the ravine marked '200' lying southeast of Andreevka; the 3rd Battalion is on its left, toward the railroad; *the 2nd Battalion moved into the second echelon, since it had been stopped by the regiment commander because it had become entangled with the combat formations of its neighbor on the right* [author's emphasis].
> … 4. The 26th Guards Airborne Rifle Regiment is moving out behind the 28th Guards Airborne on the boundary with the neighbor on the right, and will not be committed into the fighting.[25]

What information did the Soviet command have on the strength and resources of the enemy on the axis of the 5th Guards Tank Army's main advance? According to the memoirs of P. A. Rotmistrov himself, before the start of the counterstroke his staff possessed only meager intelligence information, which did not yield a clear picture of who would be opposing the Guardsmen southwest of Prokhorovka and with what forces. According to the intelligence of the *front's* headquarters, the Germans might have approximately 250-300 tanks in the sector encompassing all four of the 5th Guards Tank Army's corps. However, there were no estimates of enemy strength in front of the 18th and 29th Tank Corps, or in the area of the Oktiabr'skii State Farm. Such information began to arrive approximately one and a half hours after the launch of the counterstroke. Let's turn to the operational information of our formations and the intelligence documents, which I discovered in the files of the Central Archive of the Russian Ministry of Defense. From a combat dispatch issued by the artillery headquarters of the 42nd Guards Rifle Division:

> Through the personal observation of staff officers of the division's artillery headquarters and the resources of other units, it has been established:
>
> 1. In the division's front, the enemy has:
>   a) up to a regiment of artillery, of which up to three 75mm batteries, four 105mm batteries, and up to two 155-210mm batteries – the region of the enemy's artillery grouping has not been firmly established;
>   b) up to eight to ten mortar batteries and mortar companies;
>   c) up to 15 assault guns, the majority of which operated in the area of Oktiabr'skii State Farm;
>   d) up to two batteries of six-barreled rocket launchers [*Nebelwerfers*];
>   e) [and] up to 155 tanks of all types, including up to 40 Panzer VI ('Tiger').
> 2. In the operation of 12.07.43 ... enemy aviation was supporting the ground forces in the course of the entire day in groups of up to 30 bombers and 12-15 fighters.
> 3. The aviation and the artillery and mortar fire were primarily directed against our tanks, infantry, and the villages in the area of the front lines.
> 4. The enemy subjected the following areas to the attention of bombers: the ravine and hill north of Mikhailovka; the Mikhailovka grove and mill; north and northwest of Oktiabr'skii State Farm; and the depression west of Prokhorovka.
> 5. The enemy's small arms fire is significant.[26]

Several minutes after the start of the counterattack, scouts of the 136th Guards Rifle Regiment seized a prisoner in the area of Oktiabr'skii State Farm, *Sturmmann* Karl Wuhenpfennig of SS Division *Leibstandarte*'s II/2nd SS Panzergrenadier Regiment's 6th Company. The prisoner indicated that the division had three Panzergrenadier regiments (in reality, only two). According to the prisoner, each of these Panzergrenadier regiments was given a 2-kilometer sector of the front. The 2nd Panzergrenadier Regiment was directly defending Oktiabr'skii State Farm and Hill 252.2; behind it – from Komsomolets State Farm and Hill 241.6 – the division's panzer regiment, which was equipped with 50 tanks (15 of them Tigers), was supposed to attack toward Prokhorovka. Furthermore according to the prisoner's testimony, II Battalion had 700-800 men and consisted of six companies: a headquarters company, three rifle companies, a machine gun company, and a heavy weapons company. The latter had four anti-tank guns and three light field guns.

The 6th Company, in which the prisoner served, consisted of 125 enlisted men and 15 junior officers and officers. It was armed with 70 rifles, 12 machine guns, three heavy machine guns, as well as 15 vehicles and five motorcycles.

The prisoner confirmed that the Germans had suffered heavy losses over the recent days. According to him, the company had lost 6 killed and 30 wounded since the start of the battle, while the division had lost up to 40% of its personnel. In addition, three Tigers and 15 tanks of various types had been knocked-out. The prisoner spoke highly of the actions of our artillery, particularly of the Guards mortar regiments' *Katiushas*.

Sturmbannführer Sandig's II/2nd Panzergrenadier Regiment was located directly on Oktiabr'skii State Farm, while his 6th Company was screening the main line and conducting combat patrols. In the words of the prisoner, the SS had no advanced knowledge of our offensive. The battalion had been ordered at dawn to seize the first line of defense of the Soviet units facing the regiment.

At 1030-1045, the 5th Guards Tank Army's combined advance of four tank brigades and three batteries of the 1446th Self-propelled Artillery Regiment was halted at Hill 252.2 and the Oktiabr'skii State Farm, and a heavy exchange of fire with a well-organized anti-tank defense began. P. A. Rotmistrov understood that further advance was impossible without possession of the State Farm; therefore, he issued an order to the corps commanders for a simultaneous strike against the State Farm from two sides with all the forces available at hand. However, in the given situation it was already impossible to achieve any sort of coordination.

Learning that the 32nd Tank Brigade's 1st Battalion had reached the Komsomolets State Farm early in the fighting, I. F. Kirichenko reported this to P. A. Rotmistrov. Given the fierce resistance of the Germans, Rotmistrov seized upon this local breakthrough as a hopeful sign that the engagement had reached a turning point, and that the enemy's defenses were beginning to crumble. An instruction sent by the army commander at 1045 to the commander of the 5th Guards Mechanized Corps, Major General B. M. Skvortsov, is an indication of Rotmistrov's extremely optimistic thinking upon reading Kirichenko's message:

> The offensive of our forces is developing successfully; at 0930 12.07.43 the 29th Tank Corps and the 18th Tank Corps reached the line of the Komsomolets State Farm.
>
> I order:
>
> The Corps, with the exception of the two brigades, advanced to secure the left flank at Ryndinka and Rzhavets, to move out behind the 29th Tank Corps toward the region of Prokhorovka.
>
> Act swiftly.
>
> At approximately 0600 12.07.43 in the areas of Pokrovka and Iakovlevo, aviation spotted up to 200 tanks, moving toward the east and northeast.[27]

Within a half-hour, at 1115, a messenger was sent to Major General A. F. Popov, commander of the 2nd Tank Corps, with the following combat directive:

> The offensive of our forces is developing successfully; the 18th Tank Corps and the 29th Tank Corps have crossed the line of the Komsomolets State Farm. In the areas of Pokrovka and Iakovlevo at 0600 12.07, an aggregation of up to 200 enemy tanks was detected by aviation.
>
> I order:
>
> To assemble the corps in the area of Storozhevoe, and to be ready to develop the success to the west and attack in the direction of Shakhovo and Ryndinka.[28]

However, the high hopes placed on the slender reed of Major Ivanov's 1st Tank Battalion were not realized. Having briefly yielded the Komsomolets State Farm, the Germans counterattacked and enveloped it from the north, thereby cutting off Ivanov's battalion and the 53rd Motorized Rifle Brigade from the rest of the corps. The Germans then struck the State Farm with bombers and a heavy artillery barrage. As the veterans of the 53rd Motorized Rifle Brigade who survived the resulting slaughter later remembered, the Germans practically wiped the Komsomolets State Farm from the face of the earth.

Despite this, the Germans were unable on the first attempt to crack the skillfully arranged defenses of the State Farm, which made use of the fortifications that the Germans had abandoned. Ivanov's tanks were dug-in among the motorized riflemen's positions, which significantly enhanced the defense and enabled the defenders to hold out for some time longer.

Learning about the encirclement of elements of his brigade, Colonel A. A. Linev ordered the commander of the 2nd Tank Battalion Captain A. E. Vakulenko to detach a group of tanks to go to their assistance. Lieutenant V. S. Parshin took command of this relief force. The tankers tried to slip through the German defenses, using the same route along the rail embankment that Ivanov's T-34s had taken. However, this time the Soviet tankers ran into an ambush that the Germans had set up in the grove northeast of Komsomolets State Farm. After the war Vakulenko recalled:

> Having just moved beyond the field of rye and heading toward the [Komsomolets] State Farm, they suddenly saw a grove atop the hill literally erupt like a volcano. Ambush positions in front, behind, and almost right beside the tanks began to belch shells. The fascists concentrated a storm of fire on our tanks. Laying down a broken track, one tank came to a stop; another T-34 exploded. Over the radio I gave the command, 'To everyone, to everyone, to everyone! Smoke!' A thick shroud of smoke enveloped the tanks, and this saved many from the hostile cannons.[29]

Major P. S. Ivanov's group held out in an all-round defense for several hours, but they were outnumbered, and the enemy eventually destroyed all 15 tanks. Ivanov himself was killed. On 18 July, brother officers found his body beside his burned-out tank and committed it to the earth of the Komsomolets State Farm. The remnants of the 53rd Motorized Rifle Brigade could not withstand the Germans repeated panzer counterattacks and fell back to the southeast outskirts of Iamki.

A dash such as Ivanov's ride through the German lines requires not only military skill, knowledge of the enemy and experience, but first of all courage, a deep faith in the rightness of your cause, and most of all, a readiness to give your life for the Motherland. These qualities were possessed not only by Rotmistrov's tankers, who fought on the fields of Prokhorovka, but also by hundreds of thousands of Red Army soldiers. This readiness to sacrifice their own lives surprised the Germans and at times even gained their admiration, but it also frightened them. A country with such soldiers is invincible, and the year 1945 confirmed this.

Very many of the motorized riflemen of the 29th Tank Corps' 53rd Motorized Rifle Brigade were killed in the area of Komsomolets State Farm. According to the dispatches of its headquarters, its losses for 12 July comprised 1,122 men, including 393 dead.

At 1300, the tanks of the 181st, 32nd and 31st Tank Brigades, together with the infantry of the 136th Guards Rifle Regiment finally broke into the Oktiabr'skii State Farm. Having finally overrun the first line of anti-tank defenses on Hill 252.2, a group of 29th Tank Corps tanks poured down the hill's southwestern slopes in pursuit of the retreating enemy in the direction of the Komsomolets State Farm. But after several hundred meters of the chase, something happened which shocked their crews. Several T-34s, moving in the lead at high speed, suddenly vanished into the deep anti-tank ditch. This obstacle had been dug by local citizens while constructing the third defensive belt. Around mid-day on 11 July, SS *Leibstandarte* sappers, with several blasts, had created something like a bridge, over which the panzer regiment had crossed on their way to Hill 252.2. However, on the morning of 12 July, a group of tanks from II/1st SS Panzer Regiment was positioned not far from this passage. It is incomprehensible why our brigade and battalion commanders did not know of this barrier or the crossing. Only one thing is clear: our tankers were completely unaware of the existence of this ditch. As a result of this ill-fated obstacle, over the length of more than a kilometer several dozen Soviet tanks came to an abrupt halt on an open plain, just several hundred meters from the enemy's positions. The attack faltered, and the SS began to finish off the shock wedge of Rotmistrov's tank army with artillery and tank fire.

There exists an eyewitness account of this tragic episode by a *Sturmmann* in SS *Leibstandarte*'s panzer regiment, Wilhelm Roes. His company was located in the second echelon of his panzer battalion:

> Then our 7th Company appeared which had been in the advance guard. ... It had been almost completely overrun, and in retreating, it was drawing Russian tanks after it in close pursuit. Thus we were afraid of hitting our own tanks with our fire. Our armoured halftracks suffered the greatest losses. They had very thin armor protection. Infantry and sappers hunkered inside. The first hit would set them on fire. We saw several burning vehicles with our own eyes. All this continued for three to four hours. The T-34s committed a fatal mistake, which is indeed why I am saying that they were untrained – they approached this anti-tank ditch, the depth of which on the Russian side was 4.5 meters, while on the other side, only 1.2 meters. Just like that, they flew into this ditch at full speed and – boom! – plunged to the bottom.
>
> Our tanks would not have made it through such a scenario – their tracks wouldn't have held up to such a shock, but the T-34s kept moving. In Normandy I once fell into a pit in a tank, and I know well how someone feels after this; you never want it to happen again. And I believe, they [the Soviet tankers] were experiencing the same thing. As they were making their way out of the ditch, first their cannon appeared and their undersides became partially exposed – a very easy target for our guns. That is why they suffered heavy losses. I'm speaking, of course, only about our company and what I heard over the radio.
>
> This continued for some time. Then we couldn't see anything more through the smoke. Incidentally, when a T-34 explodes, or its ammunition, its turret goes flying off – and a smoke ring rises into the air, just like one blown by a smoker. That's just the way it was with the T-34. Indeed from these smoke rings one can see – there goes one T-34, there goes a second ... Their losses were enormous.

> The Russians, if you will, fought courageously, but coordination was lacking. In principle, with such a mass of armor they should simply have crushed us. But this didn't happen.[30]

After shooting up Kirichenko's armor at the anti-tank ditch, the Germans tried to exploit the situation and launched several counterattacks. From a 29th Tank Corps combat dispatch at 2400 on 12 July 1943:

> … after reaching the northeast outskirts of the Oktiabr'skii State Farm, the 31st Tank Brigade was held up by strong artillery and mortar fire and the ceaseless activity of enemy aviation. Four counterattacks by enemy infantry and tanks, which were trying to recapture the Oktiabr'skii State Farm, were repulsed. Losses: 20 T-34 and 18 T-70 tanks knocked out or burned-out.
>
> In formation – 3 tanks; the location and condition of the remaining tanks is being clarified.[31]

In connection with the loss of the Oktiabr'skii State Farm and the penetration of Russian tanks to the Komsomolets State Farm, the II SS Panzer Corps commander requested increased air strikes. Up to 150 Me 110 and Ju 87 aircraft were summoned to this area. A Soviet report noted: "The bombing lasted for about an hour, in groups of 7 to 37 planes. Our motorized infantry were cut off from the tanks and pinned down. The offensive was brought to a halt, but not for long."[32]

Arguments about the scale of the activity of both sides' air forces on 12 July at Prokhorovka continue to the present day. Some scholars maintain, relying on German sources, that the weather was unsuitable for flying on the morning of 12 July in the region of Prokhorovka, as a result of which the Germans didn't employ their air force there. This doesn't correspond to reality. Documents from all the formations of our army note the high activity of enemy aviation on this day. For example, there is a note that by 1400 12 July, "enemy aviation had conducted up to 1500 sorties against the corps' combat formations."[33]

In the summary of the Red Army Air Force Command, "Operations of aviation in the Belgorod defensive operation," it is observed:

> Air operations of both sides at dawn on 12 July were limited by unsatisfactory meteorological conditions. Enemy aviation with daylight operated in groups of 9 to 30 bombers against the combat formations of our forces, *concentrating their effort on the Prokhorovka axis* [author's emphasis], where up to 400 of the total number of 546 sorties were counted.
>
> … Units of the 1st Bomber Aviation Corps in the period 0800-0815 in groups of 9 to 25 Pe-2 aircraft escorted by 12-16 fighters from the 4th Fighter Aviation Corps bombed concentrations of enemy tanks and motorized infantry in the areas of Bol. Maiachki, Pokrovka, Iakovlevo, and the grove to the east
>
> … Ground attack planes from the 1st Storm Aviation Corps and the 291st Storm Aviation Division conducted no combat operations at dawn due to the

inclement weather. They only began to operate … from 1000 in groups of 12-16 aircraft covered by 12-16 fighters.

… In connection with the threat of a breakthrough by the III Panzer Corps toward Prokhorovka from the south, units of the 1st Storm Aviation Corps were redirected to operate against enemy forces in the areas of Verkh. Ol'shanets, Shliakhovoe, Melikhovo, and in the patches of woods between Verkh. Ol'shanets and Shliakhovoe.

The 291st Storm Aviation Division operated against enemy tanks and motorized infantry in the areas of Verkhopen'e, Syrtsevo, Dmitrievka, Novo-Cherkasskoe and the forest south of Dubrova, Iakovlevo and Pokrovka. Altogether, our ground attack aircraft conducted around 400 combat sorties, as the result of which a great number of enemy tanks and vehicles were destroyed or damaged, and the fire of 14 batteries was suppressed.[34]

Thus, on the Prokhorovka axis of the main assault, ground attack aircraft were almost not used at all, and air support on the battlefield seemed, to put it gently, insufficiently effective. Moreover, due to the poorly organized cooperation between the ground forces and the aviation (formations of the 2nd Air Army) there were incidents of airstrikes against our own troops. Thus, at a critical moment, when the tank battalions of the 32nd, 31st and 181st Tank Brigades, after almost five hours of heavy fighting, broke into Oktiabr'skii State Farm, at 1300 a group of our [Il-2] *Shturmoviki* dove on them, shooting up the tanks with their cannons and releasing their cluster bombs.[35]

There were cases of fratricide in units of other types of forces as well. Fire and maneuver were conducted between Soviet tank brigades and regiments belonging to different formations, and there were duels between our own artillerymen and tankers. However, friendly fire incidents in the ground forces were significantly fewer than those that involved our air force, particularly our ground attack aircraft.

The attacking wedge of the 18th and 29th Tank Corps was squeezed into the area between the natural barriers of the Psel River and the Storozhevoe forested tract, and echeloned in depth. In this narrow sector, six tank brigades, and tank and self-propelled artillery regiments were operating. This became one of the main reasons for the high losses in the first hours of the attack, and first of all from aviation. Here are some characteristic communications (jotted down on a small sheet of paper), which corps and brigade commanders sent to the 5th Guards Tank Army headquarters during the fighting:

29th Tank Corps. Losses: 25th Tank Brigade – 60% of personnel, Su-122 – 4 (left burning), Su-76 – 4 (knocked-out). Losses are primarily from enemy aviation and Tiger tanks. Our own ground attack aviation twice bombed friendly combat formations.[36]

31st Tank Brigade. At 1540 the enemy undertook a counterattack, which was beaten back. As a result of the day's fighting, the brigade has the following losses: T-34 tanks – 24, T-70 tanks – 20, 45mm guns – 1, heavy machine guns – 1, PPSh [submachine guns] – 2, rifles – 1, killed – 44 men, wounded – 39, missing in action – 18.

Ju 87 dive bombers with close fighter escort in the skies above Prokhorovka. (RGAKFD)

> Destroyed or knocked-out enemy men and material: light and medium tanks – 21, heavy Tiger tanks – 6, machine-gun nests – 17, [and] up to 600 soldiers and officers.[37]

Already after the war, smoothing out the "rough edges" to the story, P. A. Rotmistrov wrote that once the combat formations of the two sides became entangled, the artillery of both sides ceased firing. According to him, for the same reasons neither our aviation nor the enemy's aviation bombed the battlefield, although fierce clashes continued in the air, and the howl of downed and burning planes mixed with the roar of the tank battle on the earth.

However, this is far from true. From early morning, aircraft of the enemy's VIII Air Corps began to bomb the combat formations of the tank brigades, which were preparing to attack. Even before the start of the attack, combat losses among the command staff appeared due to enemy air activity. At 0800 while moving up to the 36th Separate Breakthrough Tank Regiment's line of deployment for the attack, the regiment commander Lieutenant Colonel Mitroshenko was wounded, and his radio operator and the regiment's hygiene instructor were killed by exploding bomb fragments. With the start of the attack, the bombing intensified, and Messerschmitts and Junkers literally hovered over the attackers. The units and formations of both Guards armies, taking part in the counterstroke, noted high enemy air activity.

Our aircraft appeared in small groups of five to ten fighters, which could not substantially affect the general situation in the air. There is documentary evidence to support this assertion. The summary report by the headquarters of the 5th Guards Tank Army stated, "… Enemy aviation hung over our combat formations; our aviation, and particularly fighter aviation, was insufficient."[38]

In the Kursk battle, for the first time the *Luftwaffe* operated in large groups against tanks, and it must be said that this activity was quite effective. The famous pilot Hans Rudel, who flew one of the Stukas armed with 37mm cannons, wrote: "In the first attack four tanks explode under the hammer blows of my cannons; by the evening the total rises to twelve. … the evil spell is broken, and in this aircraft we possess a weapon which speedily can be employed everywhere and is capable of dealing successfully with the formidable number of Soviet tanks."[39]

Here is a description of the application of these aircraft from the summary of combat operations of the 2nd Tank Corps' 99th Tank Brigade during the counterattack of 8 July:

> Once the 169th Tank Brigade, which was operating in front, reached the line of the Komsomolets State Farm, the enemy, firing at the tanks with artillery, heavy mortars and from Panzer VI tanks dug into the ground, began to conduct massed attacks by Ju 88 bombers and anti-tank Ju 87 dive bombers, armed with three [*sic.*] 37mm automatic cannons. The attacks intensified in step with the brigade's further advance, and by approximately 1800 8.07.43 these attacks turned into an uninterrupted assault from the air. It is possible to judge the ferocity of the Ju 87 attacks from the following fact: one Ju 87 vulture, damaged by our anti-aircraft gunners, flew directly toward a T-70 tank and struck it with all its mass. The tank was left burning, but the crew somehow survived. As a rule, the Ju 87 aircraft attacked our tanks from the rear, striking the engine compartment with their fire.[40]

The use of these types of airplanes by the enemy against tanks and motorized infantry of the 2nd Tank Corps' 4th Guards Tank Brigade and 4th Guards Motorized Rifle Brigade was observed on 12 July in the area of Kalinin as well.

After the initial effort to penetrate the enemy's defenses failed, the 5th Guards Tank Army commander, trying to find some way to revive the attack, had reduced the corps' breakthrough sector to 3-4 kilometers, thereby creating several echelons in depth, and issued the command for the tank formations to lead the attack in front of the rifle units. Rotmistrov hoped that the leading armor would be able to crush the field fortifications, hastily thrown up by the II SS Panzer Corps. Unfortunately, these hopes were not realized. As a result, the resumed attack proceeded with difficulty and did not yield the desired results. His tank army suffered large, unjustified losses in armor, and hundreds of crewmen were killed.

★ ★ ★

Colonel N. K. Volodin, commander of the 29th Tank Corps' 25th Tank Brigade, after his wounding on 12 July 1943. (Author's personal archive)

The attack of Colonel N. K. Volodin's 25th Tank Brigade ended particularly tragically. It was attacking on the opposite side of the railway, to the left of the brigades that were assaulting the Oktiabr'skii State Farm, and had the mission to pass through Storozhevoe and attack toward Ivanovskii Vyselok and Teterevino, and by the end of the day to reach the Belgorod – Oboian' highway at the village of Krapivenskie Dvory.

Units of the 183rd Rifle Division and the 2nd Tank Corps were defending at Storozhevoe, which was in our possession. However, the evening before, units of SS Panzergrenadier Division *Leibstandarte* had infiltrated the grove northeast of the small village. That night, Wisch deployed tank destroyers from the 1st SS Panzerjäger Battalion in ambush positions in the cultivated area of the Stalinskoe Branch of the [Oktiabr'skii] State Farm. The 25th Tank Brigade's tank battalions' route of advance would take them directly into these ambush positions. As the brigade's war diary testifies, our tankers moved into their start line in the area of Iamki at midnight. They were unable to conduct a normal reconnaissance and to scout out the enemy's main firing positions.

Prior to the attack, Colonel Volodin concentrated all of his brigade's T-34s in the 362nd Tank Battalion and all of his brigade's T-70s in the 25th Tank Battalion. He also attached the Su-76 and Su-122 assault guns of Captain M. S. Lunev's 1446th Self-propelled Artillery Regiment to the 362nd Tank Battalion. The 362nd Tank Battalion was to lead the attack, with the 1446th Self-propelled Artillery Regiment's assault guns trailing slightly behind and on the flanks; the 25th Tank Battalion would advance to the left and slightly behind the 362nd Tank Battalion. The infantry of his 25th Motorized

Rifle Battalion would follow the tank formations, though some of its men were mounted on the tanks.

The morning of 12 July, in response to the general signal "Steel" Volodin's 362nd and 25th Tank Battalions moved out on the attack. As they approached the cultivated area of Stalinskoe Branch, they were met with concentrated artillery fire, which separated the infantry from the tanks and pinned the infantry down. Then they then ran into the concealed elements of the 1st SS Panzerjäger Battalion, which as has been already mentioned, Wisch had specially attached to the 1st SS Panzergrenadier Regiment in order to strengthen its anti-tank defenses. I've been unable to establish the number of self-propelled guns that met the 25th Tank Brigade; it is known only that five Marder III tank destroyers of the 3rd Company under the command of SS *Oberscharführer* Kurt Sametreiter (who would receive the Knight's Cross of the Iron Cross for his successful actions in this battle) were operating here.

The 25th Tank Brigade was advancing across open ground. The leading 362nd Tank Battalion, which had no artillery support, was staggered by the fire as it closed within range of the concealed German guns. When it had become clear that the leading T-34s had run into a carefully arranged ambush and were in deep trouble, the supporting self-propelled guns rushed forward to assist the tankers. The Soviet self-propelled guns, which were lightly armored, could not attack a well-organized anti-tank defense on their own. They were supposed to remain about 400 meters behind the tanks and destroy enemy armor and revealed enemy firing positions.

With their aggressive forward move, the self-propelled guns of the 1446th Self-propelled Artillery Regiment along with some of the 25th Tank Battalion's light tanks on the left leapfrogged ahead of the 362nd Tank Battalion's T-34s. German fire now concentrated on them, and a significant number of these vehicles were destroyed before they even reached the woods. The surviving vehicles plunged into the enemy's defenses at high speed. Only a handful made it back out again. Of the 32 T-34 tanks that took part in this attack, 26 were knocked out; the self-propelled guns of both batteries were completely destroyed. The 25th Tank Battalion also suffered serious losses, without having been able to carry out the assignment.

The Soviet tankers fought with desperate courage. For example, the tank of company commander Senior Lieutenant N. A. Mishchenko took a direct hit after surging ahead of the other tanks and burst into flames. Having managed to extinguish the fire, the crew threw open the hatches and continued to fire the tank's main gun. When the battalion remnants withdrew, Mishchenko's tank became encircled by the enemy. Firing the main gun until it ran out of shells, the crew then continued to fire the tank's machine guns. As Major General A. V. Egorov (who at the time of the Kursk battle was a colonel) later recalled, the tankers killed up to 25 Nazis, and four days later managed to make their way back to their own brigade.

It is impossible to read the award citations for the crewmen of the self-propelled guns without being moved. The self-propelled gun under the command of Lieutenant V. M. Kubaevsky, with gun layer Gromov, driver-mechanic Merkulov, loader Suzdalov and breech operator Ershov was hit while approaching the woods. Continuing to fire, the crew rammed their burning vehicle into a German tank. Their self-propelled gun blew into pieces from the impact, taking with it the heroic crew. Lieutenant Kudriavtsev and driver-mechanic First Sergeant Vasil'ev, both badly wounded, brought their burning vehicle out of the battle. Lieutenant Erin's self-propelled artillery vehicle took a hit that damaged the track and knocked out an idler wheel. The foe then concentrated their fire on the immobilized vehicle. Wounded men appeared among the crew. Laying down a smokescreen, the commander undertook repairs. Likely, the Germans figured out what the crew was doing, and dropped a mortar barrage on the vehicle. Lieutenant Erin, despite being wounded by shell fragments, completed the repairs and brought the self-propelled gun back out of the battle to the corps' location.

The remnants of the 25th Tank Brigade withdrew behind the infantry's positions and took up a defense about a half-kilometer southeast of Storozhevoe. Brigade commander Colonel N. K. Volodin received a severe concussion in the battle; the commander of the 25th Motorized Rifle Battalion Major Z. P. Grigorenko was wounded and hospitalized. Major Miasnikov, the commander of the 362nd Tank Battalion, died in the flames of his burning tank. A battalion was formed from the brigade's remaining tanks, and the commander of the 25th Tank Battalion Captain Chekranov was placed in command of it.[41]

At noon, the brigade (now in reality a composite tank battalion comprised mostly of the T-70s of the 25th Tank Battalion) undertook a new attack. Passing through the formations of the 169th Tank Brigade and with its fire support, it attempted to attack Ivanovskii Vyselok, but by this time, SS Panzergrenadier Division *Leibstandarte* units had already encircled the elements of the 32nd Tank Brigade and the 53rd Motorized Rifle Brigade on the Komsomolets State Farm, and units of SS Panzergrenadier Division *Das Reich*'s left wing had set up a solid barrier in the path of Chekranov's composite battalion. Reaching a line 1 kilometer west of the village, the tankers ran into heavy fire. Operational Summary No. 5 from the 169th Tank Brigade's headquarters states that the enemy had several Tiger tanks in the first echelon of its anti-tank defense. After an hour of combat, the reduced brigade fell back to its start line.

The day's results for the brigade were very painful: it had failed to carry out its orders; of the 69 tanks which took part in the counterattack at the start, 50 were knocked-out. A mortar and a 45mm gun had been destroyed. The formation lost 158 men altogether, including 40 killed and 27 missing in action. In the course of the two attacks, three enemy tanks, one of them a heavy tank, two self-propelled guns, three anti-tank guns, two mortars and a fuel dump had been destroyed.[42]

In the 29th Tank Corps headquarters, the situation began to clarify around mid-day. At this time, the first more or less clear dispatches began to arrive. From them, the command staff gathered that by 1100, two brigades, three batteries of the 1446th Self-propelled Artillery Regiment, and the 136th Guards Rifle Regiment of the 42nd Guards Rifle Division following them, had been brought to a complete halt and were exchanging fire from static positions about a half-kilometer east of the Oktiabr'skii State Farm, while elements of the 25th Tank Brigade had begun to withdraw from the depth of the enemy's defenses and were gathering in a depression 1.5 kilometers southeast of Storozhevoe. Over these two to two and a half hours of fighting, the corps had lost more than 60% of its armor: the 32nd Tank Brigade had lost more than 63% of its armor (up to 40 tanks and around 350 men); the 25th Tank Brigade – around 70% (48 tanks); while the 31st

Tank Brigade and the 1446th Self-propelled Artillery Regiment had each lost more than 40%.

The losses in tanks were enormous, but there was something else even more terrible. Crews – living men – burned together with their combat vehicles. After the war, a veteran of the 10th Tank Corps V. T. Fedin wrote:

> Here I will allow myself to bring the readers' attention to a particular feature of the combat life of a tanker. The combat crew itself does the technical work on their tank (in contrast to, for example, the air force, where ground crews prepare the aircraft for a sortie). The crew adds the oil and pours the fuel into the gas tanks; greases the hundreds of moving parts; removes the grease from the gun barrel before a battle; lubricates the barrel after use and so forth. Therefore the tankers' uniforms were often soaked with fuel and/or motor oil. The primary fuel for the diesel engines of our tanks of that time was fuel oil. It is significantly less volatile than benzene, and remains on clothing for a long time. When a flame touches the clothing, it immediately ignites, and the likelihood of a flame licking the uniform in combat is rather high. The T-34 had three 100-liter fuel tanks on the right side, and an additional 100-liter drum with motor oil on the left side. When an armor-piercing shell penetrates the side, fuel oil or motor oil spills into the tank interior and a cascade of sparks falls on the uniform, and everything blazes up. God forbid a living being from ever having to witness a wounded, writhing person who is burning alive, or ever have to experience the same. That is why there exists among tankers a unique, unofficial measure of courage, combat maturity, and experience – the number of times you've been on fire inside a tank … It is difficult to imagine that after all this it is possible to remain among the living and not go mad. Apparently, only a Russian is capable of enduring this.[43]

Altogether in the course of 12 July, the 29th Tank Corps lost 1,991 men, including 1,033 killed and missing in action.[44] Of the 199 combat vehicles that took part in the fighting, 153 were knocked out. Of the 20 self-propelled guns, only one was serviceable after the battle, and three had been turned over for repairs. Aggregate losses for the 5th Guards Tank Army for 12 July 1943 are shown in Table 21.

Units of the 33rd Guards Rifle Corps' 9th Guards Airborne Division advanced behind the 29th Tank Corps. From the combat dispatch of the chief of staff of this division Major A Ia. Goriachev at 1800 12 July:

> 1. Enemy aviation is operating against our attacking units, shifting strikes from one flank to the other.
>
> …
>
> 3. The 28th Guards Airborne Rifle Regiment at 1400 seized the edge of the grove lying southwest of the Stalinskoe Branch of the [Oktiabr'skii] State Farm. According to a report from the deputy commander of the rifle division, Guards Colonel Grachev, the Germans lost up to 20 tanks here.
>
> By 1400, the 1st and 3rd Rifle Battalions reached the northeast edge of the woods, on the left of Storozhevoe; by 1700 they had emerged on the southern edge, but met by strong fire from the grove at Ivanovskii Vyselok and attacked by

No.	Formation and Units	Personnel		T-34	T-70	Mk-IV	SP Guns	Total	In formation 12.07.43	Participated in combat	% of armor that participated knocked out	In formation at 1300 on 13.07.43
		Total	Killed and Missing									
1	18 Tank Corps, Total	471(a)	271(a)	43	24	17	-	84	183	149	56%	33
2	110 Tank Bde	28	11	8	3	-	-	-	45	38(43)?	26%	-
3	170 Tank Bde	49	28	19	10	-	-	29	39	39	74%	-
4	181 Tank Bde	99	65	16	11	-	-	27	44	44	61%	-
5	32 Mot Rifle Bde	219	147	-	-	-	-	-	-	-	-	-
6	36 Gds Sep Hvy Tank Reg	25	7	-	-	17	-	17	19	19	89%	-
7	29 Tank Corps, Total (b)	1991	1033	109	44	-	-	153	215	199	77%	51
8	25 Tank Bde	320	140	31	24	-	-	55	73	69	80%	11
9	31 Tank Bde	101	62	24	20	-	-	44	71	67	66%	28
10	32 Tank Bde	230	100	54	-	-	-	54	64	63	86%	12
11	53 Mot Rifle Bde	1089	517	-	-	-	-	-	-	-	-	-
12	1446 SP Artillery Reg	41	24 (c)	Su-76 and Su-122			19	19	20	20	95%	1
13	2 Tank Corps, Total	124	36	18	4	-	-	22	59	52	42%	44
14	26 Tank Bde	-	-	No data available				7	14	14	50%	7
15	99 Tank Bde	-	-	7	1	-	-	8	24	20	40%	11
16	169 Tank Bde	79	36	11	3	-	-	14	18	18	78%	11
17	58 Mot Rifle Bde	45	?	-	-	-	-	-	-	-	-	-
18	15 Gds Sep Hvy Tank Reg	-	-	Did not participate in combat on this day					3	-	-	?
19	2nd Gds Tank Corps, Total	550	145	40	14	-	-	54	140	138	39%	80
20	4 Gds Tank Bde	85	34	18	4	-	-	22	47	47	47%	20
21	25 Gds Tank Bde	136	61	20	9	-	-	29	47	47	62%	14

Table 21: Aggregate Losses in the 5th Guards Tank Army, 12 July 1943

Table 21 continued

No.	Formation and Units	Personnel		T-34	T-70	Mk-IV	SP Guns	Total	In formation 12.07.43	Participated in combat	% of armor that participated knocked out	In formation at 1300 on 13.07.43
		Total	Killed and Missing									
22	26 Gds Tank Bde	40	8	-	2	-	-	2	44	44	4%	44
23	4 Gds Mot Rifle Bde	272	68	-	-	-	-	-	-	-	-	-
24	47 Gds Hvy Tank Reg	-	-	Did not participate in combat on this day				-	2	-	-	2
25	5 Gds Mechanized Corps, Total	405	?	No detailed data on losses				15	158	66	-	158
26	10 Gds Mech Bde	-	-	Did not participate in combat on this day				-	44	-	-	44
27	11 Gds Mech Bde (54 Gds Tank Reg)	354	?	No detailed data on losses				11	31	31	35%	35
28	12 Gds Mech Bde (55 Gds Tank Reg)	51	?	4	-	-	-	4	35	35	11%	?
29	24 Gds Tank Bde	-	-	Did not participate in combat on this day				-	48	-	-	51
30	1447 SP Artillery Reg	-	-	-	-	-	No losses	-	(11)	(10)	-	?
31	1 Gds Sep MC Reg	-	-	Did not participate in combat on this day				-	10	-	-	8
32	53 Gds Sep Tank Reg	22	15	9	3	-	-	12	43	38	32%	25
33	5 Gds Tank Army, Total	3,563	1,505	223	89	17	19	340 (19)	808 (32)	642 (30)	53%	399 (?)

(a) Data on personnel losses in the 18th Tank Corps have been obtained from TsAMO RF, f. 18 tk, op. 2, d. 5, l. 25.

(b) Data on the armor in formation for the 18th, 2nd and 2nd Guards Tank Corps have been obtained from TsAMO RF, f. 332, op. 4948, d. 67, l. 5; for the 29th Tank Corps – TsAMO RF, f. 29 tk, op. 1, d. 6, l.29.

(c) In the cell "Killed and missing" for the 1446th Self-propelled Artillery Regiment, only killed-in-action was given (TsAMO RF, f. 1446 sap, op. 584031, d. 1, l. 6-8).

Notes: The armor available on the morning of 13 July 1943 may be greater than the losses on 12 July 1943 would indicate when subtracted from the armor available on the morning of 12 July, due to the return overnight of vehicles from repair shops.

Tank losses in the 25th Guards Tank Brigade includes 7 T-34 and 4 T-70 tanks that became disabled on the battlefield on 12 July 1943 due to mechanical problems (TsAMO RF, f. 5. gv. TA, op. 4948, d. 70, l. 136).

Table 21 continued

Notes continued

At midnight on 12 July 1943, the 31st Guards Tank Brigade counted only 3 tanks in formation; the situation of the other tanks in the brigade was unknown to the command (TsAMO RF, f. 5 gv TA, op. 4948, d.70, l. 136).

Personnel losses in the 58th Motorized Rifle Brigade and the 12th Guards Mechanized Brigade indicate the number of dead and wounded in each brigade, and do not include the number of missing-in-action.

During the movement to a new sector on 12 July 1943, two T-70 tanks and 1 T-34 tank from the 5th Guards 'Zimovniki' Mechanized Corps (presumably from the 11th and 12th Guards Mechanized Brigades) were disabled by mine fields in the area of Rzhavets (TsAMO RF, f. 332, op. 4948, d. 41, l. 9).

The following sources correspond to each numbered row in the table:

1. TsAMO RF, f. 5 gv. TA, op. 4948, d. 75, l. 32.
2. Ibid.
3. Ibid.
4. Ibid.
5. Ibid.
6. TsAMO RF, f. 36 gv. ottp, op. 119565, d. 5, l. 94.
7. TsAMO RF, f. 332, op. 4948, d. 46.
8. TsAMO RF, f. 29tk, op. 1, d. 6, l. 92.
9. TsAMO RF, f. 31 tbr, op. 1, d. 2, l. 55.
10. TsAMO RF, f. 29tk, op. 1, d. 6, l. 92.
11. TsAMO RF, f. 53 msbr, op. 1, d. 2.
12. TsAMO RF, f. 332, op. 4948, d. 75, l. 40.
13. TsAMO RF, f. 5 gv. TA, op. 4948, d. 67, l. 12; d. 70, l. 203.
14. TsAMO RF, f. 5 gv. TA, op. 4948, d.70, l. 203 obr.
15. TsAMO RF, f. 59 gv. tbr, op. 1, d. 6, l. 24 obr.
16. TsAMO RF, f. 60 gv. tbr, op. 1, d. 14, l. 33; d. 17, l. 4.
17. TsAMO RF, f. 8 gv. tk, op. 1, d. 108, l. 207.
18. TsAMO RF, f. 8 gv. tk, op. 1, d. 233, l. 41, 41 obr.
19. TsAMO RF, f. 5 gv. TA, op. 4948, d. 75, l. 20, 28, 34.
20. TsAMO RF, f. 4 gv. tbr, op. 1, d. 26, l. 22
21. TsAMO RF, f. 25 gv. tbr, op. 1, d. 5.
22. TsAMO RF, f. 26 gv. tbr, op. 1, d. 18, l. 17.
23. TsAMO RF, f. 4 gv. msbr, op. 1, d. 21.
24. TsAMO RF, f. 3400, op. 1, d. 75, l. 34.
25. TsAMO RF, f. 5 gv. TA, op. 4948, d. 70, l. 137 obr.; f. 5 gv. TA, op. 4982, d. 23, l. 5.
26. TsAMO RF, f. 5 gv. TA, op. 4948, d. 70, l. 137 obr.
27. TsAMO RF, f. 5 gv. TA, op. 4948, d. 70, l. 15-19; op. 4982, d. 21, l. 6-10.
28. TsAMO RF, f. 55 gv. tp, op. 88261, d. 1, l. 23-25, l. 28 obr; f. 5 gv. TA, op. 4982, d. 23, l. 5.
29. TsAMO RF, f. 5 gv. TA, op. 4948, d. 70, l. 137.
30. TsAMO RF, f. 5 gv. TA, op. 4948, d. 75, l. 10a
31. TsAMO RF, f. 5 gv. TA, op. 4948, d. 70, l. 140.
32. TsAMO RF, f. 5 gv. TA, op. 4948, d. 75, l. 36.
33. Author's calculations.

A camouflaged German anti-tank gun has gotten off the first shot and destroyed a T-34 in the region of the Storozhevoe woods. (RGAKFD)

enemy ground attack aviation, the battalions became mixed up and fell back into the depth of the woods, where they reorganized and began to work over the enemy's forward positions with fire.

4. The 136th Guards Rifle Regiment had been withdrawn into the reserve northeast of Oktiabr'skii State Farm. In the area of Oktiabr'skii State Farm, a German staff vehicle was captured, containing documents and a banner. In the region of the Stalinskoe Branch, a prisoner (a Russian) indicated that the SS Division *Adolf Hitler* was operating in front of the division. At the same time he reported that he knew about the presence on our front (giving no precise location) of the 2nd [SS] Panzer Division *Das Reich* and the 9th Light Infantry Division [*sic*]. Losses of more than 50 tanks.[45]

* * *

The offensive of Major General B. S. Bakharov's 18th Tank Corps started more successfully. It had the orders to attack on the sector between the Psel River and the Oktiab'rskii State Farm (excl.) to drive the enemy from the villages on the left [southern] bank of the river and to break through to Greznoe and Malye Maiachki. After reaching this area, it was to pivot to the north in order to cut off SS Panzergrenadier Division *Totenkopf's kampfgruppe* in the bend of the river from its main forces. The army command anticipated that the villages of Prelestnoe, Andreevka and partially Mikhailovka would be in our hands, while the two key strongpoints of enemy resistance – the Oktiabr'skii and Komsomolets State Farms – were located in the attack sector of its stronger neighbor on the left. Therefore the corps, closely cooperating with the 29th Tank Corps, was to render it assistance in case the latter's attack was unable to penetrate the line Ivanovskii Vyselok – Komsomolets State Farm from the march. It was assumed that if the Germans had created a strong anti-tank barrier in the area of Hill 241.6, Bakharov's brigades would turn and strike the strongpoint in the flank from the north.

Bakharov deployed his forces with Lieutenant Colonel V. A. Puzyrev's 181st Tank Brigade in the first echelon along the river, together with Lieutenant Colonel V. D. Tarasov's 170th Tank Brigade which would attack on its left. The tankers would be supported by the 127th Guards Rifle Regiment of the 42nd Guards Rifle Division with one battalion from that division's artillery regiment. The 36th Guards Separate Heavy Tank Breakthrough Regiment had the order to advance behind the 170th Tank Brigade. Even before the offensive started, Major Plissov had to assume command of the 36th Guards Separate Heavy Tank Breakthrough Regiment after the German bomb fell near the Willys jeep of its commander, seriously wounding Lieutenant I. S. Mitroshenko.

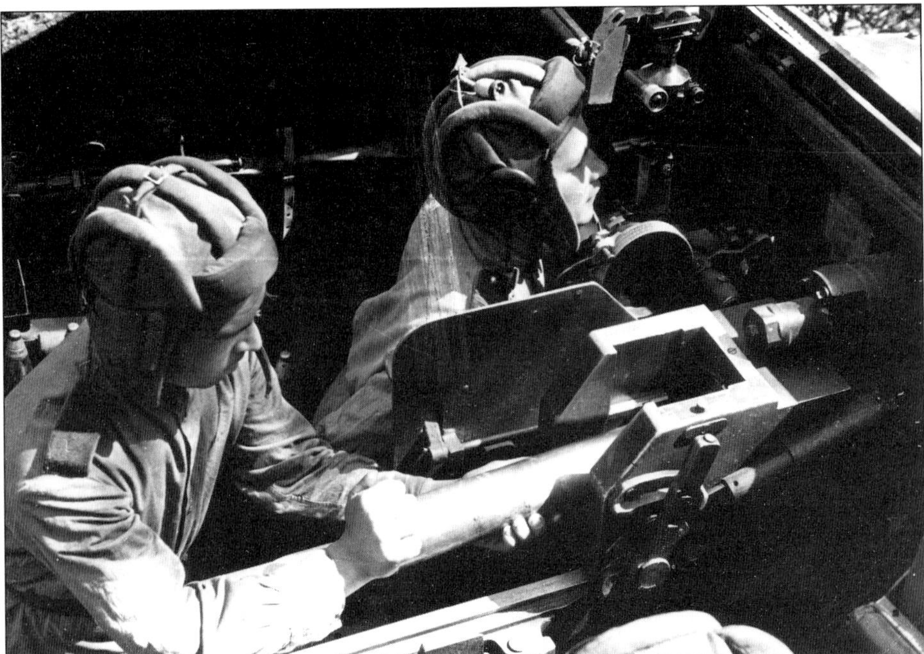

A gun layer and loader of a Soviet Su-76 self-propelled gun at work. (RGAKFD)

In the second echelon, Colonel M. E. Khvatov's 32nd Motorized Rifle Brigade moved with the corps artillery, consisting of the 80th Guards Mortar [*Katiusha*] Regiment, the 1000th Destroyer Anti-tank Artillery Regiment and the 292nd Mortar Regiment.

The 110th Tank Brigade comprised the third echelon. Its 1st and 2nd Tank Battalions were moving with infantry squads of the motorized rifle battalion mounted on their armor. Deputy corps commander Lieutenant Colonel M. G. Khliupin commanded the third echelon. The attack began as planned at 0830, with an interval of thirty minutes between the echelons. The corps attack practically struck the boundary between the two SS divisions, *Totenkopf* and *Leibstandarte*.

On the morning of 12 July, the formation numbered 149 combat-ready tanks. But for technical reasons, four Mk-IV Churchill tanks had been unable to move into position in the heavy tank regiment, and one more tank – Lieutenant Tikhostupov's – broke down at the very start of the attack. Thus, of the 36th Guards Separate Heavy Tank Breakthrough Regiment's 21 tanks, only 16 Churchills directly took part in the attack.[46]

The *Wehrmacht* command always paid close attention to the security of its formations' boundaries and flanks, and therefore the headquarters of SS Panzergrenadier Division *Totenkopf* was particularly looking after its right flank. There were legitimate concerns that the enemy was preparing to strike it with a heavy tank counterattack: according to its routine morning situation brief to II SS Panzer Corps at 0500 12 July 1943, *Leibstandarte* reported that the sounds of tank engines had been audible all night long to its front. This put the headquarters of both SS divisions on guard, and demanded increased attention to this area.

Two regiments of SS Panzergrenadier Division *Totenkopf* were operating in the bend of the Psel River, which had the assignment to expand the bridgehead across the Psel River as quickly as possible by seizing Veselyi and Hill 226.6, thereby creating conditions for a lunge in the direction of Kartashevka and Beregovoe. However, their operations had been quite complicated; firstly, by the stubborn resistance of Soviet forces, primarily the 52nd Guards Rifle Division, which the 6th Guards Army command could support with fire from mortars and *Katiushas*; and secondly, by the absence of *Totenkopf*'s armor from the bridgehead. Bridges for the tanks had been ready only by the afternoon of 11 July, but heavy rains had prevented an immediate crossing. Armor began to transfer to the right [northern] bank only late in the evening and continued all night. However, *Oberführer* Priess decided to leave part of the assault gun battalion (no less than ten vehicles) and up to a company of panzers on the left [southern] bank as his personal mobile reserve. On the morning of 12 July, this armor reserve was assembled on the right flank in the 6th SS Panzergrenadier Regiment's sector of defense, which had the following order: while supporting the 5th SS Panzergrenadier Regiment in the bridgehead, it was to parry a possible Russian tank attack from the region of Petrovka in the direction of Greznoe and to keep possession of Bogoroditskoe, where one of the two crossings for the heavy tanks was emplaced. Priess's decision to strengthen the right flank with armor proved to be far-sighted, and enabled him eventually to bring Major General B. S. Bakharov's offensive to a grinding halt by day's end.

The former commander of SS Panzergrenadier Division *Totenkopf*'s 6th SS Panzergrenadier Regiment, *Obersturmbannführer* H. Becker,[47] recalled the start of the 18th Tank Corps attack this way:

> I was at the observation post on the rooftop of a building, and I was observing the movement of our own forces through binoculars. All the division's panzers had deployed exactly according to plan and were moving out, confident in the offensive's success. At that time I noticed clouds of dust on the horizon. It was impossible to discern who was raising them, but they continued to grow in size, and soon Russian tanks began to emerge from these dust clouds. 'The Russians have advanced their reserves,' I said to my chief of staff, and I understood that now [our] offensive would be broken and that we had lost the battle for Kursk.[48]

The terrain in 18th Tank Corps' sector was cut by three deep ravines, extending from the left [southern] bank of the Psel River toward the rail line. Because of this, the brigades of the first echelon were compelled to concentrate their armor on the corps' left flank, in front of the strongly fortified anti-tank defenses on the Oktiabr'skii State Farm. The 170th Tank Brigade was the first to experience the full might of the Germans' fire. Its battalions tried to bypass the State Farm from the march at high speed, but no sooner had the tanks closed within direct fire range, when the German guns and tanks dug into the ground in the area of Oktiabr'skii State Farm opened a storm of fire. In fairly short order, the Germans inflicted serious damage to the 170th Tank Brigade's battalions. Already by noon the Brigade, still not having reached the outskirts of the State Farm, had lost up to 60% of its tanks; brigade commander Lieutenant Colonel V. D. Tarasov had burned to death within his tank, and the commander of the brigade's 1st Battalion Captain Isaev had died from wounds.[49]

With the rapidly mounting losses, already after the first forty-five to fifty minutes of fighting the corps' attack had lost momentum, followed by the loss of command and control, confusion, and finally the full suspension of the attack. These were consequences not only of the enemy's strong resistance, but also the poorly conceived plan, lacking clear assignments, which the tankers had received the evening before. It was later, after the war, that a version of this attack plan appeared in the memoirs of generals, and then in the studies of historians. The plan purported that Rotmistrov's army was involved in a counterattack upon the weakened flanks of the enemy grouping. Before the battle itself, the brigade commanders and battalion commanders read combat orders and instructions, in which it was written in black on white: "The corps on the morning of 12 July will enter into a breakthrough."

This was the mission for a Soviet tank corps, and the corps' command staffs were oriented toward just such a mission. The brigade commanders, battalion commanders and tank crews carried the same expectations: that the enemy's organized resistance in the sector would already be broken by the artillery and infantry, clearing the way for the follow-on mobile formations. They knew that it made no sense to advance the armor before a corridor had been cleared, or at least been swept of the enemy's anti-tank means.

However, the reality with which the tankers collided on the morning of 12 July was far from these expectations. Therefore when the armored vehicles reached the range of the anti-tank guns and encountered the enemy's well-organized and precisely directed anti-tank defense, the armor crews were simply stunned. Now under this storm of fire, they not only had to fight, but also first of all to make the psychological adjustment from the anticipation of a dash into the depth of the enemy's defenses to the reality of a difficult positional struggle with anti-tank defenses.

This was a particularly difficult adjustment to make for the brigade, battalion and company commanders. They were in the same predicament, under furious enemy artillery fire and bombing, as the crews of the line tanks. At the same time, however, they not only had to make the mental adjustment, but also within a few minutes to reach a correct decision, express it in a clear order and issue it to their subordinates. The outcome of the fighting, and the lives of hundreds of men, depended directly on their reaction and professionalism.

As participants of this engagement remembered, at this moment the airwaves turned into a frenzy of human emotions, and something incomprehensible happened over the radio waves. Together with the normal crackle of interference and dozens of commands and orders, the headsets picked up all those "terms of endearment," with which Russian men from all corners of the country had christened the Hanses, Fritzes, Fascists, Hitler and similar swine. The airwaves were so full of venomous Russian swearing that it seemed all this hatred might sudden turn into something material with which to strike the foe, together with the shells. As veterans later recounted, the tankers were also blistering their own leadership with their cursing for having tossed them into this furnace. Understanding that emotions had surged beyond the limits, and were not only hindering concentration, but also paralyzing the radio connections, the 18th Tank Corps in the clear demanded a halt to this hooliganism on the airwaves. The subordinate commanders and troops obeyed, but not for long …

Practically speaking, by 1100 the corps advance had been stopped by the dense, direct fire of artillery and enemy tanks. Until 1200, here and there companies and battalions attempted independent attacks, but without results. From a combat dispatch of the 18th Tank Corps headquarters sent at some point that afternoon:

> 1. The adversary is putting up stubborn resistance, and is falling back in the direction of Point 217.9 and the Komsomolets State Farm. The enemy artillery is conducting intensive fire on the corps' combat formations from the region of Greznoe.
>
> Enemy aviation conducted up to 1500 sorties on the corps' combat formations.
>
> 2. The neighbor on the left is exchanging fire for control over the Komsomolets State Farm.
>
> 3. The 18th Tank Corps is carrying out its assignment, and has reached the line: 110th Tank Brigade – 500 meters east of Mikhailovka; the 181st Tank Brigade – has occupied Oktiabr'skii State Farm, and is fighting on the line Andreevka – Hill 241.6; this message is being verified; the 170th Tank Brigade – is fighting on the line of the ravine southeast of Mikhailovka.
>
> Equipment losses: 11 Mk-IV tanks, 6 T-34 tanks and 4 T-70 tanks have been knocked-out or burned. Losses of equipment and personnel are being verified.
>
> 4. I am continuing to carry out the assignment. I request fighter air cover for the corps combat formations.
>
> 5. Command Post – northern edge of Petrovka.[50]

The combat diary of the II SS Panzer Corps reported, "Enemy tank units, attacking along the valley of the river to the south, penetrated *Adolf Hitler*'s weak flank cover and

Major (at the time of the battle Lieutenant Colonel) V. D. Tarasov, commander of the 18th Tank Corps' 170th Tank Brigade. (TsAMO)

attacked the artillery, where all the same the main portion of the hostile tanks were destroyed in close combat by fire over open sights."[51]

One must acknowledge that the lack of time for preparing the counterstroke and the insufficient cooperation between the headquarters of the 5th Guards Army and the 5th Guards Tank Army had a telling effect on the results of the combat operations – the artillerymen of the 42nd Guards Rifle Division and the 9th Guards Airborne Division did not succeed in giving substantial fire support to the attacking tank brigades of the 18th and 29th Tank Corps. After the battle, the *front* commander issued the following order on the results of the fighting on 12 July:

> In future operations, pay attention to the following:
>
> a) The power of artillery fire is not being used fully; in the rapid flow of combat, the artillery is lagging behind the infantry and tanks. In the future do not let the artillery lag behind. Suppress any resistance with massed artillery and mortar fire and coordinate the fire with the infantry weapons.
>
> b) *Many head-on attacks have been observed, and too little use has been made of maneuver to encircle the enemy* [Author's emphasis].
>
> c) Immediately eliminate the shortcoming in tactical operations; especially, thoroughly anticipate fortifying the achieved line with an all-round observation post and systems of anti-tank and antipersonnel fire in combination with engineered barriers.
>
> d) Pay attention to the better organization of mutually supporting fire.
>
> e) Report on the adopted measures.[52]

A pause settled over the offensive after the first assault failed. The mood in the brigades was depressed – everyone understood that the corps had encountered a well-organized defense, bristling with anti-tank weapons (I'll remind the reader: a panzer division had up to 100 anti-tank guns, while our tank corps had only 12). The entire field of battle was strewn with the wreckage of T-34s, T-70s and Churchills. As the tankers later recalled, the SS had registered and ranged in all the routes of attack vulnerable to tanks and had set up ambush locations. The enemy had thoroughly prepared to receive our attack. There was the sense that they had arrived here not just twenty-four hours ago, but had been there for a month already, at a minimum. And no one knew how many more combat vehicles and crew members would remain on this field …

The question arose before General Bakharov: "What's to be done?" A constant stream of reports was coming in from the brigades about the enemy's fierce resistance, the extremely heavy losses in the battalions and the limited advance. The 5th Guards Army's chief of staff Major General V. N. Baskakov, who was at army headquarters, also heard all of this clearly. They were reporting on the situation to the army commander, requesting clarification of their orders and appealing for air support. The army commander was replying: "Kirichenko has even greater losses, but he is hanging on and attacking; you also must attack, your assignment remains the same – attack!"

The recollections of the 5th Guards Tank Army's deputy chief of operations Lieutenant Colonel I. A. Dokunov relate the atmosphere and general tensions that were reigning at the 5th Guards Tank Army's observation post that day:

> … A low rise southwest of Prokhorovka. The observation post for the command staff of the 5th Guards Tank Army. Twirling one end of his mustache, General Rotmistrov is intently following the course of battle. Around him are staff officers, radio operators, and phone operators.
>
> … From the units, alarming radio dispatches began to arrive one after the other:
>
> 'Up to 100 tanks are attacking, we're exchanging heavy fire.'
>
> Another message:
>
> 'There are up to 200 enemy tanks in front of our defenses. Up to 50 tanks have bypassed our flank. I request permission to fall back. Bakharov.'
>
> Rotmistrov shouted back heatedly and with irritation, hurling the [paper] message on the parapet of the trench:
>
> 'What? Back!? Tell this forgetful fellow that a tank's gun can pivot 360° and is fully suitable for repulsing a tank attack. Not a step back! Tell him that! And tell him not to send me any more such messages. The [corps] command post will not be moved under any event! I categorically forbid it! I will check personally. Let them implement any regrouping of the corps, but without falling back. Ask him, incidentally, what his reserve is doing?'
>
> 'Comrade Commander, permit me to drive over to Bakharov and look into what's going on there, on location,' the chief of staff appealed to Rotmistrov.
>
> 'OK, Vladimir Nikolaevich [Baskakov]. Go and clarify the true situation. If necessary, make a decision in my name.'

General Baskakov drove off. Radio messages again began to arrive from the units.

'I'm suffering losses from heavy enemy artillery fire. I request air support.'

To which the commander replied:

'Tell him: Not a step back! Things are difficult for everyone, everyone is suffering losses. Strike the fascists with the least possible losses to your own troops!'

Another dispatch:

'The enemy is firing intensively from all types of weapons. There are cases of tank ramming. I request fire support. Egorov.'

'Tell him, I am seeing everything myself. The situation is equally difficult on every axis. More fire, but not a step back!'

In the afternoon, when the combat became particularly heated, the fascists conducted a new air strike on our combat formations. Now combat was unfolding on the land and in the air. Hitlerite and our own burning airplanes were plummeting to the earth from altitude in turn. Several enemy bombers exploded above the battlefield. Fragments of metal skin, fluttering in the sky, fell to the ground, literally like enormous wounded birds. In the sky, there was howling, rumbling, whistling, and the chatter of machine guns. In order to avoid hitting our own planes, our anti-aircraft gunners stopped firing at the enemy planes and switched their guns to the struggle against the enemy tanks.

Major General Baskakov reported:

'The enemy has gone on the offensive across the entire front. Bakharov is firing intensively. Of the 50 enemy tanks that had broken through, 20 have been destroyed and the remainder turned back.'

'Volodia,' the commander spoke up heatedly, 'the crisis of the battle is approaching, and you must hold out whatever the cost; not a step back! Tell Bakharov the same. We might all burn up, but not one meter back. From where are you speaking?'

'From a tank. I can see nothing, just a dense curtain of smoke. The Guardsmen are holding the line. We are standing firmly and we will continue to stand,' Baskakov concluded.

Again, bomb explosions swept across the field. The enemy had repeated an air raid on Prokhorovka. Enemy tanks continued to attack. At the cost of many tanks, left blazing on their path, a large group of tanks, with Tigers moving at the front, penetrated our defense on the left flank of the army.

Stubborn fighting began. An order was issued to bring up the reserves from the army's second echelon. The commander unfastened his tunic's collar, and wiping his high, prominent forehead with a kerchief, he asked:

'What's today's date?'

> 'The 12th of July, Comrade General,' the chief of operations on his staff Colonel F. M. Belozerov replied, smiling.
>
> 'And what a day!' Removing his glasses and wiping the lenses, the army commander added: 'We have to give credit to the enemy; he's acting in a coordinated fashion and energetically.'[53]

In order to bolster the offensive, B. S. Bakharov regrouped his forces for another effort. He decided to commit the 181st Tank Brigade and the 36th Guards Separate Heavy Tank Breakthrough Regiment into the center of his combat formations. Concerned (and not without reason) that the enemy might attempt to re-cross the Psel River from the north bank to the south, he decided call up the 110th Tank Brigade to protect the right flank of his corps, and sent the 170th Tank Brigade to protect his left. At 1200, the commander of the 110th Tank Brigade Colonel I. M. Kolesnikov was summoned to the corps command post in Petrovka. His brigade had still not entered the fighting; it had closed up to the combat formations of the 32nd Motorized Rifle Brigade east of Prelestnoe, where it received word that the corps' attack had been stopped. General Bakharov familiarized Kolesnikov with the existing situation and gave him an assignment to bring up his brigade out of the third echelon and to strengthen the corps' attack along the river in the direction of Vasil'evka and Greznoe. At the same time, he warned Kolesnikov that the enemy had made one attempt to cross to the south bank of the river that morning, and a second attempt to strike the corps' right flank could not be excluded.

While the orders were being defined more precisely, the battalion and company commanders, preparing for renewed fighting, reassembled their units in ravines and gullies, counted their losses, and the crews replenished the ammunition and topped up their tanks' fuel tanks. At 1300 Colonel Kolesnikov returned to his brigade and the 110th Tank Brigade began to move out in the direction of Mikhailovka.

Simultaneously over the radio, the corps commander issued an assignment to Lieutenant Colonel V. D. Tarasov's 170th Tank Brigade and Lieutenant Colonel V. A. Puzyrev's 181st Tank Brigade to resume the attack along the river toward Andreevka in coordination with the infantry units of the 9th Guards Airborne and the 42nd Guards Rifle Division. After seizing Andreevka, they were to pivot their front to the north.

German reconnaissance planes spotted the 110th Tank Brigade's departure from Prelestnoe and quickly summoned attack aircraft to this region. The 110th Tank Brigade's column was subjected to a most vicious bombing. In the course of it, a number of tank officers were killed and there were losses among the crews. The corps' chief of operations staff who had just arrived at the brigade, Lieutenant Colonel Oganesian, was wounded. This calamitous event delayed the brigade's arrival in its designated area for the attack.

The Oktiabr'skii State Farm was located on the boundary between the offensive sectors for the 18th Tank Corps and the 29th Tank Corps. At 1300, with the renewed push, tanks from the 29th Tank Corps finally broke into the northern portion of the State Farm with the assistance of the 170th and 181st Tank Brigades and infantry from the 42nd Guards Rifle Division and 9th Guards Airborne Division. However, this success gave no significant boost to the advance of Bakharov's corps. In the area of Hill 241.6, the SS had set up a powerful node of resistance, where a significant amount of *Leibstandarte*'s artillery regiment had been concentrated. According to information from the 42nd Guards Rifle Division's artillery commander, even 105mm and 155mm field guns had been positioned here, which strongly hindered our advance.

After cracking the German defenses on the Oktiabr'skii State Farm, the noticeably thinned battalions of the 170th Tank Brigade advanced with the 23rd Guards Airborne Rifle Regiment across the road leading from Mikhailovka to a crossing over the railroad, while Lieutenant Colonel Puzyrev's 181st Tank Brigade struck at Andreevka from Mikhailovka. The 36th Guards Separate Heavy Tank Breakthrough Regiment and the 127th Guards Rifle Regiment had been fighting here since approximately 1200, but with no success. The enemy had erected a strong barrier in their path.

In order to augment the strength of the next attack, at 1400 General Bakharov decided to introduce the first echelon of Colonel M. E. Khvatov's 32nd Motorized Rifle Brigade into the battle. It received the order to take Andreevka and to breakthrough further to Vasil'evka, with the help of the 181st Tank Brigade.

Approximately at 1430, the situation in 18th Tank Corps' sector began to sharpen substantially, as, incidentally, it did across the 5th Guards Tank Army's entire front. The SS had begun to launch short, but sharp panzer counterattacks. Hausser had guessed Bakharov's plan to drive to the bridge crossings at Bogoroditskoe and to trap a significant portion of Priess's *Totenkopf* division in the bridgehead north of the river. In order to prevent this, he issued an order to lay down a wall of artillery and *Nebelwerfer* fire on the 18th Tank Corps' assault wedge, while at the same time *Oberführer* Wisch's *Leibstandarte* launched several panzer counterattacks at its left flank.

Meanwhile, the Soviet defenders' situation north of the Psel River (in the 5th Guards Army's sector of attack) was deteriorating. Shortly after noon, *Totenkopf*'s armored group broke through the defenses of the 52nd Guards Rifle Division, overran the combat formations of the 95th Guards Rifle Division's 284th Guards Rifle Regiment as they were deploying for an attack, and emerged on the riverbank in the area of Polezhaev, thereby encircling units of the 11th Motorized Rifle Brigade in the process. From their vantage point on the high northern banks of the river, the 5th Guards Tank Army's formations were spread out before them as if on a banquet table. At 1300, 13 German tanks, including Tigers, took advantage of this favorable position, and exploiting the long-range capabilities of their guns, opened fire on the right flank and rear of our forces across the river. On the march toward Mikhailovka, Major Pleskach's leading 2nd Tank Battalion of the 110th Tank Brigade, which was advancing together with the 32nd Motorized Rifle Brigade's 2nd Motorized Rifle Battalion, was hit with concentrated tank fire from beyond the river. Simultaneously, the enemy launched two counterattacks: one with the forces of II/1st SS Panzer Regiment in the direction of Andreevka and Mikhailovka; the other – the 6th SS Panzergrenadier Regiment supported by a battalion of assault guns from the village of Kozlovka toward Vasil'evka. Thus, Bakharov's tankers and Bobrov's rifle units found themselves in a semi-circle of fire.

The situation in the 18th Tank Corps' sector was additionally complicated by the fact that by 1400, the 29th Tank Corps' attack south of the Oktiabr'skii State Farm had clearly failed: Wisch's forces had finally repulsed the 29th Tank Corps' attack on Hill 252.2; the forces of the 32nd Tank Brigade and 53rd Motorized Rifle Brigade on the

Komsomolets State Farm had been pocketed and were being reduced; and the composite battalion composed of the remnants of the 25th Tank Brigade had been thrown back to their starting positions. At the same time, *Das Reich* had pushed aside the right flank of the 2nd Guards 'Tatsinskaia' Tank Corps and had even managed to break through to the outskirts of Storozhevoe, and was steadily prying the 169th Tank Brigade and elements of the 58th Motorized Rifle Brigade out of the village.

Thus, by early afternoon the sole remaining "sore spot" in the II SS Panzer Corps's sector was the 18th Tank Corps, which was actively attacking the boundary between *Leibstandarte* and *Totenkopf*. Hausser accordingly concentrated all his effort on destroying the 18th Tank Corps' attacking units. In this situation, the 18th Tank Corps commander had no one left to count upon. All the 5th Guards Tank Army's reserves, except for two brigades of Major General Skvortsov's 5th Guards Mechanized Corps, had been exhausted, and the army commander had no strength left to render any real assistance.

An enemy attempt to cross to the south side of the Psel River in the flank of the 18th Tank Corps was thwarted by artillery fire and fire from the 18th Tank Corps' tank battalions. The enemy's panzer counterattacks on the left flank of the corps also did not develop into anything threatening. However, the general operational situation was clearly no longer in our favor. The foe had put up stiff resistance; in several sectors he had succeeded in throwing up earthworks. He had carefully arranged the anti-tank defenses, and was now conducting sharp counterattacks, in which primarily heavy tanks were participating.

A downed Ju 87 dive bomber in the zone of the 18th Tank Corps' offensive. (RGAKFD)

At 1500, Priess's headquarters reported, "In the course of the offensive at approximately 1455, we broke through to the western portion of Andreevka … In Vasil'evka, we are going on the offensive to the east."[54]

At 1430, the 36th Guards Separate Heavy Tank Breakthrough Regiment had finally reached the southwestern outskirts of Andreevka, but there it came under enemy tank fire and anti-tank fire. A bitter fight erupted with nine enemy tanks. The regiment was equipped with British Mk-IV Churchill tanks. With their short-barreled 57mm gun and thin armor, the troops had nicknamed them the "Fraternal Grave". Maneuvering under enemy fire, the two Churchills of Lieutenant Koriagin and Lieutenant Malyshev managed to close to within a half-kilometer of the German tanks and opened fire. As a result, as the regiment's combat diary informs, one Panzer IV was left burning and one Tiger was damaged. The German crews of the neighboring tanks concentrated their fire on these two impudent Churchills. Both received multiple hits and burst into flames, and the crew members received severe wounds.[55]

Having finally forced the stubborn German defenders to abandon Andreevka, the group attacking in the center of the 18th Tank Corps' combat formations (the 181st Tank Brigade, the 36th Guards Separate Heavy Tank Breakthrough Regiment, the 32nd Motorized Rifle Brigade and the 127th Guards Rifle Regiment) split up. Its main forces moved on to the west and by 1600 had reached the center of the village of Vasil'evka. But there it ran into heavy resistance from *Totenkopf*'s 6th SS Panzergrenadier Regiment.

Chief of staff of the 5th Guards Tank Army Major General V. N. Baskakov (on the left) and chief of operations Colonel F. M. Belozerov during a brief lull in the fighting in the area of Prokhorovka. (Author's personal archive)

Lieutenant Krivenko's company of Churchills was operating in concert with a battalion from the 32nd Motorized Rifle Brigade. As they moved toward the village center, they were met by well-organized fire from the vicinity of the church, where some anti-tank guns and four enemy tanks had been dug-in. In a difficult situation, exploiting every wrinkle in the terrain, the Soviet tank crews fought heroically. A shell penetrated Lieutenant Lupakhin's tank and it started to burn, but the crew continued to fire, until a fourth shell breached the front of the tank's turret and rendered the gun inoperable; driver-mechanic Junior Sergeant Staroverov was killed and the gunner Senior Sergeant Denin was wounded. With the gun now rendered inoperable, the remaining crew member abandoned the tank. Another shell struck the side of Lieutenant Pokhomov's tank and sent an armor fragment ricocheting around inside the tank, but almost miraculously none of the crew received a serious wound and they continued to fight until the day's end.

At the same time, the forces of the left wing of Bakharov's corps (the 170th Tank Brigade, part of the 181st Tank Brigade, several tanks from the 31st Tank Brigade mounting infantry from the 32nd Motorized Rifle Brigade) struck out along the gully leading from Andreevka to the southwest in the direction of Hill 241.6. The group attacked resolutely. Taking advantage of the terrain and the dense smoke of the battlefield, the tanks broke through the line of *Leibstandarte's* reconnaissance battalion and unexpectedly burst into the firing positions of the division's artillery regiment. Despite the fact that Wisch reacted swiftly to the situation and ordered SS *Sturmbannführer* Gross's II/1st SS Panzer Regiment to launch an immediate counterattack into the flank of the Russian tanks that were overrunning the artillery positions, the group could not be stopped quickly. On the side of our tankers was the factor of surprise and the confusion, arising from the complex situation in *Leibstandarte*'s sector. Within a short time, the 170th Tank Brigade was already fighting in the area of Ivanovskii Vyselok. Thus, Bakharov's brigades had managed almost fully to split the defenses of *Leibstandarte* and to emerge on its boundary with *Das Reich*, south of Komsomolets State Farm. At this moment, the crews of Major Ivanov's 1st Tank Battalion and the motorized riflemen of Lieutenant Colonel Lipichev's 53rd Motorized Rifle Brigade from the 29th Tank Corps were still fighting for their lives on the State Farm. However, the groups were unable to link up and to consolidate the success that lay so tantalizingly close.

There are several reasons for this. First, both groups were numerically small. Second, they didn't have any reliable communications between them or an experienced commander to take charge. By this time, as has already been mentioned, a number of the 170th Tank Brigade's senior officers had already been killed, including the brigade commander himself, while the staffs of the 18th and 29th Tank Corps, because of the absence of communications or organized cooperation, were not able to link the two groups from different corps operationally or to strengthen them with artillery, in order quickly to consolidate the ground gained. Third, in contrast, the command of the SS Panzer Corps had radio links with all the divisional command staffs and Hausser received a constant stream of information from the battlefield. Therefore, as soon as the success began to take shape, Hausser immediately concentrated panzer elements from both SS Panzergrenadier Division *Leibstandarte* and SS Panzergrenadier Division *Das Reich* against both of our tank groups at Komsomolets State Farm and Ivanovskii Vyselok.

In the course of this lunge into the heart of the enemy's defenses, the crew of the command tank of the 181st Tank Brigade's 2nd Battalion, led by Lieutenant I. Gusev, served as an example of self-sacrifice while saving a comrade and commander on the battlefield. When their T-34 burst into flames from a direct hit, the battalion commander Captain P. A. Skripkin, who was situated in the turret, received a severe wound. Driver-mechanic A. S. Nikolaev, loader Chernov and radio operator Zyrianov dragged their captain from the tank and carried him over to a shell crater.

On 11 August 1943, correspondent Junior Lieutenant P. Khor'kov described what happened next in an article for the 5th Guards Tank Army gazette, "*Na shturm* [Into the assault]":

> The Germans spotted the position of our tankers. A dust-colored Tiger, turning its enormous gun, moved directly toward the place, where the wounded Captain Skripkin was lying. Komsomol member Gusev in the burning tank continued to fire on the Tiger, but it kept coming and coming, drawing nearer with each second.
>
> 'Save the commander!' Nikolaev shouted to the radio operator … and leaping back into the flaming tank, he started it rolling directly at the Tiger.
>
> Nikolaev accelerated to high speed. The German tank tried to evade the conflagration flying towards it, hoping to stop it conclusively with a well-placed shot. But Nikolaev kept rushing directly at it. Suffocating in the scorched turret, he gripped the levers and saw only one thing – the Tiger – and wanted only one thing – to stop it, to save the life of his commander.

Destroyed equipment of the II SS Panzer Corps on a field southwest of Prokhorovka Station. Photo taken on 21 July 1943. (Author's personal archive)

> A column of flame and smoke rose above the spot of the collision, frightening in its force. The ruins of two wrecked tanks were wrapped in bright flame.[56]

The former chief of intelligence of the 2nd Tank Corps, at that time Lieutenant Colonel E. F. Ivanovsky recalled, "On the field at Prokhorovka, there were more than twenty incidents of a tank being used as a battering ram."[57]

In the memoir literature and in books on the Great Patriotic War, the self-sacrifice of soldiers and officers of the Red Army, including in the form of using a tank to ram an enemy tank, are seen as a manifestation of the highest patriotism. It is difficult to dispute this; however, in each individual case, the combat situation was different. Not in any way to condemn the decision of a man or woman to destroy the enemy even at the cost of life, let's heed the words of the professional tanker, Hero of the Soviet Union, Chief Marshal of the Armored Forces A. Kh. Babadzhanian[58]:

> … a tank ramming – with all its descriptive allure in the literature and writing on current affairs – was an exceptional matter. Not at all, however, because of the lack of a sufficient number of courageous men prepared to take it up. It is simply because a tank is not an airplane, and the earth is not the sky. It is fine if everything comes together, and your tank, giving a shove to the enemy tank, pushes it into a drainage ditch and it topples onto one side. More likely – you collide with it, hardly budge it from its place and, all the worse, inflict even more damage to your own tank. But of course, if your own tank is already burning and there is no salvation for you, then it is a different matter …
>
> The tank's task is to close to within a necessary range of the enemy and to fire on enemy tanks from their own gun. But to tear your own tracks on someone else's armor – that's … suicide. Even if there is a place for such a thing, then it is possible to excuse it, probably, only in the circumstance that it occurred in the very first days of the war. Subsequent experience didn't permit our tankers to carry out similarly poorly conceived acts …[59]

Not only soldiers and officers of the forward units displayed examples of courage, but also those of the special elements, without which a corps cannot operate successfully. From the combat dispatch of the chief of the 18th Tank Corps' political department, Colonel Romanov:

> … Medical orderly Sergeant Shepelenko from the 170th Tank Brigade on 12.07.43 carried 36 soldiers and their weapons from the field of battle, working twelve hours without stop. Comrade Shepelenko has been recommended for a government honor …
>
> Military doctor of the 181st Tank Brigade's 1st Tank Battalion Comrade Kruglikov on 12.07.43 at his own initiative drove into the combat zone and personally brought 20 wounded men and their weapons off the battlefield. Having rendered first aid to them, he organized their evacuation to a hospital. Comrade Kruglikov had been recommended for the Order of the Red Star.[60]

One has to have a deep sense of responsibility and professional duty, in order to leave the relatively safe rear area (where the medical services were usually located) without an order and to save human lives on the battlefield, under a storm of bullets and shell fragments. Likely, it was precisely for this humanism and their willingness to sacrifice themselves that the frontline soldiers so sincerely respected and reverently regarded the combat doctors.

From the account of the 5th Guards Tank Army's headquarters:

> By 1800 the brigades of the [18th Tank] corps had fully seized Vasil'evka and reached Kozlovka. On the line Hill 217.9 – 3 km southwest of Kozlovka – Hill 214.6, the corps encountered strong enemy fire. Assault guns, dug-in tanks, and heavy bombing from the air made the corps' further advance impossible.
>
> The corps commander ordered the units to dig in on the lines they had attained, and to organize all-round defenses – the 32nd Motorized Rifle Brigade and the 170th Tank Brigade with remnants of the 36th Guards Heavy Tank Regiment in the area: center of Vasil'evka – Mikhailovka – Prelestnoe; the 181st Tank Brigade – Petrovka; the 110th Tank Brigade – in the area (excl.) Petrovka – Beregovoe.[61]

By this time the 18th Tank Corps had advanced 7 kilometers from its start line and had penetrated more than 5 kilometers into the enemy defenses. This was the deepest penetration achieved of all the formations of the 5th Guards Tank Army on 12 July southwest of Prokhorovka.

Thus, from the very first minutes of the start of the counterattack that morning, it had started to diverge from the plan that had been worked out in the Voronezh Front headquarters. The first echelon of the 5th Guards Tank Army, delivering a powerful blow to the center of the II SS Panzer Corps southwest of Prokhorovka, had not achieved success. If before approximately 1430, its units had slowly ground forward and had seized the Oktiabr'skii State Farm and the Komsomolets State Farm and were fighting in Vasil'evka, then after that time the situation sharply changed for the worse. The adversary had figured out our plans, and with the strong fire of artillery and tanks and the support of the VIII Air Corps, had practically stopped the offensive. Soon after 1430, the II SS Panzer Corps had eliminated the 29th Tank Corps' tenuous hold over the Komsomolets State Farm, inflicting at the same time serious damage to the army's corps, after which it had begun to launch counterattacks on the flanks of the main grouping of P. A. Rotmistrov's army.

In order to augment the assault forces and to exploit albeit the only partial success in the sector of the 18th Tank Corps would require the commitment of the army's second echelon into the battle. But for a number of reasons, which will be discussed later, the 5th Guards Mechanized Corps could not be used on 12 July in this area.

★ ★ ★

The forces of General B. S. Bakharov's 18th Tank Corps conclusively went over to the defense at approximately 1900-1930. This was one of the tensest moments of the battle. On the left flank, in the sector of the 2nd Tank Corps, SS Panzergrenadier Division *Das Reich* as early as three hours before had seized Storozhevoe and, keeping constant pressure on our units, was trying to break through to Pravorot'. Rotmistrov himself personally drove to the 2nd Tank Corps command post in order to organize the defense. Having assessed the situation on the spot, Rotmistrov issued A. F. Popov an order: at 1930, from the area of Belenikhino, to attack the right flank of *Das Reich* with the strength of two tank brigades supported by motorized infantry in the direction of Ivanovskii Vyselok and the Komsomolets State Farm. At the same time, the 18th Tank Corps was supposed to attack from the opposite direction to link-up with the 2nd Tank Corps. However, Bakharov's corps failed to carry out the army commander's order.

Without exaggerations, one can assert that Bakharov had done everything within his powers to break the enemy resistance. His last attempt to overwhelm the anti-tank defense in Vasil'evka began with the commitment of the remnants of the 36th Guards Separate Heavy Tank Breakthrough Regiment into the fighting for the village at 1800. The regiment, however, was unable fundamentally to change the situation, after which it was given a new order: to halt the attack and switch to consolidating the achieved lines.

Bakharov issued this order independently, without an order from superior headquarters, although indeed under intense pressure from the serious situation he faced. This step provoked the serious dissatisfaction of the 5th Guards Tank Army's command. The subsequent order to the army on the results of the combat operations at Prokhorovka betrays this. The Military Council conspicuously avoided mention of the

Units of the 18th Tank Corps fighting on the outskirts of Vasil'evka. (RGAKFD)

Lieutenant Colonel N. P. Lipichev, commander of the 29th Tank Corps' 53rd Motorized Rifle Brigade (1945 photo). (TsAMO)

18th Tank Corps and its commander in its message that noted the combat service of the other corps commanders and all the brigade commanders of the 29th Tank Corps. It even positively mentioned Major N. A. Kurnosov, the commander of the 53rd Guards Separate Tank Regiment, the tankers of which on 12 July, without investigating the combat situation, engaged the 69th Army's 96th Tank Brigade in battle (a discussion of this fratricidal incident awaits our attention). This snub was unjustified. Judging the 18th Tank Corps' operations in this battle alone, its losses were 21% lower than that of its neighboring 29th Tank Corps, while it had made a deeper advance on the axis of the main attack.

From the first days of his corps' inclusion under the 5th Guards Tank Army's command, Boris Sergeevich Bakharov had not developed a relationship with its leadership. The army's Military Council had already on 10 July 1943 singled him out for the poor organization of the march to Prokhorovka: the unsatisfactory work of the forward detachment and the engineer units in inspecting and rebuilding bridges on the march route, and the significant number of vehicles left behind on the way. Other corps commanders showed similar failings (for example, in the 5th Guards Mechanized Corps itself), but in making this rebuke, it had failed to consider that the 18th Tank Corps was the first to reach the designated area and to move into its assigned position.

According to the testimony of the army's deputy chief of operations I. A. Dokukin, P. A. Rotmistrov was also not fully satisfied with the 18th Tank Corps commander's actions during the fighting on 12 July and therefore indeed sent his chief of staff V. N. Baskakov to him. Even though under difficult conditions, Bakharov had handled his

Captain P. A. Skripkin, commander of the 1st Tank Battalion of the 18th Tank Corps' 181st Tank Brigade, with his daughter in a 1941 photograph. (Author's personal archive)

forces professionally, his orders were fully considered, and properly responded to the demands of the situation. Sending his chief of staff to monitor the 18th Tank Corps' operations can only be seen as a demonstration of Rotmistrov's lack of confidence in the corps command and in B. S. Bakharov personally. Subsequently the relations between the two men soured totally, which immediately affected General Bakharov's career. On 25 July 1943, the State Defense Committee of the USSR relieved Major General Bakharov from command of the 18th Tank Corps for his "failure to handle his responsibilities" and reduced his post to that of deputy commander of the 9th Tank Corps.[62]

There is also reason to assume that General B. S. Bakharov was removed from his post as a result of the work of G. M. Malenkov's commission. I. V. Stalin had sent Malenkov to the Voronezh Front to investigate the circumstances of the unsuccessful counterattack on 12 July 1943. In light of everything discussed above, this supposition is fully reasonable, but it is still too early to assert with 100% confidence – many documents are still classified.

According to the testimony of officers who had the opportunity to serve under General B. S. Bakharov, he was a competent corps commander; thus it is unsurprising that already by 9 September 1943, he was promoted to command the 9th Tank Corps. Under his command, the corps took part in a number of offensive operations and particularly distinguished itself in the fighting on the Dnepr River and during the liberation of Bobruisk. He remained in this post until the day of his death in the summer of 1944 from a German anti-tank shell.

But let's return to the events of 12 July 1943. Cursory combat results of the 18th Tank Corps were summed up in Dispatch No. 38 from 13 July 1943:

> 1. The enemy in the course of the day 12.07.43 after stubborn fighting abandoned the populated points of Iamki, the Oktiabr'skii State Farm, the Komsomolets State Farm and the grove west of Teterevino; subsequently it undertook a frontal tank counterattack and an attempt to bypass [the corps] in the direction of Kozlovka, Polezhaev, using their Tiger tanks and self-propelled guns.
>
> 2. Carrying out the day's assignment – to reach the Belgorod highway, the 18th Tank Corps unexpectedly ran into well-organized, strong enemy resistance, with previously dug-in tanks and assault guns on the line of Hills 217.9 – 241.6.
>
> Suffering heavy losses, the corps with great difficulty advanced toward its designated line, but it was unable to carry out the assignment as a consequence of the aforementioned circumstances.
>
> Upon my Order No. 68, the units of the corps went over to a defense of the occupied areas:
>
> 32nd Motorized Rifle Battalion with the forward detachment tank brigade and the 36th Guards [Heavy] Tank Regiment – the area: center of Vasil'evka – Mikhailovka – Prelestnoe.
>
> 181st Tank Brigade – the area of Petrovka.
>
> 110th Tank Brigade – the area (excl.) Petrovka – Beregovoe.
>
> The artillery has been given the order to prevent the advance of enemy infantry and tanks east of the lines:
>
> a) Vasil'evka – Komsomolets State Farm.
>
> b) Psel River (northwest).
>
> Also to prevent the movement of enemy tanks on the road Veselyi – Polezhaev – Voroshilovskii State Farm.
>
> The 1694th Anti-aircraft Artillery Regiment is to cover the area of defense from enemy air attacks with its primary firing positions in the region of Beregovoe.
>
> 1. According to preliminary information, the corps suffered losses in infantry of up to 20%, in tanks of up to 30%.
>
> In the fighting today, the corps lost 8 men of the senior command and of the command staff:
>
> 1. Commander of the 170th Tank Brigade Lieutenant Colonel Tarasov – killed
> 2. Commander of 1st Battalion of the 170th Tank Brigade Captain Isaev – mortally wounded
> 3. Corps engineer Lieutenant Colonel Belov – killed
> 4. Commander of the 1st Battalion of the 181st Tank Brigade Major Garibian – wounded
> 5. Commander of the 2nd Battalion of the 181st Tank Brigade Captain Skripkin – wounded
> 6. Deputy commander of the 181st Tank Brigade Major Grigor'iants – wounded
> 7. Corps chief of operations Lieutenant Colonel Martirosov – wounded
> 8. Commander of the 414th Sapper Battalion – wounded

9. Tank losses: T-34 – 25, T-70 – 15, Churchill – 15. Losses inflicted on the enemy are still being verified.
2. Command post – southern outskirts of Beregovoe.[63]

According to revised data, over the day of fighting the 18th Tank Corps lost 84 tanks of the 149 tanks that participated in the attack; that is, more than half. Especially vital damage in armor was suffered by the tank brigades of the first echelon: the 170th Tank Brigade – 74% and the 181st Tank Brigade – 61% (see Table 21).

Thus, without going into details, in the area of Oktiabr'skii State Farm – Hill 252.2 – Lutovo, from the two corps of the 5th Guards Tank Army and the 33rd Guards Rifle Corps of the 5th Guards Army the enemy knocked-out a number of armored vehicles equivalent to that of a full-strength tank corps and half of its personnel (around 4,500 men). What were the primary reasons seen by the Soviet command for why the two major tank formations of a Guards army not only were unable to carry out their assigned missions, but also suffered such high losses having advanced only a few kilometers? A single document, which might analyze the reasons for such catastrophic consequences in detail, has not been discovered in the Central Archives of the Ministry of Defense of the Russian Federation to the present day. Nevertheless, I managed to find a number of accounts, orders and reports, in which the leadership of the 5th Guards Tank Army and of its subordinate formations offered their explanations. Thus, the Army command considered that the cause of the failure and high losses was:

A. The absence of necessary artillery (especially howitzer) and air support (the *front* had no air cover) at the start of and during the battle, the removal of the 10th Destroyer Anti-tank Artillery Brigade from army control, and the absence of the 1529th Heavy Self-propelled Artillery Regiment.
B. The change in the corps' jumping-off line [caused by the German advance on 11 July] rendered all the preparation for the artillery's deployment useless.
C. The enemy's introduction of heavy tanks of the types Tiger and "Panzer IVN" (as Soviet documents of those times sometimes labeled any updated German Panzer IV tanks) into the battle.
D. The absence of teamwork among the corps' staff officers and inability of the corps commanders to bring up forces and means quickly and expeditiously in order to consolidate ground gained and to reinforce success. As an example, there is the fighting in the area of the Komsomolets State Farm, which changed hands five times over the course of the battle, but the forces of both corps were unable to hold it.
E. The poor training and unskilled work of the middle and senior command staff, including the brigade commanders. It was observed that commanders do not know how to issue proper orders or how to explain them to subordinates. As a result, the crews know the tasks standing before the army better than they know their own platoon or company's tasks. This particularly adversely affected their actions, when communications with the battalion broke down

and brigade commanders were lost. In the fighting of 12 July at Prokhorovka, this problem became particularly acute.
F. The inability of the commander of the 18th Tank Corps General B. S. Bakharov to evaluate the situation correctly and to react to it.
G. The gun on the T-34 tank was unable to destroy the enemy's medium and heavy tanks at a range of 600 meters and greater, while the gun on enemy vehicles could damage our tanks even out to a range of 1200-1500 meters. Because of this, the formations suffered losses even during the approach stage.

The subordinate corps commands offered the following reasons:

A. The great activity of enemy aviation and the absence of air cover (in the opinion of the 18th Tank Corps).
B. The selection of the area for the jumping-off positions and the brigade's lines of deployment was incorrect (18th Tank Corps).
C. The enemy's systems of fire on its line of defense had not been suppressed during the morning artillery preparation (29th Tank Corps).
D. The enemy was able to stop the corps with a well-organized anti-tank line, bristling with anti-tank means; knocked out our tanks; and then brought up reserves and counterattacked (29th Tank Corps).
E. The artillery command of certain rifle divisions of the 5th Guards Army did not wish to help our tankers with fire during the assault on Oktiabr'skii State Farm (29th Tank Corps).

A female combat medic renders aid to a wounded mortar man while the rest of the crew continues to fire. (RGAKFD)

F. The 31st Tank Brigade stood pat and did not exploit the success of the 32nd Tank Brigade [Author's note: This was General Kirichenko's opinion, which in my view is highly questionable].
G. The corps rushed ahead and being unsupported by the neighboring 29th Corps, wound up semi-encircled and was not in a condition to develop the success (the 18th Tank Corps).

To all the aforementioned, I want to add the following. On the morning of 12 July, there were 191 T-34s and 19 Mk-IVs, which had a frontal armor thickness of 60mm and greater, in formation in Bakharov's and Kirichenko's corps. Due to the terrain, the corps' sectors were reduced to a combined 5 kilometers; consequently, the density of tanks theoretically reached the point of 42 tanks per square kilometer of front. At the same time, the density of enemy anti-tank guns (50mm-88mm) and guns, which confronted the 5th Guards Tank Army in the sector of SS Panzergrenadier Division *Leibstandarte* alone, was up to 25 gun barrels per kilometer. If though you consider the *Wespe*, *Hummel* and *Brummbär* self-propelled artillery vehicles, which also participated in localizing the penetration in the line of Wisch's division, then this number rises to 31 gun barrels per kilometer. Moreover, during the fighting it became clear that panzers of the SS Panzergrenadier Division *Totenkopf* were firing on units of the 18th Tank Corps during its attack, and the attack of the 29th Tank Corps' 25th Tank Brigade on the boundary between *Leibstandarte* and *Das Reich* had been repulsed with the assistance of *Das Reich*'s SS 2nd Panzer Regiment. Considering these additional factors, it is possible to assume that where the Soviet tank formations managed to achieve a limited success, the SS had swiftly created a density of tanks and anti-tank guns (during the counterattack) of greater than 31 gun barrels per square kilometer of the front.

I consider it hardly possible to count upon success, given such a correlation of forces. The Soviet command, likely, was unaware of such unfavorable conditions on the sector it had chosen to commit the 5th Guards Tank Army. Or perhaps they suspected it, but didn't want to believe it. The high density of anti-tank weaponry in SS Panzergrenadier Division *Leibstandarte*'s defense, which its personnel had skillfully stitched together into an integrated system of fire, indeed was one of the main reasons for the tragedy that befell Rotmistrov's two tank corps.

However, the 18th and 29th Tank Corps were only a portion of Rotmistrov's army. We'll now turn to examine how events unfolded in the attack sectors of the other corps that took part in the counterstroke. According to the 5th Guards Tank Army commander's plan, the attack of these corps was strictly connected, including in time, to the combat results of the army's main shock grouping, consisting of the 18th and 29th Tank Corps.

The 2nd Guards 'Tatsinskaia' Tank Corps was attacking on a secondary axis, but in cooperation with the 5th Guards Tank Army's 29th Tank Corps, it was to carry out a very important assignment. By 1000, the latter corps was supposed to have crushed the Germans' forward defenses between Oktiabr'skii State Farm and Iamki, split the SS Panzergrenadier Division *Leibstandarte*, and having reached Komsomolets State Farm, it was to pivot to the south. At this time, approximately between 1000 and 1100, the

2nd Guards 'Tatsinskaia' Tank Corps was supposed to go on the offensive along the Iasnaia Poliana – Kalinin – Ozerovskii – Sobachevskii axis, and with part of its forces in conjunction with the 29th Tank Corps' brigades to have encircled the enemy in the area of Storozhevoe and Iamki, while its left wing by 1700 was to penetrate to the area of Iakovlevo.

The 2nd Tank Corps and units of the 183rd Rifle Division were to destroy the encircled enemy in the area of Storozhevoe. This is just what Rotmistrov had in mind, when he sent the instruction to A. F Popov to assemble his corps in the area of Storozhevoe, once he [Rotmistrov] had received word that Kirichenko's 32nd Tank Brigade and 53rd Motorized Rifle Brigade had reached the Komsomolets State Farm.

According to Rotmistrov's grand design, while the 2nd Guards 'Tatsinskaia' Tank Corps and the 29th Tank Corps were encircling the enemy in the Storozhevoe area, the 18th Tank Corps attacking on the right flank was to have reached Greznoe, thereby cutting off the bulk of SS Panzergrenadier Division *Totenkopf* in the bend of the Psel River from the rest of the II SS Panzer Corps. This enemy group would then be destroyed by the 5th Guards Army with the support of the 18th Tank Corps, while the 29th Tank Corps and 2nd Guards Tank Corps were to continue the offensive to Iakovlevo. Thus, the 2nd Guards 'Tatsinskaia' Tank Corps had been given an important role: to drive SS Panzergrenadier Division *Das Reich* from its positions and to prevent the escape of the Germans from the "corridor" between the Psel River and Storozhevoe. However, it is difficult to understand how the *front* leadership could have failed to understand that a single tank corps could not shoulder such an ambitious assignment.

Lieutenant Colonel S. M. Bulygin's 25th Guards Tank Brigade of the 2nd Guards Tank Corps was assembled in the village of Vinogradovka. With the support of Major Zotov's 1500th Destroyer Anti-tank Artillery Regiment, it was to attack in the direction of Iasnaia Poliana and Ozerovskii. On its left, the 4th Guards Tank Brigade under the command of Colonel A. K. Brazhnikov would attack toward Kalinin. Behind and somewhat to the left of the 4th Guards Tank Brigade, Colonel V. L. Savchenko's 4th Guards Motorized Rifle Brigade was to operate in the direction of Sobachevskii and the northwestern outskirts of Luchki. The right flank of the corps was reinforced with Colonel S. K. Nesterov's 26th Guards Tank Brigade. It was to attack from the woods east of Vinogradovka, behind the 25th Guards Tank Brigade.

At the start of the counterattack, the 4th Guards Tank Brigade and 4th Guards Motorized Rifle Brigade, operating in the direction of Kalinin and Sobachevskii, were to receive fire support from the 273rd Mortar Regiment, which had deployed east of Ivanovka at midnight. After the attack start, this regiment shifted to the operational control of Colonel Savchenko. The 755th Separate Destroyer Anti-tank Artillery Battalion was assembled in Ivanovka. After the corps reached Iasnaia Poliana, the 755th Anti-tank Battalion was to move to the western edge of Belenikhino Station, to stand ready in case of necessity to render assistance to units of the corps with its anti-tank guns. The 2nd Guards 'Tatsinskaia' Tank Corps was being covered from air attacks by Major Sereda's 1695th Anti-aircraft Artillery Regiment, deployed in the villages of Ivanovka and Vinogradovka. The 2nd Guards 'Tatsinskaia' Tank Corps was also given the 16th Guards Mortar Regiment of rocket artillery as reinforcement.

In the first minutes of the battle, our units would have to overcome a heavily mined railroad embankment. Overnight before the morning of 12 July, soldiers of the 51st

Motorized Sapper Battalion together with the brigades' engineering elements had cut passages through the railroad embankment and had cleared the minefields in the path of the corps' offensive.

The morning of 12 July, the 5th Guards Tank Army headquarters received the news about the breakthrough of major forces of Army Detachment Kempf's III Panzer Corps in the 69th Army sector. At 0600, Colonel A. S. Burdeiny sent the following dispatch:

> To Vatutin, Shtevnev, Rotmistrov. The enemy has seized Rzhavets and Ryndinka with tanks, and is moving on Avdeevka and Plota. I have decided to position the 26th Guards Tank Brigade east and southeast of Plota.[64]

An hour and forty minutes later, another dispatch arrived from the 2nd Guards 'Tatsinskaia' Tank Corps headquarters:

> To Vatutin, Shtevnev, Rotmistrov. 6 enemy tanks have crossed the Northern Donets in the area of Ryndinka. After the crossing, the bridge was damaged by our sappers. The enemy is making a crossing in this area. The 26th Guards Tank Brigade has been given the assignment to destroy the tanks that have crossed and to prevent an enemy crossing in the area of Ryndinka.[65]

The departure of the 26th Guards Tank Brigade noticeably weakened the corps attack; of the corps' 141 operational tanks before the attack, 44 were removed from the sector of the offensive. This limited the possibilities of the corps commander in maneuvering his forces and reserves, the latter of which he now had practically none.

After a brief artillery barrage on the enemy's forward defenses, at 1115, three digits rang out over the airwaves: "555" – the signal for the general offensive. The tankers of the 25th Guards Tank Brigade were the first to reach the Germans' defenses, and they were immediately subjected to a salvo from *Nebelwerfer* batteries positioned near the Komsomolets State Farm and Ivanovskii Vyselok. At the same time, 20 German bombers struck the brigade's combat formations. The 25th Guards Tank Brigade was unable to break through directly to Iasnaia Poliana, so Lieutenant Colonel Bulygin directed his 1st Tank Battalion into the woods south of the village, with orders to destroy enemy artillery batteries positioned on its outskirts. At 1200, the battalion's tankers impetuously plunged into the woods and within thirty minutes took full possession of them, but they were unable to advance any farther. The SS had created a strong anti-tank defense on this axis.

A T-34 platoon from the 1st Tank Battalion, commanded by Junior Lieutenant Grazhdankin, was sent out on a reconnaissance foray. At high speed and firing from its main guns, our tankers burst into the small village of Ozerovskii. Despite the enemy's numerical superiority, the platoon commander quickly reconnoitered the area and sent a message of his findings back to the battalion commander, but decided to remain in the village and fight it out. As the result of an unequal struggle, the courageous crew was killed, but not before destroying up to ten enemy vehicles and up to a platoon of infantry, and more importantly, providing important intelligence to the brigade command.

At 1400 Colonel V. L Savchenko's motorized riflemen reached the line Ozerovskii – Sobachevskii, but there they were stopped by heavy mortar fire. Near 1500, an advance platoon of T-34s (three tanks) of the 4th Guards Tank Brigade burst into the southeastern outskirts of Kalinin, but found its path blocked by 12 enemy panzers. The platoon was wiped out, and the heavy fire from the southern outskirts of Kalinin, plus a new wave of enemy bombers, forced the 4th Guards Tank Brigade commander to halt the attack. The brigade's elements fell back to a position about 600 meters southeast of Kalinin and took up a defensive position there, leaving the 4th Guards Motorized Rifle Brigade's right flank exposed.

From a combat dispatch issued by SS Panzergrenadier Division *Das Reich*:

> 1200 [1400 Moscow time]. An enemy attack with the strength of approximately 70 tanks on I/SS Regiment *Der Führer* in the area of Iasnaia Poliana.
>
> 1350 [1550]. The attack was beaten back.
>
> 1205 [1405]. An enemy attack with 40 tanks from Belenikhino on the left flank of II/SS Regiment *Der Führer* immediately north of Kalinin, and with ten tanks on the right flank. The opponent breaks through, [but] is liquidated in a counterattack.
>
> 1540 [1740]. The panzer regiment reports: two tank attacks of the adversary on both sides of Kalinin have been repulsed; 21 enemy tanks have been knocked-out and one Martin bomber (?) destroyed.[66]

Having repulsed the 'Tatsinskaia' Tank Corps' attack, the enemy went on the offensive. Around 1500 II/SS Regiment *Deutschland* attacked Storozhevoe and cleared our defenders from the southern portion of the village and the wooded sector to the south, while another part of its forces took possession of the northern outskirts of Vinogradovka. A genuine threat arose to the positions of the corps artillery in Ivanovka and the headquarters of the 2nd Guards 'Tatsinskaia' Tank Corps in Plota. The corps commander understood that a very dangerous situation had developed.

At 1450, A. S. Burdeiny sent Rotmistrov the following dispatch:

> ... According to information from the 25th Guards Tank Brigade commander, the enemy with a force of up to 15 tanks and up to a battalion of infantry has seized Storozhevoe. 15 tanks with infantry from the direction of Teterevino are in motion toward Vinogradovka.[67]

Ten minutes later in a new dispatch, he offered updated information:

> ... According to information from the 25th Guards Tank Brigade commander, the enemy with a force of up to 6 tanks and motorized infantry has seized Storozhevoe. Up to 15 enemy tanks and a battalion of motorized infantry are moving from Ivanovskii Vyselok toward Vinogradovka. Up to a battalion of infantry with tanks are moving from Teterevino toward Vinogradovka. [Our] neighbor on the right, the 2nd Tank Corps, is showing no activity and is suffering great losses. My right flank is exposed.[68]

At about this time, a scout team captured a junior officer from the 167th Infantry Division's 339th Infantry Regiment in the vicinity of Kalinin. Based on his information, it was decided that the enemy had brought up forces from other sectors of the front. This was an incorrect conclusion, since although this regiment was part of the 167th Infantry Division, prior to 10 July it had been fighting some distance away from the rest of the division.

Under the pressure from the threat to the corps' right flank (by now the departed 26th Guards Tank Brigade was acutely missed) and likely because of the information obtained from the prisoner interrogation, Colonel Burdeiny decided to regroup his forces. Over the radio he issued an order to the 25th Guards Tank Brigade commander to halt his attack and to pull his brigade back to the vicinity of a grove southeast of Vinogradovka, giving it the assignment to cover the corps' right flank and to block further progress by the enemy. At 1700 Lieutenant Colonel Bulygin passed the order on to his subordinate units to break off the fighting and withdraw, but it wasn't simple to carry it out. An attempt to pull back directly to the indicated area was unsuccessful: enemy artillery at Vinogradovka had all the open terrain in the area under fire. The tanks had to follow a circuitous route: northern outskirts of Kalinin – southern outskirts of Ivanovka – woods east of Ivanovka – woods east of Vinogradovka.

From the daily summary of SS Panzergrenadier Division *Das Reich*:

> There are fierce attacks of infantry and tanks on the division's sector in the course of the entire day, which are being repelled by fire from all types of weapons. Local breakthroughs on the left flank of the 167th Infantry Division have been thrown back by counterattacks and are continuing to be repulsed.
>
> 1505 [1705 Moscow time]. Regiment 2 is attacking the northern part of Storozhevoe toward the east. Two "Ils" [*Shturmoviki*] have been shot down. While writing this report, fighting still continues at lower intensity. The division anticipates additional enemy tank attacks on the sector Storozhevoe – Kalinin. From the assault units and anti-aircraft batteries there are still no reports. Addendum: At 1600 [1800] Storozhevoe was occupied. The link with the division *"Adolf Hitler"* remains intact.
>
> Augmented enemy infantry units are attacking the sector of the 167th Infantry Division, with which a link has been established for a long time. Enemy air activity is very insignificant …[69]

From an order of the 167th Infantry Division's commander on 12 July:

> The enemy at 1230 [1430 Moscow time] went on the offensive with the support of numerous tanks southeast of Kalinin. The attack was repelled in cooperation with *Das Reich*'s assault gun battalion. Altogether 8 tanks were knocked-out. The enemy offensive with the strength of one regiment northeast of Luchki, in the course of which he succeeded in making a small penetration, was thrown back by a counterattack of our units and by concentrated artillery fire. The same lot befell the enemy southeast of Luchki.[70]

However, the attack on Storozhevoe and the appearance of German units on the outskirts of Vinogradovka marked only the beginning of the SS Panzergrenadier Division *Das Reich*'s offensive. It was conducted with well-organized bomber support.

As soon as *Das Reich* reached Vinogradovka, up to 40 aircraft attacked the positions of the 4th Guards Tank Brigade and the 4th Guards Motorized Rifle Brigade at Kalinin.

The joint attack of *Das Reich*'s SS Panzergrenadier Regiment *Deutschland* and SS Panzer Regiment 2 on Storozhevoe continued. The SS were plainly striving to reach Pravorot'. At the same time, the commander of the SS Panzergrenadier Regiment *Der Führer, Obersturmbannführer* S. Stadler,[71] exploiting the departure of the 4th Guards Tank Brigade from Kalinin, together with the 167th Infantry Division's 339th Infantry Regiment and with tank support, struck the exposed flank of the 4th Guards Motorized Rifle Brigade and, as follows from the "Account of combat operations of the 2nd Guards 'Tatsinskaia' Tank Corps", seized Belenikhino Station and Ivanovka.[72] However, this information is incorrect: likely, in the turmoil of the battle, preliminary information entered the staff's files. The tankers of the 4th Guards Tank Brigade and the motorized riflemen of the 4th Guards Motorized Rifle Brigade withstood the German attack and until 1800 held firmly to their occupied lines, several hundred meters from Kalinin. However, when the information arrived that the SS were now fighting in Storozhevoe, while the 25th Guards Tank Brigade had still not reached Vinogradovka, the corps commander issued the order to Colonel A. K. Brazhnikov, the commander of the 4th Guards Tank Brigade, to fall back to his previous line, Belenikhino Station – Ivanovka.

Colonel V. L. Savchenko's 4th Guards Motorized Rifle Brigade was only withdrawn two hours later; its battalions were covering the withdrawal of the 4th Guards Tank Brigade. Savchenko's formation on 12 July wound up in a very tough situation. After the tank battalions of the 4th Guards Tank Brigade departed from Kalinin, Savchenko's brigade repulsed an enemy panzer attack, after which it was subjected to an aerial attack consisting of 28 Ju 87 Stukas, 12 Macchi MC.200 Italian fighter-bombers, and 12 Ju 87 G-1 Stuka tank-hunters. This was followed by a mistaken attack of Soviet Il-2s and bombers on the brigade's combat outposts and the positions of its neighbor, the 4th Guards Tank Brigade between 1700 and 1800. The two attacks cost the 4th Motorized Rifle Brigade 272 casualties. The 1st Rifle Battalion was hit particularly hard – it losses comprised 141 killed and wounded.[73]

If until 1500 the 2nd Guards Tank Corps had still been attacking, advancing meter by meter, then after that time the situation changed. *Gruppenführer* Krüger's SS Panzergrenadier Division *Das Reich* had not only stopped the advance of the Guards corps, but was now even persistently trying to break through into its rear. A.S. Burdeiny properly evaluated the situation that was taking shape; he understood that further attacks were useless. The opponent, having set down a powerful barrier in the path of the 2nd Guards Tank Corps' offensive, was trying to turn its right flank and emerge in its rear. Weakened by the preceding fighting, stripped of one of its tank brigades, and with no support from its neighbors, the 2nd Guards 'Tatsinskaia' Tank Corps was still holding on, but the initiative had passed to the enemy. At 2000 the corps commander issued an order to halt active combat operations.

Again, documents and reports from the sector of the 2nd Guards 'Tatsinskaia' Tank Corps contain no mention of any meeting engagement of massed tank formations or any penetrating enemy attack in the course of the entire day of 12 July. The II SS Panzer Corps command, having received intelligence about the assembly of major armored formations on the corps front, sent out an order to all the division commanders to assume a defensive posture with most of their forces. As the combat operations on 12

July demonstrated, this decision of Paul Hausser, unfortunately, proved to be far-sighted and resulted in substantial losses for the Soviet forces.

The results of the 2nd Guards 'Tatsinskaia' Tank Corps offensive were far from what had been expected. Its forces were compelled to abandon the line it had achieved (falling back approximately 3-4 kilometers), while losing 54 of the 94 tanks that had taken part in the counterattack, and 533 men, including 162 killed or missing in action (Table 22).[74]

One of the major reasons for the failure of our forces in the region of Storozhevoe, Belenikhino, Kalinin and Teterevino was the fact that the Soviet command was unable to create a unified assault group from the tank brigades of the Guards corps and the rifle divisions of the 48th Rifle Corps, which was defending in this area. Cooperation was lacking between the headquarters of the 2nd Guards Tank Corps and the 183rd Rifle Division, as well as with the 5th Guards 'Stalingrad' Tank Corps' 6th Guards Motorized Rifle Brigade, which had been left in position here as far back as 9 July. As numerous documents testify, the command of the divisions and brigades were carrying out only those assignments that they had received from superior headquarters in the direct chain of command, with no cooperation with neighboring divisions or brigades. The tank corps, in its turn, operated virtually independently here from the defending rifle units in its attack sector.

The war diary of the 6th Guards Motorized Rifle Brigade for 12 July gives a clear example of this lack of coordinated action:

> The 2nd Guards Tank Corps went on the offensive in the general direction of Luchki. *The tanks burst into the outskirts of Kalinin and, lacking the proper support of infantry and artillery came back again. In order to develop the success, the 456th Motorized Rifle Battalion was thrown into the attack* [author's emphasis]. Breaking into the outskirts of Kalinin, the battalion encountered heavy artillery-mortar, machine-gun and small-arms fire. The tanks and infantry of the 2nd Guards 'T' Tank Corps fell back again, and thus the 456th Guards Motorized Rifle Battalion also withdrew to its jumping-off positions. In this combat the battalion lost 49 men killed and wounded. Two enemy aircraft were shot down by machine-gun and small-arms fire.[75]

Agreement was absent not only in the objectives, but also in the start times for the offensive. The disjointed attacks allowed the Germans to repulse each attack in turn. Thus, Major General A. S. Kostitsyn's 183rd Rifle Division, receiving the order to destroy the enemy in the Kalinin – Ozerovskii – Hill 232.0 area, went on the attack at 1310, that is, after the tank brigades of the 'Tatsinskaia' Tank Corps had already been fighting on this axis for more than three hours, had suffered major losses in equipment, and after the SS had pinned down their motorized rifle squads with *Nebelwerfer* fire. At the moment of its attack, the 183rd Rifle Division's orders no longer made any sense; rising into the attack, as had the infantry of the other units before them, its regiments were unable to take Kalinin and were pinned down on the very same lines. However, because of the lack of cooperation and agreement between the headquarters of the 2nd Guards 'Tatsinskaia' Tank Corps and the 48th Rifle Corps, no one could call off the attack. Two regiments alone of the 183rd Rifle Division – the 158th Guards and 227th

Rifle Regiments – lost 28 killed and 150 wounded in this attack, without obtaining practically any results whatsoever.

Major General V. V. Tikhomirov's 93rd Guards Rifle Division also wound up in difficult circumstances. The division attacked units of the 167th Infantry Division on the front (excl.) Teterevino – (excl.) Soshenkov, though the evening before, it had less than a half-day's worth of ammunition left, and was unable to replenish its ammunition overnight. Owing to the heroic actions of its soldiers and officers, the enemy was driven from Petrovskii. However, the relative strength of the two sides was plainly unequal. A 167th Infantry Division order from 12 July notes,

> An enemy breakthrough northeast of Smorodino was liquidated by our units with heavy losses to their side. At Soshenkov they managed to create a bridgehead on the eastern bank of the Donets River. The 627th Pioneer Battalion is blocking enemy infiltrations to the west and south toward Petrovka.

The 2nd Tank Corps was the weakest formation in the 5th Guards Tank Army. Already by 10 July it had lost half of its authorized armor; in some brigades, only one-fifth of their combat vehicles remained. Therefore Major General A. F. Popov was given the order to hold his tank corps on its present line and to cover the boundary between the 29th Tank Corps and the 2nd Guards 'Tatsinskaia' Tank Corps on its left. The plan anticipated that it would only be employed on the attack if the counterattack was making good progress. If this didn't occur, it was to defend its current line. The 2nd Tank Corps' strength in equipment and men on 10 July 1943 is shown in Table 23.

On 12 July at 0300 in connection with the delay in the start time for the offensive, Rotmistrov sent a messenger to the 2nd Tank Corps with the following combat instruction:

> To the commander of the 2nd Tank Corps.
>
> 1. [Your] task remains the same; that is to allow the combat formations of the 18th and 29th Tank Corps to pass through your lines, to be ready to exploit their success or to attack, securing the army's right flank at Sukh. Solotino.
> 2. Support the attack of the 18th and 29th Tank Corps with all available weapons.
>
> Attack start – at 0830 12.07.43.
>
> Start of artillery preparation – at 0800. Radio use authorized from 0700 12.07.43.[76]

On the night of 11 July, A. F. Popov's formation, using the military jargon of those years, had been "yanked apart" [*razdergano*]; that is, its brigades were scattered, fighting in various areas, each with its own sector, like infantry units. The 169th Tank Brigade together with a portion of the 183rd Rifle Division's 285th Rifle Regiment was defending Storozhevoe, with its tanks dug-in. That morning, Popov had also sent the 2nd Motorized Rifle Battalion of Colonel Boldyrev's 58th Motorized Rifle Brigade to the 169th Tank Brigade's commander I. Ia. Stepanov, in order to stiffen the defense at Storozhevoe.

The other two battalions of the 58th Motorized Rifle Brigade were occupying defensive positions at Iamki and on the southern edge of Prokhorovka. Lieutenant Colonel L. I. Malov's 99th Tank Brigade, which had only 19 tanks left, including nine light tanks, was fighting against a German effort to encircle it in the Vasil'evka – Andreevka area. Corps headquarters ordered it to withdraw at dawn to the area of Pravorot'. The remaining 26th Tank Brigade under the command of Colonel P. V. Piskarev was located in Grushki, where it was regrouping after four days of fighting.

Repair crews had spent the entire night of 11 July putting damaged machines back into good working order; however, the corps only had 52 tanks in formation as dawn broke on 12 July. The 2nd Tank Corps' Operational Summary No. 138 at 0700 12 July testifies to the corps' poor condition:

> …
>
> 3. The 99th Tank Brigade has: 80 active bayonets, 10 operational T-34 tanks and 4 T-34 tanks with mechanical defects, and 10 operational T-70 tanks. Losses for 11.07.43: knocked-out and burned-out T-34s – 4, T-70 – 8.
>
> Brigade headquarters – Krasnoe.
>
> 4. The 26th Tank Brigade has: 40 active bayonets, 6 operational T-34 tanks and 8 operational T-70. Losses: up to 80 men wounded and killed. … Brigade headquarters – southwest outskirts of Grushki.
>
> 5. The 169th Tank Brigade has: 85 active bayonets, 14 operational T-34 tanks and 4 operational T-70 tanks. Losses: 40 men killed and wounded; one T-34 tank burned out.
>
> Brigade headquarters – the ravine, 0.7 km east of Storozhevoe.
>
> 6. The 58th Motorized Rifle Brigade. Losses are being determined [Author's note: Several days later, the brigade headquarters reported that its losses totaled 570 men].
>
> Brigade headquarters – the ravine, 0.5 km southwest of Grushki."[77]

Lieutenant Colonel Turenkov's 15th Guards Separate Tank Breakthrough Regiment, after suffering heavy losses between 8 July and 11 July, had been withdrawn to Mochaki (2 kilometers south of Kholodnoe) for refitting. On 12 July, it had three operational Churchill tanks and seven more under repair (see Table 23).

In this condition, it was simply impossible to employ the 2nd Tank Corps. It could hardly even be used in an extreme case as a mobile reserve to strength any certain sector – and only if first its remaining tanks were gathered together in one place. That is exactly what its headquarters spent the night of 11 July trying to do, pulling together the brigades' remnants in the area Grushki – Pravorot' – Storozhevoe (south of Prokhorovka).

At 0900, corps commander Popov sent Dispatch No. 104 to the headquarters of the 5th Guards Tank Army:

> 1. Your combat order – the corps assignment for 12.07.43 – was received at 0430 12.07.43. I've started to implement it.
> 2. After the fighting of 11.07.43, the units of the corps have been given the order to bring themselves back to full order and to be ready to support the 5th Guards Tank Army's offensive with all types of weapons from their present lines, and

subsequently to develop the success in the direction: Storozhevoe, Greznoe, Sukh. Solotino.

3. The units of the corps are positioned as follows:
   58th Motorized Rifle Brigade – on the southern outskirts of Prokhorovka;
   26th Tank Brigade – Grushki;
   99th Tank Brigade – Pravorot';
   Corps headquarters – western outskirts of Pravorot'.[78]

At 1245, another messenger arrived from the army commander with an order to assemble the corps at Storozhevoe and to be prepared to develop the success of the 29th Tank Corps' forces that had reached Komsomolets State Farm, in anticipation of a possible strike on the enemy advancing from the areas of Rzhavets and Shakhovo. By this time, the 169th Tank Brigade had already been conducting a difficult defensive fight for Storozhevoe for more than two hours. There is a note by A. F. Popov on the document: "Chief of staff. For carrying out. 12.07.43 1243." His chief of staff Colonel V. V. Koshelev received the order at 1345, but received no further instructions. The order was plainly too late; between 1330 and 1430, the 5th Guards Tank Army's advance on the main axis of attack had already been conclusively stopped by the enemy.

However, the 2nd Tank Corps throughout 12 July still had two difficult fights on its hands, at Storozhevoe and in the Ivanovka – Belenikhino Station – Teterevino region. Unfortunately, the corps was defeated in both of these battles and forced to retreat, but the fighting withdrawal was orderly, and the enemy was not able to exploit the success.

An attack by units of the 2nd Guards 'Tatsinskaia' Tank Corps. (RGAKFD)

Type of Loss	10 July 43	11 July 43	12 July 43	Total over 3 Day Period
Killed	22	10	145	177
Wounded	79	35	388	502
Missing	2	15	17	34
Total Personnel Losses	103	60	550	713
Type of Equipment Losses				
Knocked-out T-70	-	-	5	5
Irrevocably destroyed T-70	-	-	9	9
Knocked-out T-34	2	-	20	22
Irrevocably destroyed T-34	-	-	20	20
Knocked-out Mk-IV	-	3	-	3
Irrevocably destroyed Mk-IV	-	2	-	2
Total tank losses	2	5	54	61
Damaged armored car	-	1	-	1
Lost 45mm anti-tank guns	1	-	7	8
Lost 76mm anti-tank guns	-	-	1	1
Lost 85mm anti-tank guns	-	4	-	4
Total anti-tank gun losses	1	4	8	13
Rifles	-	-	160	160
PPSh-41 SMGs	-	-	112	112
Light machine guns	-	-	33	33
Heavy machine guns	-	-	15	15
Anti-tank rifles	-	-	30	30
Total, small arms	-	-	290	290
Damaged vehicles	-	-	-	-
Destroyed vehicles	-	5	11	16
Destroyed motorcycles	-	1	4	5
Total transportation vehicle losses	-	6	15	21

Source: TsAMO RF, f. 5 gv. TA, op. 4948, d. 75, l. 20, 28, 34.

Table 22: Losses of Personnel and Equipment in the 2nd Guards 'Tatsinskaia' Tank Corps, 10-12 July 1943

Colonel V. L. Savchenko, commander of the 2nd Guards 'Tatsinskaia' Tank Corps' 4th Guards Motorized Rifle Brigade (1943 photo). (TsAMO)

The situation at Storozhevoe was the most difficult one. The Germans had already tried several times on 11 July to take this settlement. After several failures to take it directly, around the middle of 12 July, a portion of *Leibstandarte*'s assault group infiltrated into the woods north of Storozhevoe and seized the Stalinskoe Branch of the [Oktiabr'skii] State Farm. At the same time, part of *Das Reich* was attacking from Ivanovskii Vyselok in the effort to close a ring around the defenders in Storozhevoe. This initial attempt, though, also failed. After *Leibstandarte* managed to repel the first, most powerful attack on Oktiabr'skii State Farm, and *Totenkopf* units had successfully begun to drive back the Guards divisions in the bend of the Psel River, Hausser, trying to seize the initiative, launched attacks on the flanks of the 18th Tank Corps. Simultaneously, he undertook one more effort to take Storozhevoe with the flank units of SS Panzergrenadier Division *Das Reich*, with the aim of emerging at Pravorot'. The 169th Tank Brigade's Operational Summary No. 5 from 12 July at 1800 stated:

> 1. On the morning of 12.07.43, the enemy did not conduct active operations, limiting himself to a sharp mortar barrage on the battalion's combat formations; simultaneously, the enemy assembled submachine gunners in the woods northwest of Storozhevoe and in the woods east of Ivanovskii Vyselok. By 0730 12.07.43, up to a regiment of infantry and up to three companies of tanks, including 10 Tigers had been concentrated on the brigade's front.
>
> At 1030 12.07.43, the enemy attacked the 169th Tank Brigade with a motorized infantry [Panzergrenadier] battalion from the direction of the railroad crossing west of Storozhevoe and gained possession of the southwest edge of the forest west of Storozhevoe.

(a) Personnel, Armored Vehicles and Heavy Weapons

Unit	Personnel	Tanks			Armored Personnel Carrier	Mortars		37mm AA gun	BM-8 Katiusha	DShK-39 Hvy MG	76mm AT Gun	45mm AT Gun
		T-70	T-34	MK-4		82mm	120mm					
Corps headquarters	102	–		–	–	–	–	–	–	–	–	–
894 Sep Signals Bn	246	–	4	–	–	–	–	–	–	–	–	–
174 Sapper Bn	468	–	–	–	–	–	–	–	–	–	–	–
Sep Chemical Defense Co	47	–	–	–	–	–	–	–	–	–	–	–
207 Med-san Plt.	31	–	–	–	–	–	–	–	–	–	–	–
51 Mobile Field Bakery	60	–	–	–	–	–	–	–	–	–	–	–
26 Tank Bde	929	9	3/3*	–	2	4	–	–	–	9/2	2/2	–
99 Tank Bde	954	19	16	–	3	6	–	–	–	9/9	4	–
169 Tank Bde	1117	7/2	12/4	–	2	6	–	–	–	9/9	–	–
58 Motorized Rifle Bde	3085	–	–	–	2	28	6	–	–	–	12	12
15 Sep Gds Hvy Tank Reg	185	–	–	4/2	–	–	–	–	–	–	–	–
83 Motorcycle Bn	280	–	–	–	–	4	–	–	–	–	–	–
12 Sep AC Bn	112	11	–	–	–	–	–	–	–	–	–	–
1698 AA Artillery Reg	360	–	–	–	–	–	–	16	–	16	–	–
1502 AT Artillery Reg	260	–	–	–	–	–	–	–	–	–	–	14
269 Mortar Reg	649	–	–	–	–	–	36	–	–	–	–	–
307 Gds Mortar Bn	224	–	–	–	–	–	–	2	8	0/2	–	–
73 Mobile Repair Shop	75	–	–	–	–	–	–	–	–	–	–	–
100 Mobile Repair Shop	72	–	–	–	–	–	–	–		–	–	–
Aviation Signals Element	7	–	–	–	–	–	–	–	–	–	–	–
Total for the Corps:	9263	46/2	35/7	4/2	9	48	42	18	8	43/22	18/2	26

Table 23: Equipment and Personnel in the 69th Army's 2nd Tank Corps on 10 July 1943

Table 23 continued

(b) Small-arms and light vehicles

Unit	Anti-tank Rifles	PPSh-41 SMGs	Rifles	Machine Guns		Radio Sets	Motor Transport			
				Light	Heavy		Trucks	Tractors	Armored Cars	Motorcycles
Corps headquarters	–	42	–	1/1	–	–	–	–	–	–
894 Sep Signals Bn	–	33	117	3	–	8	49	–	10	8
174 Sapper Bn	–	122	306	4	–	–	32	–	–	3
Sep Chemical Defense Co	–	–	39	–	–	–	8	–	–	–
207 Med-san Plt.	–	10	8	–	–	–	4	–	–	–
51 Mobile Field Bakery	–	5	12	1	–	–	6	–	–	–
26 Tank Bde	24/12	160	301	20/12	4/2	10/6	72	–	–	5
99 Tank Bde	24/29	325	458	20/20	4/4	10/7	59	–	–	7
169 Tank Bde	27/28	333	400	20/20	4/4	10/8	45	–	–	7
58 Motorized Rifle Bde	81	1197	1510	110	45	28	93	–	11	13
15 Sep Gds Hvy Tank Reg	–	87	8	–	–	1	27/1	2	2/1	3
83 Motorcycle Bn	–	135	82	16	–	3/8	11	–	10	76
12 Sep AC Bn	–	78	19	–	–	1/3	9	–	22	6
1698 AA Artillery Reg	–	103	258	–	–	7	42	–	–	–
1502 AT Artillery Reg	–	141	62	5/3	–	1/1	35	–	–	–
269 Mortar Reg	–	154	382	–	–	18/10	69	–	–	–
307 Gds Mortar Bn	0/2	36	120	0/5	2	6	14	–	–	–
73 Mobile Repair Shop	–	21	41	–	–	–	8	–	–	1
100 Mobile Repair Shop	–	11	20	1	–	–	22	–	–	2
Aviation Signals Element	-	–	–	–	–		–	–	–	–
Total for Corps	156/71	2993	4143	201/61	59/10	103/43	605/1	2	55/1	131

Source: TsAMO RF, f. 332, op. 4948, d. 70, l. 130 obr.

* Note: Operational tanks/items of equipment are to the left of the slash, those under repair are to the right of the slash.

> By 1130 12.07.43 units of the brigade, with hard defensive fighting, had beaten back two attacks and were stubbornly clinging to Storozhevoe.
>
> At 1200 … the 25th Tank Brigade of the 29th Tank Corps passed through the combat formations of the battalions on the attack; units of the brigade gave fire support to the 25th Tank Brigade's attack, but reaching a line 1 km west of Storozhevoe, it encountered strong enemy resistance and deployed Tiger tanks, and at 1300 it began to fall back to the east in the direction of Storozhevoe. The enemy, having repulsed the 25th Tank Brigade attack, reached the line of the western outskirts of Storozhevoe.[79]

The Panzergrenadiers and tanks of *Das Reich*, following closely on the heels of the 25th Tank Brigade's composite battalion, attacked Storozhevoe and broke into the village at 1340. East of Storozhevoe, the 183rd Rifle Division's 285th Rifle Regiment was defending. On 11 July, the regiment commander Major A. K. Karpov reported that he had been forced to form one battalion from the survivors of the 1st and 2nd Rifle Battalions. At 1300 on 11 July, the regiment numbered just 898 soldiers and officers.[80] It had been planned that the regiment, weakened in the preceding fighting, would turn over its sector to the 9th Guards Airborne Division, but this didn't happen. Thus, the defense facing the SS attack was being held by a substantially weakened tank brigade, a shattered infantry regiment, and one battalion of the 58th Motorized Rifle Brigade that had also already suffered losses.

At 1505, up to two battalions from the SS Panzergrenadier Regiment *Deutschland* with the support of a dozen panzers attacked from the direction of Ivanovskii Vyselok

Grenadiers of the 167th Infantry Division fighting in the area of Kalinin. (RGAKFD)

Grenadiers of the 167th Infantry Division battle against attacking units of the 5th Guards Tank Army (captured photo). (RGAKFD)

and from the woods on the northern outskirts of the village. Bloody fighting went on for the next hour. The SS were striving to encircle Stepanov's tank brigade together with its attached units. The terrain in the area greatly contributed to the success of the enemy attack. Storozhevoe is almost completely surrounded by woods, and the enemy already held its southern part.

Simultaneously with *Das Reich*'s attack, the SS Panzergrenadier Division *Leibstandarte* was attacking the positions of the 183rd Rifle Division's 285th Rifle Regiment: 14 panzers and two companies of Panzergrenadiers enveloped the flanks of its 3rd Rifle Battalion, and under the pressure of superior enemy forces, the 285th Rifle Regiment was forced to fall back toward Pravorot'. Thus, the SS, by taking full control of the northern portion of the woods around Storozhevoe, had finally executed their plan – the village was now in a closing pocket. The 169th Tank Brigade had one remaining path out, through the northeastern outskirts of the village, but even this route was under fire from German tanks in the woods. According to the documents of SS Panzergrenadier Division *Das Reich*, contained in Sylvester Stadler's detailed study, our units began to pull out of the village at this point, but fighting continued on its fringes until 1700.

In the "Account of combat operations of the 169th Tank Brigade for the period 08.07.43 to 15.09.43," it is reported that the enemy didn't seize Storozhevoe until 2000. Our units were defending stubbornly, begrudgingly yielding each meter to the adversary only after hard fighting, and there was nothing like an enemy breakthrough to Pravorot'. Probably, by 2000 the last remaining pocket of resistance in the village had been crushed, but most of the defending force had already withdrawn by 1800. The

Major General V. V. Tikhomirov, commander of the 35th Guards Rifle Corps' 93rd Guards Rifle Division. (TsAMO)

169th Tank Brigade and the 2nd Motorized Rifle Battalion of the 58th Motorized Rifle Brigade dug into new positions a kilometer northeast of Storozhevoe.

But the fighting didn't cease with this. In a message to Stalin at midnight on 12 July, Vatutin wrote: "Units of the 2nd Tank Corps, which were counterattacked by a force of up to 130 tanks from the direction of Teterevino toward Storozhevoe, conducted especially bitter fighting with the enemy. The fighting for Storozhevoe is continuing at day's end."[81]

The commander of the 5th Guards Tank Army understood that the loss of Storozhevoe and Vinogradovka clearly indicated the enemy commander's intention to breakthrough to Prokhorovka from the south. As scouts reported, the SS divisions pushing toward Prokhorovka had reserves in the areas of Komsomolets State Farm, Greznoe, Teterevino and Kalinin. If events in the bend of the Psel River continued to develop in the enemy's favor, a genuine threat of the encirclement of the 5th Guards Tank Army's forces southwest of Prokhorovka would arise. Moreover, there might also be the possibility of a strike into the rear of the 69th Army's 48th Rifle Corps to link-up with Army Detachment Kempf's III Panzer Corps, which was stubbornly pushing northward from the region of Rzhavets and Ryndinka. Striving to stop the SS advance on the left flank of his army, late in the day Rotmistrov made the decision to strike SS Panzergrenadier Division *Das Reich*'s right flank.

From the account of combat operations of the 2nd Tank Corps:

> ... At 1700 the commander of the 5th Guards Tank Army arrived at corps headquarters and issued an order to the corps: at 2000 12.07.43, with one brigade

> positioned to screen the movement from the Storozhevoe direction, to assemble the main forces in Ivanovka, and to go on the offensive in the direction of Teterevino, which would facilitate the offensive of the 29th and 18th Tank Corps to the southwest.
>
> The corps commander resolved:
>
> The 169th Tank Brigade to cover the movement to Ivanovka. With the main forces consisting of the 26th Tank Brigade, the 99th Tank Brigade and the 58th Motorized Rifle Brigade with its attached units having assembled in Ivanovka, to attack the enemy in the direction of Teterevino.
>
> At 1830 the 26th Tank Brigade, the 99th Tank Brigade and the 58th Motorized Rifle Brigade with its attached units moved out of the area of Pravorot' and completed a march along the route Pravorot' – Hill 234.9 – Ivanovka; by 2000 12.07.43, the units and formations of the corps had assembled in Ivanovka and were occupying jumping-off positions for the attack.
>
> The neighboring 2nd Guards 'Tatsinskaia' Tank Corps on the left had no successes on its axis of attack in the course of the day, and was holding a line extending from Ivanovka to the south, along the rail line.[82]

Information about this attack is available not only in the corps' account, but also in the documents of the subordinate tank brigades. However, there are discrepancies between the corps' account and those of its subordinate brigades. Thus, 2nd Tank Corps staff officers report: "... the units of the corps assembled with the onset of darkness, with insufficient remaining daylight for an offensive. The corps remained in Ivanovka and conducted no combat operations before morning."[83]

However, the 99th Tank Brigade's account notes:

> At 1830 12.07.43, brigade headquarters received a combat order from the 2nd Tank Corps headquarters, from which it followed that the 99th Tank Brigade would move by the route Pravorot' – Hill 234.9 – Ivanovka to assemble by 1900 12.07.43 on the western edge of the northern part of Ivanovka, and in cooperation with the 26th Tank Brigade attack the enemy in the area of Teterevino and seize its eastern outskirts. The direction of the attack: Ivanovka – Belenikhino – eastern outskirts of Teterevino.
>
> The operations of the 2nd Tank Corps on this axis were connected with the offensive of the 18th and 29th Tank Corps in a southwest direction. The 25th Guards Tank Brigade of the 2nd Guards 'Tatsinskaia' Tank Corps was attacking to the left of the 2nd Tank Corps.
>
> The offensive began at 1920 12.07.43 and concluded at 2130 12.07.43. Further advance was impossible because of the lack of infantry and strong [enemy] artillery and mortar fire. Units of the brigade reached the depression 1 kilometer east of Point 243.1 and took up a defense. In this battle, the commander of the 290th Tank Battalion Major D'iachenko, who had been twice decorated with Orders, was killed in action.
>
> During the fighting, the following losses were inflicted on the enemy: 9 Panzer III tanks, 3 Panzer IV tanks, 4 guns and 8 vehicles with infantry were destroyed.
>
> Our losses: 7 T-34 tanks and 1 T-70 tanks were knocked-out.[84]

That the 2nd Tank Corps really did attack seems to be confirmed by a dispatch of Lieutenant Colonel Geller, chief of the 26th Tank Brigade's political department, in which he calls attention to the skill of Lieutenant Ilarionov, a T-70 tank commander in the 282nd Tank Battalion: "In the fighting of 12.07.43, Comrade Ilarionov damaged a Tiger tank, and then with three shells to its side armor, set it on fire."[85]

The brigades attacked from the march, without sufficient preparation, without infantry support and with small forces; therefore they had no success. Likely, this failure was the reason why the corps staff officers were unwilling to mention it in the corps' official account. With this, the participation of the 2nd Tank Corps in the 12 July counterstroke concluded.

11

Combat Operations in the Sector of the 5th Guards Army in the Bend of the Psel River

The counteroffensive developed in the sector of Lieutenant General A. S. Zhadov's 5th Guards Army no less easily. Its rifle units in the bend of the Psel were involved in particularly hard and bloody fighting. Two divisions of the 33rd Guards Rifle Corps – the 52nd Guards and the 95th Guards Rifle Divisions – were operating here. In addition, two battalions of 10th Tank Corps' 11th Motorized Rifle Brigade were defending Hill 226.6 with the support of the artillery battalion. The 5th Guards Army had the ambitious orders to liquidate SS Panzergrenadier Division *Totenkopf*'s bridgehead on the northern side of the river, and having forced a crossing of the river, to drive to the area of Greznoe, Malye Maiachki, Teterevino and the Komsomolets State Farm, with a subsequent advance toward the villages of Pogorelovka and Iakovlevo.

By dawn on 12 July, all seven rifle divisions and one anti-aircraft division of the 5th Guards Army had assembled at Prokhorovka, with a total of 62,800 men, 708 guns of all calibers (including anti-aircraft guns) and 1,100 mortars. In the afternoon, the 6th Guards Army's 52nd Guards Rifle Division, which was also defending in the bend of the Psel River, passed to the 5th Guards Army's operational control.

Upon reaching Prokhorovka on 11 July, the army commander had received an order to set up a solid defense with his arriving army, and it was only on the afternoon of 11 July, in the midst of the fighting that day, did an order arrive from *front* headquarters notifying Zhadov of his army's participation in the counterattack the next day. As documents reveal, the subordinate divisions didn't receive their assignments for the counterattack until that evening. As A. S. Zhadov recalled, "Only a few hours of daylight and a short summer night remained for the organization of the counterattack. Mortar and howitzer artillery brigades arrived in the evening as reinforcements, but they had extremely limited ammunition … We had no tanks at all."[1]

There were weighty reasons why the 5th Guards Army didn't receive any tanks as reinforcements – there were simply not any available. The Voronezh Front had already committed all the direct infantry support tank regiments and brigades to other sectors. The 10th Tank Corps, which had previously been part of the 5th Guards Army, had been subordinated to the 1st Tank Army back on 9 July. The only armor that the army received, if you don't include the few tanks of the 245th Separate Tank Regiment's 4th Company in the 52nd Guards Rifle Division, was Lieutenant Colonel Shapshinsky's 1440th Self-propelled Artillery Regiment from the *Stavka* Reserve, which was assigned to the 5th Guards Army on the evening of 11 July. For the duration of the counterattack, A. S. Zhadov attached it to Major General A. I. Rodimtsev's 32nd Guards Rifle Corps.[2] On 10 July the Regiment had 13 Su-76 and Su-133 self-propelled guns, but because of the lack of ammunition, it took no part in the combat operations on 12 July. Thus, the rifle units had to attack without armor and without sufficient artillery support against an SS division, having 101 combat-ready armored vehicles, its full complement of artillery, and support from *Nebelwerfer* batteries.

For the looming counterattack, Zhadov decided to concentrate his main forces on his left flank. As we have seen, the left-flank divisions of the 33rd Guards Rifle Corps (the 9th Guards Airborne and 42nd Guards Rifle Divisions) attacked between the Psel River and Storozhevoe behind the tank corps of Rotmistrov's 5th Guards Tank Army. The right-flank divisions (the 52nd Guards, 95th Guards and 97th Guards Rifle Divisions) would attack SS Panzergrenadier Division *Totenkopf*'s armored *kampfgruppe* in the river bend and the XXXXVIII Panzer Corps' 11th Panzer Division in the area of Kochetovka. The army's main task was the elimination of the German bridgehead in the area of Kliuchi and the destruction of Priess's *kampfgruppe* north of the Psel. Four of the seven divisions in the 5th Guards Army were directly involved in carrying out this assignment.

Combat Order No. 9 from the commander of the 52nd Guards Rifle Division reveals the role of the 33rd Guards Rifle Corps in the offensive:

> 1. 52nd Guards Rifle Division with a Guards mortar regiment of rocket artillery, the 649th Destroyer Anti-tank Artillery Regiment and the 133rd Separate Battalion of Anti-tank Rifles will go on the offensive in the sector: on the right – Hill 226.6 – (excl.) Prokhorovka – (excl.) Greznoe; on the left, Polezhaev – (excl.) Andreevka – (excl.) Greznoe with the task to seize Bogoroditskoe, Kozlovka and Vasil'evka.
>
> Upon carrying out the assignment, the division will go into the reserve of the 33rd Guards Rifle Corps commander.
>
> The start of the offensive 0830 12.07.43.
>
> 2. On the right – the 95th Guards Rifle Division will attack in the direction of Krasnyi Oktiabr' and Greznoe; subsequently, to the southwest; on the left – the 42nd Guards Rifle Division will attack in the direction of Andreevka, Hill 224.5, Greznoe and Mal. Maiachki.[3]

In the first hours of the offensive, the divisions of the 33rd Guards Rifle Corps in the bend of the Psel River were to pin the enemy in place. It was also assumed that the tank attack south of the Psel River would be swift, and therefore the left wing of the corps would advance more quickly and cut-off the *Totenkopf* armored *kampfgruppe* in the bridgehead from the rest of Priess's division south of the river. Having encircled the enemy in the bridgehead, the divisions on the corps' left flank were to extend the breakthrough in the direction of Greznoe, Malye Maiachki and Iakovlevo. From the north of Kochetovka, the 33rd Guards Rifle Corps' 97th Guards Rifle Division and the 32nd Guards Rifle Corps consisting of the 13th Guards Rifle Division and the 66th Guards Rifle Division were to launch a secondary attack on this same axis.

However, Hausser disrupted the entire plan with a preemptive attack of his own in the bend of the Psel River on the morning of 12 July. The point was that the enemy was not planning to sit still in its bridgehead north of the Psel, but to use it as a springboard for an attack to the east and northeast.

The main obstacle for the further advance of the II SS Panzer Corps on 12 July was the defensive strongpoint in the region of Prokhorovka. It was being held by forces of the 5th Guards Army and the 69th Army, while the major forces of the 5th Guards Tank Army were also located here. Wisch's SS Panzergrenadier Division *Leibstandarte* was still not in the position to capture Prokhorovka, because of the threats to its flanks from the villages on the southern bank of the Psel River on the left, and the Storozhevoe woods and Pravorot' on the right. Therefore in Hausser's plans for 12 July, the seizure of Hill 226.6 and the breakthrough of Priess's *kampfgruppe* to the Prokhorovka – Kartashevka road occupied a special place, since this would give him better possibilities to maneuver toward Kursk (bypassing Oboian'), or into the rear of Voronezh Front's main counterattack grouping (the 5th Guards Army and the 5th Guards Tank Army). Therefore, the initial task of Hausser's corps on the morning of 12 July was to eliminate the threats to the flanks of *Leibstandarte* and to bring all three divisions of his corps back onto line. Only then could he turn to the problem of seizing Prokhorovka. Here is a key extract from the order of the II SS Panzer Corps command for 12 July:

> *Totenkopf must go on the attack as early as possible,* immediately upon the arrival of dawn, and with panzer support advance to the northeast, first of all to reach the Prokhorovka – Kartashevka road [Author's emphasis].
>
> Secondarily it is necessary to begin the seizure of the valley of the Psel River from the southwest. Upon achieving this goal it is necessary to extend control over the Psel River valley from the north east. Support the left-flank with divisional assets.
>
> Subsequently, the division's task is to seize Veselyi and the ravine to the east of it, in order to remove the barrier on the Ol'shanka line.
>
> Aviation's main forces in the morning hours will be sent to support SS Division *Totenkopf*. Artillery spotter planes should be over the front lines at dawn.
>
> … After eliminating the flank threat on the Psel River to Division *Totenkopf*, Division *Adolf Hitler* together with units of this division [*Totenkopf*] should take Prokhorovka and Hill 252.4.[4]

In addition to building up the bridgehead and preparing for the attack on Prokhorovka, on the night of 11 July, *Totenkopf*'s command was occupied with strengthening its right wing. A group of Russian tanks with infantry from the 99th Tank Brigade were still clinging to the eastern portion of Vasil'evka on the left [southern] bank of the Psel River. *Brigadeführer* Priess believed that the Russians would bring up additional forces to this point as soon as possible, which would create a substantial threat to both of his existing crossings over the Psel River, as well as to his division as a whole. As we have seen, he astutely transferred part of his assault gun battalion (which on the evening of 11 July had 21 operational vehicles) and a significant number of panzers to the 6th SS Panzergrenadier Regiment *Theodor Eicke*, which was fighting for Vasil'evka.

The sector chosen by Priess for *Totenkopf*'s effort to break through the Soviet defenses north of the Psel River was open terrain cut by deep gullies and ravines, all dominated by two hills: 226.6 and 236.7. Possession of these heights would allow the owner not only to control the surrounding terrain, but also the possibility to observe and direct fire upon the villages lying along the river's south bank. These two hills became the focal point of the struggle on this sector north of the Psel River.

The Soviet defenses here were arranged in two echelons. Units of Lieutenant Colonel G. G. Pantiukhov's 52nd Guards Rifle Division comprised the first echelon. The 151st Guards Rifle Regiment was covering the sector running from a hill lying 500 meters north of Kliuchi to the southwestern slopes of Hill 226.6. The tactically important village of Veselyi was located in its sector. The loss of this small village and Hill 236.7 lying 2.5 kilometers north of it would give enemy access to Kartashevka and into the rear of the 5th Guards Army. The 155th Guards Rifle Regiment was defending Hill 226.6 directly, with its defenses arranged toward the southwest in the direction of Kozlovka, Vasil'evka and Andreevka. The 153rd Guards Rifle Regiment's positions extended from the southwest slopes of Hill 226.6 to Polezhaev. The 11th Motorized Rifle Brigade's 3rd Motorized Rifle Battalion had dug-in directly on the crest of Hill 226.6, while its 2nd Rifle Battalion was defending the southeastern outskirts of Vasil'evka and Andreevka, covering bridges over the Psel River.

The 95th Guards Rifle Division was in the second echelon. Its 290th Guards Rifle Regiment was located on the line: southern outskirts of Veselyi – Kliuchi – woods southeast of Kliuchi. The 284th Guards Rifle Regiment was holding the sector Hill 236.7 – Voroshilovskii State Farm – Hill 243.5. Prior to the morning of 12 July, its 287th Guards Rifle Regiment had been located northeast of Oktiabr'skii State Farm, fighting together with the 9th Guards Airborne Division's 26th Guards Airborne Regiment for possession of the State Farm and Hill 252.2. Around 0800 12 July, it had been withdrawn into the division commander's reserve in the area of Veselyi.

At 2215 11 July, Lieutenant General A. S. Zhadov brought up Colonel M. N. Smirnov's 6th Guards Airborne Division to the Sredniaia Ol'shanka – Hill 243.5 – Ostrenkii area. The 6th Guards Airborne Division provided the army a reserve force.

Such a deeply echeloned defense was necessary not only because of the importance of this axis of advance and the strength of the attacking enemy, but also due to the battered condition of two of our divisions. At 1500 11 July the depleted 52nd Guards Rifle Division had only 3,380 men, which was virtually the size of a full-strength infantry regiment.[5] The 10th Tank Corps' 11th Motorized Rifle Brigade had only 1,444 soldiers and officers reporting for duty on 6 July. Still, it had defended heroically with its small numbers. It was through the line of this brigade that the SS had been trying for several days in a row to break through beyond the Psel River. Between 1730 9 July until 2000 12 July alone, this brigade repelled 18 attacks, suffering heavy losses, especially in artillery, in the process. Thus, the most combat-capable division was the 95th Guards Rifle Division (on 10 July it had 8,781 men). The regiments of this division had fully preserved their combat capabilities even after the fighting of 11 July, because its losses on that day were insignificant.

The 5th Guards Army had several unique features, which greatly influenced the fighting on 12 July in the Psel River bend. As has already been mentioned, its rifle divisions had no supporting tank units, which placed them in an unfavorable situation. The relative forces of the two sides on this sector, which was restricted by the river, were unequal. The SS Panzergrenadier Division *Totenkopf* was clearly superior, since its 3rd SS Panzer Regiment by 0900 12 July had almost fully crossed to the northern bank of the Psel, and already by dawn some of its elements were attacking the positions of the Guardsmen even before the start of Rotmistrov's counterattack. Between 0400 and 0800, elements of the 52nd Guards Rifle's left-flank 151 Guards Rifle Regiment were fighting for its first lines of trenches. The SS succeeded in driving them out, though the position was re-established by a sharp counterattack. Parallel with this effort, the enemy was attacking the area of Veselyi, where the battalions of the 95th Guards Rifle Division were approaching to replace the 52nd Guards Rifle Division in its positions, but this it didn't manage to do. Taking advantage of its numerical superiority and the confusion in the defenders' ranks, the SS broke through our defenses in an area north and northeast of Kliuchi, and began to exploit in the directions of Hill 226.6, Polezhaev and Veselyi.

Lieutenant Colonel G. G. Pantiukhov's 52nd Guards Rifle Division had been caught in a very difficult situation. He had received an order to attack: the 155th Guards Rifle Regiment with the 2nd Battalion of the 124th Guards Artillery Regiment and the 57th Separate Destroyer Anti-tank Artillery Regiment toward Kozlovka; the 153rd Guards Rifle Regiment with the 1st Battalion of the 124th Guards Artillery Regiment and the 133rd Separate Battalion of Anti-tank Rifles, toward Bogoroditskoe and Vasil'evka; the 151st Guards Rifle Regiment, located in the second echelon, was to reinforce any success in the attack. The division was occupying the first echelon of defense on the northern bank, and the enemy's dawn attack struck when its units were in the process of turning over their sectors to the 95th Guards Division behind it. Two of its regiments, the 151st and 155th Guards Rifle Regiments, became enmeshed in very difficult fighting, at times

A counterattack by units of the 5th Guards Army's 52nd Guards Rifle Division. (RGAKFD)

Map section

Topographical maps

Note to topographical maps

These maps were adapted from 1981-1983 Soviet 1:100,000 topographical maps of the battlefield area. Unfortunately, the boundaries of the maps carve up the battlefield in an awkward way, splitting the II SS Panzer Corps' drive toward Prokhorovka between three different maps. While this makes study of the maps cumbersome, I thought it useful for the reader to have maps that locate the many villages and hamlets mentioned in the text as an aid to following the movements and orders found therein. The locations of some villages and the elevation points are only approximate.

The actual topography of the battlefield is that of a relatively flat tableland cut by numerous ravines and gullies. These ravines often served as the only natural cover on the battlefield, but after thunderstorms, often became obstacles to vehicular movement and tended to canalize the German advance along the higher ground, over which major roads and railroads ran. The highest ground on the battlefield is less than 260 meters in elevation, but Soviet fortifications made use of higher ground, and these low ridges and hills became epicenters of fierce struggles during the battle. I have marked the approximate location of some of these key elevations mentioned repeatedly in the text. There were scattered patches of woods on the battlefield, but only the woods around Storozhevoe feature prominently in the narrative.

Stuart Britton

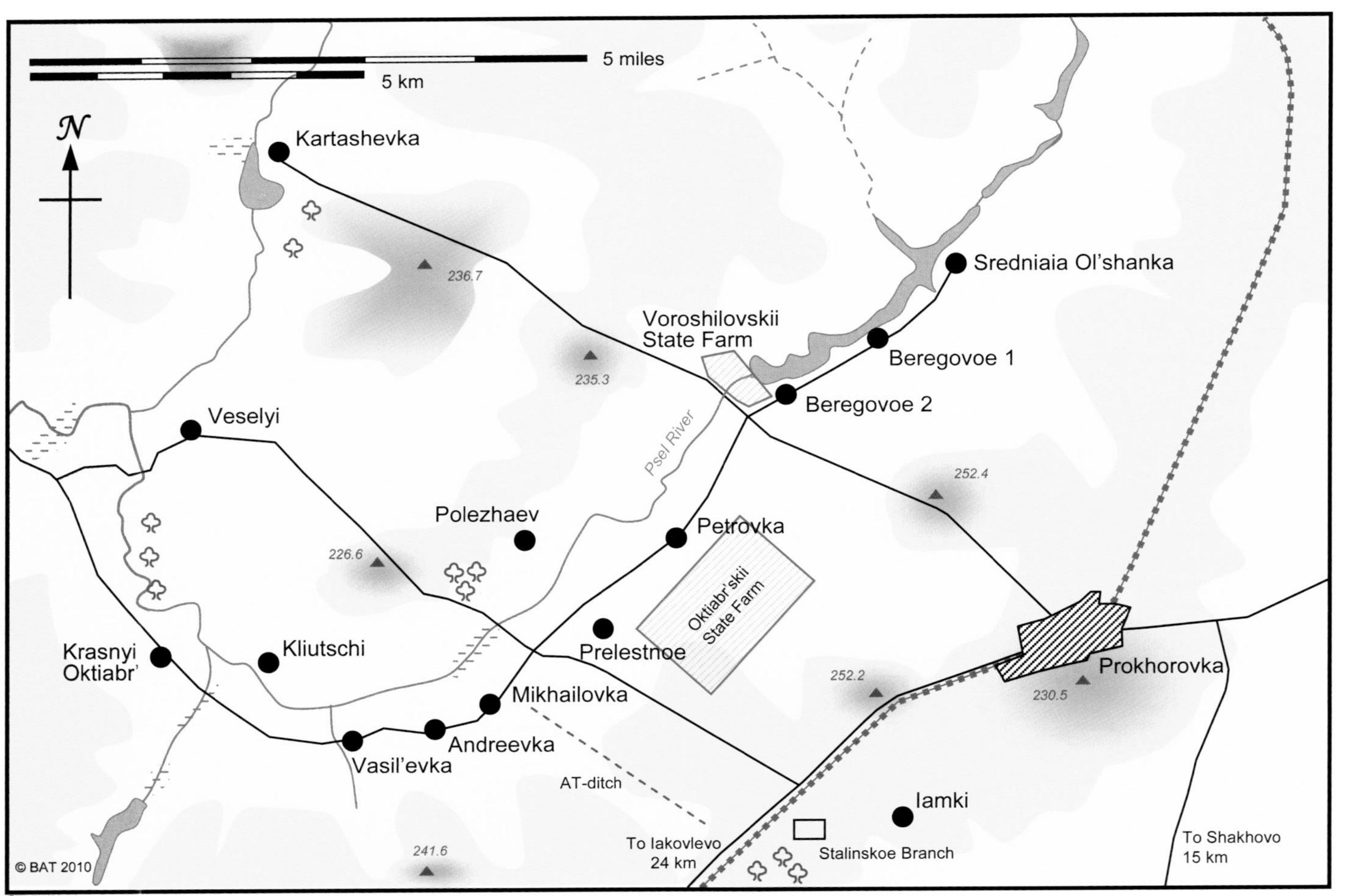

Prokhorovka-Psel River Sector

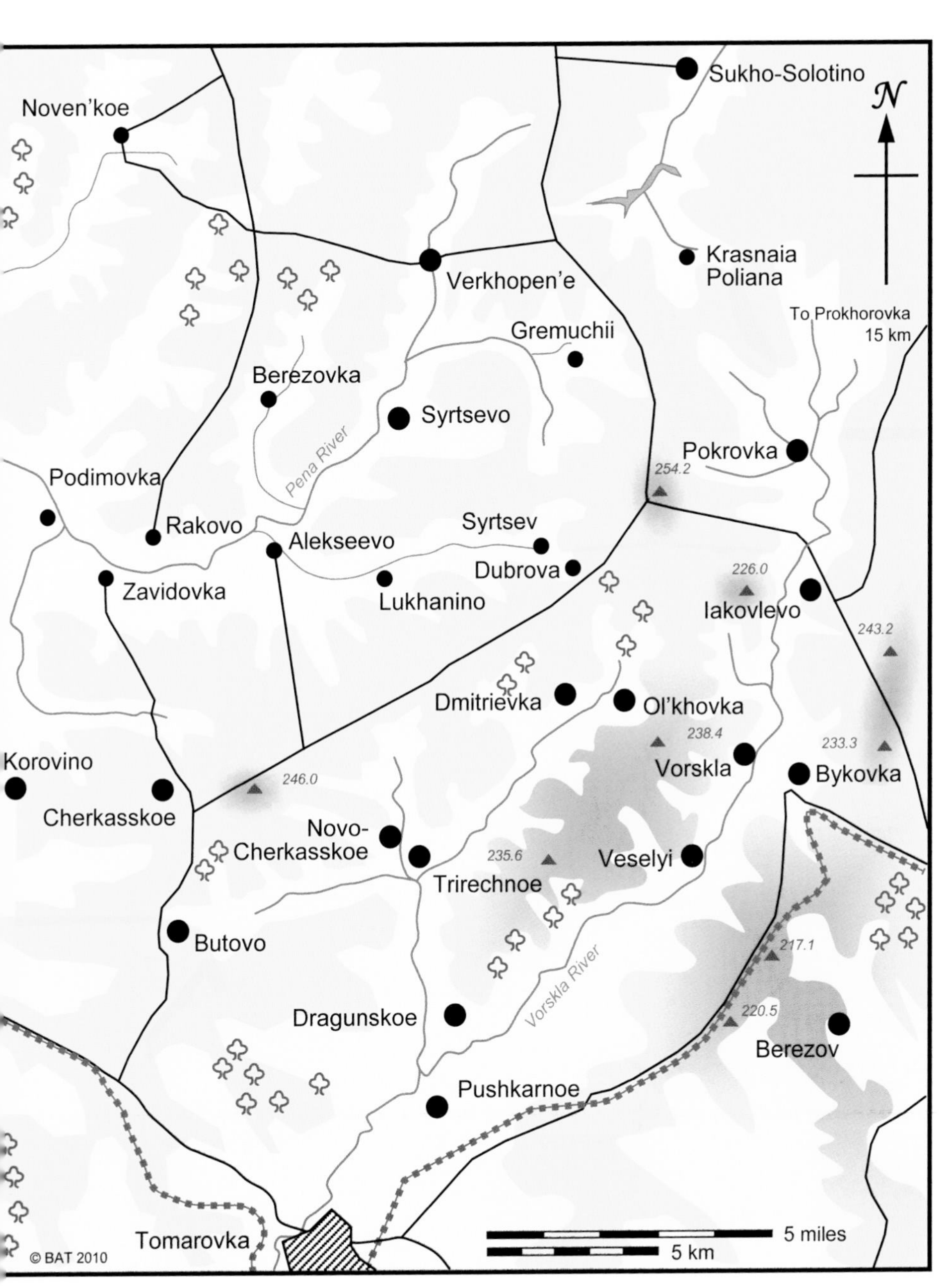

Tomarovka-Iakovlevo-Syrtsevo Sector

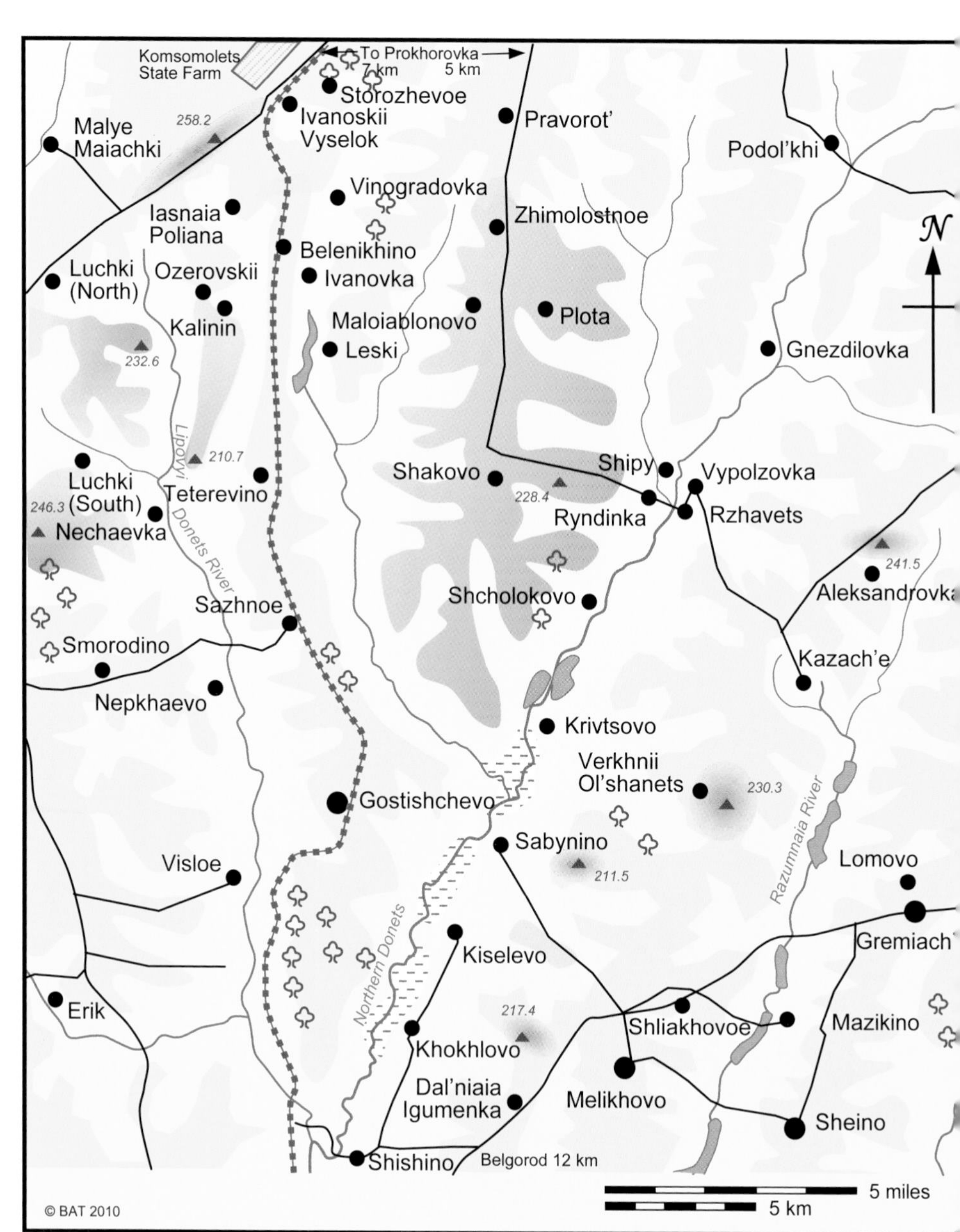

Lipovyi Donets-Northern Donets Sector

Tactical maps

Key to tactical maps

List of abbreviations and key to symbols used in maps.

German (blue) Symbols

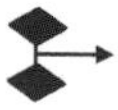

Panzer unit

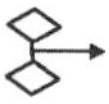

Panzergrenadier unit

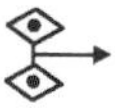

Self-propelled gun unit

Artillery or anti-tank gun battery

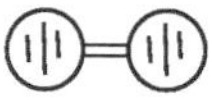

Anti-tank battalion or regiment

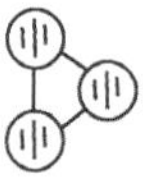

Three batteries, or an artillery battalion

Werfer regiment

Abbreviation for map	Meaning
A	Army
AK	Army Corps
AR	Artillery Regiment
CO	combat outposts
GD	*Grossdeutschland*
ID	Infantry Division
KG	*Kampfgruppe*
PzD	Panzer Division
PzK	Panzer Corps
RBn	Reconnaissance Battalion
sPzAbt	Heavy Tank Battalion
SS DR	SS Panzergrenadier Division *Das Reich*
SS LAH	SS Panzergrenadier Division *LAH* (*Leibstandarte Adolf Hitler*)
SS PzGrR	SS Panzergrenadier Regiment
SS PzK	SS Panzer Corps
SS PzR	SS Panzer Regiment
SS TK	SS Panzergrenadier Division *Totenkopf*
WfrR	Werfer Regiment

Soviet (red) Symbols

	Tank unit
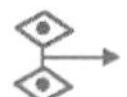	Self-propelled gun unit
	Artillery or anti-tank gun battery
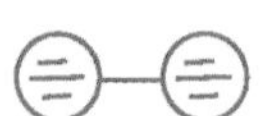	Anti-tank battalion or regiment
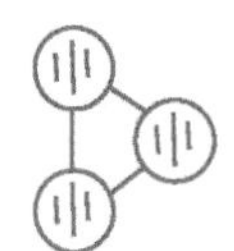	Three batteries, or an artillery battalion, normally of a rifle division's artillery regiment
	Mortar regiment
	Anti-tank ditch

Abbreviation for map	Meaning
A	Army
ABn	Artillery Battalion
AC	Army Corps
AirAR	Airborne Artillery Regiment
AirD	Airborne Division
AirR	Airborne Regiment
AR	Artillery Regiment
ATBn	Destroyer Anti-tank Artillery Battalion (or simply Anti-tank Artillery Battalion)
ATR	Destroyer Anti-tank Artillery Regiment (or simply Anti-tank Artillery Regiment)
CO	combat outposts
CR	Composite Regiment
GAR	Gun Artillery Regiment
Gds	Guards
MB	Mechanized Brigade
MC	Mechanized Corps
MoRB	Motorized Rifle Brigade
MtrBn	Mortar Battalion
MtrR	Mortar Regiment
OG	Operational Group
OP	Observation Post
RD	Rifle Division
Rkt	Rocket Artillery
RR	Rifle Regiment

SATBn	Separate Destroyer Anti-Tank Artillery Battalion (or simply Separate Anti-tank Artillery Battalion)
SATB	Separate Destroyer Anti-Tank Artillery Brigade (or simply Separate Anti-tank Artillery Brigade)
SBn	Separate Battalion
SHAR	Separate Heavy Artillery Regiment
SMoB	Separate Motorized Brigade
SMtrB	Separate Mortar Brigade
SPCo	Separate Penal Company
STC	'Stalingrad' Tank Corps
STR	Separate Tank Regiment
TA	Tank Army
TB	Tank Brigade
TC	Tank Corps
TD	Tank Division
TR	Tank Regiment

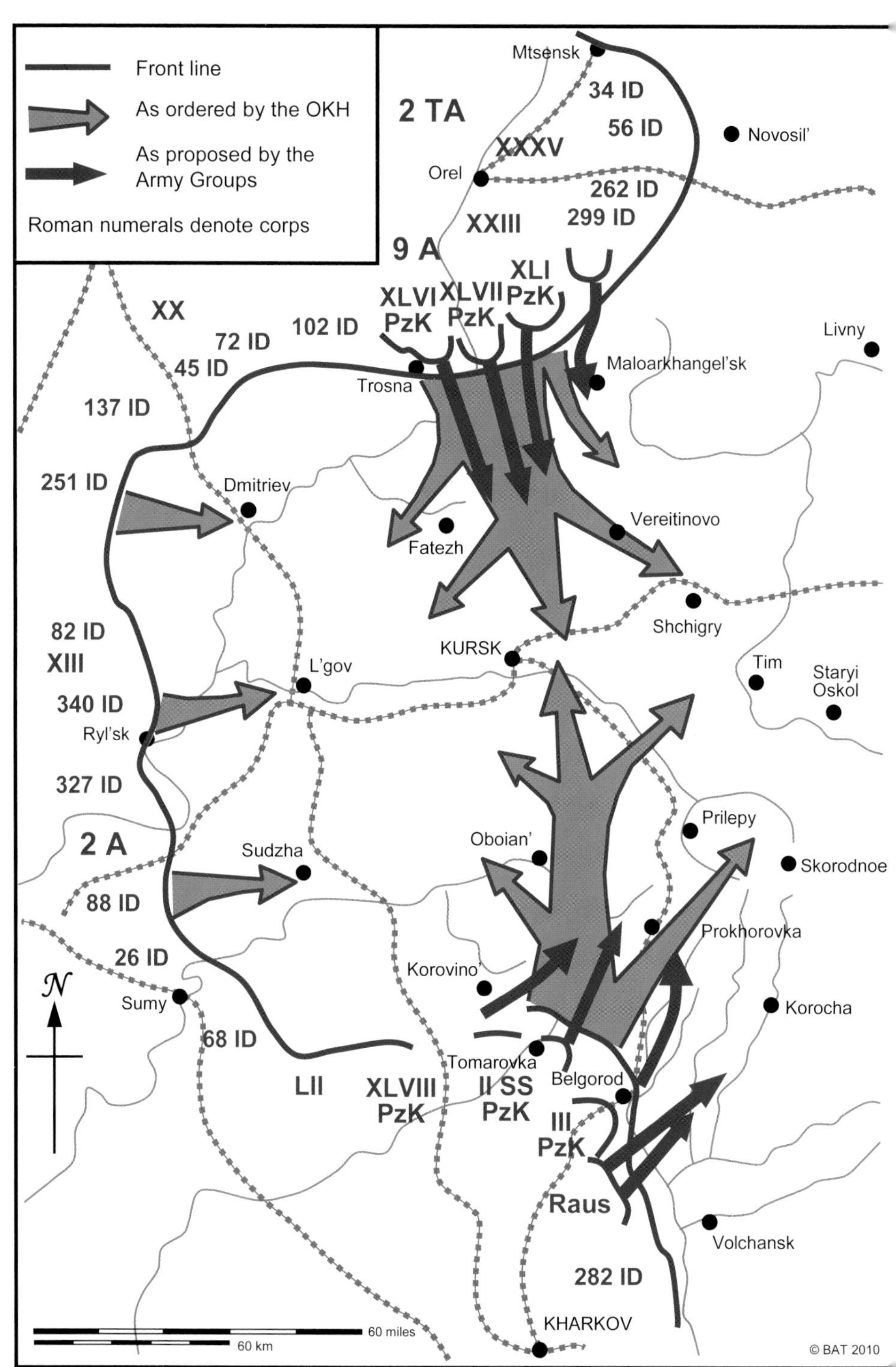

OKH Operational Order No. 6 from 15 April 1943

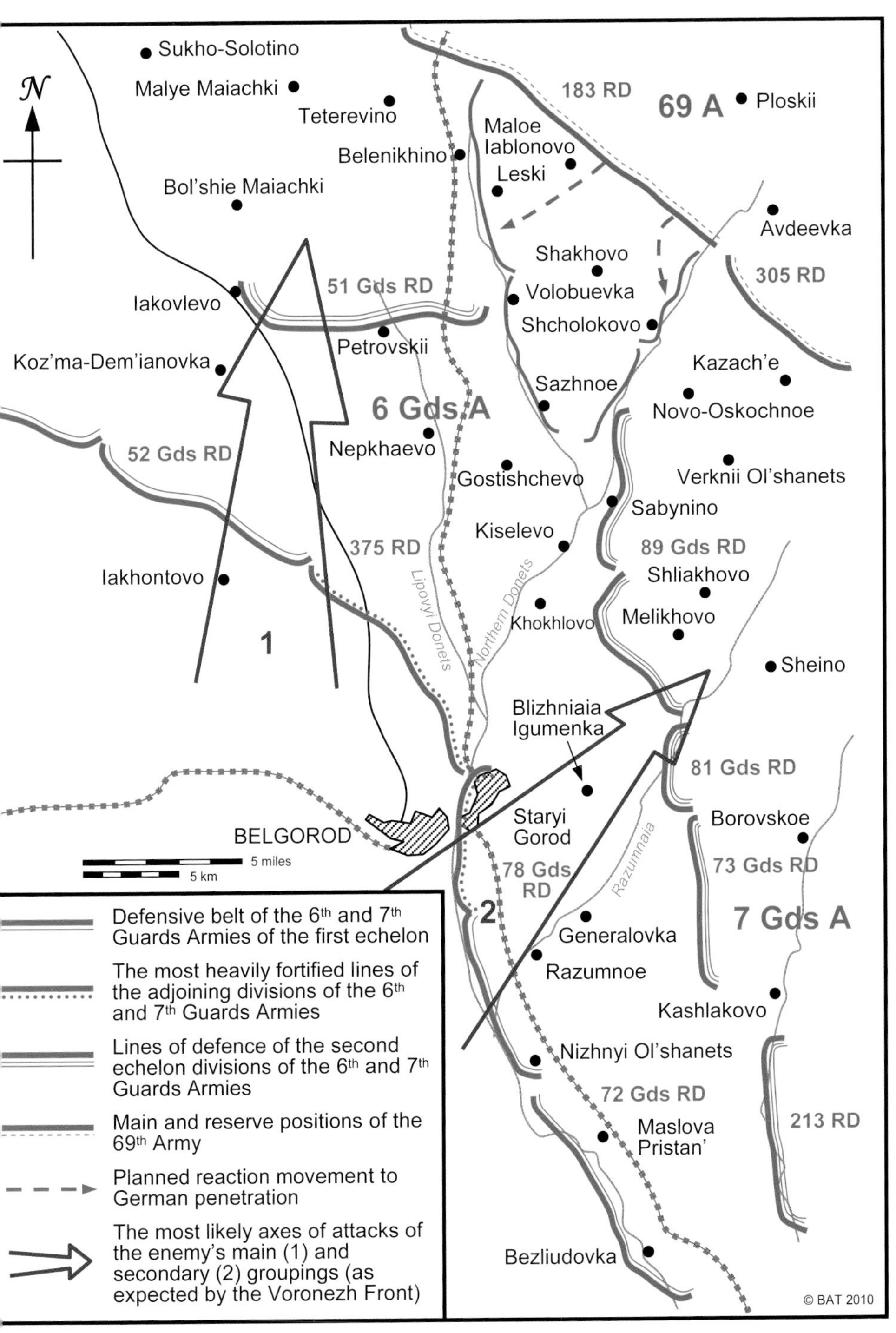

Vatutin's Plan; Voronezh Front's system of defense and the assumed directions of enemy attack

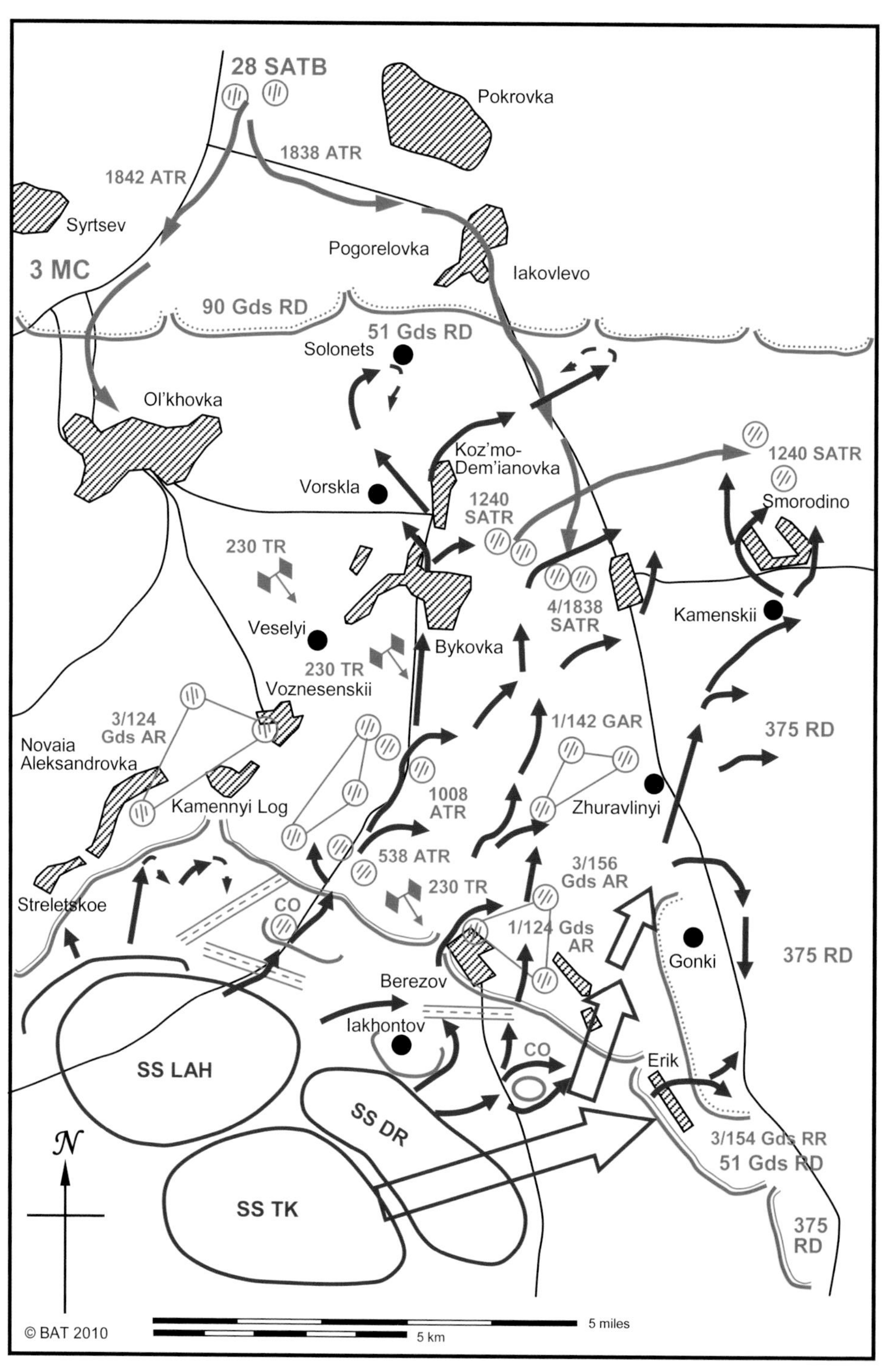

The Penetration of the 52nd Guards Rifle Division's Defenses by Divisions of the II SS Panzer Corps, 5 July 1943

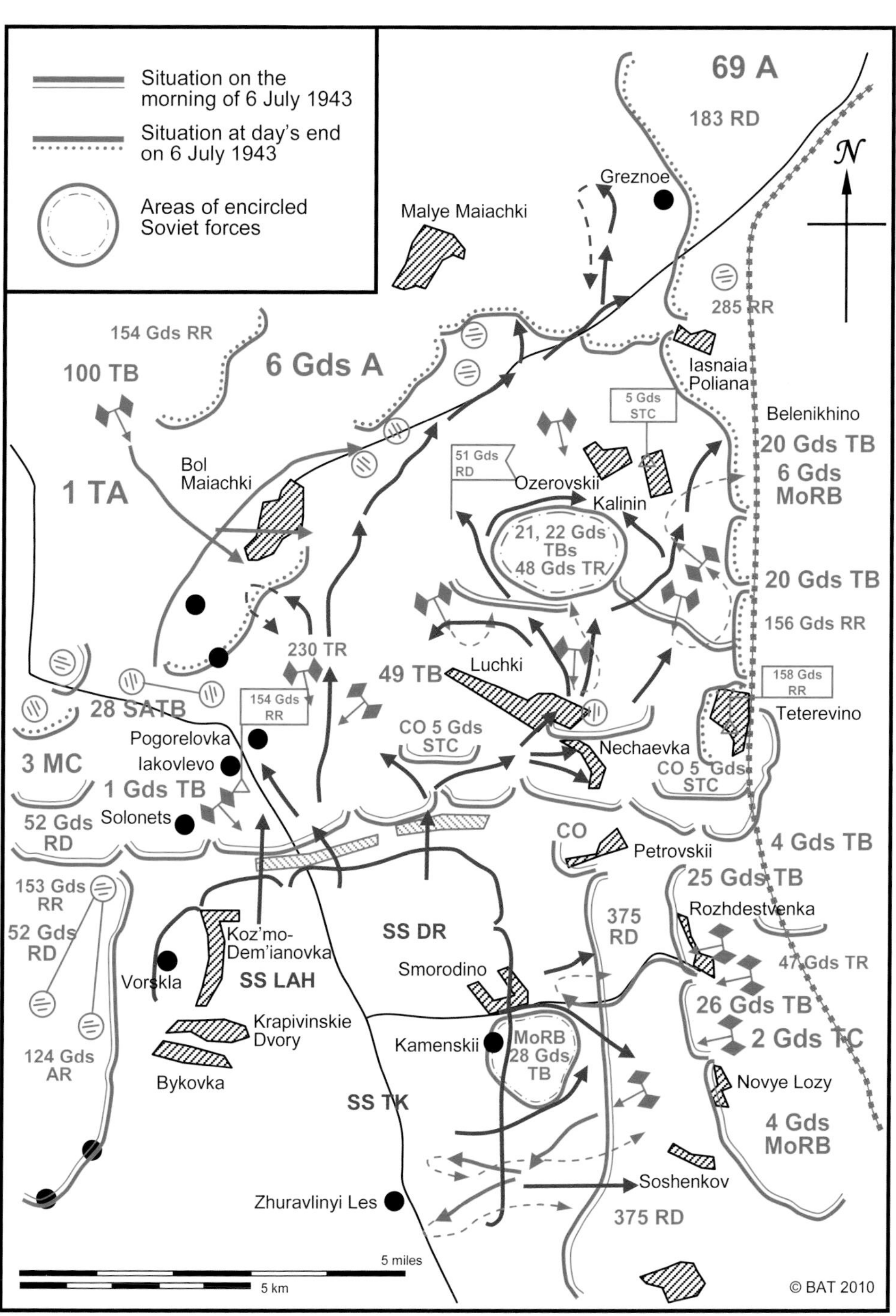

The II SS Panzer Corps' Breakthrough to the Prokhorovka Axis, 6 July 1943

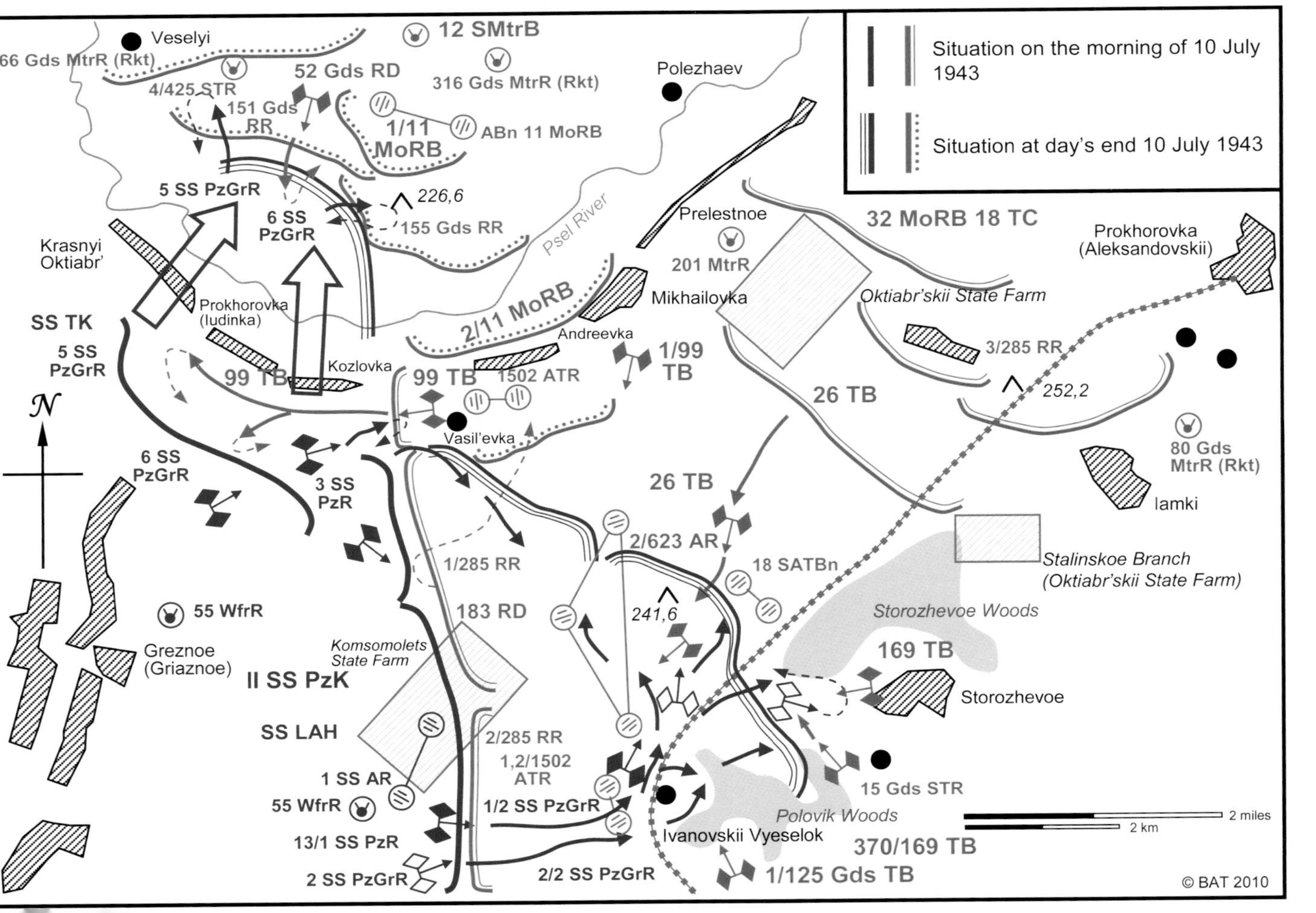

Combat Operations Southwest of Prokhorovka on 10 July 1943

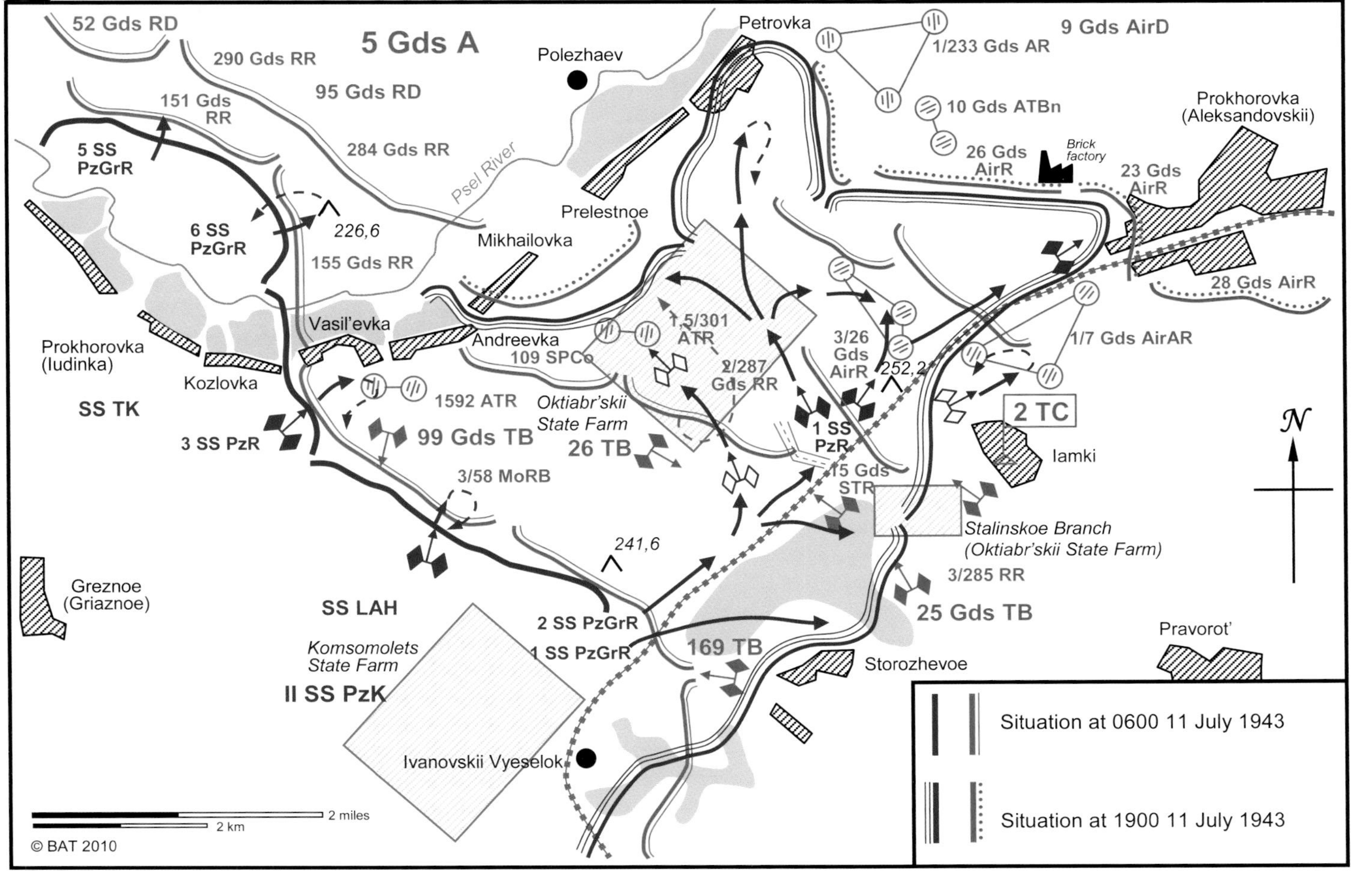

Combat Operations Southwest of Prokhorovka on 11 July 1943

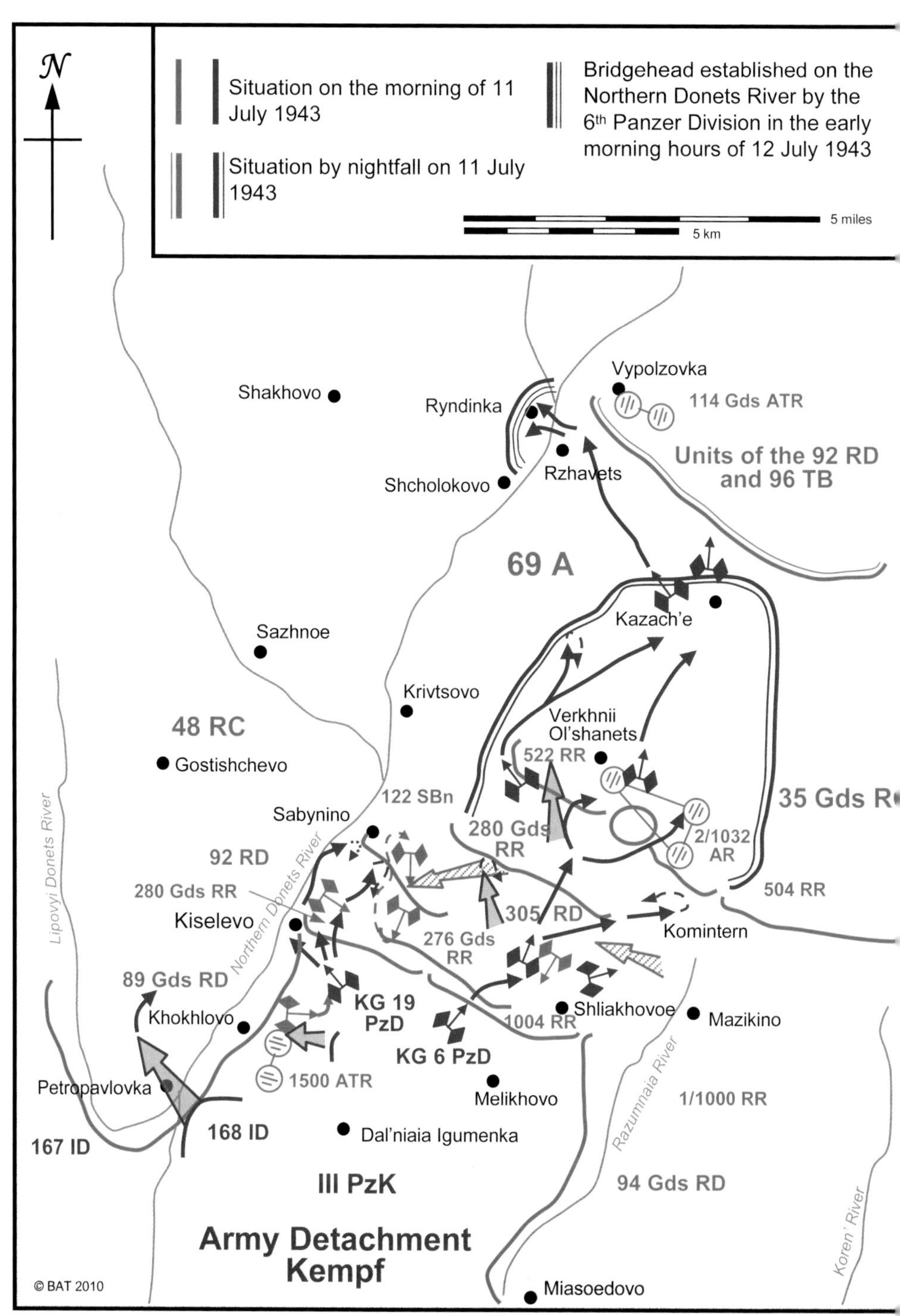

III Panzer Corps' Breakthrough of the 69th Army's Second Army-level Line on 11 July and Pre-dawn Hours of 12 July 1943

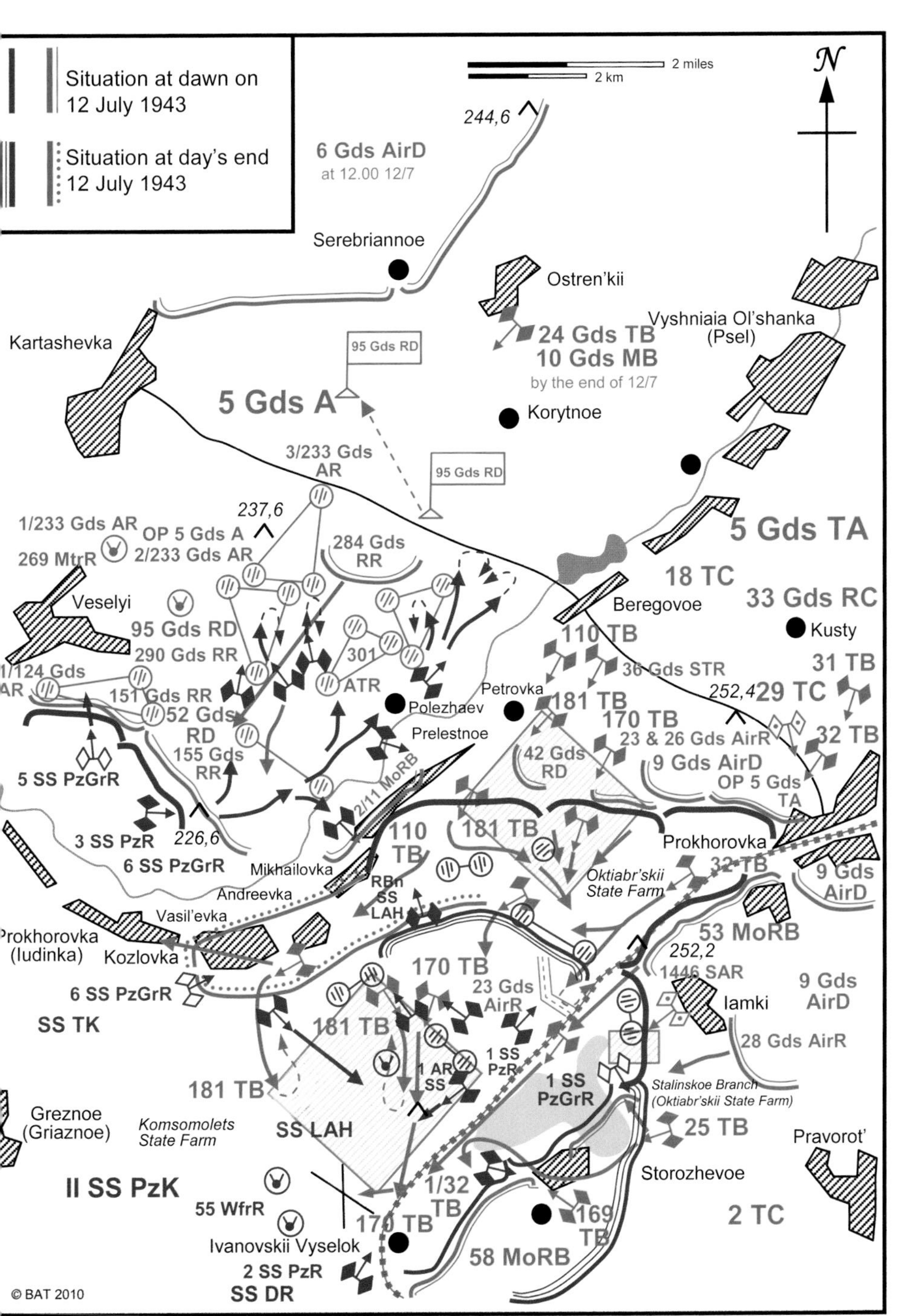

Combat Operations in the Sector of Voronezh Front's Main Counterattack Grouping on 12 July 1943

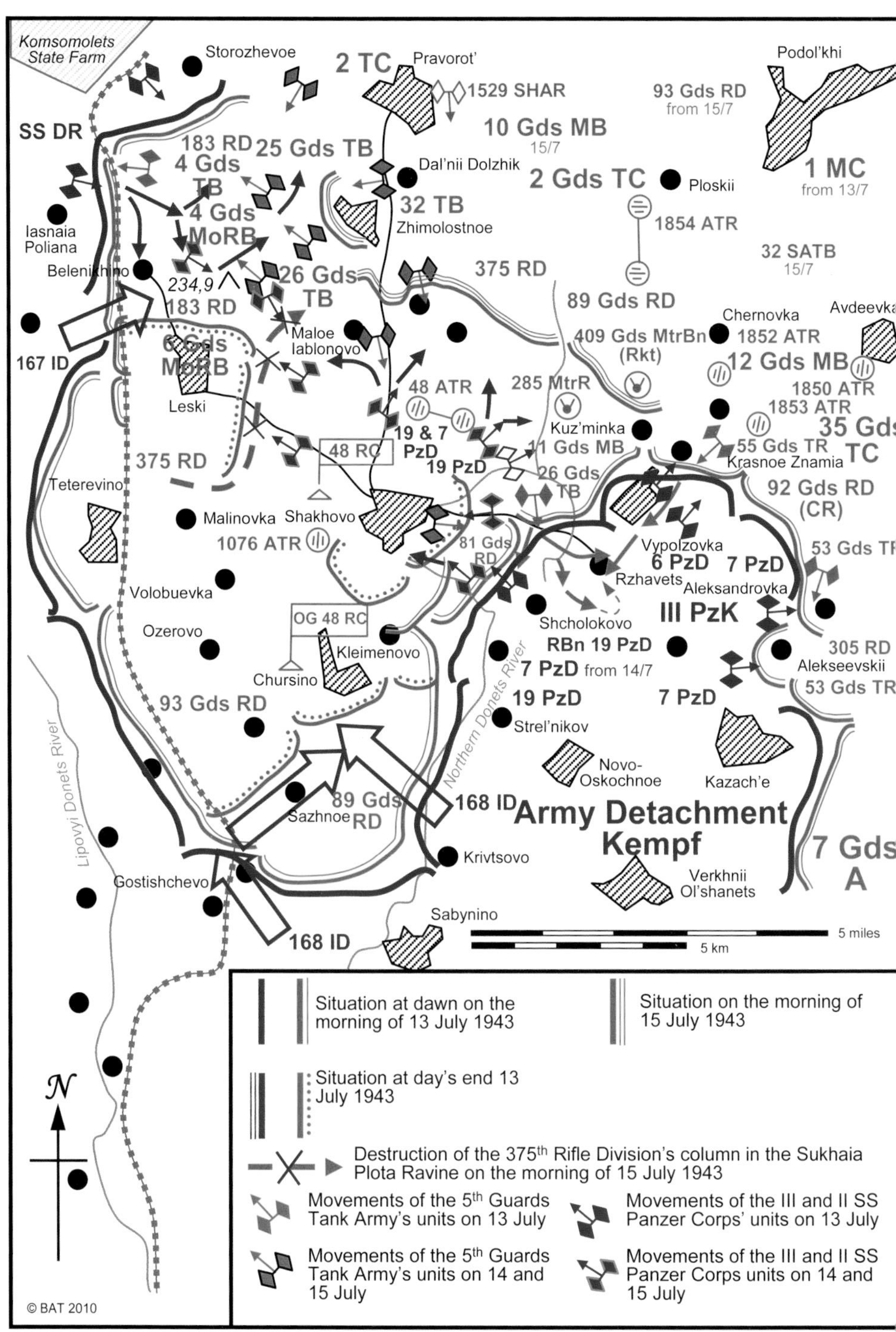

Combat Operations between the Northern Donets and Lipovyi Donets Rivers, 13-15 July 1943

reaching the point of hand-to-hand combat in the trenches. At this time, the 153rd Guards Rifle Regiment with its attached units had begun to cross the Psel River, in order to attack along the southern bank of the river. Thus, the division commander had been deprived of one-third of his division and his reserve, which was supposed to have liquidated any breakthrough by the enemy tanks. Practically speaking his division, having only one-third of its authorized strength, had been torn into two unequal parts, with the larger portion tied up in hard fighting with attacking units of the SS Panzergrenadier Division *Totenkopf*, while one regiment, which was in the process of crossing a river, was preparing to attack Mikhailovka together with the 42nd Guards Rifle Division's 126th Guards Rifle Regiment.

From SS Panzergrenadier Division *Totenkopf* dispatches:

> 0630 [0830 Moscow time]. The offensive in the direction of the barracks (west of Kliuchi), initiated at 0400 [0600] together with the panzer battalions that had crossed the evening before, is developing slowly. Very heavy artillery and *Katiusha* fire. Reports on the offensive to the northeast have still not arrived.
>
> 0705 [0905]. A very large concentration of infantry 3 kilometers east of Petrovka.
>
> 0822 [1022]. Two enemy regiments and almost 40 tanks at 0745 [0945] began moving toward Mikhailovka and the hills to the southeast.
>
> 1025 [1225]. An enemy battalion attacked from the north along the Psel River at 0900 [1100]. At 0715 [0915] the barracks were taken. The last units of the division have been passing over the bridge. The panzer regiment that crossed over the day before went on the attack at 0930 [1130] via Hill 226.6 in a northeasterly direction."[6]

SS *Totenkopf*'s main attack was launched from the area of Kliuchi and Iar Molozhavyi in the direction of Hill 226.6 and Hill 235.3 and the Beregovoe – Kartashevka road beyond. In order to secure the flanks of the breakthrough and to expand it, the SS systematically employed panzer attacks: on the left – in the direction of Veselyi and Hill 236.7, and on the right toward Polezhaev.

Here is how the chronology of events on the morning of 12 July appears, based upon the 52nd Guards Rifle Division's operational summary. At 0525 from the area of Kliuchi, the SS launched two attacks with an interval of fifteen minutes between them. The first attack to jump off involved 18 panzers with infantry support and was aimed at Veselyi and Major Baklan's 151st Guards Rifle Regiment. The second attack consisted of 15 tanks mounting infantry, and was aimed at Hill 226.6 through the sector of defense of Lieutenant Colonel A. A. Chistiakov's 155th Guards Rifle Regiment. This was the enemy's first panzer attack out of the bridgehead on the northern bank of the Psel River. Tanks with the support of Panzergrenadiers broke through the 155th Guards Rifle Regiment's front lines and drove towards Veselyi. The 95th Guards Rifle Division's journal of combat operations states:

> From the woods lying east of Kliuchi, the enemy managed to launch an attack on Veselyi with a company of submachine gunners and the support of 18 tanks [the source asserts these were Tiger tanks], and threatened to encircle the 290th

Colonel A. N. Liakhov, acting commander of the 95th Guards Rifle Division. (TsAMO)

> Guards Rifle Regiment's 1st and 3rd Battalions and the 108th Penal Company. Through the fire of artillery, mortars and anti-tank rifles, the attack of the enemy submachine gunners was beaten back.[7]

The rifle and machine-gun fire of our units pinned down the enemy's Panzergrenadiers, while the tanks that reached the outskirts of Veselyi were greeted by the fire of the 1st Battalion of the 52nd Guards Rifle Division's 124th Guards Artillery Regiment. Having lost two tanks, the SS retreated. Soldiers of the 155th Guards Rifle Regiment also helped erase the slender enemy penetration into the depths of our defenses.

Colonel A. N. Liakhov's 95th Guards Rifle Division was also caught in a difficult situation. Its rifle regiments were preparing to move into the first line of trenches occupied by the 52nd Guards Rifle Division, while the entire command staff of the artillery regiment (down to the battery commanders inclusively) headed by Major A. P. Revin was away on reconnaissance. *Totenkopf*'s attack preempted the 95th Guards Rifle Division's deployment and subsequent attack. The division's units were forced hastily to go over to the defense while under fire. In the 290th Guards Rifle Regiment, the regiment commander himself was caught in a predicament of his own creation. The division commander later accused:

> On 12 July the commander of the 290th [Guards] Rifle Regiment Zaiarny Fedor Mikhailovich removed himself from command of his regiment, driving off to the second echelon feigning illness. When the divisional command post demanded to know where he was and where his units were located, he gave an incorrect location ...[8]

Operations officers on the staff of the 5th Guards Army headquarters in their post-battle "Account of combat operations" pointed to a number of important aspects of the disorganization in Liakhov's 95th Guards Rifle Division while moving into its jumping-off positions for the planned attack. From the account of 5th Guards Army's headquarters:

> The main defects in the period of the offensive ... consisted of the lack of cooperation between the artillery and infantry of the 95th Guards Rifle Division. The units did not reach the jumping-off position for the attack in a timely fashion. Regiment commanders did not know their assignments – for example, Lieutenant Colonel Seletsky and Major Takmovtsev[9] were summoned to the command post at 0800 that morning in order to receive their orders, but by this time the fighting had already started.[10]

There is no need for a detailed explanation as to how the confusion in this sector happened on the morning of 12 July, if some regiments had already moved out to attack, while others were waiting for the return of their commanders, who had been summoned to headquarters in order to receive their combat orders. Even more, all this was occurring against the backdrop of sharp, disruptive German panzer attacks and the shaky stand of the 52nd Guards Rifle Division in the first echelon.

A second SS attack didn't follow immediately, nor did any bombing attacks. It became clear that the enemy had been only feeling out the defenses, searching for a weak spot. It had been decided apparently not to disperse strength, but instead launch a strong attack on a single location later in the day. The choice fell upon Hill 226.6.

The direct correlation between the activity shown by *Totenkopf*'s combat group north of the Psel River and the results of *Leibstandarte*'s fighting south of the river is evident. A direct communication link between their two headquarters had been established, and the command of both formations exchanged information and coordinated their operations. Up until the middle of the day, the situation in *Leibstandarte*'s sector remained unclear, so Priess temporarily suspended his attack, waiting for the results of his neighbor's fighting on the right. After 1100, it had become clear that Wisch's troops had withstood the attack of the Russian tank corps and had initiated more active operations, so Priess resumed his offensive, targeting Hill 226.6.

The 52nd Guards Rifle Division's Operational Summary No. 336 reveals:

> At 1150, having penetrated the forward defenses, 42 enemy tanks emerged at Hill 226.6, with the aim to continue the attack in the direction of Hill 236.7. Following enemy infantry were cut off from the tanks and forced to take cover, but continued to exchange fire. The majority of the enemy tanks, firing their cannons and machine guns, drove back and forth across the top of Hill 226.6 and the regiment's combat positions. Under the pressure of superior enemy forces, the regiment's elements initiated a fighting withdrawal to the north.[11]

Having overrun the defenses on Hill 226.6, the Germans exploited to the north, towards Hill 236.7. This was the commanding height in the area, which offered good visibility of the surrounding area from its crest, and especially into the Psel River valley. Therefore, the command post of the 95th Guards Rifle Division's artillery commander was situated here, and from early morning army commander Lieutenant General Zhadov was located here too. The army commander was aware of the situation in the divisions and the results of the morning fighting. Therefore, when the SS had launched their assault on Hill 226.6, he understood that a real threat of an enemy breakthrough had arisen as he watched the units of the 52nd and 95th Guards Rifle Divisions begin to retreat. So he then ordered Colonel M. N. Smirnov, the commander of his reserve 6th Guards Airborne Division, to go over to the defense with his formation along the line Nizhniaia Ol'shanka – Ostren'kii and on the heights belonging to it. Simultaneously, he ordered up the 8th Guards Airborne Artillery Regiment of this division to Hill 236.7, and deployed two batteries of the 5th Guards Destroyer Anti-tank Artillery Battalion on the crest of the hill. At 1300, these units opened fire on the attacking German tanks.

Wrote General Zhadov after the war:

> At 1215, enemy infantry and up to 100 tanks launched a counterattack in the direction of Hill 236.7. Soon, more than 40 tanks and several hundred motorcyclists had broken through in this area. Located at the observation post, which had been set-up on this very hill, I ordered the commander of the 233rd Guards Artillery Regiment Major A. P. Revin[12] to destroy the fascist tanks. In the bitter fighting, which developed on the southern slopes of the hill, the Guardsmen-artillerymen stood to the death.
>
> Located just 200-300 meters from the place of fighting, I observed it closely. Even now, I can see the sergeant, the communist, gun commander Andrei Borisovich Danilov[13] – a Siberian from Krasnoiarsk and a veteran of Stalingrad. Together with him the Ukrainian Panchenko, the Kazakh Ibraev and the Mordvinian Pankratov fought to their deaths. When the entire crew had fallen in this unequal duel with the enemy, Danilov continued a lone struggle with the attacking tanks. After the death of the neighboring gun crew, regiment commander Revin himself took position at the gun. In front of my eyes, Revin set fire to an enemy tank, while the Guardsmen-artillerymen stopped the motorcyclists with automatic fire and grenades.
>
> The scorched remains of 16 tanks with crosses on their sides remained on the battlefield, and the corpses of hundreds of motorcyclists and submachine gunners. But many warrior Guardsmen also remained to lie forever at the foot of Hill 236.7.[14]

By 1300, the SS *Totenkopf* armored *kampfgruppe* had shoved back elements of the 290th Guards and 284th Guards Rifle Regiments by 300-800 meters and had occupied their trenches north of Kliuchi and on the northern slopes of Hill 226.6. One Soviet report at that time stated grimly, "The situation had arisen, when our units had partially yielded their prepared defenses, surrendered a dominating height, and had consumed up to 80% of their ammunition, especially that of their battalion and regimental artillery."[15]

The 95th Guards Rifle Division's journal of combat operations reveals:

> At the time of the division's arrival in the region of defense, it had only a 1 to 1.5 combat load of ammunition, of which it had already expended up to one day's worth [on the morning of 12 July]. Despite requests for assistance by providing transportation for bringing up more ammunition from the army-level dumps, superior commanders rendered no assistance at all. Available trucks – ten – on 11.07.43 had been sent to the army dumps for ammunition, and the last trucks returned empty at 2200 12.07.43. All this affected the course of the battle.
>
> Moreover, our own aviation twice struck the combat formations of our infantry and artillery, as a result of which two tractors were smashed together with the artillery shells they were towing; (there are) losses in personnel.[16]

At this time, savage fighting was still continuing atop Hill 226.6. Encircled elements of the 11th Motorized Rifle Brigade were fighting desperately. Worn down in preceding fighting, the brigade was attacked by the tanks of a numerically superior enemy. The struggle was hard and bloody. German tank crews crushed entrenchments beneath the tracks of their tanks, trying to grind into the dirt anyone who could offer resistance. The brigade's artillery suffered heavy losses, and the Germans managed to split the brigade into several pieces. On 14 July 1943, the 11th Motorized Rifle Brigade's political commander Major Kovlev wrote in a dispatch:

> At 1200 12 July 1943 the enemy launched a resolute attack on our brigade's defenses, with the main blow directed at Krasnyi Oktiabr' and Hill 226.6, and hurling up to a regiment of infantry [into the attack] behind 64 tanks.
>
> After five hours of uninterrupted, bitter fighting, which included hand-to-hand combat in the trenches; exploiting the lack of steadfastness of our neighbors on the right – the 95th Guards Rifle Division's 156th Guards Rifle Regiment, and on the left – the 52nd Guards Rifle Division's 151st Guards Rifle Regiment, which exposed our flanks by falling back, the enemy succeeded in breaking into the depths of our defense with tanks and motorized infantry and in developing the offensive with attacks on our front, flanks and rear. For the next two hours, the 2nd and 3rd Motorized Rifle Battalions fought in complete encirclement, while the 1st Motorized Rifle Battalion struggled in semi-encirclement. Numerically small and weakened by the breakdown of weapons, the brigade was compelled under the cover of artillery to withdraw from the fight and turn over the defense to units of the 95th Guards Rifle Division and the 42nd Guards Rifle Division …
>
> … The men exhibited good combat training and an exceptionally high political spirit and morale in the fighting.
>
> … Alongside the positive factors in the brigade, there were manifestations of criminal cowardice. The commander of the 1st Motorized Rifle Battalion Captain Timov and his chief of staff Captain Bugarsky ran away from the command post at the very climax of the intense fighting. Battalion commander Comrade Timov lost all control over his men and wound up at the command post of a different unit, while his chief of staff Captain Bugarsky completely ran away to the rear area of his battalion, and for two days of intense combat never showed himself on the battlefield. Thanks to the fact that the battalion's deputy commander responsible

> for drilling the units assumed leadership over the battalion's fighting, the battalion continued to carry out its given assignment.
>
> An investigation into the facts surrounding the criminal cowardliness of the aforementioned commanders is being treated as a case subject to the justice of a military tribunal.[17]

Around 1300, a group of grenadiers under the cover of panzers reached the western bank of the Psel River [beyond its bend] in the vicinity of Polezhaev and tried to force a crossing into the rear of the 18th Tank Corps. However, the 18th Tank Corps foiled this attempt, though fighting here lasted for more than an hour.

SS Division *Totenkopf*'s next, even stronger attack occurred around 1500, when the advance of the 18th and 29th Tank Corps had conclusively been stopped. From the 52nd Guards Rifle Division's operational summary:

> At 1500 13 enemy tanks conducted an attack from Hill 226.6 toward Polezhaev and at 1530 approached the dirt road southwest of Polezhaev. The attack was repulsed by elements of the 153rd Guards Rifle Regiment and artillery. At 1600, 36 enemy tanks from Hill 226.6 descended into the depression north of Hill 226.6 and moving through the ravine west of Polezhaev headed toward Hill 236.7. Reaching the hill, the tanks spent an hour driving back and forth on it, and then departed into the depression west of Hill 236.7.[18]

The cited document doesn't give a clear picture of what occurred at this time in the valleys and on the hills in the bend of the river. It was written by staff officers of the 52nd Guards Rifle Division, who were observing the combat from the sidelines. This gives the readers of the operational summary the impression that the tanks, without encountering any resistance, "cruised around" the hill for an hour, and then on their own decided to depart into the depression.

This was in fact the critical moment of the day. Units of the 95th Guards Rifle Division received both attacks. Hill 236.7 was important in a tactical sense, because it dominated the area of the river bend. By this time the enemy had already taken possession of the positions of the 52nd Guards Rifle Division's regiments, and thus the main burden for holding the line of defense in the center of the army fell upon the 95th Guards Rifle Division. But unfortunately, its units could not alone withstand the enemy attack without assistance. From the account of the 5th Guards Army headquarters:

> Units of the 95th Guards Rifle Division as a result of the headquarters' loss of control during the enemy attack, having failed to repulse the enemy tank attack, spontaneously retreated to their former lines, and on 13.07.43 the division was brought back into order.[19]

The division's defense was cut into several pieces. On several isolated sectors, rifle platoons and companies were driven from their trenches, leaving others battling

In the combat positions of the 5th Guards Army's 95th Guards Rifle Division in the bend of the Psel River. (RGAKFD)

stubbornly in encirclement, with soldiers fighting hand-to-hand in their trenches. The 5th Guards Army's account observes:

> The infantry, driving back several fierce attacks, calmly continued to fight even when enemy tanks passed through their positions, and repeatedly separated the German infantry from their tanks, inflicting significant casualties. At the cost of large losses, the enemy managed to push back our units. The infantry's retreat was insufficiently organized.[20]

Only part of the opponent's forces penetrated toward Hill 236.7; the main blow of the SS was directed at Hill 235.3. It was located next to the Beregovoe – Kartashevka road, which the SS division was trying to cut. A deep gully lay in front of this hill, with branches spreading to the north and south. The gully ran from Veselyi in the direction of Beregovoe. Its deepest section fell between Veselyi and Hill 236.7. Artillery positions had been set up on the northern slopes of this hill. Between Veselyi and the Borushina gully, batteries of Major P. D. Boiko's 103rd Guards Separate Destroyer Anti-tank Artillery Battalion were dug-in.[21] Batteries of Major Bugaev's 1st Battalion of the 233rd Guards Artillery Regiment extended Boiko's line of guns. On the axis of SS Division *Totenkopf*'s main attack – in the area of Hill 235.3 – the 95th Guards Rifle Division's commander Colonel Liakhov concentrated elements of Lieutenant Colonel V. S. Nakaidze's 284th Guards Rifle Regiment, which had fallen back from the northeast slopes of Hill 226.6,

Lieutenant Colonel V. S. Nakaidze, commander of the 95th Guards Rifle Division's 284th Guards Rifle Regiment. (TsAMO)

the 2nd and 3rd Battalions of the 233rd Guards Artillery Regiment, as well as his personal reserve – the remaining batteries of Major Boiko's battalion.

Here is what remained in the memory of the 95th Guards Rifle Division's artillery commander, N. D. Sebezhko, about this difficult moment:

> I should note that this powerful strike was received for the most part by the artillery of our division. If in the sector, where the meeting tank engagement unfolded, the relative impact of the artillery was insignificant, then in our division's sector of defense, the artillery resisted the main blow of the enemy's attacking armor grouping.
>
> When the adversary began to approach the southern slopes of Hill 235.3 and the northern outskirts of Polezhaev, a real threat of a breakthrough and the enemy's emergence on the Kartashevka – Prokhorovka road had arisen, which meant as well a path into the rear of the 18th Tank Corps on the left. The critical moment had arrived.
>
> Grasping the situation that was developing, the division commander hurled all available means and reserves into the battle: the penal company, a company of submachine gunners and other elements, but most importantly, he drew all the artillery into the struggle with the enemy tanks. The entire 233rd Guards Artillery Regiment under the command of Guards Major A. P. Revin was deployed to fire over open sights. The regiment commander managed quickly to deploy and open fire with all his gun batteries, leaving behind only his howitzer batteries in their concealed firing positions. Major P. D. Boiko's 103rd Guards Separate Destroyer Anti-tank Artillery Regiment was also thrown into the battle … Major Boiko

Officers of the 95th Guards Rifle Division's 233rd Guards Artillery Regiment prepare data for firing. (RGAKFD)

was always in the thick of the fighting, skillfully handled his batteries, and by his personal example inspired the soldiers and officers under his command.[22]

The operations of the divisional and anti-tank artillery were seriously complicated by the absence of cooperation with the rifle infantry elements. This was particularly the case in the sector of the 284th Guards Rifle Regiment, which was located on the *Totenkopf* armored *kampfgruppe*'s main axis of attack, and resulted in heavy consequences. After the enemy had occupied Hill 226.6 and attacked the position of the 95th Guards Rifle Division, its continuous line of defense broke into scattered pockets of resistance. With the collapse of the 52nd Guards Rifle Division's defenses in front of them, separate platoons, companies and pieces of battalions, at times from different regiments of the 95th Guards Rifle Division, quickly took position on the first pieces of ground suitable for resistance they could find. Gaps existed between these hastily organized knots of resistance, in which the artillery batteries and battalions deployed their guns, attempting to help the infantry hold the defense. They concentrated their fire primarily on enemy tanks. In this situation, the rifle units were forced to fight on their own, trying at any cost not to let the enemy pass through their positions. At the same time, the artillery was left without any cover.

Wrote the staff officers of the 5th Guards Army in their account of the fighting:

> The absence of such infantry protection led to the situation where on the sector of the 95th Guards Rifle Division on 12.07.43, enemy submachine gunners, who had infiltrated unnoticed in the confusion of battle between the gaps in the line, advanced upon the artillery observation post and created a serious threat to the gun crews. As a result, gun crews of the 8th and part of the 9th Batteries of the 233rd Guards Artillery Regiment were killed, as well as its commander.[23]

It should be said that Major Revin's death has been described differently in various publications. The majority of authors, without bothering to check the source documents, write that Revin was killed at a gun, where he had taken the place of a fallen gun layer. This isn't correct. Already on 13 July, the 95th Guards Rifle Division artillery commander, when reporting on the losses over the period from 11 July to 13 July 1943, as well as in the 95th Guards Rifle Division's account of the fighting cited above, both stated that "the commander of the 233rd Guards Artillery Regiment, Guards Major Revin A. P., was killed at the observation post on 12.07.43."[24]

The attack, which was initiated at 1500, continued without interruption for three hours. It was apparent that the adversary had resolved to break through at any cost, and for this purpose it was first necessary to destroy our artillery. But the defenders understood the importance of the moment: many with light wounds or moderate wounds refused to leave the battlefield. The anti-tank riflemen of Senior Lieutenant P. I. Shpetny's platoon from the 95th Guards Rifle Division's 284th Guards Rifle Regiment served as a real example of fortitude in battle and heroism. The platoon was defending on one of the low hills southwest of Polezhaev. During one of the attacks, the anti-tank riflemen knocked out several tanks, but the forces were unequal. Gun crews were dying and ammunition was running out, but the enemy continued to attack. That is when the platoon commander took his final step: bleeding from wounds, with a grenade bundles in his hands, he threw himself under an enemy tank. A pillar of flame and smoke erupted from the enemy vehicle, but the brave officer was also killed. The enemy attack faltered. On the line of the heroic platoon's defense, only smoking craters remained – and the bodies of eight dead Guardsmen by their anti-tank rifles on the breastworks. For his self-sacrificial feat, Pavel Ivanovich Shpetny was posthumously awarded the title of Hero of the Soviet Union.

The rocket-launching *Katiusha* regiments rendered great assistance to our units, both during the repulse of this attack and throughout the entire day. For the Kursk battle, all of Voronezh Front's Guards mortar units were drawn together into a single operational group. It consisted of 12 mortar regiments (with 24 rocket launchers in each) and three separate battalions (eight rocket launchers in each). For greater flexibility in maneuvering, this operational group was divided into two army-level operational groups. The first was commanded by Colonel I. S. Iofa, whose headquarters were located in Skorovka. Its *Katiushas* operated in the sector of the 69th Army and the 5th Guards Tank Army. The second group under the command of Colonel Tereshonek supported the 5th and 6th Guards Armies with its fire.

A Soviet intelligence officer interrogating prisoners at a collection point. (Author's personal archive)

On 12 July, the 8th Battalion of the 66th Guards Mortar Regiment, the 444th and 445th Battalions of the 316th Guards Mortar Regiment, and the 361st Battalion of the 80th Guards Mortar Regiment directly worked over targets in the areas of Kliuchi, Veselyi and Bogoroditskoe. In total, they launched over a thousand shells during the day. The 8th Battalion of the 66th Guards Mortar Regiment launched rockets particularly intensively, expending 391 shells on the attacking panzers of *Totenkopf's* armored *kampfgruppe* in the vicinity of Veselyi alone. The Guards mortar regiments launched primarily the M-13 132mm fragmentation shells, but they struck the built-up locations of Bogoroditskoe, Kliuchi and Vasil'evka with the more powerful M-20 *fougasse* shell that carried 18.4 kilograms of explosives in its warhead. This was three times greater than the amount in the M-13 shell.

Because of the rapidly changing situation, the crews of the Guards mortar regiments had to act in extreme conditions. Often, the rocket launchers were used for firing over open sights at ranges of 800-1000 meters during the tank attack. The shock wave and wall of exploding *Katiusha* shells not only knocked out enemy armor, but set fire to it, because all the *Wermacht*'s panzers and half-tracks were equipped with benzene engines.

Nevertheless, the rocket artillery's primary target was infantry. Here are a couple of eyewitness accounts taken from German prisoners of the effectiveness of a *Katiusha* salvo on those who directly came under one. Erich Wulff, senior grenadier in the

332nd Infantry Division's 678th Infantry Regiment: "... from the rocket artillery fire our company instantly lost up to 20% of our men. I fought in many countries, but never encountered any artillery like the Russians." *Gefreiter* Erich Kohn, 678th Infantry Regiment: "The rocket artillery fire produces a terrible effect on the morale of the soldiers and extinguishes any desire to attack. Our company on the first day of the offensive sustained up to 80% casualties, half of which were due to rocket artillery fire."[25]

The Germans also made widespread use of rocket artillery in the engagement. The *Wehrmacht* was primarily equipped with 158mm and 210mm rocket launchers. As a rule, their fire was concentrated on a narrow sector of the front and was quite effective. However, these rocket launchers were significantly inferior to the Soviet models of rocket artillery in range and density of fire.

At 1600, at the height of the fighting around Polezhaev and Hills 236.7 and 235.3, the commander of the 33rd Guards Rifle Corps Major General I. I. Popov wrote the following order:

> To the commanders of the 42nd, 52nd, 95th and 97th Guards Divisions.
>
> In order to destroy the enemy tanks, operating in the region (excl.) Veselyi – Polezhaev – Hill 226.6 – Kliuchi, I order:
>
> 1. For the commander of the 42nd Guards Rifle Division to deploy 10 guns in the areas of Andreevka and Mikhailovka for firing across the valley of the Psel River from east to west.
> 2. For the commander of the 97th Guards Rifle Division to set up 10 guns in the area of Il'inskii for firing across the same valley from the northwest to the southeast.
> 3. For the commanders of the 52nd and 95th Guards Rifle Division immediately to bring up guns as closely as possible to the enemy for the destruction of enemy tanks in the Veselyi – Polezhaev – Hill 226.0 – Kliuchi area. All three points of the order are to be ready by 1800 today.
> 4. Open general fire on the enemy tanks at 1810 today at the signal – a series of red flares, launched by the 95th Guards Rifle Division's commander from Hill 236.7.
>
> The guns of the 42nd and 97th Guards Rifle Division will open fire when the targeted tanks begin to retreat from north to south across the Psel River valley.
>
> 5. After the enemy tanks begin to retreat, to give a salvo of rocket artillery and for the infantry to move forward swiftly to the northern bank of the Psel River.
> 6. All artillery groups are to have an observation post with good observers.
>
> ...
>
> 1. I place general leadership over the outlined operation on the commander of the artillery corps Guards Colonel Sobolev.[26]

Thus, by 1800 in the bend of the Psel River, the artillery of the Guards divisions were to create a cauldron of fire in the breakthrough area of SS Panzergrenadier Division *Totenkopf*'s armored *kampfgruppe*. According to the situation, depicted on the personal map of the commander of the 95th Guards Rifle Division's artillery, the enemy advance in the direction of the Prokhorovka – Kartashevka road was halted conclusively at 1730. For all practical purposes, this was the turning point in the 5th Guards Army's sector.

Although after 1800 the SS undertook a few more attacks, including tank attacks, the situation had stabilized and our units began to strengthen their current lines.

The hard combat which units of the 52nd and 95th Guards Rifle Division's endured came at a costly price. The main events unfolded in the trenches of the rifle units. The stubbornness of the Guardsmen enraged the Germans, and the panzer crews had taken vengeance on the defenders. Surviving veterans later said that the tanks had literally ironed the trenches with their treads. Having noticed a rifleman's slit trench, the tankers would drive on top of it and perform a figure-eight over it, trying to bury the soldier beneath their tracks.

As N. D. Sebezhko later recalled:

> The situation had become so critical that in order to carry out his duties, the chief of staff of the 233rd Guards Artillery Regiment Guards Captain P. P Beletsky had to deploy all the howitzer batteries to fire over open sights (by this moment the regiment commander A. P. Revin had been mortally wounded). ... These prompt and decisive steps of Guards Captain P. P. Beletsky indeed were approved as most appropriate by the division command.[27]

Only the heavy shells of the howitzers at this decisive moment could stop the advancing German armored wedge. However, things were very hard for the artillerymen of the 95th Guards Rifle Division on this day. From the 95th Guards Rifle Division's artillery staff operational summary for 2000 12 July:

> For the 233rd Guards Artillery Regiment – killed: regiment commander Guards Major Revin A. P., deputy battalion commander Guards Senior Lieutenant Lisitsyn, and commander of the 7th Battery Guards Senior Lieutenant Flius; wounded: commander of the 3rd Battalion Guards Captain Ternavsky, commander of the 1st Battery Guards Lieutenant Mikhailov, and commanders of the fire direction platoons Guards Lieutenants Efgrafov, Demshin and Busorgin. Eight junior commanders and 11 Red Army servicemen were wounded, and 11 junior officers and 22 Red Army servicemen are missing in action.[28]
>
> Armament and equipment losses: Destroyed – 5 ZIS-3 guns, 4 panoramic aiming devices, 4 azimuth compasses, 3 stereoscopes, 3 RB radios, 25 telephone sets, 33 kilometers of telephone cable, 30 carbines, 40 gas masks; Tow vehicles – 2 tractors with their trailers and 4 trucks.
>
> In the 103rd Guards Separate Destroyer Anti-tank Artillery Battalion – killed: platoon commander Guards Lieutenant Popov and 5 enlisted men; wounded: Battery commander Guards Lieutenant Mashin and 7 junior commanders and enlisted men. In equipment: the 45mm guns were destroyed by enemy fire; two Willys jeeps were damaged and require repairs.
>
> In the artillery of the rifle regiments: killed – 45mm battery commander Guards Lieutenant Gulevsky, 8 junior commanders and 14 enlisted men; wounded – 8 midlevel commanders, 12 junior commanders and 24 enlisted men.
>
> Equipment: Destroyed or crushed by enemy tanks: 45mm guns – 12, 76mm guns – 2, tow equipment – 2 trucks; 16 killed and 4 wounded horses.[29]

The rifle units of Colonel A. N Liakhov's 95th Guards Rifle Division also suffered heavy losses, especially the 284th Guards Rifle Regiment. According to the lists of killed-in-action of this regiment that I managed to discover in the Central Archives of the Ministry of Defense, on 12 July the 284th Guards Rifle Regiment lost 200 men killed, including 137 in the 1st Rifle Battalion, 51 in the 2nd Rifle Battalion and 8 in the 3rd Rifle Battalion.

The situation in the sector of the 5th Guards Army alarmed the Voronezh Front command. At 1915, Vatutin signed Order No. 036/OP:

> 1. According to a dispatch from the commander of the 5th Guards Army, the enemy with a force of up to 100 tanks and motorized infantry [Panzergrenadiers] have broken through on the northern bank of the Psel River from the Krasnyi Oktiabr' area in the direction of Hill 236.7.
>
> I order:
>
> By the combined actions of elements of the 5th Guards Army and the 5th Guards Tank Army to encircle and destroy this enemy, for which:
>
> a) the commander of the 5th Guards Army is to organize personally the destruction of this enemy, to use for this units of the 95th, 52nd and 6th Guards Rifle Divisions, as well as the army's anti-tank artillery reinforcements. ... Do not in any case allow the breakthrough of the enemy across the Ol'shanka River in the direction of Oboian' and Rzhava, or to the northeast and east.
>
> b) the commander of the 5th Guards Tank Army by the introduction of units of the 5th Mechanized Corps into the battle together with units of the 5th Guards Army is to destroy the indicated enemy;
>
> c) Report on the execution [of this order] by 2400 12.07[30]

To fulfill this order, at 2030 the commander of the 5th Guards Tank Army issued the following order:

> To the commander of the 18th Tank Corps, with copies to the 2nd Guards 'Tatsinskaia' Tank Corps, the 2nd Tank Corps, the 5th Guards 'Zimovniki' Mechanized Corps and the 29th Tank Corps.
>
> Enemy tanks are on the line: northern outskirts of Polezhaev – Hill 236.7. By this, the enemy is threatening the right flank and rear of the army.
>
> The army commander has ordered:
>
> 1. The commander of the 5th Guards 'Zimovniki' Mechanized Corps to advance the 24th Guards Tank Brigade to the area of Voroshilovskii State Farm and the northern outskirts of Polezhaev, with orders – to prevent an enemy advance to the northwest and southwest; the 10th Guards Mechanized Brigade is to deploy in the region of Ostren'kii with orders – to block the enemy to the northeast and east.
> 2. The commander of the 18th Tank Corps is to secure the deployment of the 24th Guards Tank Brigade, for which purpose it is to throw out covering forces to the northern outskirts of Petrovka and to Point 181.9.[31]

In certain publications it is asserted that supposedly it was only the attack of these two brigades that managed to halt the enemy in the 5th Guards Army sector on the evening of 12 July. This view was also put forward by P. A. Rotmistrov:

> The swift maneuver of these brigades to the their assigned areas and their decisive meeting attacks against the Hitlerite tanks that had broken through stabilized the situation on the joint flanks of the 5th Guards Tank and 5th Guards Armies. The adversary was compelled to retreat here, and then to go over to the defense.[32]

The former commander of the 5th Guards Tank Army substitutes the desirable for the real in this matter. According to the report from the headquarters of the 5th Guards Mechanized Corps, "Information on the status of units and formations of the 5th Guards 'Zimovniki' Mechanized Corps for 16.07.43," both brigades conducted no combat operations on 12 July and suffered no losses.[33] This is confirmed as well by documents of the headquarters of the 10th Guards Tank Brigade's 51st Guards Tank Regiment. According to them, on 12 July at 2145 the regiment arrived on the western outskirts of Malaia Psinka and by 2310 had taken up defensive positions there and never entered into combat.[34]

By the moment of both brigades' appearance on the battlefield, the enemy had already been stopped by the heroic defense of the units of the 52nd and 95th Guards Rifle Divisions and especially by the fire of anti-tank artillery. Tank attacks in the bend of the Psel River ceased between 2000 and 2100. However, General Zhadov was concerned about their resumption that night. Therefore, he issued the following order to Lieutenant Colonel M. N. Kamenchuk, the commander of the 14th Assault Engineer-Sapper Brigade:

> …
>
> 2. To detach one battalion each for joint operations in the sectors of the 32nd and 33rd Guards Rifle Corps;
>
> 1. To position three battalions, including the battalion operating in the 33rd Guards Rifle Corps, on the main axis vulnerable to tanks – lying between: on the left – Mikhailovka, Petrovka, Mal. Psinka, Vikhrovka; and on the right – Hills 174.0, 227.6 and Bobryshevo, with orders to block the advance of enemy tanks to the north or along the roads:
>
> a) Petrovka – Kartashevka – Verkhne-Provorotskii – Bol. Psinka – Troitskoe;
>
> b) Mal. Psinka – Sr. Ol'shanka – Troitskoe;
>
> Prepare a line for mining: Verkh. Ol'shanka – Serebrianoe and further to the south – along the Ol'shanka River to its confluence with the Psel River.
>
> Second line: Mal. Psinka – southern slopes of Hill 246.4 – Iarushka grove.
>
> … 7. Have the barriers ready in this sector by 4.00 13.07.43."[35]

On the sector of the 32nd Guards Rifle Corps, operating on the right flank of the 5th Guards Army, the offensive in essence also met with no success. Units of the 13th and 66th Guards Rifle Divisions, repulsing infantry and tank counterattacks from XXXXVIII Panzer Corps' 11th Panzer Division managed to advance only 1 to 2 kilometers in the course of 12 July. The 97th Guards Rifle Division of the 33rd Guards

Rifle Corps, which faced only enemy Panzergrenadiers without tanks, advanced 3 to 4 kilometers and then dug-in on the line it had reached. A combat dispatch from the 32nd Guards Rifle Corps at 2100 on 12 July 1943 reported the following:

> 3. The offensive undertaken by the 13th Guards Rifle Division at 1700 after artillery preparation had no success. The artillery reinforcements intended for the corps could not be used fully:
>
> a) The 1440th Self-propelled Artillery Regiment had no shells, with the exception of three guns, and only arrived in the area of operations by 2100;
>
> b) The 29th Howitzer Brigade arrived by 2100 11.07.43. It was not ready to fire even by 1100 [12 July 1943]; on the basis of verbal instructions, the deputy artillery commander of the army left without my knowledge …
>
> 4. Losses for the day: 13th Guards Rifle Division – up to 200 men killed and wounded;
>
> 66th Guards Rifle Division – around 190 men killed and wounded, exact losses are being determined.
>
> Enemy losses: 25-30 tanks knocked out or partially burned, around 150 soldiers and officers exterminated.[36]

In this fashion, in the sector selected for the counterattack by the right-flank formations of the 33rd Guards Rifle Corps, instead savage attacks by the SS Panzergrenadier Division *Totenkopf* in the bend of the Psel River had to be repulsed, and the stubborn resistance of the 11th Panzer Division at Kochetovka had to be overcome.

At 0100 13 July, a meeting of the 5th Guards Army's Military Council took place, at which the results of the two days of combat were discussed. The conclusion, drawn by the army's leadership with respect to the command of the rifle corps, was discomforting: handling of the troops required serious corrections. From the army headquarters' summary:

> … Analyzing the fighting, conducted by the army on 11 and 12 July, the Military Council came to the conclusion that many commanders of the formations and units pay insufficient attention to securing the boundaries between them, as the result of which the enemy sometimes succeeded in feeling out the boundary locations, and exploiting the lack of cooperation, in breaking through the front line and restraining the advance of our forces. I will remind the commanders of the 32nd and 33rd Guards Rifle Corps that the responsibility for the junctions lays upon them, and they must establish the responsibility for divisional boundaries. The Military Council requires the anticipation, as a rule, of positioning partial reserves, reinforced by anti-tank artillery, sappers and anti-tank mines behind the boundaries.[37]

Moreover, the headquarters of the 33rd Guards Rifle Corps and the 5th Guards Army's headquarters had lost communications with the 52nd Guards Rifle Division on 12 July. As the 5th Guards Army commander reported, the division had retreated northward, toward Ol'shanka, without orders, and the exact location of its units was still unknown. The deputy commander of the army, General M. I. Kozlov, was given an order to organize a search for the division, to establish a connection with Pantiukhov's division, to visit it and to familiarize himself with the situation that had developed. If necessary, he was to take steps to gather together whatever divisional elements he could locate.

The *front* commander was even more critical in his evaluation of the actions taken by the corps commanders. The transcript of the conversations with the commanders at 1235 on 13 July 1943 is revealing:

> N. F Vatutin:
>
> 'Comrade Zhadov, in Popov's actions [Author's note: I. I. Popov, commander of the 33rd Rifle Corps] I discern moments of panic, exaggeration of enemy forces, and totally insufficient steadiness of your troops. I doubt that 100 tanks had broken through on the northern bank of the Psel River. The dispatch about 100 tanks forced me to commit major reserves at the expense of their possible use on a more important axis.
>
> 'I am obliging you to put an end to similar cases in the future; on the other hand, the actions of your units are distinguished by their impermissible passivity. I am also obliging you to eliminate this shortcoming immediately. I am ordering you to carry out the cleansing of the northern bank of the Psel River as soon as possible and subsequently to act in close coordination with Comrade Rotmistrov's units on this sector. Unconditionally, thoroughly fortify yourself on the northern bank of the Psel River, and bring the 52nd Rifle Division back to order in accordance with GKO [State Defense Committee] Order No. 227.'
>
> A. S. Zhadov:
>
> 'In connection with the shakiness of the units, I would add first of all that of certain commanders; I have been forced to give a rebuke to corps commander Comrade Popov and to Sazonov [Author's note: Colonel A. M. Sazonov, commander of the 9th Guards Airborne Division of the 33rd Guards Rifle Corps] and a warning has been prepared.'[38]

N. F. Vatutin's nervous strain is possible to understand, but the wrath of the *front* commander is unjust. As is recorded in the daily reports of the SS Panzergrenadier Division *Totenkopf*, the division actually did have 101 armored vehicles on the morning of 12 July, including ten Tigers and 21 assault guns. In bitter fighting, General A. S. Zhadov's troops managed to knock out 46 tanks, including the ten Tigers [Editor's note: Almost all of these Tigers were recovered and returned to operational status within the next couple of days, though none on 13 July].[39] The Guardsmen stood their ground, and all further attempts by the SS to develop their offensive from the bridgehead it had seized on the northern bank of the Psel River ended in failure.

12

Combat Operations of the 69th Army and Group Trufanov of the 5th Guards Tank Army on 12 July 1943

Combat operations in the sector of the 69th Army in the region of the villages Rzhavets, Vypolzovka and Aleksandrovka had a serious influence on the results of the *front*'s main counterstroke at Prokhorovka. As has already been noted, on the afternoon and evening of 11 July, the situation on the boundary between the 69th Army's 48th Rifle Corps and 35th Guards Rifle Corps was rapidly deteriorating.

Between 1500 and 1600, the three divisions of General H. Breith's III Panzer Corps, having broken through the defenses of the 35th Guards Rifle Corps' 96th Guards and 305th Rifle Divisions in the sector Shishino – Khokhlovo – Kiselevo – Sheino – Miasoedovo, burst into the depths of the second army-level defensive belt. Colonel V. F. Trunin's 92nd Guards Rifle Division and Major General V. G. Lebedev's 96th Separate Tank Brigade, although they suffered heavy losses, nevertheless continued to struggle against the superior firepower of the enemy. But by 1900, General Walther von Hünersdorff's 6th Panzer Division, with air support, breached the center of the 92nd Guards Rifle Division's defenses and scattered its forces. Vigorously exploiting its success, the 6th Panzer Division next punched through the right wing of Lieutenant General S. G. Goriachev's 35th Guards Rifle Corps and by the onset of twilight it had seized the village of Kazach'e, which lay in the center of the second army-level defensive belt.

With the favorable turn in the situation, the division command hastened to press the advantage. Colonel Hermann von Oppeln-Bronikowski, the commander of the 6th Panzer Division's panzer group, proposed a bold night-time foray to von Hünersdorff to seize the village of Rzhavets, which was situated on the eastern bank of the Northern Donets. The plan was approved, and even before midnight had arrived, a *kampfgruppe* under the command of Major Dr. Franz Bäke moved out toward Rzhavets in a mixed column of the II/11th Panzer Regiment and the II/114th Panzergrenadier Regiment in armored half-tracks, with 503rd Heavy Panzer Battalion's Tiger tanks bringing up the rear.

Its task was a tall one. Before sunup, it not only had to reach the village of Rzhavets, but something equally important, it had to seize the bridge located there and to create at least a small bridgehead over the river. It was considered vitally important to carry out this mission. Reflecting on the previous unsuccessful experience with forcing the Northern Donets River at Belgorod, Breith believed with considerable justification that if they couldn't reach the western bank of the river from the march now, when the

Colonel M. P. Seriugin, commander of the 89th Guards Rifle Division, together with his regiment commanders reconnoiters the terrain in the area of Gostishchevo, 13 July 1943. (Author's personal archive)

Russians were stunned and in retreat, then the breaching of this river barrier might drag on for an impermissibly long time. In that case one could only dream about a breakthrough to Prokhorovka.

The attack of III Panzer Corps' left flank next to the river also had success. A *kampfgruppe* of Lieutenant General Rudolf Schmidt's 19th Panzer Division, which was operating here, passed through retreating columns of the 92nd Guards Rifle Division's 280th Guards Rifle Regiment and burst into Kiselevo at 1600, seizing a significant portion of the village. Colonel M. P. Seriugin's 89th Guards Rifle Division now entered the fighting to halt the German advance there. General S. G. Goriachev, commander of the 35th Guards Rifle Corps, immediately ordered counterattacks by the 92nd Guards Rifle Division's 276th Guards Rifle Regiment from Sabynino toward Kiselevo. These, together with the steadfast stand of the 89th Guards Rifle Division and an attack by the 96th Separate Heavy Tank Brigade, which had been falling back toward Kiselevo, all combined to stop the Germans, and on certain sectors the enemy was pushed back. Schmidt's division had been weakened in the preceding fighting, and lacked the necessary strength simultaneously to cover the left flank of the III Panzer Corps' shock group and to detach significant forces for the capture of Kiselevo. Even later after its forces had finally taken control of the area around Kiselevo, it was unable to construct a continuous line of defense, but could only fortify positions on higher pieces of ground.

Breith understood that if the Russian division bitterly defending Kiselevo was not destroyed, then the Russians' threat from this strongpoint to the III Panzer Corps' flank would only grow with the further advance of the III Panzer Corps. At the same time, he was striving to create a bridgehead on the northern bank of the Northern Donets as quickly as possible in order to drive as deeply as possible into the system of defenses of the 69th Army's 48th Rifle Corps beyond the river. Therefore, as soon as it became clear that the 19th Panzer Division's advance had begun to bog down, he immediately requested air support. At 1900, the VIII Air Corps inflicted air strikes on Kiselevo, Sabynino and the small village of Kiselev. At that moment, the 89th Guards Division's headquarters were located in Kiselev. The division's operational summary at 2200 12 July describes the effects of this attack:

> At 1900, more than 200 enemy bombers struck the combat formations and headquarters of the division. During the attack on the command post, the PNO-1 [the division's assistant chief of operations] Guards Major (illegible)-khov and the to division commander's adjutant Popyk were severely wounded; four commanders were lightly wounded; three men were killed; and two light automobiles were burned. Simultaneously the enemy attacked our line.[1]

Lacking any communications with the superior 48th Rifle Corps headquarters or his neighboring units, Colonel Seriugin, commander of the 89th Guards Rifle Division, made a flawed decision and ordered the redeployment of his headquarters to the Novo-Oskochnoe area.

Departing under the security of the training battalion, the command of the Guards division in the darkness somewhere between Rzhavets and Kurakovka ran into Major Bäke's 6th Panzer Division *kampfgruppe*, which had recently moved out of Kazach'e on the same route selected by Seriugin, but moving in the opposite direction. Tanks were in the vanguard of the German column, with the following half-tracks of Lieutenant Roembke's II/114th Panzergrenadier Regiment and the Tigers of Heavy Panzer Battalion 503. The first to encounter the enemy were soldiers of Captain N. V. Riabtsev's training battalion of the 89th Guards Rifle Division. The battalion's deputy commander, M. G. Boev, preserved his recollections of the events that followed in this dramatic account:

> The night of 11 July was exceedingly dark. The battalion had already moved out of its forward positions, and it seemed that there would not be anything to raise an alarm, though the situation did have us on guard. Riabtsev and I were moving at the head of the column, peering into the impenetrable darkness and listening intently to each sound.
>
> A messenger came galloping up and delivered an order from the division commander: 'Longer strides!'
>
> As soon as the messenger rode off, the rumbling of engines was audible from up ahead. The battalion commander took a close listen:
>
> 'Tanks. The question is: Whose tanks?'
>
> He immediately dispatched the chief of staff to report to the division commander about the tanks, and ordered the commander of the company at the head of the column to send forward a scout detachment.
>
> The returning chief of staff soon came running back and reported: 'The division commander said that there can only be our tanks in Kurakovka.'

All the same, we strained our eyes to make out what was in front of us. About 50 meters ahead, the vague silhouette of a vehicle became visible. It was one of our 'Thirty-fours.' The lead tank was cautiously crawling toward us at slow speed, with open hatches. A head popped up out of the turret hatch. 'Take the right!' – We heard a voice from the tank in perfect Russian. It had to be one of ours. We relaxed immediately and marched side by side with the tank column moving in the opposite direction, glancing carelessly at the first, second and third 'Thirty-four' as it passed us.

Then suddenly:

'Germans! ...'

Everyone turned their heads and at a distance of two paces saw white crosses on the sides of the tanks. A bitter suspicion flashed through my brain like lightning: the fascists had placed Russian traitors of the Soviet Motherland at the head of the column – 'Vlasovites.'

The battalion commander leaped to one side:

'Battalion, to battle! Employ grenades!'

The command became swallowed up by the clatter of tracks and the explosion of grenades. The 'pocket artillery' burst against the fascist armor, submachine guns rattled, and the German tankers slammed their hatches shut.

The battalion quickly switched from its marching column into a combat formation, taking position on the side of the road while continuing to hurl grenades.

... An early dawn was touching the night sky, and now the white crosses and painted predatory beasts became increasingly visible on the armor of the enemy tanks. Some of the tanks and armored half-tracks had stopped and opened fire on the cadets' defensive positions. Some distance away, Panzergrenadiers were spilling out of their half-tracks. The main force of the tank column, bypassing disabled or knocked-out vehicles, continued to roll on toward Rzhavets.

Cadet Kulakov somehow wound up among the German tanks, seemingly confused about what was going on. It was my third year of the war, and I'd never seen such a thing as what was about to happen. Only when the long barrel of a Tiger's cannon bounced in front of his eyes did he realize the situation. He snatched up an anti-tank grenade and hurled it at the rear of the departing Tiger. To glance back and see the effects of the grenade was impossible – more tanks were advancing on him. Now they had spread out into formation, several vehicles in a line. Only very little distance remained to the nearest tank, and the cadet, swinging his arm, tossed a grenade under its track and dropped to the ground. The tank suddenly pivoted on its one good track. Kulakov had no more grenades, but the tanks kept coming and coming. He made his way among the enemy vehicles, firing at the mounted infantry from his submachine gun.[2]

The enemy, taking advantage of the confusion during the night-time regrouping of the 48th Rifle Corps' divisions, penetrated into the rear of our forces, having placed captured T-34s at the head of the column. This case is indicative of the confusion and the loss of command and control both in the headquarters of the 48th Rifle Corps, as well as in the headquarters of its divisions.

Colonel M. P. Seriugin lost his head and, lacking any information about the circumstances in front of his division, should have moved his division headquarters not to the south, toward an encounter with enemy tanks, but to the northeast, toward the villages of Chursino or Shakhovo. This would have preserved command and control in his division, enabled it to hold its occupied line, and prevented it from coming under enemy tank attack. The consequences of this poor decision were heavy. The 168th Infantry Division, operating on the 19th Panzer Division's left flank, also took advantage of the confusion and forced a crossing of the Northern Donets with insignificant forces. Pushing ahead, it then seized Gostishchevo that night, a major village in the depths of the 48th Rifle Corps' defenses.

Vatutin later summarized and assessed the developments on that sector in his Order No. 000194 from 21 July 1943:

> The commander of the 89th Guards Rifle Division Guards Colonel Seriugin, without establishing communications with his neighbors and the corps command, and being unable because of this to stay suitably informed of the situation, made an incorrect decision and voluntarily abandoned the line Kalinin – Kiselevo along the Northern Donets River, which was held by the 267th Guards Rifle Regiment.
>
> Taking advantage of the withdrawal of the 267th Guards Rifle Regiment, the enemy took possession of the forest, which had been defended by this regiment, and then Gostishchevo as well, as the result of which the fulfillment of a combat order, given to another division, could not be executed.

Grenadiers of the 168th Infantry Division make a crossing of the Northern Donets River. (RGAKFD)

> Having received information about the appearance of enemy tanks in the region of Verkh. Ol'shanets, Colonel Seriugin abandoned control over the units of his division, and taking command of the training battalion, left with it for the area of Kazach'e, where he intended to set up a new command post. On the move in the direction of Kazach'e, Seriugin bumped into enemy tanks, and was pushed aside to the area of Rzhavets, where he again encountered enemy tanks and was forced to retreat. Cut-off from the units of his division, for fourteen hours he had no direction over them.[3]

The 6th Panzer Division *kampfgruppe* encircled Colonel Seriugin's small column. He ordered an all-round defense. Fighting lasted for several hours, and only by morning did the division headquarters manage to break out of the ring surrounding it and escape on foot to Plota. From here it sent a dispatch to the commander of the 48th Rifle Corps:

> At the order of the division commander, the division headquarters was being relocated to the area of Novo-Oskochnoe, and at 0200 12.07.43 the vehicle containing the division commander, his deputy and the chief of staff, as well as the vehicle containing headquarters staff, were cut off by a column of up to 300 enemy tanks. The command and staff managed to abandon their vehicles before they were destroyed by enemy tanks.
>
> By dawn, the division command, with the exception of the assistant chief of operations Guards Captain Lebedenko and the division's topographer Senior Lieutenant Levchenko, emerged from encirclement at Plota and returned to normal work …
>
> The division's special units, which were relocating together with the headquarters particularly suffered, and are being brought back to order … Losses are being determined.[4]

While the 89th Guards Rifle Division was caught in an unequal fight north of Kurakovka, the 96th Tank Brigade's 331st Tank Battalion engaged two columns of enemy tanks, numbering about 40 vehicles, in the area of Rzhavets. The Battalion's six T-34s and the crew of one gun of an anti-tank battery were pulling out of Kiselevo when they collided with the enemy column. In the subsequent night-time battle, the tankers managed to knock out nine combat vehicles of the 6th Panzer Division, and after passing through Bol. Pod'iarugi, the Battalion reached Aleksandrovka at 0400 12 July 1943, where it took up a defense.

Similar night-time clashes with the retreating forces of the 35th Guards Rifle Corps, as well as minefields and engineered obstacles, the darkness and the unfamiliar terrain – all of this prevented the adversary from fully exploiting the early morning success. The III Panzer Corps was still unable to advance quickly into the depths of the lines of General Kriuchenkin's army in a direction to the northeast.

Between 0500 and 0600 on 12 July, 6th Panzer Division's *Kampfgruppe* Bäke reached Rzhavets. By this time, the headquarters of the 69th Army had managed to strengthen the defense in this area somewhat. The "Description of Combat Operations of the 19th Panzer Division from 5 to 18 July 1943" records:

> On 11.07 units of the 6th Panzer Division attacked from the area of Melikhovo toward Rzhavets, and seized the latter location that night. They also managed to create a small bridgehead across the river around the bridge there. In connection with this, the enemy felt trapped between the 19th Panzer Division and 6th Panzer Division. Mining the routes of retreat and leaving behind strong covering elements, consisting primarily of anti-tank rifles, he began to withdraw his units on the night of 11 July from the areas of Sabynino and Sheliakovo to the western bank of the Donets River, in order to hinder there our further advance from Rzhavets and Sheliakovo across the Donets. [5]

The 168th Infantry Division's crossing of the Northern Donets, the seizure of Gostishchevo, and especially the bridgehead created by 6th Panzer Division's *kampfgruppe* at Rzhavets had great significance for both sides. As a result of these events, the potential threat of encirclement to the 48th Rifle Corps began to take on real outlines. After the capture of Rzhavets, Major General Z. Z. Rogozny's corps was caught in a closing pocket and because of the appearance of the two German bridgeheads at Gostishchevo and Rzhavets, the 48th Rifle Corps' left flank was becoming porous. Owing to the high mobility of the III Panzer Corps' *kampfgruppen*, Breith had placed the Soviet command in a very difficult situation. At the moment when Hünersdorff's 6th Panzer Division had reached the Northern Donets River, there was no longer a continuous line of defense in the sector running from a fish farm north of Krivtsovo through Shcholokovo to Rzhavets. Rather, on the afternoon of 11 July, this was in the rear of the divisions of 69th Army's first echelon, which were holding the line Shishino – Khokhlovo – Kiselevo – Shliakhovoe – Sheino – Miasoedovo.

As quite recently discovered documents testify, the first to react to the news of the German breakthrough on this sector was the leadership of the 48th Rifle Corps. Already at 2245, chief of staff Colonel Shcheglov sent the following order to Colonel P. D. Govorunenko, commander of the reserve 375th Rifle Division, which at 1300 11 July was defending on the line Zhimolostnoe – Mal. Iablonovo – Shakhovo:

> The corps commander has ordered the immediate dispatch of one battalion with two anti-tank guns to Ryndinka, in order to cover Shakhovo from the direction of Kurakovka and Rzhavets. Conduct reconnaissance in the direction of Kazach'e. Report to Shakhovo.
>
> According to unverified information, tanks have broken through at Kazach'e. Send the results of the reconnaissance to Shakhovo and the Vasil'evka ravine.[6]

There is a note on the document stating, "Sent with an officer at 0100."

Further events unfolded rapidly as the 69th Army began to pull together forces to localize the breakthrough. At 2300 Lieutenant General S. G. Goriachev, having received information about the movement of enemy tanks toward Rzhavets, shifted part of the 92nd Guards Rifle Division over the river crossing in the vicinity of Shcholokovo to the line Vypolzovka – southern outskirts of Aleksandrovka, and the 305th Rifle Division to the area of Kolomytsevo and Novo-Slobodka.

Just thirty minutes later, at 2330 the commander of the 81st Guards Rifle Division Major General I. K. Morozov issued Order No. 060:

> 1. The enemy with the support of large aviation forces and tanks has broken through the line of defense and at 2100 11.07.43 reached the line Kiselevo – Khokhlovo – 1 km south of Verkh. Ol'shanets.
> 2. The 235th Guards Rifle Regiment by 0600 12.07.43 with two battalions (the 1st and 2nd) is to occupy and firmly defend the prepared sector Krivtsovo – road leading to Verkh. Ol'shanets – southwest edge of the woods lying 500 meters southwest of Verkh. Ol'shanets.
>
> Task: Not in any case allow a breakthrough of enemy tanks and infantry in the direction of Novo-Oskochnoe. Command post – Chursino. Operations group – Novo-Oskochnoe.
> 3. The 238th Guards Rifle Regiment by 0600 12.07.43 is to occupy and firmly defend the prepared sector: eastern edge of the grove (Point 294.4) – southern outskirts of Verkh. Ol'shanets, and with a reinforced left flank, the eastern outskirts of Verkh. Ol'shanets.
>
> Task: Not to allow a breakthrough of enemy tanks and infantry in the direction of Novo-Oskochnoe. Command post – Novo-Oskochnoe.
>
> The 235th Guards Rifle Regiment is defending on the right, on the left – the 305th Rifle Division.
>
> Pay attention to the organization of reconnaissance during the approach of the units to their defensive sectors.[7]

The General Staff was intently following the situation in this region. On 12 July at 0115, Stalin issued Directive of the *Stavka* of the Supreme High Command No. 01815 to the commander of the Steppe Front General I. S. Konev:

> On the Belgorod axis the enemy with a force of up to 200 tanks with infantry has taken on units of the 69th Army and, attacking in the direction of Korocha, by the end of 11.07 emerged in the Kiselevo – Mazikino – Sheino area.
>
> The *Stavka* of the Supreme High Command has ordered:
> 1. Destroy the enemy grouping, which is moving in the direction of Korocha and further on toward the Oskol River, with the united blow of Ryzhov [Author: commander of Steppe Front's 47th Army], Obukhov [Author: commander of the Steppe Front's 3rd Guards Mechanized Corps] from the southeast and Solomatin [Author: commander of Steppe Front's 1st Mechanized Corps] from the north, for which by the end of 13.07 Ryzhov and Obukhov are to assemble in the Novyi Oskol – Velikomikhailovka – Sidorovka – Bulanovka – Slonovka area. Solomatin by the morning of 13.07 from the Solntsevo area is to move out to the area Viazovoe – Skorodnoe – Bobrovo-Dvorskoe.
> 2. Report to V. Ch. Antonov [1st Deputy Chief of the Red Army General Staff] on the time of your receipt of the current order.[8]

However, the directive spoke only of assembling the forces by the morning and end of 13 July. Until then, the enemy had to be held back by the forces of Voronezh

Front. Vatutin had no reserves: all the forces were either tied up in defensive fighting or were preparing for the counterstroke; therefore Kriuchenkin had to rely on his own means. In addition, there was an additional, even more essential factor. The directive's text speaks of the villages of Kiselevo, Mazikino and Sheino as the line that the adversary had reached by the end of 11 July. However, by that time, III Panzer Corps had already fully broken through the second army-level defensive belt and reached the rear sector in the area of Rzhavets and Vypolzovka. This information had still not reached Moscow.

General V. D. Kriuchenkin was in a very difficult situation – in addition to localizing the enemy breakthrough, in the morning forces of the 48th Rifle Corps were to participate in the counterattack of 12 July. The commander's sole reserve – the 375th Rifle Division – was part of the 48th Rifle Corps' counterattack group and on the night of 11 July was moving into the line: barracks, 2.5 km southwest of Leski – Teterevino.

After 0500 12 July, one more serious problem arose: how to halt the large-scale retreat of forces that was underway and to consolidate them on sectors of the defense. The enemy's night attacks had created panic in certain units. The divisions of the 69th Army had none of the so-called blocking detachments, since all combat-capable elements were in the front lines. In the morning hours of 12 July, this problem became very acute for the army's command. They hastily began to take extreme measures. General Kriuchenkin ordered Colonel Stroilov, the chief of the 69th Army's SMERSH [a contraction of the Russian *smert' shpionam* – "Death to spies"] counterintelligence department to organize blocking detachments from among his staff. Colonel Stroilov reported back to the 69th Army's Military Council on 17 July 1943 on the work of his blocking detachments between 12 and 17 July 1943:

> In order to fulfill the assignment of halting the rank and file and command staff of the army's formations and units, who were voluntarily abandoning the battlefield, the 69th Army's SMERSH department of counterintelligence organized 7 blocking detachments from the personnel of its separate company, with 7 men in each detachment headed by 2 operational workers.
>
> The indicated barrier detachments were positioned in the villages of Alekseevka – Prokhodnoe, Novaia Slobodka – Samoilovka, Podol'khi – Bol'shie Pod'iarugi, the hamlet of Bol'shoi – Kolomytsevo, Kashcheevo – Pogorelovka, Podkopaeva – southern outskirts of Korocha – Pushkarnoe.
>
> In the course of 12 July, 2,842 men were detained … The mass retreat of soldiers and the command staff from the battlefield, which had started at 0500 12 July 1943 … was basically stopped at 1600 of the same day and subsequently ceased completely.[9]

By dawn on 12 July, the 69th Army in the area of the German penetration was holding the following lines: Colonel A. F. Vasil'ev's 305th Rifle Division together with the 96th Separate Tank Brigade had fallen back to the area Vypolzovka – Aleksandrovka – 1st Novo-Aleksandrovskii Vyselok – Podsumki – Alekseevka – Ploskii and was digging in there; Colonel V. F. Trunin's 92nd Guards Rifle Division was straggling into the 305th Rifle Division's lines throughout the night; and Major General I. K. Morozov's

81st Guards Rifle Division was defending in the Ryndinka – Shcholokovo – Strel'nikov area. In order to strengthen the anti-tank defenses, the *front* command was forced to leave the 10th Destroyer Anti-tank Artillery Brigade with General Kriuchenkin, which had initially been detached to reinforce the 18th and 29th Corps at Prokhorovka. Its regiments hastily took up defensive positions along the line Aleksandrovka – Sviridovo – Zaiach'e – Lomovo.

According to reconnaissance information, the enemy had concentrated approximately 200 tanks in the breakthrough area. On 13 July, Rotmistrov during discussions with Vatutin mentioned that aerial reconnaissance had counted more than 400 German tanks, assembled to the south of Prokhorovka in the Verkhnii Ol'shanets – Raevka – Shliakhovoe – Melikhovo – Dal'niaia Igumenka area. But he expressed his own opinion that 300-400 vehicles might be operating in the indicated area.

On 1 July 1943, the III Panzer Corps had a total of 299 tanks of various types, including 106 tanks in the 6th Panzer Division, 112 tanks (including 13 *Flammpanzers*) in the 7th Panzer Division, and 81 tanks in the 19th Panzer Division.[10] The 6th and 7th Panzer Divisions each had one battalion of one of their Panzergrenadier regiments mounted on armored personnel carriers, while the 19th Panzer Division had only one Panzergrenadier company so equipped. The attached 503rd Heavy Panzer Battalion had 45 Tiger I tanks (three companies of 14 tanks each and three command tanks), while the attached 228th Assault Gun Battalion had 31 StuG III vehicles. Thus, at the start of Operation Citadel Breith's corps had 375 tanks and assault guns, as well as around 200 field guns and 54 *Nebelwerfers*. But in the course of the offensive thus far, his corps had suffered significant losses. As was later revealed, on the morning of 11 July the 6th

A Tiger company from the III Panzer Corps' 503rd Heavy Panzer Battalion rolls through a captured village. (RGAKFD)

Panzer Division had only 23 tanks (22% of its starting strength), while the 503rd Heavy Panzer Battalion reported 23 operational Tigers (51% of its starting strength). On the morning of 12 July, the 7th Panzer Division reported 39 (35%) operational tanks; the 19th Panzer Division counted only 14 (12%) operational tanks; and the 228th Assault Gun Battalion had 19 (61%) operational StuG III.[11]

Thus, by morning of 12 July, the III Panzer Corps had only approximately 120 tanks and assault guns operating in the area of Rzhavets, just a third of its initial number. The exaggeration of enemy armor strength in Soviet reconnaissance reports often was due to the inclusion of armored personnel carriers (the III Panzer Corps had no less than 100 of these) and ammunition carriers in the counts.

By 0600 12 July, panzers of the German 6th Panzer Division stood less than 18 kilometers south of Prokhorovka in their small bridgehead at Rzhavets. The foothold was still not secure; Soviet counterattacks managed temporarily to drive the enemy out of Rzhavets, but at 0920 50 panzers with the support of Panzergrenadiers again attacked Rzhavets from the direction of Kurakovka, and after forty minutes of hard fighting regained control of the village and once again pushed beyond the Northern Donets and even seized Ryndinka.

Working quickly to expand the bridgehead and to augment the force within it in order to resume the drive to the north, at 1115 the enemy managed to take the nearby village of Vypolzovka and continued to push Soviet forces in the direction of Avdeevka. The German breakthrough was reaching threatening proportions. Having received a report about the arrival of Hünersdorff's forward elements on the Northern Donets, General Breith ordered the 19th Panzer Division's armored group to replace the 6th

An assault gun of one of the panzer divisions of Army Detachment Kempf's III Panzer Corps crosses the Northern Donets River at Rzhavets. (RGAKFD)

Panzer Division at Rzhavets, so the latter could throw its weight behind the 7th Panzer Division's attempts to break through in the direction of 1st Novo-Aleksandrovskii Vyselok and Aleksandrovka.

Throughout the early morning hours of 12 July, sketchy and alarming reports were trickling into the headquarters of Voronezh Front about the situation in the 69th Army. Deeply concerned by the news that the Germans had seized a bridgehead over the Northern Donets at Rzhavets in the night, and might even now be lunging into the rear of the 5th Guards Tank Army through the disintegrating ranks of the 69th Army, around 0600 Vatutin was compelled to send an order to the 5th Guards Tank Army to send a portion of the army's strength to the 69th Army's sector. On the basis of this order, Rotmistrov immediately formed a composite group from units of his army and from the forces defending in the breakthrough sector in order to cover the dangerous axis, and sent an order through his chief of staff General Baskakov to his deputy Major General K. G. Trufanov, who was located in Oboian':

> To Major General Trufanov.
>
> Copies to: The commander of the 5th Guards 'Zimovniki' Mechanized Corps
> The commander of the 2nd Guards 'Tatsinskaia' Tank Corps
> The commander of the 375th Rifle Division
> The commander of the 92nd Guards Rifle Division
>
> The enemy with up to 70 tanks by 0600 12.07.43 gained possession of Ryndinka and Rzhavets, and is exploiting toward Avdeevka and Plota.
>
> The commander of the 5th Guards Tank Army has ordered:
>
> 1. You are personally to bring together under your command units of the forward detachment, the 12th and 11th Mechanized Brigades of the 5th Guards 'Zimovniki' Mechanized Corps, a regiment of the 375th Rifle Division, and units of the 92nd Guards Rifle Division and the 2nd Guards 'Tatsinskaia' Tank Corps.
> 2. With the receipt of this combat order, immediately set about the destruction of the enemy that is breaking through in the area of Ryndinka and Rzhavets.
> 3. Report every two hours on the course of executing this assignment to the army's headquarters.
>
> Basis: The order of the commander of the Voronezh Front's forces.[12]

The army's forward detachment under the command of General Trufanov immediately began moving out from Oboian' on the route Malaia Psinka – Priznachnoe – Podol'khi with the assignment to assemble in the Bol'shie Pod'iarugi – Novo-Khmelevoe area. While Trufanov was busy gathering his composite force to liquidate the breakthrough, the Germans continued to attack. The 19th Panzer Division made an attempt to lay a crossing over the Northern Donets River in the area of Shcholokovo and to transfer its tanks to the western bank, but units of the 81st Guards Rifle Division thwarted these attempts.

The first of General Trufanov's composite detachment[13] to move out toward the area of the breakthrough was Colonel S. K. Nesterov's 26th Guards Tank Brigade from the 2nd Guards 'Tatsinskaia' Tank Corps. At 0600 12 July, it had 44 combat-ready tanks, including 30 T-34 and 14 T-70.[14] Initially the brigade had assembled on the northeast fringes of the woods in the area of Vinogradovka, and was preparing to attack toward

Major General K. G. Trufanov, deputy commander of the 5th Guards Tank Army. (TsAMO)

Ozerovskii as part of the 12 July counterattack. However, with the sharp deterioration of the situation in the region of Rzhavets, at 0730 Colonel Burdeiny personally issued an order to the brigade commander to move out toward Plota. The brigade reached this village at 0830. By this time, the situation had become serious. Enemy tanks in the area of Rzhavets were continuing to exploit toward Ryndinka and Shipy. Simultaneously the 19th Panzer Division was in the process of making its attempts to force the Northern Donets in the vicinity of Shcholokovo and to seize that village. The attacks out of the Rzhavets and Shcholokovo areas were plainly directed toward Shakhovo, into the rear of first the 2nd Guards 'Tatsinskaia' Tank Corps and then the rest of the 5th Guards Tank Army.

Trufanov's composite detachment was still on the way; therefore about a half-hour after the 26th Guards Tank Brigade's arrival in Plota the corps commander Burdeiny again got in touch with its commander Colonel Nesterov and ordered him to move his brigade to Shakhovo. There he was to stop the German tanks, which were trying to reach the Ryndinka – Shakhovo road, and if necessary support Major General I. K. Morozov's 81st Guards Rifle Division in Shcholokovo with fire.

Judging by how much attention the commander of the 2nd Guards 'Tatsinskaia' Tank Corps gave this sector prior to the 12 July counterattack, the situation there was clearly troubling Burdeiny. He sent his deputy Colonel Poloskov to the brigade, who personally took part in planning the brigade's defense. At Poloskov's order, Major Dmitriev's 1st Tank Battalion with one motorized rifle company created a strongpoint of resistance on the northern slopes of Hill 228.4, straddling the Shakhovo – Ryndinka road. An anti-tank battery deployed on the eastern slopes of the same hill, while Captain Khomenko's 2nd Tank Battalion was held back as a reserve among the western outskirts of Shakhovo.

At 0955, the 11th Guards Mechanized Brigade with three battalions of the 285th Mechanized Regiment arrived from Krasnoe in the Rzhavets – Vypolzovka – Shipy area, and the 12th Guards Mechanized Brigade with ten assault guns from the 1447th Self-propelled Artillery Regiment. By 1430, all the units and elements of the composite detachment had assembled in Bol'shie Pod'iarugi, where they came under the operational control of the 69th Army's commander. Altogether, Trufanov's composite detachment had 157 tanks (of which 39 were light tanks), 15 armored cars, 21 medium anti-aircraft artillery guns, and 28 45mm and 76mm guns.[15]

Some historical studies when assessing the composition and role of the 5th Guards Tank Army's forces in the events of 12 July south of Prokhorovka Station often commit errors and exaggerations. Thus it is at times difficult to grasp what really happened there and which forces were involved. For example, in the 'Great Soviet Historical Encyclopedia' we read:

> On 12 July 1943 in the area southwest and south of Prokhorovka ... [there] occurred the greatest meeting tank engagement of the Great Patriotic War 1941-1945 between an attacking German-fascist grouping (the II SS Panzer Corps and the III Panzer Corps, altogether 700 tanks and assault guns) and the *counterattacking 5th Guards Tank Army and three tank and mechanized brigades* [Author's emphasis] (around 800 tanks and self-propelled guns). In bitter fighting that lasted the entire day, the enemy lost more than 350 tank and assault guns, more than 10,000 casualties, and was forced onto the defensive.[16]

It is easy to notice that the authors of this publication not only exaggerated the amount of enemy armor that took part in this battle and his losses, but also overestimated the strength of our own forces by incorrectly including a tank, a mechanized brigade and part of another mechanized brigade. They did not counterattack together with the 5th Guards Tank Army, but were switched to the 69th Army and took part in defensive fighting in its sector. As concerns the 5th Guards Tank Army's reserve, Trufanov's forward detachment, this esteemed publication is entirely silent. We'll try to make sense of the actions of the Soviet forces in the Shcholokovo – Rzhavets – Aleksandrovka area on 12 July, relying upon the information in archival sources.

The analysis of the documents of the 5th Guards Tank Army demonstrates that in the course of 12 July, the detachment under the command of Major General K. G. Trufanov, which by order of the army commander was supposed to include three Guards tank and mechanized brigades; a tank, an anti-tank and a motorcycle regiment; portions of the 375th and 92nd Guards Rifle Divisions and a number of other elements, never took part in the fighting that day as a unified group. At the same time, the armies' initial intelligence reports were already exaggerating the strength of the enemy opposing them.

The main cause of this fragmented participation, in conjunction with the genuinely complex operational situation, was the absence of a centralized system of command and control in the composite detachment. Major General Trufanov, who now commanded practically a corps-sized formation, did not have a headquarters or an analogous working body that could carry out the functions of a headquarters in full measure. In these circumstances, when the forces intended to comprise the composite detachment were

Major General (at the time of the battle Colonel) I. V. Shabarov, chief of staff of the 5th Guards 'Zimovniki' Mechanized Corps. (TsAMO)

Colonel S. M. Protas, acting chief of staff of the 69th Army (1948 photo). (TsAMO)

scattered across a front of 50 kilometers, from Oboian' to Aleksandrovka, the lack of a single command center played a decisive role.

The command of the 5th Guards Tank Army, as well as that of the 69th Army, which had the composite detachment under its operational control, both viewed this group of forces as a "fire brigade", hastily assembled in order to close a gap that had formed in the lines. In the given situation, control over the greater portion of General Trufanov's detachment – the tank brigade, the two mechanized brigades and the self-propelled artillery regiment, was assumed by the staff of the 5th Guards Mechanized Corps and the 2nd Guards Tank Corps. Colonel Nesterov, commander of the 26th Guards Tank Brigade, received orders and directions directly from the deputy commander of the 2nd Guards Tank Corps Colonel Poloskov, while the mechanized troops were controlled by the deputy commander of the 5th Guards Mechanized Corps Major General M. P. Lebed'.

The situation remained the same even on the following days: Rotmistrov was simultaneously issuing orders on the use of these forces to Trufanov, Lebed' and Burdeiny. At the same time, the 69th Army command was using the detachment's various elements in the interests of the defense on its sector. Nevertheless, the absence of a fully recognized and fully functioning headquarters on location with the composite detachment complicated the situation to a significant degree, and as the events of 12 July would indicate, led to major consequences.

The main burden of the struggle on 12 July with the divisions of the III Panzer Corps rested upon the brigades of the 5th Guards Tank Army and the 10th Destroyer Anti-tank Artillery Brigade. A. S. Burdeiny's tank brigade and B. M. Skvortsov's

Colonel N. V. Grishchenko, commander of the 5th Guards 'Zimovniki' Mechanized Corps' 11th Guards Mechanized Brigade. (TsAMO)

Colonel G. Ia. Borisenko, commander of the 5th Guards 'Zimovniki' Mechanized Corps' 12th Guards Mechanized Brigade. (TsAMO)

mechanized brigades proved to be reliable and steadfast formations. The 11th and 12th Guards Mechanized Brigades, as well as the 26th Guards Tank Brigade, all entered the battle earlier than the units of Trufanov's forward detachment, and played a decisive role in localizing the German breakthrough. Unfortunately, on the other hand the actions of the 53rd Guards Separate Tank Regiment on this day caused the defending divisions of the 35th Guards Rifle Corps more harm than good, but we'll get to this story later.

General Trufanov's motorcycle regiment remained in his reserve. It occupied a defense with one tank company and one battery each of 45mm and 76mm guns on a line southwest of Bol'shie Pod'iarugi – Hill 232.4 – Novo-Khmelevoe.

Colonel N. V. Grishchenko's 11th Guards Mechanized Brigade received the assignment to attack Ryndinka from the north, via Shipy and Hill 135, with the support of a mortar battalion and one regiment of the 375th Rifle Division. The enemy had deployed *Nebelwerfer* batteries on Hill 135, the fire of which were inflicting heavy casualties on our rifle units. At the same time, Hero of the Soviet Union Colonel G. Ia. Borisenko's 12th Guards Mechanized Brigade was to cooperate with units of Colonel V. F. Trunin's 92nd Guards Rifle Division to drive the Germans from Krasnoe Znamia and Vypolzovka. Meanwhile, Major N. A. Kurnosov's 53rd Guards Separate Tank Regiment was to attack over Hill 241.5 in the direction of Aleksandrovka and 1st Novo-Aleksandrovskii Vyselok.

The mechanized brigades were the first to go on the attack. Intense fighting went on for the entire day in the area of Ryndinka. By 1525 12 July, the 11th Guards Mechanized

The commander of the 11th Guards Mechanized Brigade receives a combat order. (RGAKFD)

Brigade had driven the Germans from Shipy, and at 1900 it took possession of Ryndinka. The enemy advance had been blunted, but the 19th Panzer Division *kampfgruppe* could not be dislodged from its position on the western bank of the river. Only one document has been preserved – a dispatch from the 11th Guards Mechanized Brigade's chief of the political department Colonel Drozdov – which briefly describes the course of this fighting:

> By 1130 12.07, the 11th Guards Mechanized Brigade had assembled in the indicated area and began to execute its combat assignment. The brigade has now been fighting for more than twenty-four hours. At times the enemy counterattacks, and soldiers and officers are destroying enemy equipment and personnel in hand-to-hand fighting.
>
> The brigade has been fighting under conditions of complete ignorance of the enemy's strength that has been concentrated on this sector; without sufficient attack preparation; and on an unsuitable tactical line, which has restricted the maneuver of tanks and infantry – all of this has contributed to heavy casualties in the brigade.
>
> Despite all these handicaps, the soldiers and commanders have been fighting courageously, without any manifestations of panic; incidents of cowardice have been very rarely encountered, and that fear passes after a short continuation of the fighting, and these men in a number of cases have fought well [afterwards] …

> Alongside this there are a number of shortcomings:
>
> 1) The command staff is poorly directing the fighting. It does not always skillfully assess the situation and make decisions.
>
> 2) Ground forces and the air force are cooperating poorly. On 12 July Soviet [Il-2] *Shturmoviki* twice hit our troops. At 1211, 25 aircraft took part in the bombing, and at 1230 – 30 aircraft. On the night of 12 July, a U-2 also struck our units with incendiary bombs.
>
> 3) In view of the close terrain in the sector where the brigade is fighting, the tanks do not have the ability to maneuver freely. Therefore the combat losses over the last twenty-four hours of fighting amount to 11 tanks.
>
> 4) Actions with our neighbor have been poorly coordinated. For example, at the start of combat operations, the brigade did not know that its neighbor on the right was the 26th Guards Tank Brigade.
>
> A difficult situation with ammunition is being felt. Thus, the artillery battalion is already out of fragmentation shells. The delivery [of fresh ammunition] has been made difficult by the remote location of the dumps from the front lines and the absence of the necessary number of vehicles.[17]

In the units and formations of the German Fourth Air Fleet, which was operating in this region, cooperation with the ground forces had also not been fully worked out. Here is an excerpt from the VIII Air Corps staff report, compiled on the evening of 13 July (a supplement to Fourth Air Fleet's diary of combat operations for July 1943):

> General Seidemann has reported that at 1020, our own aviation likely attacked our forces in the Rzhavets area. An investigation revealed that one of our He 111 bomber *staffel* [a *Luftwaffe* unit below the *Gruppe* level and roughly equivalent to a squadron] in poor meteorological conditions and with limited visibility, and also because of poor navigation, became lost and bombed the Rzhavets area.
>
> A military court heard the results of the investigation. As the procurator on the VIII Air Corps staff announced at 1635 of the same day, as a result of the investigation it was revealed that no one should be accused of criminal negligence, since all precautionary measures had been observed.
>
> As has been reported by the 6th Panzer Division on 13.07, enemy air activity in the region of Kazach'e inflicted appreciable losses on our forces [Author's note: regiments of the 291st Storm Aviation Division were operating here]. According to reports from the 11th Panzer Regiment, our own air force units have inflicted an even greater loss to its men and tanks.
>
> More detailed discussion of the attack on our own forces and a number of details regarding the given incident can be found in the documents of the 6th and 19th Panzer Divisions.[18]

In addition to the above I will add that judging from available information, the casualties caused by the He 111 bomber's attack on the command post of the 6th Panzer Division was significantly greater than indicated. I present only the information about human casualties in this division. Five officers were killed (including the commander of the 114th Panzergrenadier Regiment Major von Bieberstein, and the commander of its

I Battalion, Knight's Cross recipient Captain Oeckel; both mortally wounded). Total casualties were 15 killed and 49 wounded; a large part of the division's command staff was put out of action.[19]

In certain domestic and foreign publications it is maintained that the 12th Guards Mechanized Brigade's 55th Guards Tank Regiment participated in the combat operations southwest of Prokhorovka Station on 12 July. For example, A. P. Riazansky writes:

> Around noon, at the height of the tank engagement, the army commander ordered the introduction of the 12th Mechanized Brigade's 55th Guards Tank Regiment into the fighting, in order to secure the boundary between the 29th and 2nd Tank Corps … with the task to attack the enemy in the direction of the hill on Komsomolets State Farm. Deploying into its combat formations, the 55th Guards Tank Regiment attacked the enemy and engaged in intense fighting 1.5 to 2 kilometers southwest of Hill 252.2, repelling every attempt to seize this hill and to breakthrough to Prokhorovka.[20]

There is no such information in the regiment's war diary. The 5th Guards Tank Army's account of combat operations at Prokhorovka also does not support this claim. From the 12th Mechanized Brigade's 55th Guards Tank Regiment's diary of combat operations:

> … 11.07.43 the regiment was occupying a defensive sector in the area of Peresyp' and Kartashevka as part of the 12th Guards Mechanized Brigade. At 1700 an order was received about a movement to the Priznachnoe area. Completing a 50-kilometer march, the regiment assembled in the [designated area] with 20 T-34 tanks and 16 T-70 tanks; 12 tanks were lagging behind in the Nogol'noe area due to mechanical problems.
>
> At 1030 12.07.43 an order was received: as part of the brigade to operate to destroy the foe in the Shakhovo – Ryndinka area, for which the regiment was to complete a 12-kilometer march to the Aleksandrovka area. At 1100, the regiment commander issued an order to conduct the 12-kilometer march along the route Priznachnoe – Podol'khi – Avdeevka – Krasnoe Znamia, and to stop the enemy that was breaking through in the Ryndinka – Vypolzovka area.
>
> At 1300, the 2nd Tank Company upon reaching the village of Krasnyi Oktiabr' became involved in combat with tanks from the enemy's 7th and 19th Panzer Divisions. The regiment entered the fighting together with the 12th Guards Mechanized Brigade's 1st Motorized Rifle Battalion, having available 19 T-34 tanks and 16 T-70 tanks.[21]

The 12th Guards Mechanized Brigade's attack didn't yield the expected success. Fire from the German strongpoint on Hill 222.1 hindered its approach to Vypolzovka. Through the combined efforts of the brigade's tankers and self-propelled guns from Major V. F. Gaidash's 1447th Self-propelled Artillery Regiment, the 6th Panzer Division was finally driven from the hill by day's end. Borisenko's 12th Guards Mechanized Brigade managed to approach the road 2 kilometers north of Vypolzovka, where it was met with furious artillery fire and was compelled to dig-in on the defense.

The 1st and 2nd Battalions of the 375th Rifle Division's 1243rd Rifle Regiment were in defensive positions southeast of Shakhovo, with orders not to allow the enemy to pass through the crossing in the area of Ryndinka (the 3rd Rifle Battalion had been left behind in the area of Teterevino, in the sector of the offensive of the division's main forces). As Major General Trufanov's dispatch at 0555 13 July reported, the elements of the 375th Rifle Division and the 92nd Guards Rifle Division took no part in the attacks in the area of Rzhavets and Vypolzovka, because of their "small combat capabilities." They only supported the attackers with whatever fire they could generate.

The situation with the 92nd Guards Rifle Division was particularly difficult; it had been fighting since 7 July. By 9 July 1943, of its authorized strength of 10,506 men, it had only 8,430 men reporting for duty;[22] by 15 July, it had only 2,182 men reporting for duty, including only 1,552 men in the ranks.[23] Here's an excerpt from the report that the command of the 92nd Guards Rifle Division sent to the General Staff on its losses for the period 7 July to 17 July:

> Over the period of combat operations, the division lost 924 killed, 2,212 wounded, 2,499 missing in action, and 5 sick; altogether – 5,460 men.[24]
>
> … The great number of losses is explained by the fact that all three regiments were encircled on the Belgorod axis, fought their way out of encirclement, as a result of which there is a high number of missing in action."[25]

The commander Colonel V. F. Trunin's order to withdraw from the area of Kiselevo to new lines arrived at the end of 11 July, but the headquarters continued to gather elements that made their way out of encirclement until 14 July. Thus the division on the morning of 12 July had no more than strength than a rifle regiment.

The prepared defensive belt in the region played an important role in holding up the enemy. The terrain in this region is cut by deep ravines and gullies, and the western bank of the Northern Donets River is significantly higher than the eastern bank. All this contributed to the creation of a firm defense after the disorganized withdrawal across the river.

Mobile groups of the 69th Army's 328th Engineer-Sapper Battalion were operating in the area of Rzhavets and Shcholokovo. Owing to the successful work of the sappers, several German counterattacks, during which they employed heavy tanks, were thwarted. Eleven enemy armored vehicles became immobilized or destroyed in mine fields.[26] As the account of the *front*'s and the 69th Army's engineers states, based on information from prisoners and from the forward units, the Soviet troops' successful use of mines created among the enemy tankers a so-called "mine sickness" – attacks began to be conducted cautiously: having just discovered some mines, the tank crews would bring the attack to a halt and withdraw, and wait for their own sappers to clear the mines.

The attack of the 53rd Guards Separate Tank Regiment under the command of Major N. A. Kurnosov ended in a genuine tragedy. To carry out its orders, it had to advance through the 92nd Guards Rifle Division's sector of defense, but its tankers had no precise information about the layout of the infantry's positions. As a result, combat erupted between our own units. How did this occur? Let's turn to an order from the 69th Army commander:

> … Around 1700-1800 hours on 12.07, the 53rd Separate Tank Regiment began an attack in the direction of 1st Novo-Aleksandrovskii Vyselok. Moving in column toward Hill 241.5 (north of Aleksandrovka), the tanks while on the move opened fire on the combat positions of the 92nd Guards Rifle Division and tanks of the 96th Tank Brigade located in the area of Aleksandrovka. Fighting occurred between our own troops, while simultaneously our [Il-2] *Shturmoviki* shot up the positions of the 92nd Guards Rifle Division.
>
> Only after the intervention of the senior officer of the Red Army's General Staff Lieutenant Colonel Sokolov and artillery commander of the 35th Guards Rifle Corps was this battle brought to an end with great difficulty.
>
> Having passed through Aleksandrovka, the 53rd Tank Regiment began exchanging fire with enemy tanks, but after several minutes, without carrying out its assignment, it received an order to return to its start positions. The tanks of the 53rd Tank Regiment began to withdraw, drawing after them separate groups of infantry. The anti-tank artillery following behind the 53rd Tank Regiment also deployed for combat, but didn't fire on our own infantry and tanks only due to the intervention … of Lieutenant Colonel Sokolov and the 35th Guards Rifle Corps' artillery commander.
>
> The commander of the 96th Separate Tank Brigade Major General Lebedev and the commander of the 92nd Guards Rifle Division Colonel V. F. Trunin, who were located at an observation post in the area of Hill 241.5, intervened in the elimination of these disgraces too late.
>
> The tankers had not been informed about the real situation in the infantry's front lines, which led to the indicated misunderstandings.
>
> All the aforementioned occurred only because the responsible commanders, given leadership of the operation, treated that responsibility carelessly and negligently, failed to think through questions of cooperation, and failed to reconnoiter the area and the enemy …[27]

The unpleasantness for the 53rd Guards Separate Tank Regiment didn't end with this. At 1900 it received a new assignment to seize Kazach'e by nightfall. At 2000, while moving through the northern outskirts of Aleksandrovka, it was fired upon by 28 enemy tanks, including eight heavy tanks. During the battle that erupted, Major Kurnosov's tank was knocked out, and the regiment commander was severely wounded; he was subsequently sent to an army hospital. Having lost 11 tanks, the 53rd Guards Separate Tank Regiment was compelled to take covered defensive positions on the western and southwestern outskirts of Aleksandrovka.

Just as with the first attack that afternoon, this regimental attack had not been adequately prepared. Judging from everything that happened, the tankers did not have a clear picture of the situation in the attack sector or of the enemy's strength. No preliminary reconnaissance was conducted, nor had even rudimentary cooperation with its own forces defending in this area been organized. The command of the composite detachment simply didn't give the regiment any possibility to do these things before launching the attack. Its tank crews had only just emerged from their skirmish with the 96th Separate Tank Brigade, when literally within thirty to forty minutes another order to attack arrived. One more document from the 10th Separate Destroyer Anti-tank Artillery Regiment's combat diary has been preserved, which gives us a glance at the attack of Major Kurnosov's tankers from a somewhat different vantage point:

> The enemy throughout the day was erecting a crossing over the river channel in the area of Vypolzovka, and clearing passages over the anti-tank ditch and through the minefields in the region of 1st Novo-Aleksandrovskii Vyselok, seemingly unhindered by the fire of our artillery and infantry from their covered positions.
>
> At 1900, a group of 18 of our tanks came up. The enemy holding 1st Novo-Aleksandrovskii Vyselok was attacked. Because of poor reconnaissance, our units ineptly exposed their own flank. The enemy exploited this oversight, and now that the bridge and passages were ready, at the same time attacked Aleksandrovka with up to 60 tanks (the majority of which were Tiger tanks) from the directions of Vypolzovka and 1st Novo-Aleksandrovskii Vyselok.
>
> The enemy tank attack was repelled by the fire of the 4th and 3rd Batteries of the 532nd Destroyer Anti-tank Artillery Regiment and the 5th Battery of the 1245th Destroyer Anti-tank Artillery Regiment, which had only just arrived and deployed from the march.[28]

All day long, General Schmidt's 19th Panzer Division, operating in the flood plain of the Northern Donets River, had been trying to create and firmly consolidate a second bridgehead on the opposite bank. The division's "Description of Combat Operations of the 19th Panzer Division from 5 July to 18 July 1943" relates:

> 12.7 after clearing numerous minefields, the division, developing the success, pushed on to Rzhavets. Many prisoners and anti-tank rifles were captured, and several tanks (T-34 and Churchill) were destroyed. The 73rd and 74th Panzergrenadier Regiments took over the narrow bridgehead at Rzhavets from the 6th Panzer Division and expanded it. A small, fortified hill north of Shipy had a fine view of the crossing over the Donets and kept it under heavy machine gun, mortar and artillery fire; consequently, the regiments were compelled by the enemy [at times] to take cover under the water [Author's note: as stated in text].
>
> The enemy was defending the woods and hills east and southeast of Shakhovo and the hills west and northwest of Shcholokovo with major, hastily rallied units that had been defending there previously.
>
> In order to strengthen their defending units in the area of Rzhavets, the enemy brought up the 5th Guards Mechanized Corps and the 3rd Mechanized Brigade from the Voronezh line. The 3rd Mechanized Brigade made contact with our units on the Shipy – Ryndinka sector. One brigade was transferred to the east to meet the attacking SS Division *Das Reich*.[29]

The three rifle regiments of the 81st Guards Rifle Division were defending the sector Krivtsovo – Shcholokovo – Ryndinka. Units of the 19th Panzer Division twice tried to force a crossing of the river in the course of the day, but these attempts were repelled by the fire of units of the 81st Guards Rifle Division and the 26th Guards Tank Brigade;

the tankers managed to knock out five enemy tanks, leaving two of them burning. Its companies were subjected to intense artillery and mortar fire late into the evening, which killed 8 and wounded 22 men, and damaged four vehicles and one gun.[30] Thus, until midnight Schmidt's units were unable to reach Shcholokovo; the 26th Tank Brigade was firmly clinging to its positions and at the same time assisted its neighbor (the 11th Guards Mechanized Brigade) with its fire on the Vypolzovka area.

However, it must be mentioned that the III Panzer Corps' main forces were not operating around Shcholokovo. Breith on 12 July concentrated the corps' efforts for the drive through Rzhavets to the north, since a major jumping-off point had been established there – a large bridgehead had been created on the northern bank of the river, where panzers were already over the Northern Donets. All this had yet to be accomplished at Shcholokovo. Attempts to lay a crossing there in the daytime had been thwarted by our forces, thus particularly bitter fighting went on all day on 12 July around the villages of Ryndinka, Shipy and Aleksandrovskii Vyselok. Through the efforts of the 5th Guards 'Zimovniki' Mechanized Corps' brigades, the German breakthrough in these areas was localized, and Germans were even driven out of Shipy.

Nevertheless, the 19th Panzer Division continued its efforts to create a second bridgehead at Shcholokovo, in order to participate in a concentric attack on Shakhovo (from Rzhavets and Shcholokovo) right up to the onset of darkness. Around 2200, a group of Panzergrenadiers crossed the Northern Donets in boats, and infiltrated into the woods southwest of Shakhovo, drawing attention to them. A short time later, under the cover of darkness, the Germans began to erect a bridge and to transfer tanks to the

A German 81mm mortar crew prepares to fire from an orchard in Shcholokovo. (RGAKFD)

opposite bank of the Northern Donets. At dawn on 13 July, fighting at Shcholokovo flared up with renewed strength.

For the most part, the troops of the 48th Rifle Corps had fought steadfastly, securing the left flank of our shock grouping at Prokhorovka. Thanks to their stubbornness and courage, the enemy, despite all its strenuous efforts, could not exploit its success on 11 July and continued to grind away without making any real headway. However, seven days of uninterrupted bloody fighting nevertheless had a negative effect on the men in the ranks and the command staff – instances appeared where entire companies and battalions abandoned their positions.

Elements of practically all the 69th Army's divisions demonstrated instances of fragility: both those that had already been involved in hard fighting for several days in a row and were now badly tattered, and those that had only just moved into the main line of resistance. Units were observed to retreat not only when under pressure from a superior opponent, but also at moments when a few commanders displayed basic faint-heartedness. Here is just one example, which occurred in the 81st Guards Rifle Division's 235th Guards Rifle Regiment, which was defending the sector (excl.) Krivtsovo – Shcholokovo. It is taken from division commander I. K. Morozov's Order No. 083/op on 13 July 1943:

> 12.07.43 the commander of the 2nd Battalion of the 235th Guards Red Banner Rifle Regiment Guards Captain Goshtenar received an order to defend along the west bank of the Northern Donets River at the Shcholokovo fish farm and to prevent an enemy crossing of the Northern Donets River in a northwest direction.
>
> Having received the order and occupied the defense, the commander of the 2nd Battalion Goshtenar took no measures to prevent an enemy crossing. Moreover, at the appearance of an insignificant enemy force, he disgracefully abandoned the battlefield, and retreated without an order from the regiment commander. Goshtenar forgot the glorious traditions of the Stalingrad battles and shamefully fled the battlefield, while his battalion was stopped and returned to its original position by the division's chief of staff Major Svetnik and the chief of the political department Guards Lieutenant Colonel Bol'shakov, who had just arrived. Goshtenar behaved like a coward and betrayed the Motherland.
>
> I order:
>
> 1. Regiment commanders are to introduce the strictest discipline to prevent cases of abandoning their assigned sectors without orders, and to implement Order No. 227.
>
> For abandoning his assigned sector without an order and for his disgraceful flight from the battlefield, the commander of the 2nd Battalion of the 235th Guards Red Banner Rifle Regiment will be turned over for a trial by a military tribunal.[31]

The entire course of combat operations on 12 July in the region of Rzhavets and southwest of Prokhorovka Station indicates that the breakthrough in the 69th Army sector was a well-planned operation. Its final objective was supposed to be the area of Prokhorovka, where the III Panzer Corps would link up with the II SS Panzer Corps, and thereby encircle the 69th Army's 48th Rifle Corps. Despite the fact that this goal was not achieved, the III Panzer Corps managed to influence perceptibly the situation in the II SS Panzer Corps sector, by diverting significant forces to meet its attack and thereby weakening the attack of the 5th Guards Tank Army on the Prokhorovka axis. Moreover, all day on its left flank, the threat of a breakthrough and the emergence of the enemy in the 5th Guards Tank Army's rear were hanging over Rotmistrov.

By the end of 12 July the situation was becoming stabilized, but the Soviet forces were unable fully to return to the positions they had lost along the Northern Donets. However, the main task on this day had been accomplished: Breith's panzers had been halted, and the III Panzer Corps breakthrough had been temporarily localized.

I will stress: this was only a temporary success. The threat of encirclement still hung over the 48th Rifle Corps' main forces. Our command understood this. Chief of the General Staff A. V. Vasilevsky reported to I. V. Stalin on the night of 12 July:

> The threat of an enemy breakthrough from the south in the region of Shakhovo, Avdeevka and Aleksandrovka remains real for tomorrow. Through the night I am taking all measures to concentrate the entire 5th Guards Mechanized Corps, the 32nd Motorized Brigade and four regiments of anti-tank artillery there.[32]

13

The 12 July Counterattack and its Results on Supporting Directions

Lieutenant General I. M. Chistiakov's 6th Guards Army, strengthened with the 10th Tank Corps, a portion of the 5th Guards 'Stalingrad' Tank Corps and a tank group from the 1st Tank Army's 3rd Mechanized Corps, prepared to participate in the frontal counterattack with practically its full strength. Major General N. B. Ibiansky's 22nd Guards Rifle Corps was to launch the 6th Guards Army's main attack with its 90th Guards, 184th and 219th Rifle Divisions from the Chapaev – Noven'koe – Kruglik line along the Syrtsevo – Iakovlevo axis. In the area of Iakovlevo, it and the 23rd Guards Rifle Corps were supposed to link up with the 5th Guards and 5th Guards Tank Armies advancing from Prokhorovka in the direction of the Oboian' highway. This, it was assumed, would lead to the encirclement and destruction of the XXXXVIII and II SS Panzer Corps.

Major General P. P. Vakhrameev's 23rd Guards Rifle Corps with its subordinate 204th, 309th and 67th Guards Rifle Divisions were to attack from the Kruglik – Malinovoe forest line through the northern outskirts of Verkhopen'e toward Pokrovka. The 71st Guards Rifle Division was to cover the right flank of the 22nd Guards Rifle Corps, while the 51st Guards Rifle Division – after its replacement by 5th Guards Army's forces – was withdrawn into the 6th Guards Army commander's reserve.

The commanders of the 23rd Guards Rifle Corps and of the 204th, 219th and 184th Rifle Divisions personally received their orders for the counterattack from I. M. Chistiakov at 1300 11 July, while jointly surveying the battlefield from Hill 240.8. Sixth Guards Army staff officers delivered the attack orders to the 22nd Guards Rifle corps commander and the remaining division commanders slated for the counterstroke. As the day came to an end, the situation started to become complicated. Chistiakov received a communication that the 204th and 309th Rifle Divisions were to remain under the 1st Tank Army's operational control. Thus, only the single 67th Guards Rifle Division remained in the 23rd Guards Rifle Corps, and it became pointless to activate this corps in the forthcoming attack.

At the same time, the commander of the 40th Army halted the preparations underway for movement of the 184th and 219th Rifle Divisions. Lieutenant General K. S. Moskalenko didn't like the idea of depriving his army of a significant portion of its strength, and requested that these divisions remain with him during the period of the counterattack. The question was resolved only toward the morning of 12 July – Vatutin decided not to alter the already prepared plan and denied Moskalenko's request. The divisions only began pulling out of their lines at dawn at 0400 12 July, forming into marching columns within plain sight of the enemy. This hitch significantly delayed the attack of 6th Guards Army's right wing and weakened the force of the initial assault. In this situation, there is no need to speak about any sort of general, detailed plan of combat operations or the elaboration of cooperation between the 22nd Guards Rifle Corps and the tank formations. At 0830 12 July, there was still not even any skeleton staff in the jumping-off positions of the *front*'s auxiliary shock grouping (the 6th Guards and 1st Tank Armies).

According to the testimony of the commander of the 1st Tank Army Lieutenant General M. E. Katukov, Vatutin initially informed him of the prepared counterattack on 10 July (the same day as Rotmistrov). According to Katukov, Vatutin told him:

> I won't give you any big assignments for a deep penetration of the German defenses; if you only advance a kilometer or so, that's good enough. The main thing is to fix the German forces in place, to deprive them of the possibility to maneuver their reserves freely, and to prevent them from massing more strength at Prokhorovka.[1]

On the night of 10 July, *front* headquarters issued its concrete assignments. The 1st Tank Army, with four tank and one mechanized corps, and two rifle divisions with artillery as reinforcements, was first of all to prevent any further enemy advance to the north in the Kruglik – Hill 244.8 – Ol'khovatka sector. Meanwhile, two corps – Major General A. G. Kravchenko's 5th Guards 'Stalingrad' Tank Corps and Lieutenant General V. G. Burkov's 10th Tank Corps – were shifted to the army's right flank; they were to reinforce the 6th Guards Army's assault grouping (the 22nd Guards Rifle Corps) and attack to the southeast. These formations had the following specific assignments:

The 5th Guards 'Stalingrad' Tank Corps with the 21st and 22nd Guards Tank Brigades (16 T-34, nine T-70 and five Mk-IV Churchill), the 1212th (11 76mm anti-tank guns) and 222nd (eight 76mm anti-tank guns) Destroyer Anti-tank Artillery Regiments, and the 36th Guards Mortar Regiment (23 BM-13 rocket launchers) from the area of 1st Novoselovka and the Kuznetsovo forest were to attack in the direction of Hill 208.0, Sukhodol forest, Shepelevka, Lukhanino and Iakovlevo.

The 10th Tank Corps, having turned over its sector of defense on the night of 11 July to the 204th Rifle Division, moved with its main forces into the woods northwest of Noven'koe, and was to go on the attack the following morning. Its 183rd Tank Brigade together with the 727th Destroyer Anti-tank Artillery Regiment was to attack along the route: northern outskirts of Noven'koe – Tolstoe woods – Verkhopen'e – Hill 251.4, and by day's end was to occupy Krasnaia Dubrova. The 186th Tank Brigade, reinforced with the 1450th Self-propelled Artillery Regiment, was to attack behind the 183rd Tank Brigade and seize the villages of Pokrovka and Ul'ianovka. The 178th Tank Brigade with the support of the 454th Mortar Regiment was to attack Noven'koe, with a subsequent line of advance through the southern portion of the Tolstoe woods toward Hill 237.6 and Hill 254.5, and had the orders to drive the enemy from the southwestern part of Pokrovka and to seize it by the end of 12 July.[2]

Thus, the 10th Tank Corps, weakened in both armor and men, was supposed to penetrate the enemy's defenses to a depth of more than 15 kilometers. Even considering the support of the three rifle divisions, these orders were plainly unrealistic, but just as at Prokhorovka, they were made intentionally. M. E. Katukov later wrote:

> Giving the orders to Kravchenko and Burkov, we didn't limit their offensive operations to only these one or two kilometers. On the contrary, we were aiming at

> a deeper penetration of the fascists' defenses. This was done deliberately, considering a purely psychological detail. After all if you tell people that they are being sent into battle with extremely limited aims, only for the purpose of catching the enemy's attention, they will not act with the same energy, than they would if they had to break through the enemy's defenses with the intention to crush it to its full depth.[3]

The 3rd Mechanized Corps, the 31st Tank Corps, and the 204th and 309th Rifle Divisions, holding in place on their current lines, had the assignment to prevent an enemy breakthrough in case of a counterattack, and upon the retreat of the XXXXVIII Panzer Corps, were to go on the pursuit of it together with the attacking forces of the 6th Guards Army's 23rd Guards Rifle Corps. However, just minutes before the start of the attack, this order was replaced by another.

On the morning of 12 July, Colonel K. M. Baidak, commander of the 204th Rifle Division, and Colonel D. F. Dremov, commander of the 309th Rifle Division, received an order to participate in the counterattack at 0830. From the line: southern outskirts of Kalinovka – Malinovoe forest – Hill 211.9, the rifle divisions were to attack the *Grossdeutschland* Panzergrenadier and 11th Panzer Divisions with the support of a small tank group from the 3rd Tank Corps (headed by its 1st Guards Tank Brigade commander Colonel V. M. Gorelov). The situation bore strong similarities to that which developed on the Soviet side in the bend of Psel River.

It should be noted that the *front* command successfully chose both the time and place for landing the main blow by the 1st Tank Army and 6th Guards Army grouping. The point is that on their front, the Germans themselves had created suitable conditions for our attack. After the most difficult and savage fighting on the right flank of the 1st Tank Army, by the end of 11 July von Knobelsdorff's XXXXVIII Panzer Corps had pushed Group Getman[4] (6th Tank Corps, 3rd Mechanized Corps' 1st and 3rd Motorized Brigades, and the 6th Guards Army's 90th Guards Rifle Division) out of the area of the Psel River bend and had inflicted substantial damage to it. As the sun set and all through the night of 11 July, remnants of Group Getman emerged from the area of Tolstoe woods and Berezov, while officers rallied the troops and equipment was put back into order.[5] As a result of this evident success, the Fourth Panzer Army command considered that the Russians in this region were no longer in a condition to launch strong attacks and issued an order for the XXXXVIII Panzer Corps to conduct a regrouping of its forces. Division *Grossdeutschland* received an order to assemble on the Oboian' highway and to the west of it by 1500 12 July; from there it would attack together with the 11th Panzer Division in the direction of the Psel River. Meanwhile, the 3rd Panzer Division, which had been substantially weakened in the recent fighting, was to take over *Grossdeutschland*'s sector between Hill 247.0 (south of Kruglik) and the Tolstoe woods. Thus, at the moment of the start of the Soviet counterattack, the XXXXVIII Panzer Corps was in the process of regrouping. Moreover, the LII Army Corps' 332nd and 255th Infantry Divisions were to redeploy to new positions on the left flank of the 3rd Panzer Division and extending to the south and southwest. Leaping ahead, I will note that the Soviet side, judging from the archival documents that I discovered, was not able to take full advantage of such a favorable moment for an attack.

★ ★ ★

The 5th Guards 'Stalingrad' Tank Corps was the first to go on the attack at 1000 in the direction of Chapaev, with the support of only one rifle regiment from Colonel S. I. Tsukarev's 184th Rifle Division. All of the corps' remaining armor had been combined into two brigades. Colonel K. I. Ovcharenko's 21st Guards Tank Brigade took the lead with the 222nd Destroyer Anti-tank Artillery Regiment and the support of the 36th Guards Mortar Regiment's *Katiushas*. The 22nd Guards Tank Brigade was covering its left flank. The offensive developed slowly. Both the Germans and our units had densely sewn the area in the 5th Guards Tank Corps' sector with mines. The *Luftwaffe* systematically bombed the corps' tank wedge. Four T-34 and two Mk-IV Churchill tanks were destroyed by air attack – almost half of the 21st Guards Tank Brigade's total losses on this day. Our own minefield maps were inaccurate, and our sappers had to operate in broad daylight under enemy fire. Between 1300 and 1400 the 21st Guards Tank Brigade neared Chapaev, but was unable to take it from the march. By this time, the main forces of the 184th Rifle Division were beginning to approach. From the march, without preliminary preparations, the rifle regiments together with the tanks again attacked the village.

This time, overcoming fierce enemy resistance, the Red Army troops seized Chapaev. A battalion of the 332nd Infantry Division, which had been defending this area, was smashed and scattered. The Guardsmen captured several dozen prisoners, including a number of the battalion's officers, and some equipment as well. The infantry started digging in around Chapaev, while the corps's shock group advanced further in the direction of Rakovo. After three hours of combat, the tanks approached to within 1-1.5 kilometers of the western outskirts of Rakovo, but were halted there by powerful artillery and *Nebelwerfer* fire. M. E. Katukov later recalled:

> General A. G. Kravchenko tried to organize the advance of his tanks into the depth of the fascist defenses, but unsuccessfully. A torrent of fire blocked the way forward for combat vehicles.
>
> 'I cannot advance,' Andrei Grigor'evich reported over the radio, 'the Germans have increased their fire. The entire area ahead is under artillery and mortar fire … They're bombing us …'
>
> Of course, he, a fighting general accustomed to acting boldly, wanted to advance as far as possible. Tall, broad-shouldered, with a rich, deep voice and colorful speech, Kravchenko had shown himself to be a decisive commander during the fighting at Stalingrad.
>
> 'Don't advance any further,' I answered him. 'Hold your current lines. Don't advance,' I repeated to the corps commander, 'Here and there, feign an attack … Make the adversary believe that you are searching for the most vulnerable places in his defense.'[6]

Of the corps' 30 tanks, which went on the attack that morning, by the end of the day 16 had been lost, including eight T-34, five T-70 and three Mk-IV Churchill tanks.[7]

Even the more powerful 10th Tank Corps, operating on the left flank of the 5th Guards Tank Corps, could not change the situation. This corps had more than 120 tanks and self-propelled guns at the start of the day.[8] As is noted in its headquarters' account, its brigades were stopped at the Tolstoe forest, while the infantry of Major

General V. P. Kotel'nikov's 219th Rifle Division, as well of the approaching 184th Rifle Division, were quickly pinned down around 1400 by the intense fire of the enemy that had been lying in wait for them.

Recently in the Central Archives of the Russian Ministry ofDefense, I stumbled upon documents that bring into question whether the 10th Tank Corps even attempted a powerful frontal attack, since on the morning of 12 July its headquarters wasn't prepared for it and still didn't know the orders given to the corps by the 1st Tank Army command. Here is what M. E. Katukov, the 1st Tank Army commander, reported to Nikita Khrushchev, a member of Voronezh Front's Military Council, on 13 July 1943:

> At your direction, I am reporting on the results of the investigation into the commander of the 10th Tank Corps Lieutenant General Burkov's ignorance of [his] assignment for the offensive:
>
> On 11.07.43 between 1500 and 1600 hours, I personally handed the order for the 10th Tank Corps' offensive to the 10th Tank Corps' assistant chief of operations, Major Komarov. Major Komarov returned to the corps headquarters, [where] both on the map and through the written order explained the order in detail to the commander of the 10th Tank Corps Lieutenant General Burkov, who failed to organize fully the work for deploying the units in the jumping-off area, and never himself went to the command post or the army headquarters in order to clarify the orders, which prolonged the time for organizing the offensive.
>
> I request your instructions on calling the commander of the 10th Tank Corps Lieutenant General Burkov to account.[9]

A change in corps command, likely, led to the confusion in this situation. The point is that back on 9 July in the area of Orlovka, Lieutenant General V. G. Burkov had been wounded in the leg and shoulder when caught by an air attack. The chief of staff of the 10th Tank Corps had also been wounded in the attack and had been evacuated to a hospital. It is not known how severe Burkov's wounds were, or where he spent the three subsequent days – at his headquarters or in the corps' hospital, but documents show the signature of V. G. Burkov on the dispatches sent to *front* headquarters on 11 July. To what degree Vasilii Gerasimovich was physically able to handle his corps on 12 July, and exactly when the new corps commander Major General Alekseev took over the post isn't clear. Likely, having delayed in moving out, the brigades of the 10th Tank Corps nevertheless went on the attack together with the 219th Rifle Division, and exchanged fire with the enemy in the Tolstoe woods, forcing the combat outpost elements and the screening anti-tank guns of the 3rd Panzer Division and *Grossdeutschland* back to the villages in the Pena River valley.

Still, Helmuth Spaeter's history of the *Grossdeutschland* Panzer Corps reveals the impact of the Soviet attack on the German forces during their regrouping, and its disruptive effect on German plans:

> Scarcely had the Armoured Reconnaissance Battalion *GD* been relieved at Point 247.0, when at 0620 [0820 Moscow time] the enemy attacked east with strong tank and infantry forces from the area west of Kruglik – Point 254.5 and against Point 247.0. The latter position was soon lost and the Armoured Reconnaissance Battalion

A tanker from a knocked-out T-34 bandages a comrade. (RGAKFD)

> *GD* withdrew to the south. At the same time enemy armour and infantry attacked from Kalinovka against the positions of II and III Battalions, Panzergrenadier Regiment *GD*. The situation quickly became critical. II Battalion under Major Bethke, which was tied up by the enemy coming out of Kalinovka, found itself in a particularly critical situation, which temporarily forced the battalion to withdraw from its positions. ... The Battalion retook its former positions at about 1800 [20.00]. Only then did the enemy attacks subside. ...
>
> As a result of these heavy defensive battles the division's plans for a further advance to the north were initially overtaken. The units already on the move were recalled and placed in positions behind especially threatened points. ... The villages of Gertsovka and Berezovka were back in enemy hands and the danger that Soviet forces were advancing into the rear of the German attack divisions was increasing.[10]

In a few documents it is noted that Colonel G. Ia. Andriushchenko's 183rd Tank Brigade from the 10th Tank Corps even approached to within direct firing range of the center of gravity of the XXXXVIII Panzer Corps' defenses, the village of Verkhopen'e. However, it was stopped there by an enemy anti-tank screen, and then by increasingly sharp enemy counterattacks, which primarily involved Panzer IV, Panther and Tiger tanks from *Grossdeutschland's* armor brigade.[11] These tanks all had long-barreled guns, with very high muzzle velocities and armor-penetration capabilities. They presented a serious threat to our T-34s, not to mention the light T-70 tanks. Oh, how difficult it was for our soldiers and commanders to fight under such unequal terms!

Of the *Wehrmacht's* four main models of the 75mm and 88mm anti-tank and tank guns with the L/48, L/50, L/70 and L/71 barrel lengths, all were capable of penetrating 63mm to 148mm of armor at an angle of incidence of 60° from a range of 2 kilometers. But the maximum armor thickness on the T-34 Model 1942 tank, with which the 1st Tank Army was mainly equipped, was 65mm. Its own 76mm gun could only duel at relatively equal terms with the Germans' primary tank, the Panzer IV at distances up to 500 meters, since the armor of this tank ranged up to 80mm. As for the Tiger with its frontal armor of 100mm, the T-34 could only hope to knock it out with a shot from the side, and at that from close range. A graphic account of what sort of tank the Tiger was, is given by a report from the Central Front's 9th Tank Corps, which had conducted test firing on a Panzer VI Tiger that our forces had immobilized and captured:

> For firing at the tank, the 37mm light anti-aircraft artillery gun and the 45mm, 76mm and 85mm guns were selected.
>
> Firing was conducted at an immobile tank from the front and side target aspects with armor-piercing and armor-piercing discarding sabot shells of all the aforementioned guns.
>
> Results:
>
> a) From the front target aspect, not a single shell from any of the guns, fired from a range of 2000 meters, was capable of penetrating the tank's frontal armor. At a range up to 400 meters, the 45mm shell can disable the armament (gun barrel, machine gun) and jam the turret. From a range up to 400 meters, the armor-piercing 85mm shell penetrates to a depth of 12-13mm and remains embedded.
>
> b) Firing from a side target aspect, the 37mm shell doesn't penetrate the tank's armor and makes only small dents in it; from 300-400 meters it pierces the track and rollers. The 45mm armor-piercing discarding sabot shell penetrates both the side armor and the turret from ranges out to 200 meters. The armor-piercing shell ricochets off the armor.
>
> The 76mm armor-piercing shell ricochets off the armor at all ranges. It can jam the turret and leave dents in the side armor from ranges up to 300-400 meters. The 76mm armor-piercing discarding sabot shell penetrates both the side and turret armor from ranges out to 400 meters.
>
> c) The 85mm armor-piercing shell penetrates both the side and turret armor at ranges out to 1200 meters.[12]

Let's listen to a veteran of the 10th Tank Corps, Sergeant-major N. V. Kazantsev, who at the time of the Kursk battle was a T-34 driver-mechanic:

> I never rolled straight ahead, but [maneuvered] along hollows, through low-lying areas, along the reverse slopes of hillocks, and I would emerge about 300-500 meters [from the enemy tank], so that only our turret showed above the crest of the rise or some bushes, which allowed our gunners to plant a shell in the side of a Tiger unexpectedly.[13]

One more piece of testimony from P. I. Gromtsev, a former tank company commander in the same corps, who took part in the fighting at Kursk:

> At first we fired at the Tigers from around 700 meters. You'd see a hit, the armor-piercing shells would generate some sparks, but it [the tank] would keep rolling without a care, shooting up one of our tanks after another. Only the intense summer heat favored us – here and there, Tigers were erupting in flames [Gromtsev is evidently confusing the Tiger with the Panther, which did indeed occasionally exhibit this problem at Kursk]. It turned out later that fuel vapors accumulating in the tank's engine compartment were often igniting. You could directly knock out a Tiger or a Panther only from around 300 meters, and at that only with a flank shot. Back then many of our tanks were left burning, but our brigade still managed to push the Germans back a kilometre or two. But we'd just about had it, and couldn't endure any more such fighting.[14]

The attack of the 204th and 309th Rifle Divisions began somewhere between 1500 and 1600, and within an hour (approximately at 1700), the 204th Rifle Division was stopped by heavy artillery and mortar fire after advancing about 1.5 to 2.5 kilometers. However, the left-flank 309th Rifle Division was struck with a counterattack by the 11th Panzer Division's panzer regiment soon after jumping off, and was promptly hurled back to its start line. Fearing that the enemy was going over to an attack to the north, the 1st Tank Army commander at 1600 committed Group Gorelov (60 tanks of the 3rd Mechanized Corps' 1st Guards, 49th and 192nd Tank Brigades) into the fighting in the 204th Rifle Division's sector, and committed the 31st Tank Corps' 242nd and 237th Tank Brigades in support of the 309th Rifle Division. However, these were more in the form of holding attacks, and judging from Katukov's actions, he was making no effort to regroup his forces for a major push. By the end of the day, the two sides were still practically on those same lines.

When analyzing the course and outcomes of the 12 July counterattack on the operational sectors of all the armies, it is impossible to part from the thought that *front* headquarters, when launching the counterstroke, had overestimated its strength. Rather than scrupulously working out a detailed operational plan that would not only stop the enemy, but also by efficiently using its available forces, inflict substantial damage to him, the *front* headquarters left this important work to the headquarters of the armies, which by definition could not see the entire situation at the front. The armies' headquarters superficially prepared their own plans, starting from the general assignments given to their forces. The *front* command, though, didn't make any real attempt to coordinate their planning. It is precisely the *front* headquarters, which was responsible for the entire sector under its command, which should have discerned the most vulnerable spots in the enemy's lines and the most promising avenues of attack – and if necessary concentrate the forces of several formations for the assault in this area. Instead, as if entranced by the sheer quantity of armor and men at its disposal for the counterattack, the *front* command with the agreement of the General Staff busied itself with constructing plans for bludgeoning an enemy grouping that had assumed a defensive posture with frontal attacks.

One of these promising avenues, an attack along which might have permitted the encirclement of part of the enemy's attack grouping, was in the offensive sector of the 97th Guards Rifle Division of the 5th Guards Army's 33rd Guards Rifle Corps. However, like the rest of the 5th Guards Army, General I. I. Antsiferov's division attacked without tank support and without sufficient artillery support. Despite this, in contrast with its neighboring divisions in the Psel bend, the 97th Guards Rifle not only withstood the counterattacks of the 11th Panzer Division, but even managed to advance somewhat.

Its attack fell practically on the boundary between the 11th Panzer Division and SS Panzergrenadier Division *Totenkopf*. If the prospects of this line of attack had been fully appreciated in the planning stage, and the division had been reinforced with at least the three brigades of the 31st Tank Corps, which were not committed into the fighting until 1600 12 July, then the attempt to trap the SS Panzergrenadier Division *Totenkopf* north of the Psel might have been successful. At the very least, sensing the threat of a tank attack on its left flank, the *Totenkopf* command might not have been so persistent in pushing to the northeast, which without a doubt would have eased the situation of the 95th Guards Rifle Division. Unfortunately, despite the plain deficit of tank support on all the sectors of the *front*, naturally save for that in the sector of the 5th Guards Tank Army, the 31st Tank Corps, which had approximately 71 tanks in its 100th, 237th and 242nd Tank Brigades, including 53 T-34 tanks, remained mostly idle on 12 July.[15]

Unfortunately, today it is difficult to reconstruct the course of events from more than sixty years ago and to grasp their interrelations, since all the circumstances and facts, connected with the interpersonal relations among the command and leadership staff of the Voronezh Front's forces are not known. In addition, with the passing of the participants of those events, an enormous amount of information about their relationships, about possible sharp conflicts among the generals, about their friendly relations and their antipathies has been lost. Nevertheless, all these aspects had an enormous influence not only on the career rise of one or another corps commander or army commander, but also on the combat results of the troops under their command. Here is only one episode and example, which today can be expounded in detail. It is contained in a letter that Major General Kravchenko, the 5th Guards Tank Corps commander, wrote to N. F. Vatutin on 13 July 1943:

> In the bitter fighting with enemy tanks and motorized infantry [Panzergrenadiers], and without support from our neighbors on the right and left, the corps suffered large losses in tanks, but checked the enemy advance to the north. It seemed to me that the corps' glorious work, which demonstrated numerous heroic deeds, should find its reflection in the attention and concern shown to increasing its combat readiness and in preserving its veteran cadres, in which live the traditions of the Great Stalingrad battle. Such attention and concern is not visible from Lieutenant General Shtevnev, the Armored and Mechanized Forces commander.
>
> 1. On 10.07.43, an order of the 10th Tank Corps commander was received, supposedly in the name of the 1st Tank Army commander, on the transfer of the 21st and 22nd Guards Tank Brigades of my corps to the operational control of the 10th Tank Corps commander. This order was handed over supposedly at your

> direction. When checking this matter with the 1st Tank Army commander, it became clear that the latter didn't issue any sort of order on this account, and that it originated exclusively from the personal initiative of Lieutenant General Shtevnev. To deprive the corps of its veteran cadres who have been forged in battles, and to not give it a chance to inflict even more crushing blows on the enemy with its full strength – such was the conclusion of this totally unjustified order.
>
> 2. By your order of 9.07.43, the corps was to receive the 14th Tank Regiment as reinforcement. The commander of the Armored and Mechanized Forces of the V. F. [Voronezh Front] canceled your order and transferred it to the 1st Tank Army, although it was known to everyone that [this] corps, which had received the main attack of the enemy tank grouping (7, 8 and 9 July), had suffered significant losses and was in need of reinforcement more than anyone else.
>
> 3. The destroyer anti-tank artillery regiment that had been under the corps' operational control was transferred at the personal direction of the commander of the Armored and Mechanized Forces V. F. to the 10th Tank Corps, which now has two of them. The corps' tanks, lacking these guns, will unavoidably suffer losses. The reason for this transfer is incomprehensible, moreover because the corps always receives the most important combat assignments, while the 10th Tank Corps, in essence, still hasn't tasted battle. I request you to direct the commander of the Armored and Mechanized Forces of the V. F. Lieutenant General Shtevnev to show more concern, a more objective evaluation of the corps' combat work, and more attention to equipping, increasing the combat readiness and conserving the main heroic cadres of the Stalingrad corps.[16]

As concerns the 14th Tank Regiment, it was not assigned to the 5th Guards 'Stalingrad' Tank Corps for objective reasons. In all else, A. G. Kravchenko's indignation is justified. Truly, his corps during the period of most intense fighting had fought heroically and had played an important role in implementing the orders of the *front* command. Nevertheless, the attitude towards this formation on the part of certain leaders of the *front* remained, at the very least, strange. I will add a few numbers to Kravchenko's words. As an assistant to the 1st Tank Army commander Engineer-Colonel P. G. Dyner reported to the staff of the *front*'s Armored and Mechanized Forces on 16 July, on 15 July the 10th Tank Corps had 110 operational tanks, while the 5th Guards Tank Corps had only 16.[7] However, the former was withdrawn together with the other corps of the 1st Tank Army for refitting, while Major General A. G. Kravchenko's corps was assigned to the 6th Guards Army, where after repairing 14 additional tanks, it was again thrown into battle. By the conclusion of the *front*'s defensive operation, the 5th Guards 'Stalingrad' Tank Corps no longer existed as a tank corps – its strength had dropped to approximately ten tanks. Why it was considered necessary to reduce such a steadfast and battle-tested tank corps to such a condition is incomprehensible. After all, back on 18 April 1943, the *front* commanders had received *Stavka* of the Supreme High Command Directive No. 30095 on the use of Guards armies and corps in operations, in which it had been demanded "not to reduce them in any event to complete exhaustion."[18]

Thus, nothing came of the factor of surprise in the operations of the Voronezh Front's right-wing forces. Moreover, the lack of coordination and the poor organization of work in the headquarters at all levels of the Voronezh Front allowed the enemy to beat back our armies' counterattacks in turn. At the time when Rotmistrov's tankers, going on the offensive, were anticipating an attack toward Iakovlevo, into the rear of the SS divisions, the attack grouping in the Pena bulge was only still gathering its forces. Yet by the time the 5th Guards Tank Army had been halted on the "tank field" at Prokhorovka, Kravchenko's and Burkov's brigades, which had been bled white in previous fighting, supported by infantry that had been worn out by long redeployments on foot, once again went on the attack.

A similar situation occurred this day in the sector of the 7th Guards Army as well. Its 49th Rifle Corps, under the command of General Terent'ev with the 111th and 270th Rifle Divisions (bolstered with artillery units and the 201st and 27th Guards Tank Brigades) and supported by the 73rd Guards Rifle Division, received the assignment to go on the offensive on the morning of 12 July 1943 in the direction of Krutoi Log, Razumnoe and Dal'nie Peski from the jumping-off line Point 209.6 – Gremiachii – Machine Tractor Station – Hill 202.9. The objective was to emerge in the rear of Army Detachment Kempf.

The corps command, which had arrived in the 7th Guards Army only on the eve of the offensive, did not have time to organize a regrouping of the forces and to move into its start positions under the cover of darkness. The 111th Rifle Division spent the night-time hours assembling its units, and moved into its jumping-off positions piecemeal only after the sun rose on 12 July. The enemy took advantage of this situation with the 111th Rifle Division and part of the 270th Rifle Division and opened intensive *Nebelwerfer* fire. The element of surprise had been lost.[19] The 201st Tank Brigade, which had been attached to the 270th Rifle Division, had been holding a sector of the front lines, and

A German machine-gun crew demonstrating an unusual way of firing. A captured photo. (RGAKFD)

because of a delay in handing over its positions, it didn't have time to prepare for the attack.

The divisions of the 49th Rifle Corps, having advanced 2 to 3 kilometers in places, ran into bitter enemy resistance and could advance no further. They began digging in to defend the ground they had gained.

Savage fighting had lasted all day long on 12 July around the entire perimeter of the enemy's penetration into the Voronezh Front's defenses. Both sides had suffered heavy losses, and by the end of the day were consolidating their positions wherever they were located at day's end. It had become clear that the counterattack on the flanks of the II SS Panzer Corps had not achieved their goals. However, the enemy's intention to seize Prokhorovka and to create the conditions for the encirclement of the 48th Rifle Corps, as well as for a breakthrough east of Oboian' toward Kursk, had also been thwarted.

The contrasting views of the opposing sides on the events of 12 July are of doubtless interest to readers and especially to researchers. Let's begin with the daily summary report of the Fourth Panzer Army:

12.07.43
Zhuravel' woods, northwest
Daily Summary for the Army
Evaluation of the position: in the course of 12.07 the enemy launched coordinated attacks on the Fourth Panzer Army along its entire front with the forces of at least the parts of ten tank and mechanized corps and several infantry divisions. The center of gravity of the enemy attacks was on both flanks around and north of Kalinin, west of Prokhorovka, as well as west of Verkhopen'e. For this purpose, the adversary today committed two tank corps (the 18th and 29th Tank Corps) into the battle in the area of Prokhorovka, and apparently shifted the 10th Tank Corps to the area of Noven'kii [Noven'koe]. All attempts by the opponent to crush the flanks of the panzer army were beaten back in heavy defensive fighting. Attacks on the northern flank of the 167th Infantry Division, SS Division *Totenkopf*'s bridgehead, the northern front of the XXXXVIII Panzer Corps and on the LII Army Corps south of Pena were repulsed or are being repulsed through counterattacks to eliminate local penetrations.

In detail: The right flank 167th Infantry Division, crossing the Lipovyi Donets, is attacking to the north, following the left flank 168th Infantry Division. The attacks of enemy infantry from the direction of Nepkhaevo and west of Teterevino (south), as well as an attack supported by tanks against the left flank of the division were repulsed with heavy losses for the enemy. The settlement lying 2.5 kilometers northwest of Rozhdestvenka was seized by major enemy forces; measures were taken to regain control of it. The II SS Panzer Corps in the course of the entire day was repelling the fiercest attacks of numerous tanks with mounted infantry. The Corps on 12.07 up to the present moment knocked out 120 tanks. SS Division *Das Reich* repelled an attack on the position at the railway line east of Iasnaia Poliana and took Storozhevoe with its left flank, despite savage enemy resistance. The adversary attacked the positions of Panzer Division *Adolf Hitler* at the [Oktiabr'skii] state farm lying 3 km southwest of Prokhorovka and the hill to the southeast of there. In heavy combat, local penetrations were liquidated and the foe was thrown back.

Major enemy forces tried to liquidate the bridgehead of the SS Division *Totenkopf* at Bogoroditskoe. Counterattacks to the northeast and northwest were crowned with complete success. The armored group at the current moment is still engaged in a panzer battle on the hills 1 km west of Polezhaev; holding attacks against the left flank south of Ol'khovskii [Ol'khvatskii] suffered a failure. In the area of the hill 4 km west of Verkhopen'e, weakly defended because of a regrouping underway, a sudden tank attack was launched by the enemy. The 11th Panzer Division repulsed separate attacks on its right wing and in the center. The 3rd Panzer Division's armored group at the current moment is fighting with enemy tanks that have broken through 4 km west of Verkhopen'e. The panzer regiment of *Grossdeutschland* is fighting in the wooded area 2 km west of Verkhopen'e.

The LII Army Corps attacked the enemy with its right flank on a front 20 km wide with infantry and tank forces. Fighting is still going on there. The positions of the 332nd Infantry Division around Chapaev were crushed by 14 enemy tanks; orders were issued on measures for their destruction. Tank attacks on Zavidovka, as well as on the woods west of Korovino were repulsed. The enemy that had broken into Mikhailovka and Pochinok was hurled back, and the settlements were retaken by a counterattack. The foe attacked positions of the 255th Infantry Division southwest of Bubna; all attacks were repelled. The day passed quietly in the sector of the 57th Infantry Division.

The situation in the air: in connection with the weather, there was little air activity on either side.

Forward lines

The 167th Infantry Division: 1 km southwest of Gostishchevo – Soshenkov (incl.) – further without changes.

The II SS Panzer Corps: SS Division *Das Reich* – northeast corner, Kalinin – southeast corner, Iasnaia Poliana – Storozhevoe (incl.)

Adolf Hitler – without changes; *Totenkopf* – without changes, except for the armored group on the hill 1 km west of Polezhaev.

XXXXVIII Panzer Corps: 11th Panzer Division – without changes;

Units of the Division *Grossdeutschland* : 1 km southwest of Hill 243.0 – 1.5 west of Verkhopen'e.

The 332nd Infantry Division: Hill 237.6 – western outskirts of Berezovka – 1.5 km north of the woods – east of Chapaev – Chapaev (incl.).

The LII Army Corps: without changes.

All units of the 332nd Infantry Division north of the Pena have been subordinated to the XXXXVIII Panzer Corps.

Boundary line between the XXXXVIII Panzer Corps and the LII Army Corps: Alekseevka (LII Corps) – course of the Pena to Melovoe (XXXXVIII Panzer Corps).

Intentions: according to the telegram.

Weather: Cloudy, scattered rain. The condition of the roads in the II SS Panzer Corps' sector is poor; in the sector of the XXXXVIII Panzer Corps, roads are passable for all vehicles.

Special events
A visit by Field Marshal von Manstein in the middle of the day.[20]

The analysis contained in this report from the headquarters of the Fourth Panzer Army of Army Group South indicates that the adversary had a rather full picture of the Voronezh Front's force groupings. He had managed to discern the plan of the Soviet command for 12 July: with strikes against both flanks of the army to encircle its main forces.

From the report and the disposition of the Fourth Panzer Army's corps within the area of its penetration, it is clear that the main attack of the two fresh tank corps of the 5th Guards Tank Army was launched head-on against the strongest enemy grouping, which had prepared to receive the attack before continuing its offensive in a northeast direction. Therefore the Soviet forces indeed were unable to create a crisis situation on the flanks of the Fourth Panzer Army, and the local penetrations were quickly contained.

Notable is also the fact that the report contains not a single word about anything extraordinary – like a meeting tank melee involving masses of tanks. It states only that the "adversary attacked the *positions of Adolf Hitler*" (author's emphasis), which is to say that this division had in a timely fashion prepared to receive the attack of the 18th and 29th Tank Corps by fire from prepared positions.

The debut of Rotmistrov's progeny wound up to be painful and bloody. According to incomplete information, in the course of the counterstroke on 12 July the 5th Guards Tank Army lost more than 3,563 soldiers and officers, including more than 1,500 men killed or missing in action.

Without considering the losses of the 5th Guards 'Zimovniki' Mechanized Corps, 359 tanks and self-propelled guns were lost; more than 50% of them – 207 (193 tanks and 14 self-propelled guns) – were irrevocably lost. Thus, the 5th Guards Tank Army lost more than half of the armor that took part in the fighting that day. Of all the formations, the heaviest losses were sustained by the 29th Tank Corps – 153 tanks and self-propelled guns (77% of those that participated in the attack), including 103 tanks irrevocably lost. The 1446th Self-propelled Artillery Regiment, which was supporting the 29th Tank Corps in this attack, lost 19 self-propelled guns, 14 of which were totally destroyed. The 18th Tank Corps lost 84 tanks (56% of those that participated in the attack), including 35 tanks totally destroyed; the 2nd Guards 'Tatsinskaia' Corps lost 54 tanks (39% of those that participated), including 29 irrevocably lost; the 2nd Tank Corps – 22 tanks (50% of those that participated), with 11 irrevocably lost.

At 1300 hours on 13 July, the 5th Guards Tank Army had only around 400 operational tanks: the 29th Tank Corps had 51 tanks, of which 31 were light tanks; the 18th Tank Corps had 33 tanks, of which 18 were light tanks; the 2nd Guards 'Tatsinskaia' Tank Corps was in better shape with 80 tanks; the 2nd Tank Corps was down to 44 tanks; and the 5th Guards 'Zimovniki' Mechanized Corps was in the best shape of all, with 158 tanks still operational. Thus, except for Burdeiny's 2nd Guards

'Tatsinskaia' and Skvortsov's 5th Guards 'Zimovniki' Corps, the remaining corps were only capable of handling minor assignments.

For sake of comparison, and so the reader can fully grasp the scale of material losses that General Rotmistrov's 5th Guards Tank Army suffered only over the day of 12 July, I will now cite data on the armor losses in the 1st Tank Army's 3rd Mechanized Corps for the period between 6 July and 15 July 1943 inclusively. I will remind the reader that it was this corps together with units of the 6th Guards Army that received the main attack of the Fourth Panzer Army on the Oboian' axis. Thus, over ten days of most savage fighting, Krivoshein's corps lost 144 tanks irreparably destroyed, including 128 T-34 tanks, three KV tanks and 13 T-70 tanks (the losses of the 3rd Mechanized Corps are shown in more detail in Tables 25 and 26).

Chief of the General Staff Marshal A. M. Vasilevsky, who personally had to answer for the preparation and commitment of the *Stavka* Reserve's two Guards armies into the engagement, in a message to I. V. Stalin naturally tried to gloss over the situation: "... in the course of two days of fighting, Rotmistrov's 29th Tank Corps lost 60% of its tanks either irrevocably or temporarily damaged, and the 18th Tank Corps – up to 30% of its tanks."[21]

Aleksandr Mikhailovich clearly understood that in only a few hours of fighting at Prokhorovka, the combat capabilities of several fresh tank corps had been lost, if only temporarily, while the enemy still held practically all of his previous positions. It was never easy to report such a "naked" truth to Stalin, but it was also dangerous to lie, so that's why there appeared the reduced loss percentages and the "two days of fighting" in place of the actual eight to ten hours of fighting.

Now we'll take a look at the actions of the Soviet forces through the eyes of the adversary. A summary from the headquarters of the II SS Panzer Corps' intelligence department has been preserved:

> Command of the II SS Panzer Corps
> Ic. [Intelligence]
> **The enemy situation on 12.07 1943 [compiled at 2100]**
> **Enemy activities**
> In the morning the enemy attacked Kalinin with infantry and 25 tanks. In the attack on Iasnaia Poliana from 30 to 40 tanks participated, on the forested sector east of Ivanovskii Vyselok – from 18 to 20 tanks, on the position of our outposts west of Storozhevoe – infantry and tanks.
>
> Tank attacks from the area of Iamki in the direction of Hill 252.2 and southwest of Prokhorovka against the assault groups on both sides of the road to Prokhorovka. West of Prokhorovka the adversary advanced infantry and 96 tanks in a southwest direction against our outposts. The attacks led to local breakthroughs, which were liquidated with heavy losses in tanks for the enemy.
>
> Major enemy forces – 2 regiments approximately with 40 tanks – attacked our units east of Vasil'evka, through Prelestnoe, Mikhailovka, Andreevka, then, turning to the south, advanced to an area north of Komsomolets State Farm. The

situation has been restored. Obviously the enemy intention with the attack from Storozhevoe in the direction of the bend of the rail line and from the north in the direction of Komsomolets State Farm was to cut-off our forces advancing to the northeast.

In the Psel River bend, the adversary unsuccessfully attacked our line of defense west of Kliuchi from the north with major infantry forces. He repeated the attack with tank support and was again repulsed. Our offensive, in the face of strong enemy resistance, reached the Prokhorovka – Kartashevka road, excluding Polezhaev. According to aerial reconnaissance findings, the presence of 45 enemy tanks in an area east of Ivanovka is assumed (ground observers report 75 tanks); southeast of Prokhorovka, the presence of around 100 tanks has been established. Aerial reconnaissance reports a total of 109 tanks in the area between Prokhorovka and Petrovka. On the Prokhorovka – Kartashevka road, according to the information of aerial reconnaissance, around 60 tanks have been counted.

	AH	*"Reich"*	*TK*	**Total**
Prisoners	253	47	9	309
Deserters	-	41	6	47
Aircraft	1	4	-	5
Tanks	57	7	8	72
Anti-tank Guns	19	1	2	22
Anti-tank Rifles	51	17	-	68
Machine Guns	-	13	1	14
Artillery guns	-	7	-	7
Machine Pistols	-	38	5	43
Rifles	-	210	-	210
Grenade Launchers	-	2	1	3
Motorcycles	-	4	-	4
Armored Cars	-	1	-	1

AH 1st SS Panzergrenadier Division *Leibstandarte Adolf Hitler*
"Reich" 2nd SS Panzergrenadier Division *Das Reich*
TK 3rd SS Panzergrenadier Division *Totenkopf*

Table 24: Reported Enemy Losses, Prisoners and Captured Equipment (II SS Panzer Corps intelligence report July 1943)

Prisoner testimony and surveillance findings

A senior lieutenant from the 32nd Tank Brigade, 29th Tank Corps: the 29th Tank Corps, under the 5th Guards Tank Army, moved out on 5.07.1943 from Ostrogozhsk toward Sergeevka. It arrived there on 7.07.1943, and on 12.07.1943 at 0130 arrived in Prokhorovka.

Assignment: to conduct a counterattack in a southwest direction with the forces of the 32nd Tank Brigade to the right of the rail line. The 25th Tank Brigade

Unit	Rifles	Pistols and Revolvers	PPSh SMG	DP-27Ligt MG	DT Light MG	Maxim Heavy MG	Anti-tank Rifles	Machine Guns	45mm AT Gun	45mm Tank Gun	76mm AT Gun	76mm Tank Gun	82mm Mortars	120mm Mortars	KV Tanks	T-34 Tanks	T-70 Tanks
1 Guards Tank Bde	54	54	45	6	56	2	10	20	-	-	1	28	1	-	3	30	-
49 Tank Bde	37	29	48	1	80	1	2	35	-	2	-	39	2	-	-	40	2
1 Mechanized Bde	363	136	746	75	42	36	73	70	8	6	4	18	18	3	-	18	6
3 Mechanized Bde	355	49	410	63	52	32	49	50	6	-	4	26	2	3	-	26	-
10 Mechanized Bde	512	87	752	95	30	41	65	42	11	2	-	14	22	4	-	14	2
35 AT Artillery Bn	111	5	18	5	-	-	1	7	15	-	2	-	-	-	-	-	-
265 Sep Mortar Reg	44	4	23	-	-	-	7	4	-	-	-	-	-	5	-	-	-
405 Sep Gds Mortar Reg	3	-	-	-	-	-	-	-	-	-	-	-	-	-	-	-	-
34 Sep Reconnaissance Bn	-	-	2	-	·1	-	-	1		3	-	-	-	-	-	-	3
Totals	1479	364	2044	245	261	112	207	229	40	13	11	125	45	15	3	128	13

ource: TsAMO RF, f. 8 gv. tk, op. 1, d. 49, l. 27, 28.

Table 25: Equipment Losses in the Main Units of the 1st Tank Army's 3rd Mechanized Corps between 5 July and 15 July 1943

– to operate left of the railroad, together with the 31st Tank Brigade and the 53rd Motorized Rifle Brigade in the second echelon.

Replacements from Gor'kii and Ivanovo. Birth years: 1925-1926 and those returning from hospitals. Composition: 10 percent from Turkic peoples and 90 percent Russians and Ukrainians. The brigade is at full-strength.

... A military specialist school in Moscow was dissolved five days ago. The cadets were sent to the forces as sergeants. The 136th Guards Rifle Regiment of the 42nd Guards Rifle Division. The prisoner indicated that the 5th Guards Army was supposedly the former 66th Army.

The 24th Tank Brigade. The prisoner maintains that he served in the 24th Tank Brigade of the 3rd Army's 12th Tank Corps and was taken prisoner around Iamshchika (Iamki?).

In transmissions from the area of Komsomolets State Farm, the enemy is announcing his morning attacks in the direction of Storozhevoe, about attacks on the Stalinskoe Branch of the [Oktiabr'skii] State Farm, and on Komsomolets State Farm. He is reporting on the concentration of German forces at Hill 241.6 and Ivanovskii Vyselok. Closer to evening, communications followed the movement of German forces on Vinogradovka from the areas of Ivanovskii Vyselok and Teterevino. He is reporting that Storozhevoe has fallen and that the enemy is exploiting in the direction of Zhimolostnoe.

Transmissions from the area of Rzhavets are reporting the capture of Kazach'e and Vypolzovka by German forces and the enemy advance across the Northern Donets, through Ryndinka and Shipy toward Pokrovka.

Unit	Killed			Wounded			Missing			By Categories			
	Command Staff	Jr Commanders	Rank and File	Command Staff	Jr Commanders	Rank and File	Command Staff	Jr Commanders	Rank and File	Killed	Wounded	Missing	All Losses
1 Guards Tank Bde	25	61	41	25	81	85	–	–	–	127	191	–	31
49 Tank Bde	13	46	8	28	66	27	–	–	–	67	121	-	18
1 Mech Bde	37	106	212	75	282	514	17	110	318	355	871	445	167
3 Mech Bde	23	121	193	43	237	322	–	17	83	337	602	100	103
10 Mech Bde	34	111	285	49	216	347	43	260	433	330	612	100	177
35 AT Artillery Reg	-	15	19	5	18	29	-	2	4	34	52	6	92
265 Sep Mortar Reg	4	4	10	8	17	24	–	8	23	18	49	31	98
405 Gds Sep Mortar Reg	–	1	1	2	1	-	–	–	–	2	3	–	5
34 Sep Reconnaissance Bn	-	–	1	-	-	2	–	–	1	1	2	1	4
58 Sep Mortar Bn	-	1	1	-	3	6	–	–	–	2	9	-	11
27 Sep Med Bn	–	–	2	–	–	9	–	-	–	2	9	-	11
346 Sep Signals Bn	-	-	-	-	-	5	-	-	-	-	5	-	5
Total	136	466	773	235	921	1370	60	397	862	1375	2526	1319	52

Source: TsAMO RF, f. 8 mk.

Table 26: Personnel Losses in 1st Tank Army's 3rd Mechanized Corps between 5 and 15 July 1943

Transmissions from the area of Berezovka are mentioning the re-taking of Berezovka, Rakovo, Chapaev. They are demanding greater activity and further actions from the troops.

Night-time aerial reconnaissance 11.07-12.07 established movement in the direction of the front from the area of Staryi Oskol – a total of about 130 motor vehicles. From Korocha toward Prokhorovka about 25 vehicles and from the area of Kursk in a southerly direction about 120 vehicles. Major movements in the area Miropol'e – Sudzha, 335 motor vehicles in a general direction to the northeast. From an area north of Kruglik – 60 vehicles in the direction of Oboian'. In the areas of Belgorod, Volokonovka, Chernianka and Korocha – only a few solitary vehicles.

Combat reconnaissance was monitoring on 12.07 the area east of the Teterevino (south) – Pokrovka rail line. It detected an aggregation of enemy tanks west and northwest of Pokrovka and on the Prokhorovka – Kartashevka road.

General impression

The enemy intends by any means to stop our offensive south of the Psel River. He is trying to cut the supply lines of our shock groups southwest of Prokhorovka with flank attacks and to hurl back our forces north of the river bend with counterattacks.

He has transferred significant reinforcements of infantry and tanks to the areas west of Prokhorovka and north of the Psel bend, conducting the defense aggressively.

Aerial reconnaissance has also established the moving up of reserves south of Oboian', on both sides of the Belgorod – Kursk road, with the intention to avert the capture of Oboian'. Heavy traffic from the area of Miropol'e and Sudzha indicates the transfer of front reserves located there first of all to the Psel River.

The movement of the 5th Guards Tank Army allows us to assume that the front reserves north of Belgorod have already been exhausted. One can believe that even the front reserves from the sectors of neighboring military groups are moving up and entering the fighting in the Kursk area.

The II SS Panzer Corps is fighting with enemy forces composed of three Soviet tank corps and three-four rifle divisions.

Command of the Corps, Ic (Corps chief intelligence officer)[22]

The well-organized work of the II SS Panzer Corps' staff, especially of its intelligence section, merits attention, not only with the gathering of information on the enemy, but also their deep analysis of the intelligence even before it reaches the chief of staff or the corps commander. Already within twelve hours of the introduction of Rotmistrov's 5th Guards Tank Army into the battle, the chief intelligence officer had sufficient information on the army. He not only correctly assessed the situation, but also drew an accurate conclusion about our *front* reserves. To wit:

> The movement of the 5th Guards Tank Army allows us to assume that the front reserves north of Belgorod have already been exhausted. One can believe that even the front reserves from the sectors of neighboring military groups are moving up and entering the fighting in the Kursk area.

The SS estimate of the strength of our forces was also accurate: "The II SS Panzer Corps is fighting with enemy forces composed of three Soviet tank corps and three-four rifle divisions." It is just a pity that these forces, to a considerable extent, were used thoughtlessly.

Suffering great losses in armor in the course of the 12 July counterstroke, both sides worked frantically on the night of 12 July to restore the combat capabilities of their armored units. Therefore the main task standing before the command of both sides was to begin the recovery of damaged tanks as soon as it became dark. It was easier for the enemy to organize this work, since at day's end he was controlling most of the area containing the largest number of damaged or disabled armored vehicles.

Especially many of the damaged and knocked-out tanks of both sides were located in the areas of Andreevka, Hill 241.6, Oktiabr'skii State Farm and the Stalinskoe Branch of the [Oktiabr'skii] State Farm. The 29th Tank Corps alone, which was operating in the sector Oktiab'rskii State Farm – Storozhevoe (excl.), lost more than 170 tanks and self-propelled guns on 12 July, either burned-out, knocked-out, disabled by mines or immobilized by mechanical failure.

It was a difficult and hazardous matter to organize the recovery of heavy armor from the battlefield, since the majority of the vehicles were either located on ground controlled by the enemy or in no man's land. The trenches of the opposing sides were situated about 300-400 meters from each other, and any movement into no man's land was noticeable. As soon as any suspicion appeared that the enemy was trying to recover tanks, both sides would open mortar and machine-gun fire. In the course of the night of 12 July, the 31st Tank Brigade was only able to recover eight T-34 tanks from among the 44 knocked-out tanks it had left on the battlefield.

The dangers of this work are clearly illustrated in a dispatch from the 31st Tank Brigade's chief of the political section Colonel Polotsky on 14 July:

> ... During the recovery of tanks from the battlefield, the assistant commander of the 278th Tank Battalion for equipment, Engineer-Captain Sotkin was killed; two more men were killed and four wounded in the tank-riding company. One T-34 tank and one T-70 tank were recovered from the battlefield. Recovery efforts continue, despite the exceptionally difficult conditions.[23]

One must also note the thoroughness with which the Germans approached not only the organization of combat operations, but also any forthcoming troop withdrawal to previous lines. On 14 July, the Army Group South headquarters issued an order to all its subordinate formations, which contained the demand: "... All captured damaged enemy tanks, which are impossible to employ, repair or recover, must be destroyed immediately, so that they again will not fall into the enemy's hands. All officers responsible for this

The repair of vehicles in one of the field repair shops of the Voronezh Front's 69th Army. (RGAKFD)

duty must pay particular attention to this order."[24] On all sectors of the front, this order was carried out unswervingly. Major Petukhov, a General Staff officer with the 1st Tank Army had to report, "The enemy has recovered the majority of [our] damaged and destroyed equipment. Those of our tanks that he could not recover, the enemy blew up, without exception."[25]

The units of the II SS Panzer Corps also left behind only a scorched field and demolished equipment when they eventually withdrew. The headquarters of the 2nd Tank Corps reported on 16 July 1943, "… The enemy, organizing a retreat during the night, withdrew all his forces, evacuated all the damaged equipment, and torched the remaining knocked-out tanks and vehicles on the battlefield."[26]

In the Red Army, the main burden for recovering tanks and self-propelled guns and for transporting them to collection points for disabled vehicles lay on the brigades' equipment companies and the personnel of the tank battalions. Usually, the crews themselves actively participated in the recovery of their damaged tanks or self-propelled guns and then performed any routine or moderately difficult repair jobs. Kommunar tractors, and Komintern and Stalinets-2 artillery prime movers were used for this work. Mainly, however, a single T-34 or a pair of them made the recovery, because the tractors had bulky profiles, insufficient power, and no armor protection.

In contrast, the recovery and repair work in the units of Army Group South was well-organized. Each panzer regiment had a well-equipped separate tank maintenance company, while a separate Tiger battalion had its own tank maintenance platoon. These elements managed to do 95% of all the repair work on the armored vehicles, which was performed in frontline conditions.

A repair team of the SS *Das Reich* Division restores a panzer to running order. Prokhorovka axis, July 1943. (RGAKFD)

Unfortunately, it is impossible to say the same thing about the repair work in the corps formations of the 5th Guards Tank Army. At 2400 12.07.43, the headquarters of the 29th Tank Corps reported the following information in a combat dispatch:

> The brigades and battalions of the corps are engaged in recovering the wounded and equipment. In the course of the night, 3 T-34 tanks and 1 Su-122 self-propelled gun will be repaired.
>
> The recovery of damaged vehicles is being implemented by three turret-less T-34 tanks and one M-3 tank. Five teams are performing the repair work: two teams from the 32nd Tank Brigade and one from the 31st Tank Brigade, in addition to the corps repair teams. One of the corps teams is doing the repair work on self-propelled guns.[27]

Thus, of the 55 knocked-out tanks and self-propelled guns, the 29th Tank Corps was only able to repair four over the night. Naturally, at such a pace it was not easy to restore the combat capability of the corps quickly.

P. A. Rotmistrov later wrote:

> The presence in the army of only mechanical tools could not guarantee the quick restoration and repair of parts, necessary for tank repairs. The lack of welding equipment and repair workshops delayed the fabrication and rehabilitation of spare parts, and thus also the repair of tanks and self-propelled guns within set periods. Army and *front* depots of inventory for armored vehicles were located far away (150-300 kilometers), and the insufficient amount of transportation in the army's corps and brigades complicated the timely supply of components and spare parts.
>
> There were no special break-down teams in the repair units, so it was necessary to pull qualified mechanics from repair work in order to break down the tanks, which reduced the labor productivity.
>
> The mechanics' profile was quite diverse. The 83rd Army-level Repair-Recovery Battalion and the corps' mobile repair depots were staffed with qualified workers from the tank industry (the Stalingrad and Khar'kov factories), but who lacked work experience in field conditions. The tank brigades' equipment companies, on the other hand, were staffed primarily with specialists on the repair of armored vehicles under combat conditions. Such a combination of cadres on the whole produced fully satisfactory results.[28]

Major overhauls, like engine, gun, and turret replacements, were performed at the mobile repair depots of the tank corps. Each tank corps had two of these repair depots, each staffed with 70 to 80 men. For urgent repairs just 8-10 kilometers from the front lines, two army-level, three corps-level and nine brigade collection points for disabled vehicles were set up, which shared all the repair-recovery resources.

On the night of 12 July, as the 5th Guards Tank Army commander later remembered:

> The repair workers faced the task of restoring and repairing parts and components, stripped from irreparably damaged tanks and from those tanks that needed major overhauls. We had to get hold of 45 engines, 20 gear boxes and several engine and

> steering clutches. All of the recovery and repair units and teams of the separate regiments, brigades, corps and the army were mobilized to accomplish this task.[29]

To what Rotmistrov said I will add that in order to hasten the repair of the 5th Guards Tank Army's damaged armored vehicles, the *front*'s Armored and Mechanized Forces commander transferred 167 field repair depots from the 38th Army to the 5th Guards Tank Army on 14 July. This truly heroic effort produced results. Of the 420 damaged tanks in its brigades and regiments after the fighting of 12 July, 112 requiring minor or moderate repairs were restored to operation in the very first days after the battle. In addition, the *front* command took other steps to assist the army. Already by 15 July, just three days after the engagement, the 5th Guards Tank Army began to receive new tanks. The 29th Tank Corps was the first to begin to receive the new vehicles. The 31st Tank Brigade's war diary noted, "15 July … An order arrived to pick up 16 T-34 tanks at Solntsevo Station. A procurement team has been sent."

The story of the events of those days would be incomplete if I didn't touch upon the fate of our soldiers and officers who were taken prisoner; unfortunately, on 12 July there were many of them from the formations of all types of the *front*'s forces. A war without prisoners doesn't exist – this is an axiom, but even until recently it was not acceptable to speak about our prisoners as fully recognized participants in the engagements and battles of the Great Patriotic War, even though the majority of them fulfilled their military duty to the end. Plainly, Stalin's order of 1941, which decreed these people to be betrayers of the Motherland, deprived their families of government assistance (cash supplements for the loss of the main breadwinner, etc.) and subjected them to repressions, has weighed heavily on historians and publishers. Even after Stalin's death, when the mistakenness of this treatment was declared, the situation has been resistant to substantial change.

So that the reader, who didn't have to experience this war, might be able to have at least an image of the situation confronting these people, I will cite two documents relating to the period of the Prokhorovka engagement. W. Roes, the *Sturmmann* in SS Panzergrenadier Division *Leibstandarte*'s 1st Panzer Regiment, provides a story about an incident he witnessed on the evening of 12 July:

> It is a terrible memory: we were driving over to the railroad embankment; the entire field was smoking. We were sitting up front, and had gotten out our empty ammunition cases, which we had converted into boxes to hold our food. We pulled out some open-faced sandwiches (incidentally, the radio operator was responsible for obtaining food for the crew). We're eating, and singing some songs. Our commander was somewhere away at a conference. We're singing – and suddenly we hear a shot. We stood up, looked around, and caught sight of a wounded Russian, who was lying in a rut left behind by our tank. We had driven over him, across his waist and pelvis. We hadn't noticed him, because he had been lying in some sunflowers or wheat. The three of us stood over him and gazed down at him. He tried to raise his dying eyes to us. We were saying that we couldn't give him any water, or else it would finish him off. We all knew that with any stomach wound

case, one mustn't give him water. But he didn't last long anyway; after three or four minutes his head fell back and he died. Then a special team, which was collecting the injured and dead, came by and collected him.

We stood around for a while by the railroad embankment. A narrow farm road ran alongside it. At some point, a group of Russian prisoners from a Guards army or some Guards unit … I don't know which one … appeared on this road. They were wearing fine uniforms, with a multitude of Soviet stars and enameled buttons. A short *Rottenführer* [a Waffen SS rank equivalent to the *Obergefreiter* (senior lance corporal) in the *Heer*] with a submachine gun was walking along behind them. He passed right next to our tank. So we asked him: 'Aren't you afraid?' After all, he was escorting somewhere around 40 to 50 Russians. 'Afraid?' he asked right back. – 'Watch.' Then he said something in Russian. There was some sort of old shed there, still on fire. Evidently he had ordered the prisoners at the rear of the column to bring him back, I don't know, some boards or something. A couple of the prisoners actually went over to the shed, and pulled off a board. One went that way, another went this way, but our guy gave them a burst in the stomach from his submachine gun and shouted: 'Now there, just look how frightened I am!' Of course, he wasn't afraid.

As concerns prisoners … the Russian soldier fought quite bravely. But when he became a prisoner … whether they'd been fed information that we'd shoot them or something, I don't know. In general, he'd quiver like a mouse. I, for one, only saw them like that. We didn't take prisoners – tankers were forbidden to take prisoners. We'd send them back to the infantry.

In one of the groups of captured tankers there were three female radio operators. I've still never seen such proud, even haughty women, as these three. They glanced at us with such an expression, as if they were asking, 'And what have you lost in Russia?' This has been stuck in my memory.[30]

The former *Sturmmann* was surprised that defenseless people who had fallen prisoner to the SS feared for their own lives; he was forgetting what a bloody trail these "supermen" had left behind them across all the Soviet territory they had seized. Not only the *Sonderkommando* units, who were struggling against partisans and underground circles in the rear, committed atrocities, but also the combat units of the SS, when dealing with Soviet officers and soldiers that fell into their hands. After the II SS Panzer Corps retreated from the area of the Prokhorovka engagement, the Red Army found examples of SS atrocities and sadistic behavior. The deputy commander for political affairs of the 2nd Tank Corps' 83rd Separate Motorcycle Regiment sent the following dispatch on 21 July 1943:

On 20.07.43 at 1800, the battalion at the corps commander's order drove over to the area of the Sobachevskii woods. While searching the area, in a location 100-150 meters northeast of the railroad crossing at Ivanovskii Vyselok we discovered the bodies of two of our soldiers from the 1st Company's 2nd Platoon, who had been fighting west of Storozhevoe and had been mortally wounded. Komsomol member Junior Sergeant A. S. Kravtsov and non-Party member T. A. Krivonogikh, lay wounded on the battlefield and had been brutally tortured by the fascists. The

> fingers on A. S. Kravtsov's left hand, and his nose and ears had been cut off, and his head had been scalped. Sergeant T. A. Krivonogikh's lips, nose and ears had been cut off; his eyes had been gouged out; he had two bayonet wounds to the right cheek, and 6-7 bullet wounds.
>
> Nothing was found in their pockets. We buried the deceased Comrades Kravtsov and Krivonogikh 100-150 meters northeast of Ivanovskii Vyselok. More than 20 soldiers and commanders attended the burials. A document about this [case] has been compiled in the 2nd Tank Corps' Political Department.
>
> At the funerals the soldiers and command staff were once again called to a merciless struggle with the foe, in order to take revenge for the death of their comrades.[31]

The dry text of this terrible document demonstrates the true face of the enemy, with which the Red Army soldiers fought at Prokhorovka in the summer of 1943. Yet such cruel, inhumane cases only increased their resolve and strength, and their desire to defeat the German-fascist conquerors.

14

Preparations for Combat Operations on the Prokhorovka Axis from 13 July to 16 July 1943

The day of 12 July didn't bring either of the opposing sides the results that each sought. The Voronezh Front command had been able to contain the attacking panzer corps of Army Group South within the system of the three army-level defensive belts. Every enemy attempt to breach the final line and to break into operational space, like the effort to encircle a large part of the 69th Army with the forces from the II SS Panzer Corps and the III Panzer Corps, had failed.

Hoth's plan to destroy the Soviet mobile reserves and part of the 69th Army had been fully thwarted. Although Hausser's II SS Panzer Corps, through the efforts of SS Panzergrenadier Division *Totenkopf*, had managed to expand the bridgehead north of the Psel River somewhat, it has not been able to carry out the corps' main assignment: to bring all its divisions into line and, having penetrated the defense of the 5th Guards Army to its entire depth, to seize the key point – Prokhorovka Station. *Leibstandarte* had even been forced to pull back from the outskirts of the station for several kilometers. *Das Reich* had made practically no headway. Although its units had taken possession of Storozhevoe, it was unable to breakthrough to Prokhorovka from the south through Pravorot' and help its neighbors.

As before, the left flank of the Fourth Panzer Army was still dangerously exposed. Already assembled before the third and final defensive belt for a strike in the direction of Oboian', the 3rd Panzer Division and *Grossdeutschland* Division again had to hastily deploy in the bend of the Pena River and became tied up there in heavy fighting in the area of the Tolstoe forest and Berezovka. At the same time, the 11th Panzer Division not only was unable, as planned, to go on the attack, but had been compelled under the pressure of Soviet forces to retreat somewhat from its occupied line. With the aim of securing the extended left wing of Hoth's Army, von Manstein had concentrated all available forces on the west and northwest directions; that is, everything within the same second defensive belt.

Although not without great efforts, the Soviet command had nevertheless been able to halt Army Detachment Kempf's offensive after its penetration of the 69th Army's defenses, and had been able to bring the situation back under operational control. Thus, if we examine 12 July against the backdrop of the *front*'s entire defensive operation, then this day had a positive influence on its further course.

However, it is impossible to say that the Soviet side celebrated victory on this day, as Soviet historians have long tried to convince the entire world and themselves. It is more accurate to say instead that 12 July was the most tragic and, in essence, unsuccessful day not only of the Voronezh Front's defensive operation, but of the Kursk battle as a whole.

Voronezh Front had not been able to accomplish its main task – to smash the enemy grouping that had penetrated deeply into the *front*'s defenses and to seize the initiative. Moreover, the Soviet command's plan for the *front*'s counterstroke proved to be unsuccessful, because from its very start it no longer corresponded to the changed situation, or to the possibilities of the forces to fulfill their assigned missions. The 5th Guards Army and 5th Guards Tank Army were unable to bring about a fundamental change in the situation, while in the span of just a few hours the forces of their assault formations had been decimated, and on certain sectors had even abandoned the positions they had occupied that morning. Although to this day arguments continue over the number of destroyed tanks in Rotmistrov's army and Hausser's corps, it is obvious that the Guards armies suffered greater losses than the SS corps. This is an indisputable fact.

The period of combat operations between 13 and 16 July 1943 on the Voronezh Front have never been described in detail in the Soviet historical literature; it seemingly fell from the vision of scholars. This omission is intentional, done for ideological reasons. It is not simple to reconcile the readers' previous conviction, that "in the course of the greatest tank battle in history at Prokhorovka, the enemy grouping that had penetrated our defenses was fully destroyed," with the real four days of hard fighting that followed, during which the "destroyed" enemy managed to drive back the Soviet forces and to encircle the 69th Army's 48th Rifle Corps. Only due to the strenuous efforts of the command were the four divisions of this corps extracted with substantial losses and re-formed on new lines.

Even after the extremely savage fighting on 12 July, all of Army Group South's panzer corps still retained relatively high combat capabilities. For example, the II SS Panzer Corps before the start of the counterattack of 12 July had 294 operational tanks and assault guns, while the next morning due to the hard work of the repair crews, the number had fallen only to 251.

In addition, Field Marshal von Manstein still had the XXIV Panzer Corps in reserve, which had three panzer divisions: SS Panzergrenadier Division *Wiking*, and the 17th and 23rd Panzer Divisions. On 7 July, the panzer corps had 181 tanks and assault guns, and 123 field guns. This was a significant force, fully capable of allowing the continuation of Operation Citadel.

E. von Manstein later recalled:

> Group command had fought with Hitler over this corps from the very beginning of the offensive, or more accurately, from the start of preparations for it. I remember that we had always held the view that if we were to conduct Operation Citadel at all, then it was necessary to do everything to ensure the success of this undertaking, even if it meant placing the Donbas area strongly at risk. According to these beliefs, Group command, as I now recall, left only two divisions (the 23rd Panzer Division and the 16th Motorized Division) as reserves on the Mius and Donets fronts,

> anticipating the use of the XXIV Panzer Corps – initially as Group reserve – in Operation Citadel. But for this we had to appeal several times to OKH, until Hitler, who feared taking any risk in the Donbas, gave his agreement to position the corps behind Citadel's front lines. The corps, however, though being fully combat-ready, was located west of Khar'kov as OKH reserve, for which it had been withdrawn from the Group's operational control.
>
> Such was the situation, when Field Marshal Klüge and I were summoned on 13 July to the Führer headquarters. It would have been more correct, of course, if Hitler himself had visited both groups or – if he believed that the overall situation didn't permit him to leave the headquarters – if he had sent the Chief of Staff to us. But during the entire Eastern campaign, one rarely was able to persuade Hitler to travel to the front. He didn't even permit his Chief of the General Staff to do this.[1]

The conference was called for one purpose – to announce the cessation of Operation Citadel. One of the main reasons for this decision was the landing of Allied forces on Sicily. As Hitler declared, the Italians were no longer willing to fight, so Germany would have to withdraw some of its forces from the Eastern Front, in order to transfer them to southern Europe. The commander of Army Group Center, Field Marshal von Klüge, agreed with this decision.

Wrote von Manstein:

> [von Klüge] reported that Model's [Ninth] Army could no longer advance and had lost 20,000 men. Moreover, Model's group had been forced to withdraw all of its mobile formations from the Ninth Army, in order to eliminate three deep penetrations that the enemy had already created on the front of the Second Panzer Army. Already for this reason, Ninth Army's offensive could not continue and could not later be resumed.
>
> Speaking for my own Army Group, I pointed out that the battle was now at its culminating point and that to break it off at this moment would be tantamount to throwing victory away. If the Ninth Army would only pin down the enemy forces opposing it, and perhaps later resume the offensive, then we would try to smash conclusively the heavily damaged enemy units opposing us with the forces of our armies. Then the Group – as we had already reported to OKH on 12 July – would resume our attack to the north, cross with two panzer corps over the Psel east of Oboian' and having turned to the west, force the enemy forces located in the western portion of the Kursk bulge to accept battle with a reversed front. In order to secure this operation from the north and the east effectively, Group [Army Detachment] Kempf must immediately receive the XXIV Panzer Corps. Naturally, the Group's strength was only sufficient to continue the offensive to an area south of Kursk. If then the Ninth Army could not resume the offensive after overcoming the crisis in the Orel bulge, we would at least try to destroy the enemy forces then opposing us, so we could then have an easy respite. But if we only managed to damage the enemy partway, then a crisis would immediately arise not only in the Donbas, but on Citadel's front as well.
>
> Since von Klüge considered a resumption of the Ninth Army's offensive impossible, and moreover believed it necessary to return it to its starting positions,

Hitler decided – taking into account the need to withdraw forces to transfer them to the Mediterranean Sea – to discontinue Operation Citadel. In connection with the threat of an enemy offensive on the Donets front, the XXIV Panzer Corps was subordinated to the Group, but not for its free use. Hitler all the same agreed that Group South should make an attempt to smash the enemy units operating on its front, and thereby create a possibility to withdraw some of the forces that had been activated for Operation Citadel.

The Fourth Panzer Army had the task to smash fully the enemy units located south of the Psel River with short blows to the north and west. Army Detachment Kempf was to cover these attacks, operating to the east, and simultaneously cooperate with the Fourth Panzer Army to destroy the enemy that had been trapped by both armies.[2]

On the evening of 12 July, when there was still not any discussion about halting the operation, von Manstein issued a number of orders for the realization of the plan of the further offensive. Thus, at 2110 he sent an order to the commander of the XXIV Panzer Corps General Walther Nehring about the regrouping of the latter's formation to the area of Belgorod:

SS Panzer Division *Wiking* – to the area of Belgorod, and more precisely: Bolkhovets (5 km northwest of the Belgorod-Bolkhovets road – 6 km southwest of the Belgorod-Repnoe road. The 23rd Panzer Division – to the area Dolzhik – Orlovka – Bessonovka – Almazovka. The II SS Panzer Corps' security group, which is located in this sector, is to pull out immediately, concealed from enemy reconnaissance, in order to free up the space.[3]

The II SS Panzer Corps headquarters received its preliminary orders for 13 July even earlier, at 1845 12 July in a phone call from the Fourth Panzer Army's chief of operations: " … to continue enveloping operations from the north against Prokhorovka from the jumping-off point of the bridgehead and with the *Schwerpunkt* [focal point] on the left flank."[4]

At 2045, more precise written orders arrived by telegraph:

1. It is the intention of the panzer army on 13 July to fight to expand its flanks, while it is at the same time necessary to retain the positions seized along the front. The II SS Panzer Corps is immediately to begin to concentrate its forces on the northern bank of the Psel River, and then to continue enveloping operations against the tank formations in the area of Prokhorovka with the aim of encircling them. The offensive to the east around Belenikhino and further north is to continue only if the encirclement is successful.

Commander-in-chief Hoth.[5]

At 2200 on 12 July, *Obergruppenführer* Paul Hausser issued orders to his divisions. After expressing the appreciation and recognition of Field Marshal von Manstein to the divisions of the II SS Panzer Corps for their prominent successes and model conduct in battle, Hausser defined the tasks for the next day. SS Panzergrenadier Division *Totenkopf* would play the main role. It was to continue its attack to the northeast and seize the heights north of the Psel River to the Beregovoe – Kartashevka road with at least the strength of the full armored group. From this commanding position it was to seize a crossing over the Psel River to the southeast and destroy the enemy to the southeast and southwest of Petrovka in cooperation with SS Panzergrenadier Division *Leibstandarte*. Division *Leibstandarte* was to hold its current positions with its right flank and center, and convert those positions into a main line of defense, but stand ready with its left flank to go on the offensive if *Totenkopf*'s attack from the northeast was successful. *Das Reich* was to remain on the defensive, straighten out its lines in order to create additional reserves, and be prepared to send its assault guns temporarily to the 167th Infantry Division to support its counterattacks.[6]

However, in connection with the decisions taken at the conference in Hitler's Headquarters on 13 July, the objectives had changed. Army Group South went on the defensive in front of the entire Voronezh Front, with the exception of the 69th Army's sector. Fighting at Prokhorovka continued with its previous intensity, but rather than to seek the destruction of the Soviet tank corps at Prokhorovka, the II SS Panzer Corps was to attack with the aim of encircling the 48th Rifle Corps in the area between the Lipovyi Donets and Northern Donets Rivers.

For his part, the Voronezh Front commander knew that the II SS Panzer Corps had not only withstood the attack of the *front*'s powerful shock grouping, but had even gained ground in some places. The divisions of the SS Corps still retained considerable combat strength, and that meant it still had possibilities to continue the attack. While the Fourth Panzer Army was currently digging in on much of the line it had reached, this did not mean it would not attempt to achieve some more limited aims that would further cripple the Voronezh Front. Vatutin understood all this. In a coded telegram on 13 July, he reported to Stalin:

> From all the intelligence information, it has been established by the end of 12 July that in front of the Voronezh Front the enemy committed 11 tank and 1 motorized division into the fighting, of which 10 divisions are operating in the front lines, and 2 in the second echelon …
>
> … After his attempts to break through our front on the Oboian' axis were unsuccessful, the enemy switched his main attack somewhat to the east, to the Prokhorovka axis, and continues to press a secondary attack from the direction of Melikhovo toward Rzhavets and further to Prokhorovka, where he intends to link his attacks.
>
> In addition, it has been established that the enemy has grouped no less than 300 tanks in the Pokrovka – Iakovlevo area. It is not excluded that the adversary may attempt a tank attack in the direction of Luchki and Shakhovo, and further to the north. Measures have been lined out to repulse this attack.
>
> Thus, the enemy has concentrated the bulk of his mobile formations against Voronezh Front. The destruction of these mobile forces would signify a major defeat for the enemy.
>
> However, for the destruction of the enemy, a greater superiority of force is urgently necessary, since the experience of fighting has demonstrated that available forces are insufficient for a decisive encirclement and destruction of the enemy.

Front forces continue to counterattack on the primary directions on 13 July 1943.

We request the urgent reinforcement of the *front* and the transfer of Poluboiarov's 4th Guards Tank Corps and Solomatin's mechanized corps to our operational control. Authorize an additional storm aviation corps for the *front*'s aviation."

Aleksandrov,[7] Vatutin, Khrushchev[8]

Unfortunately, today the transcripts of the conversations of the *front* command with I. V. Stalin are still inaccessible for study, but judging from the decisions reached, the Supreme Commander had been expecting more substantial results from the 12 July counterstroke, and was extremely dissatisfied with the situation that had developed in Voronezh Front's sector. For the last seven days, *Stavka* Reserves had gone primarily and precisely to N. F. Vatutin. The *front* had six armies, and on 8 July it had been given an additional separate tank corps, while significant air power from the 17th Air Army had been redirected to operate in Voronezh Front's sector. Just three days before, two fresh Guards armies had arrived at Prokhorovka and gone into battle there. Yet here was another request for reserves, while von Manstein's forces kept advancing, albeit slowly.

Stalin, probably, decided that the *front* command did not have full control over the situation, and was ineptly using its forces and possibilities. After the catastrophe at Khar'kov in the spring of 1942, Stalin could also no longer trust fully the reports he was receiving from the member of the *front*'s Military Council N. S. Khrushchev. Therefore, he sent his deputy and *Stavka* representative Marshal of the Soviet Union G. K. Zhukov to look into the situation, and directed A. M. Vasilevsky to depart for the Southern Front.

Zhukov arrived at the Voronezh Front headquarters on the morning of 13 July. A conference was held at the *front* command post with the presence of Vasilevsky and Vatutin, as well as the Steppe Front commander Lieutenant General I. S. Konev. The existing situation and the results of the 12 July counterstroke were thoroughly examined. "It was decided," recalled G. K. Zhukov, "in order to obtain the best conditions for the counteroffensive of the *fronts*, to conduct the counterattack that had been started more energetically, on the heels of the retreating enemy, in order to seize the lines he had previously occupied in the area of Belgorod."[9] However, this was still a distant ambition.

An analysis of the further course of combat operations reveals that there was no continuation of the counterattack whatsoever at Prokhorovka in the period 13 to 15 July. There was neither the strength nor the means for this. However, Georgii Konstantinovich [Zhukov] had demanded a continuation of energetic counterattacks, in order not to give the enemy the possibility to regroup his forces.

The significant influence that the great losses in the 5th Guards Tank Army on 12 July had on subsequent events south of Prokhorovka on 14-15 July in the 69th Army sector must be noted. Without exaggeration one can say that the tragedy of the encirclement of the 48th Rifle Corps in the following days was a direct consequence of the destruction of the 5th Guards Army's and 5th Guards Tank Army's shock grouping. How the Soviet command employed the powerful, fully-equipped tank army was a gift for Hoth, about which he had been dreaming since May 1943, when he had planned this engagement. Having crippled two full-strength tank corps in the span of a few hours, while at the same time preserving the combat capabilities of the III Panzer Corps and the

II SS Panzer Corps without incurring substantial losses of its own, Army Group South had perceptibly eased its task to encircle the forces of General V. D. Kriuchenkin in the triangle of land between the Northern and Lipovyi Donets Rivers.

N. F. Vatutin made it the main task of his armies for 13 July to block the enemy's further advance toward Prokhorovka from the west and the south. With this aim, Voronezh Front's armies had the following orders:

- The 5th Guards Army (the 95th Guards, 42nd Guards and part of the 52nd Guards Divisions) together with the 24th Guards Tank Brigade and the 10th Guards Mechanized Brigade of the 5th Guards Mechanized Corps was to liquidate the enemy grouping on the northern bank of the Psel River with strong counterattacks;
- The 69th Army and Group Trufanov from the 5th Guards Tank Army was to destroy the forces of the III Panzer Corps, which were breaking through in the areas of Shcholokovo, Rzhavets and Ryndinka;
- The 6th Guards Army and the 1st Tank Army were to continue to conduct counterattacks with the aim of pinning down with battle the forces of the XXXXVIIII Panzer Corps and to continue to grind down the enemy's tank strength.

N. F. Vatutin understood well that after the inflicting the defeat on his *front*'s shock grouping at Prokhorovka, the Germans next step would be an attempt to encircle the 69th Army's forces between the Northern and Lipovyi Donets Rivers, or at least to drive them out of the area. After the fighting of 12 July, however, the 5th Guards Army and 69th Army were no longer able to hold their extended flank without the support of Rotmistrov's tank corps, which had been shattered in the counterattack. V. D. Kriuchenkin particularly acutely felt the lack of forces. However, the *front* commander very much wanted to hold onto the area between the two rivers, which might constitute a very suitable bridgehead for launching the forthcoming grand counteroffensive. That is why Vatutin demanded activity from his commanders. After such a large-scale slaughter on 12 July, though, Nikolai Fedorovich Vatutin didn't even suggest how his army commanders were to demonstrate this activity.

Having suffered the heaviest losses of the day before, several divisions of the Guards armies were in a noticeably battered shape. A few of them, like the 52nd Guards and 95th Guards Rifle Divisions, were totally or partially scattered, and by the morning of 13 July no one had yet been able to establish where their headquarters and commanders were located. In the 5th Guards Tank Army, the situation was even more difficult. At 1300 on 13 July, the 29th Tank Corps had only 51 operational tanks, including eight T-34 and 20 T-70 tanks in its 31st Tank Brigade; 11 T-70 tanks in its 25th Tank Brigade; and 12 T-34 tanks in the reserve 32nd Tank Brigade. The 18th Tank Corps had only 33 operational tanks, including 15 T-34 tanks and 18 T-70 tanks. The 2nd Tank Corps had 22 T-34 and 20 T-70 tanks, for a total of 42 operational tanks. The 2nd Guards 'Tatsinskaia' Tank Corps was in the best shape, with 80 operational tanks, including 45 T-34, 33 T-70 and two Mk-IV Churchill tanks. However, these numbers include the 26th Guards Tank Brigade (30 T-34, ten T-70),[10] which was located in Shakhovo and had been unable to participate in the fighting southwest of Prokhorovka. Thus, for "active operations" (to be read as "attacks"), all on the very same tank field southwest of

Prokhorovka, P. A. Rotmistrov could deploy against the SS formations on 13 July only half the armor that had been activated on 12 July.

15

Combat Operations in the Psel River Bend and Southwest of Prokhorovka – 13 July

The situation in the Psel bend as morning dawned on 13 July remained rather complicated. Lieutenant General A. S. Zhadov's 5th Guards Army had been unable to drive the enemy from the bridgehead on 12 July. On the contrary, SS Panzergrenadier Division *Totenkopf* over the day of fighting had managed to expand the bridgehead against the resistance of units of the 52nd Guards and 95th Guards Rifle Divisions, and by twilight its panzer regiment was already within direct fire range of the Prokhorovka – Kartashevka road. The main reasons for *Totenkopf*'s success were the hasty, inadequate preparations for the 5th Guards Army's counterattack and the enemy's preemptive strike, which had caught Zhadov's rifle divisions out of position and had forced them to assume a hasty defense while under attack.

However, by the end of 12 July, thanks to the efforts of the commanders of the 5th Guards Army and 5th Guards Tank Army, a sufficient amount of force, including a tank brigade, a mechanized brigade and a self-propelled artillery regiment, had been concentrated here to stymie *Totenkopf*'s further advance. Overnight, the sappers of the 14th Assault Engineer-Sapper Brigade had busily mined all the routes vulnerable to tanks, while elements of the 95th Guards Rifle Division had been rallied and put to work constructing a solid defense. Therefore, on the morning of 13 July, the situation in this area didn't cause any particular concern in the *front* command. Vatutin formulated the main task for the forces of the 5th Guards Army on this day during discussions with Zhadov at 1235 13 July:

> I warn you not to allow the army to go over prematurely to passive operations. The situation calls for activity, since the enemy has concentrated a major force of 400-500 tanks in the Verknii Ol'shanets – Kazach'e area on Kriuchenkin's southern sector, and is unquestionably preparing to attack in this direction. Measures are being taken to destroy this enemy. In these circumstances, your pressure in the north will yield a great deal. *Firstly*, because your forces will be looming over the enemy from the north; *secondly*, you will divert part of the enemy's strength onto yourself. Act with more energy and guarantee the execution of the orders given to you [emphasis in original].[1]

Even during the previous night, based upon directives he had received from *front* headquarters, Zhadov had already issued an order to his corps commanders to continue the counterattacks on 13 July. The 13th and 66th Guards Rifle Divisions of Major General A. I. Rodimtsev's right-flank 32nd Guards Rifle Corps were to seize Hill 235.9

and to drive units of the enemy's 11th Panzer Division out of Kochetovka. Tank brigades of Major General D. Kh. Chernienko's 31st Tank Corps were supposed to support the 32nd Guards Rifle Corps' attack.

Major General I. I. Popov's left-flank 33rd Guards Rifle Corps received the order with two divisions to capture Polezhaev and Hill 226.6, and if the attack developed successfully, it was to attempt to hurl the enemy from his bridgehead north of the Psel. Army intelligence reports inspired hope that this might be accomplished. The chief of the operations section of the 5th Guards Army's headquarters, Colonel Bukovsky reported at 0900 on 13 July: "[On the northern bank] up to 40-50 tanks are operating; there are many knocked-out tanks, up to two battalions worth of prisoners, but still no documents. Surveillance has established that a portion of the tanks has withdrawn to the southwest across the river. This information is being verified ..."[2]

The 5th Guards Army's intelligence section, likely, had managed to detect *Totenkopf*'s evacuation of elements of its panzer regiment from the bridgehead. According to German records, the bulk of *Totenkopf*'s panzer regiment withdrew to the southern bank of the Psel on the night of 12 July.

Colonel A. N. Liakhov's 95th Guards Rifle Division, with Colonel V. P. Karpov's 24th Guards Tank Brigade, the 10th Guards Mechanized Brigade's 51st Guards Tank

Major General A. I. Rodimtsev, commander of the 32nd Guards Rifle Corps (second from the right) reports on the operational situation to Marshal of the Soviet Union G. K. Zhukov (extreme right), while Lieutenant General A. S. Zhadov, commander of the 5th Guards Army (second from the left) looks on. Photo taken in the area of Prokhorovka, 13 July 1942. (RGAKFD)

Regiment and the 1446th Self-propelled Artillery Regiment, with additional fire support from the 18th Tank Corps' brigades south of the Psel River, was to capture Hill 226.6. The 132nd Guards Rifle Regiment of Major General A. F. Bobrov's 42nd Guards Rifle Division was ordered to seize Polezhaev, and then to participate in the assault on the key hill.

The commander of the 5th Guards Tank Army Lieutenant General Rotmistrov personally involved himself with the organization of cooperation between the units of the 5th Guards Mechanized Corps and the forces of the 33rd Guards Rifle Corps in the bend of the Psel. At 1240 he reported to N. F. Vatutin:

> In Zhadov's sector, Popov's [33rd Guards] rifle corps went on the offensive at 1100 13.07. The delay in the attack occurred because of a lack of artillery shells. I was personally with Comrade Popov in Korytnoe, where I gave the order to the 24th Tank Brigade, the 51st Tank Regiment and the artillery regiment of self-propelled artillery to go on the offensive with the infantry … at 1100 with the assignment to destroy the enemy tank grouping in the Polezhaev – Kliuchi – Hill 226.6 area. After carrying out this task, I ordered the tank brigade to withdraw to the wooded area near Korytnoe, and the mechanized brigade – to the Dumnoe area. I forbade the commitment of the motorized infantry into this battle, since Popov has enough infantry. The motorized infantry has been left in reserve in the area of Ostren'kov. I designated Colonel Shabarov, the 5th Mechanized Corps' chief of staff, to head the tank group in this sector. All instructions to the staff on this question were given at 0830 at Popov's command post in the presence of Comrade Zhadov's deputy, a major general whose last name I don't recall.[3]

The attack of the 5th Guards Army's two corps made slow progress. From the morning, the 32nd Guards Rifle Corps' artillery had begun the work of suppressing enemy firing positions, targeting first of all the dug-in tanks. At 1000 the 13th and 66th Guards Rifle Divisions went on the attack, but encountering heavy and well-organized enemy fire, managed to advance only 200-300 meters before being pinned down. For unclear reasons, the 31st Tank Corps failed to support the rifle divisions' attack; its command had received an order to hold its present lines until further special instruction. The 5th Guards Army chief of operations reported, "On this sector of our right flank, enemy aviation didn't operate today. In the same manner, our aviation also didn't operate until 0900. Units of the enemy's 11th Panzer Division are stubbornly clinging to their positions in front of Rodimtsev."[4]

The 33rd Guards Rifle Corps had more success in the bend of the Psel River. Advancing southward along the valley of the river, Colonel I. I. Antsiferov's 97th Guards Rifle Division reached the southern outskirts of Veselyi, where it became tied up in fighting with *Totenkopf* Panzergrenadiers. Supported by tanks and assault guns, the infantry of the 95th Guards Rifle Division by mid-day reached Hill 226.6. The division's war diary gives a detailed description of the advance that morning:

> In the course of 13.07.43, units of the division, running into stubborn resistance and enemy counterattacks, continued to attack in the direction: 287th Guards Rifle Regiment – Kliuchi and woods east of Kliuchi; 284th Guards Rifle Regiment

Soviet infantry fight to retake a village. The man in the foreground is firing a Degtiarev light machine gun. (RGAKFD)

– Hill 226.6; 290th Guards Rifle Regiment – echeloned behind the 287th Guards Rifle Regiment with the support of 50 tanks from the 24th Tank Brigade and the 469th Mortar Regiment.

Between 1010 and 1115, our infantry with the attached support engaged in a heavy exchange of fire with enemy infantry and tanks, and as a result threw the enemy off of Hill 226.6, having occupied the enemy's first line of trenches.

At 1118, 26 heavy enemy tanks emerged from the southeastern slopes of Hill 226.6 and 33 heavy tanks from the southwestern slopes, which outflanked our combat positions and cut off the infantry, located in the first line of trenches on the southern slopes of the hill, from the supporting tanks.

A fierce tank battle erupted, as a result of which our artillery knocked out 3 heavy and 4 medium enemy tanks and wiped out 80 Hitlerites.

At 1200, the enemy with a force of up to one infantry battalion supported by 50 tanks counterattacked our units. The valorous infantrymen, artillerymen and tank hunters, destroying enemy infantry and armor with their fire, didn't permit the enemy to take even one step into the depth of their defenses. The enemy hurled up to another infantry battalion and 30 tanks into the battle, and by 1230 he managed to push back our units and re-take Hill 226.6. The enemy sent infantry, tanks and self-propelled guns toward the wooded area east of Kliuchi and against the southern slopes of Hill 226.6, with the aim of striking our units and advancing into the depth of our defenses.

Between 1230 to 1500, the bitterest – on our part defensive – fighting took place. By 1500 under the pressure of superior enemy forces, the units of the division made a fighting withdrawal to a new line and occupied a position: the 290th Guards

Rifle Regiment – south and southeast of Veselyi; the 287th Guards Rifle Regiment – northwest slopes of Hill 226.6 to the junction of farm roads 1 kilometer north of Hill 226.6; 284th Guards Rifle Regiment – from the junction of farm roads 1 kilometer north of Hill 226.6 to the northern branch of the gully lying 2 kilometers northeast of Hill 226.6; the 24th Tank Brigade – the depression 2.5 kilometers north of Hill 226.6.

As the result of the fighting over the course of 13.07.43, 8 enemy tanks have been knocked out and more than a company of infantry destroyed by the fire of artillery, anti-tank rifles, and from tanks.

After a short lull, restoring our units back into order and bringing up ammunition, artillery and 20 tanks, the division is preparing for the attack.[5]

The 33rd Guards Rifle Corps' command summarized the day's action in Combat Dispatch No. 7 at 2200 13 July:

1. At 1000 13.07.43, the corps went on the offensive, having the individual assignment to restore the situation in the sector of the 95th Guards Rifle Division and to secure the success of further attacking operations.

2. The 97th Guards Rifle Division began the offensive from the line:

a) 289th Guards Rifle Regiment (minus two rifle battalions) – with the right flank 300 meters west of Point 209.3, the left flank – flour mill in Kochetovka;

b) 294th Guards Rifle Regiment – with the right flank at the flour mill, the left flank – reference number 117 under the designation 'Krasnyi Oktiabr';'

c) 292nd Guards Rifle Regiment (minus two rifle battalions) – in the area of Point 188.1; two rifle battalions along the left bank of the Ol'shanka River to the southern outskirts of Kartashevka, with a front facing to the southeast;

d) 104th Separate Destroyer Anti-tank Artillery Battalion – in firing positions 2 kilometers southeast of Hill 242.3.

Units of the division, coming under enemy fire, could make no advance and is exchanging fire from its current lines. During the attacks of 11.07 and 12.07.43, 200 enemy soldiers and officers were wiped out. Over the same period 1 machine gun, 1 anti-tank rifle, 1 artillery tractor, 3 fortified firing points, and a truck were destroyed; 2 mortar batteries and 3 machine guns were suppressed. One mortar, 1 machine gun and 1 submachine gun were captured.

3. 95th Guards Rifle Division at 10.00, after reorganizing and having replenished ammunition, began the offensive with the support of 50 tanks from the 24th Tank Brigade:

a) 287th Guards Rifle Regiment – in the direction of Kliuchi and the woods to the east of it;

b) 284th Guards Rifle Regiment – in the direction of Hill 226.6;

c) 290th Guards Rifle Regiment – echeloned behind the right flank of the 287th Guards Rifle Regiment.

The enemy threw 33 Panzer VI tanks against our attacking units, and simultaneously gathered force for a counterattack. Stubborn fighting developed.

At 1200, the 287th and 284th Guards Rifle Regiments managed to reach the southern slopes of Hill 226.6 and to occupy the enemy's first line of trenches.

> The adversary, seeing that the tactically advantageous Hill 226.6 had been seized, launched an enveloping counterattack from the southwest and southeast with up to a battalion of infantry and the support of 50 tanks; after stubborn fighting the enemy managed to separate our infantry in the trenches from the tanks. Bitter fighting went on from 1230 to 1700.[6]
>
> The 42nd Guards Rifle Division's 136th Guards Rifle Regiment drove the enemy out of Polezhaev and then also became enmeshed in the fighting on the southern slopes of Hill 226.6. According to information from the division headquarters, during one *Totenkopf* counterattack, six enemy tanks broke through the regiment's positions and penetrated all the way to the Prokhorovka-Kartashevka road, where they were met by the fire of the regiment's reserve elements and compelled to return to their start lines.

The enemy's II SS Panzer Corps described the day's combat north of the Psel River more laconically:

> The Corps was forced to defend its positions on 13 July against enemy counterattacks, with the main attacks falling on the left wing. The enemy's intention to eliminate the bridgehead north of Prokhorovka is plainly apparent. New in comparison with the past days is the commitment of strong infantry forces, which he is single-mindedly sending at a run against our lines, while a smaller number of attacking enemy tanks, holding back a bit, are supporting the infantry attack.

An order has been received; once again into combat! (RGAKFD)

> Attacks from the gullies east of Veselyi with a force of up to a regiment and the support of 30 tanks. The last attack at around 1500 [1700 local time] led to a penetration in our lines, which was liquidated at 1815 [2015].[7]

The persistent attacks of our infantry, supported by tanks, created a threat to the II SS Panzer Corps' left flank and forced him to cancel his planned offensive along the northern bank of the Psel River toward Prokhorovka. However, the attacks took a high toll on the participating rifle divisions.

It is a grim task to analyze the personnel losses of the 5th Guards Army's rifle divisions. From 9 to 12 July 1943 (that is, during the climax of the fighting to repel the attacks of the II SS Panzer Corps), the 95th Guards Rifle Division lost 356 men, including 91 killed or mortally wounded; the 42nd Guards Rifle Division lost a total of 421 men (killed – 58); and the 9th Guards Airborne Division – 1,600 men, including 329 killed, 103 missing in action, and four taken as prisoners. From the start of the fighting on 11 July and until 17 July inclusively, the 95th Guards Rifle Division suffered another 3,164 casualties (952 killed); the 9th Guards Airborne Division – an additional total of 2,112 casualties (including 250 killed).[8]

Thus, the 95th Guards Rifle Division incurred most of its casualties in the period between 13 and 17 July. Over these five days, the division's regiments repeatedly assaulted Hill 226.6 without sufficient preparation. That it was impossible to take this hill without powerful artillery preparation and tank support was already clear on 13 July, when the division conducted its first major assault on the hill with the support of the 24th Guards Tank Brigade and the 1446th Self-propelled Artillery Regiment. The 5th Guards Army's war diary observes:

> As a result of the operation, it was established that the enemy had constructed a company-sized strongpoint on Hill 226.6, [and was] defending it with 12-15 heavy machine guns and a company of submachine gunners with the support of two mortar batteries and a battalion of artillery.[9]

On the evening of 13 July, the 24th Guards Tank Brigade and the 1446th Self-propelled Artillery Regiment were withdrawn from the bend of the Psel, thereby depriving the 95th Rifle Division of its armor support. For 14 July, the 95th Guards Rifle Division counted only 119 shells for its 122mm howitzers, and less than a half of a daily combat load of ammunition for its 76mm field guns and its 120mm mortars. It had only 70% of a daily combat load of ammunition for its 45mm guns. However, its rifle battalions continued to assault Hill 226.6 for four more days, right up to 17 July.

Here's a description of one of the attacks, on the night of 15 July, from the 95th Guards Rifle Division's combat diary:

> On the night of 15 July, an operation was conducted to seize prisoners in the area of Hill 226.6. The prisoner snatch group consisted of the 108th and 109th Penal Companies, a company of submachine gunners from the 287th Guards Rifle Regiment, reinforced with sappers and scouts (one platoon of anti-tank rifles, 6-8 anti-tank guns from the rifle regiment, a sapper company from the 109th Separate

Rifle Battalion and two platoons from the 99th Guards Separate Scout Company; artillery group – one battalion of the 233rd Guards Artillery Regiment).

Group mission: to seize prisoners and liquidate the enemy bridgehead on the northern bank of the Psel River (Hill 226.6 – Kliuchi).

Course of operations: at 0100 the aforementioned group moved out under the cover of mortar fire.

The group of the 287th Guards Rifle Regiment with the 108th Penal Company, a platoon of sappers, three anti-tank guns, a platoon of sappers from the separate rifle battalion, and a scout platoon from the 99th Guards Separate Scout Company [attacked] in the direction of Kliuchi, where it ran into heavy machine-gun and automatic weapons fire, and artillery and mortar fire, and was pinned down, though it repeatedly tried to advance. The enemy increased his fire, and all the attempts of the operational group met with failure; it was forced to dig in on the line it had reached – 100 meters south of the road leading from Kliuchi to Polezhaev, along a front stretching from the knoll 200 meters north of Kliuchi to the northwest slopes of Hill 226.6.

The group of the 290th Guards Rifle Regiment, with a similar force composition as in the 287th Guards Rifle Regiment's group, operated in the direction of Kliuchi and the woods southeast of Kliuchi; it advanced up to 450 meters before being pinned down by heavy enemy machine-gun and artillery fire. Despite losses of up to 20 percent of its men, it attempted to break into Kliuchi with a decisive lunge. The results were not successful.[10]

The 33rd Guards Rifle Corps' operational summary at 2400 16 July tersely reported: "the forward groups [of the 95th Guards Rifle Division] as the result of night-time operations before sunrise on 16 July advanced 200-400 meters and dug in."[11] Once again, however, the infantry lacked tank support, and they were forced to withdraw after an enemy counterattack. Efforts to take the commanding Hill 226.6 continued.

In the reports of our formations, which took part in the battle of Kursk, one often encounters comments purporting that the enemy's infantry acted cowardly, lagging rather far behind the tanks, and at the leading armor's slightest pause, they would quickly fall back. However, the Germans sought to preserve their infantry; the same cannot be said about our command. In the engagement at Prokhorovka, not once did the Germans attempt a frontal attack by infantry companies without the support of tanks, aviation or artillery. In contrast, for our side such unsupported attacks were not a rarity, and the Prokhorovka engagement was no exception. This particularly fell to the lot of the 5th Guards Army's divisions. A clear example is the fruitless five-day assault on Hill 226.6.

Here is another example of how combat operations were organized in the 5th Guards Army's 33rd Rifle Corps. On the night of 11 July, in order to improve its positions, the 9th Guards Airborne Division had been ordered to attack the Oktiabr'skii State Farm from Petrovka, while units of the 95th Guards Rifle Division had received orders to attack *Totenkopf*'s bridgehead on the northern bank of the Psel. Both divisions attempted several frontal attacks without any tank support or any preliminary powerful artillery preparation. All the attacks ended in failure.

This peculiarity of our generals – the willingness to accept high casualties – was well known to the Germans. In his memoirs, the chief of staff of Fourth Panzer Army's XXXXVIII Panzer Corps General F. von Mellenthin observed:

> Regarding Russian officers in command, it is as well to know that:
>
> a) In almost every situation and every case they strictly and rigidly adhere to orders or to previous decisions. They disregard changes in the situation, the reactions of the enemy, and the losses of their own troops. Naturally this attitude has serious drawbacks, but it brings certain compensations.
>
> b) They have at their disposal almost inexhaustible resources of human material to replace casualties. The Russian Command can afford high losses and ignores them.[12]

A rather open acknowledgment on this question can be found in the memoirs of A. S. Zhadov:

> On 16 July, Marshal of the Soviet Union G. K. Zhukhov, the deputy of the Supreme Commander, arrived at our command post. He was interested in how the commitment of the army for launching the counterstroke of 12 July had been organized. On this matter, he spoke with me, with the corps commanders, and the artillery commander Major General G. V. Poluektov. Once alone with me, he expressed dissatisfaction with the way the introduction of the forces into the engagement had been handled and gave me a stern reprimand for committing a full-strength army, which had been well-prepared for carrying out combat tasks, without tank reinforcements or a sufficient quantity of artillery, and with an extremely limited amount of ammunition. In conclusion, Georgii Konstantinovich said: 'If for whatever reason the *front* headquarters has not managed to provide the army with everything necessary in a timely fashion, then you must persistently ask the *front* commander about this or in the extreme case appeal to the *Stavka*.'
>
> Incidentally, to appeal to the *Stavka* for any sort of explanations or assistance – at that time, such thoughts never even entered my mind.[13]

It is a frank admission. The army commander, who had at that time more than 62,000 men under his command, is honestly acknowledging that he did not do everything that any military commander must do in his place.

On the sector running from Vasil'evka through Oktiabr'skii State Farm and Iamki to the hill northeast of Storozhevoe, the threat of a German panzer breakthrough remained as before. Therefore Vatutin arranged a defense in depth on this sector, with the rifle units of the 5th Guards and 69th Armies primarily holding the first echelon of defense, backed by the remaining tanks of the 18th, 29th, 2nd Tank, and 2nd Guards Tank Corps in the second echelon. The 42nd Guards Rifle Division's 127th and 136th Guards Rifle Regiments were defending the sector Vasil'evka – Andreevka – Mikhailovka – Oktiabr'skii State Farm. The 9th Guards Airborne Division's 23rd and 28th Guards

Airborne Regiments were deployed between Mikhailovka (excl.) and Iamki. The 183rd Rifle Division's 285th Rifle Regiment was holding the sector between Iamki (excl.) to the hill northeast of Storozhevoe. The 9th Guards Airborne Division's 26th Guards Airborne Regiment was dug-in between a point 2 kilometers north of the Oktiabr'skii State Farm and the rail line, thereby creating a third line of defense southwest of Prokhorovka.

In contrast, from Storozhevoe (excl.) to Belenikhino Station and extending on to the eastern outskirts of Leski (incl.), tank battalions of the 2nd Guards 'Tatsinskaia' Tank Corps and the 5th Guards 'Stalingrad' Tank Corps' 6th Guards Motorized Rifle Brigade were deployed in the first echelon of defense. The 183rd Rifle Division's 227th and 295th Rifle Regiments were positioned behind them as a second echelon.[14]

It is quite difficult to trace the course of events in this area, since sporadic but bitter fighting in the vicinity of Storozhevoe went on from the late evening of 12 July into the early morning hours of 13 July. Fearing an enemy penetration through this small hamlet to Pravorot', at 0335 on 13 July, Rotmistrov issued Combat Order No. 7 to the commander of the 2nd Tank Corps:

> The enemy is displaying stubborn resistance to the offensive of the army's units. [He] has repeatedly launched counterattacks with large tank forces. By the end of 12.07.43, a group of enemy tanks broke through and seized Storozhevoe. I order:
> 1. At 0800 13.07.43 an attack to the north from your present area to take Storozhevoe, with a subsequent defense on the boundary between the 29th Tank Corps and the 2nd Guards 'Tatsinskaia' Tank Corps on the line: Storozhevoe – (excl.) Vinogradovka, to prevent an enemy breakthrough to the east.
> 2. Have in mind that the 1529th Self-propelled Artillery Regiment will support your operations from the area of Grushki, if necessary.
> 3. Report on the receipt of the given order. Report on the progress of carrying out this order every two hours, starting from 0600 13.07.43.[15]

This order didn't reach the headquarters of the 2nd Tank Corps until 0640 13 July; the order to attack arrived at the headquarters of the 99th Tank Brigade at 0800 and at the headquarters of the 58th Motorized Rifle Brigade not until 0830. Therefore the attack could not begin as ordered at 0800. According to a combat dispatch from the corps, the attack was postponed to 1030.[16]

By 1015, the tank brigades had assembled in the jumping-off area for the attack, but the 58th Motorized Rifle Brigade didn't arrive until 1400. Further traces of this attack are missing from the summary reports and combat messages of the army and the corps. In the operational summary of the 2nd Tank Corps for 13 July, issued at 1600, there is not a single word about it. However, without waiting for the motorized riflemen to show up, the tank brigades had nevertheless gone on the attack. Only in the documents of the 99th Tank Brigade and in the 69th Army's account can we find evidence of their disorganized, hasty attack on the now heavily fortified German positions in and around Storozhevoe:

> Repeated attacks by our tanks and infantry on this axis were not crowned with success. Having a superior position in the arrangement of observation posts and firing positions for artillery and mortars, and having laid minefields, the adversary

> allowed no possibility to attack Storozhevoe. Our attacking units met particularly heavy fire from the grove lying east of Ivanovskii Vyselok.[17]

Another attack was launched against the hamlet from the north and northeast with the very same result. The 69th Army's account curtly notes, "The tank brigades of the 2nd Tank Corps, lacking any infantry cover and without artillery support, halted their advance."[18]

At 1300 13 July, the 29th Tank Corps headquarters noted in its Operational Dispatch No. 76:

> The enemy is bringing up reserves, by 1200 13.07.43, up to 100 tanks and up to a regiment of infantry from the "Adolf Hitler" Motorized [Panzergrenadier] Division had assembled at the Oktiabr'skii State Farm and the Stalinskoe Branch of the [Oktiabr'skii] State Farm; in the area of Storozhevoe – up to two battalions of infantry with artillery and tanks.[19]

The only document that allows us a reliable glimpse into the plans of our command on this day is a transcript of an exchange of telegraph messages between the commander of the 5th Guards Tank Army Rotmistrov and the *front* commander Vatutin on 13 July at 1240, which I managed to discover in the Russian Federation's Central Archives of the Defense Ministry. P. A. Rotmistrov began the exchange with a report:

> On the sector of General Bakharov's 18th Tank Corps and General Kirichenko's 29th Tank Corps, it is quiet today, except for the constant bombing by enemy aviation. These corps are reorganizing today, and until the resolution of the task on my right flank in the area of Polezhaev, I don't intend to give them active assignments today. If in the case that everything is resolved quickly in the area of Polezhaev, these corps will immediately go on the offensive. Bakharov's corps, which is occupying positions in the areas of Andreevka, Mikhailovka, Prelestnoe and Petrovka, has the task to assist our right-flank tank grouping [the 24th Tank Brigade across the Psel River] with fire. Burdeiny's tank corps today is continuing to fight west of Belenikhino. General Popov's 2nd Tank Corps is attacking from the area of Ivanovka toward Ivanovskii Vyselok and Storozhevoe. The enemy has up to 60 tanks in the areas of Storozhevoe and Ivanovskii Vyselok, and is repelling all of Popov's attacks. Simultaneously, the enemy today at 0600 tried to attack Pravorot' from Storozhevoe, but had no success. His attacks were repulsed by the 169th Tank Brigade and part of the 29th Tank Corps. The general impression is that the enemy is trying to stop the offensive of our units on this sector today with his aviation, and is simultaneously preparing a major offensive for tomorrow. I repeat: This is my personal opinion, which I have derived from the enemy's behavior on the battlefield.
>
> Vatutin:
>
> 'Katukov today together with Chistiakov is continuing the offensive. It isn't clear what the enemy will do and with what strength on the Prokhorovka axis directly in front of you.

'I consider your active operations in the afternoon in the direction of Pokrovka to be absolutely necessary, in order to destroy conclusively all the local penetrations made by tanks into our defenses, to smash the enemy on this axis and to emerge in the area Greznoe – Luchki – north of Teterevino. Prepare the offensive, support it with artillery and – upon your request – with aviation. I am ordering you to do this. Are you able to report now on the start of these operations?'

Rotmistrov:

'I've just received information that my 24th Tank Brigade has reached the southern slopes of Hill 226.6. Zhadov's infantry has actually seized Veselyi and Polezhaev and is advancing behind the tanks toward the Psel River. I assume that I can begin to shift [forces] to the area of Prokhorovka and to the east at 1500. I request your permission to begin the implementation of the assignment at 1600 and to attack Greznoe and Mal. Maiachki with the forces of the 18th and 29th Tank Corps. General Popov's 2nd Tank Corps will be given a limited task to eliminate the enemy in the area of Storozhevoe, since it no longer has the strength for a larger offensive. I have in mind to give Major General Burdeiny an order to take Teterevino and to subsequently attack toward Luchki. At 1600 I will request you to support the offensive with our aviation's activities. That is all.'[20]

The *front* commander agreed with Rotmistrov's proposal and promised to give it air support. Vatutin's decision was based on the conclusions made at a conference at *front* headquarters in the presence of Marshal Zhukov. In essence, both Guards armies had been given the previous assignment – the destruction of the enemy in the salient, but just as on 12 July, the armies were unable to carry it out, simply because they lacked the strength. The 5th Guards Tank Army's Operational Summary No. 3 from 13 July at 1900 indicates the difficult situation facing its subordinate corps:

… At 1600 13.07.43, the army's forces were given an order to attack the enemy in the general direction of Komsomolets State Farm, Mal. Maiachki and Bol. Maiachki.

…

3. The 18th Tank Corps with the 80th Guards Mortar Regiment has regrouped its forces on the line Petrovka – Mikhailovka, and has received an assignment to attack in the general direction of Mal. Maiachki. Operational tanks: 15 T-34 and 18 T-70.

4. The 29th Tank Corps with the 76th Guards Mortar Regiment and the 1529th Self-propelled Artillery Regiment on the line Hill 252.2 – 0.5 km southeast of the Oktiabr'skii State Farm – Iamki – depression 1 km southeast of Storozhevoe received the assignment to attack the Komsomolets State Farm at 1600 13.07.43.

5. The 2nd Tank Corps in the area of Ivanovka has received an assignment to attack Teterevino at 1600 13.07.43 … Operational tanks: 22 T-34, 20 T-70.

6. The 2nd Guards 'Tatsinskaia' Tank Corps in the area of the nameless ridge 1.5 km west of Leski received an assignment to attack Kalinin … Operational tanks: 45 T-34, 33 T-70, 2 Mk IV [Churchill].[21]

The numbers for the 2nd Guards 'Tatsinskaia' Tank Corps includes the 30 T-34 and ten T-70 tanks of the 26th Guards Tank Brigade, which was located in Shakhovo and thus was unable to take part in the designated operation.[22] At 1300, the 29th Tank Corps had eight T-34 and 20 T-70 tanks in the 31st Tank Brigade and 11 T-70 tanks in the 25th Tank Brigade; the 32nd Tank Brigade had been withdrawn into the reserve and had 12 T-34 tanks.[23]

Judging from the cited documents, the command of the 5th Guards Tank Army on 13 July was committing on an 18-20 kilometer sector less than a full-strength tank corps into battle: 154 armored fighting vehicles, of which 94 were T-70 light tanks. This averaged to only eight or nine tanks per kilometer of front. On 12 July, this figure had been significantly higher – 50 tanks and self-propelled guns per kilometer of front.

Opposing the formations of the Guards army were the two SS Panzergrenadier Divisions *Leibstandarte* and *Das Reich*, which had a combined strength of 133 tanks, including three Tigers and 11 captured T-34 tanks, and 44 assault guns.[24] With such a correlation of forces, one couldn't count upon any real results. Probably, even the *front* command didn't have any illusions about the attack's prospects. Judging from the transcripts of Vatutin's discussions with Zhadov and Rotmistrov, the *front* commander was more concerned about the situation in the 69th Army's sector, south of Prokhorovka, where Breith's III Panzer Corps was threatening to erupt from its bridgeheads across the Northern Donets River.

The Fourth Panzer Army's report for 13 July summarizes the results of the 5th Guards Tank Army's late afternoon offensive from the German perspective:

> … The [II SS Panzer] Corps stopped for the day in order to repulse strong infantry attacks with the support of individual tanks. The *Das Reich* Division repelled an enemy attack on its right flank. At 1430 [1630 Moscow time], the division went on the attack to the east and by the onset of darkness it had seized the valley of the brook along the line Ivanovka – Vinogradovka and had broken through the enemy positions present there. Division *Adolf Hitler* repulsed numerous attacks of up to regiment strength along the Prokhorovka – Teterevino road. The assault group of the Division *Totenkopf* was forced to withdraw from the hills southwest of Polezhaev under growing enemy pressure.[25]

The forces of the two Guards armies that launched these attacks were experiencing serious ammunition shortages and difficulties with resupply. The first to begin to limit ammunition was the 5th Guards Army, already on the evening of 12 July. In its account of the operation, there is the note:

> At 1830, with the aim of restricting the expenditure of artillery shells, the army commander pointed out instances of the fruitless expenditure of artillery and mortar shells to the corps and division commanders. The formation commanders and artillery commanders have on their own initiative abandoned the battle plan and the directing of fire during enemy tank attacks. In the majority of cases (95th and 9th Guards Airborne Divisions), a disorderly fire opens on the attacking enemy tanks from all the guns, not directed by anyone who can see the tanks and without consideration for the range (of effective fire).

As a result of the indicated lack of direction, over two days of fighting only 108 enemy tanks were destroyed, with the loss of 95 guns on our side.[26]

On the morning of 13 July, the tankers delayed the attack in the Psel bend for an hour due to the lack of ammunition. At 1240, during a discussion with the *front* commander, Rotmistrov reported: "I have a very difficult situation with ammunition in my units; in particular, General Trufanov has only a quarter of a daily combat load remaining. I humbly request that you take all measures at your disposal to hurry shells to me for the tanks with 76mm guns."[27]

SS Panzergrenadier Division *Leibstandarte*'s daily summary at 1700 [1900 Moscow time] observed,

> The enemy is digging in on the line Iamki – western and southern fringes of Oktiabr'skii State Farm, and is mining sectors east of Oktiabr'skii State Farm. He has a large quantity of light and medium artillery, as well as some heavy. Frequent artillery firing has started. Attacks are more with infantry, and the strength of the opposing enemy forces has grown.[28]

Although the attacks and counterattacks of our units and formations didn't bring the desired results, they did pin down the main forces of the II SS Panzer Corps. It was unable quickly to regroup its forces for either a continuation of the offensive to the north, or for the task of encircling the 69th Army's 48th Rifle Corps on its right.

16

Combat Operations of the 69th Army in the Area of Rzhavets and Shakhovo 13-16 July

The command of Army Group South, having decided to discontinue the offensive toward Kursk, turned its main efforts toward accomplishing the limited objective of encircling and destroying the divisions of the 69th Army's 48th Rifle Corps, which were defending in the narrow projection of land between the Lipovyi Donets and the Northern Donets rivers. A two-pronged attack from Prokhorovka Station and from the areas of Rzhavets and Shakhovo would pinch off this bulge and pocket the 48th Rifle Corps. German forces were poised to carry out this plan, which the Army Group South commander had already developed by 11 July, and which he had planned to implement on 12 July. Order No. 29 from the commander of the German 167th Infantry Division General Trierenberg on 11 July gives evidence of this:

> … 2. The neighbor on the left – Panzergrenadier Division SS *Das Reich* 11.07.43 is fighting for Storozhevoe; on the morning of 12.07.43 it will attack with its left flank toward Pravorot', and then pivot to the southwest – toward Vinogradovka and Leski.
>
> 3. The 167th Infantry Division on the sector of the 315th Grenadier Regiment is attacking in the direction of the Donets River, on 12.07.43 is to hold the lines it has reached and to support the offensive of the Panzergrenadier Division SS *Reich*. With the suppression of the enemy at Leski, it is to stand ready … with its northern flank to attack in the direction of the hill east of Teterevino.[1]

On 12 July this German plan had been preempted by our counterattack. However, once the situation had become stabilized by the afternoon of 12 July, these divisions again received the order to attack with the goal of encircling the forces of the 69th Army's 48th Rifle Corps. On 13 July, the enemy primarily spent the day regrouping in order to conduct this more limited assignment. However, the III Panzer Corps simultaneously probed our defenses on its sector with strong reconnaissance forces and continued to launch holding attacks on the 69th Army from the area of Rzhavets.

The forty-eight-year old Lieutenant General V. D. Kriuchenkin was commanding the 69th Army. A veteran of the First World War and a former commander of cavalry at the division and corps level, Kriuchenkin was fresh from an accelerated course of instruction at the Military Academy of the General Staff when he took command of the 69th Army. He was a courageous commander, as evidenced by the 18 wounds and two concussions he received during the war. Unfortunately, he lacked solid professional training. In the fighting at Kursk he would be called upon to make difficult decisions …

Lieutenant General V. D. Kriuchenkin, commander of the 69th Army (on the left) and deputy Front commander General of the Army I. P. Apanasenko at an observation post. (RGAKFD)

On the morning of 14 July, an operational report issued at 0600 by the 26th Guards Tank Brigade [originally part of Burdeiny's 2nd Guards Tank Corps, but now part of Trufanov's mobile detachment] summarized the previous day's actions:

> 1. The enemy with 30 tanks and up to a regiment of infantry has crossed the Northern Donets River in the vicinity of Shcholokovo and by 0400 13.07.43 was attacking the 1st Tank Battalion along a gully lying southeast of Shakhovo.
>
> At 0800 up to two companies of enemy infantry with the support of concentrated artillery and mortar fire twice tried to attack Shakhovo from the east and northeast. A large assembly of tanks and vehicles has been observed on the west and southwest slopes of Hill 216.0 and in the area of Rzhavets.
>
> In the course of the day the enemy twice tried to attack the 11th Guards Mechanized Brigade and Shakhovo from the direction of Shcholokovo under the cover of artillery and mortar fire.
>
> At 2030 the enemy launched a vigorous attack in the direction of Ryndinka with up to 35 tanks and up to a regiment of infantry, and took possession of the village.
>
> In the course of the night of 13 July, the enemy displayed no active measures, and conducted sporadic artillery and mortar fire on the combat positions of our units. Enemy aviation periodically bombed the brigade's combat positions.[2]

The enemy's intentions were clear. The 69th Army command took measures to improve its positions and consolidate its combat formations on the axis of the enemy's main attack. Already at 1800 12 July, Lieutenant General S. G. Goriachev in fulfillment of the army commander's Order No. 00994 issued orders for the 92nd Guards Rifle Division to turn over its defenses in the Vypolzovka – Podsumki – Alekseevka – Ploskoe area to the 305th Rifle Division on the night of 12 July, and to take up positions along the line Rzhavets – Avdeevka – Verin – Pokrovka – Ryndinka. The adversary was displaying great activity in this area, and the situation demanded a speedy regrouping. The third point of Goriachev's orders called for the commander of the 92nd Guards Rifle Division to vacate its positions, assemble in the rear, and move out for the threatened sector, even before the onset of darkness and the arrival of the full 305th Rifle Division. However, part of the new sector indicated for the 92nd Guards Rifle Division was already being occupied by the Germans, and at the moment the order was signed, the 11th Guards and 12th Guards Mechanized Brigades were engaged in intense fighting there. So the 35th Guards Rifle Corps' chief of staff Colonel Tsalai had noted on Goriachev's order in his own handwriting: "If Rzhavets and Vypolzovka have not been swept clear of the enemy before the end of the day, occupy a line north of these villages with your front to the west and southeast."[3]

However, this order was issued without taking the condition of the 92nd Guards Rifle Division into consideration. The division had already suffered heavy losses, and the division commander had been forced to merge the remnants of his battalions into a single rifle regiment. At night, this composite regiment moved into the sector between Vypolzovka and Aleksandrovka, and worked until dawn digging into position, while its scout group kept watch for the enemy and cautiously probed the area of Kurakovka and 1st Novo-Aleksandrovskii Vyselok. The 305th Rifle Division moved into the line

Crews of one of the regiments of the 10th Destroyer Anti-tank Brigade hastily taking position behind the combat units of 69th Army's 92nd Guards Rifle Division, 13 July 1943. (RGAKFD)

between Podsumki and Ploskii. The situation was additionally complicated by the fact that the right flank of the 92nd Guards Rifle Division, and of the 35th Guards Rifle Corps as a whole, was exposed. Responsibility for covering it was laid upon the 11th and 12th Guards Mechanized Brigades and units of General Trufanov's mobile group. Thus, in the area of the III Panzer Corps' penetration into the rear belt of defenses, a continuous line of defense could not be organized – the 69th Army was counting upon the enemy's high losses, as well as the artillery that the *front* was planning to transfer to it, to keep its defenses intact.

Through the day and into the night of 12 July, the German III Panzer Corps conducted a regrouping of its forces and assembled the 6th, 7th and 19th Panzer Divisions on the axis of the main attack, on the line Shcholokovo – Rzhavets – Vypolzovka – Kurakovka. On the morning of 13 July, units of the 19th Panzer Division were the first to begin active operations. The division's staff account relates:

> After Major Horst with the forces of the 73rd Panzergrenadier Regiment had already late in the evening of 12.07 significantly expanded the bridgehead in an easterly direction and had occupied the hill 2 kilometers east of Shakhovo, our units deployed on the morning of 13.07 and began to expand the bridgehead to the northwest. In the breach that was being created in connection with this, the enemy attacked from the north in the sector along both sides of the Northern Donets with the strength of a newly arrived mechanized brigade led by tanks. In connection with this counterstroke, the headquarters of the 74th Panzergrenadier Regiment was cut off from its battalions, and the enemy penetrated through Ryndinka to the location of the bridge crossing, thereby severing the entire bridgehead from the eastern bank. Breaking out through enemy infantry and having knocked out one tank, the headquarters staff managed to swim across the Donets and reach the eastern bank. In so doing, control over both battalions of the 74th Regiment had become impossible and was turned over to the commander of the 73rd Regiment, Major Horst.
>
> Paying no attention to the enemy in its rear, Horst's *kampfgruppe*, which fortunately had all its heavy weapons on the western bank, successfully attacked in a northwest direction. Despite bitter resistance, the bridgehead was expanded to the grove east of Shakhovo. The 74th Panzergrenadier Regiment together with tankers managed to repulse enemy attacks from the north and east, and continuing to advance along the highway, and linked up with Horst's *kampfgruppe*. All four battalions were subsequently deployed in the night in sectors east and northeast of the woods at Shakhovo, the 74th Regiment with its front to the north, the 73rd Regiment facing west.
>
> Scouts found another crossing south of Rzhavets at Shcholokovo, over which the division managed to maintain a connection with Horst's group along this road and keep it supplied.
>
> As the result of a counterattack, our panzers on this day succeeded in clearing the bridge at Rzhavets, which was recaptured by elements of the reconnaissance battalion, and through a subsequent advance, connection was re-established with the forward units in the bridgehead.

> As a result of the advance of Horst's *kampfgruppe,* enemy units situated west of Shcholokovo, seemingly up to a regiment in strength, sensed they were encircled and made an attempt to break out to the north from a wooded area. This attack on the unprotected southern flank of Horst's group was repulsed by elements of Williken's panzer group [I/Panzer Regiment 27 of the 19th Panzer Division].[4]

The 6th Panzer Division also demonstrated great activity on this day. The 69th Army command assumed that the enemy on 13 July would try to expand the bridgehead in the area of Rzhavets, and to drive our forces back in the direction of Shipy, Krasnyi Oktiabr' and further along the west bank of the Northern Donets. Therefore it decided to employ the mechanized brigades of Trufanov's group to pin down the enemy and not permit him to create a strong armored fist in any one sector. On the evening of 12 July, a detachment had been formed from units of the 12th Guards Mechanized Brigade consisting of two tank companies from the 55th Guards Tank Regiment, the 1st Motorized Rifle Battalion, a battery of 76mm guns, a company of 120mm mortars, and an anti-tank rifle platoon. Lieutenant Colonel M. I. Gol'dberg, the commander of the 55th Guards Tank Regiment, was placed in command of this detachment. At 2200 on 12 July, these units began to move out toward Avdeevka.

At dawn on 13 July, the point unit of this column reached the village, before running into 14 enemy tanks in a depression south of Avdeevka. Fighting erupted:

> A company of T-34s under the command of Lieutenant N. P. Novak, which was following the head of the detachment's column, and the destroyer anti-tank battery quickly prepared for combat. Hurrying forward, the motorized infantry and the platoon of anti-tank rifles took position on the southern outskirts of Avdeevka. Allowing the fascists tanks to close within short range before opening fire, our T-34s and anti-tank guns shot up half the tanks, while the remaining tanks were forced to turn back. Shortly thereafter, the Hitlerites introduced their main forces into the battle.
>
> Moving out from Rzhavets, one group of tanks attacked toward Vypolzovka, while another attacked towards Avdeevka. Hot clashes erupted, involving all the elements of the detachment. Meanwhile the main forces of the column bypassed the enemy to the east and launched a heavy attack on the flank of the 6th Panzer Division. This maneuver forced the Hitlerites to abandon their attack to the north.
>
> After short but fierce fighting, the brigade seized a tactically important hill and emerged in a very favorable position. With frontal fire from this hill and flank fire from the south and southeastern fringes of Avdeevka, it knocked out several tanks. The fascists units that were attacking in the direction of Vypolzovka and Avdeevka were met with flanking fire, and from the outskirts of Avdeevka, frontal fire.
>
> One of the furious attempts of the German tanks to outflank the brigade broke up on the indestructible resolve of the Soviet warriors. The platoon of anti-tank riflemen under the command of Senior Lieutenant K. T. Pozdeev performed an unforgettably heroic deed. The platoon was covering the southern approaches to Avdeevka. Together with the commander there were 14 men. They had four anti-tank rifles, several anti-tank grenades and submachine guns. The enemy tried repeatedly to take Avdeevka. During one attack, 23 fascist tanks with submachine

gunners rushed the position occupied by the platoon at high speed. Savage but unequal fighting developed. The anti-tank riflemen fired at the tanks from point-blank range, hurled grenades at them, and mowed down the enemy infantry from their submachine guns. The Guardsmen knocked out 11 tanks during this struggle, without taking one step back and not allowing the enemy into the depths of our combat positions. In this battle, almost the entire platoon laid down their lives as brave Guardsmen, who had carried out their duty to the Motherland to the end. They demonstrated real heroism. Here are their names: Senior Lieutenant K. T. Pozdeev, Junior Sergeant I. N. Aleksandrov, Privates V. A. Sereda, G. M. Solov'ev, P. A. Ubomasov, P. A. Seregin, D. Ia. Orlovsky, M. Z. Gainutdinov, L. M. Musher, G. M. Fomichev, I. V. Medvedev, I. N. Shul'gin, I. M. Sladkikh, and P. A. Maksimov.[5]

In the fighting at Avdeevka, the tankers of Lieutenant N. P. Novak's company displayed great combat skill. As documents disclose, throughout the course of 13 July they knocked out 28 enemy tanks and assault guns; the company commander's crew destroyed five tanks, while the crew of platoon commander Lieutenant S. M. Chimakadze claimed seven. Unfortunately, both officers were killed in this savage battle of 13 July.

The enemy, adhering to well-tested methods of combat against a well-organized defense, also sought to crush the resistance of our forces with simultaneous, powerful air strikes. The 35th Guards Rifle Corps' war diary notes that the Germans conducted two mass air raids on the areas of Vypolzovka and Aleksandrovka with the participation of up to 250 Ju 87 and Ju 88 bombers.[6] During one of these attacks at 1600, the commander of the 55th Guards Tank Regiment Lieutenant Colonel Mikhail Iosifovich Gol'dberg was

A Soviet self-propelled artillery regiment on the move in the area of Rzhavets, 13 July 1943. (RGAKFD)

struck by a fragment of an exploding bomb and killed. Also killed was the commander of the 12th Guards Mechanized Brigade's 1st Motorized Rifle Battalion, Major Aleksei Filippovich Akulov, whose soldiers were defending Avdeevka together with the tankers on this day. In order to maintain firm control over the defending units, the commander of the 12th Guards Mechanized Brigade Colonel G. Ia. Borisenko immediately dispatched his deputy Colonel P. A. Mikhailenko and his chief of the political department Major P. G. Dmitriev to Avdeevka.

Despite the dogged determination of the attacking Germans, the forces of the 69th Army and Trufanov's mobile group from the 5th Guards Tank Army stood firm, and managed to hold Shipy, Avdeevka and Krasnyi Oktiabr', and by the end of the day the 12th Guards Mechanized Brigade with fire support from the 92nd Guards Rifle Division evicted units of the 6th Panzer Division from Vypolzovka, but all this success came at a heavy price: the 11th Guards Mechanized Brigade alone lost 414 men on 13 July.[7] This represented the highest loss in the brigades of the 5th Guards Mechanized Corps' over five days of fighting.

The enemy's 7th Panzer Division was also unable to break through the defense of the 35th Guards Rifle Corps in the area of Aleksandrovka. The 35th Guards Rifle Corps' account of combat operations reports:

> In the areas of the burial mounds … west of Aleksandrovka, Sviridovo and Hill 235.4, three anti-tank strongpoints were established, which had the task to prevent a breakthrough of tanks in the directions of Vypolzovka, Kazach'e and Shliakhovoe. Approaching the region of the burial mounds, enemy tanks were greeted with sharp fire from the 532nd Destroyer Anti-tank Artillery Regiment. Intense fighting broke out. The enemy tanks, unable to withstand the artillery fire, fell back to their jumping-off positions, leaving behind up to 25 knocked-out tanks. In this combat the entire 4th Battery of the 532nd Destroyer Anti-tank Artillery Regiment, which received the brunt of the enemy attack, was killed.[8]

Since the morning of 13 July, the main events on II SS Panzer Corps' front had been occurring in *Totenkopf*'s sector. The evening before, it had received the order to continue the attack to the north and northeast. However, the attacks from the divisions of General Zhadov's army had thrown these plans awry. Again, the SS Panzer Corps had been forced to go over to an active defense.

By the middle of the day, the situation suddenly changed. At 1115, Fourth Panzer Army headquarters transmitted by telephone to the chief of staff of the II SS Panzer Corps an order from General Hoth to the corps commander: after repulsing the Russian attacks in *Totenkopf*'s sector, to shift the direction of the Corps' main effort to *Das Reich*'s front. In connection with the cessation of Operation Citadel, the enemy had ultimately decided to eliminate the thorn in its side created by the Soviets' position between the Lipovyi Donets and Northern Donets, and to trap and destroy the defending 48th Rifle Corps there.

The order was immediately forwarded to *Das Reich* headquarters. The 3rd SS Panzergrenadier Regiment *Deutschland* received the order to attack from the woods south of Ivanovskii Vyselok in the direction of the northern outskirts of Belenikhino Station, while the 4th SS Panzergrenadier Regiment *Der Führer* was to attack toward the hills west of Vinogradovka to link up with the 3rd SS Panzergrenadier Regiment. Having seized the area of Belenikhino, the full division was to attack through Vinogradovka toward Pravorot'. In order to conduct the operation, the *Das Reich* command requested aerial reconnaissance in front of the division and support during the attack from its neighbor on the right, the 167th Infantry Division. Preparations for the attack went on simultaneously with the repulse of our counterattacks and against the backdrop of artillery barrages and bomb strikes. Rain fell off and on, which prevented the timely reinforcement of the division prior to its attack.

A Fourth Panzer Army communiqué for 13 July observed:

> The regrouping of the II SS Panzer Corps was impossible due to the terrible condition of the roads and the poor bridges across the Psel at Bogoroditskoe. The corps in the course of the day repulsed strong infantry attacks with the support of individual tanks. *Das Reich* repulsed enemy attacks on its right flank. At 1430 the division went on the attack to the east and with the onset of darkness seized the river valley between Ivanovka and Vinogradovka, and had penetrated the enemy positions present there.
>
> … Division *Das Reich* has the order to attack initially through Ivanovka to the east, and then to penetrate along the water barrier to the northeast and to attack Pravorot'. … Its units, trying to create suitable jumping-off positions for the attack, have advanced to the river valley north of Ivanovka and have occupied a forest mass directly to the northeast of the village. It will conduct an attack from this sector early on the morning of 14 July with that same objective.[9]

That morning of 13 July, the 183rd Rifle Division was fighting for the possession of Kalinin and Sobachevskii in *Das Reich*'s sector, but its exposed right flank eventually forced it to retreat. Having reached a patch of woods near Sobachevskii and a point east of Kalinin, the enemy infantry was stopped by heavy artillery and tank fire and forced to dig-in. The staff account of the 2nd Guards 'Tatsinskaia' Tank Corps notes:

> At 2000 13.07.43 the enemy attacked our units in Vinogradovka with up to 15 tanks and a battalion of infantry, organized into two groups. One group attacked from jumping-off positions 1 kilometer south of Ivanovskii Vyselok, the other from a point 1.5 kilometers north of the Belenikhino Machine Tractor Station. The enemy attack had air support and was strongly supported by artillery and mortar fire.
>
> With the concentrated fire of artillery, tanks and infantry of the corps' units, the enemy attack was thrown back and he returned to his start positions.
>
> As a result of the day-long fighting, the corps destroyed: 5 tanks, 3 guns, 1 mortar, 3 airplanes, 10 vehicles, 3 light machine guns, 1 heavy machine gun, 2 bunkers and 120 officers and soldiers, while suffering its own losses of 7 killed and 20 wounded; 1 T-34 tank burned out, 3 T-34 tanks and 1 T-70 tanks knocked out, 2 anti-tank guns and 3 vehicles. …[10]

Thus, in the area of Ivanovskii Vyselok, Belenikhino and Kalinin on 13 July, there were no substantial changes in the lines. However, it was clear that the enemy was gathering strength here to make a decisive attack.

The 69th Army command kept close watch on the enemy activity and clearly understood the enemy's aim. Here is an excerpt from the "Operational-tactical description of the 69th Army's defensive operation":

> In the course of fighting on 13.07, it was revealed that the enemy had formed two groupings:
>
> 1. A Southern Group – consisting of the 168th Infantry Division, the 6th Panzer Division, and elements of the 19th Panzer Division – for a strike toward Shakhovo from the areas of Rzhavets and Ryndinka.
>
> 2. A Northern Group – consisting of the Panzergrenadier Division *Das Reich*, the Panzergrenadier Division *Adolf Hitler*, and the 167th Infantry Division – for an attack from the areas of Teterevino, Iasnaia Poliana and Hill 258.2, also in the direction of Shakhovo.
>
> The task of these groupings is to encircle the forces of the 48th Rifle Corps south and southwest of Shakhovo, and to exploit in general direction to the north.[11]

Having guessed the enemy's intentions, the 69th Army commander laid out his assignments for his corps in Order No. 00107/OP from 14 July. The 48th Rifle Corps, in cooperation with the 2nd Tank Brigade, the 5th Guards Tank Army's motorized rifle brigade, the 27th Gun Artillery Brigade and a separate tank company, was to destroy the enemy in the region of Ryndinka, Rzhavets and Vypolzovka. The right flank of the 35th Guards Rifle Corps was to cooperate with the 48th Rifle Corps in this area.[12] However, because of the significant loss of equipment and men, the 69th Army was not in a condition to carry out this order.

Already by the end of 13 July, at 2330 the Voronezh Front headquarters was issuing orders to reinforce the 48th Rifle Corps, organize the defenses and prevent its encirclement. These orders placed a powerful artillery grouping at the disposal of the 48th Rifle Corps' commander, Major General Z. Z. Rogozny:

- The 69th Army's 48th Destroyer Anti-tank Artillery Regiment came under his operational control and moved into the area of Plota, there to establish a strong anti-tank line of defense.
- The 27th Gun Artillery Brigade was subordinated to the 48th Rifle Corps, and its commander Colonel Sel'nikov was ordered to deploy two battalions of 122mm guns in the Shakhovo-Vypolzovka area, with the goal of preventing an enemy breakthrough in this sector. At the same time, the main forces of the brigade were to deploy on the line Kireev-Pokrovka in order to fire on the Shcholokovo area and to prepare fire mission data for the villages of Shakhovo, Kleimenovo, Shcholokovo, Ryndinka, Rzhavets, Vypolzovka and Avdeevka. The main objective of all the brigade's units was to prevent an enemy breakthrough to the north.

- The *front*'s chief of staff Lieutenant General S. P. Ivanov also transferred the 32nd Destroyer Anti-tank Artillery Brigade to the commander of the 48th Rifle Corps. It was given the assignment to establish anti-tank strongpoints on the L'vov-Kireev-Gnezdilovka-Lutovo line, with the goal of blocking an enemy tank breakthrough to the north, northeast and northwest directions. The regiment and both brigades were only given a night to move into position and set up, and were instructed to be ready to fire at 0600 14 July.

The 69th Army's 35th Guards Rifle Corps was temporarily augmented with the transfer of units from elsewhere. It was given the 263rd Mortar Regiment (which was assigned to the 92nd Guards Rifle Division); the 290th Mortar Regiment and the 122nd Separate Battalion of Anti-tank Rifles (assigned to the 305th Rifle Division); and the 496th Mortar Regiment and the 130th Separate Battalion of Anti-tank Rifles (assigned to the 107th Rifle Division). The corps was also to receive the support of the 10th Destroyer Anti-tank Artillery Brigade (the 532nd, 1243rd and 1245th Destroyer Anti-tank Artillery Regiments), and the *Katiushas* of the 315th Guards Mortar Regiment and the 448th Separate Guards Mortar Battalion.

The 69th Army artillery commander Colonel Pyrsky instructed the artillery commander of the 35th Guards Rifle Corps on the use of these attachments:

> ...
>
> 2. Use the mortar regiments only as part of division-level mortar groups or in the extreme case as not less than a battalion to strengthen the artillery support group. Don't split up the 10th Destroyer Anti-tank Artillery Brigade; I forbid attaching it to the divisions. It must be used on the main axis [of attack] as a full brigade.
>
> 3. I demand more organized work from the staff of the 35th Guards Rifle Corps; by the end of the day, the staff must know and report to me what the corps artillery has destroyed among the enemy; what is new in the enemy's tactics; on the arrangement of its own artillery; and who and how fire missions are being decided.
>
> ... 5. I particularly demand the commander of the 10th Destroyer Anti-tank Artillery Brigade to be ready to maneuver, especially to cover Vypolzovka.[13]

The *front* commander also issued combat orders on the evening of 13 July at 2030 regarding the situation in this sector:

> The enemy (tanks and infantry) are striving to penetrate through Rzhavets and Vypolzovka to Avdeevka and Shakhovo. I order:
>
> 1. The commander of the 69th Army and the commander of the 5th Guards Tank Army through joint operations are to destroy the enemy that is breaking through, and not to allow a [full] breakthrough under any circumstances.
> 2. The commander of the 2nd Air Army with all available aircraft to continue the destruction of the enemy grouping, attacking from the areas of Kurakovka, Novo-Oskochnoe and Kazach'e.[14]

Pursuant to this order from the *front* commander, the commander of the 5th Guards Tank Army issued instructions to the commander of the 2nd Guards 'Tatsinskaia' Tank

Corps Major General A. S. Burdeiny, the deputy commander of the 5th Guards Tank Army Major General K. G. Trufanov and the deputy commander of the 5th Guards 'Zimovniki' Mechanized Corps Major General Lebed':

> Throughout the night of 12.07.43 and the morning of 13.07.43, the enemy has been moving out an SS division [*sic*] from the south in the area of Ryndinka and Rzhavets, in addition to the 19th Panzer Division and 167th Infantry Division already present there. Its forward detachment with up to 30 tanks has already seized Shcholokovo. I order:
>
> The 5th Guards Mechanized Corps' 11th Mechanized Brigade and the 2nd Guards Tank Corps' 26th Guards Tank Brigade under the command of my deputy Major General Comrade Trufanov to drive the enemy from Shcholokovo by the end of the day 13.07.43, after which the 11th Mechanized Brigade is to assume a defensive position on the west bank of the Northern Donets, while the 26th Tank Brigade is to assemble in Mal. Iablonovo.[15]

However, the enemy stubbornly clung to their occupied positions, and this order could not be carried out. According to reconnaissance findings, the enemy had concentrated up to 150 tanks by 1900 13 July in the area of the villages Ryndinka, Vypolzovka and Shcholokovo. Therefore on 14 July at 0135, the commander of the 5th Guards Tank Army issued a number of orders to his corps commanders and to Trufanov.

Major General Trufanov received the order to prevent an enemy breakthrough on the line Shakhovo – Ryndinka – Vypolzovka – Avdeevka – Bol. Pod'iarugi – Novo-Khmelevoe with the 26th Guards Tank Brigade, the 5th Guards Mechanized Corps (minus its 10th Mechanized Brigade and the 24th Tank Brigade), the 53rd Guards Separate Tank Regiment, the 1st Separate Guards Motorcycle Regiment and the 689th Destroyer Anti-tank Artillery Regiment.[16] The commander of the 2nd Guards 'Tatsinskaia' Tank Corps was instructed "… by dawn on 14.07.43 to deploy the 25th Guards Tank Brigade in the area of Mal. Iablonovo and Plota, in readiness to operate toward Avdeevka, Ryndinka and Belenikhino."[17] Rotmistrov also ordered the 5th Guards Tank Army's artillery commander "… to assemble the 32nd Destroyer Brigade in Krasnoe, where it will be held in my reserve in readiness to operate to the south in the direction of Avdeevka and to the southwest in the direction of Belenikhino."[18]

The commander of the 69th Army issued Order No. 001017/OP to outline the assignments for his subordinate formations for 14 July:

> 1. The commander of the 48th Rifle Corps, in concert with the two tank brigades and one mechanized brigade of the 5th Guards Tank Army and the 27th Gun Artillery Brigade is to destroy the enemy in the Shcholokovo – Ryndinka – Shakhovo area and to assume a strong line of defense along the western bank of the Northern Donets between Ryndinka and Shcholokovo.
>
> 2. The commander of the 5th Guards Tank Army's Mobile Group Major General Trufanov with the 1243rd, 532nd and 1853rd Destroyer Anti-tank Artillery Regiments, the 441st Separate Guards Mortar Regiment and the 348th Guards Mortar Regiment, in concert with the 48th Rifle Corps and the armor of

> the 5th Guards Tank Army is to destroy the enemy in the Ryndinka – Rzhavets – Vypolzovka area.
>
> 3. The commander of the 35th Guards Rifle Corps, through active measures on its right and left flanks, is to cooperate in the destruction of the enemy in the Ryndinka – Vypolzovka – Rzhavets area.
>
> 4. The attack will begin at 0500 14.07.43.
>
> 5. The organization of cooperation between the acting units rests upon my deputy Major General Trufanov.[19]

The commander of the 48th Rifle Corps personally organized the preparatory work to implement this order. He visited the command post of the 81st Guards Rifle Division at Shakhovo. Corps and divisional documents establish that Rogozny's plan was the destruction of the enemy southeast of Shakhovo and the recovery of the positions on the west bank of the Northern Donets at Shcholokovo and Ryndinka that had been lost by his corps. On 13 July at 2300 hours, the 48th Rifle Corps chief of staff Colonel Shcheglov sent Combat Order No. 001/OP to the commanders of the 89th and 81st Guards Rifle Divisions and the 26th Guards Tank Brigade, which laid out the essence of the operation: At dawn, the 89th Guards Rifle Division's 273rd Guards Rifle Regiment from the area northwest of Shcholokovo and the 81st Guards Rifle Division's 235th Guards Rifle Regiment from the woods northwest of Shcholokovo with the support of two tank companies of the 26th Tank Brigade were to drive the enemy from Shcholokovo.[20]

However, the effort to eliminate the enemy bridgehead on the west bank of the Northern Donets at Shcholokovo was unsuccessful. The assigned units were simply too weak. The four rifle divisions of the 48th Rifle Corps (the 81st, 89th and 93rd Guards and the 375th Rifle Divisions), which had been defending the so-called "pocket" between the Lipovyi and Northern Donets Rivers had all suffered heavy losses, and their surviving troops were extremely exhausted by the preceding days of fighting. For example, the 81st Guards Rifle Division, which was defending the vital sector between Shakhovo and Ryndinka, had only recently emerged from encirclement north of Belgorod, losing all its artillery in the process.

A combat dispatch from the commander of the 81st Guards Rifle Division Major General I. K. Morozov to the commander of the 69th Army on 13 July 1943 testifies to the division's condition:

> The 81st Guards Rifle Division has been involved in bitter and stubborn fighting between 5 – 13.07.43. The division conducted particularly heavy fighting in encirclement in the region of Belgorod. As a result of these battles, the division has lost a large number of men and a large amount of equipment.
>
> The men are physically exhausted, since while fighting in the area of Belgorod, they were without food or even water for 2-3 days.
>
> In connection with the limited quantity of motor and horse-drawn transport and the greatly extended supply lines, the division does not have the possibility to supply the units fully with ammunition and rations.
>
> In the fighting, the division has lost all of its divisional artillery and almost all of its regimental artillery. On 13.07.43 the division had up to 3,000 men reporting for duty, but part of them (approximately 20%) are unarmed.

> The division has no anti-tank means (45mm guns or anti-tank rifles), and only a few light and heavy machine guns remain.
>
> From all that has been stated above and in order to preserve the future combat capability of the division, I request the withdrawal of the division to allow the possibility for the men to recuperate. ...[21]

The following example bears witness to the difficulties of supplying the units with ammunition during the fighting. The 305th Rifle Division had been marched from Korocha into the first echelon of the 69th Army. The division was 70% below its authorized allowance of horses. Thus, when it had been forced to retreat from its previously occupied positions, it had left behind six 76mm guns and two 122mm howitzers, as well as a quarter of its ammunition, "... which we couldn't move, although we took all possible measures to do so, even to the point of giving each man a shell to carry."[22]

Levels of stress and fatigue were rising among the troops, who had experienced bloody fighting for nine days in a row without interruption and were now facing the growing threat of encirclement. The mass flight of troops from the front lines without order, which started on 12 July, had not been fully stopped. Blocking detachments on 13 July alone detained 1,841 men.[23] A special communiqué from the 69th Army's SMERSH counterintelligence department to the army's Military Council on the work of the blocking detachments between 12 and 17 July 1943 provides some details:

> ... in the process of combat operations there were cases of entire batteries and companies from the 92nd Guards and 305th Rifle Divisions and the 290th Mortar Regiment voluntarily abandoning the battlefield. For example, in the area of Novaia Slobodka on 14 July, three elements of the 305th Rifle Division were detained by a blocking detachment, specifically: a battery of 76mm guns, a howitzer battery and a sapper company.
>
> Another blocking detachment in the area of Samoilovka detained 3 mortar batteries of the 290th Mortar Regiment.
>
> A blocking detachment in the vicinity of Kashcheevo detained two wagon trains of the 92nd Guards Rifle Division, numbering 25 carts and 200 men."[24]

The army leadership tried every measure to restore order. Here's one of the first orders signed by Major General V. S. Vensky, who had only just arrived in his new post as the 69th Army's chief of staff:

> To the commanders of the 48th Rifle Corps and 35th Guards Rifle Corps.
>
> Copy to the chief of staff of the Voronezh Front.
>
> 69th Army headquarters Order No. 001028/op from 14 July 1943 at 2120.
>
> Owing to the fact that systematic control has not been organized within the units, and the personnel have not been made accountable, cases of individual

soldiers and even whole groups of soldiers leaving their combat positions with their weapons have been observed.

The Army commander has ordered:

1. Immediately establish systematic control over the personnel, which excludes possible cases of flight from the combat positions.
2. In each division, select a necessary number of thoroughly checked soldiers, and junior and senior commanders, and organize them into blocking detachments.
3. The blocking detachments must strictly keep watch, so that not a single military serviceman leaves for the rear without corresponding authorization for this. Immediately detain all military personnel who have abandoned their combat positions, organize them into teams, identify them and return them to their units.
4. Acknowledge receipt [of this order]. Begin execution of this order at 1200 15.07.43.[25]

Full control over the situation was not gained until 16 July, after the divisions of the 48th Rifle Corps were withdrawn to a new line of defense. According to the above cited SMERSH special communiqué, its blocking detachments between 12 and 17 July inclusively detained 6,956 men from the ranks and command staff, who had abandoned the battlefield or emerged from enemy encirclement, including 2,276 from the 92nd Guards Rifle Division, 1,502 from the 305th Rifle Division, 599 from the 183rd Rifle Division, 398 from the 81st Guards Rifle Division, 386 from the 89th Rifle Division, 350 from the 107th Rifle Division, 200 each from the 93rd Guards Rifle Division and the 290th Mortar Regiment, and 101 from the 375th Rifle Division, for a total of 6,228 men. The remaining 728 detained men belonged to other units and divisions. The communiqué notes that after 15 July, the number of detained men fell sharply in comparison with the first days of the blocking detachments' work.[26]

It was under these conditions that the 48th Rifle Corps commander Major General Z. Z. Rogozny had to engage the enemy. He was a well-prepared general, who back in the 1930s had graduated from two military academies. Rogozny had started the war as chief of staff to Southwest Front's 151st Rifle Corps and by February 1943 had risen to the post of chief of staff to the 69th Army; however, after the bitter results of the spring 1943 Khar'kov offensive operation, he had been removed from this post. He took command of the 48th Rifle Corps at the beginning of June 1943. During the defensive fighting at Kursk, his corps headquarters temporarily lost control over its divisions, which were nearly encircled. With considerable skill, the corps commander managed to withdraw his divisions from the threatened encirclement to a new prepared line. However, Rogozny received a formal rebuke from the *front* commander Vatutin for his "poor control" over his troops.

The brigades of the 2nd Guards 'Tatsinskaia' Tank Corps, which were also defending in the 48th Rifle Corps' sector, were in a no less difficult situation. The staff account of the 2nd Guards Tank Corps describes the situation it faced at the end of 13 July:

Major General Z. Z. Rogozny, commander of the 69th Army's 48th Rifle Corps (1945 photo). (TsAMO)

> … The corps received an order from the 5th Guards Tank Army commander to prevent an enemy breakthrough from the directions of Storozhevoe, Belenikhino, Kleimenovo, Shcholokovo and Ryndinka.
>
> … The corps commander decided to establish a firm defense on the line Vinogradovka – Belenikhino – Shakhovo – Pokrovka. On the right flank – the 4th Guards Tank Brigade, in the center – the 4th Guards Motorized Rifle Brigade, on the left flank – the 26th Guards Tank Brigade. In the Maloe Iablonovo – Plota area – the 25th Guards Tank Brigade in reserve. Artillery was centralized.
>
> … Regrouping in the night, the units at 0200 [14 July] moved into their combat sectors and set about fortifying their defenses.[27]

This account notes that by this point, the 2nd Guards Tank Corps had a total of 80 operational tanks, including 12 T-34 tanks and 16 T-70 tanks in the 4th Guards Tank Brigade; 28 T-34 tanks, 11 T-70 tanks and two Mk-IV Churchill tanks in the 26th Guards Tank Brigade, and only two T-34 tanks and nine T-70 tanks in the reserve 25th Guards Tank Brigade.[28]

According to the combat dispatches of the 69th Army, the front lines in this sector hadn't changed by the evening of 13 July. However, the situation began to deteriorate sharply on 14 July, when as we shall see, the divisions of the II SS Panzer Corps broke through our defenses in the area of Belenikhino and Vinogradovka.

In the early morning hours of 14 July, the formations of the Fourth Panzer Army initiated a simultaneous pincer attack from the north and south, with the intention of encircling the 48th Rifle Corps. Between 0400 and 0500 hours, units of the *Das Reich* and 167th Infantry Divisions (the northern grouping) went on the attack in three directions: the 3rd SS Panzergrenadier Regiment *Deutschland* attacked from Ivanovskii

Vyselok toward Vinogradovka and from Iasnaia Poliana – Kalinin area towards Belenikhino, while the 167th Infantry Division attacked towards Ivanovka and Leski from Sobachevskii.

The brigades of the 2nd Guards Tank Corps and the 183rd Rifle Division were defending here. The 4th Guards Motorized Rifle Brigade and the 4th Guards Tank Brigade were in the area of Belenikhino, and the 25th Guards Tank Brigade was still in Vinogradovka. The sector south of Belenikhino was being held by the 183rd Rifle Division's 295th and 227th Rifle Regiments. The 375th Rifle Division's 1241st Rifle Regiment and the 2nd and 3rd Rifle Battalions of the 1245th Rifle Regiment were defending Leski, Teterevino and Hill 210.7. For all these units and divisions, 14 July became one of the most difficult days of the battle. In the afternoon of 14 July, the SS in cooperation with the 167th Infantry Division managed to break the resistance of our forces in this area. Under the pressure of superior forces, our units were forced to fall back to new lines in hard and bloody fighting.

The time and circumstances of an enemy breakthrough is always an important moment, but one very difficult to analyze. Especially if as in this case several units from different divisions are defending on the targeted sector of the front. Going through the archives, it is difficult to obtain a clear and balanced determination of the causes for the breakthrough, because all the documents are based upon officers' verbal reports to higher command. Nevertheless, whatever the strength the enemy possessed and whatever the situation of the defending forces at the given moment, a breakthrough is always a critical occurrence.

Lieutenant Korchinkov, commander of a company in the 26th Guards Tank Brigade (2nd Guards 'Tatsinskaia' Tank Corps) by his tank. (Author's personal archive)

Higher headquarters or appointed commissions investigate such situations in detail. They base their findings primarily on the accounts, communications, instructions and orders of the units that came under the attack. The findings are then usually incorporated into a summary account of the operation. Today, these documents are accessible to scholars. However, when researching archival materials, one often has to acknowledge that the conclusions in these reports are not always accurate and balanced. After all, when reporting on the circumstances of the enemy's penetration into the combat positions, the officers of each unit proceeded from their own personal assessment of the situation, so at times their accounts lack objectivity. However, the work of these investigative commissions during the war was essentially a formality. So today it is not an easy matter to sort things out.

We'll try, however, to take a look at what happened on the afternoon of 14 July in the area of Belenikhino, Leski and Teterevino through the eyes of the participants in those events. Where possible, we'll supplement their stories with available combat documents.

A report from the II SS Panzer Corps states:

> ... at 0400 [0600 Moscow time], the corps went on the attack with the *Das Reich* Division in the sector south and east of Iasnaia Poliana through Belenikhino to the east, in order to seize the river southwest of Pravorot'. After savage street-fighting, which extended from 0700 [0800] to mid-day, the village [Belenikhino] fell, and the reinforced panzer regiment was able after an artillery preparation to attack the enemy flanks at 1700 [1900].[29]

On 14 July at 0300, Colonel A. K. Brazhnikov's 4th Guards Tank Brigade was supposed to turn over its sector to Colonel V. L. Savchenko's 4th Motorized Rifle Brigade, and then move to the southwestern outskirts of Vinogradovka. Having taken over Lieutenant Colonel S. M. Bulygin's 25th Guards Tank Brigade's positions there, it was to set up a defense together with the 1500th Destroyer Anti-tank Artillery Regiment. The 25th Guards Tank Brigade was then to move into the corps commander reserve on the western edge of Plota and in the eastern part of Maloe Iablonovo.

However, the unit rotation at Belenikhino was still underway when the SS struck. Major Kurchenko's 2nd Tank Battalion of the 4th Guards Tank Brigade remained in the village to strengthen the arriving 4th Guards Motorized Rifle Brigade. As the 1st Tank Battalion and motorized rifle battalion of this brigade were moving out for the march, they were attacked by the assaulting panzer group of the SS Panzergrenadier Division *Das Reich*. Fighting erupted. The Red Army tankers, having lost nine tanks, began to retreat toward Maloe Iablonovo. Enemy Panzergrenadiers, infiltrating through the woods southwest of Vinogradovka, encircled our motorized rifle battalion in the village. However, the ring wasn't solid, and the motorized riflemen emerged from it on the northwest outskirts of Ivanovka, where they linked up with the retreating elements of the 4th Guards Motorized Rifle Brigade from Belenikhino.

Fighting in the area of Belenikhino and Ivanovka continued until approximately 1800 hours, and all this time enemy aircraft intensively bombed the defenses of our forces. During one airstrike, the radio set of the 4th Guards Tank Brigade's headquarters was destroyed; communications with corps headquarters was interrupted, and control over the units had to be handled through the brigade commander's tank.

Under the pressure of superior forces, elements of the 4th Guards Tank Brigade and the 4th Guards Motorized Rifle Brigade began to retreat toward Ivanovka at approximately 1640 hours, leaving the left flank of the 25th Guards Tank Brigade in Vinogradovka exposed. The *Luftwaffe* heavily bombed this area. The weakened elements of our motorized infantry couldn't hold Ivanovka and continued to retreat toward Hill 234.9. The brigades of the 2nd Guards 'Tatsinskaia' Tank Corps, which had fallen back from Belenikhino, by 2000 had taken up a defense along the western edges of a ravine between the villages of Zhimolostnoe and Maloe Iablonovo, and on a nameless hill lying 1.5 kilometers from Zhimolostnoe. Elements of the 25th Guards Tank Brigade also arrived in this area at this time. Thus, by 2000 hours, the forces that had been driven from their lines in the area of Vinogradovka, Belenikhino and Leski halted their retreat, repulsed an enemy attack, and assumed an active defense. Scouts reported a concentration of enemy armor in the area of Belenikhino, Ivanovka and Leski, which was plainly preparing to resume the attack at the nearest possible time.

Having broken through the defenses of the 'Tatsinskaia' Tank Corps in the area of Belenikhino, the enemy obtained the possibility to attack the flanks of our rifle and motorized infantry units situated on the left of the 2nd Guards Tank Corps. From the unit diary of Colonel A. M. Shchekal's 6th Guards Motorized Rifle Brigade of the 10th Tank Corps:

> At 0900 after an artillery preparation and a massed air attack, the enemy attacked with infantry and tanks our right-hand neighbor – the 2nd Guards 'Tatsinskaia' Tank Corps, which could not withstand the blow and began to retreat toward Maloe Iablonovo and Plota, thereby exposing our right flank. The 456th Guards Motorized Rifle Battalion was outflanked on the right. The battalion had already suffered heavy losses in previous fighting, so therefore it could not offer adequate resistance to the enemy and began rolling back toward Maloe Iablonovo. During the retreat the battalion's chief of staff Senior Lieutenant Bobrochy was killed.
>
> Meanwhile, the neighboring 455th Guards Motorized Rifle Battalion [on the left] managed to hold on to its positions, and until 1800 hours both battalions continued to repulse German attacks: the 455th Guards Motorized Rifle Battalion on its sector, and the 456th Guards Motorized Rifle Battalion now at Maloe Iablonovo. After 1800 hours, both battalions fell back to Plota. In this fighting, the brigade lost 320 men killed and wounded, having destroyed 19 enemy tanks and up to 500 enemy soldiers and officers.
>
> In this combat, the gun crews of Senior Sergeants Zorin and Gedzun distinguished themselves. Repulsing enemy tank attacks, each crew knocked out two tanks. All the crews with their guns were put out of action.
>
> Reaching the area of Plota, the brigade was withdrawn into the second echelon of defense in the region of Krasnoe.[30]

On 14 July at 0400 hours, from the area of Kalinin the enemy 167th Infantry Division attacked the boundary between the 183rd and 375th Rifle Divisions in the direction of Ivanovka. It struck the flank of Major L. I. Matiushenko's 295th Rifle Regiment of the

Lieutenant General (at the time of the battle, Colonel) P. D. Govorunenko, commander of the 48th Rifle Corps' 375th Rifle Division (1940 photo). (Author's personal archive)

183rd Rifle Division. Recalled the commander of the 183rd Rifle Division's 227th Rifle Regiment, Major V. E. Sazhinov:

> In the afternoon, the situation became extremely difficult. The foe again [attacked] toward Belenikhino Station, and our right flank came under assault. Soon enemy tanks were moving along the road from Belenikhino to Ivanovka, and bitter fighting broke out, which continued for several hours. The regiment's sapper platoon managed to emplace several dozen anti-tank mines. The regiment's battery of 76mm guns, the destroyer anti-tank battery of 45mm guns, and the two companies of anti-tank riflemen fought staunchly and courageously. [Approximately] 7 or 8 [enemy] tanks were knocked out, and the enemy halted the tank attack toward Ivanovka.
>
> By evening, the enemy had outflanked the village to the north, and a large number of enemy tanks had broken through in the sector of the 295th Rifle Regiment, lunging toward Shakhovo. I managed to get in touch with the division commander and reported that the enemy had broken through, and that more than 120 enemy tanks were moving along the farm road toward Shakhovo. Within several minutes, *Katiushi* [multiple rocket launchers] and artillery deep in the rear opened a heavy fire on the enemy tanks. Twilight was gathering, and soon the fire of our artillery came to a stop. The enemy had seized Ivanovka, and we had suffered heavy losses and our badly disorganized combat formations had been nearly encircled. At night the regiment withdrew to its previous lines in the area of Novoselovka, where other units were already concentrating.[31]

Regiments of Colonel P. D. Govorunenko's 375th Rifle Division managed to prevent a further penetration of the 48th Rifle Corps' right flank. Enemy motorized infantry of the 167th Infantry Division moved out from the area of Ivanovka with the support of 20 panzers and at 1330 hours tried to seize the village of Leski. The Germans managed to infiltrate to the eastern outskirts of the village, but were halted there by the organized defense of the 1241st Rifle Regiment's 3rd Rifle Battalion. From the 69th Army's log of combat operations:

> The 375th Rifle Division was defending a line from the railroad hut (1 km north of Teterevino) through Hill 209.7 … to Teterevino. [Elements] of the division, defending between the barracks (1.5 km southwest of Leski) and Teterevino throughout the day of 14.07.43 fought stubbornly, repulsing enemy infantry and tank attacks on the right flank. The adversary, having concentrated major forces of tanks and infantry in the area of Kalinin and the woods surrounding it, went on the attack toward Ivanovka and Leski and pushed the right-hand neighbor – the 183rd Rifle Division – to the east, and seized Ivanovka and the northern outskirts of Leski.
>
> The units of the 183rd Rifle Division, defending in the area of Leski, fell back, having failed to consolidate on the hills northeast and east of Leski, which created the threat of an enemy attack on the division's flank from the north; in the afternoon of 14.07.43, the division had to fight with its flank regiment – the 1241st Rifle Regiment – refused to face the northwest and north. The enemy, encountering active resistance, did not cease to extend to the south, but exerted his main effort to the northeast, toward Hill 234.9 and Maloe Iablonovo. By the end of the day 14.07.43, he [the enemy] succeeded in reaching the western outskirts of Maloe Iablonovo with tanks and groups of submachine gunners, and thereby in crossing the narrow Sukhaia Plota ravine.
>
> The division, holding its positions on its main line, [also] became involved in bitter fighting with its two best battalions and six guns of the divisional artillery positioned east of Shakhovo, covering Shakhovo from the direction of Ryndinka and Shcholokovo. Thus, the division on 14.07.43 was dispersed and forced to repel enemy attacks not only from the front, but also from the north and east.
>
> Communications with corps headquarters on this day were being handled by radio; there were frequent interruptions in operation, and at 2200, in connection with the relocation of the corps' command post, [the signal] was completely lost.[32]

That evening, the II SS Panzer Corps reported:

> With a swift attack, at 1715 [1915 Moscow time] Ivanovka was taken, at 1825 [2025] – Hill 234.9, and the offensive continued to the northeast, where fighting continued against hostile tank forces 2.5 km west of Zhimolostnoe until darkness. The division is continuing the attack at night, in order to reach its goal of Pravorot' as quickly as possible.[33]

★ ★ ★

Fighting against the enemy's southern grouping – the 7th and 19th Panzer Divisions with the 168th Infantry Division in the area of Shcholokovo and Rzhavets, and the 6th Panzer Division on the line Vypolzovka – Hill 222.1 – Aleksandrovka – didn't cease even during the night before 14 July. The 69th Army headquarters noted in an operational summary on the morning of 14 July: "At 0100 the sixth enemy attack with a force of up 60 tanks and two infantry regiments with air support was repulsed. Vypolzovka remains in the possession of our forces."[34]

But the situation changed rapidly with the coming of dawn on 14 July. The 69th Army headquarters reported at 0815 hours:

> 1. At 0730 up to 50 tanks, including ten Panzer VI broke through in the direction of Avdeevka from Vypolzovka, followed by up to a battalion of infantry. Nine tanks have reached Hill 222.1.
>
> 2. Our artillery is engaging the tanks that have broken through. The battalion of the 12th Motorized Rifle Brigade, which was defending Vypolzovka, is falling back to the line Avdeevka – Hill 222.1.[35]

Elements of Colonel N. V. Grishchenko's 11th Guards Mechanized Brigade and Hero of the Soviet Union Colonel G. Ia. Borisenko's 12th Guards Mechanized Brigade of the 5th Guards Mechanized Corps were resisting the main attack in this region. "The tenacity of the motorized infantry of the 11th Guards and 12th Guards Mechanized Brigades, defending the line Ryndinka – Shipy – Rzhavets –Avdeevka – Hill 222.1, must be mentioned," emphasized the 5th Guards Mechanized Corps' headquarters in its report on the combat; "For example, at 1700 14.07.43 enemy tanks overran the combat positions of the 12th Guards Mechanized Brigade … [but] the infantry didn't waver and let the tanks pass through their positions."[36]

From the enemy 19th Panzer Division's description of combat operations written by the staff of this division:

> Despite desperate resistance, *Gruppe* von Meintse (*Major* von Meintse had taken over command of the 74th Panzergrenadier Regiment, replacing the severely wounded *Oberstleutnant* Richter), which had received the freed-up reconnaissance battalion, occupied Shipy that night. Shipy is located on the slope of a heavily fortified chalk hill, from where the enemy could survey the surrounding terrain out to 10 km. These positions were being held by units of a mechanized brigade, which had placed their anti-tank guns in concealed positions, while the tanks had dug-in …[37]

A captured German *Obergefreiter*, Friedrich Wörhle from the 6th Panzer Division's 4th Panzergrenadier Regiment, under preliminary interrogation later yielded the following information to the 69th Army command, as revealed in Intelligence Summary No. 9 from 16 July at 2200 hours:

> In the course of 14-15 July, the 4th Panzergrenadier Regiment took part in the fighting in the area of Hill 222.1 and Vypolzovka. Where the 11th Panzer Regiment and the 114th Panzergrenadier Regiment were operating at this time, the prisoner

> doesn't know precisely, but tanks of the 6th Panzer Division's panzer regiment took active part in the attack on Hill 222.1 together with his regiment. The prisoner knows that the 7th and 19th Panzer Divisions are operating to the left [from the vantage point of the attackers] of their 6th Panzer Division.
>
> In addition, the prisoner indicated that at the start of the offensive, the division's panzer regiment numbered around 120 vehicles. The division's Panzergrenadier regiments consist of two battalions, with three motorized rifle companies and a heavy weapons company in each battalion. One battalion in each Panzergrenadier regiment has approximately 48 halftracks. At the start of the offensive, the companies of the Panzergrenadier regiments numbered 120-130 men.
>
> Over the [recent] fighting, the losses of the division amount to around 50 tanks and halftracks. The 1st Battalion of the 4th Panzergrenadier Regiment has lost up to 75% of its halftracks. Only 25-30 men remain in the companies of this battalion.
>
> On 12.07.43 the regiment received replacements numbering 20 men per battalion, consisting primarily of previously wounded men. There are up to 100 Ukrainians and Kazakhs in the regiment, some of which are being used for scouting under the command of German officers, some of which are being used as ammo bearers and wagon drivers, and some are being used to police the area of the shallow rear.[38]

In Operational Briefing No. 00286 for 1300 hours on 14 July, the headquarters of the 69th Army observed:

> … 3. The 35th Guards Rifle Corps: units of the corps in cooperation with Major General Trufanov's mobile group continue to repulse enemy tank and infantry attacks in the direction of Krasnoe Znamia, Avdeevka, Aleksandrovka and Novo-Khmelevoe.
>
> After regrouping, the enemy with a force of up to a regiment of infantry and the support of up to 150 tanks resumed the offensive in the direction of Krasnoe Znamia, Avdeevka, Aleksandrovka and Novo-Khmelevoe. At 1200, the infantry and tank attack was repulsed. Up to 40 enemy tanks were knocked out.[39]

Six hours later, at 1900 hours 14 July, the 69th Army headquarters reported:

> The 92nd Guards Rifle Division in cooperation with Major General Trufanov's mobile group (the 11th and 12th Mechanized Rifle Brigades) has been conducting delaying, defensive fighting with the attacking enemy.
>
> By 1630 the further advance of the enemy had been stopped, and units of the division were firmly defending the line Avdeevka – Hill 222.1 – Hill 241.5. Our units knocked out 10 enemy tanks in the area of Vypolzovka.[40]

The tankers of the 53rd Guards Separate Tank Regiment under the command of Major N. A. Kurnosov fought steadfastly and courageously. The regiment was located in the second echelon, behind the units of the 92nd Guards Rifle Division and the 12th Mechanized Rifle Brigade. Upon the order of the commander of the 5th Guards

Tank Army's mobile detachment [Major General Trufanov], the day before on 13 July the 1st and 3rd Companies of the regiment had taken up a defense in the village of Aleksandrovka; the 2nd and 4th Companies – in the area of the villages of Novo-Khmelevoe, Avdeevka and Aleksandrovka. The regiment's combat diary describes the intensity of the fighting and the determination of its tank crews:

> 14 July. At 0900 the enemy began a simultaneous attack on Aleksandrovka and Avdeevka. Ten enemy tanks were destroyed in the fighting for Aleksandrovka. Under the pressure of superior enemy forces, [the regiment] was forced to abandon the village. Of the 14 tanks of the combined company [Author's note: created from the remnants of two companies], only the tank of company commander Senior Lieutenant Loginov emerged from the combat; all the remaining tanks were destroyed.
>
> The crew under the command of Junior Lieutenant Amel'chenko, which burned in their tank, fought heroically. The enemy encircled Aleksandrovka; while withdrawing from the encirclement, the commander of the 1st Tank Company Senior Lieutenant Lebedensky was killed, as were Senior Lieutenant Kutepov and Lieutenant Mishenko, who burned in their tanks together with their crews.
>
> The 2nd Tank Company under the command of Senior Lieutenant Ligman was set up in ambush in the village of Avdeevka. At 1800 an enemy tank appeared, and within radio range of our tanks, initiated negotiations. The company commander sent the tank and crew under the command of Lieutenant Kosichenko out to meet the Germans. The Germans opened fire – two more German tanks had taken up ambush positions. With their first [return] shot, Kosichenko's crew knocked out a German tank, and then a second one. But a third enemy tank concealed in some bushes damaged our tank. The shell's impact on the turret jammed the gun. The tank commander decided to drive into the enemy's positions and destroy the enemy with its machine gun and tracks. As a result of this unusual action, the tank managed to destroy up to a platoon of soldiers and capture six soldiers and one officer. After this the tankers walked back to their own unit's position.
>
> For 14 July the regiment's losses consisted of 16 T-34s, and 30 men killed and wounded. [In return] it destroyed 7 Tiger tanks, 14 medium tanks, and captured 6 soldiers and one officer.[41]

The combat operations during the day clearly demonstrated the desire of the Fourth Panzer Army command to encircle the formations of the 48th Rifle Corps. Giving the mission to the SS *Das Reich* Division to continue the attack toward Pravorot' after breaking through our defenses in the area of Belenikhino Station, the commander of the II SS Panzer Corps Paul Hausser tried from the very beginning to secure the flanks of the breakthrough and to create an outer ring of encirclement. In order to create the inner ring of the encirclement together with the 167th Infantry Division, *Das Reich* was also attacking in the direction of Leski.

In the areas of Storozhevoe and Pravorot', the tank brigades of the 2nd and 29th Tank Corps were buttressing the defense of the rifle units. Enemy intelligence knew about this, and the foe recognized that it would be unable to breakthrough to these villages from the march without large losses. Accordingly, after reaching the approaches to Maloe Iablonovo at 1910 hours on 14 July, the chief of staff of the II SS Panzer Corps received a mission order for 15 July that cardinally changed the situation: The Fourth Panzer Army was finally halting the attack toward Prokhorovka, and was now trying first of all to encircle the divisions of the 48th Rifle Corps between the Lipovyi and Northern Donets Rivers.

The new order directed the SS Panzer Corps "to concentrate all of its combat resources and panzer forces in order to crush the bitterly defending enemy north of Leski and to reach the Zhimolostnoe – Pravorot' road, at which point "it should be prepared to pivot to the south."[42] The order provided further detailed assignments:

> [The *Das Reich*] Division is to continue the offensive throughout the night of 14 July, and to seize Pravorot' and the hill north of this settlement. The hill must be held. The division will then hastily regroup for the advance of its panzer group, strengthened with grenadier units, to the south together with the SS Division *Adolf Hitler*. After the capture of Pravorot', the Division *Adolf Hitler* is to break through to Iamki and to occupy it. The left wing is to hold the present positions. The panzer group (the panzer regiment, one company of halftracks, strengthened by heavy weapons, and an artillery platoon of assault guns) is to move out at 0230 from the occupied sector and to reach, through Ivanovka, the sector west of Hill 234.9, which lies 2 km east of Ivanovka. The panzer group is directly subordinate to the commander of the II SS Panzer Corps and will together with units of the SS *Das Reich* Division breakthrough to the south. The road for the tanks from Hill 234.9 to Maloe Iablonovo should be scouted.[43]

From Order No. 32 of the 167th Infantry Division's commander, dated 14 July 1943:

> 1. The enemy is stubbornly defending its previous positions on the west bank of the Northern Donets River, west of Rozhdestvenka, and on the hills west of the Kursk – Belgorod railroad. The diversionary attacks of his infantry have been repulsed, and the heavy movement of his units and formations toward the areas of Shakhovo, Leski and Maloe Iablonovo allows us to conclude that the enemy is trying to flee from the threat of encirclement.
>
> The reinforced 339th Grenadier Regiment by the evening of 14.07.43 had reached the railroad line 2 km west of Belenikhino with its left flank. The enemy lost 67 men killed and 51 men taken prisoner.
>
> 2. Neighbors:
>
> - on the right: the 168th Infantry Division [on] 14.07.43 has reached the northern outskirts of Gostishchevo.
>
> - on the left: the SS Panzergrenadier Division *Reich*, advancing against enemy resistance, in the course of 14.07.43 emerged on the line: southern outskirts of Ivanovka – Hill 234.9, and will on 15.07.43 continue the attack in a southeastern direction.

> 3. The 167th Infantry Division is to neutralize the enemy in the area of Leski opposite the right flank of the II SS Panzer Corps, and is to assemble forces on the north [of its sector], so as to be ready to attack Leski with its reinforced left flank on 15.07.43.
>
> The boundary line for the II SS Panzer Corps: southern outskirts of Ivanovka – northern outskirts of Maloe Iablonovo. The reinforced 339th Grenadier Regiment, after replacing the II and III Battalions of the 331st Grenadier Regiment, is to take up positions to be ready on 15.07.43 to attack toward Leski with its strengthened left flank. Report to division headquarters on the readiness to attack.[44]

In addition to the four rifle divisions of the 48th Rifle Corps in the "pocket," there were formations of the 5th Guards Tank Army. The 5th Guards Mechanized Corps' 11th Guards and 12th Guards Mechanized Brigades were defending on the line of villages Shipy, Avdeevka and Vypolzovka. Casualty figures testify to the intensity of the fighting in their sector. Between 12 and 16 July, the 12th Guards Mechanized Brigade lost 244 killed and wounded, the 11th Guards Mechanized Brigade lost 1,417 men killed and wounded, including 414 on 13 July, 394 on 14 July, and 255 on 15 July.[45]

The situation of other units and formations, defending in the area between the two rivers, was no better. The 2nd Guards 'Tatsinskaia' Tank Corps, which was holding the areas of Belenikhino and Shakhovo, began the day of fighting with 80 operational tanks, but over the course of the day lost 22 tanks destroyed (of which, 11 were T-34s), and 651 men killed, wounded or missing in action.[46] The situation between the Lipovyi Donets and Northern Donets Rivers grew more alarming by the hour …

From a report by *Stavka* representative Marshal A. M. Vasilevsky to I. V. Stalin on the position of the 5th Guards Tank Army at 2100 hours on 14 July:

> The 5th Guards Mechanized Corps has been engaged in particularly stubborn fighting with three attacking enemy tank divisions along the sector of the front Shcholokovo – Vypolzovka – Avdeevka – Aleksandrovka.
>
> Between 0700 and 1400 hours, up to five enemy tank attacks have been repulsed here, primarily by our artillery, partially by our rocket artillery (firing over open sights) and tanks. On the part of the enemy, up to 200 tanks from the 19th, 6th and 7th Panzer Divisions took part. According to prisoner information, on the morning of 14 July the 19th Panzer Division had 40 tanks, the 6th Panzer Division – 80, and the 7th Panzer Division – around 100 tanks.
>
> By 1200 hours, enemy tanks had managed to break into the western part of Avdeevka and to seize Hill 222.1. The situation was fully restored at 1400 hours by a quickly organized counterattack. The enemy left 19 knocked-out tanks on our territory. The tankers and artillerymen of the 5th Guards Mechanized Corps are behaving splendidly in battle, [but] the infantry of the 92nd Rifle Division, which as a rule cannot withstand enemy tank attacks, are behaving much worse.
>
> Tank attacks undertaken by the enemy throughout the day southwest of Prokhorovka on the front Belenikhino – Teterevino have been driven back, with the exception of Belenikhino, where the enemy has penetrated into the western section of the village. Fighting is going on now to clear the enemy out of Belenikhino.

> We've initiated the withdrawal of Rotmistrov into the reserve with the aim of creating a new powerful fist. Today and tomorrow, the 29th Tank Corps will be withdrawn to the area of Pravorot' and Novoselovka.[47]

The situation of the 48th Rifle Corps in the pocket was complicated by the corps headquarters' inadequate control over its divisions. Communications with the subordinate units now and then were disrupted. The chief of signals of the 69th Army Colonel Makarov reported:

> It was almost impossible to establish an uninterrupted line of communications with the KP [command post] of the 48th Rifle Corps commander in the circumstances of that command post's frequent change of location, which is part of the corps' practice. Thus, over the last eleven hours (from 2000 12.07.43 until 0700 13.07.43), the KP has changed location 6 times (2000 12.07 – Shakhovo; 2200 12.07 – a ravine on the southern outskirts of Plota; 0330 13.07 – 2 km west of Maloe Iablonovo; 0500 – Hill 225.0; 0630 – Vasil'evka). At 0700 the headquarters left Vasil'evka – its [current] location has still not been established.
>
> This information was reported to my assistant, Comrade Maksimov, over the telephone from Plota at 0820 13.07. Major Maksimov and my deputy Lieutenant Colonel Bogdanov have been specially ordered to the area of the 48th Rifle Corps in order to establish communications with it. I consider it possible to assume that Plota is the current location of the KP of the 48th Rifle Corps commander.[48]

The establishment of communications between the headquarters of the divisions and the superior headquarters is the duty of the corps commander and chief of staff. However, in the emerging situation with communications, they were not solely guilty. The 48th Corps command post was bombed several times on 12 July, both by the *Luftwaffe* and our own air force. Thus, Major General Rogozny had been forced to change the location of his KP on the evening of 12 July after two air strikes by our own aircraft (at 1830 – 22 Il-2 and at 2030 – six Il-2) and enemy air raids. On subsequent days (13 and 14 July), his headquarters and observation post in the area of Leski was heavily bombed by our own planes and the enemy.

Lacking communications with the 48th Rifle Corps command from the evening of 12 July, the *front* chief of staff Lieutenant General Ivanov, who was personally responsible for the situation in the sector of the 69th Army, took measures to prevent the corps' loss of control over the divisions. On the night of 13 July, he operationally subordinated the 89th Guards Rifle Division and a rifle battalion of the 375th Rifle Division to the commander of the 81st Guards Rifle Division, Major General I. K. Morozov, and ordered the creation of a Detached Group of Army Forces from them, with the task to prevent an enemy breakthrough in their sector of the defense.

Unfortunately, even at such critical moments, not all officers understood their level of personal responsibility. From Order No. 084/op of 13 July by the commander of the Detached Group of Army Forces:

Despite the order of the *front*'s chief of staff … regarding the operational subordination of the forces of the 81st Guards and 89th Guards Rifle Division and a battalion of the 375th Rifle Division to the commander of the 81st Guards Rifle Division Major General Morozov, there have been attempts to reposition units and formations without my authorization. [On] 13.07.43, the chief of staff of the 89th Guards Rifle Division issued an order to the units of the 89th Guards Rifle Division to give up its occupied line and fall back, so as to take up a defense by 0630 in the sector: (excl.) Kuz'minka – Shipy – Pokrovka – Kireev – undesignated hills, without any justifications for this and without informing me. As a result, the 267th Guards Rifle Regiment, regiment commander Lieutenant Colonel Sereda, on the morning of 13.07.43 abandoned its sector of defense, and only after my interference was it stopped on the march and returned to its previous defensive positions.

I order:

Without my authorization and order, do not reposition in any case not only regiments and battalions, but even individual guns.

Any attempts by units of the division to abandon their combat sectors without my authorization will be considered a violation of my order and the order of the *front* commander, and the guilty parties will be turned over to the judgment of a military tribunal.[49]

17

The Withdrawal of the 69th Army's 48th Rifle Corps from Threatened Encirclement between the Lipovyi and Northern Donets Rivers, 15 July 1943

In the course of fighting on 13 and 14 July, the situation between the Lipovyi and Northen Donets Rivers became critical. The semi-encircled formations of the 48th Rifle Corps were experiencing ammunition shortages. In this exceptionally difficult situation, the corps headquarters was not able to maintain control over its formations and attached units. The 69th Army headquarters, on its part, could not determine the position of its divisions and thus could not organize the necessary artillery support for them.

The constant interruptions in communications and the enemy's powerful pressure on the flanks of the 48th Rifle Corps forced the 69th Army commander to create a special command group with the task to straighten out the situation in the corps. From the army's command and control staff, a special group was detached under the command of deputy commander Major General Trufanov, Military Council member Guards Major General Shchelakovsky, and an officer of the army headquarters' operational department – in order to reestablish control over the corps.

The special group departed for the village of Plota at 2000 14.07.43 in order to organize the corps' defense. At the same time, the army commander ordered:

1. To detach no less than 20 guns and set them up for firing over open sights at tanks in front of Hill 225.0 and to retake the road from Leski.
2. To detach a rifle regiment from the roster of the 375th Rifle Division and to deploy it on the western outskirts of the woods, lying southwest and west of Iamki.
3. To deploy no less than two artillery battalions of the 93rd Guards Rifle Division southwest of Shcholokovo to combat tanks.
4. To place two battalions of the 93rd Guards Rifle Division in reserve in the area of Shcholokovo.
5. To deploy no less than two artillery battalions of the 89th Guards Rifle Division in Kleimenovo.

The group's task: under no circumstances allow a further advance of enemy tanks and infantry from the directions of Leski and Shcholokovo.[1]

However, around the time this order was issued, the situation had already changed sharply. The chronology of events differs between German and Russian sources, but the essence of what happened is similarly set forth by both sides. In the documents of the II SS Panzer Corps, there is mention of a report from the III Panzer Corps that said it had already seized Shakhovo by 2130.

The headquarters of the 26th Guards Tank Brigade reported in more detail and somewhat differently about what had happened:

> 1. The enemy with one group of up to 30 tanks and up to a regiment of motorized infantry [Panzergrenadiers] from the directions of Kleimenovo and Shcholokovo by 2400 14.07.43 seized Shakhovo. Another group of up to 40 tanks with motorized infantry from the direction of Ivanovka captured Hill 234.9 and the Sloevoe grove.
>
> During the night the enemy concentrated up to 50 tanks and up to a regiment of motorized infantry in the area of Shakhovo.
>
> At 0100 15.07.43, a column of up to 50 tanks was advancing from Shakhovo toward Leski.
>
> At 0600 15.07.43, the enemy with two groups of tanks and motorized infantry was attacking Plota and Maloe Iablonovo from the south and southwest.
>
> At 0850 the enemy had taken full possession of Maloe Iablonovo and Plota, to where he has urgently been bringing up tanks and motorized infantry from the area of Shakhovo.[2]

The *Stavka* and the Voronezh Front command accurately assessed the actions of Army Group South's command. It was clear that the enemy, having failed to achieve the original goals of Operation Citadel, was now trying to achieve only more limited objectives, and at the same time was striving to secure the now inevitable withdrawal of its forces from its advanced positions.

The preparation of a general Soviet counteroffensive on the southern face of the Kursk bulge had already been initiated on 12-14 July. Orders were issued on the regrouping of the forces of General I. S. Konev's Steppe Front, and on preparations to assume the offensive. On 12 July, the 47th Army, the 3rd Guards Mechanized Corps and the 1st Mechanized Corps had begun moving out for the areas of Novyi Oskol and Velikomikhailovka. On this same day at 1655, *Stavka* Directive No. 30148 went out to the commander of the Steppe Front on assembling the 53rd Army, which would be required to march on foot, in the area of Skorodnoe by the morning of 16 July, where it would deploy together with the 1st Mechanized Corps.

For the general counteroffensive, it was extremely desirable to maintain a bridgehead in the area between the Lipovyi and Northern Donets Rivers. This salient would provide an excellent springboard for deep strikes against the right flank of the enemy's Prokhorovka grouping in the directions of Plota, Gostishchevo and Iakovlevo, as well as against the flank of Army Detachment Kempf, from the lines occupied by the 35th Guards Rifle and 48th Rifle Corps. Moreover, *Stavka*'s reserve armies were already approaching.

Therefore the commands of the 5th Guards Tank Army and the 69th Army took every possible measure to hold onto the bridgehead in the area between the rivers. However, those armies no longer had the strength. Because of heavy losses, their subordinate formations were labouring to resist the enemy attacks. On the night of 14 July, Rotmistrov sent his final reserve – the 10th Guards Mechanized Brigade – to the assistance of the 2nd Guards Tank Corps.

At 0240 hours on 15 July, Rotmistrov sent the following instructions to corps commander Major General Burdeiny:

> In connection with the current situation, as a result of which the enemy has seized the settlements of Vinogradovka and Ivanovka and reached Hill 234.9,
> I am ordering:
> 1. The 2nd Guards 'Tatsinskaia' Tank Corps is to defend Zhimolostnoe, Maloe Iablonovo, Leski and Shakhovo until the approach of the 10th Guards Mechanized Brigade.
> 2. The 10th Guards Mechanized Brigade has been given the urgent orders to move out of Novoselovka and to take up the defense of Zhimolostnoe and Maloe Iablonovo.
> 3. With the arrival of the 10th Guards Mechanized Brigade, the 2nd Guards Tank Corps is to defend Leski and prevent the advance of the enemy to Shakhovo, having in mind the further liquidation of the breakthrough group and the restoration of the situation in Ivanovka.
> 4. The entire re-grouping is to be completed by dawn of 15.07.43.
> The corps headquarters is to transfer to Novoselovka.[3]

At 0855 hours on 15 July, *front* commander Vatutin signed Order No. 248 to the commanders of the 69th, 5th Guards Tank and 2nd Air Armies for the re-capture of Shakhovo:

> A copy to the Chief of the General Staff.
> The adversary, as a result of the lack of vigilance demonstrated by the commanders of the 5th Guards Tank Army and the 69th Army, by the morning of 15.07 had seized Leski and Shakhovo, and had placed the 375th, 93rd and 89th Rifle Divisions of the 69th Army under the threat of encirclement.
> I am ordering:
> 1. Under the personal responsibility of the commander of the 5th Guards Tank Army, using all available forces, a strike in the direction of Shakhovo to seize and hold [that place], and to prevent the link-up of enemy formations attacking from the direction of Leski with the enemy in the area of Shcholokovo.
> Simultaneously, firmly defend the line Iamki – eastern bank of the ravine lying 2 km west of Pravorot' – the undesignated heights 1 km northeast of Vinogradovka – undesignated heights 2 km east of Vinogradovka – Maloe Iablonovo – Iamki – Gridino – Hill 235 – Ryndinka. Introduce the main forces of the 29th Tank Corps into the army's shock group.
> Under the personal responsibility of the commander of the 69th Army:
> a) to organize an attack in the direction of Shakhovo with the forces of the 375th, 93rd and 89th Rifle Divisions, and together with units of the 5th Guards Tank Army to destroy the enemy in the area of Shakhovo, after which it is to occupy the line Maloe Iablonovo – Point 147.0 (3 km west of Shakhovo)

– Krutoi ravine – Shakhovo – Ryndinka for a firm defense to prevent any possibility of an enemy breakthrough on this front.

The counterstrike with the goal of taking control of the Shakhovo area is to be supported with bombardment artillery.

b) before the start of the counterattack, to firmly defend the line Iamki – Gridino – Ryndinka, preventing any further enemy expansion from Shakhovo to the north, northeast or east;

c) upon seizing the area of Shakhovo, to set up an organized, occupied line of defense Maloe Iablonovo – Shakhovo – Ryndinka with units of the 48th Rifle Corps;

1. To the commander of the 2nd Air Army – destroy the enemy in the area Belenikhino, Leski and Shakhovo with all available forces.
2. Confirm receipt [of this order]. Report on issued orders.

Nikolaev [pseudonym of N. F. Vatutin]
Sergeev [pseudonym of N. S. Khrushchev]
Pavlenko [pseudonym of S. P. Ivanov][4]

This order was plainly too late. The 5th Guards Tank Army and 69th Army were no longer capable of carrying it out. The enemy had increased its pressure and the situation was rapidly deteriorating. In the given situation, there was only one choice – to withdraw the divisions of the 48th Rifle Corps from the closing pocket quickly, since they were about to be encircled. There has been preserved a draft of Combat Order No. 003/op from the 69th Army headquarters' operations group on the withdrawal of the troops from the collapsing pocket to a new line of defense. It was written in the hand of the army's chief of operations, Colonel D. N. Surzhitsem. We will cite it fully:

To the commander of the 48th Rifle Corps.

Copy: to the *front*'s chief of staff.

1. The enemy has seized Vinogradovka, Leski and Shakhovo.
2. The commander of the 48th Rifle Corps is quickly to occupy and defend the line: Zhimolostnoe – Maloe Iablonovo – Plota (excl.) – Shipy.

Assignment: Prevent a breakthrough of enemy tanks and infantry to the north and northeast. Corps headquarters – Krasnoe. On the right from Vinogradovka to Iamki and northwards – units of the 5th Guards Tank Army are defending; on the left – the 11th Motorized Rifle Brigade of the 5th Tank Army's mobile group is defending; further from Krasnoe Znamia to (excl.) Aleksandrovka, Sviridovo and to the south along the River Razumnaia to Sheino – units of the 35th Guards Rifle Corps. Boundary lines with them will be supplied.

Corps headquarters: Korocha.[5]

An official order from the commander of the 48th Rifle Corps on the withdrawal to new lines of defense has not been found. Likely, at that time the corps headquarters staff was not creating documents – there are none from this period in the files for this formation in the Russian Federation's Central Archives of the Ministry of Defense.

The commander of the 81st Guards Rifle Division Major General I. K. Morozov's Order No. 59 from 15 July 1943 at 0140 hours has been preserved. It somewhat clarifies the situation and allows us to create a chronology of the corps' withdrawal from the closing pocket:

> At the end of day 14.07.43, the enemy had assembled up to 50 tanks and a regiment of infantry on the Shakhovo axis, 6 tanks and up to a battalion of infantry east of the grove near Shcholokovo; and 18 tanks and up to a battalion of infantry on the northeast outskirts of Shakhovo. At 2000, he attacked the defending units of the division in the areas of Shakhovo and the woods west of Shcholokovo. Having a superiority of force, the enemy seized Shakhovo and the woods west of Shcholokovo.
>
> On the night of 14.07.43, the enemy from the direction of Ivanovka seized Maloe Iablonovo, as a result of which the division's units and command post became encircled.
>
> I am ordering:
>
> 1. On the basis of a verbal command from the commander of the 48th Rifle Corps at 0140 15.07.43, to begin the retreat of the division's units and command post along the route: Chursino – 1.5 km west of Shakhovo – 2 km east of Iamki – Gridino – Plota – Novoselovka – Verin – Vasil'ev – Ploskii.
>
> The place of assembly of the division's units – Podol'khi, division command post – Dolgii hill.
>
> 2. Report on the arrival of the division's units to place of assembly."[6]

The fortitude and sense of responsibility of corps commander Major General Z. Z. Rogozny should be noted. That night, in the difficult circumstances of unceasing enemy panzer attacks, he maintained his composure, and remaining within the ring of encirclement, he personally directed the division commanders during the withdrawal from encirclement to the new line of defense. The 48th Rifle Corps' headquarters operations group directly organized the withdrawal of all the divisions. Between 2100 14 July and 0200 15 July, it was located in Chursino, and then withdrew at 0500 together with the troops.[7] The withdrawal of the 48th Rifle Corps was executed in the pre-dawn hours of 15 July. The 89th Guards Rifle Division led the way, followed in turn by the 81st and 93rd Guards Rifle Divisions, with units of the 375th Rifle Division bringing up the rear. Covering elements remained in position to secure the retreat. If you calculate the passage of time from the order of the 81st Guards Rifle Division commander – 0140 – to the time it reached the regiment and battalion headquarters, and add the time required to organize the withdrawal, then it is possible that the 81st Guards Rifle Division began to move out of its positions between 0300 and 0400. By this time, the units of the leading 89th Guards Rifle Division should already have been in the process of exiting the pocket. According to a dispatch from this division's commander, Colonel M. P. Seriugin, its regiments had already started to move into the new line of defense Iamki – Gridino – Pokrovka – Kuz'minka by 0700 15 July.

Unfortunately, the withdrawal from the pocket did not proceed without complications. The 69th Army's journal of combat operations states that at dawn on 15 July, the 375th Rifle Division was still covering the withdrawal of the 81st, 89th and 93rd Guards Rifle Divisions. But at 0700, the enemy attacked from the area of Shakhovo with tank support in the direction of Maloe Iablonovo, and by 0900, forward detachments with tanks had linked up with the grouping that was attacking to the south from the area of Belenikhino.[8]

The division, leaving behind rear guard detachments, began to withdraw toward Pravorot' along the Sukhaia Plota ravine under the cover of divisional artillery and anti-tank guns, and with submachine gunners protecting the flanks. However, on the way out of the pocket it had to run a gauntlet of German fire, and its movement was hindered by a traffic jam of wagons and vehicles from the other withdrawing divisions in front of it.

In Report No. 00201 from 17.07.43 to the Military Council of the 69th Army, the commander of the 375th Rifle Division stated:

> When we reached the vicinity of the Kozinets brook, the enemy opened artillery and mortar fire on the column in combination with a storm of automatic weapons fire from the eastern and western branches of the Sukhaia Plota ravine. Deploying the units for combat, an intense exchange of fire unfolded, and with heavy losses the division broke through in the vicinity of Dal'nii Dolzhik. At 1130 the forward units broke through a ring of fire, losing a significant amount of personnel, horses and weapons. At 1200, the enemy attacked again with freshly brought up forces of infantry and tanks, blocked the Sukhaia Plota ravine (west of Maloe Iablonovo), and thus barred the way out to the remaining units of the division. The rear guard, consisting of two reinforced battalions, could not escape, and went missing, together with the commander of the 1241st Rifle Regiment Major Karlin, the commander of the 1243rd Rifle Regiment Lieutenant Colonel Frolov, signals chief Engineer-Captain Tsukasov, the two battalion commanders, and a number of mid-level commanders.
>
> The remaining personnel of the division – 3,526 men – upon moving into the new line of defense at Novoselovka quickly deployed, entrenched, and subsequently repelled two enemy attacks.[9]

The 69th Army command did whatever it could to assist the withdrawal of the 48th Rifle Corps' divisions from the pocket. For example, diversionary attacks were launched against the right flank of the enemy's III Panzer Corps. From the account of the 35th Guards Rifle Corps:

> In the early morning hours of 15.07.43, with the aim of diverting [enemy] forces from the main axis and creating panic in the enemy's rear, the 107th Rifle and 94th Guards Rifle Divisions each conducted battalion-sized operations to seize Raevka, Verkhnii Ol'shanets and Shliakhovoe. At 0200, the battalions began to attack, operating along the indicated directions. The battalion of the 107th Rifle Division, approaching Raevka, was detected by the enemy and came under concentrated artillery and mortar fire, after which it was compelled to fall back to its starting position. The battalion of the 94th Guards Rifle Division, attacking toward Shliakhovoe, reached its eastern outskirts, where its flanks were counterattacked by up to two battalions, and with fighting it withdrew to its starting position.[10]

Despite the active resistance of the enemy and the absence of reliable communications which often greatly complicated the handling of the forces, the 48th Rifle Corps managed to withdraw most of all four divisions from the pocket.

A message from the commander of the 48th Rifle Corps at 1040 on 15 July relays the condition of his divisions after the withdrawal:

> I am reporting on the grouping and the condition of the corps' forces. By morning 15.07.43, the corps' divisions, having completed a withdrawal to a line 2 km west of Pravorot' – Zhimolostnoe – Novoselovka – Gnezdilovka, took up [the following positions]:
>
> The 375th Rifle Division is in motion at approximately 1000 to the line … east of Storozhevoe – (excl.) Zhimolostnoe with a front to the west. The division has been involved in bitter fighting since the morning of 14.07.43 in the area south of Leski and Shakhovo. There are no precise figures on losses.
>
> The 93rd Guards Rifle Division at 0600 was assembling in the area of Maloe Iablonovo. The division completed its withdrawal under darkness without any particular hindrances by the enemy.
>
> The 81st Guards Rifle Division, in combat in the area of Shakhovo on 14.07.43, suffered losses, [but] precise figures on its current strength are unavailable. The division is assembling in the area of the draw east of Dal'nii Dolzhik.
>
> The 89th Guards Rifle Division at 0500 began to take up a defense on the front Novoselovka – Gnezdilovka. The division had no losses. The withdrawal was completed under conditions of darkness in complete order.
>
> The 183rd Rifle Division after combat with enemy tanks and infantry on 14.07.43 retreated from its defensive sector. Accurate information on the grouping and its condition is not available. Corps headquarters – Podol'khi.[11]

Was the 48th Rifle Corps ever fully encircled? This is not a simple question to answer, since the combat documents which I've been able to discover give a variety of responses. In the orders for 15 July and on following days (in particular, in the orders of the *front* commander), there is talk of the threat of encirclement. In the documents of the 69th Army and the 2nd Guards Tank Corps, there is frequent use of the term "semi-encirclement". The facts surrounding the withdrawal of the 48th Rifle Corps' divisions to new lines by the morning of 15 July give no clear evidence of encirclement or semi-encirclement.

In a single document of the 48th Rifle Corps – the operational summary for 1700 16 July 1943 – there is the brief statement, "The divisions of the corps after emerging from encirclement are mustering personnel and occupying a line of defense …"[12]

The rather large number of men listed as missing in action in the divisions that were in the pocket serves as indirect evidence that they were indeed actually surrounded. At the same time, there is no evidence that our units, except for the 375th Rifle Division at the tail of the withdrawing column, had to fight their way out of encirclement. Judging from everything, it is probably correct to say that the main part of our forces were able

A smashed German armored vehicle in the village of Shakhovo. (RGAKFD)

to withdraw at the last moment, before the enemy succeeded in closing shut the ring around the pocket.

On the whole, the withdrawal of three divisions of the 48th Rifle Corps from the closing pocket was conducted, despite the difficult situation, in a sufficiently organized and timely fashion. The retreat of our forces from the lines of the Lipovyi Donets and Northern Donets Rivers was predetermined by the general course of combat operations. The troops who were defending those positions fully carried out the assignment that had been given to them. However, the high losses did not allow the 48th Rifle Corps to resist the enemy any longer. The abandonment of the projection of land between the two rivers was in the final analysis to a considerable degree favorable to us: firstly, the length of the front on this sector was reduced by more than half, and as a result the army's forces were able to shorten their lines and solidify the defense; secondly, it provided the opportunity to withdraw the divisions, which had been reduced to mere regiments in fighting strength, to the rear for rest and refitting. *Most importantly, however, this was done without needless losses.*

In the course of fighting between 13 and 15 July, the 48th Rifle Corps suffered heavy losses. More detailed casualty figures in the divisions of the 48th Rifle Corps are presented in Table 27.

The large number of missing in action can be explained by the fact that the withdrawal and movement into new lines took place at night under enemy fire, and the order to the covering detachments to withdraw didn't arrive in time. Many soldiers were wounded and could not keep pace with their units, while some men simply got lost. It is likely, of course that a number of those men left behind became prisoners.

As the Germans recognize, "the SS Panzer Corps in cooperation with the III Panzer Corps closed a ring around the so-called cauldron near Belgorod. However, the Soviet 69th Army, which was operating south of Prokhorovka, withdrew, and the greater part of its forces managed to escape entrapment."[13]

The formations and units of the 5th Guards Tank Army holding the western sector of the pocket also had to undergo severe trials. According to intelligence from the 26th Guards Tank Brigade, at 0100 15 July the Germans had concentrated up to 50 tanks in the village of Shakhovo and had begun to move out in the direction of Leski. By this time, there was already no solid line of defense in this area. The 48th Rifle Corps command was withdrawing the 89th Guards, 93rd Guards and 375th Rifle Divisions from the pocket. Units of the 81st Rifle Division and elements of the 375th Rifle Division, stubbornly continuing to fight in Shakhovo, were eventually scattered by superior enemy forces. Only the brigades of the 2nd Guards Tank Corps managed to halt the enemy tank attacks. Its brigades and regiments were fighting in two areas: the Ivanovka – Vinogradovka – Maloe Iablonovo – Zhimolostnoe region, and in the villages of Shakhovo and Plota. An extract from a combat message from the 2nd Guards Tank Corps headquarters on 15 July at 0300 provides evidence on the remaining strength and condition of the brigades and regiments:

> 26th Guards Tank Brigade – 15 T-34, 9 T-70
> 4th Guards Tank Brigade – 2 T-34, 2 T-70
> 25th Guards Tank Brigade – 2 T-34, no T-70
> 47th Guards Heavy Tank Breakthrough Regiment – 2 Churchill
> 106 men killed, 126 men wounded
> Tank losses: 17 T-34, 9 T-70
>
> Conclusion: as a result of heavy combat and massed air raids, the corps has suffered significant losses in personnel and equipment. Command and control has been disrupted; the brigades, with the exception of the 26th Guards Tank Brigade, are no longer combat-worthy. I request the withdrawal of the corps behind a line of infantry and the granting of at least some time for bringing the corps' units back into order.[14]

Colonel S. K. Nesterov's 26th Guards Tank Brigade received the enemy's main attack at dawn on 15 July. It conducted a fighting withdrawal from Shakhovo to the villages of Plota and Maloe Iablonovo. By 0600 elements of the 26th Guards Tank Brigade had dug-in on the western outskirts of Maloe Iablonovo.

Units of the II SS Panzer Corps and the III Panzer Corps linked up somewhere between 0500 and 0600 hours on 15 July in the vicinity of Shakhovo. At this time, most of the defenders in the pocket had withdrawn to new lines outside the pocket.

At 0600 hours, panzer units of SS *Das Reich* and the 19th Panzer Division launched a joint operation. The positions of Colonel Nesterov's 26th Guards

Colonel S. K. Nesterov, commander of the 2nd Guards 'Tatsinskaia' Tank Corps' 26th Guards Tank Brigade. (Author's personal archive)

Tank Brigade were struck simultaneously from two directions: up to 20 tanks and a battalion of infantry attacked the southwestern outskirts of Plota, while up to 30 tanks and a battalion of infantry hit the southwestern outskirts of Maloe Iablonovo. The 1st Tank Battalion's defense in Plota was split in two, as enemy tanks cracked the line on the southwestern outskirts of the village and continued to advance toward the village center. The brigade could not withstand the pressure of the numerically superior enemy force, and its battalions began to withdraw from the two villages.

The sole remaining combat-capable corps was the 5th Guards Mechanized Corps, holding the line Zhimolostnoe – Plota – Shipy – Hill 222.2. Its 11th Guards and 12th Guards Mechanized Brigades were defending in the sector of the enemy's 6th and 7th Panzer Divisions, which were advancing from the area of Rzhavets and Avdeevka. Its 10th Guards Mechanized Brigade was in motion towards Zhimolostnoe and Maloe Iablonovo to support the buckling lines of the 2nd Guards Tank Corps. Almost all the 5th Guards Mechanized Corps' artillery units (the 104th Guards Destroyer Anti-tank Artillery Regiment, the 409th Separate Guards Rocket Artillery Battalion and others) were also still operating in the 69th Army's sector. A combat report from the 5th Guards Mechanized Corps headquarters on the morning of 15 July provides the following picture of events then unfolding:

> The 2nd Guards 'Tatsinskaia' Tank Corps is falling back in disorder to the east and northeast.
>
> The 10th Guards Mechanized Brigade has been moving up to Zhimolostnoe and Maloe Iablonovo.
>
> At 0700 up to 30 enemy tanks were attacking the southern outskirts of Plota.
>
> At 0800 enemy tanks were in motion toward Pokrovka.

At 0800, a column of up to 30 enemy tanks was detected moving toward Zhimolostnoe.

At 0840, the 10th Guards Mechanized Brigade halted and was fighting to the left of Plota, and preparing to repulse enemy tanks moving on Zhimolostnoe.

At 0830, an enemy tank column appeared, bypassing the right flank of the 11th Guards Mechanized Brigade in the direction of Pokrovka.

All is quiet on the sector of the 12th Guards Mechanized Brigade. The 24th Guards Mechanized Brigade is defending in its previous location.

The 26th [Guards] Tank Brigade is retreating in the direction of Novoselovka.[15]

Divisions	Personnel Categories	Strength on 10.07.43 (a)	Losses					
			Killed	Wounded	Missing	Sick Leave	Absent for Other Reasons (b)	Total, Men/% of Strength
93rd Gds Rifle	Command	-	25	63	308	-	-	396
	Jr Command	-	153	392	1,306	9	-	1,860
	Other Ranks	-	299	547	2,617	40	-	3,503
Total		9,426	477	1,002	4,231	49	-	5,759/61
81st Gds Rifle	Command	-	57	75	54	3	78	267
	Jr Command	-	329	272	178	4	293	1,076
	Other Ranks	-	410	795	730	4	988	2,927
Total		-	796	1,142	962	11	1,359	4,270
89th Gds Rifle	Command	-	13	16	95	3	-	127
	Jr Command	-	29	63	784	2	-	878
	Other Ranks	-	64	233	2,291	5	-	2,593
Total		8,355	106	312	3,170	10	-	3,598/43
375th Rifle	Command	-	3	26	1	-	-	30
	Jr Command	-	35	78	8	4	-	125
	Other Ranks	-	167	356	23	-	-	546
Total		7,401	205	460	32	4	-	701/9
183rd Rifle	Command	-	15	69	-	-	-	84
	Jr Command	-	123	101	-	-	-	224
	Other Ranks	-	260	732	-	-	-	992
Total		7,778	398	902	-	-	-	1,300/17
Grand Total			1,982	3,818	8,395	74	1,359	15,628

a) TsAMO RF, f. 69A, op. 10757, d. 8, l. 90, 91.

b) This column, perhaps, shows the losses suffered in the 7th Guards Army's 81st Guards Rifle Division during its withdrawal out of encirclement north of Belgorod.

Source: TsAMO RF, f. 69A, op. 10753, d. 442, l. 24.

Table 27: Losses in the 69th Army's 48th Rifle Corps, 1-16 July 1943

By 0850, the villages of Plota and Maloe Iablonovo were fully under enemy control. However, further advance by the enemy was stopped by the brigades of the 5th Guards 'Zimovniki' Mechanized Corps, especially the 10th Guards Mechanized Brigade, which had already reached and dug-in on the eastern outskirts of Zhimolostnoe and on the northern and northeastern outskirts of Plota by 0400.

Simultaneously, units of the German III Panzer Corps had attacked the right flank of the 35th Guards Rifle Corps in the direction of Vypolzovka and Novo-Khmelevoe, but these attacks were driven back. From Operational Summary No. 116 of the 5th Guards 'Zimovniki' Mechanized Corps headquarters at 2300 15 July:

> … 4. The 3rd Motorized Rifle Battalion of the 10th Guards Mechanized Brigade together with the 51st Guards Tank Regiment, supported by the 3rd Battalion of the 285th Mortar Regiment and the Brigade's artillery battalions at 1900 reached Plota and began fighting for possession of it.
>
> The 2nd Motorized Rifle Battalion of the 10th Guards Mechanized Brigade took Zhimolostnoe after stubborn fighting. As a result of the fighting, the brigade had losses: 4 T-34 tanks left burning and 9 knocked out; personnel losses are being established.
>
> 5. The 11th Guards Mechanized Brigade in the course of the day conducted stubborn defensive battles against major enemy tank and mechanized units; at 2300 it continues to hold its positions.
>
> 6. The 12th Guards Mechanized Brigade at 2000 15.07 was attacked by two battalions of infantry with the support of 14 tanks. The enemy attack was repulsed with organized artillery, machine-gun, and small-arms fire. The enemy left 2 burned-out tanks and 150 soldiers and officers behind on the battlefield.[16]

By the end of the day on 15 July, the front lines in the sector of the 69th Army had become fully stabilized. This was the final day for the enemy to gain any ground around Prokhorovka.

Assessing the results of the combat operations in the sector of the 69th Army, first of all it is necessary to stress that the army had carried out the task given to it for the defensive operation. It had prepared a sufficiently strong line of defense, which withstood all enemy attempts to crack it. In the conclusive stage of the operation, its formations in the absence of reserves and a sufficient quantity of weapons (especially tanks and artillery) and ammunition, had managed to resist superior enemy forces in the most difficult combat conditions, before making a timely retreat according to an order from above to a new defensive line.

At the same time, it is necessary to observe a number of shortcomings, which seriously and adversely affected the handling of the troops as well as their actions. This concerns first of all the miscalculations in organization. Prior to the beginning of July, the 69th Army lacked a corps headquarters. Only immediately prior to the start of the German offensive did it receive the headquarters of the 48th Rifle Corps. Major General Z. Z. Rogozny assumed command of the corps only on 4 July, just twenty-four hours before the start of the battle. Already by 6 July, the corps' troops were involved in the fighting.

Soviet artillerymen investigate a damaged and abandoned German Pz IV tank, July 1943. (RGAKFD)

One can't really speak of any sort of smooth teamwork among the officer staff of the corps headquarters, or any harmonious work with subordinate divisions' headquarters in these circumstances. In the course of fighting, there were cases of violations of command and control by units and divisions, and disruptions in communications.

It is no accident that the Voronezh Front commander's Order No. 00194 from 21 July 1943 on the imposition of disciplinary reprimands over the combat results was fully dedicated to several commanders of the 69th Army's formations. (The commander of the 89th Guards Rifle Division Colonel M. P. Seriugin was removed from his post. The reason for this decision has been discussed earlier. After an investigation of all the circumstances surrounding the combat situation and his actions, Colonel Seriugin was restored to his position. He ended the war as a major-general.)

Aware of the serious losses, which the Voronezh Front's forces had suffered in two weeks of fighting, and concerned about some possible surprise from the talented and wily von Manstein, at 1000 on 16 July Vatutin issued an order to his *front*'s forces to continue the defensive operation. Here is this order's preamble:

> With a tenacious defense by the *front*'s forces, heavy losses in personnel and equipment have been inflicted on the enemy, and the enemy's plan to seize Oboian' and Kursk has been thwarted.
>
> However, the enemy has still not abandoned offensive goals and is striving with daily attacks by main forces to bypass Oboian' on the east, as well as to expand the bridgehead he has seized.

Southwest of Prokhorovka, sappers of the Fourth Panzer Army destroying abandoned Soviet armor before the retreat, 14 July 1943. (RGAKFD)

> With the aim of decisively exhausting the strength of the attacking enemy grouping, the armies of Voronezh Front will go over to the stubborn defense of its current lines with the mission to prevent any enemy breakthrough of our defenses ...[17]

Having suffered heavy losses and having finally lost faith in victory, the Nazi forces also assumed a defensive posture. However, holding on to the area of penetration, which extended up to 90 kilometers into the Soviet lines but had a width of up to only 35 kilometers, was a risky proposition, considering the opportunities for attacks by Soviet forces at the bases of the salient. The command of Army Group South took the decision to withdraw its main forces from their advanced positions and pull them back to the lines they had occupied before the start of the offensive. The day 16 July became the final day in the Prokhorovka engagement. There were no substantial changes in the operational situation during the day. In the enemy's units and formations, typical preparations for a withdrawal were underway: rear guard groups were formed, ambush positions for heavy tanks were set up, sappers were preparing to mine roads and tank-vulnerable areas immediately upon pulling out, and the artillery received an order to open fire that evening, in order to allow the main forces to slip out of their positions quietly and begin the withdrawal.

On 16 July, the enemy also began to withdraw its rear areas back to Belgorod. That night, our aerial reconnaissance spotted the withdrawal of enemy tank units from the front lines in the direction of Belgorod and Tomarovka. Between 0700 and 1400 hours on 17 July alone, a dozen enemy columns, numbering up to 550 tanks and self-propelled guns and up to 1,000 soft vehicles, were observed moving from the area of Komsomolets State Farm in the direction of Bol'shie Maiachki and Pokrovka.[18] Under the cover of strong rear guard elements, the withdrawal of the main forces of Army Group South had begun.

This was incontrovertible evidence that Operation Citadel had failed totally. The Prokhorovka engagement was over.

Forward detachments of the 5th Guards Army and 5th Guards Tank Army did attempt to pursue. However, the enemy's covering force, which maintained constant and direct contact with our forces, continued to offer bitter resistance and even launched several spoiling counterattacks. By the end of 17 July, forward detachments of the 5th Guards Tank Army and 69th Army were occupying the Sitnoe wooded area, Komsomolets State Farm and Storozhevoe. On 18 July, by re-introducing the 18th and 29th Tank Corps into the fighting, the enemy was still only pushed back by another 4 to 5 kilometers.

Also on 18 July, the offensive of Steppe Front began, and on 20 July, the main forces of Voronezh Front went on the attack. By the end of 23 July, our forces had reached the lines they were holding at the start of the enemy offensive. Voronezh Front's defensive operation had successfully ended.

18

The Results of the Prokhorovka Engagement – Myths and Reality

The fighting for Prokhorovka began on 10 July, when the adversary, not having found success on the Oboian' axis, implemented Hoth's variant of the original plan and regrouped the divisions of the II SS Panzer Corps for a strike in the northeast direction. The Prokhorovka engagement concluded on 17 July, when our forces began the pursuit of the withdrawing enemy. Ultimate success in repelling the attack of the enemy's strongest tank grouping on the southern face of the Kursk bulge was achieved thanks to the combined efforts and courage of the men and women of the 1st and 5th Guards Tank Armies, the 5th, 6th and 7th Guards Armies, and the 69th Army, as well as units and formations of other types of forces.

Within the period of the Prokhorovka engagement, on 12 July the Voronezh Front conducted a major counterattack, the essence of which has been considered a meeting collision between opposing tank groupings. At the same time, the armor engagement at Prokhorovka (from here on I will use this long-established term to describe the action that day) is only part of the full Prokhorovka engagement, in which three Soviet armies took part, two of which were combined-arms armies.

A detailed analysis of the course of combat operations, based upon wartime archival documents, including German documents, demonstrates that many long-held views of this engagement and its results do not fully correspond to reality. In light of the research I have conducted, the conclusion of the authors of the article in the Soviet Military Encyclopedia (published in 1977) related to the Prokhorovka engagement is fully debatable: " ... *in the engagement, the complete superiority of Soviet military hardware and the Soviet military art over the military skill of the German-Fascist army was demonstrated*" [author's emphasis]. In the same article, you can find the statement: "... *Its [the counterattack's] success to a significant extent depended on the correct selection of the time to start it, and its purposeful and thorough preparation.*" [author's emphasis][1]

I have already discussed the "complete superiority" of Soviet military equipment over the German equipment in July 1943. As for the time and location for launching the counterattack with the Voronezh Front reserves, then it must be acknowledged that their selection wasn't fully successful. Vatutin and Vasilevsky had by 10 July come to the conclusion that "a decisive disruption of the German offensive and the destruction of his advanced grouping in the given circumstances can only be achieved by a powerful counterattack of the Voronezh Front's forces, reinforced with strategic reserves."[2]

This assessment was built upon the mistaken belief that the enemy, which had already been attacking for seven days, was exhausted, had suffered large losses, did not have adequate reserves, and would not have sufficient time to set up a defense. Obviously, the cause for these erroneous calculations was the poor work of battlefield reconnaissance, and as a result of this the lack of reliable intelligence about the enemy, his strength and intentions. Meanwhile, the attacking troops did not have sufficient time to prepare for the counterattack, nor did the command have experience in handling large tank formations on the defensive. The organization of the commitment of reserves into the engagement in connection with the deteriorating situation on 11 July was done in impermissible haste. A joint attack on both flanks of the enemy grouping that had deeply penetrated into our defenses did not in fact occur. In the final result, all of this led to heavy and unjustifiable losses in men, weapons, and equipment.

Some scholars accuse N. F. Vatutin of wastefully using the reserves given to him by the *Stavka*, once he had resolved upon a counterattack. In our view, this accusation is unfounded. The decision did not lie with Nikolai Fedorovich, or more accurately, with him alone. Possibly he pushed for it, but the fundamental decision to conduct a counterattack, without any doubt, was reached with the guidance of the *Stavka* and the Supreme Commander, and authorized by their personal representative on the scene, Marshal A. M. Vasilevsky. Moreover, the launching of the counterattack on 12 July had been timed to coincide with the start of an offensive by the Western and Briansk Fronts. On the *front* commander's shoulders lay the responsibility for preparing and conducting the counterattack with the application of all the forces of Voronezh Front and the *Stavka* Reserves, and of course the responsibility for its results.

When assessing the situation and taking the decision to counterattack, plainly grandiose ambitions and a lack of appreciation for the enemy's strength played telling roles (it is sufficient just to recall the disastrous offensive operations of 1942). In reality, the enemy over seven days of the offensive had indeed suffered large losses, first of all in tanks. However, the estimates of his losses, provided in Soviet dispatches and intelligence summaries, were frequently extremely exaggerated. Here, for example, is an excerpt from one dispatch: "… During the day of fighting on 9 July, the enemy advanced by 6-8 kilometers, while losing up to 295 tanks and assault guns."[3] Or: "Over one day of fighting, the Hitlerites lost 11,000 soldiers and officers, [and] 230 tanks and self-propelled guns."[4] These figures, as it turned out, proved to be very far from the genuine numbers.

Here it would be fitting to point as well to the *front*'s own intelligence summary, according to which between 5 July and 9 July, 2,460 enemy tanks and assault guns had been put out of action![5] Relying on this estimate, it meant that our forces had knocked out almost twice the number of armored vehicles that the enemy even possessed at the start of the operation! Later, when reporting on the results of the defensive operation, the Voronezh Front command calculated that the enemy had lost between 2,500 and 3,000 tanks and self-propelled guns.[6] Incidentally, we will dwell upon the actual losses suffered by both sides a little later.

The *front* command also underestimated the enemy's ability to repair damaged armor and put the vehicles back into action quickly. Although the enemy's progress was slow, he was advancing, and having possession of the tactical battlefield at the end of each day, he experienced no particular difficulties in evacuating and repairing damaged tanks. Incidentally, this experience exposed the insufficient power of Soviet anti-tank mines. As a rule, they only put a German tank out of action for a short period. The most frequent damage inflicted on a German tank by a Soviet anti-tank mine was a damaged track, or more rarely, damage to a roller. Even the fire from 45mm anti-tank guns and especially anti-tank rifles could not do much harm to the tanks. As soon as a clash ended, our intelligence organs were able to establish that the Germans were able to repair the greater portion of the damaged tanks not far behind the front lines. Thus the German panzer divisions constantly received armor replacements from the stock of repaired machines (as well as from the reserve in Akhtyrka), and thus were able to re-establish their combat capabilities quickly.

The flip side of the underestimation of the enemy's strength was the overestimation of our own capabilities. Voronezh Front received control of two fresh, fully staffed and equipped armies, one of them a tank army, in which there were approximately 700 tanks and self-propelled guns. Taking into account the 2nd Guards 'Tatsinskaia' Tank and the 2nd Tank Corps, which were subordinated to the 5th Guards Tank Army, and the 5th Guards Army, the *front*'s counterattack grouping in the area of Prokhorovka numbered more than 100,000 soldiers and officers, and more than 900 armored vehicles (though approximately one-third of them consisted of light T-70 tanks). For the first time in the war, a *front* received in the course of a defensive operation such a powerful force, possessing high mobility, firepower and shock strength – and this comprised the basis of Voronezh Front's counterattack grouping. It is not out of line to assume that the *front* command, and the *Stavka* itself, were mesmerized by such large numbers. How else to explain such a decisive aim for the counterattack, and such ambitious combat assignments as were given to the participating armies?

Stemming from the decision of the Voronezh Front commander, the goal of the counterattack, as defined, embraced nothing less than the destruction of the far-advanced enemy grouping, the restoration of the position as it stood at the start of Operation Citadel and the creation of conditions for launching a general counteroffensive. The plan envisioned enveloping attacks on the flanks of the main enemy grouping with a subsequent emergence into its rear – with the aim of the encirclement and destruction of the II SS Panzer Corps.

The expression, "History doesn't tolerate the subjunctive mood" has long ago become banal. Therefore we will not be giving advice in hindsight – whether a counterattack was even necessary, or whether it would have been better to use the strategic reserves first to strengthen the defense and repulse the enemy's attacks with defensive fire, and only then go over to active measures. We'll try to understand why the counterattack on the main axis crystallized into a head-on collision with a strong enemy tank grouping, and why it failed to reach its desired goals.

In distinction from the Central Front on the northern face of the Kursk bulge, where the first counterattack in the case of an enemy penetration had already been planned for the morning of the second or third day of the defensive operation, the Voronezh Front commander tried to throw together a counterattack with the 1st Tank Army on the morning of the second day of the battle. Fortunately, he either reconsidered or was stopped by a higher authority. Vatutin then tried to turn the situation around with counterattacks on the lengthening right flank of the enemy grouping on 6 July – with the forces of the 5th and 2nd Guards Tank Corps – and on 8 July with the forces of the 5th and 2nd Guards Tank Corps and the 2nd and 10th Tank Corps. The counterattacks failed to achieve their aim, but they did gain time to move up reserves and shift units from quiet sectors of the front in order to strengthen the threatened directions.

Until 10 July, it was still possible to consider a successful attack into the flank of the enemy's main grouping, which was continuing to attack toward Oboian'. By 11 July, however, the enemy had altered the direction of main attack and had already seized the line that had been designated for introducing the 5th Guards Tank Army into the battle.

Moreover, one must also consider that the *Wehrmacht* command always paid great attention to securing the flanks of its attacking forces when breaking through an enemy defense, especially whenever it had not yet exhausted its reserves. Back in 1941, the OKH [*Oberkommando des Heeres* – the Army High Command] Chief of Staff, Colonel General Franz Halder, while entering a report from Army Group Center about a captured Russian order into his diary, had noted: "... The Russian command is striving to cut off our panzer formations from the infantry with flank attacks. Theoretically this is a good idea; however its implementation in practice is possible only given an advantage in numbers and superiority in operational leadership ..."[7] One must give the adversary credit in knowing how to consolidate seized territory. They would set up strong anti-tank screens on the flanks of breakthrough sectors, thereby preserving operational freedom for their panzer groupings.

Thus, the enemy 167th Infantry Division on 9 July, having replaced the SS Panzergrenadier Division *Totenkopf* on the western bank of the Lipovyi Donets River, immediately started fortifying this favorable line. Our scouts spotted the German infantrymen digging trenches, emplacing mines, and setting up barbed wire.

Nevertheless, a counterattack on just this axis promised greater prospects than the location eventually selected. Owing to the overwhelming superiority in armor, one could expect a breakthrough of the 167th Infantry Division's defenses and the rapid exploitation into the rear of the enemy's Fourth Panzer Army's main forces.

Thus it was precisely after having received the mission to counterattack that P. A. Rotmistrov organized a reconnaissance with his corps commanders at 0300 11 July in the area of Shakhovo. The base of the enemy shock grouping's extended right flank was already a very enticing target. However, a counterattack here would mean that he in turn would have to expose his own flank and rear to Army Detachment Kempf's III Panzer Corps, which was doggedly pushing towards Prokhorovka from the south. These concerns were confirmed already early on the morning of 12 July, when Rotmistrov was forced to detach significant forces in order to strengthen this axis, and in the process weakened his own counterattack grouping.

In addition, one must consider the very real danger of an enemy breakthrough west of Prokhorovka. In the given situation, this could not be permitted under any circumstances. In our opinion, the *Stavka* decided not to risk withdrawing the 5th Guards Tank Army from the threatened axis on 12 July, just when the forces of Briansk Front and Western Front went on the offensive. Strategic thoughts, likely, held sway over any potential operational benefits connected with any serious risk. In the book, *Velikaia otechestvennaia voina 1941-1945: Perelom* [The Great Patriotic War 1941-1945: The Turning Point], published by the Institute of Military History, there is the following assertion:

> No small role in the failure of Voronezh Front's counterattack to destroy completely the advanced enemy grouping was played by the fear of the *Stavka*, and first of all Stalin, of deep enemy penetrations, which it always tried to halt by moving up reserves to the threatened sectors. This is exactly why the 5th Guards and 5th Guards Tank Armies were moved up from Steppe Front. As a result, the most powerful grouping of Soviet forces attacked the strongest enemy grouping, not in the flank, but rather head-on. The *Stavka*, having created a significant numerical superiority over the adversary, made no use of the advantageous configuration of the front, and undertook no attack at the base of the enemy penetration, with the aim of encircling the entire German grouping, which was operating north of Iakovlevo.[8]

Plainly, the specialists at the Institute of Military History had a basis for such a conclusion. In any case, there's little point in placing all the blame for the head-on clash with the enemy's powerful tank grouping on the commander of the 5th Guards Tank Army. There was actually little choice. In the course of discussing various plan alternatives and the results of additional reconnaissance, as Rotmistrov noted long after the war:

> … it was established that the terrain south of Prokhorovka hindered the deployment of the army's main forces and limited the maneuverability of the tank corps. In connection with this, the line of deployment was selected somewhat west and southwest of Prokhorovka (on a front of 15 kilometers), and the main blow would be launched in the direction of Luchki and Iakovlevo.[9]

In order to deploy on this line, it was necessary to squeeze into a rather narrow corridor between the railroad and the Psel River basin. The opponent, however, was also aiming at this strip of suitable tank terrain, and already on 11 July units of the SS Panzergrenadier Division *Leibstandarte* seized the advantageous ground between Hill 252.2 and the Oktiabr'skii State Farm, while units of the SS Panzergrenadier Division *Totenkopf* in the course of 11 July and early morning hours of 12 July forced a crossing of the Psel River and seized a bridgehead on its right [northern] bank. By the morning of 12 July, the adversary had also managed to push back the formations of the 1st Tank Army and 6th and 7th Armies, which complicated their participation in the counterattack.

It was already too late to change the decision, which had been adopted by the *Stavka*, in response to the changing situation, and in any case it would have been an extremely risky thing to do. There was no one who would have even dared try. The single possible axis for introducing the main forces of a tank army into an engagement on 12 July remained the narrow corridor between the swampy basin of the Psel River on one side, and the deeply cut and wooded terrain around Iamki and Storozhevoe on the other side.

It was decided to smash through the enemy's combat formations with an armored battering ram, that is to say, to strike one wedge with another wedge. For this, Rotmistrov's tank army, with the aim of ensuring a powerful initial blow, included the greater portion of its strength in the first echelon – three of the four tank corps, which together numbered up to 500 tanks and self-propelled guns (counting only the armor reported as serviceable at 1700 on 11 July 1943).

The tank brigades of the 18th and 29th Tank Corps – altogether 348 tanks – were deployed on a front of 6 kilometers on the army's main axis of attack. It was the first time in two years of war that such a density of armor, more than 50 armored vehicles per kilometer of front, had been achieved, moreover in the course of a defensive operation. The corps were handed the assignment to encircle and destroy the opposing enemy and by the end of 12 July to seize a line 20 to 25 kilometers in the depth of the Germans' positions. Yet the adversary also had three SS Panzergrenadier divisions operating on this axis, in a sector just 10-12 kilometers wide. Necessarily, there ensued a head-to-head collision of two major armored forces.

We can't proceed any further without an analysis of the size of the opposing forces and the resulting combat losses. The attention of scholars, and also simply of those interested in military history, has long been fixed on the question of just how many tanks and self-propelled guns were involved in the fighting near Prokhorovka on 12 July. Interest in this question especially grew after the publication in 1960 of P. A. Rotmistrov's memoirs. In this book, the former commander of the 5th Guards Tank Army writes:

> Prior to the engagement, Belgorod Oblast's settlement of Prokhorovka was little known to anyone, but now they know about it not only in the Soviet Union, but also abroad. Here on 12 July 1943 occurred an armor meeting engagement unparalleled in its magnitude in military history, widely known as the 'Prokhorovka bloodbath'. More than 1,500 tanks, a significant quantity of artillery, and large numbers of aircraft simultaneously took part on both sides on a small sector of terrain.[10]

Further Rotmistrov recalls, "The broad field at Prokhorovka was congested with an enormous mass of struggling tanks. On the opponent's side alone, up to 700-800 heavy, medium and light tanks took part, accompanied by a large number of self-propelled artillery."[11]

One immediately notices that the army commander has given a number for the enemy's tanks and assault guns that is much greater than that which actually took part in the clash. Incidentally, Rotmistrov didn't make up these numbers; he obtained them from the account, "Combat operations of the 5th Guards Tank Army," which was prepared by his headquarters staff and signed off by him on 30 September 1943.[12] In it, one finds the following statement about the enemy: "Seven to eight hundred tanks (from the panzer divisions [sic.] *Grossdeutschland*, *Adolf Hitler*, *Reich*, 6th, 11th and 19th Panzer Divisions) operated directly against the 5th Guards Tank Army, supported by a large quantity of bombers."[13] As we see, even the purported composition of the enemy grouping that opposed the 5th Guards Tank Army doesn't correspond to reality.

If we accept as given the numbers cited by the army commander, then if we include the actual figures for the 5th Guards Tank Army, supposedly 1,600 to 1,700 armored vehicles took part in the engagement on both sides. These numbers have always raised doubts among both military historians and the veterans of the battle. However, until recently it was very difficult to check their accuracy: the combat records of the formations and units were kept secret, and the authority of P. A. Rotmistrov had great influence on researchers.

In addition, detailed studies of the combat operations not only at Prokhorovka, but in the course of the entire Kursk battle, have still not been published. In Rotmistrov's memoirs, there was not even a brief chronology of those events, which he calls the Prokhorovka engagement. There has not been even clearly delineated boundaries for the now famous Prokhorovka field – the place where the units of the 5th Guards Tank Army and the II SS Panzer Corps met in combat.

So what sort of field is this, where supposedly 1500 tanks and self-propelled guns met in a deadly clash of armor, and which later received the name, "the Tank Field"? (Even today there is a stop on the railway here that bears the name "Tank Field". The field presents a relatively level and open expanse of terrain, stretching from Prokhorovka to the southwest, measuring approximately 90 square kilometers (6 x 15 kilometers), bordered on the right by the Psel River, and on the left, by a line of hamlets on the other side of the railroad.

The perimeter of this famous tract of ground runs as follows: Petrovka – Hill 252.4 – brick factory on the southwestern outskirts of Prokhorovka Station – Lutovo – Iamki – Storozhevoe – Kalinin – Vinogradovka – Ivanovka – Teterevino – Greznoe – Kozlovka – Bogoroditskoe – Vasil'evka – Andreevka – Mikhailovka – Prelestnoe. In the center of this field, almost on its axis, are the buildings of the Oktiabr'skii State Farm (today known as Politotdel'skii) and the Komsomolets State Farm (now known as the village of Komsomol'skoe).

Here is where the legend of the greatest meeting tank engagement of the Second World War between an attacking German panzer grouping and counterattacking Soviet forces arose, in which supposedly up to 1,500 tanks and self-propelled guns on both sides simultaneously took part. It would be worthwhile for those who believe in these numbers to stop and think: How is it possible to launch a counterattack from a defensive posture given such a correlation of tanks, if nearly half the 1,500 tanks and assault guns belonged to the enemy, and especially when the adversary has still not exhausted his offensive possibilities? In an attempt to justify these numbers, G. A. Koltunov and B. G. Solov'ev, authors of a study of the battle which came out in 1970, asserted:

> … Directly on the Prokhorovka axis from the west on a front of 15 kilometers, three enemy armored divisions were attacking with up to 500 tanks and assault guns, 100 of which were the latest models (Tigers, Panthers, Ferdinands). In this sector on the 5th Guards Tank Army's part there were (excluding General Trufanov's detachment) up to 700 tanks and self-propelled guns … The assault on Prokhorovka from the south was launched by divisions of the enemy's III Panzer Corps, in which the 6th and 19th Panzer Divisions (up to 200 tanks) were playing the primary role. These divisions were opposed by General Trufanov's group, numbering around 100 tanks. Thus, west of Prokhorovka from both sides up to 1,200 tanks and self-propelled (assault) guns took part in the battle, and south of Prokhorovka, another 300 armored vehicles. Thus, altogether up to 1,500 armored vehicles took part in the tank battle west and south of Prokhorovka.[14]

One can forgive the authors of this study – many documents from the war years were classified, and the records of the *Wehrmacht* were still unknown to them. Today we clearly know: all 90 Ferdinand assault guns were located with Army Group Center; Army Group South didn't have any, and the PzKpfw V Panthers were all with the XXXXVIII Panzer Corps operating in the sectors of the 6th Guards Army and 1st Tank Army, and took no part in the fighting at Prokhorovka. The actual number of tanks and self-propelled guns that took part in the battle at Prokhorovka (including the Tiger heavy tanks) was substantially fewer than has been commonly indicated.

Back in 1946, a group of officers on the General Staff of the Soviet Army headed by Major General N. M. Zamiatin prepared a study of the defensive operation at Kursk. In it, the authors provide the following data: "The total number of tanks of the 5th Guards Tank Army, excluding the 2nd Tank and 5th Guards Mechanized Corps, which took no direct part in the fighting on 12 July west of Prokhorovka, amounted to 533 vehicles."[15] This publication received a restricted printing and is practically unavailable to the average reader. Thus, scholars and journalists primarily used the numbers found in the much more widely available books by Rotmistrov, and Koltunov and Solov'ev.

In the work *Velikaia otechestvennaia voina Sovetskogo Soiuza* published in 1965, one can find a significantly lower estimate: 1,100 tanks and self-propelled guns took part in the engagement;[16] the 1978 edition of the Soviet Military Encyclopedia offers a figure of 1,200.[17] However it came about, this legend was perpetuated in many later publications, and continues to pass from book to book even to this day. For example, in S.Kulichkin's book *Vatutin*, published in 2001, there is the statement, "Much has been written and said about the famous tank battle at Prokhorovka, where around two thousand tanks came together in a deadly clash. The result is also known to everyone."[18]

Let us try to sort things out. First of all, we ask the following question: which event of 12 July can be considered the "meeting tank engagement" – the battle of the 18th and 29th Tank Corps against the SS Panzergrenadier Division *Leibstandarte* and elements of the SS Panzergrenadier Division *Das Reich* between the Psel River and Storozhevoe, or the counterattack of all four tank corps of the 5th Guards Tank Army, to include as well the fighting of the 2nd Tank Corps and 2nd Guards Tank Corps in the area of Teterevino, Belenikhino, Kalinin and Ozerovskii (approximately 10 kilometers from the epicenter of events, the Oktiabr'skii State Farm)?

If we follow the logic of Rotmistrov's memoirs, then it is necessary to include all the combat south of Prokhorovka – in the areas of Vypolzovka, Rzhavets, Ryndinka and Shakhovo, where the 11th and 12th Guards Mechanized Brigades of the 5th Guards Mechanized Corps, the 26th Guards Tank Brigade of the 2nd Guards Tank Corps, and the 69th Army's 53rd Guards Separate Tank Regiment and 96th Separate Tank Brigade were operating – to the Prokhorovka "meeting tank engagement". That is to say, all combat operations in those areas, where tankers of the 5th Guards Tank Army were fighting on 12 July, must be called the Prokhorovka meeting tank engagement. In doing so, the efforts and sacrifices of the rifle and artillery units and formations of the 5th Guards, 6th Guards and 69th Armies are neglected! Such an assertion not only fails to correspond with reality, it also sounds harshly dismissive with respect to the thousands of infantrymen killed in that terrible battle.

Let's dwell on terminology for a moment. In the expression, "meeting tank engagement", there are two words, "meeting" and "tank" that are important and precise. In reality, on 12 July southwest of Prokhorovka, there was a meeting tank battle between the formations of the 18th and 29th Tank Corps on the one side, and the SS Panzergrenadier Division *Leibstandarte* and elements of *Das Reich* and *Totenkopf* on the other. The scale of the battle was impressive: in the course of one day on a relatively small sector of the front, there was a clash between eight of our tank brigades and the panzer regiments and anti-tank means of two enemy divisions. There was never before anything like what happened on this day on the Prokhorovka axis and other sectors of Voronezh Front.

On the sector of the 1st Tank Army, the day was relatively quiet, because by this time all primary efforts had been shifted to Prokhorovka. Lieutenant General M. E. Katukov's army itself was exhausted and worn down; even with an order to participate in the counterattack, it was unable to put together a massed tank attack on any sort of narrow sector. The separate tank regiments and brigades of the 6th and 7th Guards Armies were also too small in size to provide any basis for including them in the group of formations, capable of conducting a tank battle on 12 July. That leaves only the 5th Guards Tank Army as the single operational Soviet army ready to launch a large tank attack.

The 5th Guards Tank Army had five corps, two of which had only come under its operational control on 11 July. It was precisely the tankers of the 18th and 29th Tank Corps that met the SS Panzergrenadier Division *Leibstandarte* head-to-head and fought pitched battles in a way that could be described as "meeting".

The combat operations of two other of the 5th Guards Tank Army's corps that took part in the counterattack, A. F. Popov's 2nd Tank Corps and A. S. Burdeiny's 2nd Guards Tank Corps, could hardly be considered "meeting battles". In particular, the 2nd Tank Corps largely remained on the defensive, while the 2nd Guards Tank Corps attacked units of the *Das Reich* Division and the 167th Infantry Division, which repelled its attacks with defensive fire from fixed positions, before undertaking more active measures, trying to turn the 2nd Guards Tank Corps' right flank. Thus, we will focus on the fighting southwest of Prokhorovka and examine it from a statistical point of view.

In numerous publications which discuss Voronezh Front's counterattack on 12 July 1943, usually there is no assessment of the correlation of forces and means between the two sides on the Prokhorovka axis or the quantitative results. This is explained by the absence of accurate data. Nevertheless, we will make the attempt on the basis of data well-known today (although it can be somewhat contradictory).

In order to assess correctly the results of the fighting and the overall engagement, it is necessary to consider not only the potential capabilities of the opposing sides, but also primarily the actual number of weapons that took part in the fighting, especially noting those that participated directly in the counterattack. For example, a significant number of tanks and even several units of the 5th Guards Tank Army for one reason or another were unable to join the fighting on 12 July. Thus, we'll immediately say that in all further calculations, only the actual number of tanks and self-propelled guns that participated in the tank engagement at Prokhorovka on 12 July will be considered. Concrete numbers have been taken from the reports of tank brigade commanders, which are confirmed by corresponding documents and are shown in Table 19. The data in this table allow a more realistic evaluation of the results of the counterattack and of the Prokhorovka engagement as a whole.

Of course, the correlation of available tanks between the two sides was of decisive significance in the Prokhorovka engagement. The 5th Guards Tank Army (including the 2nd Guards Tank and 2nd Tank Corps) had 909 tanks and 42 self-propelled guns on its roster at 1700 11 July, of which 96 tanks and five self-propelled guns were still *en route* to the assembly areas, and 24 tanks were under repair.[19] However, in the account of the 5th Guards Tank Army's combat operations in the period between 7 July and 24 July, the headquarters staff reports that the army had, together with its attached formations and units of reinforcement, 793 serviceable tanks on 12 July, including 501 T-34, 261 T-70, and 31 Mk-IV Churchill tanks; 45 self-propelled guns; 79 76mm guns and 330 45mm anti-tank guns; 495 82mm and 120mm mortars; 39 BM-13 rocket launchers; and 1,007 anti-tank rifles.[20] So this account maintains that 838 tanks and self-propelled guns took part in combat operations, beginning on 12 July (this number, obviously, doesn't include the 96 tanks that were still *en route* to the assembly areas and the 20 tanks that weren't able to be repaired by this time, though three self-propelled guns have appeared from somewhere compared to the data in Table 19).

Of course, not every unit in the 5th Guards Tank Army participated in the fighting on 12 July. According to my own calculations, based upon the numbers presented in the operational reports of the tank regiment, tank brigade and mechanized brigade commanders (which are confirmed by corresponding documents) and presented in Table 21, there were 808 serviceable tanks and 32 self-propelled guns in the units and formations of the 5th Guards Tank Army on the morning of 12 July, for a total of 840 armored vehicles. Of these 840 armored vehicles, only 642 tanks and 30 self-propelled guns took direct part in the fighting on 12 July, or 77% of the total number of serviceable machines (see Line 33, Table 21).

Army Group South numbered 1,508 tanks and assault guns (the Fourth Panzer Army – 1,089, Army Detachment Kempf – 419).[21] According to data provided by Colonel Karl-Heinz Frieser[22], a member of the *Bundeswehr*'s Military Historical Department, on the eve of the offensive the two shock groupings of Army Group South (the Fourth Panzer Army and Army Detachment Kempf) had 1,137 tanks (of which 1,043 were serviceable) and 240 assault guns (of which either 202 or 229 were serviceable; the records disagree), for a total of 1,377.[23] However, these figures do not include the assault guns in the III Panzer Corps. There was a separate battalion of 94 assault guns under Army Group South's control, but it isn't clear how many of them were used to reinforce the III Panzer Corps.[24] According to other records, the III Panzer Corps received the 223rd, 393rd and 905th Assault Gun Batteries prior to the offensive, for a total of 75 assault guns.[25]

The German historian J. Engelmann, relying upon E. von Manstein's report, maintains that the II SS Panzer Corps on 13 July had 131 tanks and assault guns remaining of its original 422; the XXXXVIII Panzer Corps correspondingly had 199 out of 520.[26] In Army Detachment Kempf's III Panzer Corps there remained 69 operational tanks and assault guns on 15 July, out of the initial 310, and in the Panther-equipped 39th Panzer Regiment of the XXXXVIII Panzer Corps, 162 Panther tanks of the starting 200.[27] Summing up, according to von Manstein's report, the two shock groupings of Army Group South had a combined 1,452 tanks and assault guns at the start of Operation Citadel. At the same time, however, the commander of Army Group

South himself, in his report upon which Engelmann relies, asserts that he had a total of 1,352 tanks and assault guns at the start of the operation, including 100 Tiger tanks and 200 Panther tanks (plainly, he is not including vehicles in the repair pool).[28]

However, we are most interested in the armored vehicles available to the formations of the II SS Panzer Corps and the III Panzer Corps that operated on the Prokhorovka axis. In the II SS Panzer Corps, with which the 5th Guards Tank Army directly collided on 12 July, at the start of the operation there were 390 tanks, including 42 Tigers and 26 captured T-34s, and 104 assault guns, for a total of 494. In the III Panzer Corps, which was reinforced with the 503rd Heavy Panzer Battalion (45 Tigers) and the 228th Separate Assault Gun Battalion, there were 344 tanks, 13 of which were flame-throwing tanks, and 31 assault guns, for a total of 375 armored vehicles.[29] Consequently, at the start of Operation Citadel the two corps numbered 869 tanks and assault guns.

In the course of the offensive, the enemy's panzer formations suffered significant losses. By the evening of 11 July, the II SS Panzer Corps had 236 tanks and 58 assault guns, for a total of 294 (60% of its initial strength).[30] By this time the corps still had 15 serviceable Tigers[31] (Karl-Heinz Frieser puts the number at 20), the superiority of which over our T-34s in the first half of 1943 is general knowledge.

Not all the divisions of the III Panzer Corps, which broke through to Rzhavets in the pre-dawn hours of 12 July, submitted reports on their available armor. According to available data, on the morning of 12 July there were 120-127 operational tanks and assault guns in the III Panzer Corps[32] (only approximately a third of its initial complement), including 23 Tigers.[33]

Thus, in the engagement at Prokhorovka on a front of about 50 kilometers, two panzer corps were operating, which possessed a total of 413-421 tanks and assault guns. According to Karl-Heinz Frieser's data, the two corps had a combined 420 tanks and assault guns on 12 July. However, let us stop there.

After introducing the 5th Guards Tank Army into the engagement on the Prokhorovka axis, our forces outnumbered the enemy's approximately twice over (840 tanks and assault guns against 413). As we see, this correlation sharply differs from the one given by Rotmistrov (800 against 700). However, this numerical superiority still had to be realized on the battlefield, and this of course depends on the ability of command to create an overwhelming superiority in strength and weapons at the proper moment on the selected axis of the main attack. Due to various reasons, only 642 tanks and 30 self-propelled guns (a total of 672) actually took part in the fighting on 12 July on our side. We must also not forget the relative qualitative superiority of the enemy's tanks.

The tank corps were given a mission to encircle and destroy a qualitatively superior enemy and by the end of 12 July to achieve a line at a depth of 20-25 kilometers. The four corps of the 5th Guards Tank Army's first echelon (the 18th, 29th, 2nd and 2nd Guards Tank Corps) numbered 571 tanks and self-propelled guns. The total correlation of forces in tanks in the sector of the 5th Guards Tank Army's offensive was 2:1 (571 versus 294) in our favor. This is plainly inadequate, given the accepted belief that the correlation should be even more to the advantage of the attacker on the assigned axis of the main assault in order to count upon any major success. Incidentally, at least one German commander believed that their forces "fought successful actions with a strength ratio of 1:5, as long as the formations involved were more or less intact and adequately equipped."[34]

The tank brigades of the 18th and 29th Tank Corps – altogether 368 tanks and assault guns – were deployed on the axis of the main attack, with a frontage of up to 6 kilometers. These corps were directly opposed by the SS Panzergrenadier Division *Leibstandarte*, which in the preceding fighting, especially on 11 July, had suffered significant losses, at least greater than those in other divisions of the SS Panzer Corps.

According to records in the former Federal Republic of Germany's military archives, the SS Panzergrenadier Division *Leibstandarte* had on the evening of 11 July only 67 serviceable tanks, 7 of which were outdated types used as command tanks, and 10 assault guns.[35] However, one must also consider the armor strength of the other two divisions, which were operating on *Leibstandarte*'s flanks. The SS Panzergrenadier Division *Das Reich*, operating on the right, had a complement of 68 tanks and 27 assault guns, for a total of 95 armored vehicles.[36] With part of its panzer regiment (no less than one-third, up to approximately 25 tanks), it was covering the right flank of *Leibstandarte*. Plainly, this *kampfgruppe* took part in the fighting against the tanks of the 29th Tank Corps, which had penetrated the German defenses at the Komsomolets State Farm.

The SS Panzergrenadier Division *Totenkopf* had 101 tanks and 21 assault guns on its combat roster on the evening of 11 July.[37] That night, the main forces of its panzer regiment crossed over the Psel River, and at 0930 attacked to the northeast out of the bridgehead it had seized. Judging from the fighting on 12 July, not less than a third of *Totenkopf*'s panzer regiment (approximately 30-35 tanks) and two-thirds of an assault gun battalion (10-15 vehicles) remained on the southern bank of the river in the attack sector of the 18th Tank Corps.

Thus, taking into consideration those elements of *Totenkopf* and *Das Reich*, the ratio in armored strength on the axis of 5th Guards Tank Army's main attack was approximately 2.5 to 1 (368 versus 147-150). Such a ratio, it would seem, allowed hope for a successful attack outcome. However, in a qualitative sense, superiority was on the side of the opponent. Firstly, 40% of the attacking echelon of our forces consisted of light T-70 tanks with their weak 45mm guns, and the 76mm assault guns based on the T-70 chassis (139 T-70 and SU-76). Secondly, approximately 40% of the combat vehicles in the SS Panzer Corps consisted of the medium Panzer IV tank with 75mm guns, which were somewhat superior to the gun on our T-34 tanks in both range and armor penetration capabilities.

Unfortunately, serious shortcomings were permitted when organizing the counterattack. For example, owing to the lack of time for preparations and the absence of reliable information on the opposing enemy forces, the artillery relied primarily on area fire. Artillery support for the attack during the battle was poorly organized; detected enemy anti-tank guns were not quickly suppressed. Insufficient cooperation among the armed branches, especially with aviation, and the poor handling of the units during the fighting were also telling. All this prevented the realization of the significant numerical advantage over the enemy in tanks, and augmented the enemy's certain qualitative superiority in weaponry. Moreover, the restricted span of the offensive sector, the right side of which was cut by ravines and gullies, led to a congested deployment (for example, the 18th Tank Corps attacked in three echelons), which in turn led to intermingling of the corps' combat formations. On one hand, this prevented the full exploitation of the Soviet tanks' superiority in mobility and maneuverability, and on the other hand, caused excessive losses from enemy artillery fire and the *Luftwaffe*.

In savage fighting, the Soviet tank corps were unable to carry out their assignments. The 18th Tank Corps, relying upon positions being held by Red Army infantry and the 2nd Tank Corps' 99th Tank Brigade, which was stubbornly fighting in encirclement in the areas of Vasil'evka and Andreevka, could only advance 4 kilometers. The more powerful 29th Tank Corps, the commander of which introduced around 200 tanks in the course of the day on a sector just 1 kilometer wide, could only advance 2 kilometers, while losing 77% of its participating armored vehicles and 1,991 men (around 20%) in the process. Moreover, in the course of the subsequent enemy counterattacks, it was driven from the line it had attained and had to abandon two tactically important points that it had temporarily seized – the Oktiabr'skii and Komsomolets State Farms.

On the axis of the 2nd Guards Tank Corps' attack (excluding the detached 26th Guards Tank Brigade), the numerical ratio in tanks was only 1.3:1 (94 tanks versus 60-70). Given such a ratio, it was difficult to expect success. Moreover, the corps' brigades attacked the enemy on an excessively broad front of around 7 kilometers. Elements of the SS *Das Reich* and the 167th Infantry Division not only repelled the corps' attack, which lost more than 50% of the participating armor, but also created a threat of a breakthrough into its rear.

The brigades of the 2nd Tank Corps (59 tanks) were covering the gap between the flanks of the 29th and 2nd Guards Tank Corps, and took no part in the general attack. In their sector, the enemy even managed to advance and capture Storozhevoe.

Thus, as a result of the meeting battle, the corps of the 5th Guards Tank Army on the axis of the main attack suffered heavy losses. By the end of 12 July, they were even forced to revert to the defense.

So, just how many tanks took part in the "famous brawl on the tank field" southwest of Prokhorovka? The analysis of combat documents and calculations indicate, that with consideration for the two tank corps of the 5th Guards Tank Army on the one side, and the SS Panzergrenadier Division *Leibstandarte* and elements of the SS Divisions *Das Reich* and *Totenkopf* of the II SS Panzer Corps on the other side, then a maximum of 368 tanks and self-propelled guns took direct part in the fighting southwest of Prokhorovka on 12 July on our side, and on the German side, not more than 150 tanks and assault guns. So altogether, a *little more than 500 tanks and assault guns* clashed southwest of Prokhorovka, and no way could it have been *1,200 armored vehicles, much less 1,500 tanks and assault guns.*

Some historians might argue that the 2nd Guards 'Tatsinskaia' Tank Corps and all of the SS Panzergrenadier Division *Das Reich* should be added to these totals. If however the 2nd Guards Tank Corps and the remaining elements of *Das Reich* can also be considered participants of the fighting on the "tank field", then the number of tanks and self-propelled guns that participated in the combat on 12 July 1943 does not exceed 700.

Three panzer divisions of the III Panzer Corps, which combined had 118-120 tanks (including 23 Tigers), launched an attack toward Prokhorovka from the south.[38] They were opposed by General K. G. Trufanov's mobile group, which consisted of the 1st Guards Separate Motorcycle Regiment, the 53rd Guards Separate Tank Regiment, the 11th and 12th Mechanized Brigades of the 5th Guards Mechanized Corps, and the 26th Guards Tank Brigade of the 2nd Guards Tank Corps – altogether 157 tanks and 11 self-propelled guns. The strength ratio in tanks on this axis was 1:1.3 in favor of the opponent. It should be stressed that there was nothing like a meeting clash of tanks on this axis on 12 July. Breith's III Panzer Corps largely spent the day focused on defending its bridgeheads across the Northern Donets. Group Trufanov failed to carry out its assignment to crush the enemy and to restore the situation on this sector. However, in cooperation with divisions of the 69th Army's 48th Rifle Corps, its attacks did manage to stabilize the situation on the 5th Guards Tank Army's left flank.

The 5th Guards Army, which participated in the counterattack and attacked without armor support, also had no success. Moreover, the adversary managed not only to retain possession of the tactically important point of Hill 226.6, but also to expand the bridgehead it had seized the day before in the bend of the Psel River, having hurled back units of the 95th Guards Rifle Division by 4 kilometers. The 24th Guards Tank Brigade (48 tanks) and the 10th Guards Mechanized Brigade (44 tanks) of the 5th Guards Mechanized Corps had to move into the 5th Guards Army's sector in order to stop the further advance of the SS Panzergrenadier Division *Totenkopf* into the rear of the 5th Guards Tank Army. This, in essence, deprived P. A. Rotmistrov of his last reserve, which could have been used instead to augment the effort on the main axis in case of success there.

To summarize, altogether on 12 July 1943, no more than 1,100 armored vehicles (642 tanks and 30 self-propelled guns on our side, and 420 tanks and assault guns on the opposing side) directly participated in the engagement southwest and south of Prokhorovka Station. The fighting continued all day long with fluctuating success; both sides suffered heavy losses and by the end of the day went over to the defense.

In the days following the 12 July counterattack, the engagement turned into an aggregation of scattered combat around the entire perimeter of the enemy's salient on the Prokhorovka axis, along a front of up to 50 kilometers. Attacks on both sides alternated with counterattacks. The adversary, unable to break through the third (and final) defensive belt, turned to more limited objectives with the aim of inflicting the heaviest possible losses on the defenders and in order to create the most satisfactory conditions for the subsequent withdrawal of its forces from the area of the salient. After the decisive collapse of the entire Operation Citadel, such a decision was the only one possible.

The evaluation of the engagement at Prokhorovka from the opposing side is of doubtless interest. Karl-Heinz Frieser, who has introduced a large amount of data on this matter based upon materials of the Government and Military Archives of the Federal Republic of Germany, and on the work of other German historians, stated:

> For the German panzer divisions, the day of 12 July proved to be very difficult, but fully successful, since they had managed to repulse a counterattack by superior Soviet tank corps. The Fourth Panzer Army's combat diary speaks of 'complete success, since not only was the Soviet offensive driven back, but the SS Panzer Corps also managed to gain more ground on this day.'[39]

Karl-Heinz Frieser added:

> If all the same one compares the German and Russian documents, first of all the situational maps, then it becomes apparent that on a front of three kilometers near Prokhorovka (between the railroad embankment and the Psel River valley), there was no collision between two complete tank armies. In essence, one panzer division fought here on the German side, and on the Soviet side – the 18th Tank Corps and units of the 29th Tank Corps.[40]

If we speak only of a head-on collision on the "tank field," then Frieser might agree: in reality, two complete tank armies didn't clash here, nor did 1,500 or even 1,200 tanks. However, in the course of the counterattack, fighting occurred in two different sectors: the first – between the Psel River valley and the villages east of the railway, on a front not less than 6-7 kilometers wide; and the second – in the sector between Ivanovskii Vyselok (excl.) and the Sukhaia Plota ravine, which was also 6-7 kilometers wide. The combined width of the two sectors comprised 12-14 kilometers. In the fighting, two SS Panzergrenadier divisions – *Leibstandarte* and *Das Reich* – took part on the German side, and on the Soviet side, three tanks corps – the 18th, 29th and the 2nd Guards Tank Corps.

Even though the counterattack failed to reach its assigned goal, so much damage was inflicted on the enemy that he was forced to abandon his intentions to continue the offensive. *This was the main result of the tank engagement of 12 July 1943 and of the counterattack as a whole.*

It is commonly known that one of the main criteria used to measure the level of development of operational art, tactics, command, staff work, and troop training is the level of losses given a known correlation of forces and means in an engagement or battle. The question of losses is a sensitive one in our [Soviet and Russian] historiography. Censorship did not permit the open publication of information about Soviet combat losses. Almost a half-century passed from the end of the war, before the veil of secrecy was finally removed from this topic – when the first statistical research on the losses of the Soviet Armed Forces in wars, combat actions and military conflicts was published under the title *Grif sekrenosti sniat* [The seal of secrecy has been removed].[41] For example, in order to explain and justify the defeat suffered by the Red Armies in the initial period of the war, the military censorship of 1944 concealed from the people a "terrible truth" – the number of tanks in the Red Army prior to the Nazi invasion!

The opening (or it is more correct to say, the partial opening) of military archives has led to a new evaluation of some events of the Great Patriotic War, as well as of the actions of famous military commanders. Not everyone likes this. Historians and researchers, who on the basis of new documentary information take a fresh look at one or another event of the past war, are frequently accused of maliciously tarnishing reputations. Meanwhile, it is no longer a secret to anyone that all too often the issuance of orders was accompanied by the words "At any cost!" These words were not written into combat and operational documents, but they were the norm, and not always made necessary by the situation. Yet just let a commander try to disobey the order!

It is necessary to look honestly, using all available sources, not only at the enemy's losses, but also our own; that is, to determine the price of victory. This in no way diminishes our victory over a strong, cruel and wily foe.

Let us try to look into the cost by which the victory at Prokhorovka was achieved, using all available information, including those in German archives, while where applicable condemning estimation errors and contradictions. Incidentally we'll note that right up to the start of the 1990s, substantiated data, confirmed by documents, on the losses of both sides over the entire period of the Prokhorovka engagement, and for 12 July in particular, had not yet been published.

First we'll try to determine the losses in armor on the German side. One of the first figures for German losses for the single day of 12 July was given by P. A. Rotmistrov in his recollections of the battle: "In the engagement at Prokhorovka, the 5th Guards Tank Army destroyed around 400 enemy tanks (including 70 Tigers), 88 guns, 70 mortars, 83 machine guns, more than 300 vehicles carrying troops or cargo, and more than 3,500 soldiers and officers."[42] A few pages later, Rotmistrov gives a more precise figure: "For the entire period of fighting from 12 July to 16 July 1943, 459 enemy tanks were destroyed by the forces of the 5th Guards Tank Army in combination with the combined arms formations."[43] On the losses in his own army, the army commander is silent. Only at the end of the book, when speaking about the work of the army's recovery and repair service, does Rotmistrov note: "On the first days of the meeting tank engagement alone, the army's repair pool consisted of approximately 420 tanks, of which 112 had insignificant damage, which were repaired on the spot and the vehicles were returned to service."[44] (Later the army commander offers a clarification: "... over the first two days of the meeting tank engagement.")

In his book *Stal'naia gvardiia* released in 1984, Rotmistrov corrected earlier published figures: "On 12 July alone in fighting with the 5th Guards Tank Army, the enemy lost more than 350 tanks and more than 10,000 men killed."[45] On the losses of his army – again there is nothing, except for a general statement: "We also lost a lot of tanks, especially light [tanks], and many courageous Guardsmen were killed in the furious clashes." Such an approach by the army commander to important information raises doubt and suspicion toward the numbers he offers. Incidentally, this is not at all Rotmistrov's fault – one can sense the hand of the military censor here, without whose approval at that time not a single book could be published. Relying upon declassified documents of the units and formations of the 5th Guards Tank Army, it is possible to speak about the armor losses in its corps and brigades at various points of the engagement with a greater amount of confidence.

As concerns the enemy, then, here the discrepancies in the statistical data are quite high. Over the past decades, several interesting investigations into German losses have emerged. Western historians display especially great interest in this topic; in their works, they give a variety of figures for the total losses in the German panzer corps during the Kursk offensive, including the losses in the II SS Panzer Corps and the III Panzer Corps for 12 July. All these figures come from one source – Germany's Federal Military Archive. Here are a few examples:

• N. Zetterling and A. Frankson assert that over the 13 days [of Operation Citadel] (from 5 July to 17 July 1943), the formations of Army Group South lost 190 tanks and assault guns, while the II SS Panzer Corps and III Panzer Corps between 11 July and 17 July lost 17 and 37 armored vehicles respectively.[46]

• The German scholar K.-H. Frieser maintains that in the fighting on 12 July, the three SS divisions lost five tanks irreparably damaged, while an additional 42 tanks and 12 assault guns required lengthy repairs.[47]

• In a 2001 article published in the Russian *Voenno-Istoricheskii Zhurnal* [Military History Journal] as a response to Frieser's assertion, Colonel I'lin gives the following data: Army Group South between 5 and 16 July lost a total of 175 armored vehicles, including 161 tanks and 14 assault guns, while the II SS Panzer Corps for the single day of 12 July supposedly lost 130 tanks and 23 assault guns, for a total of 153 vehicles.[48]

• According to data provided by J. Engelmann, of the 294 serviceable tanks and assault guns that the II SS Panzer Corps fielded on the evening of 11 July, by 13 July 1943 only 131 tanks and assault guns remained operational – thus, the losses of the corps for 12 July comprised 163 armored vehicles.[49]

Several reasons explain such a wide divergence in figures. First is the way the *Wehrmacht* calculated combat losses. The Germans regarded as lost only those combat vehicles that were completely destroyed or left abandoned to the enemy – all remaining tanks were assigned to the repair pool. In documents, damaged armor were assigned to a different category, either long-term or short-term repairs. Accordingly, if one considers that the Germans controlled the battlefield at Prokhorovka right up to the afternoon of 17 July, then they were able to recover all of their knocked-out armor and return those that could be repaired to eventual action. Only the few armored vehicles that could not be returned to service were counted as destroyed. Meanwhile, the enemy blew up all of our equipment that was left on the battlefield during our withdrawal. This fact gives rise to the seemingly absurd assertion that the German side lost only five tanks at Prokhorovka on 12 July. Moreover, how should we consider badly damaged tanks, not considered as lost in the engagement, but assigned to long-term repair, when they were sent back to Germany for a lengthy period, after the fighting at Prokhorovka had been concluded?

Let's again return to the data provided by J. Engelmann: in the II SS Panzer Corps on 13 July, there were 131 serviceable tanks and assault guns remaining of the 422 with which it had started Operation Citadel. In Army Group Kempf's III Panzer Corps, according to Engelmann, on 15 July there remained 69 operational tanks and assault guns out of the initial 310.[50] Thus, as it turns out, of the 294 serviceable tanks and assault guns in the II SS Panzer Corps on the evening of 11 July, 163 armored vehicles were lost to the corps in the fighting on 12 July as damaged or destroyed. This figure is just a little larger than the one offered by Il'in above (153).The III Panzer Corps lost approximately 51 to 58 tanks between 12 July and 14 July. If we assume that on 12 July, the day of heaviest fighting, the losses comprised no less than 30 to 35 tanks and assault guns (60% of the losses between 12 and 14 July), and 15 (50%) of these were totally destroyed, then we can estimate that the II SS Panzer Corps and the III Panzer Corps together *lost 193 tanks and assault guns on 12 July (including 20 that were unable to be repaired and put back into service). This amounts to 47% of the 414 serviceable tanks and assault guns available on the evening of 11 July.*

No less difficult problems arise when trying to calculate enemy losses in personnel. It is very difficult to determine the real combat and numerical strength of the hostile formations that were opposing our forces. I've thus far been unable to locate precise troop strength data. General figures, indicated for assessing the strength ratios of the fronts, are inadequate for calculating losses. Figures for so-called ration strength (*Vepflegungsstarken*) for 1 July 1943 can give us some idea of the II SS Panzer Corps troop strength. These indicate how many men were on rations in the corps' divisions. However, these include non-combat personnel, such as the so-called *Hiwis* (*hilfswillige* – volunteer assistants from former military prisoners and Nazi supporters), men under military detention, and even civilians who were providing service to the combat units.

Altogether on 1 July 1943, there were 82,836 individuals in the II SS Panzer Corps obtaining rations. In the three Panzergrenadier divisions of the Corps, 72,960 rations were allotted for the divisions' own personnel rosters, 4,164 for the *Hiwis*, and 5,712 for the personnel of attached units, who were on the divisions' rations.

In addition to the troops and officers reporting for duty, the rosters (*Liststarke*) of the divisions counted also the wounded and sick, those on leave, and those sent elsewhere on temporary assignment, who might return to the unit within eight weeks. Moreover, the Germans had a category for the combat strength of the formation (or unit), that is, the number of men who were participating directly in combat. This combat strength (*Gefechtstarke*) included military personnel of various types of forces (infantry, armor, artillery, engineer, and reserve units and elements), but excluded service, transport and repair personnel. At the same time, the Germans sometimes used a category *Kampfstarke*, which included only men who participated directly in combat – the riflemen and those supporting them. The combat strength or battle strength excluded the wounded, sick and those on leave or on temporary assignment elsewhere. Finally, there was the category of the combat strength on the day of reporting (*Tagesstarke*). As the basis for calculating losses, we have selected to use the daily reports on combat strength and the attrition of personnel.

Thus, according to German records, on 1 July the 2nd SS Panzergrenadier Division *Das Reich* had 20,654 personnel on rations, including 1,576 *Hiwis* and 660 men in attached units. The combat strength of the division numbered 7,350 men (36% of the ration strength). On 4 July, the 3rd Panzer Division numbered respectively 14,141 and 5,170 (37%) and the 167th Infantry Division – 17,837 and 6,776 men (38%). The 19th Panzer Division had a ration strength of 13,221 on 1 July. In passing we'll note that our intelligence had quite accurate estimates of the enemy divisions' combat strengths at the start of the operation. For example, *Das Reich*'s combat strength was put at 7,000 men, and the 167th Infantry Division's strength was estimated at 8,300 men (for the divisions of the II SS Panzer Corps, the average error was only in the range of 200-500 men).

Using the above associations, we can calculate the approximate combat strength of the II SS Panzer Corps as 36% of its ration strength of 82,836, or 26,265 men. According to our intelligence estimates at the start of the operation, the corps' strength was 23,800 – 25,000 men. Similar information for Army Group Kempf's III Panzer Corps, unfortunately, is not in our possession.

It must be remembered that in the course of fighting, non-combat personnel were often deployed in the combat units as replacements. Moreover, the divisions also had field replacement battalions (in Russian terminology, reserve or spare battalions). For example, the SS *Das Reich* Division on 30 August 1943 had 13,592 men on rations, but 5,692 (42%) of these men were considered combatants, which indicates that the proportion of men in the combat strength calculation increased at times of heavy combat. The SS *Totenkopf* Division on 1 July 1943 distributed 23,800 individual rations; on 10 July this number dropped to 20,830, and on 20 July, to 19,630. Likely, the reduction in this number between 1 July and 20 July 1943 by 4,170 was connected not only with the release of civilian assistants and the flight of *Hiwis*, but also with combat losses.

The II SS Panzer Corps on 12 July lost 149 killed, 660 wounded, and 33 missing, for a total of 842 soldiers and officers. Between 10 July and 16 July (over seven days), it lost 4,178 men (approximately 16% of its combat strength), including 755 killed, 3,351 wounded and 68 missing.[51]

The III Panzer Corps on the approaches to Prokhorovka in the period between 12 July and 16 July 1943 lost approximately 2,790 men, and a total of 8,489 men between 5 July and 20 July 1943.[52] Calculating from the cited data, both corps combined (three Panzergrenadier divisions and one infantry division of the II SS Panzer Corps and three panzer and two infantry divisions of the III Panzer Corps) in the course of the Prokhorovka engagement between 10 July 1943 and 17 July 1943 lost approximately 7,000 soldiers and officers. Altogether the II SS Panzer Corps lost 8,095 men from 5 July to 20 July 1943 (SS *Leibstandarte* Division – 2,896; SS *Das Reich* Division – 2,802; and troops under corps headquarters – 69), of which 1,467 (18%) were killed, and 166 (2%) were missing.[53]

Erich von Manstein asserts that in the course of the offensive, both of his armies – Fourth Panzer Army and Army Detachment Kempf – suffered a combined 20,720 casualties, of which 3,330 were killed.[54] All the divisions, except for one panzer division (possibly, the 19th Panzer Division), remained combat-worthy. If von Manstein's numbers are correct, then 80% of all the losses in Army Group South would have come from the II SS Panzer Corps and the III Panzer Corps. It follows that the remaining three corps and the units under direct control by army headquarters could have lost at most only 4,136 men, which cannot be true. The XXXVIII Panzer Corps alone lost 6,541 in killed, wounded and missing between 4 July and 20 July.[55] In passing we'll note that the German side frequently understated their losses. In addition, generally speaking commanders and military chiefs in their memoirs rarely lost any engagements or battles. In case of failure, they have tried in every way to minimize the harm suffered.[56]

However, one must still pay the enemy credit where it is due: in the *Wehrmacht's* units, the recovery, repair and return to service of damaged army equipment was highly organized. For this purpose, each German panzer regiment had a repair company, and separate panzer battalions had repair platoons. For example, the service platoon of the 502nd Battalion of Tiger tanks, which had an authorized strength of 40 Tigers, over two years of combat operations managed to put 102 damaged Tiger tanks back into action.

Another example speaks to the enemy's impressive repair capabilities. Within several days after launching the offensive, the number of tanks in the Fourth Panzer Army and Army Detachment Kempf had dropped to approximately 40% of their initial strength (primarily the vehicles were rendered unserviceable ostensibly because of mechanical problems). But when the seven days of fighting for Prokhorovka had ended, the number of combat-capable tanks had not only not decreased, but had even increased somewhat – to 46% of initial strength.[57] This indicates that the number of knocked-out tanks during the week of fighting was less than the number of tanks returning from repairs.[58]

It is also possible to follow the enemy's flow of losses and repair work by the example of the combat use of the Panzer V Panther tanks in the operation. On 5 July, there were 184 serviceable Panthers remaining; on 6 July – 166; on 7 July – 40; and on 10 July – just 38. By 21 July, of the 200 initial Panthers at the start of Citadel, only 41 (20%) remained combat-ready; 85 of the Panthers were in the repair pool, while 16 had been sent away for major overhaul. Fifty-eight of the Panthers were written off as unrecoverable losses, and of these, 49 were demolished by explosives when the Germans withdrew.[59]

The exaggeration of German armor losses by the Soviet authors of memoirs and military historians is connected with the desire to emphasize the successes of the Soviet forces, and in so doing, justify the heavy losses on our side. One should also recall that all sorts of weapons were firing at the German tanks most of the time, and when one indicated it had been struck (by halting or erupting in flames), each firing tank crew or gun crew claimed credit for it (one mustn't forget as well the NKO's Order No. 38 on incentive bonuses for knocked-out enemy armor!). Meanwhile, the headquarters staff conscientiously and dutifully added up all the reported figures. In addition, obviously, destroyed armored half-tracks, of which there were many in the panzer divisions, became included in the count of knocked-out armor. At least one of the Panzergrenadier regiments in each of the SS Panzergrenadier divisions was equipped with 48 armored half-tracks. On the attack they were covered by the panzers and advanced behind them. For some reason, only a line for destroyed infantry-carrying trucks appears in the accounts of our forces, a fact which suggests that the armored half-tracks were considered in the same class as tanks and assault guns!

Similar exaggerations appear with respect to destroyed Tigers, which we have seen throughout this study. For example, German sources categorically deny any tanks of this type were total losses on 12 July. It is possible that our troops were confusing the Panzer IV-H, which also had a long-barreled gun with a prominent muzzle brake, with the Panzer VI Tiger (notably, on some occasions these tanks were referred to as "Tiger Type IV").

According to statistical research conducted after the war, the Red Army lost more tanks and self-propelled guns than any other type of weapon or equipment during the years of the war. The figures are colossal: 96,500 combat vehicles! This number represents 427% of the amount of armor available at the start of 1941, and 73% of the total supplied during the war. During the war, the acting Red Army daily lost an average of 68 tanks and self-propelled guns; on days of operations this figure grew to 90-290, and on days of major engagements – 70-90. For purposes of comparison, one can look at incomplete data for German losses by the end of the war. They amount to 42,700 armored vehicles.[60] Let us now try to look into the losses of our forces during the Prokhorovka engagement.

The wide divergence in the figures for the losses in armor on both sides is largely explained by the desire to inflate the enemy's losses while correspondingly lowering your own side's losses. In every publication in the open Soviet press, in which losses were given in the Prokhorovka engagement, though at times the figures may have changed, the enemy losses were always reported to be higher than our own. Even the latest edition (1999) of the Military Encyclopedia maintains that the Germans lost 360 tanks and self-propelled guns on 12 July, while the 5th Guards Tank Army lost 350.[61]

In one of the 5th Guards Tank Army's summary reports in the course of operation, it is stated that on 12 July 1943, the Army lost 300 tanks and self-propelled guns.[62]

However, similar evidence on losses was kept in classified archives and was not publicly known.

In 1993, the 50-year withholding period concerning the Red Army's operational documents from the battle of Kursk expired, and the figure for the 5th Guards Tank Army's unrecoverable losses began to appear in publications – 323 tanks and self-propelled guns. This information is contained in a 5th Guards Tank Army headquarters' document, "Findings on the condition, losses and captured material of the units and formations of the 5th Guards Tank Army on 16 July 1943," which was prepared on 17 July 1943 and signed by the chief of staff Major General V. N. Baskakov and his deputy, Lieutenant Colonel Torgalo. Aggregate data for the period 12-16 July (inclusively) for all five tank and mechanized corps, which took part in the Prokhorovka engagement, are shown in Table 28. Unfortunately, the document doesn't isolate the losses on 12 July, so it is difficult to put together a precise and clear picture of the combat worthiness of the army's corps and the condition of their equipment after the so-called meeting engagement of 12 July. However, without this snapshot of the 5th Guards Tank Army's condition, it is impossible to understand the logic driving the course of events after 12 July.

On the basis of operational documents from the headquarters of the tank regiments, tank brigades and mechanized brigades that took part in the counterattack, I've managed to compile a composite table of the losses of the formations and units of the 5th Guards Tank Army for 12 July. Unfortunately, only incomplete returns are available for the 5th Guards Mechanized Corps on 12 July, so there was no possibility to establish the losses on 12 July of that corps (in the Russian Federation's Central Archives of the Ministry of Defense, all the operational and combat documents for the formations of this corps have still not been unearthed). Referring back to Table 21, with only incomplete data for the 5th Guards Mechanized Corps, records indicate that the 5th Guards Tank Army lost 359 tanks and self-propelled guns on this day. Thus, in one day, the army lost 53% of the tanks and self-propelled guns that took part in the counterattack.

Again referring to Table 21, with the additional information on irrevocably destroyed armor that could not fit within the confines of the table, the losses of the individual corps that were involved in the fighting on the "tank field" over the single day of 12 July comprised the following: the 29th Tank Corps – 153 tanks and self-propelled guns (77% of those that took part in the attack), including 103 tanks that were irrecoverably destroyed; the 1446th Self-Propelled Artillery Regiment – 19 self-propelled guns, of which 14 were irrevocably destroyed; the 18th Tank Corps – 84 tanks (56%), including 35 irrevocably destroyed; the 2nd Guards Tank Corps – 54 tanks (39%), including 29 irrevocably destroyed; and the 2nd Tank Corps – 22 tanks (50%), with 11 irrevocably destroyed.[63]

Altogether the four tank corps of the 5th Guards Tank Army lost 340 tanks and 19 self-propelled guns, of which 193 and 14 (207), respectively, were irrecoverably destroyed. The total losses of the II SS Panzer Corps and the III Panzer Corps on 12 July likely amounted to 193 tanks and assault guns, including 20 that were written-off as total losses. According to German historians, the II SS Panzer Corps lost 153-163 tanks and assault guns, including five that were written-off, and another 55 that required major repair.

	29 Tank Corps	18 Tank Corps	2 Gds Tank Corps	2 Tank Corps	5 Gds Mechanized Corps	Units directly under Army HQ	Total
In Formation							
T-34 tanks	42	45	35	31	57	15	225
T-70 tanks	47	44	18	32	33	6	180
Churchills	-	9	-	5	-	-	14
Su-122s	4	-	-	-	9	-	13
Su-76s	6	-	-	-	6	-	12
Vehicles	777	911	471	459	645	330	3,593
122mm guns	-	-	-	-	-	19	19
76mm guns	23	21	16	15	44	-	119
45mm guns	26	30	10	16	31	26	139
85mm AA	-	-	-	-	-	15	15
37mm AA	5	16	15	24	-	40	100
120mm mortars	39	40	40	38	44	-	201
82mm mortars	44	56	20	36	65	6	227
M13 Rocket	-	-	-	-	7	24	31
En Route or Under Repair							
T-34 tanks	14	26	28	23	46	6	143
T-70 tanks	5	7	17	13	13	1	56
Churchills	-	1	-	6	-	-	7
Su-122s	-	-	-	-	3	-	3
Su-76s	-	-	-	-	3	-	3
85mm AA	-	-	6	-	-	-	6
37mm AA	-	-	-	3	-	-	3
76mm guns	-	-	5	5	1	-	11
45mm guns	-	-	8	1	1	-	10
120mm mortars	-	-	4	-	2	-	6
82mm mortars	-	-	3	7	5	-	15
Irrecoverable Losses							
T-34 tanks	60	32	38	10	59	23	222
T-70 tanks	31	12	24	5	14	3	89
Churchills	-	11	-	1	-	-	12
Su-122s	8	-	-	-	-	-	8
Su-76s	3	-	-	-	-	-	3
Vehicles	25	31	95	44	26	19	240
122mm guns	-	-	-	-	-	1	1

Table 28: Findings on the status, losses and captured material of the units and formations of the 5th Guards Tank Army on 16 July 1943

Table 28 continued

	29 Tank Corps	18 Tank Corps	2 Gds Tank Corps	2 Tank Corps	5 Gds Mechanized Corps	Units directly under Army HQ	Total
76mm guns	1	3	3	4	3	-	14
45mm guns	6	2	12	12	15	6	53
85mm AA	-	-	6	-	-	-	6
37mm AA	-	-	1	-	-	5	6
122mm mortars	3	2	9	4	4	-	22
82mm mortars	5	2	9	9	4	-	29
Personnel Losses							
Killed	656	179	807	123	1,122	53	2,940
Wounded	1,017	426	833	247	928	59	3,510
Missing	447	163	53	425	67	2	1,157
Enemy Destroyed							
Soldiers and Officers	3,780	1,190	2,755	1,373	5,432	390	14,920
Tanks	85	92	73	48	213	41	552
Inc. Tigers	14	21	11	9	22	16	93
Artillery batteries	6	1	10	8	14	6	45
Mortar batteries	7	5	6	-	9	2	29
Vehicles	132	56	139	76	354	12	769
Aircraft	8	6	10	6	5	24	59
Ammo dumps	6	3	-	-	1	-	10

Source: TsAMO RF, f. 203, op. 2851, d. 24, l. 451-455.

One can also try to compare the overall losses of the opposing sides in armor for the day of 12 July. According to data provided by scholars of the Russian Institute of Military History, the 5th Guards Tank Army lost a total of approximately 500 tanks and self-propelled guns damaged or destroyed.[64] Unfortunately, the source for this estimate is not given. Possibly, this number includes the 420 damaged vehicles in the repair pool, with the exception of 112 tanks that required only minor repair (207 irrevocably destroyed + 308 requiring major repairs = 515). In this case, the ratio of losses in tanks and self-propelled guns on the "tank field" corresponds to 2.5:1 in favor of the Germans.

A thought rises involuntarily: was it really worth that cost to launch a frontal assault on the enemy's chosen ground and strongest point? The events of 12 July proved that the enemy lost little of his attacking capabilities and instead greatly scrambled the cards held by the Voronezh Front command, having ruined the careful preparation of the Soviet forces for a major counterattack following the halting of the German offensive. Perhaps in retrospect it would have been better to demonstrate patience and to continue to adhere to the adopted plan of a deliberate defense – to continue to whittle down von Manstein's panzers with defensive fire and from ambush positions? At the same time this would have also created suitable conditions for subsequent active operations. After all, time was on our side …

In this case, the result obtained by a counterattack (after blocking an enemy breakthrough into the operational depth) might have been obtained with immeasurably fewer losses in men, weapons and equipment. However, who could have taken upon himself the responsibility for changing a decision already adopted by the *Stavka*?

An indirect sign of I. V. Stalin's dissatisfaction with the developments on the Voronezh Front and the results of the counterattack was the appointment on 13 July of G. K. Zhukov as *Stavka* representative together with A. M. Vasilevsky (who was sent to the Southwest Front to organize and oversee that *front*'s counteroffensive). N. S. Khrushchev recalls:

> Zhukov arrived at Voronezh Front's headquarters. Together, the two of us decided to travel to the area of Prokhorovka, to Rotmistrov's tank army. We arrived at the headquarters' location, directly on the field of battle in a wooded belt … There were no kind of services there – just Rotmistrov himself and some staff officers with their communications support. A road had been laid down to their location. But we were warned that [the road] was under enemy fire and being heavily bombed. Zhukov and I sped through the danger zone and didn't experience any real danger.
>
> … There were a lot of knocked-out tanks visible on the fields – both the enemy's and our own. A disagreement arose over the evaluation of losses: Rotmistrov said that he could see more wrecks of enemy tanks, while I spotted more of our own. Incidentally, it was natural to see one or the other. There were sizeable losses on both sides.[65]

G. K. Zhukov, having familiarized himself with the situation, and with the actions of the enemy and of our own forces in the area of Prokhorovka, came to the conclusion that it was necessary to continue the counterattack more energetically, in order to pin the enemy's forces in place. The analysis of combat operations in the region of Prokhorovka between 13 July and 16 July show that in reality, there was no such continuation of the counterattack. There was no longer enough force or means for this. Efforts instead were directed primarily at preventing the encirclement and destruction of the 69th Army's 48th Rifle Corps. Still Zhukov, with his characteristic energy and resolve, continued to press for ceaseless attacks and counterattacks along the entire length of the German salient, in order to fix the enemy's forces in place and to prevent a regrouping of his units. Thus the 5th Guards Army unsuccessfully tried several times to liquidate *Totenkopf*'s bridgehead across the Psel River.

According to a 5th Guards Tank Army headquarters staff report on 16 July 1943, the data from which were shown in Table 28, the written-off losses in armor for the Army to that point of the Prokhorovka engagement amounted to 323 tanks and 11 self-propelled guns. However, on this same day, due to armored vehicles returned from repairs and replacements the Army had received, it now had 419 tanks and 25 self-propelled guns ready for duty (see Table 28).[66] Thus, within just a matter of days after the 12 July clash, the 5th Guards Tank Army's combat-readiness had primarily been restored.

The sharp increase (by more than two times) in the tank army's written-off armor in comparison with the report for 12 July 1943 – 323 tanks versus 189 – calls attention to itself. It is possible to explain this increase by the following: previously uncounted losses of the 5th Guards Mechanized Corps (73 tanks), which had experienced bitter fighting for the four days between 12 July and 16 July in the area of Rzhavets and Vypolzovka, had by then been added to the 5th Guards Tank Army's total losses. The losses of the 18th and 29th Tank Corps, which had continued to experience skirmishes in the area of Prokhorovka in the days following 12 July, were also added to the total. It is possible as well that the losses of the 29th Tank Corps' 31st and 32nd Tank Brigades, which had been compelled on 12 July to leave behind knocked-out tanks on the Oktiabr'skii and Komsomolets State Farms, had by this time been clarified. It is known that German formation and unit commanders had a strict order to demolish knocked-out Russian armored vehicles, if they were unable to be evacuated from the battlefield. The difference of 235 tanks and self-propelled guns between the 12 July and 16 July 1943 loss reports reflects the written-off losses of the 5th Guards Tank Army's four corps for the period 13-16 July, against 153 of the enemy's armored vehicles (a loss ratio of 1.5 : 1 in favor of the opponent).

However, a tank army and a tank corps are first of all the men (and women) crewing the combat vehicles, without which a tank is not a tank. Only thanks to the resolve, heroism and selflessness of the Soviet fighting tankers was it possible to withstand and repulse the powerful assault of the well-armed and well-equipped divisions of the German Fourth Panzer Army and Army Detachment Kempf. Members of every nationality of the former Soviet Union were represented on the battlefields at Kursk. For example, in the fighting around Prokhorovka among the 44,000 soldiers and officers of the 5th Guards Tank Army (excluding the 2nd Guards and 2nd Tank Corps) were representatives of more than 36 nationalities of the Soviet Union (see Table 29). Primarily they consisted of Russians (74%), Ukrainians (11.7%), and Belorussians (1.8%). The severe tests of war could not shake the friendship between the peoples of our great Motherland, despite Hitler's best efforts. Table 30 shows the age and education profile of the personnel of the 5th Guards Tank Army as of 5 July 1943.

The counterattack, conducted against the enemy under such unfavorable conditions, and the subsequent fighting near Prokhorovka cost the 5th Guards Tank Army dearly in men. In fighting between 12 July and 18 July 1943, the Army lost a total of 9,945 men, including 2,845 soldiers and officers killed, and 2,046 missing in action. Comparable figures as of 16 July were 7,107 total casualties, with 2,240 killed and 1,157 missing in action. The composite losses of the 5th Guards Tank Army are shown in Table 31. Table 32 displays the 18th Tank Corps' losses in personnel for the more limited period of 12-14 July 1943.

The 5th Guards Army in fighting between 9 July and 17 July lost a total of 16,118 men, of which 2,677 were killed and 4,900 went missing in action. The losses in personnel of the rifle formations of this army in the Prokhorovka engagement are shown in Table 33.

The 52nd Guards Rifle Division, which had been transferred from the 6th Guards Army, suffered the heaviest losses in the 5th Guards Army – 5,451 [Editor's note: the author has excluded the 4 individuals listed as a casualty "for other reasons" from his casualty total for the 5th Guards Army] soldiers and officers, including 558 killed, and a whopping 3,796 missing in action. It was precisely this division, defending initially in the first and main defensive belt, which received the main attack of the enemy panzer

Nationality	Command staff	Junior Command Staff	Rank and File	Total	% of Total
Russian	4,520	10,806	17,734	33,060	74.1
Ukrainian	1,210	1,542	2,485	5,237	11.7
Tatar	78	331	744	1,153	2.6
Belorussian	202	247	346	795	1.8
Jewish	323	176	208	707	1.6
Chuvash	44	164	446	654	1.5
Mordvin	34	111	293	438	0.9
Kazakh	29	82	294	405	0.9
Uzbek	13	71	231	315	0.7
Maritsian	14	71	144	229	0.5
Udmurt	7	62	154	223	0.5
Armenian	43	40	100	183	0.4
Bashkir	14	22	146	182	0.4
Georgian	19	38	93	150	0.3
Komi	9	59	56	124	0.3
Azeri	14	24	67	105	0.2
Kirghiz	3	18	55	76	0.2
Dagestan nationalities	8	19	27	54	0.1
Tadzhik	3	10	40	53	0.1
Buriat	1	19	32	52	0.1
Turkmen	2	10	33	45	0.1
Ossetian	13	10	22	45	0.1
Karelian	3	10	24	37	< 0.1
Moldavian	4	12	15	31	< 0.1
Kalmyk	1	3	26	30	< 0.1
Polish	2	6	11	19	< 0.1
Kabardinian and Balkar	3	3	3	9	< 0.1
Latyshi and Latgaltsy	2	-	7	9	< 0.1
Greek	3	2	2	7	< 0.1
Bulgarian	2	1	3	6	< 0.1
Finnish	-	-	6	6	< 0.1
Lithuanian	2	1	2	5	< 0.1
Chechen-Ingush	-	3	1	4	< 0.1
Estonian	-	2	1	3	< 0.1
Others	13	57	103	173	0.4
Total	6,645	14,032	23,948	44,625	100

Note: The table includes data for the 18th and 29th Tank Corps and the 5th Guards Mechanized Corps and all units under Army control on 5 July 1943, and include those personnel temporarily absent in hospitals for which data was available.
Source: TsAMO RF, f. 5 gv. TA, op. 4952, d. 5, l. 8, 8 obr; f. 18 tk, op. 1, d. 93, l. 89.

Table 29: Nationalities in the 5th Guards Tank Army, 5 July 1943

divisions on the first day of the battle. However, note that it continued to play a key role in defending the Psel River against *Totenkopf*'s advance!

In the 69th Army, the greatest losses were from the 183rd Rifle Division (which had only 2,562 men reporting for duty) and the 92nd Guards Rifle Division (2,182 men reporting for duty). The losses of the 69th Army's 48th Rifle Corps totaled 15,628 (see Table 34).

Thus, the formations and units of the Red Army that took part in the Prokhorovka engagement lost more than 42,000 soldiers and officers as casualties. Not less than half this number consisted of killed or missing in action.

Presently, it is not possible to determine exactly the enemy's human losses in the fighting for Prokhorovka. We have previously come up with an estimate of around 7,000 casualties between the II SS Panzer Corps and the III Panzer Corps for the engagement for the period 10 July to 17 July 1943. Undoubtedly, however, the estimates of enemy

Year of Birth (age)	Command staff		Junior Command Staff		Rank and File		Total	% of Total
	Reporting for duty	In hospital	Reporting for duty	In hospital	Reporting for Duty	In hospital		
1925-1922 (18-21 years)	1,465	5	3,556	12	5,456	20	10,514	23.6
1921-1917 (22-26 years)	1,673	12	3,537	15	3,726	23	8,986	20.1
1916-1912 (27-31 years)	1,678	9	3,226	9	4,291	33	9,246	20.7
1911-1907 (32-36 years)	943	9	1,998	2	4,354	23	7,329	16.4
1906-1902 (37-41 years)	549	-	1,148	2	3,635	6	5,340	12.0
1901-1897 (42-46 years)	203	2	368	-	1,505	4	2,082	4.7
1896 and older (47 years/older)	96	1	157	-	872	3	1,129	2.5
Army Total:	6,607	38	13,990	40	23,839	112	44,626	100.0
Education Levels in Years of Schooling								
Higher (10 years or more)	3,317	18	1,248	4	1,006	6	5,599	12.5
Middle School (7-9 years)	2,350	14	3,741	15	3,639	16	9,775	21.9
Primary (1-6 years)	940	6	8,997	21	18,533	89	28,586	64.0
Illiterate	-	-	4	-	661	1	666	1.5
Army Total:	6,607	38	13,990	40	23,839	112	44,626	100.0

Note: The table includes data (on 5 July 1943) for the 18th and 29th Tank Corps, the 5th Guards Mechanized Corps, and all the units subordinate to Army headquarters, including all those temporarily absent in hospitals for which data were available.

Source: TsAMO RF, f. 5 gv. TA, op. 4952, d. 5, l.7, 8; f. 18 tk, op. 1, d. 93, l. 89.

Table 30: Age and Education Level of Personnel of the 5th Guards Tank Army as of 1-5 July 1943

Formation or Unit	Killed or Mortally Wounded	Wounded with Evacuation to Hospital	Missing-in-Action	Illness with Evacuation to Hospital	Other Reasons	Total Losses	Of which, command staff	Of which, junior command staff	Of which, rank and file	Irreplaceable Losses
2 Tank Corps	371	850	1,054	4	1	2,280	221	626	1,433	1,425
2 Gds Tank Corps	679	1,202	17	38	1	1,937	222	671	1,044	696
18 Tank Corps	241	607	171	33	4	1,056	130	366	560	412
29 Tank Corps	739	1,054	450	6	-	2,249	201	868	1,180	1,189
5 Gds Mech Corps	690	1,132	345	3	2	2,172	192	818	1,162	1,035
6 AA Artillery Div	20	70	-	-	-	90	13	19	58	20
1 Gds Sep MC Reg	1	11	-	-	-	12	-	2	10	1
53 Gds Tank Reg	26	22	2	1	-	51	16	35	-	28
689 AT Artillery Reg	7	20	-	-	-	27	1	9	17	7
678 Howitzer Art Reg	10	35	7	-	-	52	1	5	46	17
76 Gds Mortar Reg	11	8	-	-	-	19	3	5	11	11
Total losses:	2,759	5,011	2,046	85	8	9,945	1,000	3,424	5,526	4,841

Source: TsAMO RF, f. 5 gv. TA, op. 4952, d. 7, l. 3.

Table 31: Casualties in the Formations and Units of the 5th Guards Tank Army, 12-18 July 1943

Formation or Unit	Killed or Mortally Wounded	Wounded with Evacuation to Hospital	Missing-in-Action	Illness with Evacuation to Hospital	Other Reasons	Total Losses	Of which, command staff	Of which, junior command staff	Of which, rank and file	Irreplaceable Losses
Headquarters	1	1	-	-	-	2	2	-	-	1
419 Sep Signals Bn	-	4	-	-	-	4	-	2	2	0
115 Sep Sapper Bn	1	2	-	6	-	9	1	2	6	1
110 Tank Bde	8	64	3	7	1	83	15	22	46	11
170 Tank Bde	7	55	5	14	-	81	15	30	36	12
181 Tank Bde	67	50	33	-	-	150	29	71	50	100
32 Mot Rifle Bde	85	313	122	-	-	520	34	152	334	207
36 Sep Gds Hvy Tank Reg	3	19	-	-	-	22	8	14	-	3
1000 AT Artillery Reg	5	15	-	-	-	20	4	9	7	5
292 Sep Mortar Reg	1	3	-	-	-	4	2	1	1	1
1694 AA Artillery Reg	1	-	-	-	-	1	-	-	1	1
Total:	179	526	163	27	1	896	110	303	483	342

Source: TsAMO RF, f. 5 gv. TA, op. 4952, d.7, l. 104.

Table 32: Personnel Losses in the 18th Tank Corps, 12-14 July 1943

Divisions	Killed or Mortally Wounded	Wounded with Evacuation to Hospital	Missing-in-Action	Illness with Evacuation to Hospital	Other Reasons	Total Losses	Of which, command staff	Of which, junior command staff	Of which, rank and file	Irreplaceable Losses
6 Gds Airborne	16	54	-	80	-	150	6	45	102	16
13 Gds Rifle	307	1,079	128	52	3	1,569	106	461	999	435
66 Gds Rifle	348	1,692	20	21	13	2,094	108	553	1,420	368
97 Gds Rifle	246	1,328	-	-	-	1,574	94	276	1,204	246
Total, 32 Gds Rifle Corps (a)	917	4,153	148	153	16	5,387	314	1,335	3,725	1,065
9 Gds Airborne	250	1,467	377	8	10	2,112	149	681	1,272	627
52 Gds Airborne	558	1,033	3,796	64	4	5,455	385	1,544	3,522	4,354
95 Gds Airborne	952	1,633	579	-	-	3,164	203	992	1,969	1,531
Total, 33 Gds Rifle Corps	1,760	4,133	4,752	72	14	10,731	737	3,217	6,763	6,512
Total, Army	2,677	8,286	4,900	225	30	16,118	1,051	4,552	10,488	7,577

(a) Editor's note: There were erroneous totals in the original reports for the 32nd Guards Rifle Corps. For example, the report gives 901 as killed in action or mortally wounded for the Corps, 4,099 for those wounded and evacuated to a hospital, and only 73 for those who were sick and evacuated to a hospital. I have corrected the totals, and the corrected subtotals for the 32nd Rifle Corps, when added with the subtotals for the 33 Guards Rifle Corps, do yield correct Army totals for the categories. However, the subcategories by rank do not add up to the total casualties for the 32nd Guards Rifle Corps.

Source: TsAMO RF, f. 5 gv. A, op. 4855, d.20, l. 4.

Table 33: Personnel Losses in the Divisions of the 5th Guards Army, 5-17 July 1943

Division	Strength on 10 July 1943 (a)	Losses							
		Killed	Wounded	Missing	Absent due to illness	Absent for other reasons (b)	Total Losses	% of Starting Strength	Irrecoverable losses/% of Total Losses
93 Gds Rifle	9,426	477	1,002	4,231	49	-	5,759	61	4,708/82
81 Gds Rifle	-	796	1,142	962	11	1,359	4,270	-	1,758/41
89 Gds Rifle	8,355	106	312	3,170	10	-	3,598	43	3,276/91
375 Rifle	7,401	205	460	32	4	-	701	9	237/34
183 Rifle	7,778	398	902	-	-	-	1,300	17	391/30
Corps Total		1,982	3,818	8,395	74	1,359	15,628	-	10,377/66

(a) The data for each division's strength as of 10 July 1943 comes from TsAMO RF, f. 69A, op. 10757, d. 8, l. 90, 91.

(b) The 1,359 officers and soldiers listed as "Absent for other reasons" for the 7th Guards Army's 81st Guards Rifle Division possibly shows the losses for this division when escaping encirclement north of Belgorod.

Source: TsAMO RF, f. 69 A, op. 10753, d. 442, l. 24.

Table 34: Losses in the Divisions of the 69th Army's 48th Rifle Corps, 1-16 July 1943

casualties as found in the reports of the Voronezh Front and its subordinate armies were greatly exaggerated. One can reach this conclusion through a comparison of Russian and German sources.

Thus, in the 5th Guards Tank Army's report from 17 July 1943 (see Table 28), enemy losses were presented: 15,620 soldiers and officers and 552 tanks destroyed, including 93 Tigers (it is interesting to ponder the question of who did the counting and how they did so, since the battlefield between 10 and 17 July remained under enemy control). The readers can on their own assess the reliability of these figures. Don't forget that the other Soviet armies submitted similar reports.

In contrast, the summary estimate of the combat and numerical strength of the opponent's units that went on the attack on the Tomarovka axis on 4 July 1943, compiled by Voronezh Front's intelligence department, was actually very close to the actual enemy strength. This intelligence estimate put the enemy grouping's total strength at 122,000 men [through a mathematical error, which are not uncommon in these reports, the actual estimate of the enemy's total strength was 112,000 men] and 1,240 armored vehicles. These estimates just slightly overstated enemy troop strength, but the estimated number of armored vehicles was actually quite close to the real number of armor in Army Group South, disregarding its reserves.

The German formations that operated on the Prokhorovka axis numbered 66,460 men, including 33,800 men in the three Panzergrenadier divisions of the II SS Panzer Corps plus the 167th Infantry Division, and 32,660 men in the three panzer divisions of the III Panzer Corps plus the 168th Infantry Division.[67] It is possible that with attached units, the numerical strength of this grouping approached 100,000 men.

★ ★ ★

As far as is known, no one ever blamed the *Front* commander for the failure of the counterattack to reach its objectives. However, the armor losses suffered by the 5th Guards Tank Army in the fighting at Prokhorovka provoked the wrath of the Supreme High Commander, Stalin. Here's how P. A. Rotmistrov himself spoke about this after the war in a conversation with Doctor of Historical Sciences F. D. Sverdlov:

> '… I. V. Stalin, when he learned about our losses, became enraged: after all, the tank army according to the *Stavka* plan had been assigned to take part in the counteroffensive aimed at Khar'kov. But now it again required significant replacements. The Supreme Commander was on the verge of removing me from my post and about to send me before a tribunal. A. M. Vasilevsky told me this. Yet he gave Stalin a detailed report about the situation and a recapitulation of the disruption of the entire German summer offensive operation. Stalin calmed down somewhat and never again returned to this matter.' Incidentally, giving me a sly smile, Rotmistrov noted that the *Front* commander and General of the Army N. F. Vatutin had recommended him for the Order of Suvorov 1st Degree, but on this occasion, he didn't receive the Order.[68]

It is known that I. V. Stalin directed the formation of a commission under the direction of a member of the State Defense Committee and Secretary of the Party's Central Committee, G. M. Malenkov, with the task to analyze the reasons of the counterattack's failure and of the 5th Guards Tank Army's high casualties and losses in equipment. It is known that Stalin almost never created such commissions after victories (victors in Russia from time immemorial have never been judged). For example, such a commission was set up after Stalingrad, where the heavy losses were caused by the

Candidate Politburo member G. M. Malenkov, whom I. V. Stalin delegated with the task of ascertaining the causes of the failures and high losses at Prokhorovka. (RGAKFD)

exceptionally difficult situation. Another investigative commission examined Vitebsk, where from 29 December 1943 to 5 March 1944, the 33rd Army conducted three so-called local operations, losing over 90,000 casualties (19,520 in killed alone), but failed to crack the enemy's defenses. The extent of advance in each operation consisted of only 8 to 12 kilometers, 3 to 4 kilometers, and 2 to 6 kilometers correspondingly.

The materials of Malenkov's commission are still preserved in the Communist Party of the Soviet Union's Central Committee archives, and are inaccessible to an ordinary scholar. However, its main finding is known: the commission labeled the combat operations of 12 July 1943 at Prokhorovka a model of an unsuccessfully conducted operation. Traces of the commission's work can be found in the numerous accounts and reports of various chiefs (some of which have been previously presented in this book), where at times they offer a forthright critique of the decisions and actions of the commanders and of the formations and units subordinate to them.

There were several causes for the high losses, suffered by the forces of the Voronezh Front. First and foremost, there was the lack of sufficient experience among the military commanders in the use and handling of such an enormous formation as a tank army in a defensive operation (especially when the 5th Guards Tank Army was reinforced with two additional tank corps immediately prior to its commitment into the battle). This is the root cause of many of the shortcomings in the organization of the combat operations: the hasty commitment into the battle and the weak work of reconnaissance and intelligence. As a result, the effectiveness of the preparatory artillery barrage and subsequent artillery support was low. Cooperation between the artillery and the forces operating in front of it was poor, as was the level of cooperation between the attacking corps and divisions during the battle. Air support was also poorly coordinated with the ground forces.

Unfortunately, even the experience with using tank units and formations acquired over the first two years of the war, as summarized in NKO Order No. 325 from 16 October 1942 was ignored. This Order demanded the elimination of the following shortcomings in the use of tanks:

> …
>
> 2. Tanks are being thrown against the enemy's defense without sufficient artillery support. The artillery prior to the start of the attack is not suppressing the enemy's anti-tank means in the forward edge of defense … On the approach to the enemy's front lines, the tanks are met with the enemy's anti-tank and artillery fire and suffer heavy losses. Tank and artillery commanders are not coordinating their actions in place through [the use of] terrain features and lines, and are not establishing signals for requesting and cancelling artillery fire missions. Artillery commanders, supporting the tank attack, direct their artillery fire from distant locations and are not employing radio-equipped tanks in the role of mobile forward artillery observation posts.
>
> 3. Tanks are being introduced into battle hastily, without the tankers' reconnoitering the terrain in the enemy's front lines, without studying the terrain in the depth of the enemy's positions, and without carefully analyzing the enemy's system of fire. Tank commanders, lacking time to organize the tank attack, fail to inform the tank crews of the assignment, as a result of which without knowledge

of the enemy and terrain, the tanks attack tentatively. … The tanks are not maneuvering on the battlefield, are not using the terrain to make a concealed approach and unexpected strike on the flank or rear, and are most often attacking the enemy head-on.

4. Tanks are not carrying out their primary assignment of destroying enemy infantry, but are being diverted into combat against enemy tanks and artillery. The established practice of opposing enemy tank attacks with our tanks and getting tied-up in tank battles is incorrect and harmful.

5. The combat operations of tanks are not receiving adequate air cover, aerial reconnaissance, or aerial direction. The air force, as a rule, is not escorting tank formations into the depth of the enemy's defenses, and the combat operations of the air force are not coordinated with the tank attacks.

6. There is poor organization of command and control over the tanks on the battlefield. Inadequate use of radios is being made as a means of control. Commanders of tank brigades and corps, located at their command posts, are detached from their subordinate combat forces, do not observe the actions of the tanks, and have no influence on the course of battle. Commanders of companies and battalions, moving at the head of their combat formations, do not have the possibility to observe the tanks and to direct the fighting of their subordinate elements, and thus turn into ordinary tank commanders, while the units, lacking any direction, become lost and confused on the battlefield, suffering needless losses.

If we did not know the date of this document, then it is fully possible to conclude that this is a brief and concise description, in the military style, of that which occurred at Prokhorovka in the 5th Guards Tank Army's sector of attack on 12 July 1943. The shortcomings noted in NKO Order No. 375 had not been eliminated by the time of Prokhorovka, even though almost a full year had passed since the order was issued.

The most serious grievances should be lodged against the weak tactical reconnaissance prior to the engagement at Prokhorovka. Corps and brigade commanders, especially tank commanders, paid little attention to organizing the work of the reconnaissance branch, and scout commanders were not employed according to their intended purpose even at the most critical stages of the fighting. In the tank formations, it was considered senseless to conduct reconnaissance prior to selecting the points and directions of attack. Therefore, the timely flow of information from the combat units operating at the front had not been established. The matter descended to the point of combat between friendly units.

During the battle of Kursk, *front* artillery played a major role in repulsing the enemy's attack. At the start of the enemy offensive, a sufficient quantity of ammunition had been issued to the firing positions – from four to five days' worth of ammunition instead of the typical one and a half to two days' worth. However, in the course of Voronezh Front's defensive operation, the compulsory withdrawal of troops under the pressure of superior German forces led to the frequent shifting of firing positions, which in turn caused the loss of ammunition at the most critical moments of the fighting due to the lack of sufficient motorized transport.

The strength of the Soviet artillery fire in the course of the operation can be judged from the following numbers. Voronezh Front, which had a third fewer artillery pieces and mortars than Central Front, expended 417 train carloads of ammunition, whereas the Central Front fired 1,079 train carloads, which is 2.5 times greater.[69] Such a large difference can likely be explained by the difficulties in organizing the maneuver of the artillery units and in transporting ammunition to defending units on the enemy's main lines of attacks. On the Central Front, the main fighting occurred in a smaller area – the adversary penetrated only to a depth of 10 kilometers. On Voronezh Front, four armies took part in the fighting to repel the enemy attacks, and two more armies were subsequently added to it. Here, the enemy managed to penetrate to a depth of 35 kilometers into our forces' defenses.

At the same time, the fact should not be overlooked that the 5th Guards Tank Army's introduction into battle lacked sufficient artillery preparation. Approximately 190 guns of a caliber greater than 76mm, including 66 122mm, 152mm and 203mm howitzers from the Long Range Artillery Group conducted the artillery preparation. A portion of these forces (the 93rd Gun Artillery Regiment of the 27th Separate Heavy Gun Brigade, the 216th Guards Mortar Regiment, and the 2nd Battalion of the 678th Guards Artillery Regiment) were used not only for the preparatory fire in the sector of the 18th and 29th Tank Corps, but also in that of the 2nd Guards 'Tatsinskaia' Tank Corps. Thus, on a front of approximately 10 kilometers, the average density of guns comprised a maximum of 19 to 20 guns per kilometer of front. Unfortunately, the effectiveness of the fire of the artillery grouping was significantly reduced due to the lack of information on the locations of enemy troop concentrations and the poorly organized cooperation between army headquarters and the additional artillery from the Long-Range Artillery Group.

Given the facts, the following assertion by Lieutenant General Varentsov, the artillery commander of Voronezh Front, seems at the very least strange:

> For liquidating the threat in the area of Prokhorovka on 12 July, a counterattack by three of our tank corps was undertaken. The artillery support was organized by me. The 5th Guards and 69th Armies were called upon for the artillery role in the counterattack. A Long-range Artillery Group was created. ... *The operation after my artillery preparation was crowned with success – the enemy was thrown back several kilometers from Prokhorovka on the first day* [Author's emphasis].[70]

Aircraft from the 2nd and 17th Air Armies cooperated with the ground forces in repelling the enemy's attacks. However, their direct support for our attacking tank formations during the counterattack on 12 July was largely ineffective. The absence of air controllers in the first echelon units and of reliable communications with army headquarters, much less with the corps headquarters, was telling. Incidentally, in the report on the use of aviation on 12 July it is noted: 'The aerial combat operations on both sides were restricted on this day from the morning due to unfavorable meteorological conditions.'[71]

Not more than 50% of the total number of Soviet aircraft sorties was used to support the ground forces directly on the battlefield – an insufficient number. The Red Army Air Force's efforts were not concentrated on the main axis. Our aviation had managed to win superiority in the air only by 10 July. Prior to this, air cover for the ground forces was inadequate. Perhaps this is why company commanders were afraid to place air identification panels to mark their positions, in order to avoid enemy air strikes. Moreover, in connection with the fires and dense smoke from burning vehicles hanging over the battlefield, as well as the mingling of combat formations and rapid movement of the formations and units, there were repeated instances of mistaken air strikes against our own forces.

The shortcomings in the organization of the combat operations, and the relative absence of coordination in force operations do not at all diminish the significance of the victory obtained at Prokhorovka. Soviet troops even in a most unsatisfactory situation stood up to and stopped a strong foe.

When evaluating the role and significance of the Prokhorovka engagement, one must not ignore the fact that the forces of Voronezh Front faced a significantly more powerful enemy grouping than did those of Central Front.[72] It was precisely here, in front of Voronezh Front, that the enemy concentrated the *Wehrmacht's* best panzer and Panzergrenadier divisions. Neither before nor after the Kursk battle did the Nazis assemble such a powerful tank grouping. General-Field Marshal Erich von Manstein, an experienced and highly capable commander, commanded Army Group South. The operation itself had been very carefully prepared. As General F. von Mellenthin recalled after the war in his own memoirs, not a single operation had been prepared so thoroughly and comprehensively.

Doubtlessly, the Prokhorovka engagement was the culminating moment of the Kursk defensive operation on the southern face of the Kursk bulge, after which the intensity of the fighting sharply decreased. Unfortunately, in many publications about the Kursk battle, a rather widespread logical fallacy is committed, either inadvertently or deliberately: *post hoc ergo propter hoc* (after this, therefore because of this). Already on 11 July, the day before the armor clash at Prokhorovka, the *Wehrmacht* command, having learned of the offensives of the Western and Briansk Fronts (interpreting the preliminary reconnaissance-in-force probes on a broad front as the start of an offensive) came to the conclusion: "In view of the fact that to achieve a rapid success is impossible, now there can only be talk of inflicting the greatest damage to the enemy with the fewest possible of our own losses."[73]

Moreover in our view, the events entitled "the Prokhorovka engagement" should not be considered equivalent to the events labeled as "the Prokhorovka tank engagement of 12 July". The tank engagement comprised only a part, although indeed the most important part, of the Prokhorovka engagement. The repulse of Army Group South's powerful attack and the great damage inflicted on the *Wehrmacht's* armored forces, were achieved as a result of the combined efforts of troops of Voronezh Front with the reinforcements from *Stavka* Reserve.

In connection with this, it is interesting to compare how P. A. Rotmistrov and G. K. Zhukov evaluated the significance of the tank clash on 12 July. We'll recall the words of the 5th Guards Tank Army's commander:

> Here on 12 July 1943 there occurred the meeting tank engagement, widely known as the Prokhorovka bloodbath, which is incomparable in the history of wars for its

scale. On a small sector of terrain, more than 1,500 tanks, a significant quantity of artillery and major numbers of aircraft participated simultaneously from both sides.

And further:

The grand tank engagement at Prokhorovka, which unfolded on 12 July 1943 has entered military history as the culminating stage of the defense of Soviet forces at Kursk. As a result of the attack launched by the 5th Guards Tank Army in cooperation with other forces, the main enemy grouping, attacking toward Prokhorovka, was smashed. The day 12 July became a day of crisis for the German offensive. The fascist command was compelled to cancel the offensive and go over to defense.[74]

In light of the analysis presented in this book, the results of the 12 July Prokhorovka counterattack and the success of the 5th Guards Tank Army appear to be much more modest, especially given the comparison of combat losses suffered by the two sides. The Deputy of the Supreme High Commander G. K. Zhukov asserts:

In his memoirs the former commander of the 5th Guards Tank Army P. A. Rotmistrov writes as if the 5th Guards Tank Army played the decisive role in the destruction of Army Group South's armored forces. *This is immodest and not at all correct* [Zhukov's emphasis]. The forces of the 6th and 7th Guards and the 1st Tank Army, supported by artillery from *Stavka* Reserve and an air army ground down and bled white the foe in the fighting between 4 and 12 July. The 5th Guards Tank Army had only to deal with an already extremely weakened enemy grouping, which had lost faith in the possibility of a successful struggle with the Soviet forces.[75]

Here's the opinion of a man who spent many years studying the Prokhorovka engagement. Lieutenant Colonel (reserve) V. N. Lebedev, a scientific scholar of the Belgorod Regional Museum, writes:

After all … at Prokhorovka the 5th Guards Tank Army over three days of fighting destroyed 150 enemy tanks, and not the 400, as claimed by the commander of the 5th Guards Tank Army. … Moreover, each day of fighting prior to 12 July had been more savage than that at Prokhorovka. How is it possible to ignore the [preceding] events that occurred on the Oboian' axis north of Belgorod, where the fascists' plan for a breakthrough to Kursk were thwarted and where the fascists' main forces on the southern flank of the bulge were ground down? Finally, the soldiers and commanders of General Chistiakov's 6th Guards Army and General Katukov's 1st Tank Army together with units of other types of forces in the most savage fighting, suffering enormous losses and demonstrating unparalleled heroism, placed a barrier across the road to Kursk for the fascists! [Yet] the press, radio and television have boiled down the success of the Soviet forces to the success of the 5th Guards Tank Army.[76]

In reality, it is perhaps already time to reject loud words when evaluating the tank engagement at Prokhorovka: what results is an 'engagement' within the framework of another engagement, or even more absurdly, a 'battle' in the course of the Kursk battle! Even the word "bloodbath" in the light of new, never before published data on losses can give rise fully to unpleasant associations …

It is no accident that serious articles of recent times no longer use the terms 'meeting tank engagement at Prokhorovka'. Now Prokhorovka is discussed as a meeting battle of tank formations.[77] After all, following the introduction of the 5th Guards Tank Army into the engagement, Soviet corps formations fought against enemy divisions.

An evaluation of the engagement from the German side, which the aforementioned German historian K.-H. Frieser voices, is interesting: "… Today it can be stated: the meeting tank engagement at Prokhorovka on 12 July was won by neither the Germans nor the Soviets, since neither side managed to fulfill its assigned objective."[78]

Our German friend K.-H. Frieser is trying to confuse the issue. In reality, the Soviet forces counterattacking at Prokhorovka could not fully carry out their assignment, because it was simply unrealistic for them to do so, given the existing correlation of forces involved in the engagement. However, the main task of the defender is the repulse of an enemy attack, and this assignment our forces indeed carried out: they prevented a German breakthrough into the operational space in the rear of Voronezh Front, preserved the operational resilience of the defense and inflicted such losses on the enemy that it was compelled to suspend the continuation of the offensive on the main axis. After all, such a decisive breakthrough is what von Manstein had planned for 12 July via a regrouping of his forces. The enemy did not achieve this goal. *Thus in sum, the forces of Voronezh Front won the engagement at Prokhorovka, and then successfully completed the defensive operation, having created the conditions for a decisive counteroffensive* [Author's emphasis].

After the forces of the Western and Briansk Fronts went on the offensive on 12 July, it had become finally clear that Army Group South's offensive operation had reached a dead end. On 13 July 1943, the day after the 5th Guards Tank Army's counterattack at Prokhorovka, Hitler made the decision to halt Operation Citadel.

Manstein maintains that Hitler, having prevented him from employing the XXIV Panzer Corps – Army Group South's operational reserves – at the decisive moment of the engagement, deprived him of a deserved victory. Engelmann seconds von Manstein's assertion, declaring that the offensive at Kursk was "an engagement, interrupted midway, and a victory, given away not long before its achievement."[79] However, by this time the preparations of the Soviet Southern Front for an offensive against the German First Panzer Army was already known to the enemy, and once launched it created a serious threat to the southern flank of von Manstein's forces.

The impact of the Soviet counterattack at Prokhorovka on enemy planning is clear. After 12 July von Manstein thought only about conducting limited operations with limited objectives: the encirclement of the formations of 69th Army's 48th Rifle Corps, and then in the future, about an attack to the northwest, with the aim of encircling the forces of the 40th Army.

However, even had it obtained a clear breakthrough at Prokhorovka on 12 July, it isn't clear that Army Group South could have continued Operation Citadel. As soon as the Soviet Southwestern and Southern Fronts on 17 July went on the offensive (which yielded on the first day a breakthrough of a well-prepared German defense along the

Mius River and the seizure of a bridgehead by Southern Front), that same evening von Manstein ordered the withdrawal of the II SS Panzer Corps from the battle, in order to send it to the threatened axis. On 18 July, Army Detachment Kempf's III Panzer Corps was also withdrawn for redeployment elsewhere.

As concerns the assertion that the tank engagement at Prokhorovka was the largest tank battle of the Second World War, then it also seems dubious in light of the previously discussed information in this book. It is known that in the course of the border battles in the area of Brody, Berestechko and Dubno (an area of approximately 60 by 40 kilometers [24 by 36 miles]), the Soviet command from 26 to 29 July 1941 conducted a counterattack with five mechanized corps of the Southwestern Front (the 8th, 9th, 15th, 19th and 22nd Mechanized Corps, a total of about 5,000 tanks) against the enemy's attacking First Panzer Group and parts of the Sixth Army (with a total of around 1,000 tanks).[80] Unfortunately, our forces, despite some isolated successes, suffered a major defeat there, losing 2,648 tanks in the process. For the next two years, the Nazis liked to drive foreign correspondents to these fields and show them the enormous cemetery of our armor.[81] This engagement has largely been forgotten. Even if it is mentioned in Russia, then again no figures on combat losses are given. Truthfully, as has been said, "Victory has many parents, but a defeat is always an orphan."

However it might have been, Soviet forces won the engagement at Prokhorovka. Victory was achieved due to the resolve and courage of the soldiers and officers of all types of forces [Author's emphasis]. Victory in this fighting, which became the culminating stage of the battle on the southern face of the Kursk bulge, foreordained the success of Voronezh Front's defensive operation as a whole.

In the course of defensive fighting, the troops of the Voronezh and Central Fronts ground down and bled white the foe's shock groupings, which lost according to Soviet estimates approximately 100,000 men, more than 1,200 tanks and assault guns, approximately 850 artillery pieces and mortars, and more than 1,500 aircraft.[82] Enemy losses in the course of the entire Kursk battle (including the counteroffensives by Voronezh and Central Fronts after halting the German advance) comprised more than 500,000 soldiers and officers, 3,000 guns and mortars, more than 1,500 tanks and assault guns, and more than 3,700 airplanes.[83] These figures are undoubtedly grossly inflated; according to German sources, the *Wehrmacht's* ground forces lost 474,702 men on the entire Eastern Front in July-August 1943. Even so, German losses were unquestionably heavy.[84]

In works published in Germany, also including in the memoirs of former commander of Army Group South E. von Manstein, it is said that in the course of the fighting at Orel, Kursk, Belgorod and Khar'kov, German forces lost approximately 200,000 soldiers and officers. According to captured German documents, during the period of the Soviet counteroffensive after Kursk, the forces of Army Group South and Army Group Center, which were operating on the Belgorod-Kursk and Orel directions respectively, lost 113,900 men killed, missing or wounded. Thus, losses in the period of the German offensive might comprise 80,000 to 100,000 men.[85]

The victory at Kursk cost the Soviet people dearly. For the nineteen days between 5 to 23 July 1943 the losses of Voronezh Front alone comprised 27,542 men killed or missing (5% of initial strength) and 46,350 men wounded or sick, for a total of 73,892 (13.8% of the *front*'s strength prior to the battle). Let us compare: Central Front over the eleven days of the defensive operation lost a total of 33,897 men (4.6%), of which 15,336 (2%) were killed or missing; Steppe Front over the fifteen days between 9 and 23 July lost 70,058 men, of which 27,452 were killed or missing.[86]

Thus, the Voronezh and Steppe Fronts, which operated on the southern face of the Kursk bulge, together lost approximately 144,000 men killed, wounded or missing in the course of the defensive operation. In the defensive fighting at Kursk, the forces of all three *fronts* – Voronezh, Central and Steppe – lost 177,847 men, 1,614 tanks and assault guns, 3,929 artillery pieces and mortars, and 459 airplanes.[87]

In the course of bitter fighting, the troops of Central and Voronezh Fronts first weakened, and then stopped the offensive by the German-fascist shock groupings and created favorable possibilities for the transition to a counteroffensive. The Red Army managed not only to withstand the powerful attack of German forces, but also in the following counteroffensive to hurl the enemy back by 150 kilometers to the south and southwest, thereby creating the prerequisites for a grand offensive by Soviet forces that took them across the Dnepr River.

Thus, Hitler's attempt to seize the strategic initiative in the war was thwarted. Germany was no longer able to replace fully all the losses that it suffered at Kursk. At Kursk, the Soviet armed forces took the strategic initiative and held it until the end of the war.

The victory at Kursk was achieved owing to the courage and selflessness of the Soviet warriors, and their exceptional resolve and readiness for self-sacrifice for the sake of crushing the foe. In addition, they went on the attack not at all because of any fear of the blocking detachments, as certain publicists and "historians" try to suggest today;

The burial of fallen soldiers and officers in one of Voronezh Front's rifle divisions (July 1943). (Author's personal archive)

they were motivated by feelings of patriotism, love for the Motherland, and hatred for the enemy.

In the Western press, they sometimes call Operation Citadel and the Kursk battle "insignificant episodes in the war", the importance of which have been exaggerated by Soviet propaganda. Such thinking cannot stand up to critical analysis. In the Kursk defensive operation, the German command's plan to encircle and destroy a more than million-man grouping of Soviet forces was foiled, and Hitler lost the strategic initiative on the Eastern Front for good.

A statement by Heinz Guderian, Germany's General Inspector of Armored Forces, serves as the best response to such historians:

> As a result of the failure of the '*Zitadelle*' [Citadel] offensive, we suffered a decisive defeat. The armored forces ...because of the heavy losses in men and equipment were for a long time withdrawn from combat ... and no longer had any quiet days on the Eastern Front. The initiative had fully gone over to the adversary."[88]

The German historian W. Goerlitz on the same subject observed that "the major battle at Kursk ... was for the German army the beginning of a precipitous crisis."[89]

On the other hand, some Western historians try to explain the collapse of Operation Citadel by the landing of the Anglo-American allies on Sicily on 10 July 1943, which supposedly compelled Hitler to withdraw the SS Panzer Corps in order to send it to southern Italy. Here, the attempt to rehabilitate the *Wehrmacht* command for all its errors in preparing and conducting the offensive, and to place all the blame on Hitler, is being overlooked. The decision to halt Operation Citadel was made on 13 July 1943 – and the transfer of the SS Panzer Corps to the West was all the same delayed. In the final result it was withdrawn from the battle only on 17 July, and even then remained on the Eastern Front in order to respond to the numerous crises that arose in the course of the Soviet offensive after Kursk.

One more important result of the combat operations in the Kursk battle and Prokhorovka engagement should be noted. It taught valuable lessons to the Red Army and its commanders in using tanks and self-propelled guns effectively in the new and greatly changed conditions of the second period of the Great Patriotic War. The combat experience drawn from Kursk was extremely important for the personnel of the tank formations and for the Soviet generals and marshals, but also for the leadership of the country and for the designers and builders of armored vehicles. Already within several days of the conclusion of the fighting at Kursk, a large conference was conducted at one of the tank factories that included the command of the Red Army's Armored and Mechanized Forces, government officials responsible for armaments and the tank industry, and staff from the leading design bureaus. The purpose of the conference was to accelerate work on a fundamental modernization of the main Soviet tank, the T-34/76, which was showing itself to be inferior to the latest German designs. Already by February-March 1944, new "34s" began to appear in the acting army: the T-34/85.

This design eliminated the main shortcomings in the previous main model: in addition to a more powerful 85mm main gun in a new three-man turret and better optics, the thickness of the front armor on the hull and turret was doubled from 45mm to 90mm. After this modification indeed was born the T-34 that entered history as the best medium tank of the war.

It was a rather rare case: within the span of a half-year, not only was the acquired experience processed and analyzed, but also an extensive modification of the tank was implemented, its factory and field testing completed, and the vehicle had been moved into production. However, let the reader not be misled by this rapid development in armor. One and a half years of war preceded it, in which thousands of crews had paid with their own lives and blood due to the shortcomings of existing combat vehicles.

That the most numerous Soviet T-34/76 tank had no advantage over the new main tank of the German army, the Panzer IV, had become obvious already during the combat operations in the bend of the Don River in the summer of 1942. Here's an extract from a German document – "A Report on the Tactical Use of German and Soviet Tank Units in Practice (compiled on the combat experience of the 23rd Panzer Division in the course of Operation Blue)":

> …
>
> 6.
>
> a) T-34. This tank was superior to all German tanks prior to the appearance in the spring of 1942 of the German long-barreled tank guns, the 50mm Kw L/60 and the 75mm Kw L/43, and now it is inferior to them. The Russian T-34, which had attacked German tanks in several armor engagements and suffered heavy losses, having impaled themselves on the fire of the new guns, now prefers to avoid battle when possible and to retreat.
>
> b) KV-1. The Russian KV-1 and KV-1s with increased armor are often used in place of the T-34. Since these tanks are not usually employed in mass, their destruction was not a particularly difficult problem.[90]

After being up-gunned, the German tanks could destroy ours from a range out to 1.5 kilometers, while the 76mm gun of the T-34 had to close to within 500-600 meters to be effective. It isn't difficult to imagine the psychological condition of the tank crew, which was aware of this frightening arithmetic. At a conference at the end of August 1943, the People's Commissar of the Tank Industry V. A. Malyshev observed: "Boiling it down to basics, the adversary has a reach out to one and a half kilometers, while we have one of only a half-kilometer. It is immediately necessary to equip the T-34 with a more powerful gun."[91]

Yet this was already after the battle of Kursk, while in the summer of 1942, the Soviet command evaluated the actions of tank crews, who strove not to close within direct fire range of an enemy gun, as cowardice and an attempt to avoid fulfilling the military oath. Moreover, given the high armor losses at the front, the State Defense Committee was demanding from industry and the rear units a significant expansion in the production of armor and an increased output of tanks. The rush unavoidably led to factory defects, and a low level of training of the specialists. All of this taken together, alongside the lack of sufficient experience in handling the forces on the part of formation headquarters, did not improve the situation in our country's armored forces. Responsibility for the system that had arisen was laid upon scapegoats. On 10 August 1943, I. V. Stalin signed an Order of the Supreme High Command, which stated:

> Our tank units and formations often suffer very large losses, where losses in armor due to technical malfunctions exceed combat losses: for example, on the Stalingrad front, over six days of fighting, twelve of our tank brigades, having a significant superiority in tanks, artillery and aircraft over the enemy, lost 326 tanks out of 400, of which approximately 200 were due to mechanical breakdowns, the majority of which were left abandoned on the battlefield. Analogous examples are evident on other fronts as well.
>
> I consider such an impermissibly high percentage of tanks, lost due to technical defects, unbelievable. The *Stavka* is seeing here the presence of hidden sabotage and wrecking on the part of a certain number of tankers, who are trying to avoid battle and abandoning the tank on the battlefield by searching for isolated minor bugs in the tanks or deliberately creating them. At the same time, the disgraceful state of the technical monitoring of the equipment in the tank units and of supervision over each tank's fulfillment of the combat task assigned to it contributes to this criminal, intolerable phenomenon in the army.[92]

Such shameful phenomena as cowardice and the unsteadiness of troops did not bypass a single army, but the Soviet tankers in their majority were models of bravery and skill. Even the foe recognized these qualities in the aforementioned German document, "A Report on the Tactical Use of German and Soviet Tank Units in Practice (compiled on the combat experience of the 23rd Panzer Division in the course of Operation Blue)":

> The combat spirit of the Russian tankers is fantastic: several tanks become immobile, receive 5-6 direct hits, but their crews do not surrender and continue to fire. For the destruction of such vehicles we have to send special groups of demolition engineers. The Russians fight to the last shell and cartridge.[93]

For the sake of justice, it must be noted that there was a number of objective reasons that prevented the modernization of the T-34. The span of time, when the Red Army lacked a tank which would answer the demands of battle, lasted for approximately a year and a half, between the summer of 1942 and the beginning of 1944. This was a watershed period for the entire war – a period of the most colossal battles and engagements.

Attempts to alter the situation were undertaken from the beginning of 1943. A number of measures were adopted and implemented to counter enemy armor before the start of the Kursk battle: in particular, with respect to the introduction of self-propelled guns and the strengthening of anti-tank artillery, but the main problem – a comprehensive modernization of the T-34/76 – could not be resolved. Thus in the summer campaign, the Red Army was compelled to use primarily not a qualitative, but a quantitative superiority in tanks. This became one of the causes of the huge armor losses in the period of combat operations in the cauldron around Kursk.

Shortly after the end of the battle, on 20 August 1943 the commander of the 5th Guards Tank Army Lieutenant General P. A. Rotmistrov had to send a memorandum for the record to Deputy of People's Commissariat of Defense Marshal G. K. Zhukov, in which it was noted:

> Commanding tank units from the first days of the Patriotic War, I am compelled to report to you that our tanks today have lost their superiority over enemy tanks in armor and armament. The main gun, armor and accuracy of fire of the German tanks have become much superior, and only the exceptional courage of our tankers, and the great density of artillery in the tank units have prevented the enemy from fully exploiting the superiority of his tanks. The German tanks' powerful weapon, strong armor and excellent optical equipment place our tankers in a plainly unfavorable position. The effectiveness of employing our tanks is being strongly reduced, while their losses are increasing. ... Thus, upon colliding with German tanks units that have switched to a defensive posture, we as a rule suffer enormous losses in tanks and have no success. ... On the basis of our T-34 tank – the finest tank in the world at the start of the war – in 1943 the Germans have managed to produce a still more advanced Panzer V Panther tank, which in essence is a copy of our T-34 tank, but which in its qualities stands significantly higher than the T-34 tank, especially in armament ...
>
> I, as an avid patriot of the tank forces, request that you, Comrade Marshal of the Soviet Union, break down the conservatism and conceit of our tank designers and producers, and with all urgency raise the question of the massed production of new tanks, superior in their combat qualities and design to the currently existing types of German tanks, already by the winter of 1943.[94]

Such a harsh tone was justified – the delay in modernizing the primary tank cost our forces dearly. The letter of the army commander was not the first from the acting army: more than once, representatives of the *Stavka* and the General Staff, having arrived from the front, also reported on this matter. Therefore immediately after the Kursk battle, the leadership placed the resolution of this problem on the front burner. As a result, on 23 January 1944, the T-34/85 arrived to equip the Red Army – a combat vehicle that significantly strengthened the armored forces of the Red Army and played an important role in the battles of the concluding stage of the Great Patriotic War.

The victory at Kursk had an enormous military and political influence. It marked a fundamental turning point in the course of the war on the entire Soviet-German front, and contributed to the creation of more favorable conditions for the operations of our allies in Italy, which led to its withdrawal from the war on the side of Germany. Under the influence of the successful summer offensive after Kursk, the prestige of the Soviet Union as the leading force in the anti-Hitler coalition was strengthened.

Appendix I

Thoughts on the Nature and Proper Designation of the Combat at Prokhorovka

Much has been written about the July fighting of 1943 in the 10 to 18 kilometer (6 to 11 mile) area around Prokhorovka Station. Commonly this period, or more often just 12 July 1943, is called either the tank battle (or even – slaughter) at Prokhorovka, or the Prokhorovka battle, or sometimes – the counterattack on the Prokhorovka staging area. In order to understand this terminology, I will offer the following definitions:

> A **battle** (*bitva*) is the decisive collision of the main forces of the opposing sides, which is connected to a local theater of combat operations and the culmination of an entire campaign. Large battles are capable of bringing about a change, a turning point in the war, of altering fundamentally the correlation of forces of the opposing sides …[1]
>
> Thus, we can immediately set aside the term "battle" as it applies to the fighting at Prokhorovka: Under this definition, there could be not be any sort of "battle" within the framework of the larger Battle of Kursk. Neither the main forces of Voronezh Front nor of Army Group South were ever concentrated in the region of Prokhorovka. The largest grouping that appeared here on the Soviet side before 12 July consisted of two fresh Guards Armies (a tank and a combined arms army), as well as two separate tank corps, four rifle divisions of the 69th Army, and one from the 6th Guards Army. At this time, the Voronezh Front had a total of seven combined arms and tank armies, and also three separate tank corps. The adversary brought up two corps of the six that he possessed, to the two regions southwest and south (Rzhavets-Shcholokovo) of Prokhorovka. No portentous questions of the entire war were settled here.

> An **engagement** (*srazhenie*) is an element of a separate operation, an aggregation of the most important and tough combats between major troop formations – from the army-level and higher – which are often of a prolonged nature, and are directed at achieving one goal, carrying out one operational assignment, and fixed to one time and space. In the course of an engagement, the situation for one of the sides is less foreseen, especially when one of the opponents imposes the given situation on the other side. Thus in the course of an engagement, combat operations are always aimed at *seizing the initiative and take on an extremely sharp character.* The outcome of an engagement remains unclear until the last moment, since both sides strain to the utmost to gain the victory.[2]

In the given case of Prokhorovka, this definition is more suitable. As has been noted above, the combat operations at Prokhorovka took place within the framework of a larger defensive operation of Voronezh Front, which extended from 5 to 23 July 1943; that is to say they were an element of the overall battle, just as were the combat operations on the Oboian' and Korocha directions, and not of an independent, separately planned operation. At the same time, by the amount of forces involved, the length of time, and most importantly, by their results, these combat operations stood out. The enemy made no further advances beyond Prokhorovka, and it was from this place that he began his retreat.

Unquestionably, if the enemy had been able to carry out the assignments that had been given to it in Operation Citadel, the initiative in the summer campaign could have gone over to the *Wehrmacht*. Therefore both sides strained to their utmost, and the combat actions in the engagement for possession of Prokhorovka took on a sharp and rather extended character (the first stage continued for five days, the second stage, for seven). As a result of these factors, the commander of Voronezh Front had been forced to commit two Guards Armies from the *Stavka* Reserve into the battle, both of which had been originally intended to be withheld in order to participate in a grand counteroffensive, at the moment when the Germans had exhausted their strength. This gave a particular bitterness to the entire engagement.

In the framework of the Voronezh Front's defensive operation, its command used various combat techniques; primarily – a deeply echeloned defense by rifle and artillery units, and secondarily – massed armor counterattacks. Three such counterattacks were undertaken with the forces of several tank corps: on 6, 8 and 12 July 1943. The last counterattack occurred already as part of the Prokhorovka engagement, and was stronger than the previous ones, because on this sector southwest of Prokhorovka Station, the main forces of two Guards Armies – Lieutenant General A. S. Zhadov's 5th Guards Army and Lieutenant General P. A. Rotmistrov's 5th Guards Tank Army – were introduced into the battle simultaneously.

The day of 12 July was the climax of the engagement, its turning point. General N. F. Vatutin activated all his available force and resources. In the course of the counterattack, which lasted for practically the entire day, a number of tank combats occurred with the involvement of artillery and infantry. The most significant of them was the fighting in the sector between the Psel River and the farm village of Storozhevoe, which became later known as the "tank field", in which four tank corps and units from three rifle divisions and one airborne division took part. The counterattack did not achieve its basic goal; the enemy was not routed, but the further advance of the II SS Panzer Corps beyond Prokhorovka was finally halted.

Notes

1 V. V. Pokhlebkin, *Velikaia voyna i nesostoyavshiisia mir. 1941-1945-1994* [The Great war and the unsettled peace. 1941-1945-1994]. (Moscow: Art-biznes-tsentr, 1997), 186.

2 Ibid., 182.

Appendix II

German Order of Battle in the Battle of Kursk

Belgorod-Oboian-Kursk Axis, 1 July 1943

ARMY GROUP SOUTH (Field Marshal Erich von Manstein)
Fourth Panzer Army (Colonel General Hermann Hoth)
XXXXVIII Panzer Corps (General Otto von Knobelsdorff)
3d Panzer Division (Lieutenant General Westhoven)
6th Panzer Regiment
3d Panzergrenadier Regiment
394th Panzergrenadier Regiment
75th Panzer Artillery Battalion
3d Motorcycle Battalion
3d Panzer Reconnaissance Battalion
39th Panzer Engineer Battalion
543d Anti-tank Battalion
314th Anti-aircraft (Flak) Detachment
(Strength 90 tanks)

11th Panzer Division (Major General Micki)
15th Panzer Regiment
110th Panzergrenadier Regiment
111th Panzergrenadier Regiment
119th Panzer Artillery Regiment
61st Motorcycle Battalion
61st Panzer Reconnaissance Battalion
231st Panzer Engineer Battalion
61st Anti-tank Battalion
277th Anti-aircraft Detachment
(Strength 113 tanks)

167th Infantry Division (Lieutenant General Trierenberg)
315th Infantry Regiment
331st Infantry Regiment
339th Infantry Regiment
167th Artillery Regiment
167th Reconnaissance Battalion
167th Anti-tank Battalion

Panzergrenadier Division *Grossdeutschland* (Lieutenant General Hoernlein)
Grossdeutschland Panzer Regiment
Grossdeutschland Panzergrenadier Regiment
Grossdeutschland Fusilier Regiment
Grossdeutschland Artillery Regiment

Grossdeutschland Panzer Reconnaissance Battalion
Grossdeutschland Anti-tank Battalion
Grossdeutschland Panzer Engineer Battalion
Grossdeutschland Panzer Anti-aircraft Battalion
Grossdeutschland Assault Gun Battalion
(Strength 132 tanks and 35 assault guns)
10th Panzer Brigade (Panther)
39th Panzer Regiment
51st Panzer Detachment
(Strength 100 tanks)
52d Panzer Detachment
(Strength 100 tanks)

132d Artillery Command (Arko)
144th Artillery Command (Arko)
70th Artillery Regiment
Mortar Detachment, 3d Battalion, 109th Mortar Regiment
101st Heavy Howitzer Detachment
842d Cannon Detachment (100mm)
911th Assault Gun Detachment
(Strength 31 assault guns)
515th Pioneer Regiment
48th Pioneer Battalion (mot)
1st Pioneer Lehr (Training) Battalion (mot)
616th Army Anti-aircraft (Flak) Battalion
(Corps strength 535 tanks and 66 assault guns)

II SS Panzer Corps (SS Obergruppenführer Paul Hausser)
1st SS Panzergrenadier Division *Leibstandarte Adolf Hitler*
(SS Brigadeführer Wisch)
1st SS Panzer Regiment
1st SS Panzergrenadier Regiment
2d SS Panzergrenadier Regiment
1st SS Panzer Artillery Regiment
1st SS Panzer Reconnaissance Battalion
1st SS Anti-tank Battalion
1st SS Panzer Engineer Battalion
1st SS Anti-aircraft Battalion
(Strength 106 tanks and 35 assault guns)

2d SS Panzergrenadier Division *Das Reich* (SS Gruppenführer Kruger)
2d SS Panzer Regiment
3d SS Panzergrenadier Regiment *Deutschland*
4th SS Panzergrenadier Regiment *Der Führer*
2d SS Panzer Artillery Regiment
2d SS Panzer Reconnaissance Battalion
2d SS Anti-tank Battalion
2d SS Panzer Engineer Battalion
2d SS Anti-aircraft Battalion
(Strength 145 tanks and 34 assault guns)

3d SS Panzergrenadier Division *Totenkopf* (SS Brigadeführer Priess)

3d SS Panzer Regiment
5th SS Panzergrenadier Regiment *Thule*
6th SS Panzergrenadier Regiment *Theodor Eicke*
3d SS Panzer Artillery Regiment
3d SS Panzer Reconnaissance Battalion
3d SS Anti-tank Battalion
3d SS Panzer Engineer Battalion
3d SS Anti-aircraft Battalion
(Strength 139 tanks and 35 assault guns)

122d Artillery Command (Arko)
1st Field Howitzer Detachment, 861st Artillery Regiment (mot)
1st Field Howitzer Detachment, 3d Battalion, 818th Artillery Regiment (mot)
3d Smoke Troop
55th Werfer (Engineer Mortar) Regiment
1st Werfer Lehr (Training) Regiment
680th Pioneer Regiment
627th Pioneer Battalion (mot)
666th Pioneer Battalion (mot)
(Corps strength 390 tanks and 104 assault guns)

VIII Air Corps

(Army strength 223,907 men, 925 tanks, and 170 assault guns)

Army Detachment Kempf (General Werner Kempf)
III Panzer Corps (General Hermann Breith)
6th Panzer Division (Major General von Hunersdorf)
11th Panzer Regiment
4th Panzergrenadier Regiment
114th Panzergrenadier Regiment
76th Panzer Artillery Regiment
82d Motorcycle Battalion
6th Panzer Reconnaissance Battalion
41st Anti-tank Battalion
57th Panzer Engineer Battalion
298th Anti-aircraft Detachment
(Strength 117 tanks)

7th Panzer Division (Lieutenant General Freiherr von Funck)
25th Panzer Regiment
6th Panzergrenadier Regiment
7th Panzergrenadier Regiment
78th Panzer Artillery Battalion
58th Motorcycle Battalion
7th Panzer Reconnaissance Battalion
42d Anti-tank Battalion
58th Panzer Engineer Battalion
296th Anti-aircraft Detachment
(Strength 112 tanks)

19th Panzer Division (Lieutenant General Rudolf Schmidt)

27th Panzer Regiment
73d Panzergrenadier Regiment
74th Panzergrenadier Regiment
19th Panzer Artillery Regiment
19th Motorcycle Battalion
19th Panzer Reconnaissance Battalion
19th Anti-tank Battalion
19th Panzer Engineer Battalion
272d Anti-aircraft Detachment
(Strength 70 tanks)

168th Infantry Division (Major General Charles de Beaulieu)
417th Infantry Regiment
429th Infantry Regiment
442d Infantry Regiment
248th Artillery Regiment
168th Reconnaissance Battalion
248th Anti-tank Battalion

54th Werfer (Engineer Mortar) Regiment
503d Heavy Panzer Detachment (Tiger)
(Strength 45 tanks)
99th Anti-aircraft (Flak) Regiment
153d Anti-aircraft (Flak) Regiment
674th Pioneer Regiment
70th Pioneer Battalion
651st Pioneer Battalion
601st Pioneer Regiment
127th Pioneer Battalion (1 co.)
531st Pioneer Bridge Battalion
3d Artillery Command
612th Artillery Regiment
228th Assault Gun Detachment
(Strength 25 assault guns)
2d Battalion, 71st Artillery Regiment (150mm)
857th Heavy Artillery Detachment (210mm)
2d Battalion, 62d Artillery Regiment (105mm)

(Corps strength 344 tanks and 25 assault guns)

Fourth Air Fleet (CO, General Dessloch)

Note All figures denote on-hand tank and assault guns strengths. Operational (serviceable) strengths were somewhat less.

Source: David M. Glantz, 2010. Note that this is a truncated order of battle, concentrating on those formations and units that were active in the German offensive toward Prokhorovka. Formations and units on secondary sectors are not included, unless they were transferred to armies or corps in the relevant area of analysis.

Appendix III

Red Army Order of Battle in the Battle of Kursk

Belgorod-Oboian-Kursk Axis, 1 July 1943

VORONEZH FRONT (Commander, Army General N. F. Vatutin)
Commissar, Lieutenant General N. S. Khrushchev
Chief of Staff, Lieutenant General S. P. Ivanov
6th Guards Army (Commander, Lieutenant General I. M. Chistiakov)
Commissar, Major General P. I. Krainov
Chief of Staff, Major General V. A. Penkovsky

22d Guards Rifle Corps (Major General N. B. Ibiansky)
67th Guards Rifle Division (Major General A. I. Baksov)
196th Guards Rifle Regiment
199th Guards Rifle Regiment
201st Guards Rifle Regiment
138th Guards Artillery Regiment (Lieutenant Colonel M. I. Kidrianov)
73d Guards Separate Anti-tank Artillery Battalion
71st Guards Rifle Division (Colonel I. P. Sivakov)
210th Guards Rifle Regiment
213th Guards Rifle Regiment
219th Guards Rifle Regiment
151st Guards Artillery Regiment
76th Guards Separate Anti-tank Artillery Battalion
134th Separate Anti-tank Rifle Battalion (attached)
136th Separate Anti-tank Rifle Battalion (attached)
90th Guards Rifle Division (Colonel V. G. Chernov)
268th Guards Rifle Regiment
272d Guards Rifle Regiment
274th Guards Rifle Regiment
193d Guards Artillery Regiment

23d Guards Rifle Corps (Major General P. P. Vakhrameev (to 21.7), Major General N. T. Tavartkiladze (from 22.7)
51st Guards Rifle Division (Major General N. T. Tavartkiladze (to 20.7), Colonel I. M. Sukhov (from 21.7)
154th Guards Rifle Regiment
156th Guards Rifle Regiment
158th Guards Rifle Regiment
122d Guards Artillery Regiment (Major M. N. Uglovsky)
52d Guards Rifle Division (Major General. I. M. Nekrasov)
151st Guards Rifle Regiment (Lieutenant Colonel I. F. Iudich)
153d Guards Rifle Regiment
155th Guards Rifle Regiment

124th Guards Artillery Regiment
57th Guards Separate Anti-tank Artillery Battalion
375th Rifle Division (Colonel P. D. Govorunenko) (to 35GRC on 8.7) (to 69A on 10.7)
1241st Rifle Regiment
1243d Rifle Regiment
1245th Rifle Regiment
193d Artillery Regiment (Lieutenant Colonel P. T. Gubarev)
89th Guards Rifle Division (Colonel I.A. Pigin) (to 69A on 10.7)
267th Guards Rifle Regiment
270th Guards Rifle Regiment
273d Guards Rifle Regiment
196th Guards Artillery Regiment
96th Tank Brigade (Major General V. G. Lebedev (to 15.7), Colonel A. M. Popov (from 16.7) (attached to 52GRD) (to 69A on 10.7).
228th Tank Battalion
331st Tank Battalion
230th Separate Tank Regiment (attached to 52GRD)
245th Separate Tank Regiment (attached to 67GRD)
1440th Self-Propelled Artillery Regiment (76mm) (attached to 67GRD)
60th Separate Armored Train Battalion
27th Gun Artillery Brigade (to 69A on 10.7 and 5GTA on 11.7)
93d Gun Artillery Regiment (122mm) (attached to 375RD)
142d Gun Artillery Regiment (152mm) (attached to 52GRD)
33d Gun Artillery Brigade (to 1TA on 8.7)
163d Gun Artillery Regiment (attached to 67 and 71GRDs)
159th Gun Artillery Regiment (attached to 67GRD)
628th Separate Gun Artillery Regiment (attached to 71GRD)
27th Anti-tank Artillery Brigade (Lieutenant Colonel N. D. Chevola) (attached to 71GRD on 6.7)
1837th Anti-tank Artillery Regiment (Major N. E. Plysiuk)
1839th Anti-tank Artillery Regiment (Major Ia. E. Kuvshinov)
1841st Anti-tank Artillery Regiment (Major V. G. Gashkov)
28th Anti-tank Gun Artillery Brigade (attached to 52GRD on 6.7)
1838th Anti-tank Artillery Regiment
1840th Anti-tank Artillery Regiment
1842d Anti-tank Artillery Regiment
493d Anti-tank Artillery Regiment (attached to 71GRD on 5.7)
496th Anti-tank Artillery Regiment (attached to 71 and 67GRDs on 6.7)
538th Anti-tank Artillery Regiment (from 1TA in April) (attached to 52GRD on 6.7)
611th Anti-tank Artillery Regiment (attached to 67GRD)
694th Anti-tank Artillery Regiment (attached to 375RD)
868th Anti-tank Artillery Regiment (attached to71GRD)
1008th Anti-tank Artillery Regiment (Lieutenant Colonel Kotenko) (from 1TA in April) (attached to 52GRD on 6.7)
1240th Anti-tank Artillery Regiment (attached to 375RD)
1666th Anti-tank Artillery Regiment (attached to 71GRD)
1667th Anti-tank Artillery Regiment (attached to 375RD)
263d Mortar Regiment (attached to 375RD) (to 69A on 13.7)
295th Mortar Regiment (attached to 71GRD)
5th Guards Mortar Regiment (Lieutenant Colonel L. Z. Parnovsky) (two battalions to 67GRD and one to 52 GRD)

16th Guards Mortar Regiment (Lieutenant Colonel Ia. T. Petrakovsky) (attached to 375RD) (to 5GTA on 11.7)
79th Guards Mortar Regiment (two battalions to 375RD and one to 67GRD) (to 6TC, 1TA on 6.7)
314th Guards Mortar Regiment (attached to 22GRC)
316th Guards Mortar Regiment (from 1TA in April)
26th Anti-aircraft Artillery Division (Colonel A. E. Florenko)
1352d Anti-aircraft Artillery Regiment
1357th Anti-aircraft Artillery Regiment
1363d Anti-aircraft Artillery Regiment
1369th Anti-aircraft Artillery Regiment
1487th Anti-aircraft Artillery Regiment
205th Separate Engineer Battalion
540th Separate Engineer Battalion

(Army strength 79,900 men, 1,682 guns and mortars, 92 MRLs, and 155 tanks and SP guns).

31st Anti-tank Artillery Brigade (from 7GA on 8.7) (to 69A on 13.7)
184th Rifle Division (from 40A on 12.7)
219th Rifle Division (from 40A on 12.7)

7th Guards Army (Commander, Lieutenant General M. S. Shumilov)
Commisar, Major General Z. T. Serdiuk
Chief of Staff, Major General G. S. Lukin

24th Guards Rifle Corps (Major General N. A. Vasil'ev)
15th Guards Rifle Division (Major General Vasilenko)
44th Guards Rifle Regiment (Major I. A. Usikov)
47th Guards Rifle Regiment (Major I. I. Bat'ianov)
50th Guards Rifle Regiment
43d Guards Artillery Regiment
36th Guards Rifle Division (Major General M. I. Denisenko)
104th Guards Rifle Regiment (Major P. A. Il'ichev)
106th Guards Rifle Regiment (Major I. A. Zaitsev)
108th Guards Rifle Regiment (Major I. P. Moiseev)
65th Guards Artillery Regiment
39th Guards Separate Anti-tank Artillery Battalion (Captain N. A. Borisov)
(Strength 8,013 men)
72d Guards Rifle Division (Major General A. I. Losev)
222d Guards Rifle Regiment
224th Guards Rifle Regiment
229th Guards Rifle Regiment
155th Guards Artillery Regiment (Major Resenuk)

25th Guards Rifle Corps (Major General G. B. Safiullin)
73d Guards Rifle Division (Colonel S. A. Kozak)
209th Guards Rifle Regiment (Lieutenant Colonel G. P. Slatov)
211th Guards Rifle Regiment (Major P. N. Petrov)
214th Guards Rifle Regiment (Major V. I. Davidenko)
153d Guards Artillery Regiment (Major A. A. Nikolaev)

78th Guards Rifle Division (Major General A. V. Skvortsov)
223d Guards Rifle Regiment (Major S. A. Arshinov)
225th Guards Rifle Regiment (Major D. S. Khorolenko)
228th Guards Rifle Regiment (Major I. A. Khitsov)
158th Guards Artillery Regiment
81st Guards Anti-tank Artillery Battalion
(Strength 7,854 men)
81st Guards Rifle Division (Colonel I. K. Morozov) (to 35GRC on 8.7) (to 69A on 10.7)
233d Guards Rifle Regiment
235th Guards Rifle Regiment
238th Guards Rifle Regiment
173d Guards Artillery Regiment
213th Rifle Division (Colonel I. E. Buslaev)
585th Rifle Regiment
702d Rifle Regiment
793d Rifle Regiment
671st Artillery Regiment
27th Guards Tank Brigade (Colonel M. V. Nevzhinsky (to 18.8), Colonel N. M. Brizhinov (from 19.8) (attached to 24GRC)
201st Tank Brigade (Colonel (Major General on 16.7) A. I. Taranov) (attached to 24GRC) (to 78GRD on 6.7)
295th Tank Battalion
296th Tank Battalion
148th Separate Tank Regiment (attached to 24GRC) (to 69A on 10.7)
167th Separate Tank Regiment (attached to 25GRC) (to 73GRD on 6.7)
262d Separate Tank Regiment (attached to 25GRC)
1438th Self-Propelled Artillery Regiment (122mm) (attached to 25GRC) (to 73GRD on 6.7)
1529th Self-Propelled Artillery Regiment (152mm) (attached to 24GRC)
34th Separate Armored Train Battalion
38th Separate Armored Train Battalion
109th Guards Gun Artillery Regiment (attached to 24GRC)
161st Guards Gun Artillery Regiment (attached to 25GRC)
265th Guards Gun Artillery Regiment (attached to 25GRC) (to 73GRD on 6.7)
30th Anti-tank Artillery Brigade (army reserve, attached to 78GRD, 25GRC on 6.7) (to 69A on 10.7)
1844th Anti-tank Artillery Regiment
1846th Anti-tank Artillery Regiment
1848th Anti-tank Artillery Regiment
114th Guards Anti-tank Artillery Regiment (Lieutenant Colonel N. Shubin) (attached to 25GRC)
115th Guards Anti-tank Artillery Regiment (Lieutenant Colonel N. Koziarenko) (attached to 36GRD, 24GRC) (to 69A on 13.7)
1669th Anti-tank Artillery Regiment (attached to 36GRD on 5.7 and 78 GRD on 6.7)
1670th Anti-tank Artillery Regiment
1st Anti-tank Rifle Battalion (attached to 24GRC)
2d Anti-tank Rifle Battalion (attached to 81GRD)
3d Anti-tank Rifle Battalion
4th Anti-tank Rifle Battalion (attached to 78GRD)
5th Anti-tank Rifle Battalion (attached to 24GRC)
290th Mortar Regiment (attached to 25GRC) (to 69A on 13.7)
5th Anti-aircraft Artillery Division (Colonel M. A. Kudriasov)

670th Anti-aircraft Artillery Regiment
743d Anti-aircraft Artillery Regiment
1119th Anti-aircraft Artillery Regiment
1181st Anti-aircraft Artillery Regiment
162d Guards Anti-aircraft Artillery Regiment
258th Guards Anti-aircraft Artillery Regiment
60th Engineer-Sapper Brigade (Colonel D. Sh. Tsepeniuka)
175th Separate Engineer Battalion
329th Separate Engineer Battalion (Major A. I. Sychev) (to 73GRD on 6.7)
(Army strength 76,800 men, 1,573 guns and mortars, 47 MRLs, and 246 tanks and SP guns).

★ ★ ★

97th Guards Mortar Regiment (from *front* on 4.7) (attached to 81GRD, 25GRC) (to 72GRD on 6.7)
309th Guards Mortar Regiment (from *front* on 5.7) (to 78GRD on 6.7)
315th Guards Mortar Regiment (from *front* on 4.7) (attached to 25GRC) (to 69A on 13.7)
443d Guards Mortar Battalion (to 81GRD on 5.7)
477th Guards Mortar Battalion (to 81GRD on 5.7)
31st Anti-tank Artillery Brigade (from *front* on 6.7) (to 73GRD on 6.7) (to6GA on 8.7)

69th Army (Commander, Lieutenant General V. D. Kriuchenkin)
Commissar, Major General A. V. Shchelakovsky
Chief of Staff, Colonel S. M. Protas

48th Rifle Corps (Major General Z. Z. Rogoznyi)
107th Rifle Division (Major General P. M. Bezhko) (to 35GRC on 10.7)
504th Rifle Regiment
516th Rifle Regiment
522d Rifle Regiment
1032d Artillery Regiment
183d Rifle Division (Major General A.S. Kostitsyn (to 24.7), Colonel I. D. Vasilevsky (from 25.7)
227th Rifle Regiment
285th Rifle Regiment
296th Rifle Regiment
623d Artillery Regiment (Major I. N. Sadovnikov)
305th Rifle Division (Colonel A. F. Vasil'ev) (to 35GRC on 10.7)
1000th Rifle Regiment
1002d Rifle Regiment
1004th Rifle Regiment
830th Artillery Regiment

49th Rifle Corps (Major General G. P. Terentev) (to 7GA on 7.7)
111th Rifle Division (Lieutenant Colonel A. N. Petrushin)
399th Rifle Regiment
468th Rifle Regiment
532d Rifle Regiment
286th Artillery Regiment
270th Rifle Division (Colonel I. P. Beliaev)
973d Rifle Regiment
975th Rifle Regiment
977th Rifle Regiment

810th Artillery Regiment
1661st Anti-tank Artillery Regiment
496th Mortar Regiment
225th Guards Anti-aircraft Artillery Regiment
322d Separate Anti-aircraft Artillery Battalion
328th Separate Engineer Battalion

(Army strength 52,000 men and 889 guns and mortars)

35th Guards Rifle Corps (from *front* on 5.7)
92d Guards Rifle Division
94th Guards Rifle Division
93d Guards Rifle Division (from *front* on 7.7)
81st Guards Rifle Division (from 7GA on 10.7)
89th Guards Rifle Division (from 6GA on 10.7)
10th Anti-tank Artillery Brigade (from Southwestern Front on 10.7) (to 5GTA on 11.7) (from 5GTA on 13.7)
375th Rifle Division (from 6GA on 10.7)
2d Guards Tank Corps (from 1TA on 10.7)
96th Tank Brigade (from 6GA on 10.7)
148th Separate Regiment (from 7GA on 10.7)
30th Anti-tank Artillery Brigade (from 7GA on 10.7)
27th Gun Artillery Brigade (from 6GA on 10.7) (to 5GTA on 11.7) (returned on 13.7)
32d Anti-tank Artillery Brigade (from 40A on 13.7)
36th Anti-aircraft Artillery Division (from *front* reserve on 13.7)
1385th Anti-aircraft Artillery Regiment
1391st Anti-aircraft Artillery Regiment
1397th Anti-aircraft Artillery Regiment
1399th Anti-aircraft Artillery Regiment
80th Guards Mortar Regiment (from 5GTA on 13.7)
1076th Anti-tank Artillery Regiment (from 2GTC on 13.7)
31st Anti-tank Artillery Brigade (from 6GA on 13.7)
115th Guards Mortar Regiment (from 7GA on 13.7)
1658th Anti-tank Artillery Regiment (from 38A on 13.7)
315th Guards Mortar Regiment (from 7GA on 13.7)
293d Mortar Regiment (from 6GA on 13.7)
290th Mortar Regiment (from 7GA on 13.7)
48th Anti-tank Artillery Regiment (from 2TC on 13.7)
638th Anti-tank Artillery Regiment (on 13.7) (from another AT brigade)
1510th Anti-tank Artillery Regiment (on 13.7) (from another AT brigade)

1st Tank Army (Commander, Lieutenant General M. E. Katukov)
Commissar, Major General N. K. Popel
Chief of Staff, Major General M. A. Shalin

3d Mechanized Corps (Major General S. M. Krivoshein)
1st Mechanized Brigade (Colonel F. P. Lipatenkov)
14th Tank Regiment
3d Mechanized Brigade (Colonel A. Kh. Babadzhanian)
16th Tank Regiment
10th Mechanized Brigade (Colonel I. I. Iakovlev)

17th Tank Regiment (Major I. N. Boiko)
1st Guards Tank Brigade (Colonel V. M. Gorelov)
49th Tank Brigade (Lieutenant Colonel A. F. Burda)
58th Motorcycle Battalion
35th Anti-tank Artillery Regiment
265th Mortar Regiment
405th Separate Guards Mortar Battalion
34th Separate Armored Car (Reconnaissance) Battalion
(Corps strength 250 tanks)

6th Tank Corps (Major General A. L. Getman)
22d Tank Brigade (Colonel N. G. Vedenichev)
1st Tank Battalion
?? Tank Battalion
112th Tank Brigade (Colonel M. T. Leonov)
124th Tank Battalion (Major F. P. Borid'ko)
125th Tank Battalion (Major P. I. Orekhov)
200th Tank Brigade (Colonel N. V. Morgunov)
191st Tank Battalion
192d Tank Battalion
6th Motorized Rifle Brigade (Colonel I. P. Elin)
85th Motorcycle Battalion
1461st Self-Propelled Artillery Regiment (76mm) (to 40A on 5.7)
538th Anti-tank Artillery Regiment (Major V. I. Barkovsky) (to 6GA in April)
1008th Anti-tank Artillery Regiment (Major I. K. Kotenko) (to 6GA in April)
270th Mortar Regiment
40th Separate Armored Car (Reconnaissance) Battalion
(Corps strength 179 tanks on 6.7 and 52 tanks on 18.7)

79th Guards Mortar Regiment (from 6GA on 6.7)

31st Tank Corps (Major General D. Kh. Chernienko)
100th Tank Brigade (Colonel N. M. Ivanov (to 21.7), Major V. M. Potapov (from 22.7)
1st Tank Battalion (Captain. P. F. Kunchenko)
2d Tank Battalion (Captain. M. G. Marilov)
237th Tank Brigade (Major N. P. Protsenko)
1st Tank Battalion (Captain N. M. Godin)
2d Tank Battalion
242d Tank Brigade Lieutenant (Colonel V. P. Sokolov)
1st Tank Battalion
2d Tank Battalion
31st Separate Armored Car (Reconnaissance) Battalion
210th Anti-tank Rifle Battalion
(Corps strength 43 T-34 and 12-17 T-60 and T-70 tanks per brigade for a total of 196 (155 T-34 and 41 T-60 and T-70) tanks.

753d Anti-tank Artillery Battalion (on 10.7)
316th Guards Mortar Regiment (attached to 6GA in April)
8th Anti-aircraft Artillery Division (Colonel I. G. Kamen'sky)
797th Anti-aircraft Artillery Regiment

848th Anti-aircraft Artillery Regiment
978th Anti-aircraft Artillery Regiment
1063d Anti-aircraft Artillery Regiment
71st Separate Motorized Engineer Battalion
267th Separate Motorized Engineer Battalion
385th Signal Aviation Regiment (19 PO-2)
83d Signal Regiment
35th Auto Transport Regiment
6th Repair-Reconstruction Battalion
7th Repair-Reconstruction Battalion
(Army strength 40,000 men, 419 guns and mortars, 56 MRLs, 646 tanks and SP guns, and several thousand vehicles)

2d Guards Tank Corps (from *front* on 5.7)
5th Guards Tank Corps (from *front* on 5.7)
29th Anti-tank Artillery Brigade (from 38A on 7.7) (attached to 31TC)
180th Separate Tank Brigade (from 38A on 7.7)
192d Separate Tank Brigade (from 38A on 7.7)
111th Guards Howitzer Artillery Regiment (from 38A on 7.7)
222d Anti-tank Artillery Regiment (from 38A on 7.7)
1244th Anti-tank Artillery Regiment (from 40A on 7.7) (attached to 31TC)
66th Guards Mortar Regiment (from 38A on 7.7)
754th Anti-tank Artillery Battalion (from 38A or 40A on 8.7)
756th Anti-tank Artillery Battalion (from 38A or 40A on 8.7)
138th Anti-tank Rifle Battalion (from 38A or 40A on 8.7)
139th Anti-tank Rifle Battalion (from 38A or 40A on 8.7)
86th Separate Tank Brigade (from 40A on 8.7)
33d Gun Artillery Brigade (from 6GA on 8.7)
4th Guards Anti-tank Artillery Regiment (from 40A on 8.7)
12th Anti-tank Artillery Regiment (from 40A on 8.7)
36th Guards Mortar Regiment (from *front* on 8.7)
10th Tank Corps (from Steppe Front on 8.7)
309th Rifle Division (from 40A on 8.7) (to 40A on 12.7)
59th Separate Tank Regiment (from 40A on 8.7)
60th Separate Heavy Tank Regiment (from 40A on 8.7)
203d Separate Tank Regiment (from *front* on 8.7)
483d Anti-tank Artillery Regiment (from 38A on 8.7)
869th Anti-tank Artillery Regiment (from 40A on 8.7)
14th Anti-tank Artillery Brigade (from *front* on 8.7)
9th Anti-aircraft Artillery Division (from 40A on 8.7)
204th Rifle Division (from *front* on 10.7)

2d Air Army (Commander, Lieutenant Gen. S. A. Krasovsky)

Front subordination

35th Guards Rifle Corps (Major General S. G. Goriachev) (to 69A on 5.7)
92d Guards Rifle Division (Colonel V. F. Trunin (to 10.8), Colonel A. N. Petrushin (from 11.8) (to 69A on 5.7)
276th Guards Rifle Regiment
280th Guards Rifle Regiment
282d Guards Rifle Regiment

197th Guards Artillery Regiment (Colonel S. I. Shapovalov)
93d Guards Rifle Division (Major General V. V. Tikhomirov) (to 48RC on 7.7)
278th Guards Rifle Regiment
281st Guards Rifle Regiment
285th Guards Rifle Regiment
198th Guards Artillery Regiment
94th Guards Rifle Division (Colonel I. G. Russkikh) (to 69A on 5 July, returned to 35GRC on 8.7)
283d Guards Rifle Regiment
286th Guards Rifle Regiment
288th Guards Rifle Regiment
199th Guards Artillery Regiment
(Corps strength 35,000 men and 620 guns and mortars)

81st Guards Rifle Division (from 7GA on 8.7, returned to 48RC, 69A on 10.7)
375th Rifle Division (from 6GA on 8.7, returned to 48RC, 69A on 10.7)
305th Rifle Division (from 69A on 10.7)
107th Rifle Division (from 69A on 10.7)
1510th Anti-tank Artillery Regiment (45mm) (corps reserve on 13.7)

2d Guards Tank Corps (Major General A. S. Burdeiny) (to 1TA on 5.7, 69A on 10.7, and 5GTA on 11.7)
4th Guards Tank Brigade (Colonel A. K. Brazhnikov)
25th Guards Tank Brigade (Lieutenant Colonel S. M. Bulygin)
26th Guards Tank Brigade (Colonel S K. Nesterov)
4th Guards Motorized Rifle Brigade
47th Guards Tank Regiment
1500th Anti-tank Artillery Regiment
755th Separate Anti-tank Artillery Battalion
273d Mortar Regiment
1695th Anti-aircraft Artillery Regiment
19th Separate Armored Car (Reconnaissance) Battalion
79th Separate Motorcycle Battalion
(Strength 200 tanks on 5.7 and 100 tanks on 11.7)

1076th Anti-tank Artillery Regiment (from *front* on 7.7) (to 69A on 13.7)

5th Guards Tank Corps (Major General A. G. Kravchenko) (to 1TA on 5.7)
20th Guards Tank Brigade (Lieutenant Colonel P. F. Okhrimenko)
21st Guards Tank Brigade (Colonel K. I. Ovcharenko)
22d Guards Tank Brigade (Colonel F. A. Zhilin)
6th Guards Motorized Rifle Brigade
48th Guards Tank Regiment
1499th Anti-tank Artillery Regiment
454th Mortar Regiment
1696th Anti-aircraft Artillery Regiment
23d Separate Armored Car (Reconnaissance) Battalion
80th Separate Motorcycle Battalion
(Strength 200 tanks)
?? Battalion, 203d Separate Heavy Tank Regiment

1528th Howitzer Artillery Regiment (29th Howitzer Artillery Brigade)
522d High-Powered Howitzer Artillery Regiment (to 5GTA on 11.7)
1148th High-Powered Howitzer Artillery Regiment (to 5GTA on 11.7)
14th Anti-tank Artillery Brigade (to 1TA on 8.7)
    1177th Anti-tank Artillery Regiment
    1207th Anti-tank Artillery Regiment
    1212th Anti-tank Artillery Regiment
31st Anti-tank Artillery Brigade (to 7GA on 6.7 and 6GA on 8.7)
    1849th Anti-tank Artillery Regiment
    1851st Anti-tank Artillery Regiment
    1853d Anti-tank Artillery Regiment
1076th Anti-tank Artillery Regiment (Lieutenant Colonel Kalinin) (to 2GTC on 7.7)
1689th Anti-tank Artillery Regiment (to 40A on 5.7)
12th Mortar Brigade
469th Mortar Regiment
36th Guards Mortar Regiment (to 1TA on 8.7)
80th Guards Mortar Regiment (Lieutenant Colonel Samchenko) (to 5GTA on 11.7)
97th Guards Mortar Regiment (Lieutenant Colonel M. M. Chumak) (to 7GA on 4.7)
309th Guards Mortar Regiment (to 7GA on 5 July)
315th Guards Mortar Regiment (Lieutenant Colonel A. F. Ganiushkin) (to 7GA on 4.7)
22d Guards Separate Anti-aircraft Battalion
4th Engineer-Mine Brigade
5th Engineer-Mine Brigade
42d Engineer Brigade (*Spetznaz*)
6th Pontoon-Bridge Brigade
13th Guards Miners Battalion
6th Pontoon-Bridge Battalion
20th Pontoon-Bridge Battalion

1529th Self-Propelled Artillery Regiment (from *RGK* in July)
36th Anti-aircraft Artillery Division (from *RGK* in July)
    1385th Anti-aircraft Artillery Regiment
    1391st Anti-aircraft Artillery Regiment
    1397th Anti-aircraft Artillery Regiment
    1399th Anti-aircraft Artillery Regiment
204th Rifle Division (from 38A on 8.7)
13th Artillery Penetration Division (Major General D. M. Krasnokutsky) (from Briansk Front after 20.7) (to 5GA by 1.8)
    42d Light Artillery Brigade
    47th Howitzer Artillery Brigade
    88th Heavy Howitzer Artillery Brigade
    91st Heavy Howitzer Artillery Brigade (to 27A by 1.8)
    101st High Power Howitzer Artillery Brigade
    17th Mortar Brigade
17th Artillery Penetration Division (7th Artillery Penetration Corps) (from Briansk Front after 20.7)
    37th Light Artillery Brigade
    39th Gun Artillery Brigade
    50th Gun Artillery Brigade
    92d Heavy Gun Artillery Brigade
    108th Gun Artillery Brigade

22d Mortar Brigade
(*Front* strength 625,591 men, 8,718 guns and mortars, 272 MRLs, 1,704 tanks and SP guns, 272 MRLs, and 900 aircraft)

★ ★ ★

SOUTHWESTERN FRONT (Commander, Army General R. Ia. Malinovsky)
2d Tank Corps (Major General A. F. Popov) (to SWF on 8.7 and 5GTA on 11.7)
26th Tank Brigade
99th Tank Brigade (Lieutenant Colonel L. I. Malov) (KIA on 11.7)
169th Tank Brigade
58th Motorized Rifle Brigade
83d Motorcycle Battalion
48th Anti-tank Artillery Regiment (to 69A on 13.7)
1502d Anti-tank Regiment
269th Mortar Regiment
1698th Anti-aircraft Regiment
307th Guards Mortar Battalion
(Strength 168 tanks on 8.7 and 100 tanks on 12.7)

STEPPE MILITARY DISTRICT (STEPPE FRONT on 9.7)
5th Guards Army (to Voronezh Front on 8.7)
Commander, Lieutenant General A. S. Zhadov
Commissar, Major General A. M. Krivulin
Chief of Staff, Major General N. I. Liamin

32d Guards Rifle Corps (Major General A. I. Rodimtsev)
13th Guards Rifle Division (Major General G. V. Baklanov)
34th Guards Rifle Regiment (Lieutenant Colonel D. I. Panikhin)
39th Guards Rifle Regiment (Lieutenant Colonel A. K. Shchur)
42d Guards Rifle Regiment (Lieutenant Colonel A. V. Kolesnik)
32d Guards Artillery Regiment (Lieutenant Colonel A. V. Klebanovsky)
66th Guards Rifle Division (Major General A. V. Iakushin)
145th Guards Rifle Regiment
193d Guards Rifle Regiment
195th Guards Rifle Regiment
135th Guards Artillery Regiment
6th Guards Airborne Division (Colonel M. N. Smirnov)
14th Guards Airborne Regiment
17th Guards Airborne Regiment
20th Guards Airborne Regiment
8th Guards Airborne Artillery Regiment

33d Guards Rifle Corps (Major General I. I. Popov (to 30.8), Major General M. I. Kozlov (from 31.8)
95th Guards Rifle Division (Colonel A. N. Liakhov)
284th Guards Rifle Regiment (Lieutenant Colonel V. S. Nakaidze)
287th Guards Rifle Regiment (Lieutenant Colonel F. M. Zaiarny)
290th Guards Rifle Regiment
233d Guards Artillery Regiment (Lieutenant Colonel A. P. Revin)
103d Guards Separate Anti-tank Battalion
97th Guards Rifle Division (Colonel I. I. Antsiferov)
289th Guards Rifle Regiment (Lieutenant Colonel P. R. Pansky)

292d Guards Rifle Regiment (Lieutenant Colonel V. S. Savinov)
294th Guards Rifle Regiment
232d Guards Artillery Regiment
104th Guards Separate Anti-tank Artillery Battalion (Major I. D. Rudenko)
9th Guards Airborne Division (Colonel A. M. Sazonov)
23d Guards Airborne Regiment (Lieutenant Colonel N. M. Nazarov)
26th Guards Airborne Regiment (Lieutenant Colonel G. M. Kashpersky)
28th Guards Airborne Regiment (Major V. A. Ponomarev)
7th Guards Artillery Regiment (Major V. K. Valuev)
10th Guards Anti-tank Artillery Battalion
42d Guards Rifle Division (Major General F. A. Bobrov)
127th Guards Rifle Regiment
132d Guards Rifle Regiment
136th Guards Rifle Regiment
75th Guards Artillery Regiment

10th Tank Corps (Major General V. G. Burkov) (to *front* on 7.7 and 1TA on 8.7)
178th Tank Brigade (Major K. M. Pivorarov)
183d Tank Brigade (Colonel G. Ia. Andriushchenko (to 15.8), Lieutenant Colonel M. K. Akopov (from 15.8)
186th Tank Brigade (Lieutenant Colonel A. V. Ovsiannikov)
11th Motorized Rifle Brigade (Colonel P. G. Borodkin)
1450th Self-Propelled Artillery Regiment (122m/76mm) (Lieutenant Colonel L. M. Lebedev)
30th Separate Armored Car (Reconnaissance) Battalion
77th Motorcycle Battalion
727th Anti-tank Regiment (Lieutenant Colonel V. S. Shonichev)
(20 76mm guns)
287th Mortar Regiment (Lieutenant Colonel V. F. Druzhinin)
(36 120mm mortars)
1693d Anti-aircraft Regiment (Major N. A. Shumilov)
(16 37mm AA guns)
(Corps strength 164 tanks (99 T-34, 64 T-70, 1 KV), 21 SP-guns (12 SU-122, 9 SU-76)
301st Anti-tank Artillery Regiment (attached to 33GRC) (to 95GRD on 12.7)
1322d Anti-tank Artillery Regiment
308th Guards Mortar Regiment
29th Anti-aircraft Artillery Division (Colonel Ia. M. Liubimov (to 23.7), Colonel M. A. Vialov (from 24.7)
1360th Anti-aircraft Artillery Regiment
1366th Anti-aircraft Artillery Regiment
1372d Anti-aircraft Artillery Regiment
1374th Anti-aircraft Artillery Regiment
256th Separate Engineer Battalion
431st Separate Engineer Battalion
(Army strength 80,000 men, 1,953 guns and mortars, 133 MRLs, and185 tanks and SP guns)

5th Guards Tank Army (to Voronezh Front on 11.7)
Commander, Lieutenant General P. A. Rotmistrov
Commissar, Major General P. G. Grishin
Chief of Staff, Major General V. N. Baskakov

5th Guards Mechanized Corps (Major General B. M. Skvortsov)

10th Guards Mechanized Brigade (Colonel I. B. Mikhailov)
51st Guards Tank Regiment (Colonel D. Ia. Klinfeld)
11th Guards Mechanized Brigade (Colonel N. V. Grishchenko)
54th Guards Tank Regiment (Lieutenant Colonel V. Riazantsev)
12th Guards Mechanized Brigade (Colonel G. Ia. Borisenko)
55th Guards Tank Regiment (Lieutenant Colonel M. Gol'dberg)
24th Guards Tank Brigade (Lieutenant Colonel V. P. Karpov (to 29.7), Colonel T. A. Akulovich (30.7-11.8), Lieutenant Colonel V. P. Karpov (from 12.8)
4th Guards Separate Armored Car (Reconnaissance) Battalion (Captain N. A. Shtykoi)
2d Guards Motorcycle Battalion (Captain. V. P. Kuz'min)
1447th Self-Propelled Artillery Regiment (85mm) (Major V. F. Gaidash)
104th Guards Anti-tank Artillery Regiment (57mm) (Major F. Z. Babachenko)
285th Mortar Regiment (Major S. S. Belen'kovo)
737th Separate Anti-tank Artillery Battalion
409th Separate Guards Mortar Battalion (Captain. N. A. Kolupaev)
(Strength 212 tanks and 16 SP guns; tank regiment strength – 32 T-34, 16-17 T-70 each; and tank brigade strength, 63 T-34 each)

29th Tank Corps (Major General I. F. Kirichenko)
25th Tank Brigade (Colonel N. K. Volodin)
31st Tank Brigade (Colonel S. F. Moiseev (to 8.8), Colonel A. A. Novikov (from 9.8)
32d Tank Brigade (Colonel A. A. Linev (KIA on 25.8), Colonel K. K. Vorob'ev (from 26.8)
53d Motorized Rifle Battalion (Lieutenant Colonel N. P. Lipichev)
1446th Self-Propelled Artillery Regiment 85mm) (Captain. M. S. Lunev)
38th Separate Armored Car (Reconnaissance) Battalion
75th Motorcycle Battalion
108th Anti-tank Artillery Regiment
271st Mortar Battalion
747th Separate Anti-tank Battalion
(Strength 170 tanks and 21 SP guns)

76th Guards Mortar Regiment (attached on 5.7)
53d Guards Separate Tank Regiment (Major N. A. Kurnosov) (to Group Trufanov on 11.7) (Strength 21 tanks)
1549th Self-Propelled Artillery Regiment (152mm)
1st Separate Guards Motorcycle Regiment (Lieutenant Colonel V. A. Dokudovsky) (to Group Trufanov on 11.7)
678th Howitzer Artillery Regiment (to Group Trufanov on 11.7)
689th Anti-tank Artillery Regiment (Major I. S. Guzhvy) (to Group Trufanov on 11.7)
76th Guards Mortar Regiment
6th Anti-aircraft Artillery Division (Colonel G. P. Mezhinsky)
146th Anti-aircraft Artillery Regiment (attached to 5GMC)
366th Anti-aircraft Artillery Regiment (attached to 29TC)
516th Anti-aircraft Artillery Regiment
1062d Anti-aircraft Artillery Regiment
4th Separate Signal Regiment (Lieutenant Colonel A. M. Gorbachev)
994th Light Bomber Aviation Regiment
377th Separate Engineer Battalion
18th Tank Corps (Major General B. S. Bakharov) (from *RVK* on 7.7)
110th Tank Brigade (Lieutenant Colonel M. G. Khliupin)

170th Tank Brigade (Lieutenant Colonel V. D. Tarasov (to 13.7), Lieutenant Colonel A. I. Kazakov (14.7-7.8), Colonel N. P. Chunikin (from 8.8)
181st Tank Brigade (Lieutenant Colonel V. A. Puzyrev (to 15.8), Lieutenant Colonel A. F. Shevchenko (from 16.8)
32d Motorized Rifle Brigade (Lieutenant Colonel I. A. Stukov (KIA on 13.7), Colonel M. E. Khvatov (from 13.7)
36th Guards Separate Tank Regiment (Heavy)
1000th Anti-tank Artillery Regiment
736th Separate Anti-tank Artillery Battalion
292d Mortar Regiment
1694th Anti-aircraft Artillery Regiment
29th Separate Armored Car (Reconnaissance) Company
78th Separate Motorcycle Battalion
(Strength 190 tanks)

(Army strength 37,000 men, and 593 tanks and 37 SP guns on 6.7)

2d Tank Corps (Major General A. F. Popov) (from SWF on 8.7, to 5GTA on 11.7)
1529th Self-propelled Artillery Regiment (from *RVK* and Voronezh Front on 11.7) (attached to 29TC)
522d High Power Howitzer Artillery Regiment (from Voronezh Front on 11.7)
148th High Power Howitzer Artillery Regiment (from Voronezh Front on 11.7)
148th Gun Artillery Regiment (from Voronezh Front on 11.7)
93d Gun Artillery Regiment (from Voronezh Front on 11.7)
16th Guards Mortar Regiment (Lieutenant Colonel Ia. T. Tsetrakovsky) (from 6GA, Voronezh Front on 11.7)
80th Guards Mortar Regiment (Lieutenant Colonel. I. Samchenko) (from Voronezh Front on 11.7) (to 69A on 13.7)
10th Anti-tank Artillery Brigade (57mm) (from 69A on 11.7) (one regt to 18TC, remainder to 2GTC) (to 69A on 13.7)
532d Anti-tank Artillery Regiment
1243d Anti-tank Artillery Regiment
1245th Anti-tank Artillery Regiment
27th Gun Artillery Brigade (from 6GA on 11.7) (to 69A on 13.7)
(5GTA strength on 11.7, with 2GTC and 2TC 793 tanks and 37 SP guns, including 501 T-34, 261 T-70, and 31 Mk. IV Churchill tanks).

Note Denotes on-hand tank and self-propelled gun strengths. Operational (serviceable) strengths were somewhat less.

Source: David M. Glantz, 2010. Note that this is a truncated order of battle, concentrating on those formations and units that defended against the German offensive toward Prokhorovka. Formations and units on secondary sectors are not included, unless they were transferred to armies or corps in the relevant area of analysis.

Notes

Chapter 1

1 Nikolai Fedorovich Vatutin, General of the Army (1943) was born 16 December 1901 in the village of Chepukhino in Kursk (today Belgorod) Oblast into the large family of a middle-class peasant, who eventually had eight other children. Because of his relatively advantageous social position, Vatutin received a good education. In 1913 he completed his primary education in a village school, then two years of schooling at a district school in the city of Valuika and three years at a trade school in Urazovo. Before 1917 he lived in his father's family and worked in agriculture.

He was mobilized for service in the Workers' and Peasants' Red Army in April 1920. In 1920-1921, in the ranks of the Red Army he participated in the fighting against Makhno's band and that of Ataman Belenky on the land of Lugansk, Poltava and Khar'kov Oblasts. He graduated from the Poltava Infantry School in 1922, the Kiev Higher Unified Military School in 1924, and the prestigious Frunze Military Academy in 1929. He commanded a squad, a platoon, and then a company. He began staff work in June 1929, and served as an assistant to the 7th Rifle Division's chief of operations in the city of Chernigov, as assistant chief of operations in the North Caucasus Military District (in Rostov), the chief of staff of the 28th Mountain Rifle Division (in Ordzhonokidze), and the chief of staff of the Siberian Military District in Novosibirsk. After graduation from the General Staff Academy in July 1937, he was appointed deputy chief of staff of the Kiev Special Military District, and rose to chief of staff of the Kiev Special Military District in November 1938. Between 26 July 1940 and 13 February 1941, he was a deputy chief of the General Staff and simultaneously the chief of the Operations Branch. Between 13 February 1941 and 30 June 1941, Vatutin was the first deputy chief of the General Staff for operational matters and the arrangement of rear services. On 30 June 1941, he became the Northwestern Front's chief of staff. In the middle of July 1942, at his personal request and with the support of A. M. Vasilevsky, he was appointed by Stalin to command the Voronezh Front, then was transferred to the Southwestern Front. Under his command, this *front* achieved signal successes in the Stalingrad battle, for which on 7 December 1942, Vatutin received the command rank of colonel general. On 12 February 1943, Vatutin became a General of the Army and was honored with the Order of Suvorov, First Degree. On 28 March 1943, he again took command of the Voronezh Front.

N. F. Vatutin was one of the most well-trained and promising generals in the cohort of *front* commanders. Among the notable characteristics of his style of leadership were the deep and thorough preparation of his operations, his energy and ability to organize powerful tank thrusts into the depth of the enemy's defenses, and his purposefulness. The General had a calm and well-balanced personality. As N. S. Khrushchev recalled, Vatutin was a very decent and modest man. He was distinguished by his respectful treatment of his subordinates, in work he sought to give them the opportunity to show their talents and to display initiative. However, he had difficult relations with I. V. Stalin. The Supreme Commander more than once, often justifiably, pointed out Vatutin's errors in handling his *front*, and expressed dissatisfaction with his leadership methods. In particular, there is evidence that Stalin harshly criticized Vatutin's actions in the Kursk defensive fighting, the subsequent counteroffensive, as well as in the Korsun-Shevchenko operation, although he did award Nikolai Fedorovich the Order of Kutuzov, First Degree for his role at Kursk. However, right up to Vatutin's tragic death, Stalin never decorated him with the Gold Star of Hero of the Soviet Union, nor promoted him to the highest military command rank of Marshal of the Soviet Union, even though N. F. Vatutin fully deserved these honors.

N. F. Vatutin died on 15 April 1944 in a Kiev hospital from a wound he had suffered in an ambush set by Ukrainian nationalist partisans in the 60th Army's sector on 29 February 1944.

2 I. V. Porod'ko (ed.), *Kurskaia bitva* [The Battle of Kursk], (Moscow: Nauka, 1970), 520-521.

3 Werner Kempf, General of Panzer Troops; born on 9 March 1886 in Königsberg. He participated in the First World War, rising to the rank of captain by the war's end. In the period between the wars, he served in a number of staff positions, including as an inspector of motorized units. After receiving the rank of colonel on 1 April 1935, he was appointed commander of the 4th Panzer Brigade. At the beginning of 1939, he was awarded the first general's rank – major general – and became the commander of Division Kempf (which later became the 10th Panzer Division), while on 1 October

of that year he became commander of the 6th Panzer Division. On 31 July 1940, he was promoted to lieutenant general, and on 1 April 1941, General of Panzer Troops. On 1 June 1941, he took command of the XXXXVIII Panzer Corps. He participated in battles on the Soviet-German front, and later became commander of the Eighth Army and Army Detachment Kempf. At the end of August 1943, after abandoning Khar'kov against orders, Hitler removed him from command of the Eighth Army and transferred him to command *Wehrmacht* forces in East European countries (on the roster of Army Group North). He was awarded the Knight's Cross (1940) and Oak Leaves (1942). He died in West Germany in 1964.

4 Steven H. Newton, *Kursk: The German View* (New York: Da Capo Press, 2002), p. 185.

5 Hermann Hoth was born on 12 April 1885 in Neuruppin. He began serving in the Kaiser's army at 19 years of age, and within a year, in 1905, he received his first officer's rank, lieutenant. He participated in the First World War, and after its end, he remained in the army during the Weimar period. In the 1920s, he didn't serve in any important posts. On 1 February 1932, he was promoted to the rank of colonel and given command of the 17th Infantry Regiment; later, he became the military commandant in the city of Liubeck. A noticeable rise in his career came after the Nazis came to power. In October 1934, Hoth became a general and was placed in command of the 18th Infantry Division. Within two years, on 1 October 1936, Hoth received the rank of lieutenant general. In October 1938, Hoth became a General of Infantry and took command of the XV Army Corps (mot.). In this position he participated in his first campaign of the Second World War – the invasion of Poland. His formation, which was subordinated to the Tenth Army, managed to shatter the Polish forces defending Warsaw and to take that city, for which he received the Knight's Cross from Hitler. Next his corps took part in the occupation of France. At the time of Germany's invasion of the Soviet Union, Lieutenant-General Hoth was commanding the Third Panzer Group (which later became the Third Panzer Army) of Army Group Center. Already by 28 June, his forces had entered Minsk and continued to advance successfully toward Polotsk. For his part in the encirclement of significant forces of the Red Army in the "Smolensk Pocket", he was awarded the Knight's Cross with Oak Leaves. In October 1941, he was transferred to command the Seventeenth Army, and then on 1 June 1942, he took command of the Fourth Panzer Army. In the course of the battle for Stalingrad, part of his army together with von Paulus's Sixth Army was encircled and destroyed. In the course of the Kursk operation, Hoth's army was the strike formation of Army Group South, but it met with failure. For battles in the Ukraine, on 15 October 1943, he was awarded with the Knight's Cross with Oak Leaves and Swords, but within just two weeks, on 30 September, he was sent into retirement by Hitler.

A number of Western scholars rank Hoth among that unarguably talented group of panzer commanders of the *Wehrmacht*, such as Guderian and Rommel. Hoth was a strict and resolute military commander. He had the ability to assess an operational situation soberly, to defend his views on conducting combat operations stubbornly before command superiors, and then consistently put his idea into practice. At the same time, however, he committed a number of serious miscalculations. At the Nuremburg trials after the war, Hoth was accused of war crimes and sentenced to fifteen years in prison. The Allies released him early in April 1954. He passed away in West Germany in 1970.

6 Newton, *Kursk,* p. 366.

7 Newton, *Kursk*, pp. 78-79.

8 Porod'ko, *Kurskaia bit'va,* p. 516.

9 *Sovershenno sekretno! Tol'ko dlya komandovaniye!* [Top secret! Only for command!] (Moscow: Nauka, 1967), pp. 504-505.

10 *Velikaia Otechestvennaia voina 1941-1945. Perelom. Tom 2* [The Great Patriotic War 1941-1945. The Turning Point. Volume 2] (Moscow: Nauka, 1998), p. 257.

11 *Velikaia Otechestvennaia voina*, p. 260.

Chapter 2

1 Prokhorovka, a station of the South East Rail Road, situated between the cities of Belgorod and Kursk, was founded in 1868. The station was actually located in the village of Aleksandrovskii, which had been the administrative center of the Prokhorovskii District of Kursk Oblast since 1928. For over 100 years, the settlement and the station within it had carried different names. In 1968, the Aleksandrovskii workers' settlement of city type was renamed Prokhorovka. At the end of the 1950s, there was another village situated on the left bank of the River Psel about 12 kilometers southwest of the station that also carried the name Prokhorovka, or Iudinka.

The combat operations that took place in July 1943 on the territory of the Prokhorovskii District, as well as of the Korochanskii, Ivnianskii, Belenikhinskii and Sazhnoskii Districts, entered the history of

World War II as the battle of Prokhorovka. In 1954, Prokhorovskii District became part of Belgorod Oblast. After a territorial reorganization, the Prokhorovskii District absorbed the Belenikhinskii District and part of the Sazhnoskii District, which was split up among several districts. It was also given part of the Ivnianskii District. In this way, the entire area of the Prokhorovka battlefield now lies within the boundaries of Prokhorovskii District. On 26 April 1995, by decree of the Russian President, the "Prokhorovka Field" State Military-Historical Park Museum was created on the site of the battle.

2 TsAMO RF, f. 203, op. 2845, d. 227, l. 3-5, 8, 9.
3 A. Kh. Babadzhanian, *Dorogami pobeda* [Along the roads of victory] (Moscow: Voenizdat, 1981), p. 126.
4 TsAMO RF, f. 236, op. 2673, d. 120, l. 219,220.
5 TsAMO RF, f. 426, op. 1073, d. 84, l. 164.
6 G. A. Koltunov and B. G. Solov'ev, *Kurskaia bitva* [The Kursk battle] (Moscow: Voenizdat, 1970), p. 70.
7 TsAMO RF, f. 240, op. 2795, d. 36.

Chapter 3

1 P. A. Rotmistrov, *Tankovoe srazhenie pod Prokhorovkoi* [Tank battle at Prokhorovka] (Moscow: Voenizdat, 1960), p. 10.
2 P. A. Rotmistrov, *Stal'naia gvardiia* [Steel guard] (Moscow: Voenizdat, 1984), p. 123.
3 *Stalingradskaia epopeia* [Stalingrad epic] (Moscow: "Zvonnitsa – MG"), p. 167.
4 A. I. Radzievsky, *Tankovyi udar* [Tank attack] (Moscow: Voenizdat, 1974), p. 27.
5 All the basic biographical data on Soviet officers and generals, used in this book, have been taken from the personnel cards of the officers' staff of the Red Army, which are stored at the Russian Federation's Central Archive of the Ministry of Defense (TsAMO RF).
6 Rotmistrov, *Stal'naia gvardiia,* pp. 168-169.
7 Rotmistrov, *Stal'naia gvardiia,* p. 169.
8 TsAMO RF, f. 18 tk, op.1, d. 23, l. 4.
9 TsAMO RF, *lichnoe delo* [personal records] of B. S. Bakharov
10 Radzievsky, *Tankovyi udar*, p. 28.
11 TsAMO RF, f. 332, op. 4948, d. 1.
12 Ibid.
13 TsAMO RF, f. 5 gv. TA, op. 4978, d.1, l. 20.
14 TsAMO RF, f. 203, op. 2851, d. 22, l. 104.
15 P. A. Rotmistov, *Tankovoe srazheniye pod Prokhorovkoi*, p. 12.
16 TsAMO RF, f. 203, op. 2851, d. 22.
17 A. I. Gribkov, *Vstrecha s polkovodtsami* [Meetings with commanders] (Moscow: Mysl', 1999), pp. 127-128.

Chapter 4

1 E. von Manstein, *Uteriannye pobed* [Lost victories] (Moscow: Voenizdat), p. 442.
2 Chistiakov Ivan Mikhailovich (1900-1979), Colonel General (1944), Hero of the Soviet Union (1944). From March 1941, he was commanding a rifle corps in the Far Eastern Front, but after November – the commander of the 64th Separate Rifle (Naval) Brigade. From January 1942, he was a Major General, commander of the 8th Guards Rifle Division, and then the 2nd Guards Rifle Corps in Northwestern Front and Kalinin Front. He distinguished himself in the battle of Stalingrad, in the course of which he was commanding the 1st Guards Army, and after 15 October 1942 – 21st Army, which in April 1943 became the 6th Guards Army under Voronezh Front. Chistiakov commanded this army until the end of the Great Patriotic War. In the period of the Kursk defensive operation, the troops of the 6th Guards Army received the main attack of the German Army Group South and stood their ground. In August – September 1945, he commanded the 25th Army, which under Far Eastern Front took part in the destruction of the Kwantung Army during the war with Japan.
3 Koltunov and Solov'ev, *Kurskaia bitva,* p. 516.
4 Ibid.
5 Glantz and House, *The Battle of Kursk* (Lawrence KS: University Press of Kansas, 1999), pp. 350-351.
6 NARA, T. 354, R 605, f. 162, 167, 169, 171.
7 TsAMO RF, f. 1163, op. 1, d. 47, l. 159.
8 TsAMO RF, f. 236, op. 2673, d. 120, l. 205.
9 D. Khazanov and V. Gorbach, *Aviatsiia v bitve nad Orlovsko-kurskoi dugoi* [Aviation in the battle above the Orel-Kursk bulge] (Moscow, Del'ta PG, 2004), p. 111.

10 N. K. Popel', *Tanki povernuli na zapad* [Tanks turned to the west] (Moscow: Izdatel'stvo AST, 2001), pp. 131, 141.
11 On 5 July, the 538th Destroyer Anti-tank Artillery Regiment had in operation 20 45mm guns, while the 1008th Destroyer Anti-tank Artillery Regiment had 24 76mm guns.
12 TsAMO RF, f. 11 gv. tk, op. 1, d. 26, l. 155 obr.
13 TsAMO RF, f.203, op. 2843, d. 431, l. 10.
14 TsAMO RF, f. 52 gv. sd, op. 1, d. 41, l. 43.
15 S. Stadler, *Die Offensive gegen Kursk 1943: II. SS-Panzerkorps als Stosskeil im Grosskampf* (Osnabrück: Munin, 1980), p. 41.
16 TsAMO RF, f. 6 gv. A, op. 5113, d. 235, l. 20.
17 Stadler, *Die Offensive gegen Kursk 1943*, p. 41.
18 TsAMO RF, f. 9700, op. 1, d. 3, l. 4, 5.
19 TsAMO RF, f. 6 gv. A, op. 5113, d. 235, l. 20.
20 Stadler, *Die Offensive gegen Kursk 1943*, p. 38.
21 TsAMO RF, 5 gv. tk, op. 1, d. 12, l. 23-31.
22 TsAMO RF, f. 203, op. 2777, d. 75, l. 333-334.
23 TsAMO RF, f. 8 gv. mk, op. 1, d. 37, l. 5.
24 Koltunov and Solov'ev, *Kurskaia bitva*, p. 161.

Chapter 5

1 M. E. Katukov, *Na ostrie glavnogo udara* [On the point of the main attack] (Moscow: Voenizdat, 1974), p. 220.
2 TsAMO RF, f. 8 gv. mk, op. 2. d. 37, l. 5.
3 TsAMO RF, f. 203, op. 2845, d. 227, l. 14.
4 M. E. Katukov, *Na ostrie glavnogo udara*, pp. 220, 222.
5 TsAMO RF, f. 51 gv. sd, op. 1, d. 69, l. 16.
6 TsAMO RF, f. 1163, op. 1, d. 179, l. 7.
7 According to the records of Headquarters, Voronezh Front, on 5 July 1943 the division's strength had reached 8,950 men. TsAMO RF, f.203, op. 2843, d. 426, l. not numbered.
8 Filipp Timofeevich Sushkov, Lieutenant Colonel (dating 3 January 1943) was born 12 August 1906 in the village of Peschatka in Kursk Oblast's Novo-Oskol'skii District. He was drafted by the Red Army in 1928. In 1932, after graduating from the Moscow Infantry School, he was sent to the Far East, where he served until the middle of December 1941. He rose from platoon commander to the assistant chief of staff of 59th Rifle Corps' 4th Rifle Brigade. From 15 April 1942 he was commander of the 93rd Rifle Regiment of the 76th Rifle Division, which was then reformed into the 154th Guards Rifle Regiment of the 51st Guards Rifle Division. On 13 January 1944, he was designated deputy commander of the 51st Guards Rifle Division. He perished on 30 July 1944.
9 TsAMO RF, f. 1163, op. 1, d. 179, l. 11.
10 Ibid., l. 17.
11 N. Zetterling and A. Frankson, *Kursk 1943: A Statistical Analysis* (London: Cass, 2000), Table A 6.4 – 6.6, pp. 187-188.
12 TsAMO RF, f. 5 gv. tk, op. 1, d. 7, l. 140.
13 Ibid.
14 Chernienko Dmitrii Khrisanovich (sometimes seen as Khristoforovich in documents) (1901-1943), Major General of Tank Forces (1943). From July 1940 – chief of operations in the headquarters of the 4th Mechanized Corps in the Kiev Special Military District. He took part in defensive battles in the Southwestern Front in the vicinities of Poltava and Khar'kov in October 1941 as commander of the 10th Tank Brigade with the 38th Army and the 21st Army. From May 1942, he was commander of the 1st Tank Corps' 49th Tank Brigade of Briansk Front.
15 TsAMO RF, 5 gv. tk, op. 1, d. 8, l. 192-194.
16 Ibid.
17 TsAMO RF, f. 5 gv. tk, op. 1, d. 7, l. 2.
18 TsAMO RF, f. 5 gv. tk, op. 1, d. 7, l. 203.
19 TsAMO RF, f. 5 gv. tk, op. 1, d. 8, l. 197.
20 Materials of the Federal Government Institute of Culture's State Military Historical Prokhorovka Battlefield Museum, recollections of I. S. Vakromeev.
21 This total includes the losses of the two rifle battalions, which fought in the sectors of the 52nd Guards

Rifle Division and the 375th Rifle Division.

22 TsAMO RF, f. 3400, op. 1, d. 31, l. 8.

23 TsAMO RF, f. 285 sp, op. 46981s, d. 1, l. 128ob – 131.

24 TsAMO RF, f. 48k, op. 1, d. 44.

25 TsAMO RF, f. 48k, op. 1, d. 17.

26 TsAMO RF, f. 236, op. 2673, d. 6, l. 45.

27 Vakhrameev, Pavel Prokop'evich (1901 – ?), Major General (1943). In the Red Army from 1920. A participant in the Soviet – Polish War. In 1938, he graduated from the M. V. Frunze Military Academy. At the start of the Great Patriotic War, he was the chief of staff of the 235th Rifle Division, which from the first days fought as part of the Northwestern Front. In September 1941 he was appointed commander of the 23rd Rifle Division, with which he fought at Stalingrad. From April 1943, he was the commander of the 6th Guards Army's 23rd Guards Rifle Corps. After the Kursk battle, he commanded the 93rd Rifle Corps, but in November 1944 he was again removed from command under the accusations of "his inability to provide combat leadership of the corps, lack of initiative, and personal lack of discipline." He distinguished himself during the forced crossing of the Oder and the Elbe Rivers, and for his skillful leadership of the 61st Army's 89th Rifle Corps in 1945 he was awarded the Order of the Red Banner and the Order of Lenin. He was released into the reserves in 1950.

28 Such a quick personnel decision, even for wartime conditions, was probably dictated not only by the severity of the situation, but also a personal factor. As evidence, N. S. Khrushchev wrote the following about Vatutin: "This general was a bit peculiar in a way. His peculiarity lay in the fact that he was almost a tee-totaller. I never saw him once even drinking wine. In addition, he was very able-bodied." (Khrushchev N. S., *Vospominaniya* [Memoirs] (Moscow: Vagrius, 1977), 135). So naturally, Nikolai Fedorovich didn't like it when his subordinates abused alcohol, while General Vakhrameev was just one of those commanders. This had an effect on not only the combat operations of his corps. In the TsAMO RF, there is a Declaration by a signals officer with the headquarters of the Front's Armored and Mechanized Forces, who was present at the 5th Guards Tank Corps command post on 6 July at the moment of the German breakthrough. He was a witness to how the commander of the 23rd Guards Rifle Corps [Vakhrameev], being not entirely sober, threatening arrest, demanded that the tank corps commander [Kravchenko] start an attack, and then arrested the signals officer who witnessed the episode for refusing to give a similar order in the name of the Armored and Mechanized Forces headquarters.

29 *Komandiry korpusov v Velikoi Otechestvennoi voyne 1941-1945: Kratkii biograficheskii slovar'* [Corps commanders in the Great Patriotic War 1941-1945: A Short biographical reference] (Moscow, 1995), p. 7.

30 TsAMO RF, f. 203, op. 2843, d. 489, l. 22.

31 TsAMO RF, f. 31tk, op. 1, d. 1, l. 46.

32 The 52nd Guards Division's commander, Colonel I. M. Nekrasov, had been wounded in the fighting on 6 July 1943, and had been sent to the division's hospital. The Guards formation's chief of staff, Lieutenant Colonel G. G. Pantiukhov, had been temporarily appointed to carry out the duties of divisional commander while Nekrasov recovered.

33 Stadler, *Die Offensive gegen Kursk*, p. 57.

34 Stadler, *Die Offensive gegen Kursk*, pp. 61-62, 64.

35 The urgent delivery of shaped charge shells from Moscow to the army depots of Voronezh Front between 7 and 10 July was secured by a convoy from the 3rd Battalion of the 14th Motor Vehicle Regiment of the *Stavka*'s 2nd Motor Vehicle Brigade, which consisted of 106 trucks. Guards Captain Shilov, commander of the 3rd Battalion, led the convoy. TsAMO RF, f. 203, op. 2849, d. 83, l. 172.

36 N. S. Khruschchev, *Vospominaniya*, p. 158.

37 TsAMO RF, 5gv. tk, op. 1, d. 8, l. 136-138.

38 TsAMO RF, f. 203, op. 2777, d. 75, l. 357-359.

39 TsAMO RF, 8 gv. tk, op. 1, d. 105, l. 10 obr.

40 TsAMO RF, 59 gv tbr, op. 1, d. 6, l. 21, 22 obr.

41 TsAMO RF, f. 48 sk, op. 1, d. 44, l. 49.

42 TsAMO RF, f. 203, op. 2777, d. 75, l. 362.

43 I. M. Chistiakov, *Sluzhim otechestvu* [We serve the fatherland] (Moscow: Voenizdat, 1975), pp. 153-154.

44 Stadler, *Die Offensive gegen Kursk*, p. 67.

45 Ibid., 69.

46 TsAMO RF, f. 48 sk, op. 1, d. 17, l. 9.

47 TsAMO RF, f. 208, op. 2843, d. 461, l. 143obr.
48 Koltunov and Solov'ev, *Kurskaia bitva*, p. 155.

Chapter 6

1 TsAMO RF, f. 203, op. 51360, d. 16, l. 342-343.
2 TsAMO RF, f. 203, op. 2777, d. 75, l. 364-368.
3 Rotmistrov, *Stal'naia gvardiia*, pp. 175-177.
4 TsAMO RF, f. 332, op. 4948, d. 31, l. 34.
5 Author's personal archives.
6 A. S. Zhadov, *Chetyre goda voiny* (Moscow: Voenizdat, 1978), pp. 88-89.
7 Ibid., p. 90.

Chapter 7

1 Stadler, *Die Offensive gegen Kursk*, p. 81.
2 Ibid., pp. 81-82.
3 Rudolf Lehmann, *The Leibstandarte III* (Winnipeg: J. J. Fedorowicz Publishing, 1990), pp. 224-225.
4 Zhadov, *Chetyre goda voiny*, p. 8.
5 TsAMO RF, f. 203, op. 2843, d. 461, l. 50.
6 TsAMO RF, f. 203, op. 2777, d. 86, l. 163-164.
7 TsAMO RF, f. 332, op. 4948, d. 31.
8 G. A. Oleinikov, *Prokhorovskoe srazhenie (iul' 1943)* [Prokhorovka engagement (July 1943)] (Saint Petersburg: Nestor, 1998), pp. 26-28.
9 TsAMO RF, f. 42 gv. sd, op. 1, d. 5, l. 124.
10 TsAMO RF, f. 5 gv. tk, op. 1, d. 8, l. 193.
11 Ibid., l. 197.
12 The 183rd Rifle Division had been formed in 1940 in the region of Riga from units of the former Latvian Army. From 24 June 1941 as part of the 24th Rifle Corps, it was in the reserve of the Northwestern Front, and then became involved in heavy defensive fighting on the Leningrad axis. In the course of 1941, its units were twice encircled, in August and September, on the Kalinin Front. Between 18 January and 17 February 1942, it again fought in encirclement in the 29th Army's sector. In January 1943, becoming part of Voronezh Front's 40th Army, it participated in the Voronezh – Kastornoe offensive; in February, it had liberated the Prokhorovka district and Prokhorovka Station, the city of Belgorod (for the first time), and the city of Khar'kov.

From 4 April 1943, Kostitsyn's division became part of the 69th Army and remained in Voronezh Front's second echelon of defense in the vicinity of Prokhorovka Station (its headquarters was situated in Krasnoe). Prior to the start of the Battle of Kursk, the 183rd Rifle Division numbered a total of 7,981 men. During the Prokhorovka engagement, its units were located on the axis of the II SS Panzer Corps' main attack and suffered heavy losses in personnel – 5,328 men. By 24 July 1943, only 2,652 men reported for duty in the division.

From 2 October 1942, Major General (from 21 April 1943) Aleksei Stepanovich Kostitsin commanded the formation. On 24 July 1943, he died when a large-caliber mortar shell directly struck his bunker. He was buried in the city of Novyi Oskol of Belgorod Oblast.

13 TsAMO RF, f. 285 sp, op. 46981, d. 1, l. 103.
14 TsAMO RF, f. 183 sd, op. 1, d. 8, l. 19-20.
15 TsAMO RF, f. 48 sk, op. 1, d. 2, l. 9.
16 TsAMO RF, f. 203, op. 2834, d. 461, l. 51.
17 TsAMO RF, f. 3407, op. 1, d. 59, l. 9.
18 TsAMO RF, f. 3407, op. 1, d. 59, l. 10.
19 TsAMO RF, f 8 gv. tk, op. 1, d. 105, l. 8.
20 Hugo Krass was born on 25.01.1911 in Witten-am-Ruhr into a large family. As the eldest son, he was compelled to quit his schooling early and go to work in order to help support the family. He served in the SA, but in 1935 he joined the SS. After completing the SS Junker School in Braunschweig, he was transferred into *Leibstandarte "Adolf Hitler"*. As a platoon commander in an anti-tank company, he took part in the invasion of Poland. During the campaign in France, he commanded a motorcycle platoon. Later in the Balkan campaign, he was now commanding the 2nd Company of *Leibstandarte*'s reconnaissance battalion. He particularly distinguished himself during the seizure of Rostov-on-Don, and on 29.12.1941 he was awarded the German Cross in Gold. In the summer of 1942, after the reforming of the SS Division *Leibstandarte*, he was appointed commander of I/2nd Motorized Infantry

Regiment. For his part in the fighting for Khar'kov, on 28.03.1943 he was awarded the Knight's Cross. In connection with Wisch's appointment to the command of the division, at the beginning of July 1943, Krass took over Wisch's former regiment. On 24.01.1944, Krass received the Knight's Cross with Oak Leaves. On 05.01.1944, Krass was severely wounded. From 13.11.1944 until the end of the war, Krass commanded the 12th SS Panzer Division *Hitlerjugend*. On 08.05.1945 near Linz, Austria, Krass surrendered to American forces together with his division. His final military rank was *Brigadeführer* and Major General of SS Forces. He remained in a military prisoner camp until 1948, when he was released. He died on 20.02.1980 in the Federal Republic of Germany.

21 Stadler, *Die Offensive gegen Kursk*, pp. 87-88.

22 TsAMO RF, f. 3407, op. 1, d. 59, l. 13.

23 TsAMO RF, f. 15 gv. ottp, op. 376854, d. 1, l. 35, 36.

24 TsAMO RF, f. 52 gv. sd, op. 1, d. 37, l. 348.

25 Stadler, *Die Offensive gegen Kursk*, p. 87.

26 Ibid.

27 *Bitva pod Kurskom. Oboronitel'noe srazheniye (iul' 1943)* [The Battle of Kursk. The defensive engagement (July 1943)] (Moscow: Voenizdat, 1946), pp. 195-196.

28 Over the four days, the regiment lost four tanks, including three tanks that had been destroyed by artillery fire, and another tank by a direct air strike. (TsAMO RF, f. 245 otp, op. 180438s, d. 2, l. 4).

29 Stadler, *Die Offensive gegen Kursk*, p. 89.

30 TsAMO RF, f. 81 gv. sd, op. 1, d. 7, l. 293.

31 Prior to May 1943, the 227th Rifle Regiment had been occupying the forward sector of defenses in the region Novoselovka – Kireev – L'vov – Shcholokovo, but then had been pulled back to the line of the Sazhenskii Donets River in the Sazhnoe – Volobuevka – Chursino region.

32 Files of the FGUK GVIMZ "PP" [Federal State Institute of Culture's "State Military Historical Museum "Prokhorovka Field", Book 28, 1971.

33 The 58th Motorized Rifle Brigade on the morning of 10 July 1943 numbered 3,189 men, 1,151 rifles, 1,218 PPSh-41 submachine guns, 108 light machine guns, 45 heavy machine guns, nine large-caliber DShK machine guns, 83 anti-tank rifles, 12 45mm anti-tank guns, 12 76mm anti-tank guns, 29 82mm mortars, six 120mm mortars, 95 motor vehicles, 13 motorcycles (of which eight were operational); 11 BA-64 light armor cars, and two armored personnel carriers. (TsAMO RF. f. 28 gv. msbr, op. 1, d. 8, l. 266.

34 TsAMO RF, f. 28 gv. msbr, op. 1, d. 8, l. 285.

35 TsAMO RF, f. 28 gv. msbr, op. 1, d. 3, l. 457.

36 TsAMO RF, f. 287 gv. sp, op. 215370 s, d. 1, l. 91, 92.

37 Vladimir Il'ich Solov'ev (1913 – ?), a lieutenant colonel as of 1943, was born in the village of Guliai-Pole in Zaporozh'e Oblast. Prior to volunteering for the Red Army in 1935, he worked as a metal toolmaker. After graduating from the Khar'kov Infantry School in 1937, he commanded a machine gun company and a training rifle platoon. As commander of a rifle company in the 95th Rifle Division, he took part in the Soviet-Finnish [Winter] War, where he was wounded. In July 1941 he was appointed commander of a rifle battalion in Southwestern Front's 226th Rifle Division. From May 1942, he was the deputy commander, and from November 1942, the commander of the 226th Rifle Division's 987th Rifle Regiment (which was later reformed into the 287th Guards Rifle Regiment). Solov'ev was a participant in the battle for Stalingrad. After the fighting in the Kursk bulge, he carried out the duties of commander of the 294th Guards Rifle Regiment of the 97th Guards Rifle Division in the 5th Guards Army. From March 1944 and until the end of the war, he commanded the 97th Guards Rifle Division's 292nd Guards Rifle Regiment. He was honored with two Orders of the Red Banner, three Orders of the Red Star, and the Orders of Aleksandr Nevsky and the Patriotic War, 1st Degree. He retired from active service in 1953.

38 TsAMO RF, f. 5 gv. A, op. 4852, d. 38, l. 53.

39 TsAMO RF, f. 900, op. 1, d. 10, l. 4.

40 TsAMO RF, f. 301 gv. lap, op. 363039a, d. 1, l. 320.

41 TsAMO RF, f. 28 gv. msbr, op. 1, d. 8, l. 287.

42 E. F. Ivanovsky, *Ataku nachinali tankisty* (Moscow: Voenizdat, 1984), pp. 127-128.

43 TsAMO RF, f. 1433, op. 1, d. 10, l. 78.

44 Savelii Il'ich Chernyshev was born in 1919 in the village of Zhadino in Kursk Oblast. He completed ten years of schooling, before joining the Red Army in 1937. In 1939 he graduated from the 1st Moscow Artillery Specialist School. He began active service in the operational army in June 1941. For his service in the battle of Kursk, by order of the 69th Army's commander, he was awarded the Order of Aleksandr

Nevsky. He ended the war in the position of chief of staff of the 140th Rifle Division's 371st Artillery Regiment.

45 The collection, *V ogne Kurskoi bitvy. Iz vospominanii uchastnikov boev* [In the fire of the Kursk battle. From the recollections of participants in the fighting] (Kursk: Kurskoe knizhnoe izdanie, 1963), 335.

46 Stadler, *Die Offensive gegen Kursk*, p. 95.

47 Files of the FGUK GVIMZ "PP." Book 28, 1971, recollections of V. E. Sazhinov.

48 TsAMO RF, f. 58 gv. msbr, op. 1, d. 8, l. 290.

49 Files of the FGUK GVIMZ "PP," recollections of veterans of the 9th Guards Airborne Division.

50 At this moment, J. Peiper was the commander of III/2nd Panzergrenadier Regiment of the SS Panzergrenadier Division *Leibstandarte*.

51 Martin Gross was born on 15 April 1911 in the city of Frankfurt-am-Main. Serving with SS units, he took part in the seizure of the Sudeten region of Czechoslovakia, and the occupation of Poland and France. As part of the panzer regiment of SS Division *Leibstandarte*, he particularly distinguished himself in the fighting for Khar'kov in the spring of 1943 (receiving the German Cross in Gold) and at Kursk. On 22 July 1943, he received the Knight's Cross to the Iron Cross. The write up for this award noted his resolve and stubbornness in the course of the most vicious fighting at Prokhorovka on 12 July 1943, when his panzer battalion was at the epicenter of the counterattack from two corps of the 5th Guards Tank Army. In the summer of 1944, he formed the SS Panzer Brigade *Gross*, but already in September of the very same year, it was dissolved. At the beginning of November 1944, he was promoted to the rank of SS *Obersturmbannführer*. From the beginning of 1945 and until Germany's capitulation, Gross commanded a panzer regiment in the 12th SS Panzer Division *Hitlerjügend*. He surrendered to American forces. Gross passed away in 1984 in Germany.

52 TsAMO RF, f. 3407, op. 1, d. 59, l. 13.

53 Author's personal archive.

54 Files of the FGUK GVIMZ "PP." Book 28, 1971. Recollections of V. E. Sazhinov.

55 TsAMO RF, f. 9 gv. vdd, op. 1, d. 4, l. 54.

56 Files of the FGUK GVIMZ "PP," recollections of veterans of the 9th Guards Airborne Division.

57 TsAMO RF, f. 33 gv. sk, op. 1, d. 79, l. 12, 13.

58 TsAMO RF, f. 8 gv. tk, op. 1, d. 234, l. 4.

59 Files of the FGUK GVIMZ "PP," recollections of veterans of the 9th Guards Airborne Division.

60 TsAMO RF, f. 287gv. sp, op. 215370s, d. 1, l. 108.

61 The combat and equipment strength of the 287th Guards Rifle Regiment's 2nd Rifle Battalion on 24 June 1943 was as follows: Personnel – 474 men; rifles – 265; Tokarev semi-automatic rifles – 55; PPSh submachine guns – 49; machine guns – 70; anti-tank rifles – nine; anti-tank guns – two; mortars – 14. (TsAMO RF, f. 5gv. A, op. 4852, d. 38, l. 72, 72 obr.)

62 Stadler, *Die Offensive gegen Kursk*, p. 95.

63 Werner Ostendorff was born in Königsberg on 15 August 1903. He entered military service in 1925, and received the rank of *Oberleutnant*. He joined the SS in 1935, and served as an instructor at the SS Officer Cadet School at Bad-Tölz. As part of SS units, he participated in the campaigns in Poland and France, and from the first days of the German invasion of the Soviet Union on the Eastern Front. On 13 September 1941 he was awarded the Knight's Cross to the Iron Cross. Between February and June 1942, Ostendorff commanded a *kampfgruppe* of the SS Division *Das Reich*, and then was appointed chief of staff of the SS Corps. On 5 May 1942, he received the German Cross in Gold. On 20 October 1943, Ostendorff received command of the 17th SS Panzergrenadier Division *Götz von Berlichengen*. At the beginning of 1944, Ostendorff received a severe wound, but after recovering he returned to the division. In the middle of November 1944, Ostendorff was relieved of command of the formation and given a staff position as chief of staff of the Army Group Upper Rhine. On 1 December 1944, he received his final military rank as Lieutenant-General of SS Forces. But already on 29 January 1945, Ostendorff was appointed to command the 2nd SS Panzer Division *Das Reich*. In the course of fighting in Hungary, he received another severe wound on 9 March 1945, from which he died on 5 May 1945. On 6 May 1945, he was posthumously awarded the Oak Leaves to the Iron Cross.

64 Lehmann, *The Leibstandarte* III, pp. 224-226.

65 P. A. Rotmistrov, *Stal'naia gvardiia* [The Steel guard] (Moscow: Voenizdat, 1984), p. 182.

66 Editor's Note: This eyewitness is referring to the Soviet PTAB (*protivotankovaia aviabomba*) 2.5, an anti-tank cluster bomblet first used at Kursk. The PTAB 2.5 weighed 2.5 kg, with 1.5 kg of high explosives in a shaped charge warhead. An Il-2 could carry over 200 of these anti-tank bomblets, which could theoretically penetrate 60-70 mm of tank armor – sufficient to penetrate the top armor of even heavy tanks. However, at Kursk the pilots were not familiar with the weapon, and most often dropped

them from altitudes too low for the fuses to have time to arm, causing the bombs to fail to detonate. Thus, they were not an effective tank-killer at Kursk. However, this new weapon generated many myths about their effectiveness at Kursk, where they supposedly left hundreds of burned-out German tanks behind after their use. This eyewitness's statement is an example of this. Again, the reader should exercise great caution with respect to Soviet combat reports and eyewitness accounts from this period. I want to thank Boris Kavelerchik for bringing this information to my attention.

67 Files of the FGUK GVIMZ "PP," recollections of I. S. Vakhrameev.
68 TsAMO RF, f. 203, op. 2843, d. 461, l. 58, 59.
69 Ibid.
70 On 14 July 1943, Major General V. S. Bensky was appointed chief of staff of the 69th Army and took over the position.
71 TsAMO RF, f. 203, op. 2777, d. 86, l. 273.
72 A. S. Zhadov, *Chetyre goda voiny*, p. 91.
73 TsAMO RF, f. 426, op. 10753, d. 82, l. 16.
74 TsAMO RF, f. 332, op. 4948, d. 70, l. 132.
75 Fedor Ivanovich Terekhov (1906-1980), major. After graduating from the Briansk Machine-building Institute, Terekhov worked as a foreman, then as a shop manager at the Novokramatorskii Machine-building Factory. In 1941, he volunteered for a Communist division which was forming in the Donbas. The autumn of that same year, Terekhov fought on the Southwestern Front at Khar'kov and Belgorod as a member of the 226th Rifle Division (which subsequently became the 95th Guards Rifle Division). In November 1942 he was appointed chief of staff of the 226th Rifle Division's artillery. Terekhov was a veteran of the Stalingrad battle. After fighting in the Kursk bulge, he participated in the liberation of the Ukraine in his position as chief of staff of the division's artillery. He was severely wounded in 1944 and discharged from the army in 1945. Terekhov was decorated with the Orders of the Red Banner, the Patriotic War, the Red Star, and medals.
76 TsAMO RF, f. 426, op. 10753, d. 82, l. 25.
77 I. Ia. Samchuk and P. G. Skachko, *Atakuiut desantniki* [Paratroopers Attack], (Moscow: Voenizdat), p. 31.
78 Files of the FGUK GVIMZ "PP," recollections of veterans of the 9th Guards Airborne Division, V. Kazakov.
79 Ibid., recollections of veterans of the 9th Guards Airborne Division, F. A. Galaganov.
80 This document is presently on display in the Museum of the History of the Prokhorovka Tank Engagement at the State Military-Historical Museum "Prokhorovka field".
81 TsAMO RF, f. 33 gv. sk, op. 1, d. 8, l. 5.
82 Files of the FGUK GVIMZ "PP." Book 28, 1971, recollections of V. E. Sazhinov.
83 TsAMO RF, f. 3400, op. 1, d. 23, l. 101 obr.
84 Stadler, *Die Offensive gegen Kursk*, p. 100.

Chapter 8

1 W. Haupt, *Srazheniia gruppy armii "Iug"* [The Battles of Army Group South] (Moscow: Iazua, 2006), p. 295.
2 Sergei Georgievich Goriachev (1897-1983), lieutenant general. In the period before the war, he rose from platoon commander to the command of a rifle division. At the start of the Great Patriotic War, he commanded the Northwestern Front's 23rd Rifle Division. After completing courses at the Military Academy of the General Staff, in September 1942 Goriachev was appointed commander of the 7th Rifle Corps. He commanded this formation until the end of the war. The corps as part of the 64th Army took active part in the battle of Stalingrad, for which in early 1943 it was reformed as the 35th Guards Rifle Corps.
3 TsAMO RF, f. 35 gv. sk, op. 1, d. 44, l. 7.
4 TsAMO RF, f. 38, op. 9027, d. 46, l. 153 obr.
5 TsAMO RF, f. 375 sd, op. 1, d. 23, l. 39.
6 TsAMO RF, f. 38, op. 9027, d. 46, l. 153 obr, 154.
7 TsAMO RF, f. 375 sd, op. 1, d. 23, l. 40.
8 TsAMO RF, f. 38, op. 9027, d. 46, l. 7, 8.
9 TsAMO RF, f. 35 gv sk, op. 1, d. 44, l. 9-11.
10 TsAMO RF, f. 38, op. 9027, d. 46, l. 8.
11 TsAMO RF, f. 35 gv. sk, op. 1, d. 44.
12 TsAMO RF, f. 203, op. 2851, d. 54, l. 422.

Chapter 9

1 TsAMO RF, f. 203, op. 2843, d. 452, l. 52.
2 Ibid., l. 50.
3 TsAMO RF, f. 1 TA, op. 3109, d. 10, l. 10.
4 TsAMO RF, f. 203, op. 2843, d. 452, l. 71.
5 *Istoriia Velikoi Otechestvennoi voiny Sovetskogo Soiuza* [History of the Great Patriotic War of the Soviet Union] (Moscow: Voenizdat, 1961), p. 272.
6 Rotmistrov, *Stal'naia gvardiia*, pp. 179-181.
7 *V ogne Kurskoi bitvy. Iz vospominanii uchastnikov*, p. 313.
8 TsAMO RF, f. 48 sk, op. 1, d. 15, l. 26, 26 obr.
9 TsAMO RF, f. 332, op. 4948, d. 31, l. 44-45.
10 TsAMO RF, 42 gv. sd, op. 1, d. 5, l. 125.
11 TsAMO RF, f. 33, op. 4948, d. 70, l. 5.
12 TsAMO RF, f. 29 tk, op.1, d. 1, l. 8, 9.
13 TsAMO RF, f. 18 tk, op.1, d. 23, l. 9.
14 A. I. Radzievsky, *Tankovyi udar*, p. 113.
15 The 1529th Self-propelled Artillery Regiment, equipped with the SU-152, was formally subordinated to Rotmistrov on 11 July 1943, but in fact it remained in the sector of the 7th Guards Army until 12 July.
16 *V ogne Kurskoi bitvy. Iz vospominanii uchastnikov*, p. 298.
17 Iosif Semenovich Iofa (1915-1974), colonel, Hero of the Soviet Union (1944). Iofa began the war in July 1941 on the Western Front and participated in the fighting on the Berezina and Dnepr. In 1942, the *Katiusha* battalion under his command served under the 62nd Army at Stalingrad. From April 1943 until the end of the war, Iofa commanded a Guards mortar regiment of rocket artillery.
18 TsAMO RF, f. 332, op. 4948, d. 31, l. 44-45.
19 TsAMO RF, f. 3420, op.1, d. 59, l. 56, 57.
20 TsAMO RF, f. 3415, op. 1, d. 23, l. 11, 12.
21 TsAMO RF, f. 5 gv. TA, op. 4848, d. 1, l. 7, 8.
22 N. S. Khrushchev, *Vospominaniia* [Recollections] (Moscow: Vagrius), p. 162.
23 Even today, the role of Chief of the General Staff Marshal of the Soviet Union A. M. Vasilevsky in the decision to launch the counterstroke and its preparation has not been fully evaluated. Unfortunately, little is known about the mutual relations and joint work of Nikolai Fedorovich Vatutin and Aleksandr Mikhailovich Vasilevsky. Therefore, probably, it is not out of place to mention an episode that occurred during the preparations for the Stalingrad counteroffensive. K.K. Rokossovsky discusses it his memoirs.

I will remind the reader that Vatutin and Vasilevsky were well-known to each other through their mutual service on the General Staff before the war. In 1940, Vatutin had been Chief of the Operations Branch, while Vasilevsky had been his deputy. Then the situation changed: in May 1942, Vatutin was now Vasilevsky's deputy, as Vasilevsky by that time was heading the General Staff. From 9 July 1943 at Stalin's order, Marshal Vasilevsky was present with the Voronezh Front as a *Stavka* representative. Thus, Rokossovsky wrote:

> In order to resolve several questions of cooperation, I again had to visit the command post of the Southwestern Front commander General Vatutin, where the Chief of the General Staff Vasilevsky was also present. The behavior of both seemed strange to me. I had the impression that Vasilevsky was in the role of *front* commander, as he was deciding a number of serious questions connected with the forthcoming operations of this *front*, often without consulting the actual commander. For his part, Vatutin factually speaking was not even fulfilling the role of chief of staff: he walked repeatedly to the telegraph, conducted conversations through the telegraph and over the phone; he was gathering reports, and reporting on them to Vasilevsky. All those questions, which I had intended to discuss with Vatutin, I had to talk about with Vasilevsky. Source: K.K. Rokossovsky, *Soldatskii dolg* [Soldier's duty] Moscow: Voenizdat, pp. 237-238.)

24 *V ogne Kurskoi bitvy. Iz vospominanii uchastnikov*, pp. 298-299.
25 On 12 July, the 2nd Air Army counted 96 ground attack aircraft, 140 bombers and 266 fighters.
26 TsAMO RF, f. 69A, op. 10753, d. 410, l. 14.
27 TsAMO RF, f. 426, op. 10753, d. 65, l. 18.
28 Ibid., l. 15.
29 TsAMO RF, f. 332, op. 4948, d. 31.
30 TsAMO RF, f. 203, op. 2849, d. 83, l. 169.
31 A. S. Zhadov, *Chetrye goda voiny*, p. 97.

32 K. S. Moskalenko, *Bitva na Kurskoi duge* [Battle at the Kursk bulge] (Moscow: Nauka, 1975), p. 63, 64.
33 Lieutenant General Andrei Dmitrievich Shtevnev had been assigned to this post on 7 June 1943. A veteran of the Russian Civil War, as deputy commander of Stalingrad Front for tank forces, Shtevnev had participated in the fighting on the approaches to Stalingrad. He was killed in action on 29 January 1944.
34 TsAMO RF, f. 203 (BT and MV), op. 2831, d. 22, l. 245.
35 TsAMO RF, f. 203 (BT and MV), op. 2381, d. 22, l. 245, 263, 263 obr.

Chapter 10

1 TsAMO RF, f. 25 tbr, op. 1, d. 4, l. 37.
2 Stadler, *Die Offensive gegen Kursk*, pp. 79, 80.
3 Ibid., p. 92.
4 Ibid., p. 97.
5 Files of the FGUK "GVIMZ 'PP'", recollections of veterans of the 9th Guards Airborne Division, K. V. Kazakov.
6 TsAMO RF, f. 31 tbr, op. 1, d. 19, l. 282.
7 P. Ia. Egorov, I. V. Krivoborsky, I. K. Ivlev and A. I. Rogalevich, *Dorogami pobedy (boevoi put' 5-i gv. tankovoi armii)* [Along the roads of victory (the combat path of the 5th Guards Tank Army)] (Moscow: Voenizdat, 1960), pp. 32-33.
8 TsAMO RF, f. 5 gv. TA, op. 4948, d. 75, l. 10a.
9 Ibid.
10 TsAMO RF, f. 332, op. 4948, d. 69, l. 11.
11 TsAMO RF, f. 332, op. 4948, d. 1, l. 9, 12, 13.
12 TsAMO RF, f. 332, op. 4948, d. 1, l. 15.
13 Rotmistrov, *Stal'naia gvardiia*, p. 186.
14 TsAMO RF, f. 203, op. 2843, d. 491, l. 61.
15 F. Kurowski, *500 tankovykh atak* [500 tank attacks] (Moscow: Iauza/EKSMO, 2007). Editor's note: von Ribbentrop's account has been published in English in Franz Kurowski's *Panzer Aces: German Tank Commanders of WWII* (Winnipeg, CA: J. J. Fedorowicz Publishing, Inc. 1992; 2004 edition published by Stackpole Books of Mechanicsburg, PA), pp. 178-180.
16 Author's personal archive.
17 Files of the FGUK GVIMZ "PP," recollections of veterans of the 9th Guards Airborne Division, I. M. Fomichev.
18 Stadler, *Die Offensive gegen Kursk*, p. 101.
19 TsAMO RF, f. 332, op. 4948, d. 46.
20 TsAMO RF, f. 332, op. 4948, d. 70, l. 130.
21 TsAMO RF, f. 332, op. 4948, d. 1, l. 10.
22 Stadler, *Die Offensive gegen Kursk*, p. 102.
23 V. P. Beketov (ed.), Collection "*Prokhorovskoe pole* [Prokhorovka field]", (Belgorod: Izdatel'skii dom "V. Shapovalov", 1998), pp. 311-312.
24 TsAMO RF, f. 42 gv. sd, op.1, d. 8, l. 328.
25 TsAMO RF, f. 9 gv. vdd, op. 1, d. 4, l. 57.
26 TsAMO RF, f. 42 gv. sd, op.1, d. 79, l. 1.
27 TsAMO RF, f. 332, op. 4948, d. 31, l. 16.
28 TsAMO RF, f. 3407, op. 1, d. 59, l. 16.
29 Collection "*Prokhorovskoe pole*," pp. 311-312
30 Author's personal archive.
31 TsAMO RF, f. 332, op. 4948, d. 70, l. 136.
32 TsAMO RF, f. 3420, op. 1, d. 31, l. 62.
33 TsAMO RF, f. 3415, op. 1, d. 26, l. 9.
34 *Deistviia aviatsii v Belgorodskoi oboronitel'noi operatsii. Otchet Upravleniia VVC Krasnoi Armii* [Operations of aviation in the Belgorod defensive operation. Summary of the Air Force Command of the Red Army] (Moscow: Voenizdat, date unknown)
35 TsAMO RF, f. 332, op. 4948, d. 70, l. 136.
36 TsAMO RF, f. 332, op. 4948, d. 70, l. 146.
37 Ibid.
38 TsAMO RF, f. 332, op. 4948, d. 1, l. 10.
39 Hans-Ulrich Rudel, *Stuka Pilot*, (New York: Ballantine Books, 1971), pp. 85-86.

40 TsAMO RF, f. 59 gv. tbr, op. 1, d. 6, l. 21 obr.
41 TsAMO RF, f. 25 tbr, op. 1, d. 4, l. 37 obr.
42 TsAMO RF, f. 3420, op. 1, d. 8, l. 63.
43 V. D. Fetin, "*Prokhorovka (55 let tomu nazad na Kurskoi duge)*" ["Prokhorovka (55 years ago at the Kursk bulge)], Gazeta "Duel'," No. 25 (72), 1998, p. 6.
44 TsAMO RF, f. 332, op. 4948, d. 80, l. 7.
45 TsAMO RF, f. 9 gv. vdd, op. 1, d. 4, l. 57.
46 TsAMO RF, f. 36 gv. ttpp, op. 581422, d. 1, l. 5; f. 36 gv. ttpp, op. 119565, d. 5, l. 94.
47 Helmut Becker was born on 12 June 1902 in Alt-Ruppin, Brandenburg. He joined the *Reichswehr* in 1920, but after twelve years, having risen only to the rank of a junior officer, he was released from service. Becker joined the SS in 1933 and became a protégé of Theodore Eicke, the inspector of concentration camps and former commandant of Dachau. He began serving in *Totenkopf*'s militarized formation in 1935. As a company commander, and then a battalion commander, Becker participated in the occupation of Austria, the Sudeten, Poland and France. He served on the Eastern Front as part of *Totenkopf* from 1941. When the division was encircled at Demiansk in 1942, Becker displayed great combat capabilities and martial qualities. After *Totenkopf* withdrew from the pocket, he was appointed commander of the 6th Motorized Regiment, which in 1943 after Eicke's death carried his name. On 26 September 1942, Becker earned the German Cross in Gold. Even by the measures of the code of honor for SS officers, Becker was a singular figure: he possessed great personal bravery, and between September 1943 and September 1944, he received two high honors – the Knight's Cross of the Iron Cross and the Knight's Cross with Oak Leaves. However, at the same time, he was accused of immoral acts connected with orgies and prostitutes. On 21 June 1944 he became commander of the SS Panzer Division *Totenkopf*. This was the final post of his military career. On 9 May 1945 together with remnants of his division, Becker surrendered to the American Third Army in Austria. After some time, the Americans turned Becker over to the Soviet Union as a war criminal. In 1947 Becker was sentenced to 25 years imprisonment, but five years later he was condemned of sabotage and executed in 1953.
48 M. Bagrin, *Put' generala* [A general's path] (Moscow: Voenizdat, 1953), p. 214.
49 TsAMO RF, f. 18 tk, op. 1, d.27, l. 45; f. 332, op. 4948, d. 70, l. 150.
50 TsAMO RF, f. 3415, op. 1, d. 26, l. 9.
51 Stadler, *Die offensive gegen Kursk*, p. 100.
52 TsAMO RF, f. 42 gv. sd, op. 1, d. 76, l. 237.
53 *V ogne Kurskoi bitvy*, p. 313, 317.
54 Stadler, *Die Offensive gegen Kursk*, p. 104.
55 TsAMO RF, f. 36 gv. otpp, op. 581422, d. 5, l. 8.
56 TsAMO RF, f. 332, op. 4948, d. 2, l. 31 obr.
57 Ivanovsky, *Ataku nachinali tankisty*, p. 131.
58 A participant in the Kursk battle, on 6 and 7 July 1943 Babadzhanian was commanding the 3rd Mechanized Brigade in the 1st Tank Army's 3rd Mechanized Corps, which was located at the focal point of XXXXVIII Panzer Corps attack. On 7 July Babadzhanian broke his leg and spent the rest of the battle in a hospital.
59 A. Kh. Babadzhanian, *Dorogami pobed* [Along the roads of victory] (Moscow: Molodaia gvardiia, 1981), pp. 124-125.
60 TsAMO RF, f. 18 tk, op. 1, d. 98, l. 60 obr.
61 TsAMO RF, f. 332, op. 4948, d.8, l. 1-9.
62 Archival reference TsAMO RF No. 2/75366 from 11.02.2003.
63 TsAMO RF, f. 332, op. 4948, d. 70, l. 150.
64 TsAMO RF, f. 3400, op. 1, d. 31, l. 67.
65 Ibid., l. 68.
66 Stadler, *Die Offensive gegen Kursk*, p. 102.
67 TsAMO RF, f. 3400, op. 1, d. 31, l. 71.
68 Ibid., l. 72.
69 Stadler, *Die Offensive gegen Kursk,* p. 102.
70 TsAMO RF, f. 500, op. 121477, d. 639, l. 8.
71 Sylvester Stadler was born in Fohnsdorf (Austria-Hungary). He actively participated in the Nazi movement in Austria. After the *Anschluss* he joined the SS. During the campaigns in Poland and France, he was already commanding a battalion in Regiment *Der Führer*. Stadler distinguished himself in the operation to retake Khar'kov in February-March 1943, for which on 6.04.43 he was awarded the Knight' Cross. On 23.04.43 he was appointed to command *Das Reich*'s SS Panzergrenadier Regiment

4. After Kursk, he received the Knight's Cross with Oak Leaves. From 10.07.44 (with a two month interruption), he commanded the 9th SS Panzer Division *Hohenstaufen*. *Brigadeführer* and Major General of SS Troops Stadler surrendered to American forces in Austria on 08.05.45. After the war, on the basis of archival materials, he prepared and published the book *Die Offensive gegen Kursk 1943. II SS-Panzerkorps als Stosskeil im Grosskampf*, which is the most complete source on the II SS Panzer Corps' role in the Kursk battle. Stadler passed away in Bavaria on 23 August 1995.

72 TsAMO RF, f. 3400, op. 1, d. 32, l. 104 obr.
73 TsAMO RF, f. 4 gv. msbr, op. 1, d. 21; f. 4 gv. tbr, op. 1, d. 4, l. 14.
74 TsAMO RF, f. 5 gv. TA, op. 4948, d. 75, l. 20, 28, 34.
75 TsAMO RF, f. 6 gv. msbr, op. 1, d. 4, l. 65.
76 TsAMO RF, f. 332, op. 4948, d. 70, l. 203, 203 obr.
77 Ibid., l. 138.
78 Ibid.
79 TsAMO RF, f. 60 gv. tbr, op. 1, d. 14, l. 33.
80 TsAMO RF, f. 183 sd, op. 1, d. 59, l. 10.
81 TsAMO RF, f. 203, op. 2843, d. 431, l. 65.
82 TsAMO RF, f. 8 gv. tk, op. 1, d. 81, l. 5,6.
83 Ibid, l. 6.
84 TsAMO RF, f. 59 gv. tbr, op. 1, d. 6, l. 24, 24 obr.
85 TsAMO RF, 8 gv. tk, op. 1, d. 233, l. 71 obr.

Chapter 11

1 A. S. Zhadov, *Chetyre goda voiny*, pp. 91, 94.
2 Aleksei Il'ich Rodimtsev (1905-1977), Colonel General (1961), Twice Hero of the Soviet Union (1937, 1945). In 1941 he commanded the 5th Airborne Brigade on the Southwestern Front, then the 87th Rifle Division (from January 1942, the 13th Guards Rifle Division), which became famous in the fighting for Murmaev Kurgan in Stalingrad with the 62nd Army. From May 1943 and until the end of the war, Rodimstsev commanded the 5th Guards Army's 32nd Guards Rifle Corps.
3 TsAMO RF, f. 1165, op. 1, d. 32, l. 94.
4 Stadler, *Die Offensive gegen Kursk*, pp. 97, 98.
5 TsAMO RF, f. 1165, op. 1, d. 37, l. 342.
6 Stadler, *Die Offensive gegen Kursk*, pp. 100, 101.
7 TsAMO RF, f. 95 gv. sd, op. 1, d. 25, l. 107.
8 TsAMO RF, f. 95 gv. sd, op. 2, d. 59, l. 168.
9 Guards Lieutenant Colonel N. P. Seletsky was chief of staff of the 95th Guards Rifle Division's 290th Guards Rifle Regiment; Guards Major V. V. Takmovtsev was chief of staff of the 95th Guards Rifle Division's 284th Guards Rifle Regiment.
10 TsAMO RF, 5 gv. A, op. 4852, d. 83, l. 16.
11 TsAMO RF, f. 52 gv. sd, op. 1, d. 37, l. 340.
12 Aleksandr Petrovich Revin (1910-1943), Colonel (1942). According to the memories of men who served with him and the dispatches of the 95th Guards Rifle Division's artillery staff, the commander of the 233rd Guards Artillery Regiment held the rank of Guards major. However, on the registration-service card, preserved in the TsAMO RF, there is a note about the awarding of the rank of lieutenant colonel to A. P. Revin on 9.10. 1942. After finishing artillery school in 1933, Revin was the assistant chief of staff in the 135th Light Artillery Regiment. At the outbreak of the Great Patriotic War, he was the chief of staff of the 32nd Howitzer Artillery Regiment. From October 1941, as the chief of staff to the 21st Army's 806th Artillery Regiment, he took part in the fighting on the Southwestern Front. In February 1943, Revin was appointed chief of the artillery of the 24th Separate Rifle Brigade on the Don Front. From 30.05. 1943, he was the commander of the 233rd Guards Artillery Regiment of the 95th Guards Rifle Division. On 12.07.43, he was mortally wounded while attempting to withdraw from the regiment's observation post. His remains lie in the village of Petrovka of the Prokhorovskii District.
13 Andrei Borisovich Danilov (1908-1943), Sergeant, gun commander in the 95th Guards Rifle Division's 233rd Guards Artillery Regiment. On 12.8.43 near Sukhino in Khar'kov Oblast, for three hours he conducted an unequal fight against enemy tanks. After the death of his crew, he took over the roles of gun layer and loader, disabled two tanks and inflicted large damage to the enemy's personnel. He died from his wounds on 19.09.43 and was buried in the village of Khorunzhei in Khar'kov Oblast's Bogodukhskii District. On 24.12.43 he was awarded the title Hero of the Soviet Union (posthumously).
14 Zhadov, *Chetyre goda voiny*, p. 98.

15 TsAMO RF, f. 1267, op. 1, d. 25, l. 105.
16 TsAMO RF, f. 95 gv. sd, op. 1, d. 25, l. 106 obr.
17 Captain Timov was killed in Nagol'noe on 14 July 1943 during a bombing raid. As for Captain Bugarsky, no further information on his fate was found. TsAMO RF, f. 10 tk, op. 1, d. 78, l. 77, 78.
18 TsAMO RF, f. 52 gv. sd, op. 1, d. 37, l. 340.
19 TsAMO RF, f. 5 gv. A, op. 4852, d. 83, l. 31.
20 Ibid., l. 16, 17.
21 Pavel Dem'ianovich Boiko (1902-1975), Major. Veteran of the Russian Civil War. At the front from 1941, a participant of the fighting on the Southwestern Front. In the autumn of 1942, he was appointed to command 226th Rifle Division's separate destroyer anti-tank battalion, which was later reformed as the 103rd Guards Separate Destroyer Anti-tank Artillery Battalion. He was a participant in the Stalingrad fighting. For his personal courage, Boiko was decorated with two Orders of the Red Banner, and with Orders of the Patriotic War 1st Degree and the Red Star.
22 TsAMO RF, f. 38 A, op. 9027, d. 46, l. 154 obr.
23 TsAMO RF, f. 5 gv. A, op. 4852, d. 99, l. 45.
24 TsAMO RF, f. 33 gv. sk, op. 1, d. 76, l. 10.
25 TsAMO RF, f. 236, op. 2673, d. 120, l. 221, 222.
26 TsAMO RF, f. 42 gv. sd, op. 1, d. 76, l. 239.
27 Files of the FGUK GVIMZ "PP," recollections of N. D. Sebezhko.
28 In addition to this, at the end of the summary it is noted in pencil that an additional junior commander and three enlisted men were killed in the 233rd Guards Artillery Regiment.
29 TsAMO RF, f. 33 gv. sk, op. 1, d. 78, l. 10.
30 TsAMO RF, f. 203, op. 2843, d. 301, l. 252.
31 TsAMO RF, f. 332, op. 4948, d. 31, l. 37.
32 Rotmistrov, *Stal'naia gvardiia*, pp. 190, 192.
33 TsAMO RF, f. 5 gv. TA, op. 4948, d. 80, l. 15, 16.
34 TsAMO RF, f. 51 gv. tp, op. 396517 s, d. 1, l. 29, 31.
35 TsAMO RF, f. 328, op. 4852, d. 100, l. 61.
36 TsAMO RF, f. 328, op. 4852, d. 83.
37 TsAMO RF, f. 5 gv. A, op. 4852, d. 83, l. 17, 18.
38 TsAMO RF, f. 203, op. 2843, d. 461, l. 64, 64 obr.
39 N. Zetterling and A. Frankson, *Kursk 1943: A Statistical Analysis* (London: Frank Cass, 2000), p. 188.

Chapter 12

1 TsAMO RF, f. 89 gv. sd, op. 1, d. 22, l. 11.
2 M. G. Boev, *Zvezdnyi chas Belgoroda* [Stellar hour of Belgorod] (Belgorod: Vezelitsa, 1998), pp. 72, 73.
3 Files of the FGUK GVIMZ "PP".
4 TsAMO RF, f. 89 gv. sd, op. 1, d. 22, l. 11.
5 TsAMO RF, f. 38 A, op. 9027, d. 46, l. 154 obr.
6 TsAMO RF, f. 375 sd, op. 1, d. 23, l. 41a.
7 TsAMO RF, f. 81 gv. sd, op. 1, d. 5, l. 275.
8 TsAMO RF, f. 148 a, op. 3763, d. 130, l. 190.
9 *Ognennaia duga: Kurskaia bitva glazami Lubianki* [The fiery bulge: the Kursk battle through the eyes of the Lubianka], p. 61.
10 Zetterling and Frankson, *Kursk 1943*, p. 31.
11 Ibid., pp. 188, 189,
12 TsAMO RF, f. 332, op. 4948, d. 19, l. 39.
13 The 5th Guards Tank Army's forward detachment under the command of the army's deputy commander Major General Trufanov received the title "composite detachment" on 12 July after the two mechanized brigades of the 5th Guards 'Zimovniki' Mechanized Corps and the one tank brigade of the 2nd Guards 'Tatsinskaia' Tank Corps were included in it. One often encounters it under this designation in the staff documents of the 5th Guards Tank Army. But in the dispatches and orders of the 69th Army, this group is referred to as the "mobile detachment of the 5th Guards Tank Army."
14 TsAMO RF, f. 26 gv. tbr, op. 1, d. 20, l. 15.
15 TsAMO RF, f. 332, op. 4948, d. 70, l. 103, 128, 129, 131; f. 332, op. 4948, d. 75, l. 10a, 10a obr.
16 *Bol'shaia sovetskaia istoricheskaia entsiklopediia* [Great Soviet Historical Encyclopedia] Volume 21 (Moscow, 1975), p. 160.
17 TsAMO RF, f. 5 gv. TA, op. 4982, d. 21, l. 6, 7.

18 V. Gorbach and D. Khazanov, *Aviatsiia v bitve nad Orlovsko-Kursk dugoi* [Aviation in the battle over the Orel-Kursk bulge] (Moscow: Moskva 2004], p. 169.
19 Kurowski, *Panzer Aces*, p. 55.
20 A. P. Riazansky, *V ogne tankovykh srazhenii* [In the fire of tank engagements] (Moscow: Nauka, 1975), pp. 70-71.
21 TsAMO RF, f. 55 gv. tp, op. 88261, d.1, l. 23-25, 28 obr.
22 TsAMO RF, f. 92 gv. sd, op.1, d. 13, l. 108.
23 TsAMO RF, f. 426, op. 10753, d. 43, l. 14.
24 On 13 July 1943, the commander of the 69th Army issued an order that removed Colonel Trunin from command of the 92nd Guards Rifle Division "for inept leadership of the division in the course of fighting between 10 and 12 July 1943, having permitted the loss of equipment and the division's flight from the battlefield on two occasions." (TsAMO RF, f. 48 sk, op. 1, d. 2, l. 17). Documents from the investigation of such great losses in the division are today still secret; therefore it is difficult to judge the fairness of the accusations against the division commander. Moreover it is known that in the war years, including in the period of Voronezh Front's defensive operation in July 1943, there were cases when division commanders were removed from their posts without any solid justifications. Only one thing can be stated with confidence: by the summer of 1943, Colonel V. F. Trunin didn't have sufficient experience to command a formation like a division. One only has to look at his personal service record, which is preserved in the TsAMO RF.
25 TsAMO RF, f. 92 gv. sd, op. 1, d. 13, l. 134.
26 TsAMO RF, f. 69 A, op. 10753, d. 410, l. 15.
27 TsAMO RF, f. 48 sk, op.1, d. 2, l. 17.
28 TsAMO RF, f. 10 iptabr, op. 1, d. 28, l. 8 obr., 9 obr.
29 TsAMO RF, f. 38 A, op. 9027, d. 46, l. 154 obr, 155.
30 TsAMO RF, f. 26 gv. tbr, op. 1, d. 20, l. 18.
31 On 19.7.43, the commander of the 81st Guards Rifle Division canceled this order, because "the retreat of the 2nd Battalion from the lines it was occupying did not entail any consequences, since it was stopped in time … In the following days the 2nd Battalion and Guards Captain Goshtenar personally fought selflessly with the foe and demonstrated courage and bravery, which atoned for his guilt before the Motherland." (TsAMO RF, f. 81 gv. sd, op. 1, d. 5, l. 276).
32 A. M. Vasilevsky, *Delo vsei zhizni* [Matter of a lifetime] Volume 2, 6th ed. (Moscow: Politizdat, 1989), p. 28.

Chapter 13

1 *Na ostrie glavnogo udara*, p. 236.
2 TsAMO RF, f. 10 tk, op. 1, d. 17, l. 2.
3 Katukov, *Na ostrie glavnogo udara*, pp. 236-237.
4 Major General Andrei Lavrent'evich Getman commanded the 1st Tank Army's 6th Tank Corps, but due to the increasingly complicated situation, received an order on the night of 8 July 1943 to assume temporary command of all the formations of the 1st Tank Army and 6th Guards Army defending in the bend of the Psel River.
5 Nevertheless, the 6th Tank Corps had an order to cover the northwest flank of the counterattack. Given the satisfactory development of the attack, the corps was withdrawn into the reserve for rest and refitting.
6 Katukov, *Na ostrie glavnogo udara*, p. 237.
7 TsAMO RF, f. 5 gv. tk, op. 1, d. 7, l. 144.
8 TsAMO RF, f. 10 tk, op. 1, d. 15, l. 6a.
9 TsAMO RF, f. 203, op. 2843, d. 325, l. 179.
10 Helmuth Spaeter, *The History of the Panzerkorps Grossdeutschland*, Vol. 2 (Winnipeg: J. J. Fedorowicz Publishing, 1995), pp. 129-130.
11 On 6 July 1943, the XXXXVIII Panzer Corps commander had consolidated the 10th Panzer Brigade's two battalions of Panthers and *Grossdeutschland*'s panzer regiment into a single formation under the command of *Oberst* Graf Strachwitz, and after his wounding on 10 July, of *Hauptmann* von Wietersheim.
12 TsAMO RF, NSB inv. No. 9989, s. 89.
13 V. T. Fedin, "Prokhorovka (55 let tomu nazad na Kurskoi duge" ["Prokhorovka (55 years ago on the Kursk bulge"] Gazeta "Duel", 1998, No. 25 (72), p. 6.
14 Ibid.
15 This estimate uses data for the 100th Tank Brigade as of 1100 13 July 1943. TsAMO RF, f. 31 tk, op.

1, d. 1, l. 8; f. 31 tk, op. 1, d. 5, l. 85.
16 TsAMO RF, f. 5 gv. Stk, op. 1, d. 7, l. 179.
17 TsAMO RF, f. 203, op. 2843, d. 325, l. 6.
18 TsAMO RF, f. 148a, op. 3763, d. 142, l. 90, 91.
19 TsAMO RF, f. 7 gv. A, op. 5312, d. 183, l. 11.
20 Stadler, *Die Offensive gegen Kursk*, pp. 107-108.
21 Vasilevsky, *Delo vsei zhizni*, p. 321.
22 Stadler, *Die Offensive gegen Kursk*, pp. 107-108.
23 TsAMO RF, f. 31 gv. tbr, op. 4982, d. 29, l. 8.
24 Stadler, *Die Offensive gegen Kursk*, p. 125.
25 TsAMO RF, f. 8 gv. mk, op. 1, d. 37, l. 6.
26 TsAMO RF, f. 8 gv. tk, op. 1, d. 81, l. 7 obr.
27 TsAMO RF, f. 29 tk, op. 1, d. 6, l. 93.
28 P. A. Rotmistrov, *Tankovoe srazhenie pod Prokhorovkoi* [Tank engagement at Prokhorovka] (Moscow: Voenizdat, 1960), pp. 102-103.
29 Ibid., p. 101.
30 Author's personal archive.
31 TsAMO RF, f. 8 gv. tk, op. 1, d. 233, l. 209.

Chapter 14

1 E. von Manstein, *Poteriannye pobedy* [Lost victories] (Moscow: Voenizdat, date unknown), p. 447. Editor's note: The English language version of Manstein's book, *Lost Victories*, is an abridged version of the German original. As the translator noted, it was "necessary to excise a number of passages from the original version." The passage that Zamulin cites from the Russian version is evidently one of these passages, as I could not locate it in the 2004 English version. See Manstein, *Lost Victories* (Methuen & Co. Ltd, 1958; MBI Publishing Company, 2004), p. 549.
2 Ibid., pp. 447-448.
3 Stadler, *Die Offensive gegen Kursk*, p. 104.
4 Ibid., p. 103.
5 Ibid.
6 Ibid., p. 104.
7 The pseudonym of A. M. Vasilevsky.
8 TsAMO RF, f. 203, op. 2843, d. 489, l.68.
9 G. K. Zhukov, *Vospominaniia i razmyshleniia* [Memoirs and reflections] (Moscow: APN, 1969), p. 489.
10 TsAMO RF, f. 26 gv. tbr, op. 1, d. 20, l. 16 obr.

Chapter 15

1 TsAMO RF, f. 203, op. 2843, d. 461, l. 64 obr.
2 TsAMO RF, f. 203, op. 2843, d. 461, l. 59, 60.
3 TsAMO RF, f. 203, op. 2843, d. 461, l. 62, 63.
4 TsAMO RF, f. 203, op. 2843, d. 461, l. 59, 60.
5 TsAMO RF, f. 95 gv. sd, op. 1, d. 25, l. 105, 105 obr.
6 TsAMO RF, f. 5 gv. A, op. 4855, d. 58, l. 77.
7 Stadler, *Die Offensive gegen Kursk*, p. 109.
8 TsAMO RF, f. 5 gv. A, op. 4855, d. 20, l. 5.
9 TsAMO RF, f. 5 gv. A, op. 4852, d. 58, l. 77.
10 TsAMO RF, f. 95 gv. sd, op. 1, d. 25, l. 106 obr.
11 TsAMO RF, f. 33 gv. sk, op. 1, d. 8, l. 16.
12 F. W. von Mellenthin, *Panzer Battles: A Study of the Employment of Armor in the Second World War* (Norman, OK: University of Oklahoma Press, 1956; Konecky and Konecky, 1956), p. 234.
13 Zhadov, *Chetyre gody voiny*, pp. 97-98.
14 TsAMO RF, f. 33 gv. sk, op. 1, d. 8, l. 8, 8 obr; f. 42 gv. sd, op. 1, d. 6, l. 208.
15 TsAMO RF, f. 332, op. 4948, d. 31, l. 53.
16 TsAMO RF, f. 332, op. 4948, d. 70, l. 160.
17 TsAMO RF, f. 59 gv. tbr, op. 1, d. 6, l. 24 obr.
18 TsAMO RF, f. 69 A, op. 10753, d. 410, l. 9.
19 TsAMO RF, f. 29 tk, op. 1, d. 6, l. 94.
20 TsAMO RF, f. 203, op. 2843, d. 461, l. 62-63.

21 TsAMO RF, f. 332, op. 4948, d. 67, l. 5.
22 TsAMO RF, f. 26 gv. tbr, op. 1, d. 20, l. 16 obr.
23 TsAMO RF, f. 29 tk, op. 1, d. 6, l. 94.
24 V.N. Zamulin and L. N. Lopukhovsky, 'Prokhorovskoe srazhenie: Mify i real'nost' [Prokhorovka engagement: Myths and reality], *Voenno-istoricheskii arkhiv*, No. 2, 2003: 13.
25 Stadler, *Offensive gegen Kursk*, p. 111.
26 TsAMO RF, f. 5 gv. A, op. 4852, d. 83, l. 24.
27 TsAMO RF, f. 203, op. 2843, d. 461, l. 62-63.
28 Stadler, *Offensive gegen Kursk*, p. 116.

Chapter 16

1 TsAMO RF, f. 500, op. 12477, d. 639, l. 18.
2 TsAMO RF, f. 26 tbr, op. 1, d. 20, l. 18.
3 TsAMO RF, f. 35 gv. sk, op. 1, d. 26, l. 85.
4 B. V. Sokolov, *Razvedka: Tainy Vtoroi mirovoi voiny* [Intelligence: Secrets of the Second World War] (Moscow: AST, 2002), pp. 358-359.
5 A. P. Riazansky, *V ogne tankovykh srazhenii* [In the fire of tank engagements] (Moscow: Nauka, 1975), pp. 77-78.
6 TsAMO RF, f. 35 gv. sk, op. 1, d. 44, l. 10.
7 TsAMO RF, f. 5 gv. ta, op. 4948, d. 80, l. 16.
8 Ibid.
9 Stadler, *Offensive gegen Kursk*.
10 TsAMO RF, f. 3400, op. 1, d. 23, l. 104, 104 obr.
11 TsAMO RF, f. 69A, op. 10753, d. 410, l. 9.
12 Ibid.
13 TsAMO RF, f. 426, op. 10753, d. 100, l. 66, 67.
14 TsAMO RF, f. 203, op. 2777, d. 75, l. 409.
15 TsAMO RF, f. 332, op. 4948, d. 31, l. 57.
16 Ibid., l. 58.
17 Ibid., l. 60.
18 Ibid., l. 59.
19 TsAMO RF, f. 48 sk, op. 1, d. 2, l. 3.
20 TsAMO RF, f. 48 sk, op. 1, d. 17.
21 TsAMO RF, f. 48 sk, op. 1, d. 2, l. 21.
22 *Ognennaia duga. Kurskaia bitva glazami Lybianki* [Circle of fire. The Kursk battle through the eyes of the Lubianka] (Moscow: 2003), p. 61.
23 Ibid.
24 Ibid.
25 TsAMO RF, f. 426, op. 10753, d. 43, l. 13, 13 obr.
26 *Ognennaia duga*, pp. 60-61.
27 TsAMO RF, f. 3400, op. 1, d. 23, l. 106-108.
28 Ibid., l. 108.
29 Stadler, *Offensive gegen Kursk,* p. 118.
30 TsAMO RF, f. 6 gv. msbr, op. 1, l. 65 obr, 66.
31 Files of the State Military Historical Museum of Prokhorovka Field, Book 28, 1971.
32 TsAMO RF, f. 69 A, op. 10753, d. 390, l. 28, 29.
33 Stadler, *Offensive gegen Kursk,* 118.
34 TsAMO RF, f. 426, op. 10753, d. 43, l. 36.
35 Ibid., l. 49.
36 TsAMO RF, f. 332, op. 4948, d. 42, l. 8.
37 TsAMO RF, f. 38A, op. 9027, d. 46, l. 9-10.
38 TsAMO RF, f. 426, op. 10765, d. 13, l. 11 obr.
39 TsAMO RF, f. 426, op. 10753, d. 43, l. 48.
40 Ibid., l. 22.
41 TsAMO RF, f. 53 gv. otp, op. 354813 s, d. 1, l. 21.
42 Stadler, *Offensive gegen Kursk*, p. 122.
43 Ibid.
44 TsAMO RF, f. 500, op. 12477, d. 639, l. 14-15.

45 TsAMO RF, f. 332, op. 4948, d. 80, l. 19.
46 TsAMO RF, f. 3400, op. 1, d. 23, l. 106 obr.
47 TsAMO RF, f. 203, op. 2777, d. 75, l. 414, 415.
48 TsAMO RF, f. 426, op. 10753, d. 43, l. 8.
49 TsAMO RF, f. 81 gv. sd, op. 1, d. 5, l. 277.

Chapter 17

1 TsAMO RF, f. 426, op. 10753, d. 410, l. 11, 12.
2 TsAMO RF, f. 26 gv. tbr, op. 1, d. 18, l. 27.
3 TsAMO RF, f. 332, op. 4948, d. 31, l. 65.
4 TsAMO RF, f. 203, op. 2843, d. 301, l. 258-259.
5 TsAMO RF, f. 1, op. 2, l. 23, 24.
6 TsAMO RF, f. 81 gv. sk, op. 1, d. 5, l. 284.
7 TsAMO RF, f. 48 sk, op. 1, d. 17, l. 36.
8 TsAMO RF, f. 69A, op. 10753, d. 390, l. 32.
9 Ibid., l. 32-33.
10 TsAMO RF, f. 35 gv. sk, op. 1, d. 44, l. 16.
11 TsAMO RF, f. 69A, op. 10753, d. 442, l. 24.
12 Ibid.
13 Address of Karl-Heinz Frieser to the Military-Historical Conference in Moscow on 12 July 1993, the 50th Anniversary of the engagement at Prokhorovka. See the conference proceedings, p. 15.
14 TsAMO RF, f. 3400, op. 1, d. 31, l. 103.
15 TsAMO RF, f. 5 gv. TA, op. 5948, d. 75. l. 66.
16 Ibid., l. 67.
17 TsAMO RF, f. 203, op. 2777, d. 75, l. 437.
18 TsAMO RF, f. 203, op. 51360, d. 5, l. 103, 105.

Chapter 18

1 *Sovetskaia voennaia entsiklopediia* [Soviet military encyclopedia], Volume 6 (Moscow: Voenizdat, 1977), p. 612.
2 TsAMO RF, f. 203, op. 51360, d. 3, l. 252.
3 TsAMO RF, f. 335, op. 5113, d. 235, l. 33.
4 TsAMO RF, f. 203, op. 51354, d. 18, l. 8.
5 TsAMO RF, f. VorF [Voronezh Front] (Intelligence department), op. 2874, d. 60.
6 TsAMO RF, f. 236, op. 2673, d. 6, l. 48.
7 *Sovershenno sekretno! Tol'ko dlia komandovaniia!*, [Totally secret! Only for the command!] (Moscow: Nauka, 1967), pp. 502-506.
8 Institute of Military History, *Velikaia otechestvennaia voina 1941-1945: Perelom* [Great Patriotic War 1941-1945: The Turning Point] (Moscow: Nauka, 1998), p. 288.
9 Rotmistrov, *Tankovoe srazhenie*, p. 49.
10 Ibid., p. 7.
11 Ibid., p. 72.
12 TsAMO RF, f. 332, op. 4948, d. 19, l. 8.
13 Ibid., l. 5.
14 Koltunov and Solov'ev, *Kurskaia bitva*, p. 174.
15 General Staff study, *Kurskaia bitva, oboronitel'noe srazhenie (1943)* [Kursk battle, the defensive engagement (1943)] (Moscow: Voenizdat, 1946), p. 192.
16 *Velikaia otechestvennaia voina Sovetskogo Soiuza, 1941-1945* [Great Patriotic War of the Soviet Union, 1941-1945] (Moscow: Voenizdat, 1965), p. 244.
17 *Sovetskaia voennaia entsiklopediia* [Soviet military encyclopedia] Vol. 4 1978, p. 538.
18 S. Kulichkin, *Vatutin* (Moscow: Voenizdat, 2001), p. 262.
19 TsAMO RF, f. 5 gv. TA, op. 4948, d. 67, l. 12.
20 TsAMO RF, f. 5 gv. TA, op. 4948, d. 18, l. 7, 8.
21 Zetterling and Frankson, *Kursk 1943*, Table 2.1, p.18
22 Colonel Karl-Heinz Frieser, Doctor of History, who presented reports at military-historical conferences in Moscow on 12 July 1993 and in Ingolstadt (Germany) in September of the same year, revealed many previously unknown facts and documents to scholarly study.
23 Bundesarchiv-Militärarchiv [BA-MA] Study P-114 V. c. Part & Anhang. Tabelle 111, p. 119.

24 Ibid.
25 H. Müller-Hillebrand, *Das Deutsche Heer1933-1945* [The German Army 1933-1945] Vol. 3, (Frankfurt a. M.: Mittler, 1969).
26 J. Engelmann, *Zitadelle: Die größte Panzerschlacht im Osten 1943* [Citadel: The Greatest Panzer Battle in the East 1943] (Friedburg: Podzun Pallas, 1980), p. 71.
27 Ibid., p. 71, 148, 151.
28 Manstein, *Uteriannye pobedy*, p. 575.
29 Zetterling and Frankson, *Kursk 1943*, Tables 3.5 and 3.6, pp. 30-31.
30 Based on German archives and as published in V. N. Zamulin and L. N. Lopukhovsky, "Prokhorovskoe srazheniye. Mify i real'nost'" ("The Prokhorovka Engagement. Myths and Reality"), *Voenno-istoricheskii arkhiv*, no. 3, 2003, pp. 79-80. [Editor's note: Based upon the same German archives, this matches the total number of operational tanks and assault guns given by Zetterling and Frankson, *Kursk 1943*, p. 103, though Zetterling and Frankson do not break out the number of assault guns from the number of tanks.]
31 Zetterling and Frankson, *Kursk 1943*, Table A6.4, Table A6.5 and Table A6.6, pp. 187-188.
32 Zetterling and Frankson, *Kursk 1943,* Table A6.7, A6.8, A6.9, pp. 188-189.
33 Editor's Note: Presumably, the author here is referring to the 23 Tiger tanks reported as operational in the 503rd Heavy Panzer Battalion on the morning of 11 July, not 12 July. Unfortunately, no report is available on the number of operational Tiger tanks in this battalion on the morning of 12 July. See Zetterling and Frankson, *Kursk 1943*, Table A6.10, p. 190.
34 Major General F. W. von Mellenthin, *Panzer Battles*, p. 306.
35 Zetterling and Frankson, *Kursk 1943*, Table A6.4, p. 187
36 Ibid., Table A6.5, p. 187.
37 Ibid., Table A6.6, p. 188.
38 Frieser, Address to the Kursk military-historical conference in Moscow 12 July 1993, "The German offensive at Kursk: Illusions and Legends," p. 15.
39 BA-MA: Study P-114 c. 1, Part. V.S. 154 auch BA-MA: RH 21-4/ 104. p. 152.
40 Frieser, Address to the Kursk military-historical conference in Moscow 12 July 1993, "The German offensive at Kursk: Illusions and Legends," p. 15.
41 G. Krivosheev, V. Andronikov and P. Burikov, *Grif sekretnosti sniat* [The seal of secrecy has been removed] (Moscow: Voenizdat, 1993).
42 Rotmistrov, *Tankovoe srazhenie*, p. 86.
43 Ibid., p. 94.
44 Ibid., p. 100.
45 Rotmistrov, *Stal'naia gvardiia*, p. 203.
46 Zetterling and Frankson, *Kursk 1943*, p. 122 and 108.
47 BA-MA: RH 10, 64, Blatt 48; as cited by Frieser, Address to the Kursk military-historical conference in Moscow 12 July 1993, "The German offensive at Kursk: Illusions and Legends," p. 15.
48 Il'in, "Mozhno li bylo, poteriav pyat' tankov, proigrat' srazhenie pod Prokhorovkoi?" ("Was it possible, having lost five tanks, to lose the Prokhorovka engagement?") *Voenno-istoricheskii zhurnal*, No. 6, 2001, p. 70.
49 Engelmann, *Zitadelle*, p. 151.
50 Engelmann, *Zitadelle*, p. 151.
51 Data on the combat losses suffered by the II SS Panzer Corps are calculated from the information in Table A10.9 in Zetterling and Frankson, *Kursk 1943*, p. 207.
52 Ibid., p. 108 and 110n.22.
53 Ibid., Table A10.9, p. 207.
54 Manstein, *Poteriannye pobedy,* p. 535.
55 Zetterling and Frankson, Table 8.2, p. 115.
56 V. N. Zamulin and L. N. Lopukhovsky, "Mif i real'nost'" ["Myth and reality"] *Voenno-istoricheskii arkhiv*, No. 3, 2003, pp. 103-105.
57 BA-MA: Study P-114 c. Part. S. 100, 128, 130.
58 Frieser, Address to the Kursk military-historical conference in Moscow 12 July 1993, "The German Offensive at Kursk: Illusions and Legends," p. 22.
59 *TankoMaster*, No. 5, 1999, p. 32, 34.
60 All these data on total losses during the war come from V. V. Pokhlebkin, *Velikaia voina i nesostoiavshiy mir* [The great war and the unsettled peace], pp. 339, 342.
61 *Voennaia entsiklopediia* [Military encyclopedia] Vol. 4 (Moscow: Voenizdat, 1999), p. 360.

62 TsAMO RF, f. 332, op. 4948, d. 51, l. 7.
63 TsAMO RF, f. 332, op. 4948, d. 6.
64 *Velikaia otechestvennaia voina 1941-1945. Tom 2. Perelom*, p. 269.
65 Khrushchev, *Vospominaniia*, pp. 161-162.
66 TsAMO RF, f. 203, op. 2851, d. 24, l. 451-455.
67 TsAMO RF, f. VorF, razv. otdel., op. 2874, d. 60.
68 F. D. Sverdlov, *Neizvestnoe o sovetskikh polkovodtsakh* [The Unknown about Soviet Commanders] (Moscow, 1995), p. 95.
69 In the quantity of artillery, Central Front exceeded the Voronezh Front (which was anticipating the attack of a more powerful enemy grouping) by approximately 33% (excluding later reinforcements): the two fronts had 10,900 and 8,200 artillery pieces and mortars respectively. (N. A. Antipenko, *Na glavnom napravlenii* [On the Main Axis] (Moscow: Nauka, 1967), pp. 114-115.
70 TsAMO RF, f. 203, op. 2843, d. 421, l. 20.
71 Air operations in the Belgorod defensive operation. Command of the Red Army's Air Force (Moscow, 1945), p. 56.
72 According to German data, Army Group Center's Ninth Army, which operated against Central Front, likely had 523 tanks and around 300 assault guns, including 90 Ferdinand heavy assault guns. BA-MA RH 10/64, Blatt 24.
73 KTV/OKW Bd. 111. Hb 11. S. 769.
74 P. A. Rotmistrov, *Tankovoe srazhenie*, p. 104.
75 G. K. Zhukov, *Vospominaniia i razmyshleniia* [Reminiscences and Reflections] (Moscow: Novsosti, 1990), p. 57.
76 Cited by A. M. Samsonov, *Znat' i pomnit'. Smotret' pravde v glaza* [To know and to remember. To look truth in the eyes] (Moscow, 1989), p. 170.
77 *Velikaia Otechestvennaia voina, 1941-1945*, Tom 2 Perelom [Turning Point], p. 271.
78 Frieser, 'Address to the Kursk political-historical conference in Moscow,' p. 15; Ernst Klink, *Das Gesetz des Handels* (Stuttgart, 1966), p. 243; Janusz Piekalkiewicz, *Unternehmen Zitadelle* (Bergisch Gladbach: Lubbe, 1983), p. 201.
79 Engelmann, *Zitadelle*, p. 5.
80 *Voenno-istoricheskii Arkhiv* [Military-history Archive], no. 10, 2001, p. 48.
81 Ibid., Volume 17, no. 2, p. 94.
82 *Istoriia Vtoroi mirovoi voiny, 1939-1945* [History of the Second World War, 1939-1945] (Moscow: Voenizdat, 1976), Table 7, p. 178.
83 F. Hahn, *Waffen und Geheimwaffen des deutchen Heeres, 1933-1945*. Volume 2 (Koblenz: Bernard & Graefe, 1987), p. 317.
84 *Voennaia Entsiklopediia, Tom 4* [Military Encyclopedia, Volume 4] (Moscow: Voenizdat, 1999), p. 360.
85 *Velikaia Otechestvennaia Voina 1941-1945, Tom 2 Perelom*, p. 257.
86 Krivosheev, *Grif sekretnosti*, p. 188.
87 Ibid., p. 370.
88 H. Guderian, *Vospominaniia soldata* [A Soldier's Memoirs] (Moscow, 1954), p. 296.
89 As cited by A. M. Vasilevsky, *Delo vsei zhizni*, p. 324.
90 M. Kolomiets and A. Smirnov, "Boi v izluchine Dona" ["Fighting in the Don River bend"] *Zhurnal Frontovaia Illiustratsiia*, no. 6 (2002), p. 75.
91 *Zhurnal Modelist-Konstruktor* [Journal Modeler-Builder], no. 5 (2002), p. 31.
92 TsAMO RF, f. 5 gv. tk, op. 1, d. 7, l. 4.
93 Kolomiets and Smirnov, "Boi v izluchine Dona," p. 75.
94 *Zhurnal Vokrug sveta* [Journal around the World], no. 4 (2003), p. 134.

Bibliography

The majority of this work is based on archival sources, notably those at the Central Archive of the Russian Federation's Ministry of Defense (referenced TsAMO within the notes), as well as materials of the Federal Government Institute of Culture's State Military Historical Prokhorovka Battlefield Museum. For a fuller discussion of archive sources see the Introduction.

Anon., *Bitva pod Kurskom. Oboronitel'noe srazheniye (iul' 1943)* [The Battle of Kursk. The defensive engagement (July 1943)] (Moscow: Voenizdat, 1946)

Anon., *Deistviia aviatsii v Belgorodskoi oboronitel'noi operatsii. Otchet Upravleniia VVC Krasnoi Armii* [Operations of aviation in the Belgorod defensive operation. Summary of the Air Force Command of the Red Army] (Moscow: Voenizdat, n.d.)

Anon., *Komandiry korpusov v Velikoi Otechestvennoi voyne 1941-1945: Kratkii biograficheskii slovar'* [Corps commanders in the Great Patriotic War 1941-1945: A Short biographical reference] (Moscow, 1995)

Anon., *Ognennaia duga. Kurskaia bitva glazami Lybianki* [Circle of fire. The Kursk battle through the eyes of the Lubianka] (Moscow: 2003)

Anon., *Sovershenno sekretno! Tol'ko dlya komandovaniye!* [Top secret! Only for command!] (Moscow: Nauka, 1967)

Babadzhanian, A. Kh., *Dorogami pobeda* [Along the roads of victory] (Moscow: Voenizdat, 1981)

Bagrin, M., *Put' generala* [A general's path] (Moscow: Voenizdat, 1953)

Beketov, V.P. (ed.), *Prokhorovskoe pole* [Prokhorovka field], (Belgorod: Izdatel'skii dom 'V. Shapovalov', 1998)

Boev, M. G., *Zvezdnyi chas Belgoroda* [Stellar hour of Belgorod] (Belgorod: Vezelitsa, 1998)

Chistiakov, I. M., *Sluzhim otechestvu* [We serve the fatherland] (Moscow: Voenizdat, 1975

Egorov, P. Ia., I. V. Krivoborsky, I. K. Ivlev & A. I. Rogalevich, *Dorogami pobedy (boevoi put' 5-i gv. tankovoi armii)* [Along the roads of victory (the combat path of the 5th Guards Tank Army)] (Moscow: Voenizdat, 1960)

Engelmann, J., *Zitadelle: Die größte Panzerschlacht im Osten 1943* [Citadel: The Greatest Panzer Battle in the East 1943] (Friedburg: Podzun Pallas, 1980)

Fetin, V. D., 'Prokhorovka (55 let tomu nazad na Kurskoi duge)' [Prokhorovka (55 years ago at the Kursk bulge)], *Duel'*, No. 25 (72), 1998

Frieser, K.-H., 'The German offensive at Kursk: Illusions and Legends' (address to the Kursk military-historical conference in Moscow 12 July 1993)

Glantz, D. M. & J. M. House, *The Battle of Kursk* (Lawrence KS: University Press of Kansas, 1999)

Gribkov, A. I., *Vstrecha s polkovodtsami* [Meetings with commanders] (Moscow: Mysl', 1999)

Guderian, H., *Vospominaniia soldata* [A Soldier's Memoirs] (Moscow, 1954)
Hahn, F., *Waffen und Geheimwaffen des deutchen Heeres, 1933-1945*. Volume 2 (Koblenz: Bernard & Graefe, 1987)
Haupt, W., *Srazheniia gruppy armii "Iug"* [The Battles of Army Group South] (Moscow: Iazua, 2006)
Il'in, Colonel Iu. V., 'Mozhno li bylo, poteriav pyat' tankov, proigrat' srazhenie pod Prokhorovkoi?' (Was it possible, having lost five tanks, to lose the Prokhorovka engagement?) *Voenno-istoricheskii zhurnal*, No. 6, 2001
Institute of Military History (eds.), *Velikaia otechestvennaia voina 1941-1945: Perelom* [Great Patriotic War 1941-1945: The Turning Point] (Moscow: Nauka, 1998)
Ivanovsky, E. F. *Ataku nachinali tankisty* (Moscow: Voenizdat, 1984)
Katukov, M. E., *Na ostrie glavnogo udara* [On the point of the main attack] (Moscow: Voenizdat, 1974)
Khazanov, D. & V. Gorbach, *Aviatsiia v bitve nad Orlovsko-kurskoi dugoi* [Aviation in the battle above the Orel-Kursk bulge] (Moscow, Del'ta PG, 2004)
Khrushchev N. S., *Vospominaniya* [Memoirs] (Moscow: Vagrius, 1977)
Klink, E., *Das Gesetz des Handels – Die Operation Zitadelle 1943* (Stuttgart, 1966)
Kolomiets, M. & A. Smirnov, 'Boi v izluchine Dona' [Fighting in the Don River bend] *Frontovaia Illiustratsiia*, no. 6 (2002)
Koltunov, G. A. & B. G. Solov'ev, *Kurskaia bitva* [The Kursk battle] (Moscow: Voenizdat, 1970)
Krivosheev, G., V. Andronikov & P. Burikov, *Grif sekretnosti sniat* [The seal of secrecy has been removed] (Moscow: Voenizdat, 1993)
Kulichkin, S., *Vatutin* (Moscow: Voenizdat, 2001)
Kurowski, F., *500 tankovykh atak* [500 tank attacks] (Moscow: Iauza/EKSMO, 2007)
Lehmann, R., *The Leibstandarte III* (Winnipeg: J. J. Fedorowicz Publishing, 1990)
Manstein, E. von, *Uteriannye pobed* [Lost victories] (Moscow: AST, 2007)
Mellenthin, F. W. von, *Panzer Battles: A Study of the Employment of Armor in the Second World War* (Norman, OK: University of Oklahoma Press, 1956)
Moskalenko, K. S., *Bitva na Kurskoi duge* [Battle at the Kursk bulge] (Moscow: Nauka, 1975)
Müller-Hillebrand, H., *Das Deutsche Heer1933-1945* [The German Army 1933-1945] Volume 3, (Frankfurt a. M.: Mittler, 1969)
Newton, S. H., *Kursk: The German View* (New York: Da Capo Press, 2002)
Oleinikov, G. A., *Prokhorovskoe srazhenie (iul' 1943)* [Prokhorovka engagement (July 1943)] (Saint Petersburg: Nestor, 1998)
Piekalkiewicz, J., *Unternehmen Zitadelle* (Bergisch Gladbach: Lubbe, 1983)
Pokhlebkin, V. V., *Velikaia voina i nesostoiavshiy mir* [The great war and the unsettled peace] (Moscow: ABS, 1997)
Popel', N. K., *Tanki povernuli na zapad* [Tanks turned to the west] (Moscow: Izdatel'stvo AST, 2001)
Radzievsky, A. I., *Tankovyi udar* [Tank attack] (Moscow: Voenizdat, 1974)
Riazansky, A. P., *V ogne tankovykh srazhenii* [In the fire of tank engagements] (Moscow: Nauka, 1975
Rotmistrov, P. A., *Tankovoe srazhenie pod Prokhorovkoi* [Tank engagement at Prokhorovka] (Moscow: Voenizdat, 1960)

Rotmistrov, P. A., *Stal'naia gvardiia* [Steel guard] (Moscow: Voenizdat, 1984)
Rudel, H.-U., *Stuka Pilot* (New York: Ballantine Books, 1971)
Samchuk, I. Ia. & P. G. Skachko, *Atakuiut desantniki* [Paratroopers Attack], (Moscow: Voenizdat)
Samsonov, A. M., *Znat' i pomnit'. Smotret' pravde v glaza* [To know and to remember. To look truth in the eyes] (Moscow, 1989)
Sokolov, B. V., *Razvedka: Tainy Vtoroi mirovoi voiny* [Intelligence: Secrets of the Second World War] (Moscow: AST, 2002)
Soviet General Staff, *Kurskaia bitva, oboronitel'noe srazhenie (1943)* [Kursk battle, the defensive engagement (1943)] (Moscow: Voenizdat, 1946)
Spaeter, Helmuth, *The History of the Panzerkorps Grossdeutschland* Volume 2 (Winnipeg: J. J. Fedorowicz Publishing, 1995)
Stadler, S., *Die Offensive gegen Kursk 1943: II. SS-Panzerkorps als Stosskeil im Grosskampf* (Osnabrück: Munin, 1980)
Sverdlov, F. D., *Neizvestnoe o sovetskikh polkovodtsakh* [The Unknown about Soviet Commanders] (Moscow, 1995)
Various authors, *Bol'shaia sovetskaia istoricheskaia entsiklopediia* [Great Soviet Historical Encyclopedia] Volume 21 (Moscow, 1975)
Various authors, *Istoriia Velikoi Otechestvennoi voiny Sovetskogo Soiuza* [History of the Great Patriotic War of the Soviet Union] (Moscow: Voenizdat, 1961)
Various authors, *Istoriia Vtoroi mirovoi voiny, 1939-1945* [History of the Second World War, 1939-1945] (Moscow: Voenizdat, 1976)
Various authors, *Sovetskaia voennaia entsiklopediia* [Soviet military encyclopedia], Volume 6 (Moscow: Voenizdat, 1977)
Various authors, *Velikaia Otechestvennaia voina 1941-1945. Perelom. Tom 2* [The Great Patriotic War 1941-1945. The Turning Point. Volume 2] (Moscow: Nauka, 1998)
Various authors, *Velikaia otechestvennaia voina Sovetskogo Soiuza, 1941-1945* [Great Patriotic War of the Soviet Union, 1941-1945] (Moscow: Voenizdat, 1965)
Various authors, *Vogne Kurskoi bitvy. Iz vospominanii uchastnikov boev* [In the fire of the Kursk battle. From the recollections of participants in the fighting] (Kursk: Kurskoe knizhnoe izdanie, 1963)
Vasilevsky, A. M., *Delo vsei zhizni* [Matter of a lifetime] Volume 2 (Moscow: Politizdat, 1989, 6th edition)
Zamulin, V.N. & L. N. Lopukhovsky, 'Prokhorovskoe srazhenie: Mify i real'nost' [Prokhorovka engagement: Myths and reality], *Voenno-istoricheskii arkhiv*, No. 2, 2003
Zetterling, N. & A. Frankson, *Kursk 1943: A Statistical Analysis* (London: Cass, 2000)
Zhadov, A. S., *Chetyre goda voiny* (Moscow: Voenizdat, 1978)
Zhukov, G. K., *Vospominaniia i razmyshleniia* [Memoirs and reflections] (Moscow: APN, 1969)

Index

Occasionally, orders, reports and accounts will use differing ranks when referring to the same officer. This is likely due to promotions that took place shortly before or after the battle. The author sought not to pinpoint the actual rank of an officer at the time of the battle, so this index presents the different ranks under which several officers appear in the text.

Related titles published by Helion & Company

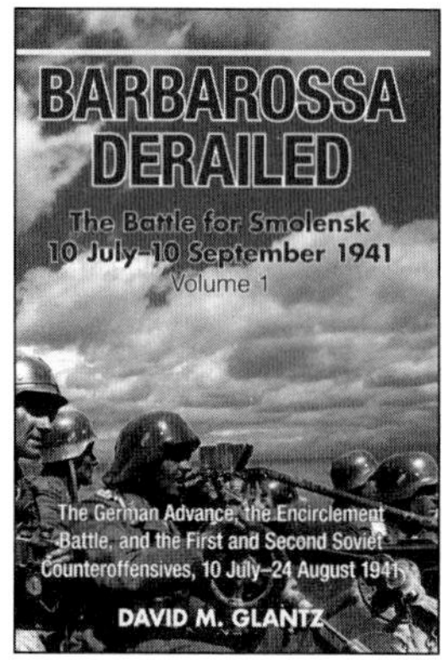

Barbarossa Derailed: The Battle for Smolensk 10 July-10 September 1941 Volume 1: The German Advance, The Encirclement Battle, and the First and Second Soviet Counteroffensives, 10 July-24 August 1941
David M. Glantz
656 pages Hardback
ISBN 978-1-906033-72-9

Secrets of the Cold War. US Army Europe's Intelligence & Counterintelligence activities against the Soviets during the Cold War
Leland C. McCaslin
200 pages Hardback
ISBN 978-1-906033-91-0

A selection of forthcoming titles

The Oder Front 1945 Volume 1. Generaloberst Gotthard Heinrici, Heeresgruppe Weichsel and Germany's Final Defense in the East, 20 March-4 May 1945
A. Stephan Hamilton ISBN 978-1-906033-87-3

Barbarossa Derailed: The Battle for Smolensk 10 July-10 September 1941 Volume 2: The German Offensives on the Flanks and the Third Soviet Counteroffensive, 25 August-10 September 1941
David M. Glantz ISBN 978-1-906033-90-3

With the Courage of Desperation. Germany's defence of the southern sector of the Eastern Front 1944-45
Rolf Hinze ISBN 978-1-906033-86-6

SS Armour in Normandy. The Combat History of SS Panzer Regiment 12 and SS Panzerjäger Abteilung 12, Normandy 1944, based on their original war diaries
Norbert Számvéber ISBN 978-1-907677-24-3

HELION & COMPANY
26 Willow Road, Solihull, West Midlands B91 1UE, England
Telephone 0121 705 3393 Fax 0121 711 4075
Website: http://www.helion.co.uk